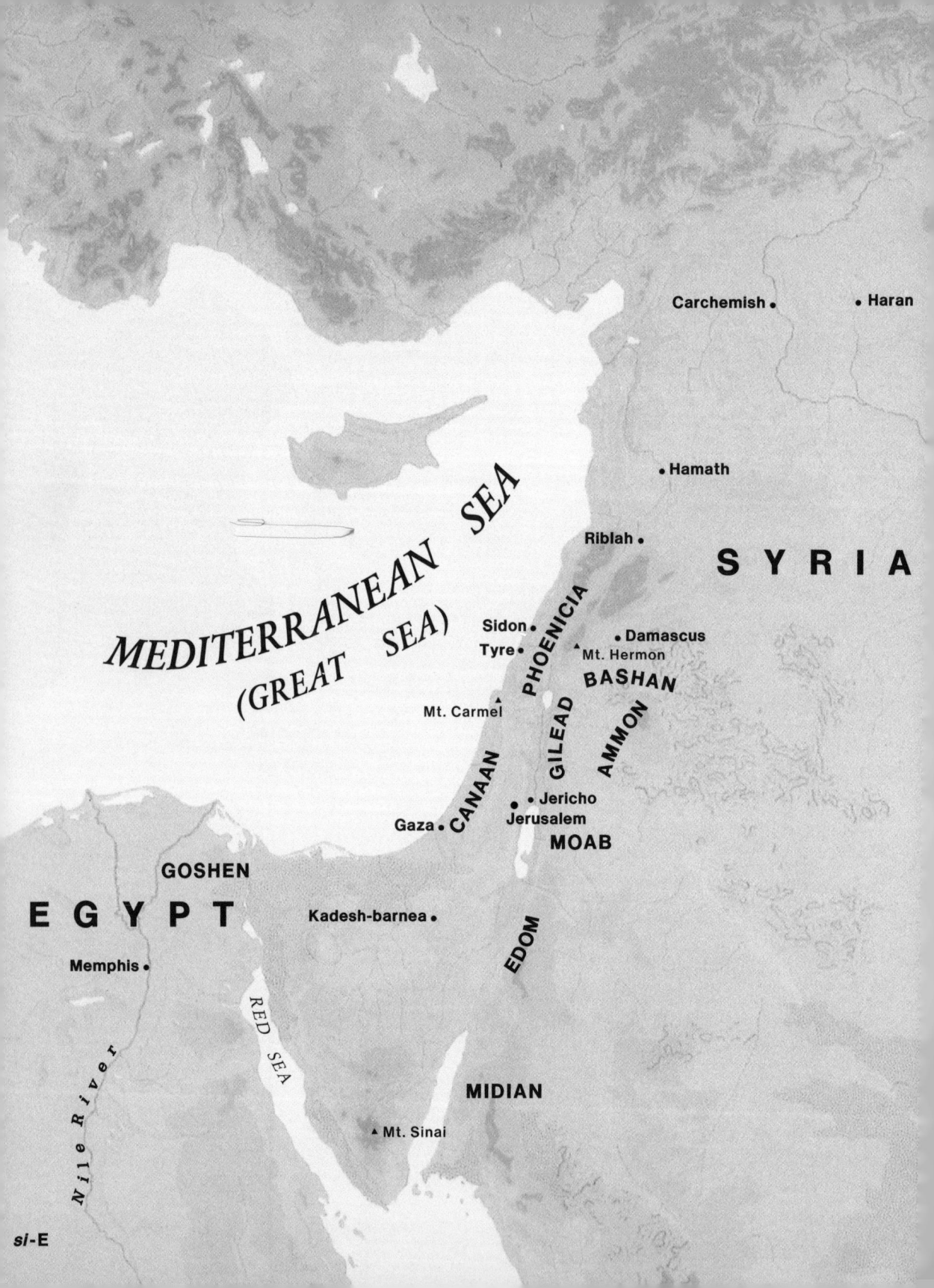

Carchemish • • Haran

• Hamath

Riblah • **S Y R I A**

MEDITERRANEAN SEA
(GREAT SEA)

Sidon • PHOENICIA
Tyre • • Damascus
Mt. Hermon ▲

Mt. Carmel • BASHAN

CANAAN GILEAD AMMON

• Jericho
Gaza • • Jerusalem

MOAB

GOSHEN

E G Y P T Kadesh-barnea •

EDOM

Memphis •

RED SEA

MIDIAN

▲ Mt. Sinai

Nile River

si-E

CASPIAN SEA

• Nineveh

A S S Y R I A

Asshur •

Tigris River

Euphrates River

M E D I A

Ecbatana •

B A B Y L O N I A

Babylon •

P E R S I A

• Shushan

CHALDEA

Ur •

E L A M

PERSIAN GULF

"All Scripture Is Inspired of God and Beneficial"

"All Scripture is inspired of God and beneficial
for teaching, for reproving, for setting things straight,
for disciplining in righteousness, that the man of God may be
fully competent, completely equipped for every good work."
—2 Timothy 3:16, 17.

Publishers
WATCHTOWER BIBLE AND TRACT SOCIETY OF NEW YORK, INC.
INTERNATIONAL BIBLE STUDENTS ASSOCIATION
Brooklyn, New York, U.S.A.

1990 Printing in English:
2,000,000 Copies

Unless otherwise indicated, Scripture quotations are from the modern-language
New World Translation of the Holy Scriptures—With References, 1984 Edition

Inside cover maps, front and back, are based on maps copyrighted by
Pictorial Archive (Near Eastern History) Est. and Survey of Israel

"All Scripture Is Inspired of God and Beneficial"
English (*si*-E)

Made in the United States of America

CONTENTS

CONTENTS

Studies on the Inspired Scriptures and Their Background

Charts, Maps, and Illustrations

NOTE: All quotations from the classical authors are from the Loeb Classical Library, unless otherwise indicated.

"All Scripture Is Inspired of God and Beneficial"

"ALL Scripture is inspired of God." These words at 2 Timothy 3:16 identify God, whose name is Jehovah, as the Author and Inspirer of the Holy Scriptures. How satisfyingly delightful the inspired Scriptures are! What an amazing fund of true knowledge they provide! They are indeed "the very knowledge of God" that has been sought after and treasured by lovers of righteousness in all ages.—Prov. 2:5.

2 One of these seekers of knowledge was Moses, the visible leader and organizer of God's nation of Israel, who said that divine instruction was as refreshing "as the dew, as gentle rains upon grass and as copious showers upon vegetation." Then there was David, valiant fighter and upholder of Jehovah's name, who prayed: "Instruct me, O Jehovah, about your way. I shall walk in your truth." There was peaceful Solomon, builder of one of the most glorious structures ever to stand on this earth, the house of Jehovah in Jerusalem, who evaluated godly wisdom in these words: "Having it as gain is better than having silver as gain and having it as produce than gold itself. It is more precious than corals, and all other delights of yours cannot be made equal to it."—Deut. 32:2; Ps. 86:11; Prov. 3:14, 15.

3 Jesus, the Son of God, set the highest value on God's word, declaring, "Your word is truth." To his followers he said: "If you remain in my word, you are really my disciples, and you will know the truth, and the truth will set you free." (John 17:17; 8:31, 32) Powerful indeed is this word that Jesus received from his Father. It is God's word. After his death and resurrection and his ascension to Jehovah's own right hand in the heavens, Jesus made further revelation of his Father's word, including a delightful description of God's blessings for mankind in the Paradise earth. Following that, God instructed the apostle John: "Write, because these words are faithful and true." All the words of the inspired Scriptures are "faithful and true," bringing immeasurable benefits to those who heed them.—Rev. 21:5.

4 How do these benefits come about? The complete expression of the apostle Paul at 2 Timothy 3:16, 17 supplies the answer: "All Scripture is inspired of God and beneficial for teaching, for reproving, for setting things straight, for disciplining in righteousness, that the man of God may be fully competent, completely equipped for every good work." The inspired Scriptures, then, are beneficial for teaching right doctrine and right conduct, setting things straight in our minds and lives, and reproving and disciplining us so that we may walk humbly in truth and righteousness. By submitting ourselves to the teaching of God's Word, we may become "God's fellow workers." (1 Cor. 3:9) There is no greater privilege on earth today than for one to be busy in God's work as the 'fully competent and completely equipped man of God.'

FIRM FOUNDATION FOR FAITH

5 For one to be a fellow worker with God, faith is needed. Faith is not to be confused with the watered-down credulity that is so prevalent today. Many people think that any kind of belief—sectarian, evolutionary, or philosophical—is sufficient. However, the man of God must "keep holding the pattern of healthful words . . . with the faith and love that are in connection with Christ Jesus." (2 Tim. 1:13) His faith must be real and alive, for "faith is the assured expectation of things hoped for, the evident demonstration of realities though not beheld." It must be grounded in a firm belief in God and his rewards for those who please him. (Heb. 11:1, 6) This faith is to be obtained only through diligent study of God's Word, the Bible. It is founded in deep love for the Bible and for the God of the Bible, Jehovah, and for his Son, Jesus Christ. There is only one such living faith, even as there is only one Lord, Jesus Christ, and one God and Father of all, Jehovah.—Eph. 4:5, 6.

6 We need to know what God's Word is and where it came from as well as its authority and

---

1. How does the Bible identify its Author, and what kind of knowledge do the Scriptures provide?
2. How did Moses, David, and Solomon evaluate godly wisdom?
3. What value do Jesus and God himself place on the divine word?

---

4. For what are the inspired Scriptures beneficial?
5. What is faith, and how only may it be obtained?
6. True faith is of what quality?

purpose and its power for righteousness. Gaining appreciation of its glorious message, we will have faith. Moreover, we shall come to love the Bible and its Author so fervently that nothing will ever be able to stifle that faith and love. It is the Scriptures, which include the sayings of Jesus Christ, that build a firm foundation for faith. True faith will be of the kind that will endure test and bitter trial, persecutions, and the materialistic advances and philosophies of a godless society. It will triumph gloriously right through into God's new world of righteousness. "This is the conquest that has conquered the world, our faith."—1 John 5:4.

⁷ In order to gain and hold on to faith, we need to apply ourselves to building love and appreciation for God's Word, the inspired Scriptures. The Scriptures are God's incomparable gift to mankind, a storehouse of spiritual treasures whose depth of wisdom is unfathomable and whose power for enlightening and stimulating to righteousness exceeds that of all other books ever written. As we dig down to gain knowledge of God's Word, we will be led to exclaim with the apostle Paul: "O the depth of God's riches and wisdom and knowledge!" To know the inspired Scriptures and their Author is to enter into the pathway of eternal joy and pleasantness.—Rom. 11:33; Ps. 16:11.

JEHOVAH—A COMMUNICATING GOD

⁸ In speaking of the glory of Jehovah's name, David exclaimed: "You are great and are doing wondrous things; you are God, you alone." (Ps. 86:10) Jehovah has done many "wondrous things" for mankind on earth, and among these is the communicating of his Word to them. Yes, Jehovah is a communicating God, a God who lovingly expresses himself for the benefit of his creatures. How thankful we should be that our Creator is no aloof potentate, shrouded in mysteries and unresponsive to the needs of lovers of righteousness on earth! As he will also do in the new world to come, Jehovah resides even now with those who exercise faith and love toward him, in the relation of a kind Father communicating good things to his inquiring children. (Rev. 21:3) Our heavenly Father is not like the demon gods, who must be represented by fearsome dumb idols. Gods of metal and stone have no fatherly relationship with their benighted worshipers. They can communicate nothing of benefit to them. Truly, "those making them will become just like them."—Ps. 135:15-19, 1 Cor. 8:4-6.

⁹ Jehovah is the "God merciful and gracious,

slow to anger and abundant in loving-kindness and truth." (Ex. 34:6) Out of the abundance of his loving-kindness, he has communicated an abundance of truth to mankind. This is all sound counsel for the guidance of mankind and includes prophecy to lighten one's paths to future blessings. "For all the things that were written aforetime were written for our instruction, that through our endurance and through the comfort from the Scriptures we might have hope." (Rom. 15:4) Out of the realms above, from heaven itself, has come reliable communication to instruct mankind, who are in the realms below.—John 8:23.

¹⁰ Jehovah has never communicated in an unknown tongue but always in the language of mankind, the living tongue of his faithful witnesses. (Acts 2:5-11) To Adam, Noah, Abraham, Moses, and the Hebrew prophets, Jehovah spoke in mankind's first language, now known as Hebrew. Hebrew continued to be used for as long as it could be understood, even as late as the time of Saul of Tarsus, to whom the resurrected Jesus spoke in that language. (Acts 26:14) When the Aramaic language of the Chaldeans took hold among the Israelites in exile, some communications then came from God in Aramaic, for the people understood that language. (Ezra 4:8–6:18; 7:12-26; Dan. 2:4b–7:28) Later, when Greek was the international language and the principal language of his witnesses, Jehovah's communications were made and preserved in that tongue. The sayings preserved in the Bible are Jehovah's communication, spoken always in a living tongue for the benefit of humble, truth-loving men on earth.

¹¹ Jehovah is the Creator of the mind and of the speech organs, including the tongue, mouth, and throat, which form all the intricacies of speech sounds for each of the many systems of language. Thus, it may be said that Jehovah is the Former of all language. His authority over the language of mankind was demonstrated by his miracle performed at the Tower of Babel. (Ex. 4:11; Gen. 11:6-9; 10:5; 1 Cor. 13:1) No language is strange to Jehovah. Not only did he give man the original Hebrew language but, by his creation of the mind and the speech organs, he also provided the basis for Aramaic and Greek and for all of the some 3,000 languages now being spoken by mankind.

THE LANGUAGE OF TRUTH

¹² Regardless of the system of human language used by Jehovah, in all instances he has communicated in the language of truth, not in religious

---

7. What rewards come with the finding of Bible wisdom?
8. (a) Why should we be thankful that Jehovah is a communicating God? (b) In what way does he contrast with the demon gods?
9. What kind of communication has come from God in the realms above?

10. In what tongues has Jehovah made communication, and why?
11. Why may it be said that Jehovah is the Former of all language?
12, 13. (a) How has Jehovah made his communications easy to understand? (b) Give examples.

mysticisms. It is a language simple and easy to understand. (Zeph. 3:9) Earthly man can easily understand three-dimensional matters, that is, objects that have height, breadth, and length and that are set in the stream of time. Therefore, Jehovah has represented invisible things by using typical representations that the mind of man can comprehend. As an example, there was the tabernacle designed by God and erected by Moses in the wilderness. Under inspiration Paul used its three-dimensional symbols to explain glorious realities that are of heaven itself.—Heb. 8:5; 9:9.

¹³ Another example: Jehovah, who is spirit, does not literally sit on a thronelike chair in heaven. However, to us mere men, bound by visible realities, God expresses himself by using such a visible symbol to convey understanding. When he commences heavenly court proceedings, it is just as when a king on earth begins proceedings by taking his seat on a throne.—Dan. 7:9-14.

EASILY TRANSLATED

¹⁴ Since the Bible has been written in these down-to-earth, easily understandable terms, it is possible to translate its symbols and actions clearly and accurately into most modern-day languages. The original power and force of truth are preserved in all translations. Simple everyday words, such as "horse," "war," "crown," "throne," "husband," "wife," and "children," communicate accurate thought clearly in every language. This is in contrast with human philosophical writings, which often do not lend themselves to accurate translation. Their complicated expressions and up-in-the-air terminology often cannot be conveyed precisely in another tongue.

¹⁵ The Bible's power of expression is far superior. Even when God communicated judgment messages to nonbelievers, he did not use philosophical language but, rather, everyday symbols. This is shown at Daniel 4:10-12. Here the kingdom of the self-glorifying pagan king was described in some detail under the symbol of a tree, and then, by means of actions involving this tree, future happenings were accurately foretold. All of this is clearly conveyed in translations into other languages. Jehovah has lovingly made communications in this way in order that "the true knowledge will become abundant." How wonderfully this has aided in the understanding of prophecy in this "time of the end"!—Dan. 12:4.

LINE OF COMMUNICATION

¹⁶ Someone may ask, What has been the means of communication? This may well be illustrated by a modern-day example. Communications lines have (1) the utterer, or originator, of the message; (2) the transmitter; (3) the medium through which the message passes; (4) the receiver; and (5) the hearer. In telephone communications we have (1) the telephone user originating the communication; (2) the telephone transmitter, which converts the message into electrical impulses; (3) the telephone lines carrying the electrical impulses to the destination; (4) the receiver reconverting the message from impulses to sounds; and (5) the hearer. Likewise in heaven (1) Jehovah God originates his utterances; (2) then his official Word, or Spokesman—now known as Jesus Christ—often transmits the message; (3) God's holy spirit, the active force that is used as the medium of communication, carries it earthward; (4) God's prophet on earth receives the message; and (5) he then publishes it for the benefit of God's people. Just as on occasion today a courier may be sent to deliver an important message, so Jehovah at times chose to use spirit messengers, or angels, to carry some communications from the heavens to his servants on the earth.—Gal. 3:19; Heb. 2:2.

PROCESS OF INSPIRATION

¹⁷ The expression "inspired of God" is translated from the Greek *the·o'pneu·stos,* meaning "God-breathed." (See 2 Timothy 3:16, first footnote.) It is God's own spirit, his active force, that he has 'breathed' on faithful men, causing them to compile and write the Sacred Scriptures. This process is known as inspiration. The prophets and other faithful servants of Jehovah who became subject to inspiration had their minds borne along by means of this active force. This means that they received messages, including pictures of purpose, from God and that these became firmly fixed in the circuits of their minds. "For prophecy was at no time brought by man's will, but men spoke from God as they were borne along by holy spirit." —2 Pet. 1:21; John 20:21, 22.

¹⁸ While these men of God were awake and fully conscious or while they were asleep in a dream, his spirit firmly implanted the message emanating from the divine origin of the line of communication. Upon receiving the message, the prophet had the responsibility of relaying it in word form to others. When Moses and other faithful prophets return in the resurrection, they will no doubt be able to confirm the accuracy of the preserved records of their writings, for their appreciative re-created minds will likely still hold the original

---

14, 15. Why is the Bible, in contrast with human philosophical writings, easily translatable into other tongues? Illustrate.

16. How may Jehovah's channel of communication be outlined?

17. What Greek word is translated "inspired of God," and how does its meaning help us to understand the process of inspiration?

18. How deeply were the inspired messages impressed on their human receivers?

communications clearly in memory. In like manner, the apostle Peter was so deeply impressed by the vision of the transfiguration that he could write vividly concerning its magnificence more than 30 years later.—Matt. 17:1-9; 2 Pet. 1:16-21.

THE AUTHOR AND HIS FINGER

19 Human authors have used fingers to write, in ancient times by means of a pen or stylus and in modern times by means of a pen, typewriter, or computer. What has been produced through these fingers is said to have been authored by the mind of their owner. Did you know that God has a finger? This is so, for Jesus spoke of God's spirit as His "finger." When Jesus cured a demon-possessed man so that he regained his power of speech and his sight, religious foes blasphemed the means by which Jesus had cured the man. According to Matthew, Jesus said to them: "If it is by means of God's spirit that I expel the demons, the kingdom of God has really overtaken you." (Matt. 12:22, 28) Luke adds to our understanding by quoting Jesus as saying on a like occasion: "If it is by means of God's finger I expel the demons, the kingdom of God has really overtaken you." (Luke 11:20) On an earlier occasion, the magic-practicing priests of Egypt were forced to admit that the plagues on Egypt were an exhibition of Jehovah's superior power, acknowledging: "It is the finger of God!" —Ex. 8:18, 19.

20 In harmony with these uses of the word "finger," it can be appreciated that "God's finger" has great power and that this designation well applies to his spirit as he used it in the writing of the Bible. So the Scriptures inform us that by means of "God's finger," he wrote the Ten Commandments on the two tablets of stone. (Ex. 31:18; Deut. 9:10) When God used men to write the various books of the Holy Bible, his symbolic finger, or spirit, was likewise the directive force behind the pen of those men. God's holy spirit is unseen, but it has been active in a marvelous way, with the visible, tangible result that mankind has received the treasured gift of God's Word of truth, *His* Bible. There is no question that the Bible's Author is Jehovah God, the heavenly Communicator.

THE INSPIRED COLLECTION BEGINS

21 As has been seen, Jehovah "proceeded to give Moses two tablets of the Testimony, tablets of stone written on by God's finger." (Ex. 31:18) This writing comprised the Ten Commandments, and it is of interest that this document officially presents

the divine name, Jehovah, eight times. In the same year, 1513 B.C.E., Jehovah commanded Moses to start making permanent records. So began the writing of the Sacred Scriptures. (Ex. 17:14; 34: 27) God also commanded Moses to construct "the ark of the testimony," or "the ark of the covenant," a chest of beautiful workmanship in which the Israelites were to preserve this most treasured communication. (Ex. 25:10-22; 1 Ki. 8:6, 9) The design of the Ark, and of the tabernacle that housed it, was supplied by Jehovah; and the chief artisan and builder, Bezalel, was filled "with the spirit of God in wisdom, in understanding and in knowledge and in every sort of craftsmanship" in order to complete his work according to the divine pattern.—Ex. 35:30-35.

22 In making known his purposes, God "spoke on many occasions and in many ways" over a long period of time. (Heb. 1:1) The penmen who wrote down his Word did so from 1513 B.C.E. to about 98 C.E., or during about 1,610 years. The one Author, Jehovah God, used about 40 of these scribes, or human secretaries. All these cowriters were Hebrews and thus members of the nation "entrusted with the sacred pronouncements of God." (Rom. 3:2) Eight of them were Christian Jews who knew Jesus either personally or through his apostles. The inspired Scriptures written before their time had borne witness concerning the coming of the Messiah, or Christ. (1 Pet. 1:10, 11) Although called from many walks of life, these earthly Bible writers, from Moses to the apostle John, all shared in upholding the sovereignty of Jehovah God and proclaiming his purposes in the earth. They wrote in Jehovah's name and by the power of his spirit.—Jer. 2:2, 4; Ezek. 6:3; 2 Sam. 23:2; Acts 1:16; Rev. 1:10.

23 Several of these writers include in their records compilations from eyewitness documents made by earlier writers, not all of whom were inspired. Moses, for example, may have compiled parts of Genesis from such eyewitness accounts, as Samuel may have done in writing the book of Judges. Jeremiah compiled First and Second Kings, and Ezra wrote First and Second Chronicles, largely in this way. The holy spirit guided these compilers in determining which portions of older human documents should be incorporated, thus authenticating these compilations as being reliable. From the time of their compilation forward, these extracts from older documents became part of the inspired Scriptures.—Gen. 2:4; 5:1; 2 Ki. 1:18; 2 Chron. 16:11.

---

19. What is God's "finger," as proved by what scriptures?
20. How has God's "finger" operated, and with what result?
21. (a) How did the writing of the Scriptures commence? (b) In what way did Jehovah provide for their preservation?

22. (a) Who is the Author of the inspired Scriptures, and how long did the writing take? (b) Who were the cowriters of the Bible, and what is known about them?
23. What earlier records did some Bible writers use, and how did these become inspired Scripture?

24 In what order did the 66 Bible books come to us? What part of the endless stream of time do they cover? After describing the creation of the heavens and the earth and the preparation of the earth as man's home, the Genesis account takes up the beginnings of human history from the creation of the first man in 4026 B.C.E. The Sacred Writings then narrate important events down until shortly after 443 B.C.E. Then, after a gap of more than 400 years, they pick up the account again in 3 B.C.E., taking it on to about 98 C.E. Thus, from a historical viewpoint, the Scriptures span a period of 4,123 years.

25 The chart on page 12 will assist in the understanding of the background of the Bible writers and the sequence in which the Bible writings came to us.

THE COMPLETE "BOOK" OF DIVINE TRUTH

26 The Sacred Scriptures, as a collection from Genesis to Revelation, form one complete book, one complete library, all inspired by the one Supreme Author. They should not be divided into two parts, so that one part is given less value. The Hebrew Scriptures and the Christian Greek Scriptures are essential to each other. The latter supplements the former to make the one complete book of divine truth. The 66 Bible books, *all together,* form the one library of the Holy Scriptures.—Rom. 15:4.

27 It is a mistake of tradition to divide God's written Word into two sections, calling the first section, from Genesis to Malachi, the "Old Testament," and the second section, from Matthew to Revelation, the "New Testament." At 2 Corinthians 3:14 the popular *King James Version* tells of the "reading of the old testament," but here the apostle is not referring to the ancient Hebrew Scriptures in their entirety. Nor does he mean that the inspired Christian writings constitute a "new testament [covenant]." The apostle is speaking of the Law covenant, which was recorded by Moses in the Pentateuch and which makes up only a part of the pre-Christian Scriptures. For this reason he says in the next verse, "when Moses is read." The Greek word rendered "testament" in the *King James Version* has uniformly been rendered "covenant" in many modern translations.—Matt. 26: 28; 2 Cor. 3:6, 14, *New World Translation of the Holy Scriptures, Revised Standard Version, American Standard Version.*

28 That which has been recorded and preserved as the Holy Scriptures is not to be tampered with. (Deut. 4:1, 2; Rev. 22:18, 19) The apostle Paul writes on this point: "However, even if we or an angel out of heaven were to declare to you as good news something beyond what we declared to you as good news, let him be accursed." (Gal. 1:8; see also John 10:35.) All of Jehovah's word of prophecy must be fulfilled in due course. "So my word that goes forth from my mouth will prove to be. It will not return to me without results, but it will certainly do that in which I have delighted, and it will have certain success in that for which I have sent it."—Isa. 55:11.

EXAMINING THE SCRIPTURES

29 In the following pages, the 66 books of the Sacred Scriptures are examined in turn. The setting of each book is described, and information is given concerning the writer, the time of writing, and in some cases the period covered. Proof is also presented to show that the book is authentic and that it rightly belongs as part of the inspired Scriptures. This proof may be found in the words of Jesus Christ or in the inspired writings of other servants of God. Very often the authenticity of the book is shown by undeniable fulfillments of Bible prophecy or by internal evidence from the book itself, such as its harmony, honesty, and candor. Supporting evidence may be taken from archaeological finds or reliable secular history.

30 As the contents of each book are described, the endeavor is to make the powerful message of the Bible writer stand out in such a way as to instill in the heart of the reader a deep love for the inspired Scriptures and their Author, Jehovah God, and thus to enhance appreciation for the living message of God's Word with all its practicalness, harmony, and beauty. The contents of the book are set out under paragraph subheadings. This is for convenience in study and does not mean that these are arbitrary subdivisions for the books of the Bible. Each book is in itself an entity, making a valuable contribution to the understanding of the divine purposes.

31 In concluding each book, the discussion points out why this portion of the inspired Scriptures is "beneficial for teaching, for reproving, for setting things straight, for disciplining in righteousness." (2 Tim. 3:16) The fulfillments of prophecy, where these are indicated by the inspired testimony of later Bible writers, are considered. In each

---

24, 25. (a) What period of history is covered in the Bible? (b) Point out some interesting facts found in the chart on page 12.
26. In what way are the Scriptures one complete book?
27. Why are the expressions "Old Testament" and "New Testament" misnomers?

28. What assurance is given as to Bible prophecies?
29. In this book, as each Bible book is examined in turn, what introductory information is provided?
30. In what way are the contents of each Bible book presented?
31. (a) What information is presented to show why each book is beneficial? (b) What glorious theme is kept to the fore throughout the discussions of Bible books?

instance, the book's contribution to developing the overall theme of the Bible is shown. The Bible is no myth. It contains the only living message for mankind. From the first book, Genesis, to the last book, Revelation, the inspired Scriptures testify to the purpose of the Creator of the universe, Jehovah God, to sanctify his name by the Kingdom ruled by his Seed. Therein lies the glorious hope for all lovers of righteousness.—Matt. 12:18, 21.

³² After considering the 66 Bible books themselves, we devote some space to giving background information on the Bible. This includes studies on the geography of the Promised Land, the timing of the events of the Bible, Bible translations, archaeological and other supporting evidences of the authenticity of the Bible, and proof of the Bible catalog. Other valuable information and tables also

appear in this section. All of this is designed to heighten appreciation for the Bible as the most practical and beneficial book on earth today.

³³ The divine Author has spoken to mankind at great length. He has shown great depth of love and fatherly interest in what he has done for his children on earth. What a remarkable collection of inspired documents he has provided for us in the Holy Scriptures! Truly, these form a treasure beyond compare, an extensive library of 'divinely breathed' information, far exceeding in wealth and in scope the writings of mere men. Devotion to the study of God's Word will not become "wearisome to the flesh," but, rather, it will bring eternal benefits to those knowing "the saying of Jehovah [that] endures forever."—Eccl. 12:12; 1 Pet. 1: 24, 25.

---

32. What information is provided to heighten appreciation for the Bible?

33. How might the Bible be described, and of what benefit is a study of it?

THE BIBLE'S INSPIRED PENMEN AND THEIR WRITINGS

(In Date Order)

Order	Writers	Occupations	Writings Completed	Writings
1.	Moses	Scholar, shepherd, prophet, leader	1473 B.C.E.	Genesis; Exodus; Leviticus; Job; Numbers; Deuteronomy; Psalm 90 (possibly also 91)
2.	Joshua	Leader	c. 1450 B.C.E.	Joshua
3.	Samuel	Levite, prophet	before c. 1080 B.C.E.	Judges; Ruth; part of First Samuel
4.	Gad	Prophet	c. 1040 B.C.E.	Part of First Samuel; Second Samuel (both with Nathan)
5.	Nathan	Prophet	c. 1040 B.C.E.	See above (with Gad)
6.	David	King, shepherd, musician	1037 B.C.E.	Many of the Psalms
7.	Sons of Korah			Some of the Psalms
8.	Asaph	Singer		Some of the Psalms
9.	Heman	Wise man		Psalm 88
10.	Ethan	Wise man		Psalm 89
11.	Solomon	King, builder, wise man	c. 1000 B.C.E.	Most of Proverbs; The Song of Solomon; Ecclesiastes; Psalm 127
12.	Agur			Proverbs chapter 30
13.	Lemuel	King		Proverbs chapter 31
14.	Jonah	Prophet	c. 844 B.C.E.	Jonah
15.	Joel	Prophet	c. 820 B.C.E.(?)	Joel
16.	Amos	Herdsman, prophet	c. 804 B.C.E.	Amos
17.	Hosea	Prophet	after 745 B.C.E.	Hosea
18.	Isaiah	Prophet	after 732 B.C.E.	Isaiah
19.	Micah	Prophet	before 717 B.C.E.	Micah
20.	Zephaniah	Prince, prophet	before 648 B.C.E.	Zephaniah
21.	Nahum	Prophet	before 632 B.C.E.	Nahum
22.	Habakkuk	Prophet	c. 628 B.C.E.(?)	Habakkuk
23.	Obadiah	Prophet	c. 607 B.C.E.	Obadiah
24.	Ezekiel	Priest, prophet	c. 591 B.C.E.	Ezekiel
25.	Jeremiah	Priest, prophet	580 B.C.E.	First and Second Kings; Jeremiah; Lamentations
26.	Daniel	Prince, ruler, prophet	c. 536 B.C.E.	Daniel
27.	Haggai	Prophet	520 B.C.E.	Haggai
28.	Zechariah	Prophet	518 B.C.E.	Zechariah
29.	Mordecai	Prime minister	c. 475 B.C.E.	Esther
30.	Ezra	Priest, copyist, administrator	c. 460 B.C.E.	First and Second Chronicles; Ezra
31.	Nehemiah	Court official, governor	after 443 B.C.E.	Nehemiah
32.	Malachi	Prophet	after 443 B.C.E.	Malachi
33.	Matthew	Tax collector, apostle	c. 41 C.E.	Matthew
34.	Luke	Physician, missionary	c. 61 C.E.	Luke; Acts
35.	James	Overseer (brother of Jesus)	before 62 C.E.	James
36.	Mark	Missionary	c. 60-65 C.E.	Mark
37.	Peter	Fisherman, apostle	c. 64 C.E.	First and Second Peter
38.	Paul	Missionary, apostle, tentmaker	c. 65 C.E.	First and Second Thessalonians; Galatians; First and Second Corinthians; Romans; Ephesians; Philippians; Colossians; Philemon; Hebrews; First and Second Timothy; Titus
39.	Jude	Disciple (brother of Jesus)	c. 65 C.E.	Jude
40.	John	Fisherman, apostle	c. 98 C.E.	Revelation; John; First, Second, and Third John

1

Genesis

Writer: **Moses**
Place Written: **Wilderness**
Writing Completed: **1513 B.C.E.**
Time Covered: **"In the beginning" to 1657 B.C.E.**

IMAGINE picking up a book of only 50 short chapters and finding in the first page or two the only accurate account of the earliest history of man and a record showing the relationship of man to God, his Creator, as well as to the earth with its myriads of creatures! In those few pages, you gain, too, a deep insight into God's purpose in putting man on earth. Reading a little farther, you discover why man dies and the reason for his present troubled condition, and you are enlightened regarding the real basis for faith and for hope, even regarding identifying God's instrument for deliverance—the Seed of promise. The remarkable book that contains all these things is Genesis, the first of the 66 books of the Bible.

2 "Genesis" means "Origin; Birth," the name being taken from the Greek *Septuagint* translation of the book. In the Hebrew manuscripts, the title is the opening word, *Bere'·shith'*, "in the beginning" (Greek, *en ar·khei'*). Genesis is the first book of the Pentateuch (an Anglicized Greek word meaning "five rolls" or "fivefold volume"). Evidently this was originally one book called the Torah (Law) or "the book of the law of Moses" but was later divided into the five rolls for easier handling. —Josh. 23:6; Ezra 6:18.

3 Jehovah God is the Author of the Bible, but he inspired Moses to write the book of Genesis. From where did Moses get the information he recorded in Genesis? Some could have been received directly by divine revelation and some, under the direction of holy spirit, through oral transmission. It is also possible that Moses possessed written documents preserved by his forefathers as precious, valuable records of the origins of mankind.*

4 It was possibly in the wilderness of Sinai in 1513 B.C.E. that Moses, under inspiration, completed his writing. (2 Tim. 3:16; John 5:39, 46, 47) Where did Moses obtain the information for the last part of Genesis? Since his great-grandfather Levi was the half brother of Joseph, these details would be accurately known within his own family. Levi's life may even have overlapped that of Moses' father, Amram. Further, Jehovah's spirit would again assure the correct recording of this portion of the Scriptures.—Ex. 6:16, 18, 20; Num. 26:59.

5 There is no question as to who wrote Genesis. "The book of the law of Moses" and similar references to the first five books of the Bible, of which Genesis is one, are to be found often from the time of Moses' successor, Joshua, onward. In fact, there are some 200 references to Moses in 27 of the later Bible books. Moses' writership has never been questioned by the Jews. The Christian Greek Scriptures make frequent mention of Moses as the writer of "the law," the crowning testimony being that of Jesus Christ. Moses wrote at Jehovah's direct command and under His inspiration.—Ex. 17:14; 34:27; Josh. 8:31; Dan. 9:13; Luke 24: 27, 44.

6 Some skeptics have asked, But how were Moses and his predecessors able to write? Was not writing a later human development? Writing evidently had its start early in human history, perhaps before the Deluge of Noah's day, which occurred in 2370 B.C.E. Is there any evidence of man's early ability to write? While it is true that archaeologists have assigned dates earlier than 2370 B.C.E. to certain clay tablets that they have excavated, such dates are merely conjectural. However, it should be noted that the Bible clearly shows that the building of cities, the development of musical instruments, and the forging of metal tools had their start long before the Deluge. (Gen. 4:17, 21, 22) Reasonably, then, men would have had little difficulty in developing a method of writing.

---

* *Insight on the Scriptures,* Vol. 1, pages 919-20; Vol. 2, page 1212.

---

1. What are some of the vital topics covered in Genesis?
2. What is the meaning of the name Genesis, and of what is it the first part?
3. (a) Who is the Author of Genesis, but who wrote it? (b) How may Moses have obtained the information he included in Genesis?
4. (a) Where and when did Moses complete his writing? (b) How could Moses have obtained the material he incorporated in the last part of Genesis?

---

5. What internal Bible evidence proves Moses' writership?
6. What suggests that writing had its start early in human history?

[7] In many other respects, Genesis has proved to be amazingly consistent with proved facts. It is only Genesis that gives a true and factual account of the Flood and its survivors, though accounts of a deluge and survival by humans (in many cases as a result of being preserved in a vessel) are found in the legends of many branches of the human family. The Genesis account also locates the beginnings of the dwellings of the different branches of mankind, stemming from the three sons of Noah —Shem, Ham, and Japheth.* Says Dr. Melvin G. Kyle, of Xenia Theological Seminary, Missouri, U.S.A.: "That from a central point, somewhere in Mesopotamia, the Hamitic branch of the race migrated to the south-west, the Japhetic branch to the north-west, and the Semitic branch 'eastward' toward the 'land of Shinar' is indisputable."#

[8] The authenticity of Genesis as part of the divine record is shown also by its internal harmony, as well as by its complete agreement with the remainder of the inspired Scriptures. Its candor reflects a writer who feared Jehovah and loved truth and who unhesitatingly wrote of the sins of both the nation and those prominent in Israel. Above all, the unswerving accuracy with which its prophecies have come to fulfillment, as will be shown toward the end of this chapter, marks Genesis as an outstanding example of a writing inspired by Jehovah God.—Gen. 9:20-23; 37:18-35; Gal. 3:8, 16.

CONTENTS OF GENESIS

[9] **Creation of the heavens and the earth, and the preparation of the earth for human habitation** (1:1–2:25). Reaching back evidently through billions of years of time, Genesis opens with impressive simplicity: "In the beginning God created the heavens and the earth." Significantly, this opening sentence identifies God as the Creator and his material creation as the heavens and the earth. In majestic, well-chosen words, the first chapter continues on to give a general account of the creative work relative to the earth. This is accomplished in six time periods called days, each beginning with an evening, when the creative work for that period is undefined, and ending in the brightness of a morning, as the glory of the creative work

becomes clearly manifest. On successive "days" appear the light; the expanse of the atmosphere; dry land and vegetation; the luminaries to divide day and night; fish and fowl; and land animals and finally man. God here makes known his law governing kinds, the impassable barrier making it impossible for one kind to evolve into another. Having made man in His own image, God announces His threefold purpose for man on earth: to fill it with righteous offspring, to subdue it, and to have in subjection the animal creation. The seventh "day" is blessed and pronounced sacred by Jehovah, who now proceeds 'to rest from all his work that he has made.' The account next gives a close-up, or magnified view, of God's creative work as regards man. It describes the garden of Eden and its location, states God's law of the forbidden tree, relates Adam's naming of the animals, and then gives the account of Jehovah's arranging the first marriage by forming a wife from Adam's own body and bringing her to Adam.

[10] **Sin and death enter the world; "seed" foretold as deliverer** (3:1–5:5). The woman eats the forbidden fruit and persuades her husband to join her in rebellion, and so Eden becomes defiled through disobedience. God immediately points to the means by which his purpose will be accomplished: "And Jehovah God proceeded to say to the serpent [Satan, the invisible instigator of the rebellion]: ' . . . And I shall put enmity between you and the woman and between your seed and her seed. He will bruise you in the head and you will bruise him in the heel.'" (3:14, 15) Man is expelled from the garden, to live in pain and sweatful toil among thorns and thistles. Finally, he must die and return to the ground from which he had been taken. Only his offspring may hope in the promised Seed.

[11] The ravages of sin continue outside Eden. Cain, the first man-child born, becomes the murderer of his brother Abel, a faithful servant of Jehovah. Jehovah banishes Cain to the land of Fugitiveness, where he brings forth offspring later wiped out by the Deluge. Adam now has another son, Seth, who becomes father to Enosh; at this time men begin to call on the name of Jehovah in hypocrisy. Adam dies at 930 years of age.

[12] **Wicked men and angels ruin the earth; God brings the Deluge** (5:6–11:9). The genealogy through Seth is here given. Outstanding among these descendants of Seth is Enoch, who sanctifies Jehovah's name by "walking with the true God."

---

* *Insight on the Scriptures,* Vol. 1, pages 328-9.
# *Biblical History in the Light of Archaeological Discovery,* 1934, D. E. Hart-Davies, page 5.

---

7. What secular evidence is there of a global deluge and of three branches to the human race, as described in the Bible account?
8. What other types of evidence testify to the authenticity of Genesis?
9. (a) What is related in the opening chapter of Genesis concerning creation by God? (b) What added details does the second chapter give concerning man?

---

10. How does Genesis explain the origin of sin and death, and what important purpose is here made known?
11. How do the ravages of sin continue outside Eden?
12. How does the earth come to be ruined in the days of Noah?

(5:22) The next man of notable faith is Enoch's great-grandson Noah, born 1,056 years after Adam's creation. During this time something occurs to increase the violence in the earth. Angels of God forsake their heavenly habitation to marry the good-looking daughters of men. This unauthorized cohabitation produces a hybrid race of giants known as the Nephilim (meaning "Fellers"), who make a name, not for God, but for themselves. Jehovah therefore announces to Noah that He is going to wipe out man and beast because of the continuing badness of mankind. Only Noah finds favor with Jehovah.

[13] Noah becomes father to Shem, Ham, and Japheth. As violence and ruination continue in the earth, Jehovah reveals to Noah that He is about to sanctify His name by means of a great flood, and He commands Noah to build an ark of preservation, giving him detailed building plans. Noah promptly obeys and gathers his family of eight persons, together with beasts and birds; then, in the 600th year of his life (2370 B.C.E.), the Flood begins. The downpour continues for 40 days, until even the tall mountains are covered by as much as 15 cubits (c. 22 ft) of water. When, after one year, Noah is finally able to lead his family out of the ark, his first act is to offer a great sacrifice of thanksgiving to Jehovah.

[14] Jehovah now blesses Noah and his family and commands them to fill the earth with their offspring. God's decree gives permission to eat meat but demands abstinence from blood, which is the soul, or life, of the flesh, and requires the execution of a murderer. God's covenant nevermore to bring a deluge upon the earth is confirmed by the appearance of the rainbow in the heavens. Later, Ham shows disrespect for Jehovah's prophet Noah. Learning of this, Noah curses Ham's son Canaan, but he adds a blessing showing that Shem will be specially favored and that Japheth also will be blessed. Noah dies at 950 years of age.

[15] Noah's three sons carry out God's command to multiply, producing 70 families, the progenitors of the present human race. Nimrod, grandson of Ham, is not counted in, evidently because he becomes "a mighty hunter in opposition to Jehovah." (10:9) He sets up a kingdom and starts to build cities. At this time all the earth has one language. Instead of scattering over the earth to populate and cultivate it, men decide to build a city and a tower with its top in the heavens so that they can

make a celebrated name for themselves. However, Jehovah thwarts their intention by confusing their language, and so scatters them. The city is called Babel (meaning "Confusion").

[16] **God's dealings with Abraham** (11:10–25:26). The important line of descent from Shem to Terah's son Abram is traced, supplying also the chronological links. Instead of seeking a name for himself, Abram exercises faith in God. He leaves the Chaldean city of Ur at God's command and, at 75 years of age, crosses the Euphrates on his way to the land of Canaan, calling on the name of Jehovah. Because of his faith and obedience, he comes to be called "Jehovah's friend [lover]," and God establishes his covenant with him. (Jas. 2:23; 2 Chron. 20:7; Isa. 41:8) God protects Abram and his wife during a brief stay in Egypt. Back in Canaan, Abram shows his generosity and peaceableness by allowing his nephew and fellow worshiper, Lot, to select the best part of the land. Later, he rescues Lot from four kings who have captured him. Then, returning from the fight, Abram meets Melchizedek, king of Salem, who as priest of God blesses Abram, and to whom Abram pays tithes.

[17] God later appears to Abram, announcing that He is Abram's shield and enlarging on the covenant promise by revealing that Abram's seed will become as the stars of heaven for number. Abram is told that his seed will suffer affliction for 400 years but will be delivered by God, with judgment upon the afflicting nation. When Abram is 85 years old, Sarai his wife, still childless, gives him her Egyptian maidservant Hagar that he may have a child by her. Ishmael is born and is viewed as the possible heir. However, Jehovah purposes differently. When Abram is 99 years old, Jehovah changes his name to Abraham, changes Sarai's name to Sarah, and promises that Sarah will bear a son. The covenant of circumcision is given to Abraham, and he immediately has his household circumcised.

[18] God now announces to His friend Abraham His determination to destroy Sodom and Gomorrah because of their heavy sin. Angels of Jehovah warn Lot and help him to flee from Sodom with his wife and two daughters. However, his wife, lingering to look at the things behind, becomes a pillar of salt. In order to procure offspring, Lot's daughters get their father intoxicated with wine, and through intercourse with him, they bear two

---

13. How does Jehovah now sanctify his name?
14. What does Jehovah now command and covenant, and what events fill out Noah's life?
15. How do men attempt to make a celebrated name for themselves, and how does Jehovah thwart their intention?

16. (a) Why is the genealogy of Shem important? (b) How does Abram come to be called "Jehovah's friend," and what blessings does he receive?
17. How does God enlarge his covenant, and what is revealed concerning Abram's seed?
18. What noteworthy happenings climax Lot's life?

sons, who become the fathers of the nations of Moab and Ammon.

19 God protects Sarah from contamination by Abimelech of the Philistines. The promised heir, Isaac, is born when Abraham is 100 years old and Sarah about 90. Some five years after this, the 19-year-old Ishmael pokes fun at Isaac, the heir, resulting in the dismissal of Hagar and Ishmael, with God's approval. Some years later, God tests Abraham by commanding him to sacrifice his son Isaac on one of the mountains of Moriah. Abraham's great faith in Jehovah does not waver. He attempts to offer up his son and heir but is stopped by Jehovah, who provides a ram as a substitute sacrifice. Jehovah again confirms His promise to Abraham, saying that He will multiply Abraham's seed like the stars of heaven and the grains of sand that are on the seashore. He shows that this seed will take possession of the gate of his enemies and that all nations of the earth will certainly bless themselves by means of the Seed.

20 Sarah dies at the age of 127 and is buried in a field that Abraham buys from the sons of Heth. Abraham now sends his chief household servant to obtain a wife for Isaac from the country of his relatives. Jehovah guides the servant to the family of Nahor's son Bethuel, and arrangements are made for Rebekah to return with him. Rebekah goes willingly, with her family's blessing, and becomes the bride of Isaac. Abraham, on his part, takes another wife, Keturah, who bears him six sons. However, he gives these gifts and sends them away and makes Isaac his sole heir. Then, at the age of 175, Abraham dies.

21 As Jehovah had foretold, Isaac's half brother Ishmael becomes the head of a great nation, founded upon his 12 chieftain-sons. For 20 years Rebekah remains barren, but Isaac keeps on entreating Jehovah, and she gives birth to twins, Esau and Jacob, of whom Jehovah had told her the older would serve the younger. Isaac is now 60 years old.

22 **Jacob and his 12 sons** (25:27–37:1). Esau becomes a lover of hunting. Failing to appreciate the covenant with Abraham, he returns from the hunt one day and sells his birthright to Jacob for a mere swallow of stew. He also marries two Hittite women (and later an Ishmaelite), who become a source of bitterness to his parents. With his mother's assistance, Jacob disguises himself as Esau in

order to obtain the firstborn's blessing. Esau, who had not revealed to Isaac that he had sold the birthright, now plans to kill Jacob when he learns of what Jacob has done, so Rebekah advises that Jacob flee to Haran to her brother Laban. Before Jacob leaves, Isaac blesses him again and instructs him to take as a wife, not a pagan, but someone from his mother's household. At Bethel, on his way to Haran, in a dream he sees Jehovah, who reassures him and confirms the covenant promise toward him.

23 At Haran, Jacob works for Laban, marrying his two daughters, Leah and Rachel. Though this polygamous marriage is brought on him by a trick of Laban, God blesses it by giving Jacob 12 sons and a daughter through the wives and their two maidservants, Zilpah and Bilhah. God sees to it that the flocks of Jacob increase greatly and then instructs him to return to the land of his forefathers. He is pursued by Laban, but they make a covenant at the place called Galeed and The Watchtower (Hebrew, ham·Mits·pah'). Resuming the journey, Jacob is reassured by angels and grapples at night with an angel, who finally blesses him and changes his name from Jacob to Israel. Jacob peacefully negotiates a meeting with Esau and travels on to Shechem. Here his daughter, Dinah, is violated by the Hivite chieftain's son. Her brothers Simeon and Levi take revenge by slaughtering the men of Shechem. This displeases Jacob because it gives him, as a representative of Jehovah, a bad name in the land. God tells him to go to Bethel to make an altar there. On the trek out of Bethel, Rachel dies while bearing to Jacob his 12th son, Benjamin. Reuben violates Rachel's maidservant, Bilhah, the mother of two of Jacob's sons, and for this he forfeits the birthright. Soon afterward Isaac dies, at 180 years of age, and Esau and Jacob bury him.

24 Esau and his household move to the mountainous region of Seir, the accumulated wealth of Esau and Jacob being too great to permit their dwelling together any longer. The lists of Esau's offspring as well as the sheiks and the kings of Edom are given. Jacob continues dwelling in Canaan.

25 **To Egypt for the preservation of life** (37: 2–50:26). Because of Jehovah's favor and some dreams that he causes Joseph to have, the older brothers come to hate Joseph. They scheme to kill him but instead sell him to some passing Ishmaelite merchants. Dipping Joseph's striped garment

---

19. What test does Abraham meet successfully in connection with the Seed, and what does Jehovah further reveal in confirming His promise?
20. What care does Abraham exercise in providing Isaac with a wife, and how is Isaac made sole heir?
21. How do Isaac and Rebekah come to have twin sons?
22. How do Esau and Jacob view the covenant with Abraham, and with what results?

---

23. (a) How does Jacob come to have 12 sons? (b) How does Reuben forfeit the birthright?
24. Why do Esau and his household move to the mountainous region of Seir?
25. What events lead to Joseph's becoming a slave in Egypt?

in the blood of a goat, they present it to Jacob as evidence that the young lad of 17 has been killed by a wild beast. Joseph is taken to Egypt and sold to Potiphar, the chief of Pharaoh's bodyguard.

[26] Chapter 38 digresses momentarily to give the account of the birth of Perez to Tamar, who, by strategy, causes Judah her father-in-law to perform the marriage due toward her that should have been performed by his son. This account again underlines the extreme care with which the Scriptures record each development leading to the production of the Seed of promise. Judah's son Perez becomes one of the ancestors of Jesus. —Luke 3:23, 33.

[27] Meanwhile, Jehovah blesses Joseph in Egypt, and Joseph becomes great in Potiphar's household. However, difficulty pursues him when he refuses to reproach God's name by fornication with Potiphar's wife, so he is falsely accused and thrown into prison. There he is used by Jehovah in interpreting the dreams of two fellow prisoners, Pharaoh's cupbearer and his baker. Later, when Pharaoh has a dream that greatly worries him, Joseph's ability is called to his attention, so that he is quickly brought to Pharaoh from his prison hole. Giving the credit to God, Joseph interprets the dream as forecasting seven years of plenty, to be followed by seven years of famine. Pharaoh recognizes "the spirit of God" upon Joseph and appoints him prime minister to handle the situation. (Gen. 41:38) Now 30 years of age, Joseph administers wisely by storing up foodstuffs during the seven years of plenty. Then during the worldwide famine that follows, he sells the grain to the people of Egypt and of other nations who come to Egypt for food.

[28] Eventually Jacob sends his ten older sons to Egypt for grain. Joseph recognizes them, but they do not recognize him. Holding Simeon as hostage, he demands that they bring their youngest brother back with them on the next trip for grain. When the nine sons return with Benjamin, Joseph reveals himself, expresses forgiveness toward the ten guilty ones, and instructs them to get Jacob and move to Egypt for their welfare during the famine. Accordingly, Jacob, with 66 of his offspring, moves down to Egypt. Pharaoh gives them the best of the land, the land of Goshen, in which to dwell.

[29] As Jacob draws close to death, he blesses Ephraim and Manasseh, the sons of Joseph, and then calls his own 12 sons together to tell them what will happen to them "in the final part of the days." (49:1) He now gives in detail a series of prophecies, all of which have since come to remarkable fulfillment.* Here he foretells that the scepter of rulership will remain in the tribe of Judah until the coming of Shiloh (meaning "He Whose It Is; He to Whom It Belongs"), the promised Seed. After thus blessing the heads of the 12 tribes and giving commands concerning his own future burial in the Land of Promise, Jacob dies at the age of 147 years. Joseph continues to care for his brothers and their households until his own death at 110 years of age, at which time he expresses his faith that God will again bring Israel into their land and requests that his bones too be taken to that Land of Promise.

WHY BENEFICIAL

[30] As the beginning of the inspired Word of God, Genesis is of inestimable benefit in introducing the glorious purposes of Jehovah God. What a basis it provides for understanding the later Bible books! Within its broad scope, it describes the beginning and end of the righteous world in Eden, the development and disastrous flushing out of the first world of ungodly people, and the rise of the present evil world. Outstandingly, it sets the theme for the entire Bible, namely, the vindication of Jehovah through the Kingdom ruled by the promised "seed." It shows why man dies. From Genesis 3:15 forward—and especially in the record of God's dealings with Abraham, Isaac, and Jacob—it holds forth the hope of life in the new world under the Kingdom of the Seed. It is beneficial in pointing out the proper objective for all mankind—to be integrity keepers and sanctifiers of Jehovah's name. —Rom. 5:12, 18; Heb. 11:3-22, 39, 40; 12:1; Matt. 22:31, 32.

[31] The Christian Greek Scriptures make reference to every prominent event and person recorded in the book of Genesis. Moreover, as shown throughout the Scriptures, the prophecies recorded in Genesis have been unerringly fulfilled. One of these, the "four hundred years" of affliction on Abraham's seed, commenced when Ishmael mocked Isaac in 1913 B.C.E. and ended with the deliverance from Egypt in 1513 B.C.E.# (Gen. 15:

---

* *The Watchtower,* 1962, pages 360-74, 392-408.
# *Insight on the Scriptures,* Vol. 1, pages 460-1, 776.

---

26. Why is the account of Perez' birth important?
27. How does Joseph become prime minister of Egypt?
28. What events surround the moving of Jacob's household to Egypt?
29. What important series of prophecies does Jacob make on his deathbed?

30. (a) What basis does Genesis provide for understanding the later Bible books? (b) To what proper objective does Genesis point?
31. By reference to the accompanying chart, show that Genesis contains (a) meaningful prophecies and (b) valuable principles.

13) Examples of other meaningful prophecies and their fulfillment are shown in the accompanying chart. Also of immense benefit in building faith and understanding are the divine principles first stated in Genesis. The prophets of old, as well as Jesus and his disciples, frequently referred to and applied passages from the book of Genesis. We will do well to follow their example, and a study of the accompanying chart should assist in this.

[32] Genesis very clearly reveals God's will and purpose concerning marriage, the proper relationship of husband and wife, and the principles of headship and family training. Jesus himself drew on this information, quoting both the first and second chapters of Genesis in his one statement: "Did you not read that he who created them from the beginning made them male and female and said, 'For this reason a man will leave his father and his mother and will stick to his wife, and the two will be one flesh'?" (Matt. 19:4, 5; Gen. 1:27; 2:24) The record in Genesis is essential in providing the genealogy of the human family and also in calculating the time that man has been on this earth.—Gen., chaps. 5, 7, 10, 11.

[33] Also of real benefit to the student of the Scriptures is the study of patriarchal society that Genesis affords. Patriarchal society was the community form of family government that operated among God's people from Noah's day until the Law was given at Mount Sinai. Many of the details incorporated in the Law covenant were already being practiced in patriarchal society. Such principles as community merit (18:32), community responsibility (19:15), capital punishment as well as sanctity of blood and of life (9:4-6), and God's hatred of the glorifying of men (11:4-8) have affected mankind throughout history. Many legal practices and terms throw light on later events, even down to the days of Jesus. Patriarchal law governing the custody of persons and property

GENESIS—INSPIRED AND BENEFICIAL

Genesis Texts	Principle	References From Other Writers
1:27; 2:24	Sacredness, permanence of marriage bond	Matt. 19:4, 5
2:7	Man is a soul	1 Cor. 15:45
2:22, 23	Headship	1 Tim. 2:13; 1 Cor. 11:8
9:4	Sacredness of blood	Acts 15:20, 29
20:3	Adultery wrong	1 Cor. 6:9
24:3; 28:1-8	Marry only believer	1 Cor. 7:39
28:7	Obedience to parents	Eph. 6:1

Prophecies Fulfilled and Prophetic Parallels

12:1-3; 22:15-18	Identification of Abraham's Seed	Gal. 3:16, 29
14:18	Melchizedek typifies Christ	Heb. 7:13-15
16:1-4, 15	Pictorial meaning of Sarah, Hagar, Ishmael, Isaac	Gal. 4:21-31
17:11	Pictorial meaning of circumcision	Rom. 2:29
49:1-28	Jacob's blessing on the 12 tribes	Josh. 14:1–21:45
49:9	Lion that is of the tribe of Judah	Rev. 5:5

Other Texts Used by Prophets, Jesus, and Disciples—In Illustration, in Application, or as Example—Further Proving Authenticity of Genesis

1:1	God created heaven and earth	Isa. 45:18; Rev. 10:6
1:26	Man made in God's image	1 Cor. 11:7
1:27	Man made, male and female	Matt. 19:4; Mark 10:6
2:2	God rested on seventh day	Heb. 4:4
3:1-6	Serpent deceived Eve	2 Cor. 11:3
3:20	All mankind from original pair	Acts 17:26
4:8	Cain killed Abel	Jude 11; 1 John 3:12
4:9, 10	Abel's blood	Matt. 23:35
Chaps. 5, 10, 11	Genealogy	Luke, chap. 3
5:21	Enoch	Jude 14
5:29	Noah	Ezek. 14:14; Matt. 24:37
6:13, 17-20	Flood	Isa. 54:9; 2 Pet. 2:5
12:1-3, 7	Abrahamic covenant	Gal. 3:15-17
15:6	Faith of Abraham	Rom. 4:3; Jas. 2:23
15:13, 14	Sojourn in Egypt	Acts 7:1-7
18:1-5	Hospitality	Heb. 13:2
19:24, 25	Sodom and Gomorrah destroyed	2 Pet. 2:6; Jude 7
19:26	Wife of Lot	Luke 17:32
20:7	Abraham a prophet	Ps. 105:9, 15
21:9	Ishmael taunts Isaac	Gal. 4:29
22:10	Abraham attempts to offer up Isaac	Heb. 11:17
25:23	Jacob and Esau	Rom. 9:10-13; Mal. 1:2, 3
25:32-34	Esau sells birthright	Heb. 12:16, 17
28:12	Ladder of communication with heaven	John 1:51
37:28	Joseph sold into Egypt	Ps. 105:17
41:40	Joseph made prime minister	Ps. 105:20, 21

(Gen. 31:38, 39; 37:29-33; John 10:11, 15; 17:12; 18:9) and the manner of conveying property (Gen. 23:3-18), as well as the law governing the inheritance of one who received the right of the firstborn (48:22), must be known if we are to have the background needed to gain a clear understanding of the Bible. Other practices of patriarchal society incorporated in the Law were sacrifices, circumcision (given first to Abraham), the making of covenants, brother-in-law marriage (38:8, 11, 26), and the use of oaths to confirm a matter.—22:16; 24:3.*

[34] Genesis, the opening book of the Bible, pro-

---

32. What important information does Genesis contain on marriage, genealogy, and the count of time?
33. Name some principles and practices of patriarchal society that are important to understanding the Bible.

---

* *The Watchtower*, 1952, pages 432-45.

---

34. What lessons, valuable to Christians, may be learned through the study of Genesis?

vides many lessons in integrity, faith, faithfulness, obedience, respect, good manners, and courage. Here are a few examples: Enoch's faith and courage in walking with God in the face of violent enemies; Noah's righteousness, faultlessness, and implicit obedience; Abraham's faith, his determination, and his endurance, his sense of responsibility as a family head and teacher of God's commands to his children, his generosity, and his love; Sarah's submissiveness to her husband-head and her industriousness; Jacob's mildness of temper and his concern for the promise of God; Joseph's obedience to his father, his moral uprightness, his courage, his good conduct in prison, his respect for superior authorities, his humility in giving glory to God, and his merciful forgiveness of his brothers;

the consuming desire of all these men to sanctify Jehovah's name. These exemplary traits stand out in the lives of those who walked with God during the long period of 2,369 years from the creation of Adam to the death of Joseph, as covered in the book of Genesis.

[35] Truly, the account in Genesis is beneficial in building up faith, presenting as it does such magnificent examples of faith, that tested quality of faith that reaches out for the city of God's building and creation, his Kingdom government that he long ago began to prepare through his Seed of promise, the leading sanctifier of Jehovah's great name.—Heb. 11:8, 10, 16.

---

35. In building faith, to what does Genesis point forward?

Bible Book Number 2
Exodus

Writer: **Moses**

Place Written: **Wilderness**

Writing Completed: **1512 B.C.E.**

Time Covered: **1657-1512 B.C.E.**

THE soul-stirring accounts of momentous signs and miracles that Jehovah performed in delivering his name people from the afflictions of Egypt, his organizing of Israel as his special property as "a kingdom of priests and a holy nation," and the beginning of Israel's history as a theocratic nation—these are the highlights of the Bible book of Exodus. (Ex. 19:6) In Hebrew it is called *We'el'leh shemohth'*, meaning "Now these are the names," or simply *Shemohth'*, "Names," according to its first words. The modern-day name comes from the Greek *Septuagint,* where it is called *E'xo·dos,* which has been Latinized to *Exodus,* meaning "Going Forth" or "Departure." That Exodus is a continuation of the account in Genesis is shown by the opening word, "Now" (literally, "And"), and by the relisting of the names of Jacob's sons, as taken from the fuller record of Genesis 46:8-27.

[2] The book of Exodus reveals God's magnificent name, JEHOVAH, in all the brilliance of its glory

and sanctity. As he proceeded to demonstrate the depth of meaning of his name, God told Moses, "I SHALL PROVE TO BE WHAT I SHALL PROVE TO BE," and added that he should tell Israel, "I SHALL PROVE TO BE [Hebrew: אהיה, *'Eh·yeh'*, from the Hebrew verb *ha·yah'*] has sent me to you." The name JEHOVAH (יהוה, *YHWH*) comes from the kindred Hebrew verb *ha·wah'*, "become," and actually means "He Causes to Become." Certainly Jehovah's mighty and fearsome acts that he now proceeded to bring to pass in behalf of his people, Israel, magnified and clothed that name in a resplendent glory, making it a memorial "to generation after generation," *the name* to be revered for an eternity of time. It is of all things most beneficial that we know the wonderful history surrounding that name and that we worship the only true God, the One who declares, "I am Jehovah."*—Ex. 3: 14, 15; 6:6.

[3] Moses is the writer of Exodus, as is indicated

---

1. (a) What are the highlights of Exodus? (b) What names have been given Exodus, and of what account is it a continuation?

2. What does Exodus reveal concerning the name JEHOVAH?

---

* Exodus 3:14, footnote; *Insight on the Scriptures,* Vol. 2, page 12.

---

3. (a) How do we know that Moses was the writer of Exodus? (b) When was Exodus written, and what period does it cover?

by its being the second volume of the Pentateuch. The book itself registers three instances of Moses' making a written record at the direction of Jehovah. (17:14; 24:4; 34:27) According to Bible scholars Westcott and Hort, Jesus and the writers of the Christian Greek Scriptures quote or refer to Exodus more than 100 times, as when Jesus said: "Moses gave you the Law, did he not?" Exodus was written in the wilderness of Sinai, in the year 1512 B.C.E., a year after the sons of Israel had left Egypt. It covers a period of 145 years, from the death of Joseph in 1657 B.C.E. to the erection of the tabernacle of Jehovah's worship in 1512 B.C.E. —John 7:19; Ex. 1:6; 40:17.

4 Considering that the events of Exodus occurred about 3,500 years ago, there is a surprising amount of archaeological and other external evidence testifying to the accuracy of the record. Egyptian names are correctly used in Exodus, and titles mentioned correspond to Egyptian inscriptions. Archaeology shows that it was a custom of the Egyptians to allow foreigners to live in Egypt but to keep separate from them. The waters of the Nile were used for bathing, which calls to mind that Pharaoh's daughter bathed there. Bricks have been found made with and without straw. Also, in Egypt's heyday magicians were prominent.—Ex. 8:22; 2:5; 5:6, 7, 18; 7:11.

5 Monuments show that the Pharaohs personally led their charioteers into battle, and Exodus indicates that the Pharaoh of Moses' day followed this custom. How great must have been his humiliation! But how is it that ancient Egyptian records make no reference to the Israelites' sojourn in their land or to the calamity that befell Egypt? Archaeology has shown that it was the custom for a new Egyptian dynasty to erase anything uncomplimentary in previous records. They never recorded humiliating defeats. The blows against the gods of Egypt—such as the Nile god, the frog god, and the sun god—which discredited these false gods and showed Jehovah to be supreme, would not be suited to the annals of a proud nation.—14: 7-10; 15:4.*

6 Moses' 40 years of service as a shepherd under Jethro acquainted him with living conditions and locations of water and food in the area, thus well qualifying him to lead the Exodus. The exact route of the Exodus cannot be traced with certainty today, since the various sites mentioned in the

account cannot be definitely located. However, Marah, one of the early encampments in the Sinai Peninsula, is usually identified with 'Ein Hawwara, 50 miles SSE of modern Suez. Elim, the second encampment location, is traditionally identified with Wadi Gharandel, about 55 miles SSE of Suez. Interestingly, this modern site is known as a watering place with vegetation and palms, calling to mind the Biblical Elim, which had "twelve springs of water and seventy palm trees."* The authenticity of Moses' account, however, is not dependent upon archaeologists' corroboration of the various sites along the way.—15:23, 27.

7 The account of the construction of the tabernacle on the plains before Sinai fits in with local conditions. One scholar stated: "In form, structure, and materials, the tabernacle belongs altogether to the wilderness. The wood used in the structure is found there in abundance."# Whether it is in the field of names, customs, religion, places, geography, or materials, the accumulation of external evidence confirms the inspired Exodus account, now about 3,500 years old.

8 Other Bible writers referred to Exodus constantly, showing its prophetic significance and value. Over 900 years later, Jeremiah wrote of "the true God, the great One, the mighty One, Jehovah of armies being his name," who proceeded to bring his people, Israel, out of Egypt "with signs and with miracles and with a strong hand and with a stretched-out arm and with great fearsomeness." (Jer. 32:18-21) More than 1,500 years later, Stephen based much of the stirring testimony that led to his martyrdom on the information in Exodus. (Acts 7:17-44) The life of Moses is cited for us as an example of faith at Hebrews 11:23-29, and Paul makes other frequent references to Exodus in setting forth examples and warnings for us today. (Acts 13:17; 1 Cor. 10:1-4, 11, 12; 2 Cor. 3: 7-16) All of this helps us to appreciate how the parts of the Bible are interwoven one with another, each portion sharing in the revelation of Jehovah's purpose in a way that is beneficial.

CONTENTS OF EXODUS

9 **Jehovah commissions Moses, emphasizing His own Memorial Name** (1:1–4:31). After naming the sons of Israel who have come down into Egypt, Exodus next records the death of Joseph. In

---

* Insight on the Scriptures, Vol. 1, pages 532, 535; Archaeology and Bible History, 1964, J. P. Free, page 98.

4, 5. What archaeological evidence supports the Exodus account?
6. With what locations are the Israelites' early encampments generally identified?

---

* Insight on the Scriptures, Vol. 1, pages 540-1.
# Exodus, 1874, F. C. Cook, page 247.

---

7. What other evidence, including the tabernacle construction, confirms Exodus as inspired?
8. How is Exodus shown to be interwoven with the rest of the Scriptures as inspired and beneficial?
9. Under what circumstances is Moses born and reared?

time a new king arises over Egypt. When he sees that the Israelites keep on "multiplying and growing mightier at a very extraordinary rate," he adopts repressive measures, including forced labor, and tries to reduce Israel's male population by ordering the destruction of all newborn male children. (1:7) It is under these circumstances that a son is born to an Israelite of the house of Levi. This child is the third in the family. When he is three months old, his mother hides him in a papyrus ark among the reeds by the bank of the Nile River. He is found by the daughter of Pharaoh, who likes the boy and adopts him. His own mother becomes his nursemaid, and as a result, he grows up in an Israelite home. Later on he is brought to Pharaoh's court. He is named Moses, meaning "Drawn Out [that is, saved out of water]."—Ex. 2:10; Acts 7:17-22.

[10] This Moses is interested in the welfare of his fellow Israelites. He kills an Egyptian for mistreating an Israelite. As a result, he has to flee, and so he comes into the land of Midian. There he marries Zipporah the daughter of Jethro, the priest of Midian. In time Moses becomes father to two sons, Gershom and Eliezer. Then, at the age of 80, after he has spent 40 years in the wilderness, Moses is commissioned by Jehovah for a special service in sanctification of Jehovah's name. One day while shepherding Jethro's flock near Horeb, "the mountain of the true God," Moses sees a thornbush that is aflame but is not consumed. When he goes to investigate, he is addressed by an angel of Jehovah, who tells him of God's purpose to bring His people "the sons of Israel out of Egypt." (Ex. 3:1, 10) Moses is to be used as Jehovah's instrument in freeing Israel from Egyptian bondage.—Acts 7:23-35.

[11] Moses then asks how he is to identify God to the sons of Israel. It is here, for the first time, that Jehovah makes known the real meaning of his name, associating it with his specific purpose and establishing it as a memorial. "This is what you are to say to the sons of Israel, 'I SHALL PROVE TO BE has sent me to you . . . Jehovah the God of your forefathers, the God of Abraham, the God of Isaac and the God of Jacob, has sent me to you.'" His name, Jehovah, identifies him as the one who will cause his purposes in connection with his name people to come to pass. To this people, the descendants of Abraham, he will give the land promised to their forefathers, "a land flowing with milk and honey."—Ex. 3:14, 15, 17.

[12] Jehovah explains to Moses that the king of Egypt will not let the Israelites go free but that He will first have to strike Egypt with all His wonderful acts. Moses' brother, Aaron, is given to him as spokesman, and they receive three signs to perform to convince the Israelites that they come in the name of Jehovah. While on the way to Egypt, Moses' son has to be circumcised to prevent a death in the family, reminding Moses of God's requirements. (Gen. 17:14) Moses and Aaron gather the older men of the sons of Israel and inform them of Jehovah's purpose to bring them out of Egypt and to take them to the Promised Land. They perform the signs, and the people believe.

[13] **The blows on Egypt** (5:1–10:29). Moses and Aaron now go in to Pharaoh and announce that Jehovah, the God of Israel, has said: "Send my people away." In a scornful tone, proud Pharaoh replies: "Who is Jehovah, so that I should obey his voice to send Israel away? I do not know Jehovah at all and, what is more, I am not going to send Israel away." (5:1, 2) Instead of freeing the Israelites, he imposes harder tasks on them. However, Jehovah renews his promises of deliverance, again tying this in with the sanctification of his name: "I am Jehovah . . . I shall indeed prove to be God to you . . . I am Jehovah."—6:6-8.

[14] The sign Moses performs before Pharaoh, by having Aaron throw down his rod to become a big snake, is imitated by the magic-practicing priests of Egypt. Although their snakes are swallowed up by Aaron's big snake, still Pharaoh's heart becomes obstinate. Jehovah now proceeds to bring ten successive heavy blows upon Egypt. First, their river Nile and all the waters of Egypt turn to blood. Then a plague of frogs comes upon them. These two blows are imitated by the magic-practicing priests, but the third blow, that of gnats on man and beast, is not. The priests of Egypt have to recognize that this is "the finger of God." However, Pharaoh will not send Israel away. —8:19.

[15] The first three blows come upon Egyptians and Israelites alike, but from the fourth one on, only the Egyptians are afflicted, Israel standing distinct under Jehovah's protection. The fourth blow is heavy swarms of gadflies. Then comes pestilence upon all the livestock of Egypt, followed

---

10. What events lead to Moses' being commissioned for special service?
11. In what special sense does Jehovah now make known his name?

12. What does Jehovah explain to Moses as to freeing the Israelites, and how do the people accept the signs?
13. What results from Moses' first encounter with Pharaoh?
14. How are the Egyptians compelled to recognize "the finger of God"?
15. Which blows afflict only the Egyptians, and why only does Jehovah permit Pharaoh to continue?

by boils with blisters on man and beast, so that even the magic-practicing priests are unable to stand before Moses. Jehovah again lets Pharaoh's heart become obstinate, declaring to him through Moses: "But, in fact, for this cause I have kept you in existence, for the sake of showing you my power and in order to have my name declared in all the earth." (9:16) Moses then announces to Pharaoh the next blow, "a very heavy hail," and here the Bible registers for the first time that some among Pharaoh's servants fear Jehovah's word and act on it. The eighth and ninth blows —an invasion of locusts and a gloomy darkness— follow in quick succession, and the obstinate, enraged Pharaoh threatens Moses with death if he tries to see his face again.—9:18.

16 The Passover and striking of the firstborn (11:1–13:16). Jehovah now declares, "One plague more I am going to bring upon Pharaoh and Egypt"—the death of the firstborn. (11:1) He orders that the month of Abib be the first of the months for Israel. On the 10th day, they are to take a sheep or a goat—a male, one year old, unblemished—and on the 14th day, they are to kill it. On that evening they must take the blood of the animal and splash it on the two doorposts and the upper part of the doorway, and then they must stay inside the house and eat the roasted animal, of which not one bone is to be broken. There is to be no leaven in the house, and they must eat in haste, dressed and equipped for marching. The Passover is to serve as a memorial, a festival to Jehovah throughout their generations. It is to be followed by the seven-day Feast of Unfermented Cakes. Their sons must be fully instructed in the meaning of all of this. (Later, Jehovah gives further instructions concerning these feasts, and he commands that all firstborn males belonging to Israel, both men and beasts, must be sanctified to him.)

17 Israel does as Jehovah commands. Then disaster strikes! At midnight Jehovah kills all the firstborn of Egypt, while passing over and delivering the firstborn of Israel. "Get out from the midst of my people," shouts Pharaoh. And 'the Egyptians begin to urge the people' to get away quickly. (12: 31, 33) The Israelites do not leave empty-handed, for they ask for and receive from the Egyptians articles of silver and of gold and clothing. They march out of Egypt in battle formation, to the number of 600,000 able-bodied men, together with their families and a vast mixed company of non-Israelites, as well as a numerous stock of

animals. This marks the end of 430 years from Abraham's crossing of the Euphrates to enter the land of Canaan. This is indeed a night to be memorialized.—Ex. 12:40, second footnote; Gal. 3:17.

18 Jehovah's name sanctified at the Red Sea (13:17–15:21). Guiding them by day in a pillar of cloud and by night in a pillar of fire, Jehovah leads Israel out by way of Succoth. Again Pharaoh grows obstinate, chasing them with his chosen chariots of war and trapping them, so he thinks, at the Red Sea. Moses reassures the people, saying: "Do not be afraid. Stand firm and see the salvation of Jehovah, which he will perform for you today." (14:13) Jehovah then makes the sea go back, forming an escape corridor through which Moses leads the Israelites safely to the eastern shore. Pharaoh's mighty hosts rush in after them, only to be trapped and drowned in the returning waters. What a climactic sanctification of Jehovah's name! What grand cause for rejoicing in him! That rejoicing is then expressed in the Bible's first great song of victory: "Let me sing to Jehovah, for he has become highly exalted. The horse and its rider he has pitched into the sea. My strength and my might is Jah, since he serves for my salvation. . . . Jehovah will rule as king to time indefinite, even forever." —15:1, 2, 18.

19 Jehovah makes Law covenant at Sinai (15: 22–34:35). In successive stages, as guided by Jehovah, Israel travels toward Sinai, the mountain of the true God. When the people murmur about the bitter water at Marah, Jehovah makes it sweet for them. Again, when they murmur about the lack of meat and bread, he provides them quail in the evening and the sweetish manna, like dew on the ground, in the morning. This manna is to serve as bread for the Israelites for the next 40 years. Also, for the first time in history, Jehovah orders the observance of a rest day, or sabbath, having the Israelites pick up twice the quantity of manna on the sixth day and withholding the supply on the seventh. He also produces water for them at Rephidim and fights for them against Amalek, having Moses record His judgment that Amalek will be completely wiped out.

20 Moses' father-in-law, Jethro, then brings him his wife and two sons. The time has now come for better organization in Israel, and Jethro contributes some good practical counsel. He advises Moses not to carry the whole load himself but to appoint capable, God-fearing men to judge the people as chiefs of thousands, hundreds, fifties,

16. What does Jehovah command concerning the Passover and the Feast of Unfermented Cakes?
17. What events mark this as a night to be memorialized?

18. What climactic sanctification of Jehovah's name takes place at the Red Sea?
19. What events mark the journey toward Sinai?
20. How is better organization effected?

and tens. Moses does this, so that now only the difficult cases come to him.

[21] Within three months after the Exodus, Israel camps in the wilderness of Sinai. Jehovah here promises: "And now if you will strictly obey my voice and will indeed keep my covenant, then you will certainly become my special property out of all other peoples, because the whole earth belongs to me. And you yourselves will become to me a kingdom of priests and a holy nation." The people vow: "All that Jehovah has spoken we are willing to do." (19:5, 6, 8) Following a period of sanctification for Israel, Jehovah comes down on the third day upon the mountain, causing it to smoke and tremble.

[22] Jehovah then proceeds to give the Ten Words, or Ten Commandments. These stress exclusive devotion to Jehovah, while forbidding other gods, image worship, and the taking up of Jehovah's name in a worthless way. The Israelites are commanded to render service six days and then to keep a sabbath to Jehovah, and to honor father and mother. Laws against murder, adultery, stealing, testifying falsely, and covetousness complete the Ten Words. Then Jehovah goes on to set judicial decisions before them, instructions for the new nation, covering slavery, assault, injuries, compensation, theft, damage from fire, false worship, seduction, mistreatment of widows and orphans, loans, and many other matters. Sabbath laws are given, and three annual festivals are arranged for the worship of Jehovah. Moses then writes down the words of Jehovah, sacrifices are offered, and half the blood is sprinkled on the altar. The book of the covenant is read to the people, and after they again attest their willingness to obey, the rest of the blood is sprinkled on the book and on all the people. Thus Jehovah makes the Law covenant with Israel through the mediator, Moses.—Heb. 9:19, 20.

[23] Moses then goes up to Jehovah in the mountain to receive the Law. For 40 days and nights, he is given many instructions concerning the materials for the tabernacle, the details of its furnishings, minute specifications for the tabernacle itself, and the design for the priestly garments, including the plate of pure gold, inscribed "Holiness belongs to Jehovah," on Aaron's turban. The installation and service of the priesthood are de-

tailed, and Moses is reminded that the Sabbath will be a sign between Jehovah and the sons of Israel "to time indefinite." Moses is then given the two tablets of the Testimony written on by the 'finger of God.'—Ex. 28:36; 31:17, 18.

[24] In the meantime the people become impatient and ask Aaron to make a god to go ahead of them. Aaron does this, forming a golden calf, which the people worship in what he calls "a festival to Jehovah." (32:5) Jehovah speaks of exterminating Israel, but Moses intercedes for them, though he shatters the tablets in his own blazing anger. The sons of Levi now stand up on the side of pure worship, slaughtering 3,000 of the revelers. Jehovah also plagues them. After Moses implores God to continue leading his people, he is told he may glimpse the glory of God and is instructed to carve two additional tablets on which Jehovah will again write the Ten Words. When Moses goes up into the mountain the second time, Jehovah proceeds to declare to him the name of Jehovah as He goes passing by: "Jehovah, Jehovah, a God merciful and gracious, slow to anger and abundant in loving-kindness and truth, preserving loving-kindness for thousands." (34:6, 7) Then he states the terms of his covenant, and Moses writes it down as we have it today in Exodus. When Moses comes down from Mount Sinai, the skin of his face emits rays because of Jehovah's revealed glory. As a result, he has to put a veil over his face.—2 Cor. 3:7-11.

[25] **Construction of the tabernacle** (35:1–40:38). Moses then calls Israel together and transmits Jehovah's words to them, telling them that the willinghearted have the privilege of contributing to the tabernacle and the wisehearted the privilege of working on it. Soon it is reported to Moses: "The people are bringing much more than what the service needs for the work that Jehovah has commanded to be done." (36:5) Under Moses' direction workmen filled with Jehovah's spirit proceed to build the tabernacle and its furnishings and to make all the garments for the priests. One year after the Exodus, the tabernacle is completed and erected on the plain before Mount Sinai. Jehovah shows his approval by covering the tent of meeting with his cloud and by filling the tabernacle with his glory, so that Moses is not able to enter the tent. This same cloud by day and a fire by night mark Jehovah's guidance of Israel during all their journeyings. It is now the year 1512 B.C.E., and here the record of Exodus ends,

---

21. What promise does Jehovah next make, but on what conditions?

22. (a) What commandments are contained in the Ten Words? (b) What other judicial decisions are set before Israel, and how is the nation taken into the Law covenant?

23. What instructions does Jehovah provide Moses in the mountain?

---

24. (a) What sin do the people commit, and with what result? (b) How does Jehovah next reveal his name and glory to Moses?

25. What does the record relate concerning the tabernacle and the further manifestation of Jehovah's glory?

with the name of Jehovah gloriously sanctified through his marvelous works performed in behalf of Israel.

WHY BENEFICIAL

26 Preeminently, Exodus reveals Jehovah as the great Deliverer and Organizer and the Fulfiller of his magnificent purposes, and it establishes our faith in him. This faith is increased as we study the many references to Exodus in the Christian Greek Scriptures, indicating fulfillments of many features of the Law covenant, the assurance of a resurrection, Jehovah's provision to sustain his people, precedents for Christian relief work, counsel on consideration for parents, requirements for gaining life, and how to view retributive justice. The Law was finally summarized in two commands regarding the showing of love for God and fellowman.—Matt. 22:32—Ex. 4:5; John 6:31-35 and 2 Cor. 8:15—Ex. 16:4, 18; Matt. 15:4 and Eph. 6:2—Ex. 20:12; Matt. 5:26, 38, 39—Ex. 21: 24; Matt. 22:37-40.

27 At Hebrews 11:23-29 we read of the faith of Moses and his parents. By faith he left Egypt, by faith he celebrated the Passover, and by faith he led Israel through the Red Sea. The Israelites got baptized into Moses and ate spiritual food and drank spiritual drink. They looked forward to the spiritual rock-mass, or Christ, but still they did not have God's approval, for they put God to the test and became idolaters, fornicators, and murmurers. Paul explains that this has an application for Christians today: "Now these things went on befalling them as examples, and they were written for a warning to us upon whom the ends of the systems of things have arrived. Consequently let him that thinks he is standing beware that he does not fall."—1 Cor. 10:1-12; Hebrews 3:7-13.

28 Much of the deep spiritual significance of Exodus, together with its prophetic application, is given in Paul's writings, especially in Hebrews chapters 9 and 10. "For since the Law has a shadow of the good things to come, but not the very substance of the things, men can never with the same sacrifices from year to year which they offer continually make those who approach perfect." (Heb. 10:1) We are interested, therefore, in knowing the shadow and understanding the reality. Christ "offered one sacrifice for sins perpetually." He is described as "the Lamb of God." Not a bone of this "Lamb" was broken, just as in the type. The apostle Paul comments: "Christ our passover has been sacrificed. Consequently let us keep the festival, not with old leaven, neither with leaven of badness and wickedness, but with unfermented cakes of sincerity and truth."—Heb. 10:12; John 1:29 and 19:36—Ex. 12:46; 1 Cor. 5:7, 8—Ex. 23:15.

29 Jesus became the Mediator of a new covenant, as Moses had been mediator of the Law covenant. The contrast between these covenants is also clearly explained by the apostle Paul, who speaks of the 'handwritten document of decrees' having been taken out of the way by Jesus' death on the torture stake. The resurrected Jesus as High Priest is "a public servant of the holy place and of the true tent, which Jehovah put up, and not man." The priests under the Law rendered "sacred service in a typical representation and a shadow of the heavenly things" according to the pattern that was given by Moses. "But now Jesus has obtained a more excellent public service, so that he is also the mediator of a correspondingly better covenant, which has been legally established upon better promises." The old covenant became obsolete and was done away with as a code administering death. Those Jews not understanding this are described as having their perceptions dulled, but those believers who appreciate that spiritual Israel has come under a new covenant can "with unveiled faces reflect like mirrors the glory of Jehovah," being adequately qualified as its ministers. With cleansed consciences these are able to offer up their own "sacrifice of praise, that is, the fruit of lips which make public declaration to his name."—Col. 2:14; Heb. 8: 1-6, 13; 2 Cor. 3:6-18; Heb. 13:15; Ex. 34:27-35.

30 Exodus magnifies Jehovah's name and sovereignty, pointing forward to a glorious deliverance of the Christian nation of spiritual Israel, to whom it is said: "You are 'a chosen race, a royal priesthood, a holy nation, a people for special possession, that you should declare abroad the excellencies' of the one that called you out of darkness into his wonderful light. For you were once not a people, but are now God's people." Jehovah's power as demonstrated in gathering his spiritual Israel out of the world to magnify his name is no less miraculous than the power he showed in behalf of his people in ancient Egypt. In keeping Pharaoh in existence to show him His power and in order that His name might be declared, Jehovah foreshadowed a far greater testimony to be accomplished

---

26. (a) How does Exodus establish faith in Jehovah? (b) How do references to Exodus in the Christian Greek Scriptures increase our faith?
27. Of what benefit to the Christian is the historical record in Exodus?
28. How have the shadows of the Law and the Passover lamb been fulfilled?

---

29. (a) Contrast the Law covenant with the new covenant. (b) What sacrifices do spiritual Israelites now offer to God?
30. What did the deliverance of Israel and the magnifying of Jehovah's name in Egypt foreshadow?

through His Christian Witnesses.—1 Pet. 2:9, 10; Rom. 9:17; Rev. 12:17.

³¹ Thus, we can say from the Scriptures that the nation formed under Moses pointed forward to a new nation under Christ and to a kingdom that will never be shaken. In view of this, we are encouraged to "render God sacred service with

---

31. What does Exodus foreshadow as to a kingdom and Jehovah's presence?

godly fear and awe." Just as Jehovah's presence covered the tabernacle in the wilderness, so he promises to be eternally present with those who fear him: "Look! The tent of God is with mankind, and he will reside with them, and they will be his peoples. And God himself will be with them. . . . Write, because these words are faithful and true." Exodus is indeed an essential and beneficial part of the Bible record.—Ex. 19:16-19—Heb. 12: 18-29; Ex. 40:34—Rev. 21:3, 5.

Bible Book Number 3

Leviticus

Writer: **Moses**
Place Written: **Wilderness**
Writing Completed: **1512 B.C.E.**
Time Covered: **1 month (1512 B.C.E.)**

THE most common name for the third book of the Bible is Leviticus, which comes from *Leu·i·ti·kon´* of the Greek *Septuagint* by way of the Latin *Vulgate's "Leviticus."* This name is fitting, even though the Levites are given only passing mention (at 25:32, 33), for the book consists chiefly of the regulations of the Levitical priesthood, which was chosen from the tribe of Levi, and the laws that the priests taught the people: "For the lips of a priest are the ones that should keep knowledge, and the law is what people should seek from his mouth." (Mal. 2:7) In the Hebrew text, the book is named from its opening expression, *Wai·yiq·ra´*, literally, "And he proceeded to call." Among the later Jews, the book was also called Law of the Priests and Law of Offerings. —Lev. 1:1, footnote.

² There is no question but that Moses wrote Leviticus. The conclusion, or colophon, states: "These are the commandments that Jehovah gave Moses." (27:34) A similar statement is found at Leviticus 26:46. The evidence previously noted that proves that Moses wrote Genesis and Exodus also supports his writership of Leviticus, as the Pentateuch evidently was originally one scroll. Moreover, Leviticus is joined to the preceding books by the conjunction "and." The strongest testimony of all is that Jesus Christ and other inspired servants of Jehovah frequently quote or refer to the laws and principles in Leviticus and attribute them to Moses.—Lev. 23:34, 40-43 —Neh. 8:14, 15; Lev. 14:1-32—Matt. 8:2-4; Lev.

12:2—Luke 2:22; Lev. 12:3—John 7:22; Lev. 18:5—Rom. 10:5.

³ What time period does Leviticus cover? The book of Exodus concludes with the setting up of the tabernacle "in the first month, in the second year, on the first day of the month." The book of Numbers (immediately following the Leviticus account) opens with Jehovah's speaking to Moses "on the first day of the second month in the second year of their coming out of the land of Egypt." It follows, therefore, that not more than a lunar month could have elapsed for the few events of Leviticus, most of the book consisting of laws and regulations.—Ex. 40:17; Num. 1:1; Lev. 8:1–10:7; 24:10-23.

⁴ When did Moses write Leviticus? It is reasonable to conclude that he kept a record of events as they took place and wrote down God's instructions as he received them. This is implied by God's command to Moses to write down the doom of the Amalekites right after Israel had defeated them in battle. An early date is also suggested by certain matters in the book. For example, the Israelites were commanded to bring animals that they wanted to use for food to the entrance of the tent of meeting for slaughtering. This command would be given and recorded shortly after the installation of the priesthood. Many instructions are given for guiding the Israelites during their wilderness journey. All of this points to Moses' writing Leviticus during 1512 B.C.E.—Ex. 17:14; Lev. 17:3, 4; 26:46.

---

1. (a) Why is the name Leviticus fitting? (b) What other names have been given to Leviticus?
2. What evidence supports Moses' writership?

---

3. What time period is covered by Leviticus?
4. When was Leviticus written?

⁵ Why was Leviticus written? Jehovah had purposed to have a holy nation, a sanctified people, set apart for his service. From the time of Abel, faithful men of God had been offering sacrifices to Jehovah, but first with the nation of Israel did Jehovah give explicit instructions regarding sin offerings and other sacrifices. These, as explained in detail in Leviticus, made the Israelites aware of the exceeding sinfulness of sin and impressed upon their minds how displeasing it made them to Jehovah. These regulations, as part of the Law, served as a tutor leading the Jews to Christ, showing them the need of a Savior and at the same time serving to keep them as a people separate from the rest of the world. Especially did God's laws regarding ceremonial cleanness serve the latter purpose. —Lev. 11:44; Gal. 3:19-25.

⁶ As a new nation journeying toward a new land, Israel needed proper direction. It was still less than a year from the Exodus, and the living standards of Egypt as well as its religious practices were fresh in mind. Marriage of brother and sister was practiced in Egypt. False worship was carried on in honor of many gods, some of them animal gods. Now this large congregation was on its way to Canaan, where life and religious practices were even more degrading. But look again at the encampment of Israel. Swelling the congregation were many who were pure or part Egyptian, a mixed multitude who were living right in among the Israelites and who had been born of Egyptian parents and were raised and schooled in the ways, religion, and patriotism of the Egyptians. Many of these had undoubtedly indulged in detestable practices in their homeland only a short time before. How necessary that they now receive detailed guidance from Jehovah!

⁷ Leviticus bears the stamp of divine inspiration throughout. Mere humans could not have devised its wise and just laws and regulations. Its statutes regarding diet, disease, quarantine, and treatment of dead bodies reveal a knowledge of facts not appreciated by worldly men of medicine until thousands of years later. God's law regarding animals unclean for eating would protect the Israelites while they traveled. It would safeguard them against trichinosis from pigs, typhoid and paratyphoid from certain kinds of fish, and infection from animals found already dead. These practical laws were to direct their religion and their lives that they might remain a holy nation and reach

and inhabit the Promised Land. History shows that the regulations provided by Jehovah gave the Jews a definite advantage over other peoples in the matter of health.

⁸ The fulfillment of the prophecies and types in Leviticus further proves its inspiration. Both sacred and secular history record the fulfillment of the Leviticus warnings about the consequences of disobedience. Among other things, it foretold that mothers would eat their own children because of famine. Jeremiah indicates that this was fulfilled at the destruction of Jerusalem in 607 B.C.E., and Josephus tells of its happening at the city's later destruction, in 70 C.E. The prophetic promise that Jehovah would remember them if they repented found its fulfillment in their return from Babylon in 537 B.C.E. (Lev. 26:29, 41-45; Lam. 2:20; 4:10; Ezra 1:1-6) Further testifying to the inspiration of Leviticus are quotations other Bible writers make from it as inspired Scripture. In addition to those previously noted in establishing Moses as the writer, please see Matthew 5:38; 12:4; 2 Corinthians 6:16; and 1 Peter 1:16.

⁹ The book of Leviticus consistently magnifies Jehovah's name and sovereignty. No less than 36 times its laws are credited to Jehovah. The name Jehovah itself appears, on an average, ten times in each chapter, and time and again obedience to God's laws is inculcated by the reminder, "I am Jehovah." A theme of *holiness* runs throughout Leviticus, which mentions this requirement more often than any other Bible book. The Israelites were to be holy because Jehovah is holy. Certain persons, places, objects, and periods of time were set apart as holy. For example, the Day of Atonement and the Jubilee year were set aside as seasons of special observance in the worship of Jehovah.

¹⁰ In line with its emphasis on holiness, the book of Leviticus stresses the part that the shedding of blood, that is, the sacrifice of a life, played in the forgiveness of sins. The animal sacrifices were limited to creatures that were both domestic and clean. For certain sins confession, restoration, and the payment of a penalty were required in addition to a sacrifice. For still other sins, the penalty was death.

CONTENTS OF LEVITICUS

¹¹ Leviticus consists mostly of legislative writ-

---

5. What purpose was served by the laws concerning sacrifices and ceremonial uncleanness?
6. Why was detailed guidance from Jehovah now a special need?
7. In what way do the regulations of Leviticus bear the stamp of divine authorship?

8. How do the prophetic contents of Leviticus further prove inspiration?
9. How does Leviticus magnify Jehovah's name and holiness?
10. What is stressed in connection with sacrifices, and what penalties for sin are noted?
11. How may Leviticus be outlined?

ing, much of which is also prophetic. In the main the book follows a topical outline and may be divided into eight sections, which follow one another quite logically.

[12] **Regulations for sacrifices** (1:1–7:38). The various sacrifices fall into two general categories: *blood,* consisting of cattle, sheep, goats, and fowl; and *bloodless,* consisting of grain. The *blood* sacrifices are to be offered as either (1) burnt, (2) communion, (3) sin, or (4) guilt offerings. All four have these three things in common: The offerer must himself bring it to the entrance of the tent of meeting, he must lay his hands upon it, and then the animal is to be slaughtered. Following the sprinkling of the blood, the carcass must be disposed of according to the kind of sacrifice. Let us now consider the *blood* sacrifices in turn.

[13] (1) Burnt offerings may consist of a young bull, ram, goat, or pigeon or of a turtledove, depending upon the means of the offerer. It is to be cut in pieces and, except for the skin, is to be burned in its entirety upon the altar. In the case of a turtledove or a pigeon, the head must be nipped off but not severed, and the crop and feathers must be removed.—1:1-17; 6:8-13; 5:8.

[14] (2) The communion sacrifice may be either a male or a female, of the cattle or of the flocks. Only its fatty parts will be consumed upon the altar, a certain portion going to the priest and the rest being eaten by the offerer. It is well termed a communion sacrifice, for by it the offerer shares a meal, or has communion, as it were, with Jehovah and with the priest.—3:1-17; 7:11-36.

[15] (3) A sin offering is required for unintentional sins, or sins committed by mistake. The type of animal offered depends upon whose sin is being atoned for—that of the priest, the people as a whole, a chieftain, or an ordinary person. Unlike the voluntary burnt and communion offerings for individuals, the sin offering is mandatory.—4:1-35; 6:24-30.

[16] (4) Guilt offerings are required to cover personal guilt due to unfaithfulness, deception, or robbery. In some instances guilt requires confession and a sacrifice according to one's means. In others, compensation equivalent to the loss plus 20 percent and the sacrifice of a ram are required. In this section of Leviticus dealing with the offerings, the eating of blood is emphatically and repeatedly forbidden.—5:1–6:7; 7:1-7, 26, 27; 3:17.

[17] The *bloodless* sacrifices are to consist of grain and are to be offered either whole roasted, coarse ground, or as fine flour; and they are to be prepared in various ways, such as baked, done on a griddle, or fried in deep fat. They are to be offered with salt and oil and at times with frankincense, but they must be wholly free of leaven or honey. With some sacrifices a portion will belong to the priest.—2:1-16.

[18] **Installation of the priesthood** (8:1–10:20). The time now comes for a great occasion in Israel, the installation of the priesthood. Moses handles it in all its detail, just as Jehovah commanded him. "And Aaron and his sons proceeded to do all the things that Jehovah had commanded by means of Moses." (8:36) After the seven days occupied with the installation, there comes a miraculous and faith-strengthening spectacle. The whole assembly is present. The priests have just offered up sacrifice. Aaron and Moses have blessed the people. Then, look! "Jehovah's glory appeared to all the people, and fire came out from before Jehovah and began consuming the burnt offering and the fatty pieces upon the altar. When all the people got to see it, they broke out into shouting and went falling upon their faces." (9:23, 24) Indeed, Jehovah is worthy of their obedience and worship!

[19] Yet there are transgressions of the Law. For example, Aaron's sons Nadab and Abihu offer illegitimate fire before Jehovah. "At this a fire came out from before Jehovah and consumed them, so that they died before Jehovah." (10:2) In order to offer acceptable sacrifice and enjoy Jehovah's approval, people and priest alike must follow Jehovah's instructions. Right after this, God gives the command that priests must not drink alcoholic beverages while serving at the tabernacle, implying that intoxication may have contributed to the wrongdoing of Aaron's two sons.

[20] **Laws on cleanness** (11:1–15:33). This section deals with ceremonial and hygienic cleanness. Certain animals, both domestic and wild, are unclean. All dead bodies are unclean and cause those who touch them to become unclean. The birth of a child also brings uncleanness and requires separation and special sacrifices.

[21] Certain skin diseases, such as leprosy, also cause ceremonial uncleanness, and cleansing is to apply not only to persons but even to clothing and houses. Quarantining is required. Menstruation

---

12. What kinds of blood sacrifices are there, and how must they be offered?
13-16. (a) Outline the requirements for (1) burnt offerings, (2) communion sacrifices, (3) sin offerings, and (4) guilt offerings. (b) In connection with blood sacrifices, what is repeatedly forbidden?

17. How are bloodless sacrifices to be offered?
18. With what faith-strengthening spectacle is the installation of the priesthood climaxed?
19. What transgression takes place, followed by what?
20, 21. What regulations cover cleanness and proper hygiene?

and seminal emissions likewise result in uncleanness, as do running discharges. Separateness is required in these cases, and on recovery, in addition, the washing of the body or offering of sacrifices or both are required.

[22] **Day of Atonement** (16:1-34). This is an outstanding chapter, for it contains the instructions for Israel's most important day, the Day of Atonement, which falls on the tenth day of the seventh month. It is a day to afflict the soul (most likely by fasting), and on it no secular work will be permitted. It begins with the offering of a young bull for the sins of Aaron and his household, the tribe of Levi, followed by the offering of a goat for the rest of the nation. After the burning of incense, some of the blood of each animal is to be brought, in turn, into the Most Holy of the tabernacle, to be sprinkled before the Ark's cover. Later the animal carcasses must be taken outside the camp and burned. On this day a live goat is also to be presented before Jehovah, and upon it all the sins of the people are to be pronounced, after which it is to be led off into the wilderness. Then two rams must be offered as burnt offerings, one for Aaron and his household and the other for the rest of the nation.

[23] **Statutes on blood and other matters** (17:1–20:27). This section sets out many statutes for the people. Once again blood is prohibited in one of the most explicit statements on blood to be found anywhere in the Scriptures. (17:10-14) Blood may properly be used on the altar, but not for eating. Detestable practices, such as incest, sodomy, and bestiality, are forbidden. There are regulations for the protection of the afflicted, the lowly, and the alien, and the command is given, "You must love your fellow as yourself. I am Jehovah." (19:18) The social and economic well-being of the nation is guarded, and spiritual dangers, such as the worship of Molech and spiritism, are outlawed, with death as the penalty. Again God emphasizes separateness for his people: "And you must prove yourselves holy to me, because I Jehovah am holy; and I am proceeding to divide you off from the peoples to become mine."—20:26.

[24] **The priesthood and festivals** (21:1–25:55). The next three chapters deal chiefly with Israel's formal worship: the statutes governing the priests, their physical qualifications, whom they may marry, who may eat holy things, and the requirements for sound animals to be used in sacrifices. Three

national seasonal feasts are commanded, providing occasions to "rejoice before Jehovah your God." (23:40) As one man, the nation in this way will turn attention, praise, and worship to Jehovah, strengthening its relationship with him. These are feasts to Jehovah, annual holy conventions. The Passover, along with the Festival of Unfermented Cakes, is set for early spring; Pentecost, or the Festival of Weeks, follows in the late spring; and the Atonement Day and eight-day Festival of Booths, or of Ingathering, are in the fall.

[25] In chapter 24, instruction is given concerning the bread and oil to be used in the tabernacle service. There follows the incident in which Jehovah rules that anyone abusing "the Name"—yes, *the* name Jehovah—must be stoned to death. He then states the law of punishment in kind, "eye for eye, tooth for tooth." (24:11-16, 20) In chapter 25, regulations are found regarding the year-long Sabbath, or rest year, to be held every 7th year and the Jubilee every 50th year. In this 50th year, liberty must be proclaimed in all the land, and hereditary property that was sold or surrendered during the past 49 years must be restored. Laws protecting the rights of the poor and of slaves are given. In this section the number "seven" appears prominently—the seventh day, the seventh year, festivals of seven days, a period of seven weeks, and the Jubilee, to come after seven times seven years.

[26] **Consequences of obedience and disobedience** (26:1-46). The book of Leviticus reaches its climax in this chapter. Jehovah here lists the rewards for obedience and the punishments for disobedience. At the same time, he holds out hope for the Israelites if they humble themselves, saying: "I will remember in their behalf the covenant of the ancestors whom I brought forth out of the land of Egypt under the eyes of the nations, in order to prove myself their God. I am Jehovah."—26:45.

[27] **Other statutes** (27:1-34). Leviticus concludes with instructions on handling vow offerings, on the firstborn for Jehovah, and on the tenth part that becomes holy to Jehovah. Then comes the brief colophon: "These are the commandments that Jehovah gave Moses as commands to the sons of Israel in Mount Sinai."—27:34.

WHY BENEFICIAL

[28] As a part of the inspired Scriptures, the book of Leviticus is of great benefit to Christians today. It is of wonderful help in appreciating Jehovah, his

---

22. (a) Why is chapter 16 outstanding? (b) What is the Atonement Day procedure?
23. (a) Where do we find one of the Bible's most explicit statements on blood? (b) What other regulations follow?
24. What does Leviticus outline as to priestly qualifications and seasonal feasts?

25. (a) How is it shown that "the Name" must be held in honor? (b) What regulations involve the number "seven"?
26. In what does Leviticus reach its climax?
27. How does Leviticus conclude?
28. Of what benefit is Leviticus to Christians today?

attributes, and his ways of dealing with his creatures, as he so clearly demonstrated with Israel under the Law covenant. Leviticus states many basic principles that will always apply, and it contains many prophetic patterns, as well as prophecies, that are faith strengthening to consider. Many of its principles are restated in the Christian Greek Scriptures, some of them being directly quoted. Seven outstanding points are discussed below.

²⁹ (1) *Jehovah's sovereignty.* He is the Lawgiver, and we as his creatures are accountable to him. Rightly he commands us to be in fear of him. As the Universal Sovereign, he brooks no rivalry, be that in the form of idolatry, spiritism, or other aspects of demonism.—Lev. 18:4; 25:17; 26:1; Matt. 10:28; Acts 4:24.

³⁰ (2) *Jehovah's name.* His name is to be kept holy, and we dare not bring reproach upon it by words or by actions.—Lev. 22:32; 24:10-16; Matt. 6:9.

³¹ (3) *Jehovah's holiness.* Because he is holy, his people must also be holy, that is, sanctified, or set apart for his service. This includes keeping separate from the godless world around us.—Lev. 11:44; 20:26; Jas. 1:27; 1 Pet. 1:15, 16.

³² (4) *The exceeding sinfulness of sin.* It is God who determines what is sin, and we must strive against it. Sin always requires an atoning sacrifice. In addition, it also requires of us confession, repentance, and making amends to the extent possible. For certain sins there can be no forgiveness.—Lev. 4:2; 5:5; 20:2, 10; 1 John 1:9; Heb. 10:26-29.

³³ (5) *The sanctity of blood.* Because blood is sacred, it may not be taken into the body in any form. The only use permitted for blood is as an atonement for sin.—Lev. 17:10-14; Acts 15:29; Heb. 9:22.

³⁴ (6) *Relativity in guilt and punishment.* Not all sins and sinners were considered in the same light. The higher the office, the greater the responsibility and penalty for sin. Willful sin was punished more severely than unintentional sin. Penalties were often graded according to ability to pay. This principle of relativity also applied in fields other than sin and punishment, such as in ceremonial uncleanness.—Lev. 4:3, 22-28; 5:7-11; 6:2-7; 12:8; 21:1-15; Luke 12:47, 48; Jas. 3:1; 1 John 5:16.

³⁵ (7) *Justice and love.* Summing up our duties toward our fellowman, Leviticus 19:18 says: "You must love your fellow as yourself." This takes in everything. It precludes showing partiality, stealing, lying, or slandering, and it requires showing consideration to the handicapped, the poor, the blind, and the deaf.—Lev. 19:9-18; Matt. 22:39; Rom. 13:8-13.

³⁶ Also proving that Leviticus is outstandingly "beneficial for teaching, for reproving, for setting things straight, for disciplining in righteousness" in the Christian congregation are the repeated references made to it by Jesus and his apostles, notably Paul and Peter. These called attention to the many prophetic patterns and shadows of things to come. As Paul noted, "the Law has a shadow of the good things to come." It sets forth "a typical representation and a shadow of the heavenly things."—2 Tim 3:16; Heb. 10:1; 8:5.

³⁷ The tabernacle, the priesthood, the sacrifices, and especially the annual Atonement Day had typical significance. Paul, in his letter to the Hebrews, helps us to identify the spiritual counterparts of these things in relation to "the true tent" of Jehovah's worship. (Heb. 8:2) The chief priest Aaron typifies Christ Jesus "as a high priest of the good things that have come to pass, through the greater and more perfect tent." (Heb. 9:11; Lev. 21:10) The blood of the animal sacrifices foreshadows the blood of Jesus, which obtains "everlasting deliverance for us." (Heb. 9:12) The innermost compartment of the tabernacle, the Most Holy, into which the high priest entered only on the annual Day of Atonement to present the sacrificial blood, is "a copy of the reality," "heaven itself," to which Jesus ascended "to appear before the person of God for us."—Heb. 9:24; Lev. 16:14, 15.

³⁸ The actual sacrificial victims—sound, unblemished animals offered as burnt or sin offerings—represent the perfect unblemished sacrifice of the human body of Jesus Christ. (Heb. 9: 13, 14; 10:1-10; Lev. 1:3) Interestingly, Paul also discusses the feature of the Atonement Day where the carcasses of animals for the sin offering were taken outside the camp and burned. (Lev. 16:27) "Hence Jesus also," writes Paul, "suffered outside the gate. Let us, then, go forth to him outside the camp, bearing the reproach he bore." (Heb. 13: 12, 13) By such inspired interpretation, the ceremonial procedures outlined in Leviticus take on added significance, and we can indeed begin to comprehend how marvelously Jehovah there

---

29-31. How does Leviticus emphasize respect for Jehovah's (a) sovereignty, (b) name, and (c) holiness?
32-34. What principles are outlined as to (a) sin, (b) blood, and (c) relative guilt?
35. How does Leviticus sum up our duties toward our fellowman?

---

36. What proves Leviticus to be beneficial for the Christian congregation?
37. What fulfillments of types are described in Hebrews?
38. How were the typical sacrifices fulfilled in Jesus?

made awesome shadows pointing forward to realities that could be made plain only by the holy spirit. (Heb. 9:8) Such proper understanding is vital for those who are to benefit by the provision for life that Jehovah makes through Christ Jesus, the "great priest over the house of God."—Heb. 10:19-25.

³⁹ Like Aaron's priestly household, Jesus Christ as High Priest has underpriests associated with him. These are spoken of as "a royal priesthood." (1 Pet. 2:9) Leviticus clearly points to and explains the sin-atoning work of Jehovah's great

---
39. How does Leviticus blend in with "all Scripture" in making known Jehovah's Kingdom purposes?

High Priest and King and the requirements laid upon the members of His household, who are spoken of as "happy and holy" and as being 'priests of God and of the Christ and ruling as kings with him for the thousand years.' What blessings that priestly work will accomplish in lifting obedient mankind up to perfection, and what happiness that heavenly Kingdom will bring by restoring peace and righteousness to the earth! Surely, we must all thank the holy God, Jehovah, for his arranging for a High Priest and King and a royal priesthood to declare abroad His excellencies in sanctification of His name! Truly, Leviticus blends in wonderfully with "all Scripture" in making known Jehovah's Kingdom purposes.—Rev. 20:6.

Bible Book Number 4

Numbers

Writer: **Moses**

Place Written: **Wilderness and Plains of Moab**

Writing Completed: **1473 B.C.E.**

Time Covered: **1512-1473 B.C.E.**

THE events of the Israelites' wilderness trek have been recorded in the Bible for our benefit today.* As the apostle Paul said: "Now these things became our examples, for us not to be persons desiring injurious things." (1 Cor. 10:6) The vivid record in Numbers impresses upon us that survival depends on sanctifying Jehovah's name, obeying him under all circumstances, and showing respect for his representatives. His favor does not come because of any goodness or merit in his people but out of his great mercy and undeserved kindness.

² The name Numbers has reference to the numbering of the people that took place first at Mount Sinai and later on the Plains of Moab, as recorded in chapters 1-4 and 26. This name has been carried over from the title *Numeri* in the Latin *Vulgate* and is derived from *A·rith·moi´* in the Greek *Septuagint.* However, the Jews more fittingly call the book *Bemidh·bar´,* which means "In the Wilderness." The Hebrew word *midh·bar´* indicates an open place, empty of cities and towns. It was in the wilderness to the south and to the east of Canaan that the events of Numbers took place.

---
* *Insight on the Scriptures,* Vol. 1, pages 540-2.

---
1. Why were the events of Numbers recorded, and what do they impress on us?
2. To what does the name Numbers refer, but what more fitting title did the Jews give to the book?

³ Numbers was evidently part of the original fivefold volume that included the books from Genesis to Deuteronomy. Its first verse opens with the conjunction "and," tying it in with what went before. Thus, it must have been written by Moses, the writer of the preceding records. This is also clear from the statement in the book that "Moses kept recording," and by the colophon, "These are the commandments and the judicial decisions that Jehovah commanded by means of Moses."—Num. 33:2; 36:13.

⁴ The Israelites had departed from Egypt a little more than a year previously. Taking up the account in the second month of the second year after the Exodus, Numbers covers the next 38 years and nine months, from 1512 to 1473 B.C.E. (Num. 1:1; Deut. 1:3) Though not fitting into this time period, the events related at Numbers 7:1-88 and 9:1-15 are included as background information. The earlier portions of the book were no doubt written as the events occurred, but it is evident that Moses could not have completed Numbers until toward the end of the 40th year in the wilderness, early in the calendar year 1473 B.C.E.

⁵ There can be no doubt as to the authenticity of

---
3. What proves Moses' writership of Numbers?
4. What period of time is covered by Numbers, and when was the book completed?
5. What features testify to the authenticity of Numbers?

the account. Of the generally arid land in which they journeyed, Moses said that it was a "great and fear-inspiring wilderness," and it is true even today that the scattered inhabitants are constantly on the move in search of pastures and water. (Deut. 1:19) Furthermore, the detailed instructions concerning encampment of the nation, the order of march, and the trumpet signals to govern camp affairs testify that the account was indeed written "in the wilderness."—Num. 1:1.

⁶ Even the fearful report of the spies when they returned from their expedition into Canaan, to the effect that "the fortified cities are very great," is borne out by archaeology. (13:28) Modern-day discoveries have shown that the inhabitants of Canaan at that time had consolidated their hold by a series of forts stretching across the country in several places, from the Low Plain of Jezreel in the north to Gerar in the south. Not only were the cities fortified but they were usually built on the tops of hills, with towers rising above their walls, making them most impressive to people like the Israelites, who had lived for generations in the flat land of Egypt.

⁷ Nations of the world are prone to whitewash their failures and magnify their conquests, but with an honesty that bespeaks historical truth, the Numbers account tells that Israel was completely routed by the Amalekites and by the Canaanites. (14:45) It straightforwardly confesses that the people proved faithless and treated God without respect. (14:11) With remarkable candor, God's prophet Moses exposes the sins of the nation, of his nephews, and of his own brother and sister. Nor does he spare himself, for he tells of the time that he failed to sanctify Jehovah when water was provided at Meribah, so that he forfeited the privilege of entering the Promised Land.—3:4; 12:1-15; 20:7-13.

⁸ That the account is a genuine part of the Scriptures that are inspired by God and beneficial is borne out by the fact that nearly all its major events, as well as many other details, are directly referred to by other Bible writers, many of whom highlight their significance. For example, Joshua (Josh. 4:12; 14:2), Jeremiah (2 Ki. 18:4), Nehemiah (Neh. 9: 19-22), Asaph (Ps. 78:14-41), David (Ps. 95:7-11), Isaiah (Isa. 48:21), Ezekiel (Ezek. 20:13-24), Hosea (Hos. 9:10), Amos (Amos 5:25), Micah (Mic. 6:5), Luke in his record of Stephen's discourse (Acts 7:36), Paul (1 Cor. 10:1-11), Peter (2 Pet. 2:15, 16), Jude (Jude 11), and John in recording Jesus' words to the Pergamum congregation (Rev. 2:14), all draw on the record in Numbers, as did Jesus Christ himself.—John 3:14.

⁹ What purpose, then, does Numbers serve? Truly its account is of more than historical value. Numbers emphasizes that Jehovah is the God of order, requiring exclusive devotion of his creatures. This is vividly impressed on the reader's mind as he observes the numbering, testing, and sifting of Israel and sees how the nation's disobedient and rebellious course is used to emphasize the vital need to obey Jehovah.

¹⁰ The record was preserved for the benefit of the generations to come, just as Asaph explained, "that they might set their confidence in God himself and not forget the practices of God but observe his own commandments" and that "they should not become like their forefathers, a generation stubborn and rebellious, a generation who had not prepared their heart and whose spirit was not trustworthy with God." (Ps. 78:7, 8) Over and over again, the events of Numbers were recounted in the psalms, which were sacred songs among the Jews and so were often repeated as being beneficial to the nation.—Psalms 78, 95, 105, 106, 135, 136.

CONTENTS OF NUMBERS

¹¹ Numbers logically falls into three parts. The first of these, concluding at chapter 10, verse 10, covers events taking place while the Israelites were still encamped at Mount Sinai. The next part, concluding with chapter 21, tells what happened during the next 38 years and a month or two more, while they were in the wilderness and until they arrived at the Plains of Moab. The final part, through chapter 36, is concerned with events on the Plains of Moab as the Israelites prepared for their entry into the Promised Land.

¹² **Events at Mount Sinai** (1:1–10:10). The Israelites have already been in the mountainous region of Sinai for about a year. Here they have been molded into a closely knit organization. At Jehovah's command a census is now taken of all the men 20 years old and upward. The tribes are found to range in size from 32,200 able-bodied men in Manasseh up to 74,600 in Judah, making a total of 603,550 men qualified to serve in the army of Israel, besides the Levites and the women and children—a camp perhaps numbering three million or more. The tent of meeting is situated, along with the Levites, in the center of the camp. In assigned places on each side are camped the other Israelites, in three-tribe divisions, each tribe having instructions as to the order of march when the camp is to move. Jehovah issues

---

6. How do archaeological finds support Numbers?
7. What stamp of honesty does Numbers bear?
8. How do other Bible writers testify to the inspiration of Numbers?

---

9. What does Numbers emphasize concerning Jehovah?
10. For whose benefit was Numbers preserved, and why?
11. Into what three parts may the contents of Numbers be divided?
12. How large is the Israelite encampment at Sinai, and how is the camp organized?

the instructions, and the record says: "The sons of Israel proceeded to do according to all that Jehovah had commanded Moses." (2:34) They obey Jehovah and show respect for Moses, God's visible representative.

¹³ The Levites are then set apart for Jehovah's service, as a ransom for the firstborn of Israel. They are divided into three groups, according to their descent from the three sons of Levi: Gershon, Kohath, and Merari. Locations in the camp and service responsibilities are determined on the basis of this division. From 30 years of age on, they are to do the heavy work of transporting the tabernacle. To get the lighter work done, provision is made for others to serve, starting at 25 years of age. (This was reduced in David's time to 20 years of age.) —1 Chron. 23:24-32; Ezra 3:8.

¹⁴ That the camp may be kept pure, instructions are given for quarantining those who become diseased, for making atonement for acts of unfaithfulness, for resolving cases in which a man might become suspicious of the conduct of his wife, and for assuring right conduct on the part of those set apart by vow to live as Nazirites to Jehovah. Since the people are to have the name of their God upon them, they must deport themselves in accord with his commandments.

¹⁵ Filling in some details from the previous month (Num. 7:1, 10; Ex. 40:17), Moses next tells of the contributions of materials made by the 12 chieftains of the people over a period of 12 days from the time of the inauguration of the altar. There was no competition or seeking of self-glory in it; each one contributed exactly what the others did. All must now keep in mind that over these chieftains, and over Moses himself, there is Jehovah God, who speaks instructions to Moses. They must never forget their relationship to Jehovah. The Passover is to remind them of Jehovah's wondrous deliverance from Egypt, and they celebrate it here in the wilderness at the appointed time, one year after leaving Egypt.

¹⁶ In the same way that he had directed Israel's movement out of Egypt, Jehovah continues to lead the nation in its travels by a cloud that covers the tabernacle of the tent of the Testimony by day and by the appearance of fire there by night. When the cloud moves, the nation moves. When the cloud remains over the tabernacle, the nation remains encamped, whether for a few days or a month or longer, for the account tells us: "At the order of Jehovah they would encamp, and at the order of Jehovah they would pull away. They kept their obligation to Jehovah at the order of Jehovah by means of Moses." (Num. 9:23) As the time for departure from Sinai draws near, trumpet signals are arranged both to assemble the people and to direct the various divisions of the encampment on their wilderness trek.

¹⁷ **Events in the wilderness** (10:11–21:35). At last, on the 20th day of the second month, Jehovah lifts the cloud from over the tabernacle, thus signaling Israel's departure from the region of Sinai. With the ark of Jehovah's covenant in their midst, they set out for Kadesh-barnea, some 150 miles to the north. As they march by day, Jehovah's cloud is over them. Each time the Ark goes out, Moses prays to Jehovah to arise and scatter his enemies, and each time it comes to rest, he prays for Jehovah to return "to the myriads of thousands of Israel." —10:36.

¹⁸ However, trouble arises in the camp. On the trip north to Kadesh-barnea, there are at least three occasions of complaining. To quell the first outbreak, Jehovah sends a fire to consume some of the people. Then "the mixed crowd" set Israel to bemoaning that they no longer have as food the fish, cucumbers, watermelons, leeks, onions, and garlic of Egypt, but only manna. (11:4) Moses becomes so distressed that he asks Jehovah to kill him off rather than let him continue as male nurse to all this people. Considerately, Jehovah takes away some of the spirit from Moses and puts it upon 70 of the older men, who proceed to assist Moses as prophets in the camp. Then meat comes in abundance. As had happened once before, a wind from Jehovah drives in quail from the sea, and the people greedily seize great supplies, selfishly hoarding them. Jehovah's anger blazes against the people, striking down many because of their selfish craving.—Ex. 16:2, 3, 13.

¹⁹ The troubles continue. Failing properly to view their younger brother, Moses, as Jehovah's representative, Miriam and Aaron find fault with him over his wife, who has recently come into the camp. They demand more authority, comparable to that of Moses, though "the man Moses was by far the meekest of all the men who were upon the surface

_____

13. According to what arrangement are the Levites assigned to service?
14. What instructions are given to ensure the purity of the camp?
15. (a) In connection with the inauguration of the altar, what contributions were made? (b) What relationship must Israel remember, and of what is the Passover to remind them?
16. How does Jehovah lead the nation, and what trumpet signals are arranged?

_____

17. Describe the procedure of march.
18. What complaining breaks out on the way to Kadesh-barnea, and how does Jehovah adjust theocratic procedure in the camp?
19. How does Jehovah deal with the faultfinding of Miriam and Aaron?

of the ground." (Num. 12:3) Jehovah himself sets the matter straight and lets it be known that Moses occupies a special position, striking Miriam, who was likely the instigator of the complaint, with leprosy. Only by Moses' intercession is she later healed.

20 Arriving at Kadesh, Israel camps at the threshold of the Promised Land. Jehovah now instructs Moses to send spies to scout out the land. Entering from the south, they travel north clear to "the entering in of Hamath," walking hundreds of miles in 40 days. (13:21) When they return with some of the rich fruitage of Canaan, ten of the spies faithlessly argue that it would be foolish to go up against so strong a people and such great fortified cities. Caleb tries to quiet the assembly with a favorable report, but without success. The rebellious spies strike fear into the Israelites' hearts, claiming the land to be one that "eats up its inhabitants" and saying, "All the people whom we saw in the midst of it are men of extraordinary size." As murmurings of rebellion sweep through the camp, Joshua and Caleb plead, "Jehovah is with us. Do not fear them." (13:32; 14:9) However, the assembly begins to talk of pelting them with stones.

21 Then Jehovah intervenes directly, saying to Moses: "How long will this people treat me without respect, and how long will they not put faith in me for all the signs that I performed in among them?" (14:11) Moses implores him not to destroy the nation, as Jehovah's name and fame are involved. Jehovah therefore decrees that Israel must continue to wander in the wilderness until all those registered among the people, from 20 years old and up, have died off. Of the registered males, only Caleb and Joshua will be permitted to enter the Land of Promise. In vain the people try to go up on their own initiative, only to suffer a terrible defeat meted out by the Amalekites and the Canaanites. What a high price the people pay for their disrespect of Jehovah and his loyal representatives!

22 Truly, they have much to learn in the way of obedience. Fittingly, Jehovah gives them additional laws highlighting this need. He lets them know that when they come into the Promised Land, atonement must be made for mistakes, but the deliberately disobedient must be cut off without fail. Thus, when a man is found gathering wood in violation of the Sabbath law, Jehovah commands: "Without fail the man should be put to death." (15:35) As a reminder of the commandments of Jehovah and the importance of obeying them, Jehovah instructs that the people wear fringes on the skirts of their garments.

23 Nevertheless, rebellion breaks out again. Korah, Dathan, Abiram, and 250 prominent men of the assembly gather in opposition to the authority of Moses and Aaron. Moses puts the issue to Jehovah, saying to the rebels: 'Take fire holders and incense and present them before Jehovah, and let him choose.' (16:6, 7) Jehovah's glory now appears to all the assembly. Swiftly he executes judgment, causing the earth to split apart to swallow up the households of Korah, Dathan, and Abiram, and sending out a fire to consume the 250 men, including Korah, offering the incense. The very next day, the people begin to condemn Moses and Aaron for what Jehovah did, and again He scourges them, wiping out 14,700 complainers.

24 In view of these events, Jehovah commands that each tribe present a rod before him, including a rod with Aaron's name for the tribe of Levi. The next day Aaron is shown to be Jehovah's choice for the priesthood, for his rod alone is found to be in full bloom and bearing ripe almonds. It is to be preserved in the ark of the covenant "for a sign to the sons of rebelliousness." (Num. 17:10; Heb. 9:4) After further instructions for the support of the priesthood by means of tithes and concerning the use of cleansing water with the ashes of a red cow, the account returns us to Kadesh. Here Miriam dies and is buried.

25 Again at the threshold of the Land of Promise the assembly gets to quarreling with Moses because of the lack of water. Jehovah counts it as quarreling with Him, and He appears in His glory, commanding Moses to take the rod and bring out water from the crag. Do Moses and Aaron now sanctify Jehovah? Instead, Moses twice strikes the crag in anger. The people and their livestock get water to drink, but Moses and Aaron fail to give the credit to Jehovah. Though the heartbreaking wilderness journey is almost over, they both incur Jehovah's displeasure and are told they will not enter the Land of Promise. Aaron dies later on Mount Hor, and his son Eleazar takes over the duties of high priest.

26 Israel turns to the east and seeks to go through the land of Edom but is rebuffed. While making a long detour around Edom, the people get into trouble again as they complain against God and Moses. They are tired of the manna, and they are thirsty. Because of their rebelliousness Jehovah sends poisonous serpents among them, so that many die. At last, when Moses intercedes, Jehovah instructs him

---

20, 21. What events give rise to Jehovah's decree that Israel must wander 40 years in the wilderness?
22. In what ways is the importance of obedience emphasized?

23. What is the outcome of the rebellion of Korah, Dathan, and Abiram?
24. What sign does Jehovah perform to end the rebelliousness?
25. How do Moses and Aaron fail to sanctify Jehovah, and with what result?
26. What events mark the detour around Edom?

to make a fiery copper serpent and place it on a signal pole. Those who have been bitten but who gaze at the copper serpent are spared alive. Heading north, the Israelites are impeded, in turn, by the belligerent kings Sihon of the Amorites and Og of Bashan. Israel defeats both of these in battle, and Israel occupies their territories to the east of the Rift Valley.

[27] **Events on the Plains of Moab** (22:1–36:13). In eager anticipation of their entry into Canaan, the Israelites now gather on the desert plains of Moab, north of the Dead Sea and to the east of the Jordan across from Jericho. Seeing this vast encampment spread out before them, the Moabites feel a sickening dread. Their king Balak, in consultation with the Midianites, sends for Balaam to use divination and put a curse on Israel. Although God directly tells Balaam, "You must not go with them," he wants to go. (22:12) He wants the reward. Finally he does go, only to be stopped by an angel and to have his own she-ass miraculously speak to rebuke him. When at last Balaam gets around to making pronouncements about Israel, God's spirit impels him, so that his four proverbial utterances prophesy only blessings for God's nation, even foretelling that a star would step forth out of Jacob and a scepter would rise out of Israel to subdue and destroy.

[28] Having infuriated Balak by his failure to curse Israel, Balaam now seeks the king's good graces by suggesting that the Moabites use their own females in enticing the men of Israel to share in the lewd rites involved in the worship of Baal. (31:15, 16) Here, right on the border of the Promised Land, the Israelites begin to fall away to gross immorality and the worship of false gods. As Jehovah's anger blazes forth in a scourge, Moses calls for drastic punishment of the wrongdoers. When Phinehas, son of the high priest, sees the son of a chieftain bring a Midianite woman into his tent right inside the camp, he goes after them and kills them, striking the woman through her genital parts. At this, the scourge is halted, but not before 24,000 die from it.

[29] Jehovah now commands Moses and Eleazar to take a census of the people again, as had been done nearly 39 years earlier at Mount Sinai. The final count shows that there has been no increase in their ranks. On the contrary, there are 1,820 fewer men registered. None remain that had been registered at Sinai for army service, except Joshua and Caleb. As Jehovah had indicated would happen, all of them had died in the wilderness. Jehovah next gives instructions concerning the division of the land as an inheritance. He repeats that Moses will not enter the Land of Promise because of his failure to sanctify Jehovah at the waters of Meribah. (20:13; 27:14, footnotes) Joshua is commissioned as successor to Moses.

[30] Through Moses, Jehovah next reminds Israel of the importance of His laws concerning sacrifices and feasts and of the seriousness of vows. He also has Moses settle the account with the Midianites because of their part in seducing Israel over Baal of Peor. All the Midianite males are slain in battle, along with Balaam, and only virgin girls are spared, 32,000 of these being taken captive along with plunder that includes 808,000 animals. Not one Israelite is reported missing in battle. The sons of Reuben and of Gad, who raise livestock, ask to settle in the territory east of the Jordan, and after they agree to help in conquering the Promised Land, the request is granted, so that these two tribes, together with half the tribe of Manasseh, are given this rich tableland as their possession.

[31] After a review of the stopping places on the 40-year journey, the record again focuses attention on the need for obedience to Jehovah. God is giving them the land, but they must become His executioners, driving out the depraved, demon-worshiping inhabitants and destroying every last trace of their idolatrous religion. The detailed boundaries of their God-given land are stated. It is to be divided among them by lot. The Levites, who have no tribal inheritance, are to be given 48 cities with their pasture grounds, 6 of these to be cities of refuge for the unintentional manslayer. Territory must remain within the tribe, never being transferred to another tribe by marriage. If there is no male heir, then the daughters who receive an inheritance—for example, the daughters of Zelophehad—must marry within their own tribe. (27:1-11; 36:1-11) Numbers concludes with these commandments of Jehovah through Moses and with the sons of Israel poised at last to enter the Land of Promise.

WHY BENEFICIAL

[32] Jesus referred to Numbers on several occasions, and his apostles and other Bible writers clearly demonstrate how meaningful and beneficial its record is. The apostle Paul specifically compared

---

27. How does Jehovah overrule Balak's plans in connection with Balaam?
28. What subtle snare is brought on Israel at Balaam's suggestion, but how is the scourge halted?
29. (a) What is revealed by the census at the end of the 40th year? (b) What preparation is now made for entry into the Promised Land?

30. How is the account with the Midianites settled, and what territory assignment is made east of the Jordan?
31. (a) On entering the land, how must Israel continue to show obedience? (b) What instructions are given regarding tribal inheritances?
32. In what ways are Jesus and his sacrifice typified in Numbers?

Jesus' faithful service to that of Moses, which is largely recorded in Numbers. (Heb. 3:1-6) In the animal sacrifices and in the sprinkling of the ashes of the young red cow of Numbers 19:2-9, we again see pictured the far grander provision for cleansing through the sacrifice of Christ.—Heb. 9:13, 14.

³³ Similarly, Paul showed that the bringing forth of water from the rock in the wilderness is full of meaning for us, saying: "They used to drink from the spiritual rock-mass that followed them, and that rock-mass meant the Christ." (1 Cor. 10:4; Num. 20: 7-11) Fittingly, it was Christ himself who said: "Whoever drinks from the water that I will give him will never get thirsty at all, but the water that I will give him will become in him a fountain of water bubbling up to impart everlasting life."—John 4:14.

³⁴ Jesus also made direct reference to an incident recorded in Numbers that foreshadowed the marvelous provision that God was making through him. "Just as Moses lifted up the serpent in the wilderness," he said, "so the Son of man must be lifted up, that everyone believing in him may have everlasting life."—John 3:14, 15; Num. 21:8, 9.

³⁵ Why were the Israelites sentenced to wander 40 years in the wilderness? For lack of faith. The apostle Paul gave powerful admonition on this point: "Beware, brothers, for fear there should ever develop in any one of you a wicked heart lacking faith by drawing away from the living God; but keep on exhorting one another each day." Because of their disobedience and because of their faithlessness, those Israelites died in the wilderness. "Let us therefore do our utmost to enter into [God's] rest, for fear anyone should fall in the same pattern of disobedience." (Heb. 3:7–4:11; Num. 13:25–14:38) In warning against ungodly men who speak abusively of holy things, Jude referred to Balaam's greed for reward and to Korah's rebellious talk against Jehovah's servant Moses. (Jude 11; Num. 22:7, 8, 22; 26:9, 10) Balaam was also referred to by Peter as one "who loved the reward of wrongdoing," and by the glorified Jesus in his revelation through John as one who 'put before Israel a stumbling block of idolatry and fornication.' Certainly the Christian congregation today should be warned against such unholy ones.—2 Pet. 2:12-16; Rev. 2:14.

³⁶ When immorality arose in the Corinthian congregation, Paul wrote them about "desiring injurious things," referring specifically to Numbers. He admonished: "Neither let us practice fornication, as some of them committed fornication, only to fall, twenty-three thousand of them in one day." (1 Cor. 10:6, 8; Num. 25:1-9; 31:16)* What about the occasion when the people complained that obeying God's commands entailed personal hardship and that they were dissatisfied with Jehovah's provision of the manna? Concerning this, Paul says: "Neither let us put Jehovah to the test, as some of them put him to the test, only to perish by the serpents." (1 Cor. 10:9; Num. 21:5, 6) Then Paul continues: "Neither be murmurers, just as some of them murmured, only to perish by the destroyer." How bitter the experiences of Israel as a result of their murmuring against Jehovah, his representatives, and his provisions! These things that *"went on befalling them as examples"* should stand forth as a clear warning to all of us today, so that we may *go on* serving Jehovah in the fullness of faith.—1 Cor. 10:10, 11; Num. 14:2, 36, 37; 16:1-3, 41; 17:5, 10.

³⁷ Numbers also provides the background against which many other Bible passages can be better understood.—Num. 28:9, 10—Matt. 12:5; Num. 15:38—Matt. 23:5; Num. 6:2-4—Luke 1:15; Num. 4:3—Luke 3:23; Num. 18:31—1 Cor. 9:13, 14; Num. 18:26—Heb. 7:5-9; Num. 17:8-10—Heb. 9:4.

³⁸ What is recorded in Numbers is indeed inspired of God, and it is beneficial in teaching us the importance of obedience to Jehovah and respect for those whom he has made overseers among his people. By example, it reproves wrongdoing, and by happenings with prophetic import, it directs our attention to the One whom Jehovah has provided as the Savior and Leader of His people today. It provides an essential and instructive link in the record leading to the establishment of Jehovah's righteous Kingdom in the hands of Jesus Christ, the one He appointed as Mediator and High Priest.

---

33. Why is the bringing forth of water in the wilderness of interest to us today?
34. How did Jesus show that the copper serpent had prophetic meaning?
35. (a) Against what should Christians be on guard, as illustrated by the Israelites in the wilderness, and why? (b) In their letters, to what examples of greed and rebellion did Jude and Peter refer?

---

* *Insight on the Scriptures,* Vol. 1, page 233.

---

36. Against what injurious practices did Paul warn, and how may we today benefit by his counsel?
37. Illustrate how Numbers helps us to understand other Bible passages.
38. In what particular ways is the book of Numbers beneficial, and to what does it direct our attention?

Deuteronomy

Writer: **Moses**
Place Written: **Plains of Moab**
Writing Completed: **1473 B.C.E.**
Time Covered: **2 months (1473 B.C.E.)**

THE book of Deuteronomy contains a dynamic message for Jehovah's people. After wandering in the wilderness for 40 years, the sons of Israel now stood on the threshold of the Land of Promise. What lay ahead of them? What were the peculiar problems that they would face on the other side of the Jordan? What would Moses finally have to say to the nation? We may also ask, Why is it beneficial for us today to know the answers to these questions?

2 The answers are to be found in the words that Moses spoke and that he recorded in the fifth book of the Bible, Deuteronomy. Though it restates much from the earlier books, Deuteronomy is important in its own outstanding way. Why so? It adds emphasis to the divine message, being provided at a time in the history of Jehovah's people when they really needed dynamic leadership and positive direction. They were about to enter the Promised Land under a new leader. They needed encouragement to go forward, and at the same time they needed divine warning to enable them to take the right course leading to Jehovah's blessing.

3 In accord with the need, Moses was moved mightily by Jehovah's spirit to make a forthright appeal to Israel to be obedient and faithful. Throughout the entire book, he emphasizes that Jehovah is the Most High God, who exacts exclusive devotion and who desires his people to 'love him with all their heart and all their soul and all their vital force.' He is "the God of gods and the Lord of lords, the God great, mighty and fear-inspiring, who treats none with partiality nor accepts a bribe." He tolerates no rivalry. To obey him means life, to disobey, death. Jehovah's instruction, as given in Deuteronomy, was just the preparation and counsel that Israel needed for the momentous tasks that lay ahead of them. It is also the kind of admonition we need today so that we may keep walking in the fear of Jehovah, sanctifying his name in the midst of a corrupt world.—Deut. 5:9, 10; 6:4-6; 10:12-22.

4 The name Deuteronomy comes from the title in the Greek Septuagint translation, *Deu·te·ro·no'mi·on,* which combines *deu'te·ros,* meaning "second," with *no'mos,* meaning "law." It therefore means "Second Law; Repetition of the Law." This comes from the Greek rendering of the Hebrew phrase in Deuteronomy 17:18, *mish·neh' hat·toh·rah',* correctly rendered 'copy of the law.' Despite the meaning of the name Deuteronomy, however, this Bible book is *not* a second law nor a mere repetition of the Law. Instead, it is an *explanation* of the Law, exhorting Israel to love and obey Jehovah in the Promised Land that they would soon be entering.—1:5.

5 This being the fifth roll, or volume, of the Pentateuch, the writer must have been the same as for the preceding four books, namely, Moses. The opening statement identifies Deuteronomy as "the words that Moses spoke to all Israel," and later expressions, such as "Moses wrote this law" and "Moses wrote this song," clearly prove his writership. His name appears nearly 40 times in the book, usually as authority for the statements made. The first person, referring to Moses, is used predominantly throughout. The closing verses were added after Moses' death, most likely by Joshua or by Eleazar the high priest.—1:1; 31:9, 22, 24-26.

6 When did the events of Deuteronomy take place? At the outset, the book itself states that "in the fortieth year, in the eleventh month, on the first of the month, Moses spoke to the sons of Israel." On completion of the record in Deuteronomy, the book of Joshua takes up the account three days before the crossing of the Jordan, which was "on the tenth of the first month." (Deut. 1:3; Josh. 1:11; 4:19) This leaves a period of two months and

---

1. What questions may be asked in connection with Israel's entry into the Promised Land?
2. In what outstanding way is Deuteronomy important?
3. What does Moses emphasize throughout Deuteronomy, and why is this important to us today?

4. What is the meaning of the name Deuteronomy, and what is the purpose of the book?
5. What proves that Moses was the writer of Deuteronomy?
6. (a) What time period is covered by Deuteronomy? (b) By when was the book practically complete?

one week for the events of Deuteronomy. However, 30 days of this nine-week period were spent mourning the death of Moses. (Deut. 34:8) This means that practically all the events of Deuteronomy must have occurred in the 11th month of the 40th year. By the close of that month, the writing of the book must also have been practically complete, with Moses' death coming early in the 12th month of the 40th year, or early in 1473 B.C.E.

⁷ The proofs already submitted for the authenticity of the first four books of the Pentateuch hold also for Deuteronomy, the fifth book. It is also one of the four books in the Hebrew Scriptures most often cited in the Christian Greek Scriptures, the others being Genesis, Psalms, and Isaiah. There are 83 of these citations, and only six of the books in the Christian Greek Scriptures omit alluding to Deuteronomy.*

⁸ Jesus himself gives the strongest testimony in support of Deuteronomy. At the outset of his ministry, he was three times tempted by the Devil, and three times he came back with the answer, "It is written." Written where? Why, in the book of Deuteronomy (8:3; 6:16, 13), which Jesus quoted as his inspired authority: "Man must live, not on bread alone, but on every utterance coming forth through Jehovah's mouth." "You must not put Jehovah your God to the test." "It is Jehovah your God you must worship, and it is to him alone you must render sacred service." (Matt. 4:1-11) Later, when the Pharisees came testing him with regard to God's commandments, Jesus quoted in reply "the greatest and first commandment" from Deuteronomy 6:5. (Matt. 22:37, 38; Mark 12:30; Luke 10:27) Jesus' testimony conclusively stamps Deuteronomy as authentic.

⁹ Moreover, the events and statements in the book fit exactly the historical situation and surroundings. The references to Egypt, Canaan, Amalek, Ammon, Moab, and Edom are faithful to the times, and place-names are accurately stated.# Archaeology continues to bring to light proof upon proof as to the integrity of Moses' writings. Henry H. Halley writes: "Archaeology has been speaking so loudly of late that it is causing a decided reaction toward the conservative view [that Moses wrote the Pentateuch]. The theory that writing was unknown in Moses' day is absolutely explod-

ed. And every year there are being dug up in Egypt, Palestine and Mesopotamia, evidences, both in inscriptions and earth layers, that the narratives of the [Hebrew Scriptures] are true historical records. And 'scholarship' is coming to have decidedly more respect for the tradition of Mosaic authorship."* Thus, even external evidence supports Deuteronomy, as well as the rest of the Pentateuch, as being a genuine, authentic record made by God's prophet Moses.

CONTENTS OF DEUTERONOMY

¹⁰ The book is mainly composed of a series of discourses that Moses delivered to the sons of Israel on the Plains of Moab opposite Jericho. The first of these concludes in chapter 4, the second runs to the end of chapter 26, the third continues through chapter 28, and another discourse extends to the end of chapter 30. Then, after Moses makes final arrangements in view of his approaching death, including the commissioning of Joshua as his successor, he records a most beautiful song to Jehovah's praise, followed by a blessing on the tribes of Israel.

¹¹ **Moses' first discourse** (1:1–4:49). This provides a historical introduction to what follows. Moses first reviews Jehovah's faithful dealings with His people. Moses is telling them to go in and take possession of the land promised to their forefathers Abraham, Isaac, and Jacob. He recounts how Jehovah coordinated the activity of this theocratic community at the outset of the wilderness trek by having him, Moses, select wise, discreet, and experienced men to act as chiefs of thousands, of hundreds, of fifties, and of tens. There was splendid organization, watched over by Jehovah, as Israel "went marching through all that great and fear-inspiring wilderness."—1:19.

¹² Moses now recalls their sin of rebellion when they heard the report of the spies returning from Canaan and complained that Jehovah hated them because, they charged, He had brought them up out of Egypt only to abandon them to the Amorites. For their lack of faith, Jehovah told that evil generation that none of them, except Caleb and Joshua, would see the good land. At this they again behaved rebelliously, getting all heated up and making their own independent assault on the enemy, only to have the Amorites chase them like a swarm of bees and scatter them.

---

* See the list of "Quotations from the Old Testament" in *The New Testament in Original Greek*, by B. F. Westcott and F. J. A. Hort, 1956, pages 601-18.
# Deuteronomy 3:9, footnote.

7. What shows that Deuteronomy is authentic?
8. What conclusive testimony by Jesus bears out the authenticity of Deuteronomy?
9. What external evidence vindicates Deuteronomy?

---

* *Halley's Bible Handbook*, 1988, Henry H. Halley, page 56.

10. Of what is Deuteronomy composed?
11. How does Moses introduce his first discourse?
12. What events surrounding the initial spying out of Canaan does he next recall?

[13] They traveled in the wilderness down toward the Red Sea, and during 38 years, all the generation of the men of war died off. Jehovah then commanded them to cross over and take possession of the land north of the Arnon, saying: "This day I shall start to put the dread of you and the fear of you before the peoples beneath all the heavens, who will hear the report about you; and they will indeed be agitated and have pains like those of childbirth because of you." (2:25) Sihon and his land fell to the Israelites, and then Og's kingdom was occupied. Moses assured Joshua that Jehovah would fight for Israel in the same way in overcoming all the kingdoms. Moses then asked God if he himself might by any means pass over to the good land beyond the Jordan, but Jehovah continued to refuse this, telling him to commission, encourage, and strengthen Joshua.

[14] Moses now lays great emphasis on God's Law, warning against adding to or taking away from His commandments. Disobedience will bring disaster: "Only watch out for yourself and take good care of your soul, that you may not forget the things that your eyes have seen and that they may not depart from your heart all the days of your life; and you must make them known to your sons and to your grandsons." (4:9) They saw no form when Jehovah stated the Ten Words to them under fearsome circumstances in Horeb. It will be ruination to them if they now turn to idolatry and image worship, for, as Moses says, "Jehovah your God is a consuming fire, a God exacting exclusive devotion." (4:24) He it was who had loved their forefathers and had chosen them. There is no other God in the heavens above or on the earth beneath. Obey Him, Moses exhorts, "that you may lengthen your days on the soil that Jehovah your God is giving you, always."—4:40.

[15] After concluding this powerful speech, Moses proceeds to set apart Bezer, Ramoth, and Golan as cities of refuge to the east of the Jordan.

[16] **Moses' second discourse** (5:1–26:19). This is a call to Israel to hear Jehovah, who spoke with them face-to-face at Sinai. Note how Moses restates the Law with some necessary adjustments, thus adapting it for their new life across the Jordan. It is no mere recounting of regulations and ordinances. Every word shows that the heart of Moses is full of zeal and devotion to his God. He speaks for the welfare of the nation. Obedience to the Law is stressed throughout—obedience from a loving heart, not by compulsion.

[17] First, Moses repeats the Ten Words, the Ten Commandments, and tells Israel to obey them, not turning to the right or to the left, that they may lengthen their days in the land and that they may become very many. "Listen, O Israel: Jehovah our God is one Jehovah." (6:4) Heart, soul, and vital force must be given to loving Him, and Israel must teach their sons and tell them of the great signs and miracles that Jehovah performed in Egypt. There are to be no marriage alliances with the idolatrous Canaanites. Jehovah has chosen Israel to become his special property, not because they are populous, but because he loves them and will keep the sworn statement he made with their forefathers. Israel must shun the snare of demon religion, destroy the images out of the land, and hold to Jehovah, truly "a great and fear-inspiring God."—7:21.

[18] Jehovah humbled them for 40 years in the wilderness, teaching them that man lives, not by manna or bread, but by every expression of Jehovah's mouth. During all those years of correction, their clothing did not wear out, nor did their feet become swollen. Now they are about to enter a land of wealth and plenty! However, they must guard against the snares of materialism and self-righteousness and remember that Jehovah is 'the giver of power to make wealth' and the dispossessor of the wicked nations. (8:18) Moses then recounts occasions when Israel provoked God. They must remember how Jehovah's anger blazed against them in the wilderness, with plague and fire and slaughter! They must remember their ruinous worship of the golden calf, which resulted in Jehovah's hot anger and the remaking of the tablets of the Law! (Ex. 32:1-10, 35; 17:2-7; Num. 11:1-3, 31-35; 14:2-38) Surely they must now serve and cling to Jehovah, who has loved them for their fathers' sakes and had constituted them "like the stars of the heavens for multitude."—Deut. 10:22.

[19] Israel must keep "the whole commandment," and they must without fail obey Jehovah, loving him as their God and serving him with all their heart and all their soul. (11:8, 13) Jehovah will back them up and reward them if they obey him. However, they must apply themselves and diligently teach their sons. The choice before Israel is clearly stated: Obedience leads to blessing, disobe-

---

13. On what basis did Moses assure Joshua of victory?
14. What emphasis does Moses place on God's Law and on exclusive devotion?
15. What arrangement for cities of refuge is made east of the Jordan?
16. What does Moses' second discourse stress?

17. How must Israel reciprocate the love that Jehovah has shown them?
18. Against what does Moses exhort the Israelites to guard themselves?
19. What choice is clearly stated, and what laws are outlined for the nation?

dience to malediction. They must not "walk after other gods." (11:26-28) Moses then outlines specific laws affecting Israel as they move in to take possession of the Land of Promise. There are (1) laws touching religion and worship; (2) laws relating to administration of justice, government, and war; and (3) laws regulating the private and social life of the people.

²⁰ (1) *Religion and worship* (12:1–16:17). When the Israelites enter the land, every vestige of false religion—its high places, altars, pillars, sacred poles, and images—must be absolutely destroyed. Israel must worship only in the place where Jehovah their God chooses to put his name, and there they must rejoice in him, all of them. Regulations on the eating of meat and sacrifices include repeated reminders that they must not eat blood. "Simply be firmly resolved not to eat the blood . . . You must not eat it, in order that it may go well with you and your sons after you, because you will do what is right in Jehovah's eyes." (12:16, 23-25, 27; 15:23) Moses now launches into an outspoken condemnation of idolatry. Israel must not even inquire into the ways of false religion. If a prophet is proved to be false, he must be put to death, and apostates —even one's dear relative or friend, yes, even entire cities—must likewise be devoted to destruction. Next come regulations on clean and unclean food, the payment of tenths, and the care of the Levites. The interests of debtors, the poor, and bond slaves are to be lovingly protected. Finally, Moses reviews the annual festivals as times to thank Jehovah for his blessing: "Three times in the year every male of yours should appear before Jehovah your God in the place that he will choose: in the festival of the unfermented cakes and in the festival of weeks and in the festival of booths, and none should appear before Jehovah empty-handed."—16:16.

²¹ (2) *Justice, government, and war* (16:18–20: 20). First of all, Moses gives the laws affecting judges and officers. Justice is the important thing, bribes and perverted judgment being hateful to Jehovah. The procedures in establishing evidence and handling legal cases are outlined. "At the mouth of two witnesses or of three witnesses the one dying should be put to death." (17:6) Laws are stated concerning kings. Provision is made for the priests and Levites. Spiritism is outlawed as "detestable to Jehovah." (18:12) Looking far into the future, Moses declares: "A prophet from your own midst, from your brothers, like me, is what Jehovah your God will raise up for you—to him you people should listen." (18:15-19) However, a

false prophet must die. This section closes with laws concerning cities of refuge and the avenging of blood, as well as qualifications for military exemptions and the rules of war.

²² (3) *Private and social life* (21:1–26:19). Laws touching the everyday life of the Israelites are set forth on such matters as a person found slain, marriage to captive women, the right of the firstborn, a rebellious son, the hanging of a criminal on a stake, evidence of virginity, sex crimes, castration, illegitimate sons, treatment of foreigners, sanitation, payment of interest and vows, divorce, kidnapping, loans, wages, and harvest gleanings. The limit for beating a man is to be 40 strokes. A bull must not be muzzled while threshing. The procedure for brother-in-law marriage is outlined. Accurate weights must be used, for injustice is detestable to Jehovah.

²³ Before concluding this fervent discourse, Moses recalls how Amalek struck the weary Israelites from the rear as they fled from Egypt, and Moses commands Israel to "wipe out the mention of Amalek from under the heavens." (25:19) When they enter into the land, they must offer the firstfruits of the soil with rejoicing, and they must also offer the tithes with the thankful prayer to Jehovah: "Do look down from your holy dwelling, the heavens, and bless your people Israel and the soil that you have given us, just as you swore to our forefathers, the land flowing with milk and honey." (26:15) If they carry out these commandments with all their heart and soul, Jehovah, on his part, will 'put them high above all the other nations that he has made, resulting in praise and reputation and beauty, while they prove themselves a people holy to Jehovah their God, just as he has promised.' —26:19.

²⁴ **Moses' third discourse** (27:1–28:68). In this the older men of Israel and the priests are associated with Moses as he recites at length Jehovah's curses for disobedience and the blessings for faithfulness. Dire warnings are given concerning the fearful results of unfaithfulness. If Israel as his holy people keep listening to the voice of Jehovah their God, they will enjoy wonderful blessings, and all the peoples of the earth will see that Jehovah's name is called upon them. However, if they fail in this, Jehovah will send upon them "the curse, confusion and rebuke." (28:20) They will be stricken by loathsome disease, by drought, and by famine; their enemies will pursue and enslave

---

20. What points highlight the laws concerning worship?
21. What laws are given relating to justice, and what important prophecy does Moses utter?

22. Laws governing what private and social matters are discussed?
23. What does Moses show will result when God's people obey His commandments?
24. What blessings and cursings does the third discourse set before Israel?

them, and they will be scattered and annihilated out of the land. These curses, and more, will come upon them if they "will not take care to carry out all the words of this law that are written in this book so as to fear this glorious and fear-inspiring name, even Jehovah, [their] God."—28:58.

25 **Moses' fourth discourse** (29:1–30:20). Jehovah now concludes a covenant with Israel at Moab. This incorporates the Law, as restated and explained by Moses, that will guide Israel as they enter the Land of Promise. The solemn oath accompanying the covenant drives home the nation's responsibilities. Finally, Moses calls the heavens and the earth to witness as he places before the people life and death, the blessing and the malediction, and exhorts: "You must choose life in order that you may keep alive, you and your offspring, by loving Jehovah your God, by listening to his voice and by sticking to him; for he is your life and the length of your days, that you may dwell upon the ground that Jehovah swore to your forefathers Abraham, Isaac and Jacob to give to them."—30:19, 20.

26 **Commissioning of Joshua, and Moses' song** (31:1–32:47). Chapter 31 relates how, after writing the Law and giving instructions concerning the regular public reading of it, Moses commissions Joshua, telling him to be courageous and strong, and then how Moses prepares a memorial song and completes the writing of the words of the Law and arranges for it to be placed at the side of the ark of the covenant of Jehovah. After that, Moses speaks the words of the song to all the congregation as a final exhortation.

27 How appreciatively does Moses' song open, identifying the refreshing Source of his instruction! "My instruction will drip as the rain, my saying will trickle as the dew, as gentle rains upon grass and as copious showers upon vegetation. For I shall declare the name of Jehovah." Yes, attribute greatness to "our God," "the Rock." (32:2-4) Make known his perfect activity, his just ways, and his faithfulness, righteousness, and uprightness. It was shameful that Israel acted ruinously, though Jehovah encircled them in an empty, howling desert, safeguarding them as the pupil of his eye and hovering over them as an eagle over its fledglings. He made his people fat, calling them Jeshurun, "Upright One," but they incited him to jealousy with strange gods and became "sons in whom there is no faithfulness." (32:20) Vengeance and

retribution are Jehovah's. He puts to death and makes alive. When he sharpens his glittering sword and his hand takes hold on judgment, he will indeed pay back vengeance to his adversaries. What confidence this should inspire in his people! As the song says in climax, it is a time to "be glad, you nations, with his people." (32:43) What worldly poet could ever approach the exalted beauty, power, and depth of meaning of this song to Jehovah?

28 **Moses' final blessing** (32:48–34:12). Moses is now given final instructions concerning his death, but he is not yet through with his theocratic service. First, he must bless Israel, and in doing this, he again extols Jehovah, the King in Jeshurun, as beaming forth with his holy myriads. By name the tribes receive individual blessings, and then Moses praises Jehovah as the eminent One: "A hiding place is the God of ancient time, and underneath are the indefinitely lasting arms." (33:27) From a heart brimming with appreciation, he then speaks his final words to the nation: "Happy you are, O Israel! Who is there like you, a people enjoying salvation in Jehovah?"—33:29.

29 After viewing the Land of Promise from Mount Nebo, Moses dies, and Jehovah buries him in Moab, his tomb being unknown and unhonored to this day. He lived to be 120 years of age, but "his eye had not grown dim, and his vital strength had not fled." Jehovah had used him to perform great signs and miracles, and as the final chapter reports, there had not yet "risen up a prophet in Israel like Moses, whom Jehovah knew face to face."—34:7, 10.

WHY BENEFICIAL

30 As the concluding book of the Pentateuch, Deuteronomy ties together all that has gone before in declaring and sanctifying the great name of Jehovah God. He alone is God, exacting exclusive devotion and tolerating no rivalry by demon gods of false religious worship. In this day, all Christians must give earnest attention to the great principles underlying God's law and obey him so that they will be free of his curse as he sharpens his glittering sword for execution of vengeance on his adversaries. His greatest and first commandment must become the guidepost in their lives: "You must love Jehovah your God with all your heart and all your soul and all your vital force."—6:5.

31 The rest of the Scriptures frequently refer to

---

25. (a) What covenant does Jehovah now conclude with Israel? (b) What choice does Moses place before the people?
26. What final arrangements does Moses make before his death?
27. What powerful message is contained in Moses' song?

28. How is Jehovah exalted in Moses' final blessing?
29. In what ways was Moses outstanding?
30. How does Deuteronomy provide a fitting conclusion to the Pentateuch?
31. How do other inspired scriptures draw on Deuteronomy in enriching appreciation for God's purposes?

Deuteronomy to enrich appreciation for the divine purposes. In addition to his quotations in answering the Tempter, Jesus made many other references. (Deut. 5:16—Matt. 15:4; Deut. 17:6—Matt. 18:16 and John 8:17) These continue into Revelation, where the glorified Jesus finally warns against adding to or taking away from the scroll of Jehovah's prophecy. (Deut. 4:2—Rev. 22:18) Peter quotes from Deuteronomy in clinching his powerful argument that Jesus is the Christ and the Prophet greater than Moses whom Jehovah promised to raise up in Israel. (Deut. 18:15-19—Acts 3:22, 23) Paul quotes from it with reference to rewards for workers, thorough investigation at the mouth of witnesses, and the instruction of children.—Deut. 25:4—1 Cor. 9:8-10 and 1 Tim. 5:17, 18; Deut. 13:14 and 19:15—1 Tim. 5:19 and 2 Cor. 13:1; Deut. 5:16—Eph. 6:2, 3.

[32] Not only the writers of the Christian Scriptures but also God's servants of pre-Christian times drew instruction and encouragement from Deuteronomy. We do well to follow their example. Consider the implicit obedience of Moses' successor, Joshua, in devoting conquered cities to destruction during the invasion of Canaan, taking no spoil as did Achan. (Deut. 20:15-18 and 21:23—Josh. 8:24-27, 29) Gideon's elimination of those "afraid and trembling" from his army was in obedience to the Law. (Deut. 20:1-9—Judg. 7:1-11) It was out of faithfulness to the law of Jehovah that the prophets in Israel and Judah spoke boldly and courageously in condemnation of backsliding nations. Amos provides an excellent example of this. (Deut. 24:12-15—Amos 2:6-8) Indeed, there are literally hundreds of examples tying Deuteronomy in with the rest of God's Word, thus showing that it is an integral and beneficial part of the harmonious whole.

[33] The very essence of Deuteronomy breathes praise to the Sovereign God, Jehovah. It stresses throughout: 'Worship Jehovah; render him exclusive devotion.' Though the Law is no longer binding upon Christians, its underlying principles have not been abrogated. (Gal. 3:19) How much true Christians can learn from this dynamic book of God's law, with its progressive teaching, candor, and simplicity of presentation! Why, even the nations of the world have recognized the excellence of Jehovah's supreme law, writing many of the regulations of Deuteronomy into their own lawbooks. The accompanying table gives interesting

examples of laws that they have drawn on or applied in principle.

[34] Moreover, this explanation of the Law points to and heightens appreciation of God's Kingdom. How so? While on earth the King-Designate, Jesus Christ, was thoroughly acquainted with the book and applied it, as his skillful references to it show. In spreading his Kingdom rule over all the earth, he will govern according to the right *principles* of this same "law," and all who come to bless themselves in him as the Kingdom "seed" will have to obey these principles. (Gen. 22:18; Deut. 7:12-14) It is beneficial and advantageous to start obeying them now. Far from being out-of-date, this 3,500-year-old "law" speaks to us today in dynamic tones, and it will keep on speaking right on into the new world under God's Kingdom. May Jehovah's name continue to be sanctified among his people in the application of all the beneficial instruction of the Pentateuch, which so gloriously reaches its climax in Deuteronomy—certainly an inspired and inspiring part of "all Scripture"!

34. What connection is there between this "Repetition of the Law" and God's Kingdom?

SOME LEGAL PRECEDENTS IN DEUTERONOMY*

	Chapters and Verses
I. Personal and family laws	
A. Personal relations	
1. Parents and children	5:16
2. Marriage relations	22:30; 27:20, 22, 23
3. Laws of divorce	22:13-19, 28, 29
B. Property rights	22:1-4
II. Constitutional laws	
A. Qualifications and duties of the king	17:14-20
B. Military regulations	
1. Exemptions from military service	20:1, 5-7; 24:5
2. Minor officers	20:9
III. The judiciary	
A. Duties of judges	16:18, 20
B. Supreme court of appeal	17:8-11
IV. Criminal laws	
A. Crimes against the state	
1. Bribery, perverting justice	16:19, 20
2. Perjury	5:20
B. Crimes against morality	
1. Adultery	5:18; 22:22-24
2. Unlawful marriage	22:30; 27:20, 22, 23
C. Crimes against the person	
1. Murder and assault	5:17; 27:24
2. Rape and seduction	22:25-29
V. Humane laws	
A. Kindness toward animals	25:4; 22:6, 7
B. Consideration for the unfortunate	24:6, 10-18
C. Building safety code	22:8
D. Treatment of dependent classes, including slaves and captives	15:12-15; 21:10-14; 27:18, 19
E. Philanthropic provisions for the needy	14:28, 29; 15:1-11; 16:11, 12; 24:19-22

* *Israel's Laws and Legal Precedents*, 1907, C. F. Kent, pages vii through xviii; see also *Insight on the Scriptures*, Vol. 2, pages 214-20.

32. In what respect are Joshua, Gideon, and the prophets fine examples for us?
33. (a) How does Deuteronomy breathe praise to Jehovah? (b) What does the accompanying table show as to the worldly nations' recognition of principles of God's law?

Joshua

Writer: **Joshua**
Place Written: **Canaan**
Writing Completed: **c. 1450 B.C.E.**
Time Covered:
1473–c. 1450 B.C.E.

THE year is 1473 B.C.E. The scene is most dramatic and thrilling. The Israelites, encamped on the Plains of Moab, are poised for their entry into Canaan, the Promised Land. That territory on the other side of the Jordan is inhabited by numerous petty kingdoms, each with its own private army. They are divided among themselves and weakened through years of corrupt domination by Egypt. Yet, to the nation of Israel, the opposition is formidable. The many fortified walled cities, such as Jericho, Ai, Hazor, and Lachish, have to be taken if the land is to be subdued. A critical time lies ahead. Decisive battles must be fought and won, with Jehovah himself entering in with powerful miracles in behalf of his people, in order to fulfill his promise to settle them in the land. Unquestionably, these stirring events, so outstanding in Jehovah's dealings with his people, will have to be recorded, and that by an eyewitness. What better man could there be for this than Joshua himself, the one appointed by Jehovah as successor to Moses!—Num. 27:15-23.

2 The choice of Joshua, both as leader and as a recorder of the events about to take place, is most appropriate. He has been a very close associate of Moses throughout the previous 40 years in the wilderness. He has been "the minister of Moses from his young manhood on," showing him to be qualified as a spiritual as well as a military leader. (Num. 11:28; Ex. 24:13; 33:11; Josh. 1:1) In the year Israel left Egypt, 1513 B.C.E., he was captain of the armies of Israel in the defeat of the Amalekites. (Ex. 17:9-14) As the loyal companion of Moses and a fearless army commander, he was the natural choice to represent the tribe of Ephraim when one man was chosen from each tribe for the dangerous mission of spying out Canaan. His courage and faithfulness on that occasion assured his entry into the Promised Land. (Num. 13:8; 14:6-9, 30, 38) Yes, this man Joshua, the son of Nun, is "a man in whom there is spirit," a man who "followed Jehovah wholly," a man "full of the spirit of wisdom." No wonder that "Israel continued to serve

Jehovah all the days of Joshua."—Num. 27:18; 32:12; Deut. 34:9; Josh. 24:31.

3 From the standpoint of his experience, training, and tested qualities as a true worshiper of Jehovah, Joshua was certainly in position to be used as one of the writers of the 'Scriptures inspired by God.' Joshua is no mere legendary figure but a real-life servant of Jehovah. He is mentioned by name in the Christian Greek Scriptures. (Acts 7:45; Heb. 4:8) It is logical that just as Moses was used to write concerning the events of his lifetime, so his successor, Joshua, would be used to write down the events that he himself witnessed. That the book was written by someone who witnessed the events is shown by Joshua 6:25. Jewish tradition credits Joshua with writership, and the book itself states: "Then Joshua wrote these words in the book of God's law."—Josh. 24:26.

4 At the time of Jericho's destruction, Joshua placed a prophetic curse on the rebuilding of the city, which had a remarkable fulfillment in the days of Ahab king of Israel, some 500 years later. (Josh. 6:26; 1 Ki. 16:33, 34) The authenticity of the book of Joshua is further established by the many references that later Bible writers make to the events recorded in it. Time and again, the psalmists refer to these (Ps. 44:1-3; 78:54, 55; 105:42-45; 135:10-12; 136:17-22), as do Nehemiah (Neh. 9:22-25), Isaiah (Isa. 28:21), the apostle Paul (Acts 13:19; Heb. 11:30, 31), and the disciple James (Jas. 2:25).

5 The book of Joshua covers a period of over 20 years, from the entry into Canaan in 1473 B.C.E. to approximately 1450 B.C.E., in which year Joshua probably died. The very name Joshua (Hebrew, *Yehoh·shu´a´*), meaning "Jehovah Is Salvation," is most fitting in view of Joshua's role as visible leader in Israel during the conquest of the land. He

---

3. What proves that Joshua was a real-life servant of Jehovah, as well as the writer of the book bearing his name?
4. How has the authenticity of the book of Joshua been proved both by the fulfillment of prophecy and by the testimony of later Bible writers?
5. (a) What period is covered by the book of Joshua? (b) Why is the name Joshua appropriate?

---

1. What situation confronts Israel in 1473 B.C.E.?
2. Why is the choice of Joshua, both as leader and as recorder, appropriate?

gave all the glory to Jehovah as Deliverer. In the *Septuagint* the book is called *I·e·sous'* (the Greek equivalent of *Yehoh·shu'a'*), and from this the name Jesus has been derived. In his fine qualities of courage, obedience, and integrity, Joshua was truly a splendid prophetic type of "our Lord Jesus Christ."—Rom. 5:1.

CONTENTS OF JOSHUA

⁶ The book falls into four natural sections: (1) crossing into the Promised Land, (2) the conquest of Canaan, (3) apportioning the land, and (4) Joshua's farewell exhortations. The entire account is vividly told and packed with thrilling drama.

⁷ **Crossing into the Promised Land** (1:1–5:12). Knowing of the tests ahead, Jehovah gives assurance and sound counsel to Joshua at the outset: "Only be courageous and very strong . . . This book of the law should not depart from your mouth, and you must in an undertone read in it day and night, in order that you may take care to do according to all that is written in it; for then you will make your way successful and then you will act wisely. Have I not commanded you? Be courageous and strong . . . for Jehovah your God is with you wherever you go." (1:7-9) Joshua gives credit to Jehovah as the real Leader and Commander and immediately sets about preparing to cross the Jordan as commanded. The Israelites accept him as Moses' successor, and they pledge loyalty. Onward, then, to the conquest of Canaan!

⁸ Two men are dispatched to spy out Jericho. Rahab the harlot seizes the opportunity to demonstrate her faith in Jehovah by hiding the spies at the risk of her life. In return, the spies swear that she will be spared when Jericho is destroyed. The spies carry back the report that all the inhabitants of the land have grown disheartened because of the Israelites. The report being favorable, Joshua moves immediately to the Jordan River, which is at flood stage. Jehovah now gives tangible evidence that he is backing up Joshua and that, just as in Moses' time, there is "a living God" in the midst of Israel. (3:10) As the priests carrying the ark of the covenant step into the Jordan, the waters from upstream are heaped up, allowing the Israelites to pass over on dry ground. Joshua takes 12 stones from the middle of the river as a memorial and sets another 12 stones in the river, where the priests are standing, after which the priests pass over and the waters return to flood stage.

⁹ Once across, the people encamp at Gilgal, between the Jordan and Jericho, and here Joshua sets up the memorial stones as a witness to the generations to come and "in order that all the peoples of the earth may know Jehovah's hand, that it is strong; in order that you may indeed fear Jehovah your God always." (4:24) (Joshua 10:15 indicates that thereafter Gilgal may have been used as a base camp for some time.) It is here that the sons of Israel are circumcised, since there had been no circumcising during the wilderness journey. The Passover is celebrated, the manna ceases, and at last the Israelites begin to eat the produce of the land.

¹⁰ **Conquest of Canaan** (5:13–12:24). Now the first objective lies within striking distance. But how to take this "tightly shut up" walled city of Jericho? (6:1) Jehovah himself details the procedure, sending the "prince of the army of Jehovah" to instruct Joshua. (5:14) Once a day for six days, the armies of Israel must march around the city, with the men of war in the lead, followed in procession by priests blowing rams' horns and others carrying the ark of the covenant. On the seventh day, they must go around seven times. Joshua faithfully relays the orders to the people. Exactly as commanded, the armies march around Jericho. No word is spoken. There is no sound but the tramping of feet and the blowing of horns by the priests. Then, on the final day, after the completion of the seventh circuit, Joshua signals them to shout. Shout they do, "a great war cry," and the walls of Jericho fall down flat! (6:20) As one man, they rush the city, capture it, and devote it to fiery destruction. Only the faithful Rahab and her household find deliverance.

¹¹ Then on westward to Ai! Confidence in another easy victory turns to dismay, as the men of Ai put to rout the 3,000 Israelite soldiers sent up to capture the city. What has happened? Has Jehovah forsaken them? Joshua anxiously inquires of Jehovah. In reply Jehovah discloses that contrary to his command to devote everything in Jericho to destruction, someone in the camp has disobeyed, stealing something and hiding it. This uncleanness must be removed from the camp before Israel can continue to prosper with Jehovah's blessing. Under divine guidance, Achan, the evildoer, is discovered, and he and his household are stoned to death. With Jehovah's favor restored, the Israelites now move against Ai. Once again Jehovah himself reveals the strategy to be used. The men of Ai are lured out of their walled city and find

---

6. Into what natural sections does the book of Joshua fall?
7. What encouragement and counsel does Jehovah give Joshua?
8. (a) How does Rahab demonstrate faith? (b) How does Jehovah show himself to be "a living God" in the midst of Israel?

---

9. What next happens at Gilgal?
10. How does Jehovah instruct Joshua concerning the capture of Jericho, and what dramatic action follows?
11. How is the initial reverse at Ai remedied?

themselves trapped in an ambush. The city is captured and devoted to destruction with all its inhabitants. (8:26-28) No compromise with the enemy!

[12] In obedience to Jehovah's command through Moses, Joshua next builds an altar in Mount Ebal and writes on it "a copy of the law." (8:32) Then he reads the words of the Law, together with the blessing and the malediction, to the assembly of the entire nation as they stand, half in front of Mount Gerizim and half in front of Mount Ebal. —Deut. 11:29; 27:1-13.

[13] Alarmed at the speedy progress of the invasion, a number of the petty kingdoms of Canaan unite in an effort to halt Joshua's advance. However, when 'the Gibeonites hear what Joshua has done to Jericho and Ai, they act with shrewdness.' (Josh. 9:3, 4) Under pretense of being from a land distant from Canaan, they enter into a covenant with Joshua "to let them live." When the ruse is discovered, the Israelites honor the covenant but make the Gibeonites "gatherers of wood and drawers of water," like the 'lowest slaves,' thus fulfilling in part Noah's inspired curse on Canaan, the son of Ham.—Josh. 9:15, 27; Gen. 9:25.

[14] This defection of the Gibeonites is no small matter, for "Gibeon was a great city . . . greater than Ai, and all its men were mighty ones." (Josh. 10:2) Adoni-zedek, king of Jerusalem, sees in this a threat to himself and the other kingdoms in Canaan. An example must be made to stop further desertion to the enemy. So Adoni-zedek and four other kings (those of the city kingdoms of Hebron, Jarmuth, Lachish, and Eglon) organize and war against Gibeon. Honoring his covenant with the Gibeonites, Joshua marches all night to their aid and routs the armies of the five kings. Once again Jehovah enters into the fight, using superhuman powers and signs, with devastating results. Mighty hailstones rain down from heaven, killing more of the enemy than the swords of the Israelite army. And then, wonder of wonders, 'the sun keeps standing still in the middle of the heavens and does not hasten to set for about a whole day.' (10:13) Thus, mopping-up operations can be completed. The worldly-wise may try to discount this miraculous event, but men of faith accept the divine record, well aware of Jehovah's power to control the forces of the universe and direct them according to his will. For a fact, "Jehovah himself was fighting for Israel."—10:14.

[15] After slaying the five kings, Joshua devotes Makkedah to destruction. Passing on quickly to the south, he utterly destroys Libnah, Lachish, Eglon, Hebron, and Debir—cities in the hills between the Salt Sea and the Great Sea. By now news of the invasion has spread the length of Canaan. Up in the north, the alarm is sounded by Jabin, king of Hazor. Far and wide, to both sides of the Jordan, he sends out the call to mass for united action against the Israelites. As they encamp by the waters of Merom, below Mount Hermon, the assembled forces of the enemy are "as numerous as the grains of sand that are on the seashore." (11:4) Again Jehovah assures Joshua of victory and outlines the battle strategy. And the result? Another crushing defeat for the enemies of Jehovah's people! Hazor is burned with fire, and its allied cities and their kings are devoted to destruction. Thus Joshua extends the area of Israelite domination through the length and breadth of Canaan. Thirty-one kings have been defeated.

[16] **Apportioning the land** (13:1–22:34). Despite these many victories, with many key fortified cities destroyed and with organized resistance broken for the time being, "to a very great extent the land yet remains to be taken in possession." (13:1) However, Joshua is now close to 80 years of age, and there is also another big job to be done—that of apportioning the land as inheritances for nine full tribes and the half tribe of Manasseh. Reuben, Gad, and half the tribe of Manasseh have already received their inheritance of land to the east of the Jordan, and the tribe of Levi is to receive none, "Jehovah the God of Israel" being their inheritance. (13:33) With the help of Eleazar the priest, Joshua now makes the assignments to the west of the Jordan. The 85-year-old Caleb, eager to fight Jehovah's enemies to the last, requests and is assigned the Anakim-infested region of Hebron. (14:12-15) After the tribes receive their inheritances by lot, Joshua requests the city of Timnahserah in the mountains of Ephraim, and this is given him "at the order of Jehovah." (19:50) The tent of meeting is set up at Shiloh, which is also in the mountainous region of Ephraim.

[17] Six cities of refuge for the unintentional manslayer are set aside, three on each side of the Jordan. Those to the west of the Jordan are Kedesh in Galilee, Shechem in Ephraim, and Hebron in the hill country of Judah. Those on the east are Bezer in Reuben's territory, Ramoth in Gilead, and Golan

---

12. What divine command does Joshua next carry out?
13. What results from the Gibeonites' acting "with shrewdness"?
14. How does Jehovah demonstrate at Gibeon that he is fighting for Israel?

15. Describe the course of the invasion and its climax at Hazor.
16. What assignments of land are made?
17. What provision is made for cities of refuge and for cities of residence for the Levites?

in Bashan. These are given "a sacred status." (20:7) Forty-eight cities with their pasture grounds are assigned by lot from the tribal allocations as cities of residence for the Levites. These include the six cities of refuge. Thus Israel "proceeded to take possession of [the land] and to dwell in it." Just as Jehovah had promised, so "it all came true."—21: 43, 45.

¹⁸ The men of war from the tribes of Reuben and Gad and from the half tribe of Manasseh, who have continued with Joshua up to this time, now return to their inheritances across the Jordan, carrying with them Joshua's exhortation to faithfulness and his blessing. On the way, as they come close to the Jordan, they erect a great altar. This precipitates a crisis. Since the appointed place for Jehovah's worship is at the tent of meeting in Shiloh, the western tribes fear treachery and disloyalty, and they prepare for battle against the supposed rebels. However, bloodshed is averted when it is explained that the altar is not for sacrifice but only to serve as "a witness between us [Israel to the east and to the west of the Jordan] that Jehovah is the true God."—22:34.

¹⁹ **Joshua's farewell exhortations** (23:1–24:33). 'And it comes about many days after Jehovah has given Israel rest from all their enemies all around, when Joshua is old and advanced in days,' that he calls all Israel together for inspiring farewell exhortations. (23:1) Humble to the end, he gives Jehovah all the credit for the great victories over the nations. Let all now continue faithful! "Be very courageous to keep and to do all that is written in the book of the law of Moses by never turning away from it to the right or to the left." (23:6) They must shun the false gods and 'be on constant guard for their souls by loving Jehovah their God.' (23: 11) There must be no compromise with the remaining Canaanites, no marriage or interfaith alliances with them, for this will bring down Jehovah's blazing anger.

²⁰ Assembling all the tribes at Shechem and calling out their representative officers before Jehovah, Joshua next relates Jehovah's personal account of His dealings with His people from the time He called Abraham and brought him into Canaan until the conquest and occupation of the Land of Promise. Again Joshua warns against false religion, calling on Israel to "fear Jehovah and serve him in faultlessness and in truth." Yes, "serve Jehovah"! Then he states the issue with utmost clarity: "Choose for yourselves today whom

you will serve, whether the gods that your forefathers . . . served or the gods of the Amorites in whose land you are dwelling. But as for me and my household, we shall serve Jehovah." With conviction reminiscent of Moses, he reminds Israel that Jehovah "is a holy God; he is a God exacting exclusive devotion." So, away with the foreign gods! The people are thus stirred to declare as one man: "Jehovah our God we shall serve, and to his voice we shall listen!" (24:14, 15, 19, 24) Before dismissing them, Joshua makes a covenant with them, writes these words in the book of God's law, and sets up a great stone as a witness. Then Joshua dies at the good old age of 110 years and is buried in Timnath-serah.

WHY BENEFICIAL

²¹ As you read Joshua's farewell exhortations concerning faithful service, does it not stir your heart? Do you not echo the words of Joshua that he uttered more than 3,400 years ago: "As for me and my household, we shall serve Jehovah"? Or if you serve Jehovah under conditions of trial or isolation from other faithful ones, do you not draw inspiration from Jehovah's words to Joshua, uttered at the beginning of the march into the Land of Promise: "Only be courageous and very strong"? Moreover, do you not find inestimable benefit in following His admonition to 'read [the Bible] in an undertone day and night, in order to make your way successful'? Surely, all who follow such wise counsel will find it outstandingly beneficial.—24: 15; 1:7-9.

²² The events so vividly recorded in the book of Joshua are more than just ancient history. They highlight godly principles—preeminently that implicit faith and obedience to Jehovah are vital to his blessing. The apostle Paul records that by faith "the walls of Jericho fell down after they had been encircled for seven days," and that because of faith "Rahab the harlot did not perish with those who acted disobediently." (Heb. 11:30, 31) James likewise cites Rahab as a beneficial example for Christians in producing works of faith.—Jas. 2:24-26.

²³ The unusual supernatural events recorded at Joshua 10:10-14, when the sun kept motionless and the moon stood still, as well as the many other miracles that Jehovah performed in behalf of his people, are powerful reminders of Jehovah's ability and purpose to bring a final extermination of all wicked opposers of God. Gibeon, the scene of battle both in Joshua's time and in David's time, is

---

18. What crisis develops between the eastern and the western tribes, but how is this resolved?
19, 20. (a) What farewell exhortations does Joshua give? (b) What issue does he put before Israel, and how does he emphasize the right choice for Israel to make?

21. What wise admonition in the book of Joshua is of outstanding benefit today?
22. What essential qualities of true worship are highlighted?
23. What powerful reminders are contained in Joshua?

connected by Isaiah with Jehovah's rising up in agitation for this extermination, "that he may do his deed—his deed is strange—and that he may work his work—his work is unusual."—Isa. 28: 21, 22.

²⁴ Do the events of Joshua point forward to God's Kingdom? Certainly they do! That the conquest and settlement of the Promised Land are to be tied in with something far greater was indicated by the apostle Paul: "For if Joshua had led them into a place of rest, God would not afterward have spoken of another day. So there remains a sabbath resting for the people of God." (Heb. 4:1, 8, 9) They

---

24. How does the book of Joshua tie in with the Kingdom promises, and what assurance does it give that these will 'all come true'?

press onward to make sure of their "entrance into the everlasting kingdom of our Lord and Savior Jesus Christ." (2 Pet. 1:10, 11) As shown by Matthew 1:5, Rahab became an ancestress of Jesus Christ. The book of Joshua thus provides another vital link in the record leading down to the production of the Kingdom Seed. It provides firm assurance that Jehovah's Kingdom promises will come to certain fulfillment. Speaking of God's promise made to Abraham, Isaac, and Jacob and repeated to the Israelites, their descendants, the record states concerning Joshua's day: "Not a promise failed out of all the good promise that Jehovah had made to the house of Israel; it all came true." (Josh. 21:45; Gen. 13:14-17) Likewise, with Jehovah's "good promise" concerning the righteous Kingdom of heaven—it shall all come true!

Bible Book Number **7** **Judges**		**Writer: Samuel**
		Place Written: **Israel**
		Writing Completed: **c. 1100 B.C.E.**
		Time Covered: **c. 1450–c. 1120 B.C.E.**

HERE is a page of Israel's history that is packed full of action, alternating between disastrous entanglements with demon religion and Jehovah's merciful deliverances of his repentant people by divinely appointed judges. Faith-inspiring are the mighty deeds of Othniel, Ehud, Shamgar, and the other judges who followed. As the writer of Hebrews said: "The time will fail me if I go on to relate about Gideon, Barak, Samson, Jephthah, . . . who through faith defeated kingdoms in conflict, effected righteousness, . . . from a weak state were made powerful, became valiant in war, routed the armies of foreigners." (Heb. 11:32-34) To round out the number of 12 faithful judges of this period, there are also Tola, Jair, Ibzan, Elon, and Abdon. (Samuel is not usually counted among the judges.) Jehovah fought the judges' battles for them, and spirit enveloped them as they performed their deeds of prowess. They gave all the credit and glory to their God.

² In the *Septuagint* the book is called *Kri·tai´*, and in the Hebrew Bible, it is *Sho·phetim´*, which is translated "Judges." *Sho·phetim´* is derived from

the verb *sha·phat´*, meaning to "judge, vindicate, punish, govern," which well expresses the office of these theocratic appointees of "God the Judge of all." (Heb. 12:23) They were men raised up by Jehovah on specific occasions to deliver his people from foreign bondage.

³ When was Judges written? Two expressions in the book help us to find the answer. The first is this: "But the Jebusites keep on dwelling . . . in Jerusalem down to this day." (Judg. 1:21) Since King David captured "the stronghold of Zion" from the Jebusites in the eighth year of his reign, or in 1070 B.C.E., Judges must have been written before that date. (2 Sam. 5:4-7) The second expression occurs four times: "In those days there was no king in Israel." (Judg. 17:6; 18:1; 19:1; 21:25) Hence, the record was written down at a time when there *was* a "king in Israel," that is, after Saul became the first king in 1117 B.C.E. It must therefore be dated between 1117 and 1070 B.C.E.

⁴ Who was the writer? Unquestionably, he was a devoted servant of Jehovah. It is Samuel who stands out alone as the principal advocate of Jehovah's worship at this time of transition from the

---

1. In what ways was the period of the judges noteworthy?
2. In what way is the Hebrew name of the book of Judges appropriate?

3. When was Judges written?
4. Who was the writer of Judges?

judges to the kings, and he is also the first of the line of faithful prophets. As such, Samuel would be the logical one to record the history of the judges.

⁵ How long a period does Judges cover? This can be calculated from 1 Kings 6:1, which shows that Solomon began to build the house of Jehovah in the fourth year of his reign, which was also "the four hundred and eightieth year after the sons of Israel came out from the land of Egypt." ("Four hundred and eightieth" being an ordinal number, it represents 479 full years.) The known time periods included in the 479 years are 40 years under Moses in the wilderness (Deut. 8:2), 40 years of Saul's reign (Acts 13:21), 40 years of David's reign (2 Sam. 5:4, 5), and the first 3 full years of Solomon's reign. Subtracting this total of 123 years from the 479 years of 1 Kings 6:1, there remain 356 years for the period between the entry of Israel into Canaan and the start of Saul's reign.* The events recorded in the book of Judges, extending largely from the death of Joshua down to the time of Samuel, cover about 330 years of this 356-year period.

⁶ The authenticity of Judges is beyond doubt. The Jews have always recognized it as part of the Bible canon. Writers of both the Hebrew and the Christian Greek Scriptures have drawn on its record, as at Psalm 83:9-18; Isaiah 9:4; 10:26; and Hebrews 11:32-34. In candor, it hides nothing of Israel's shortcomings and backsliding, while at the same time it exalts the infinite loving-kindness of Jehovah. It is Jehovah, and no mere human judge, who receives the glory as Deliverer in Israel.

⁷ Further, archaeological finds support the genuineness of Judges. Most striking are those on the nature of the Baal religion of the Canaanites. Apart from the Bible references, little was known of Baalism until the ancient Canaanite city of Ugarit (the modern Ras Shamra on the Syrian coast opposite the northeast tip of the island of Cyprus) was excavated, beginning in 1929. Here, Baal religion was revealed as featuring materialism, extreme nationalism, and sex worship. Each Canaanite city evidently had its Baal sanctuary as well as shrines known as high places. Inside the shrines, there may have been images of Baal, and near the altars outside were to be found stone pillars—perhaps phallic symbols of Baal. Detestable human sacrifices bloodied these shrines. When the Israelites became contaminated by Baalism, they likewise offered up their sons and daughters. (Jer. 32:35) There was a sacred pole representing Baal's mother, Asherah. The fertility goddess, Ashtoreth, Baal's wife, was worshiped by lewd sex rites, both men and women being kept as "consecrated" temple prostitutes. It is no wonder that Jehovah had commanded extermination for Baalism and its bestial adherents. "Your eye must not feel sorry for them; and you must not serve their gods."—Deut. 7:16.*

CONTENTS OF JUDGES

⁸ The book divides logically into three sections. The first two chapters describe the conditions in Israel at the time. Chapters 3 through 16 describe the deliverances of the 12 judges. Chapters 17 through 21 then describe some events involving internal strife in Israel.

⁹ **Conditions in Israel at the time of the judges** (1:1–2:23). The tribes of Israel are described as they spread out to settle in their assigned territories. However, instead of completely driving out the Canaanites, they put many of them to forced labor, permitting them to dwell among the Israelites. Therefore Jehovah's angel declares, "They must become snares to you, and their gods will serve as a lure to you." (2:3) Thus, when a new generation arises that does not know Jehovah or his works, the people soon abandon him to serve the Baals and other gods. Because Jehovah's hand is against them for calamity, they get "in very sore straits." Because of their stubbornness and refusal to listen even to the judges, Jehovah does not drive out a single one of the nations he has left to test Israel. This background is an aid in understanding subsequent events.—2:15.

¹⁰ **Judge Othniel** (3:1-11). In distress because of their captivity to the Canaanites, the sons of Israel begin to call on Jehovah for aid. He first raises up Othniel as judge. Does Othniel judge by human power and wisdom? No, for we read: "The spirit of Jehovah now came upon him" to subdue Israel's enemies. "After that the land had no disturbance for forty years."—3:10, 11.

---

* Most modern translations testify that the "about four hundred and fifty years" of Acts 13:20 do not correspond to the period of the judges but precede it; they would seem to cover the period from Isaac's birth in 1918 B.C.E. to the division of the Land of Promise in 1467 B.C.E. (*Insight on the Scriptures*, Vol. 1, page 462) The order in which the judges are mentioned in Hebrews 11:32 is different from that in the book of Judges, but this fact does not necessarily indicate that the events in Judges do not follow in chronological sequence, for certainly Samuel did not follow David.

5. How may the time period of Judges be calculated?
6. What proves the authenticity of Judges?
7. (a) How does archaeology support the record in Judges? (b) Why did Jehovah rightly decree extermination for Baal worshipers?

---

* *Insight on the Scriptures*, Vol. 1, pages 228-9, 948.

8. Into what sections does Judges logically divide?
9. What background is provided by the two opening chapters of Judges?
10. By what power does Othniel judge, and with what result?

[11] **Judge Ehud** (3:12-30). When the sons of Israel have been subject to Moab's king Eglon for 18 years, Jehovah again hears their calls for aid, and he raises up Judge Ehud. Gaining secret audience with the king, left-handed Ehud snatches his homemade sword from beneath his cloak and kills Eglon by plunging the sword deep into fat Eglon's belly. Israel rallies quickly to Ehud's side in the fight against Moab, and the land again enjoys God-given rest, for 80 years.

[12] **Judge Shamgar** (3:31). Shamgar saves Israel by striking down 600 Philistines. That the victory is by Jehovah's power is indicated by the weapon he uses—a mere cattle goad.

[13] **Judge Barak** (4:1–5:31). Israel next becomes subject to the Canaanite king Jabin and his army chief, Sisera, who boasts of having 900 chariots with iron scythes. As Israel again begins to cry out to Jehovah, He raises up Judge Barak, ably supported by the prophetess Deborah. So that Barak and his army may have no cause to boast, Deborah makes known that the battle will be by Jehovah's direction, and she prophesies: "It will be into the hand of a woman that Jehovah will sell Sisera." (4:9) Barak calls together men of Naphtali and Zebulun to Mount Tabor. His army of 10,000 then descends to do battle. Strong faith wins the day. 'Jehovah begins to throw Sisera and all his war chariots and all the camp into confusion,' overwhelming them by a flash flood in the valley of Kishon. "Not as much as one remained." (4:15, 16) Jael, wife of Heber the Kenite, to whose tent Sisera flees, climaxes the slaughter by nailing Sisera's head to the ground with a tent pin. "Thus God subdued Jabin." (4:23) Deborah and Barak exult in song, extolling the invincible might of Jehovah, who caused even the stars to fight from their orbits against Sisera. Truly, it is a time to "bless Jehovah"! (5:2) Forty years of peace follow.

[14] **Judge Gideon** (6:1–9:57). The sons of Israel again do what is bad, and the land is devastated by the raiding Midianites. Jehovah, through his angel, commissions Gideon as judge, and Jehovah himself adds assurance with the words, "I shall prove to be with you." (6:16) Gideon's first courageous act is to break down Baal's altar in his home city. The combined armies of the enemy now cross over into Jezreel, and 'Jehovah's spirit envelops Gideon' as he summons Israel to battle. (6:34) By the test of exposing a fleece to the dew on the threshing floor, Gideon receives a twofold sign that God is with him.

[15] Jehovah tells Gideon that his army of 32,000 is too large and that the size may give cause for human bragging about victory. The fearful are first sent home, leaving but 10,000. (Judg. 7:3; Deut. 20:8) Then, by the water-drinking test, all but an alert and watchful 300 are eliminated. Gideon spies out the Midianite camp at night and is reassured when he hears a man interpret a dream to mean that "this is nothing else but the sword of Gideon . . . The true God has given Midian and all the camp into his hand." (Judg. 7:14) Gideon worships God and then sets his men in three bands around the Midianite camp. The calm of night is suddenly shattered by the trumpeting of horns, by the dashing to pieces of large water jars, by the flashing of torches, and by Gideon's 300 shouting, "Jehovah's sword and Gideon's!" (7:20) The enemy camp breaks into pandemonium. The men fight one against another and take to flight. Israel gives chase, slaughtering them and killing their princes. The people of Israel now ask Gideon to rule over them, but he refuses, saying, "Jehovah is the one who will rule over you." (8:23) However, he makes an ephod out of the war booty, which later comes to be overly venerated and hence becomes a snare to Gideon and his household. The land has rest for 40 years during Gideon's judgeship.

[16] Abimelech, one of Gideon's sons by a concubine, usurps power after Gideon's death, and he murders his 70 half brothers. Jotham, Gideon's youngest son, is the only one to escape, and he proclaims Abimelech's doom from atop Mount Gerizim. In this parable about the trees, he likens Abimelech's "kingship" to that of a lowly bramble. Abimelech soon gets caught up in internal strife in Shechem and is humiliated in death, being killed by a woman when she makes a direct hit with a millstone thrown from the tower of Thebez, smashing his skull.—Judg. 9:53; 2 Sam. 11:21.

[17] **Judges Tola and Jair** (10:1-5). These are next to effect deliverances in Jehovah's power, judging for 23 and 22 years respectively.

[18] **Judge Jephthah** (10:6–12:7). As Israel persists in turning to idolatry, Jehovah's anger again blazes against the nation. The people now suffer oppression by the Ammonites and the Philistines.

---

11. How does Jehovah use Ehud in bringing deliverance to Israel?

12. What shows that Shamgar's victory is by God's power?

13. What dramatic events are climaxed by the victory song of Barak and Deborah?

14, 15. What sign of Jehovah's backing does Gideon receive, and how is this backing further emphasized in the final defeat of the Midianites?

16. What doom befalls the usurper Abimelech?

17. What does the record tell of Judges Tola and Jair?

18. (a) What deliverance does Jephthah bring? (b) What vow to Jehovah does Jephthah faithfully perform? How?

Jephthah is recalled from exile to lead Israel in the fight. But who is the real judge in this controversy? Jephthah's own words supply the answer: "Let Jehovah the Judge judge today between the sons of Israel and the sons of Ammon." (11:27) As Jehovah's spirit now comes upon him, he vows that on returning from Ammon in peace, he will devote to Jehovah the one who shall first come out of his house to meet him. Jephthah subdues Ammon with a great slaughter. As he returns to his home in Mizpah, it is his own daughter who first comes running to meet him with joy at Jehovah's victory. Jephthah fulfills his vow—no, not by pagan human sacrifice according to Baal rites, but by devoting this only daughter to exclusive service in Jehovah's house to His praise.

[19] The men of Ephraim now protest that they were not called on to fight against Ammon, and they threaten Jephthah, who is compelled to drive them back. In all, 42,000 Ephraimites are slaughtered, many of them at the fords of the Jordan, where they are identified by their failure to pronounce the password "Shibboleth" correctly. Jephthah continues to judge Israel for six years.—12:6.

[20] **Judges Ibzan, Elon, and Abdon** (12:8-15). Though little is mentioned concerning these, the periods of their judging are stated as seven, ten, and eight years respectively.

[21] **Judge Samson** (13:1–16:31). Once again Israel falls captive to the Philistines. This time it is Samson whom Jehovah raises up as judge. His parents devote him as a Nazirite from birth, and this requires that no razor shall ever come upon his hair. As he grows up, Jehovah blesses him, and 'in time Jehovah's spirit starts to impel him.' (13:25) The secret of his strength lies, not in human muscle, but in power supplied by Jehovah. It is when 'Jehovah's spirit becomes operative upon him' that he is empowered to slay a lion with his bare hands and later to repay Philistine treachery by striking down 30 of their number. (14:6, 19) As the Philistines continue to act treacherously in connection with Samson's betrothal to a Philistine girl, Samson takes 300 foxes and, turning them tail to tail, puts torches between their tails and sends them out to burn the grainfields, vineyards, and olive groves of the Philistines. Then he accomplishes a great slaughter of the Philistines, "piling legs upon thighs." (15:8) The Philistines persuade his fellow Israelites, men of Judah, to bind Samson and deliver him to them, but again 'Jehovah's

spirit becomes operative upon him,' and his fetters melt, as it were, from off his hands. Samson strikes down a thousand Philistines—"one heap, two heaps!" (15:14-16) His weapon of destruction? The moist jawbone of an ass. Jehovah refreshes his exhausted servant by causing a miraculous spring of water to break forth at the scene of battle.

[22] Samson next lodges a night at a prostitute's house in Gaza, where the Philistines quietly surround him. However, Jehovah's spirit again proves to be with him as he arises at midnight, pulls out the doors of the city gate and the side posts, and carries them clear to the top of a mountain facing Hebron. After this he falls in love with the treacherous Delilah. A willing tool of the Philistines, she nags him until he discloses that his Nazirite devotion to Jehovah, as symbolized in his long hair, is the real source of his great strength. While he sleeps, she has his hair snipped off. This time it is in vain that he awakes to do battle, for "it was Jehovah that had departed from him." (16:20) The Philistines grab him, bore out his eyes, and set him to grinding as a slave in their prison house. As it comes time for a great festival in honor of their god Dagon, the Philistines bring Samson out to provide amusement for them. Failing to attach value to the fact that his hair is again growing luxuriantly, they allow him to be stationed between the two mighty pillars of the house used for the worship of Dagon. Samson calls on Jehovah: "Lord Jehovah, remember me, please, and strengthen me, please, just this once." Jehovah *does* remember him. Samson grasps the pillars and 'bends himself with power'—Jehovah's power—'and the house goes falling, so that the dead that he puts to death in his own death come to be more than those he put to death during his lifetime.'—16:28-30.

[23] We now come to chapters 17 through 21, which describe some of the internal strife that unhappily plagues Israel during this time. These events take place quite early in the period of the judges, as is indicated by mention of Jonathan and Phinehas, grandsons of Moses and Aaron, as being still alive.

[24] **Micah and the Danites** (17:1–18:31). Micah, a man of Ephraim, sets up his own independent religious establishment, an idolatrous "house of gods," complete with a carved image and a Levite priest. (17:5) Tribesmen of Dan come by on their way to seek an inheritance in the north. They plunder Micah of his religious paraphernalia and priest, and they march far north to destroy the

---

19. What events lead to the "Shibboleth" test?
20. Which three judges next receive mention?
21, 22. (a) What mighty acts does Samson perform, and by what power? (b) How is Samson overcome by the Philistines? (c) What events culminate in Samson's greatest feat, and who remembers him in this hour?

23. What events are recounted in chapters 17 through 21, and when did they take place?
24. How do some Danites set up an independent religion?

unsuspecting city of Laish. In its place they build their own city of Dan and set up Micah's carved image. Thus, they follow the religion of their own independent choice all the days that Jehovah's house of true worship continues in Shiloh.

25 **Benjamin's sin at Gibeah** (19:1–21:25). The next recorded event gives rise to Hosea's later words: "From the days of Gibeah you have sinned, O Israel." (Hos. 10:9) Returning home with his concubine, a Levite from Ephraim lodges overnight with an old man in Gibeah of Benjamin. Good-for-nothing men of the city surround the house, demanding to have intercourse with the Levite. However, they accept his concubine instead and abuse her all night. She is found dead on the threshold in the morning. The Levite takes her body home, carves it into 12 pieces, and sends these into all Israel. The 12 tribes are thus put to the test. Will they punish Gibeah and so remove the immoral condition from Israel? Benjamin condones this vile crime. The other tribes congregate to Jehovah at Mizpah, where they resolve to go up by lot against Benjamin at Gibeah. After two sanguinary setbacks, the other tribes succeed by an ambush and practically annihilate the tribe of Benjamin, only 600 men escaping to the crag of Rimmon. Later, Israel regrets that one tribe has been chopped off. Occasion is found to provide wives for the surviving Benjamites from among the daughters of Jabesh-gilead and of Shiloh. This closes out a record of strife and intrigue in Israel. As the concluding words of Judges repeat, "In those days there was no king in Israel. What was right in his own eyes was what each one was accustomed to do."—Judg. 21:25.

WHY BENEFICIAL

26 Far from being merely a record of strife and bloodshed, the book of Judges exalts Jehovah as the great Deliverer of his people. It shows how his incomparable mercy and long-suffering are expressed toward his name people when they come to him with repentant hearts. Judges is most beneficial in its forthright advocacy of Jehovah's worship and its powerful warnings concerning the folly of demon religion, interfaith, and immoral

associations. Jehovah's severe condemnation of Baal worship should impel us to stand clear of the modern-day equivalents of materialism, nationalism, and sexual immorality.—2:11-18.

27 An examination of the fearless and courageous faith of the judges should stir in our hearts a like faith. No wonder they are mentioned with such glowing approval at Hebrews 11:32-34! They were fighters in sanctification of Jehovah's name, but not in their own strength. They knew the source of their power, Jehovah's spirit, and they humbly acknowledged it. Likewise, we today can take up "the sword of the spirit," God's Word, confident that God will empower us as he did Barak, Gideon, Jephthah, Samson, and the others. Yes, in overcoming mighty obstacles, with the help of Jehovah's spirit, we can be as strong spiritually as Samson was physically if we but pray to Jehovah and lean upon him.—Eph. 6:17, 18; Judg. 16:28.

28 The prophet Isaiah refers to Judges in two places to show how Jehovah will, without fail, shatter the yoke that His enemies place upon his people, just as he did in the days of Midian. (Isa. 9:4; 10:26) This reminds us also of the song of Deborah and Barak, which concludes with the fervent prayer: "Thus let all your enemies perish, O Jehovah, and let your lovers be as when the sun goes forth in its mightiness." (Judg. 5:31) And who are these lovers? Showing them to be the Kingdom heirs, Jesus Christ himself used a similar expression at Matthew 13:43: "At that time the righteous ones will shine as brightly as the sun in the kingdom of their Father." Thus, the book of Judges points forward to the time when the righteous Judge and Kingdom Seed, Jesus, will exercise power. By means of him, Jehovah will bring glory and sanctification to His name, in harmony with the psalmist's prayer concerning the enemies of God: "Do to them as to Midian, as to Sisera, as to Jabin at the torrent valley of Kishon . . . that people may know that you, whose name is Jehovah, you alone are the Most High over all the earth."—Ps. 83: 9, 18; Judg. 5:20, 21.

---

25. How is internal strife in Israel climaxed at Gibeah?
26. What powerful warnings in Judges apply also in this day?

---

27. How may we today profit by the good example of the judges?
28. How does the book of Judges point forward to the sanctification of Jehovah's name through the Kingdom Seed?

Bible
Book
Number **8**

Writer: **Samuel**
Place Written: **Israel**
Writing Completed: **c. 1090 B.C.E.**
Time Covered: **11 years of
judges' rule**

Ruth

THE book of Ruth is a delightful drama that blossoms into the beautiful love story of Boaz and Ruth. However, it is no mere love idyll. Its purpose is not to entertain. The book highlights Jehovah's purpose to produce a Kingdom heir, and it exalts His loving-kindness. (Ruth 1:8; 2:20; 3:10) The expansive quality of Jehovah's love is seen in his selecting a Moabitess, a former worshiper of the pagan god Chemosh, who converted to the true religion, to become an ancestress of Jesus Christ. Ruth is one of four women mentioned by name in the genealogy from Abraham to Jesus. (Matt. 1:3, 5, 16) Ruth, along with Esther, is one of the two women after whom Bible books are named.

2 "Now it came about in the days when the judges administered justice . . . " With these opening words, the book of Ruth launches into its thrilling narrative. From these words it is understood that the book itself was written later, in the time of the kings of Israel. However, the events related in the book covered a period of about 11 years in the time of the judges. Though the name of the writer is not stated, very likely it was Samuel, who also appears to have written Judges and who was the outstanding faithful figure at the start of the period of the kings. Since the closing verses indicate that David was already becoming prominent, this would place the writing at about 1090 B.C.E. Samuel, who was well acquainted with Jehovah's promise of "a lion" from the tribe of Judah, and who had been used by Jehovah in anointing David of that tribe to be king in Israel, would be deeply interested in making a record of the genealogy down to David.—Gen. 49:9, 10; 1 Sam. 16:1, 13; Ruth 1:1; 2:4; 4:13, 18-22.

3 The canonical authority of Ruth has never been challenged. Sufficient confirmation of it was given when Jehovah inspired the listing of Ruth in the genealogy of Jesus at Matthew 1:5. Ruth has always been recognized by the Jews as part of the Hebrew canon. It is not surprising, then, that fragments of the book have been found among the other canonical books in the Dead Sea Scrolls that were discovered starting in 1947. Moreover, Ruth harmonizes completely with Jehovah's Kingdom purposes as well as with the requirements of the Law of Moses. Though marriage with idol-worshiping Canaanites and Moabites was forbidden to the Israelites, this did not exclude foreigners such as Ruth who embraced Jehovah's worship. In the book of Ruth, the law on repurchase and brother-in-law marriage is observed in all its detail.—Deut. 7:1-4; 23:3, 4; 25:5-10.

CONTENTS OF RUTH

4 **Ruth's decision to stick with Naomi** (1:1-22). The story opens during a season of famine in Israel. A man of Bethlehem, Elimelech, crosses the Jordan with his wife, Naomi, and two sons, Mahlon and Chilion, to settle for a time in the land of Moab. There the sons marry Moabite women, Orpah and Ruth. Tragedy breaks the family circle, first in the death of the father, and later in the death of his two sons. Three childless, widowed women are left, with no seed to Elimelech. Hearing that Jehovah has again turned his attention to Israel by giving his people bread, Naomi decides to journey back to her native Judah. The daughters-in-law set out with her. Naomi pleads with them to return to Moab, petitioning Jehovah's loving-kindness in providing them with husbands from their own people. Finally Orpah "returned to her people and her gods," but Ruth, sincere and strong in her conversion to the worship of Jehovah, sticks with Naomi. Her decision is beautifully expressed in the words: "Where you go I shall go, and where you spend the night I shall spend the night. Your people will be my people, and your God my God. Where you die I shall die, and there is where I shall be buried. May Jehovah do so to me and add to it if anything but death should make a separation between me and you." (1:15-17) However, the widowed and childless Naomi, whose name means

---

1. (a) Why is the book of Ruth more than just a love story? (b) What special mention is given Ruth in the Bible?
2. When did the events of Ruth take place, when was the book written, and by whom?
3. What facts confirm the canonicity of Ruth?

---

4. What decision faces Ruth, and what does her choice indicate as to her form of worship?

"My Pleasantness," suggests for herself the name Mara, meaning "Bitter."

⁵ **Ruth gleans in the field of Boaz** (2:1-23). On arrival in Bethlehem, Ruth obtains Naomi's permission to glean in the barley harvest. Boaz, the owner of the field, an elderly Jew and near kinsman of her father-in-law, Elimelech, notices her. Though God's law grants her gleaner's rights, Ruth shows meekness by asking permission to work in the field. (Lev. 19:9, 10) This is readily granted, and Boaz tells her to glean only in his field with his young women. Saying that he has heard of her loyal conduct toward Naomi, he encourages her with the words: "May Jehovah reward the way you act, and may there come to be a perfect wage for you from Jehovah the God of Israel, under whose wings you have come to seek refuge." (Ruth 2:12) That evening Ruth generously shares the fruits of her labor with Naomi and explains that her success in gleaning is due to the goodwill of Boaz. Naomi sees in this the hand of Jehovah, saying: "Blessed be he of Jehovah, who has not left his loving-kindness toward the living and the dead. . . . The man is related to us. He is one of our repurchasers." (2:20) Yes, Boaz is a near relative, who can legally raise up offspring for Naomi in the name of the dead Elimelech. Ruth continues to glean in the fields of Boaz until the barley harvest and the wheat harvest come to an end.

⁶ **Boaz, as repurchaser, marries Ruth** (3:1–4: 22). Having grown too old herself for bearing offspring, Naomi now instructs Ruth to substitute for her in marriage by repurchase. At such an important season, it was customary for the landowner personally to supervise the winnowing out of the grain, which was done in the evening in order to catch the breezes that blew after a hot day. Boaz would be sleeping at the threshing floor, and that is where Ruth finds him. She comes quietly to him, uncovers him at his feet, and lies down. On his awaking at midnight, she identifies herself and, in compliance with the customary procedure followed by women when claiming the right to brother-in-law marriage, requests that he spread his skirt over her.* Boaz declares, "Blessed may you be of Jehovah, my daughter," and commends her for not going after the young men out of passion or greed. Far from being one who would make a proposal of impure relationship, Ruth makes a reputation as "an excellent woman." (3: 10, 11) However, as he now tells her, there is

another repurchaser more closely related than himself; he will consult with this one in the morning. Ruth keeps lying at his feet until early morning. Then he presents her with a gift of grain, and she returns to Naomi, who anxiously inquires about the outcome.

⁷ Boaz goes up early to the city gate to seek the repurchaser. Taking ten of the older men of the city as witnesses, he gives this next of kin first opportunity to purchase all that had belonged to Elimelech. Will he do this? His immediate answer is yes when it appears that he can increase his wealth. However, when he learns of the requirement that he perform brother-in-law marriage with Ruth, he becomes fearful for his own inheritance and then legally signifies his refusal by drawing off his sandal. In the Bible record he remains nameless, receiving only dishonorable mention as "So-and-so." Before the same witnesses, Boaz then purchases Ruth as his wife. Is this for any selfish reason? No, but that "the name of the dead man may not be cut off." (4:1, 10) All the onlookers ask Jehovah's blessing on this loving arrangement, and wonderful indeed does that blessing prove to be! Ruth bears a son to Boaz in his old age, and Naomi becomes nurse to the child. He is called "a son . . . to Naomi" and is named Obed. —4:17.

⁸ The closing verses of Ruth give the genealogy from Perez, through Boaz, to David. Some critics have argued that not all the generations are listed, as the time span is too great for so few persons. Is this true? Or was each one blessed with great longevity and with a son in his old age? The latter conclusion could be the correct one, emphasizing that the production of the promised Seed is by Jehovah's arrangement and undeserved kindness, and not by the natural power of man. On other occasions Jehovah exercised his power in a similar way, as with the births of Isaac, Samuel, and John the Baptizer.—Gen. 21:1-5; 1 Sam. 1:1-20; Luke 1:5-24, 57-66.

WHY BENEFICIAL

⁹ This delightful record is certainly beneficial, helping lovers of righteousness to build strong faith. All the principals in this exciting drama showed outstanding faith in Jehovah, and they "had witness borne to them through their faith." (Heb. 11:39) They became fine examples for us today. Naomi exhibited deep confidence in the loving-kindness of Jehovah. (Ruth 1:8; 2:20) Ruth

---

* *Insight on the Scriptures,* Vol. 2, page 829.

5. What fine qualities does Ruth display, and how does Boaz encourage her?
6. How does Ruth request marriage by repurchase, and what response does Boaz make?

7. How does Boaz negotiate the marriage, and what blessing results?
8. What further indicates that the production of the Seed of promise is by Jehovah's arrangement?
9. In what respects are the principal persons in the drama of Ruth fine examples for us today?

willingly left her homeland to pursue the worship of Jehovah; she proved herself to be loyal and submissive, as well as a willing worker. It was Boaz' keen appreciation of Jehovah's law and his humble acquiescence in doing Jehovah's will, as well as his love for the faithful Naomi and the industrious Ruth, that led him to perform his privilege of marriage by repurchase.

[10] Jehovah's provision of marriage, and in this instance marriage by repurchase, was used to his honor. Jehovah was the Arranger of the marriage of Boaz and Ruth, and he blessed it according to his

---

10. Why should the record in Ruth strengthen our confidence in the Kingdom promises?

loving-kindness; he used it as a means of preserving unbroken the royal line of Judah leading to David and finally to the Greater David, Jesus Christ. Jehovah's watchful care in producing the Kingdom Heir according to his legal provision should strengthen our assurance and make us look forward with confidence to the fulfillment of all the Kingdom promises. It should stimulate us to be busy in the modern-day harvest work, confident of a perfect wage from Jehovah, the God of spiritual Israel, under whose 'wings we have come to seek refuge' and whose Kingdom purposes are advancing so gloriously to their complete fulfillment. (2:12) The book of Ruth is another essential link in the record leading up to that Kingdom!

Bible Book Number 9

1 Samuel

Writers: **Samuel, Gad, Nathan**
Place Written: **Israel**
Writing Completed: **c. 1078 B.C.E.**
Time Covered:
  c. 1180–1078 B.C.E.

IN THE year 1117 B.C.E., there came a momentous change in Israel's national organization. A human king was appointed! This happened while Samuel was serving as Jehovah's prophet in Israel. Though Jehovah had foreknown and foretold it, still the change to a monarchy, as demanded by the people of Israel, came as a stunning blow to Samuel. Devoted as he had been to Jehovah's service from birth, and filled as he was with reverential recognition of Jehovah's kingship, Samuel foresaw disastrous results for his fellow members of God's holy nation. Only at Jehovah's direction did Samuel give in to their demands. "Upon that Samuel spoke to the people about the rightful due of the kingship and wrote it in a book and deposited it before Jehovah." (1 Sam. 10:25) Thus there came to an end the era of the judges, and there began the era of human kings that would see Israel rise to unprecedented power and prestige, only to fall finally into disgrace and divorcement from Jehovah's favor.

[2] Who would qualify to make the divine record of this momentous period? Fittingly, Jehovah chose the faithful Samuel to start the writing. Samuel means "Name of God," and he was indeed

outstanding as an upholder of Jehovah's name in those days. It appears that Samuel wrote the first 24 chapters of the book. Then, at his death, Gad and Nathan took up the writing, completing the last few years of the record down to Saul's death. This is indicated by 1 Chronicles 29:29, which reads: "As for the affairs of David the king, the first ones and the last, there they are written among the words of Samuel the seer and among the words of Nathan the prophet and among the words of Gad the visionary." Unlike Kings and Chronicles, the books of Samuel make practically no reference to earlier records, and thus David's contemporaries Samuel, Gad, and Nathan are confirmed as the writers. All three of these men held positions of trust as prophets of Jehovah and were opposed to the idolatry that had sapped the strength of the nation.

[3] The two books of Samuel were originally one roll, or volume. Samuel was divided into two books when this part of the Greek *Septuagint* was published. In the *Septuagint,* First Samuel was called First Kingdoms. This division and the name First Kings were adopted by the Latin *Vulgate* and continue in Catholic Bibles to this day. That First and Second Samuel originally formed one book is shown by the Masoretic note to 1 Samuel 28:24,

---

1. What great change in the organization of the nation of Israel came in 1117 B.C.E., and what conditions were to follow thereafter?
2. Who wrote First Samuel, and what were their qualifications?

3. (a) How did First Samuel come to be a separate Bible book? (b) When was it completed, and what period does it cover?

which states that this verse is in the middle of the book of Samuel. The book appears to have been completed about 1078 B.C.E. Hence First Samuel likely covers a period of a little more than a hundred years, from about 1180 to 1078 B.C.E.

⁴ Evidence abounds as to the accuracy of the record. Geographic locations fit the events described. Interestingly, Jonathan's successful attack on a Philistine garrison at Michmash, which led to the complete rout of the Philistines, was repeated in World War I by a British Army officer, who reportedly routed the Turks by following the landmarks described in Samuel's inspired record. —14:4-14.*

⁵ However, there are even stronger proofs of the inspiration and authenticity of the book. It contains the striking fulfillment of Jehovah's prophecy that Israel would ask for a king. (Deut. 17:14; 1 Sam. 8:5) Years later, Hosea confirmed its record, quoting Jehovah as saying, "I proceeded to give you a king in my anger, and I shall take him away in my fury." (Hos. 13:11) Peter implied that Samuel was inspired when he identified Samuel as a prophet who had 'plainly declared the days' of Jesus. (Acts 3:24) Paul quoted 1 Samuel 13:14 in briefly highlighting the history of Israel. (Acts 13: 20-22) Jesus himself stamped the account as authentic by asking the Pharisees in his day: "Have you not *read* what David did when he and the men with him got hungry?" He then related the account of David's asking for the showbread. (Matt. 12:1-4; 1 Sam. 21:1-6) Ezra also accepted the account as genuine, as already mentioned. —1 Chron. 29:29.

⁶ This being the original account of David's activities, every mention of David throughout the Scriptures confirms the book of Samuel as being part of God's inspired Word. Some of its events are even referred to in superscriptions of the psalms of David, as at Psalm 59 (1 Sam. 19:11), Psalm 34 (1 Sam. 21:13, 14), and Psalm 142 (1 Sam. 22:1 or 1 Sam. 24:1, 3). Thus, the internal evidence of God's own Word testifies conclusively to the authenticity of First Samuel.

CONTENTS OF FIRST SAMUEL

⁷ The book covers in part or entirely the life spans of four of Israel's leaders: Eli the high priest,

Samuel the prophet, Saul the first king, and David who was anointed to be the next king.

⁸ **Eli's judgeship and the youthful Samuel** (1:1– 4:22). As the account opens, we are introduced to Hannah, the favorite wife of Elkanah, a Levite. She is childless and is scorned on this account by Elkanah's other wife, Peninnah. While the family is making one of its yearly visits to Shiloh, where the ark of Jehovah's covenant is located, Hannah prays fervently to Jehovah for a son. She promises that if her prayer is answered, she will devote the child to the service of Jehovah. God answers her prayer, and she bears a son, Samuel. As soon as he is weaned, she brings him to the house of Jehovah and places him in the care of the high priest, Eli, as one 'lent to Jehovah.' (1:28) Hannah then expresses herself in a jubilant song of thanksgiving and happiness. The boy becomes "a minister of Jehovah before Eli the priest."—2:11.

⁹ All is not well with Eli. He is old, and his two sons have become good-for-nothing scoundrels who do "not acknowledge Jehovah." (2:12) They use their priestly office to satisfy their greed and immoral lusts. Eli fails to correct them. Jehovah therefore proceeds to send divine messages against the house of Eli, warning that "there will not come to be an old man in your house" and that both of Eli's sons will die on the one day. (1 Sam. 2: 30-34; 1 Ki. 2:27) Finally, He sends the boy Samuel to Eli with an ear-tingling judgment message. Thus young Samuel is accredited as prophet in Israel.—1 Sam. 3:1, 11.

¹⁰ In due course Jehovah executes this judgment by bringing up the Philistines. As the tide of battle turns against Israel, the Israelites, shouting loudly, bring the ark of the covenant from Shiloh to their army encampment. Hearing the shouting and learning that the Ark had been brought inside the Israelite camp, the Philistines strengthen themselves and win a startling victory, completely routing the Israelites. The Ark is captured, and Eli's two sons die. His heart atremble, Eli hears the report. At mention of the Ark, he falls backward off his seat and dies of a broken neck. Thus ends his 40-year judgeship. Truly, "Glory has gone away from Israel," for the Ark represents Jehovah's presence with his people.—4:22.

¹¹ **Samuel judges Israel** (5:1–7:17). Now the Philistines too have to learn to their great sorrow that the ark of Jehovah must not be used as a magic charm. When they take the Ark into Dagon's temple at Ashdod, their god falls flat on his face.

---

* The Romance of the Last Crusade, 1923, Major Vivian Gilbert, pages 183-6.

4. How has the accuracy of the record in First Samuel been supported?
5. How do Bible writers testify to the genuineness of First Samuel?
6. What other internal Bible evidence shows First Samuel to be authentic?
7. The history contained in the book concerns the lives of which leaders in Israel?

8. What are the circumstances of Samuel's birth and of his becoming "a minister of Jehovah"?
9. How does Samuel come to be prophet in Israel?
10. How does Jehovah execute judgment on Eli's house?
11. How does the Ark prove to be no magic charm?

On the next day Dagon again falls down flat at the threshold, this time with his head and both palms cut off. This starts the superstitious Philistine practice of 'not treading upon the threshold of Dagon.' (5:5) The Philistines hurry the Ark off to Gath and then to Ekron but all to no avail! Torments come in the form of panic, piles, and a plague of rodents. The Philistine axis lords, in final desperation as the death toll mounts, return the Ark to Israel on a new wagon drawn by two cows that were giving suck. At Beth-shemesh disaster befalls some of the Israelites because they look upon the Ark. (1 Sam. 6:19; Num. 4:6, 20) Finally, the Ark comes to rest in the house of Abinadab in the Levite city of Kiriath-jearim.

¹² For 20 years the Ark remains in the house of Abinadab. Samuel, grown to manhood, urges Israel to put away the Baals and the Ashtoreth images and to serve Jehovah with all their heart. This they do. As they gather to Mizpah to worship, the axis lords of the Philistines seize the opportunity for battle and catch Israel off guard. Israel calls on Jehovah through Samuel. A loud noise of thunder from Jehovah throws the Philistines into confusion, and the Israelites, strengthened by sacrifice and by prayer, gain a smashing victory. From that time on, 'the hand of Jehovah continues to be against the Philistines all the days of Samuel.' (7:13) However, there is no retirement for Samuel. All his life he keeps judging Israel, making a yearly circuit from Ramah, just north of Jerusalem, to Bethel, Gilgal, and Mizpah. In Ramah he builds an altar to Jehovah.

¹³ **Israel's first king, Saul** (8:1–12:25). Samuel has grown old in Jehovah's service, but his sons do not walk in their father's ways, for they accept bribes and pervert judgment. At this time the older men of Israel approach Samuel with the demand: "Now do appoint for us a king to judge us like all the nations." (8:5) Greatly disturbed, Samuel seeks Jehovah in prayer. Jehovah answers: "It is not you whom they have rejected, but it is I whom they have rejected from being king over them. . . . And now listen to their voice." (8:7-9) First, however, Samuel must warn them of the dire consequences of their rebellious request: regimentation, taxation, loss of freedom, and eventually bitter sorrow and crying to Jehovah. Undeterred in their wishes, the people demand a king.

¹⁴ Now we meet Saul, a son of Kish of the tribe of Benjamin and by far the handsomest and tallest man in Israel. He is directed to Samuel, who honors him at a feast, anoints him, and then introduces him to all Israel at an assembly at Mizpah. Though Saul at first hides among the luggage, he is finally presented as Jehovah's choice. Samuel once again reminds Israel of the rightful due of kingship, writing it in a book. However, it is not until his victory over the Ammonites, which relieves the siege at Jabesh in Gilead, that Saul's position as king is strengthened, so the people confirm his kingship at Gilgal. Samuel again exhorts them to fear, serve, and obey Jehovah, and he calls on Jehovah to send a sign in the form of unseasonal thunders and rain in harvesttime. In a frightening demonstration, Jehovah shows his anger at their rejection of him as King.

¹⁵ **Saul's disobedience** (13:1–15:35). As the Philistines continue to harass Israel, Saul's courageous son Jonathan strikes down a Philistine garrison. To avenge this, the enemy sends a huge army, 'like the sand of the seashore' for number, and they encamp at Michmash. Unrest sweeps the Israelite ranks. 'If only Samuel would come to give us Jehovah's direction!' Impatient at waiting for Samuel, Saul sins by presumptuously offering up the burnt sacrifice himself. Suddenly Samuel appears. Brushing aside Saul's lame excuses, he pronounces Jehovah's judgment: "And now your kingdom will not last. Jehovah will certainly find for himself a man agreeable to his heart; and Jehovah will commission him as a leader over his people, because you did not keep what Jehovah commanded you."—13:14.

¹⁶ Jonathan, zealous for Jehovah's name, again attacks a Philistine outpost, this time with only his armor-bearer, and they quickly strike down about 20 men. An earthquake adds to the enemy's confusion. They are routed, with Israel in full pursuit. However, the full force of the victory is weakened by Saul's rash oath forbidding the warriors to eat before the battle is over. The men tire quickly and then sin against Jehovah by eating freshly killed meat without taking time to drain the blood. Jonathan, on his part, has refreshed himself from a honeycomb before hearing of the oath, which he boldly denounces as a hindrance. He is redeemed from death by the people because of the great salvation he has performed in Israel.

¹⁷ Now it comes time to carry out Jehovah's judgment on the despicable Amalekites. (Deut. 25:17-19) They are to be completely wiped out. Nothing is to be spared, man or beast. No spoil is to be

---

12. What blessings result from Samuel's advocacy of right worship?
13. How does Israel come to reject Jehovah as King, and of what consequences does Samuel warn?
14. How does Saul come to be established in the kingship?

15. What presumptuous sin leads to Saul's failure?
16. Saul's rashness results in what difficulties?
17. What further rejection of Saul follows his second serious sin?

taken. Everything must be devoted to destruction. However, Saul disobediently preserves Agag, the Amalekite king, and the best of the flocks and herds, ostensibly to sacrifice to Jehovah. This so displeases the God of Israel that he inspires Samuel to express a second rejection of Saul. Disregarding Saul's face-saving excuses, Samuel declares: "Does Jehovah have as much delight in burnt offerings and sacrifices as in obeying the voice of Jehovah? Look! To obey is better than a sacrifice . . . Since you have rejected the word of Jehovah, he accordingly rejects you from being king." (1 Sam. 15: 22, 23) Saul then reaches out to beseech Samuel and rips the skirt off his coat. Samuel assures him that Jehovah will just as surely rip the kingdom from Saul and give it to a better man. Samuel himself picks up the sword, executes Agag, and turns his back on Saul, never to see him again.

18 **David's anointing, his valor** (16:1–17:58). Jehovah next directs Samuel to the house of Jesse in Bethlehem of Judah to select and anoint the future king. One by one the sons of Jesse pass in review but are rejected. Jehovah reminds Samuel: "Not the way man sees is the way God sees, because mere man sees what appears to the eyes; but as for Jehovah, he sees what the heart is." (16:7) Finally, Jehovah indicates his approval of David, the youngest, described as "ruddy, a young man with beautiful eyes and handsome in appearance," and Samuel anoints him with oil. (16:12) Jehovah's spirit now comes upon David, but Saul develops a bad spirit.

19 The Philistines again make inroads into Israel, putting forward their champion, Goliath, a giant towering to the height of six cubits and a span (about 9.5 ft). He is so monstrous that his coat of mail weighs about 125 pounds and the blade of his spear about 15 pounds. (17:4, 5, 7) Day after day this Goliath blasphemously and contemptuously challenges Israel to choose a man and let him come out and fight, but none reply. Saul quakes in his tent. However, David comes to hear the Philistine's taunts. With righteous indignation and inspired courage, David exclaims: "Who is this uncircumcised Philistine that he has to taunt the battle lines of the living God?" (17:26) Rejecting Saul's armor because he had never tried it before, David goes out to do battle, equipped only with a shepherd's staff, a sling, and five smooth stones. Regarding a match with this young shepherd boy as beneath his dignity, Goliath calls down evil on David. The confident reply rings out: "You are coming to me with a sword and with a spear and with a javelin, but I am coming to you with the

name of Jehovah of armies." (17:45) One well-aimed stone is flung from David's sling, and the champion of the Philistines crumples to the ground! Running to him, in full view of both armies, David draws the giant's sword and uses it to cut off its owner's head. What a great deliverance from Jehovah! What rejoicing in the camp of Israel! Now that their champion is dead, the Philistines take to flight, with the jubilant Israelites in hot pursuit.

20 **Saul's pursuit of David** (18:1–27:12). David's fearless action in behalf of Jehovah's name opens up a wonderful friendship for him. This is with Jonathan, who is the son of Saul and is the one naturally in line for the kingdom. Jonathan comes "to love him as his own soul," so that the two conclude a covenant of friendship. (18:1-3) As David's fame comes to be celebrated in Israel, Saul angrily seeks to kill him, even while giving him his daughter Michal in marriage. Saul's enmity grows more and more insane, so that at last David has to make his escape with Jonathan's loving assistance. The two weep at parting, and Jonathan reaffirms his loyalty to David, saying: "May Jehovah himself prove to be between me and you and between my offspring and your offspring to time indefinite." —20:42.

21 In his flight from the embittered Saul, David and his small band of famished supporters come to Nob. Here the priest Ahimelech, on receiving assurance that David and his men are clean from women, permits them to eat the holy showbread. Now armed with the sword of Goliath, David flees to Gath in Philistine territory, where he feigns insanity. Then he goes on to the cave of Adullam, then to Moab, and later, at the advice of Gad the prophet, back to the land of Judah. Fearful of an uprising in favor of David, the insanely jealous Saul has Doeg the Edomite slaughter the priestly population of Nob, only Abiathar escaping to join David. He becomes priest for the group.

22 As a loyal servant of Jehovah, David now wages effective guerrilla warfare against the Philistines. However, Saul continues his all-out campaign to get David, gathering his men of war and hunting him "in the wilderness of En-gedi." (24:1) David, the beloved of Jehovah, always manages to keep one step ahead of the pursuers. On one occasion he has opportunity to strike down Saul, but he refrains, simply cutting off the skirt of Saul's coat in evidence that he has spared his life. Even this harmless act strikes David at heart, for he feels he

---

18. On what basis does Jehovah choose David?
19. What early victory does David gain in Jehovah's name?

20. How does Jonathan's attitude toward David contrast with that of Saul?
21. What events mark David's flight from Saul?
22. How does David demonstrate loyalty to Jehovah and respect for His organization?

has acted against the anointed of Jehovah. What fine respect he has for Jehovah's organization!

²³ Though Samuel's death is now recorded (25:1), his successor scribe keeps the account moving. David requests that Nabal, of Maon in Judah, provide food for him and his men in return for their befriending Nabal's shepherds. Nabal only 'screams rebukes' at David's men, and David sets out to punish him. (25:14) Realizing the danger, Nabal's wife, Abigail, secretly takes provisions to David and appeases him. David blesses her for this discreet act and sends her back in peace. When Abigail informs Nabal of what has taken place, his heart is stricken, and ten days later he dies. David himself now marries the gracious and beautiful Abigail.

²⁴ For a third time, Saul takes up the fanatic pursuit of David, and once again he experiences David's mercy. "A deep sleep from Jehovah" falls upon Saul and his men. This enables David to enter the camp and take Saul's spear, but he refrains from thrusting out his hand "against the anointed of Jehovah." (26:11, 12) David is forced a second time to flee to the Philistines for refuge, and they give him Ziklag as a place of dwelling. From here he keeps up his sorties against others of Israel's enemies.

²⁵ **Saul's suicidal end** (28:1–31:13). The axis lords of the Philistines move a combined army to Shunem. Saul, in a countermove, takes up his position at Mount Gilboa. He frantically seeks guidance but can get no answer from Jehovah. If only Samuel could be contacted! Disguising himself, Saul commits another grave sin when he goes to seek out a spirit medium at En-dor, behind the Philistine lines. Finding her, he begs her to contact Samuel for him. Anxious to jump to conclusions, Saul assumes that the apparition is the dead Samuel. However, "Samuel" has no comforting message for the king. Tomorrow he will die, and true to Jehovah's words, the kingdom will be taken from him. In the other camp, the axis lords of the Philistines are going up to the battle. Seeing David and his men among them, they become suspicious and send them home. David's men arrive back in Ziklag just in time! A raiding band of Amalekites has made off with the family and possessions of David and his men, but David and his men give chase, and all are recovered without harm.

²⁶ Battle is now joined at Mount Gilboa. Israel suffers a disastrous defeat, and the Philistines get control of strategic areas of the land. Jonathan and other sons of Saul are slain, and the mortally wounded Saul kills himself with his own sword—a suicide. The victorious Philistines hang the bodies of Saul and his three sons on the walls of the city of Beth-shan, but they are removed from this disgraceful position by the men of Jabesh-gilead. The calamitous reign of Israel's first king has reached its disastrous end.

WHY BENEFICIAL

²⁷ What a history is contained in First Samuel! Starkly honest in every detail, it exposes at once both the weakness and the strength of Israel. Here were four leaders in Israel, two who heeded the law of God and two who did not. Note how Eli and Saul were failures: The former neglected to act, and the latter acted presumptuously. On the other hand, Samuel and David showed a love for Jehovah's way from their youth on, and they prospered accordingly. What valuable lessons we find here for all overseers! How necessary for these to be firm, watchful of cleanness and order in Jehovah's organization, respectful of his arrangements, fearless, even-tempered, courageous, and lovingly considerate of others! (2:23-25; 24:5, 7; 18:5, 14-16) Note also that the two who were successful had the advantage of a good theocratic training from their youth upward and that they were courageous from an early age in speaking Jehovah's message and guarding the interests entrusted to them. (3:19; 17:33-37) May all youthful worshipers of Jehovah today become young "Samuels" and "Davids"!

²⁸ Clearly to be remembered among all the beneficial words of this book are those that Jehovah inspired Samuel to utter in judgment of Saul for his failure to "wipe out the mention of Amalek from under the heavens." (Deut. 25:19) The lesson that 'obedience is better than sacrifice' is repeated in various settings at Hosea 6:6, Micah 6:6-8, and Mark 12:33. (1 Sam. 15:22) It is essential that we today benefit from this inspired record by fully and completely obeying the voice of Jehovah our God! Obedience in recognizing the sanctity of blood is also drawn to our attention at 1 Samuel 14:32, 33. Eating flesh without properly draining the blood was regarded as "sinning against Jehovah." This also applies to the Christian congregation, as is made plain at Acts 15:28, 29.

²⁹ The book of First Samuel illustrates the pitiful

---

23. How does Abigail make peace with David and finally become his wife?
24. How does David again spare Saul's life?
25. What third grave sin does Saul commit?
26. How does the calamitous reign of Israel's first king end?

27. (a) Wherein did Eli and Saul fail? (b) In what respects are Samuel and David fine examples for overseers and for youthful ministers?
28. How is obedience stressed, and what counsel of First Samuel is repeated later by other Bible writers?
29. First Samuel illustrates the consequences of what national error on the part of Israel, with what warning to self-willed persons?

error of a nation that came to view God's rule from heaven as impractical. (1 Sam. 8:5, 19, 20; 10: 18, 19) The pitfalls and futility of human rulership are graphically as well as prophetically portrayed. (8:11-18; 12:1-17) Saul is shown at the outset to be a modest man who had God's spirit (9:21; 11:6), but his judgment darkened and his heart became bitter as love of righteousness and faith in God diminished. (14:24, 29, 44) His early record of zeal was annulled by his later acts of presumptuousness, disobedience, and infidelity to God. (1 Sam. 13:9; 15:9; 28:7; Ezek. 18:24) His lack of faith bred insecurity, festering into envy, hate, and murder. (1 Sam. 18:9, 11; 20:33; 22:18, 19) He died as he had lived, a failure to his God and to his people, and as a warning to any who might become "self-willed" as he did.—2 Pet. 2:10-12.

30 However, there is the contrast of the good. For example, note the course of the faithful Samuel, who served Israel all his life without fraud, partiality, or favor. (1 Sam. 12:3-5) He was eager to obey from his boyhood on (3:5), polite and respectful (3:6-8), dependable in performing his duties (3:15), unswerving in his dedication and devotion (7:3-6; 12:2), willing to listen (8:21), ready to uphold Jehovah's decisions (10:24), firm in his judgment regardless of personalities (13: 13), strong for obedience (15:22), and persistent in fulfilling a commission (16:6, 11). He was also one having a favorable report from others. (2:26; 9:6) Not only should his youthful ministry encourage young ones to take up the ministry today (2:11, 18) but his continuance without retirement to the end of his days should uphold those weary with age. —7:15.

31 Then there is the splendid example of Jonathan. He showed no hard feelings over the fact that David was anointed to the kingship that he might have inherited. Rather, he recognized David's fine qualities and made a covenant of friendship with him. Similar unselfish companionships can be most upbuilding and encouraging among those today who faithfully serve Jehovah.—23: 16-18.

32 For women, there is the example of Hannah, who accompanied her husband regularly to the place of Jehovah's worship. She was a prayerful, humble woman, who gave up companionship with her son to keep her word and show appreciation for Jehovah's kindness. Wonderful indeed was her reward in seeing him embark on a lifetime of fruitful service to Jehovah. (1:11, 21-23, 27, 28) Further, there is the example of Abigail, who displayed a womanly submission and sensibleness that won David's praise, so that later she became his wife.—25:32-35.

33 David's love for Jehovah is movingly expressed in the psalms that David composed while being hounded in the wilderness by Saul, the backsliding "anointed of Jehovah." (1 Sam. 24:6; Ps. 34:7, 8; 52:8; 57:1, 7, 9) And with what heartfelt appreciation did David sanctify Jehovah's name as he hurled defiance at the taunter Goliath! "I am coming to you with the name of Jehovah of armies . . . This day Jehovah will surrender you into my hand, . . . and people of all the earth will know that there exists a God belonging to Israel. And all this congregation will know that neither with sword nor with spear does Jehovah save, because to Jehovah belongs the battle, and he must give you men into our hand." (1 Sam. 17:45-47) David, the courageous and loyal "anointed one" of Jehovah, magnified Jehovah as God of all the earth and the only true Source of salvation. (2 Sam. 22:51) May we ever follow this fearless example!

34 What has First Samuel to say about the development of God's Kingdom purposes? Ah, this brings us to the real highlight of this Bible book! For it is here that we meet David, whose name probably means "Beloved." David was loved of Jehovah and chosen as the "man agreeable to his heart," the one fit to be king in Israel. (1 Sam. 13:14) Thus the kingdom passed to the tribe of Judah, in harmony with Jacob's blessing at Genesis 49:9, 10, and the kingship was due to remain in the tribe of Judah until the Ruler to whom the obedience of all people belongs should come.

35 Moreover, David's name is associated with that of the Kingdom Seed, who was also born in Bethlehem and was of David's line. (Matt. 1:1, 6; 2:1; 21:9, 15) That one is the glorified Jesus Christ, "the Lion that is of the tribe of Judah, the root of David," and "the root and the offspring of David, and the bright morning star." (Rev. 5:5; 22:16) Reigning in Kingdom power, this "son of David" will show all the steadfastness and courage of his illustrious forebear in fighting God's enemies to their downfall and sanctifying Jehovah's name in all the earth. How strong our confidence in this Kingdom Seed!

---

30. What qualities of Samuel may be cultivated with profit by modern-day ministers?
31. In what was Jonathan a fine example?
32. What fine traits are to be observed in the women Hannah and Abigail?

---

33. David's fearless love and loyalty should impel us to what course?
34. How do Jehovah's Kingdom purposes further unfold in connection with David?
35. How did David's name come to be associated with that of the Kingdom Seed, and what qualities of David will that Seed yet show?

10

2 Samuel

Writers: **Gad and Nathan**
Place Written: **Israel**
Writing Completed: **c. 1040 B.C.E.**
Time Covered:
1077–c. 1040 B.C.E.

THE nation of Israel was in despair over the disaster of Gilboa and the resulting inroads by the victorious Philistines. The leaders of Israel and the flower of its young men lay dead. In this setting the young "anointed of Jehovah," David the son of Jesse, moved fully onto the national scene. (2 Sam. 19:21) Thus commences the book of Second Samuel, which might well be called a book of Jehovah and David. Its narrative is filled with action of every sort. We are carried from the depths of defeat to the pinnacle of victory, from the distresses of a strife-torn nation to the prosperity of a united kingdom, from the vigor of youth to the wisdom of advanced years. Here is the intimate account of David's life as he sought to follow Jehovah with all his heart.* It is an account that should cause searchings of heart on the part of every reader that he may strengthen his own relationship and standing with his Creator.

2 Actually, Samuel's name is not even mentioned in the record of Second Samuel, the name being given to the book apparently because of its having been originally one roll, or volume, with First Samuel. The prophets Nathan and Gad, who completed the writing of First Samuel, continued on in writing all of Second Samuel. (1 Chron. 29:29) They were well qualified for this task. Gad had been with David when he was a hunted outlaw in Israel, and toward the end of David's 40-year reign, he was still actively associated with the king. Gad was the one used to pronounce Jehovah's displeasure on David for unwisely numbering Israel. (1 Sam. 22:5; 2 Sam. 24:1-25) Overlapping and extending beyond the period of Gad's lifetime was the activity of Nathan the prophet, a close associate of David. It was his privilege to make known Jehovah's significant covenant with David, the covenant for an everlasting kingdom. He it was who courageously and under inspiration pointed

out David's great sin involving Bath-sheba and the penalty for it. (2 Sam. 7:1-17; 12:1-15) Thus Jehovah used Nathan, whose name means "[God] Has Given," and Gad, whose name means "Good Fortune," to record the inspired and beneficial information in Second Samuel. These unassuming historians did not seek to preserve memory of themselves, as no information is given of their ancestry or personal lives. They sought only to preserve the record inspired by God, for the benefit of future worshipers of Jehovah.

3 Second Samuel takes up the narrative of accurate Bible history following the death of Saul, Israel's first king, and carries it along to near the end of David's 40-year reign. Thus, the period covered is from 1077 B.C.E. to about 1040 B.C.E. The fact that the book does not record David's death is strong evidence that it was written about 1040 B.C.E., or just prior to his death.

4 For the same reasons put forth with regard to First Samuel, the book of Second Samuel must be accepted as part of the Bible canon. Its authenticity is beyond question. Its very candor, not glossing over even King David's sins and shortcomings, is a strong circumstantial evidence in itself.

5 However, the strongest evidence for the authenticity of Second Samuel is to be found in the fulfilled prophecies, particularly those relating to the Kingdom covenant with David. God promised David: "Your house and your kingdom will certainly be steadfast to time indefinite before you; your very throne will become one firmly established to time indefinite." (7:16) Jeremiah, even in the evening of the kingdom of Judah, mentioned the continuity of this promise to the house of David with the words: "This is what Jehovah has said, 'There will not be cut off in David's case a man to sit upon the throne of the house of Israel.'" (Jer. 33:17) This prophecy has not gone unfulfilled, for Jehovah later brought forth from Judah "Jesus

---

* *Insight on the Scriptures*, Vol. 1, pages 745-7.

1. Against what background does Second Samuel open, and how does its account develop?
2. (a) How did the book come to be called Second Samuel? (b) Who were the writers, what were their qualifications, and what record only did they seek to preserve?

3. What period is covered by Second Samuel, and when was its writing completed?
4. For what reasons must Second Samuel be accepted as part of the Bible canon?
5. What is the strongest reason for accepting Second Samuel as inspired Scripture?

Christ, son of David," as the Bible clearly testifies. —Matt. 1:1.

CONTENTS OF SECOND SAMUEL

⁶ **Early events of David's reign** (1:1–4:12). Following Saul's death at Mount Gilboa, an Amalekite fugitive from the battle comes hurrying to David at Ziklag with the report. Hoping to curry favor with David, he fabricates the story that it is he himself who took Saul's life. Instead of commendation, the Amalekite receives only the reward of death, for he has condemned himself by testifying to striking "the anointed of Jehovah." (1:16) The new king, David, now composes a dirge, "The Bow," in which he laments the death of Saul and of Jonathan. This rises to a beautiful climax in its touching expression of David's overflowing love for Jonathan: "I am distressed over you, my brother Jonathan, very pleasant you were to me. More wonderful was your love to me than the love from women. How have the mighty ones fallen and the weapons of war perished!"—1:17, 18, 26, 27.

⁷ At Jehovah's direction, David and his men move their households to Hebron in the territory of Judah. Here the elders of the tribe come to anoint David as their king in 1077 B.C.E. General Joab becomes the most prominent of David's supporters. However, as a rival for the kingship over the nation, Ish-bosheth, a son of Saul, is anointed by Abner, the chief of the army. There are periodic clashes between the two opposing forces, and Abner kills a brother of Joab. Finally, Abner defects to David's camp. To David he takes Saul's daughter Michal, for whom David long ago paid the marriage price. However, in revenge for the slaying of his brother, Joab finds an occasion for killing Abner. David is greatly distressed at this, disclaiming any responsibility. Soon thereafter Ish-bosheth himself is murdered as he is "taking his noonday siesta."—4:5.

⁸ **David king in Jerusalem** (5:1–6:23). Though he has already ruled as king in Judah for seven years and six months, David now becomes undisputed ruler, and representatives of the tribes anoint him as king over all Israel. This is his third anointing (1070 B.C.E.). One of David's first acts as ruler of the entire kingdom is to capture the stronghold of Zion in Jerusalem from the entrenched Jebusites, surprising them by way of the water tunnel. David then makes Jerusalem his capital city. Jehovah of armies blesses David, making him greater and greater. Even Hiram, rich king of Tyre, sends David valuable cedars and also workmen to construct a house for the king. David's family increases, and Jehovah prospers his reign. There are two more encounters with the warlike Philistines. In the first of these, Jehovah breaks through the enemy for David at Baal-perazim, giving him the victory. In the second, Jehovah performs another miracle by making a "sound of a marching in the tops of the baca bushes," indicating that Jehovah is going ahead of Israel to rout the armies of the Philistines. (5:24) Another outstanding victory for Jehovah's forces!

⁹ Taking 30,000 men with him, David sets out to bring the ark of the covenant from Baale-judah (Kiriath-jearim) to Jerusalem. As it is being brought along with great music and rejoicing, the wagon on which it is riding gives a lurch, and Uzzah, who is walking alongside, reaches out to steady the sacred Ark. "At that Jehovah's anger blazed against Uzzah and the true God struck him down there for the irreverent act." (6:7) The Ark comes to rest at the house of Obed-edom, and during the next three months, Jehovah richly blesses the household of Obed-edom. After three months David comes to take the Ark in the right manner the rest of the way. With joyful shouting, music, and dancing, the Ark is brought into David's capital. David gives vent to his great joy in dancing before Jehovah, but his wife Michal takes exception to this. David insists: "I will celebrate before Jehovah." (6:21) In consequence Michal remains childless until her death.*

¹⁰ **God's covenant with David** (7:1-29). We now come to one of the most important events in David's life, one that is directly connected with the central theme of the Bible, the sanctification of Jehovah's name by the Kingdom under the promised Seed. This event arises out of David's desire to build a house for the ark of God. Living in a beautiful house of cedars himself, he indicates to Nathan his desire to build a house for Jehovah's ark of the covenant. Through Nathan, Jehovah reassures David of His loving-kindness toward Israel and establishes with him a covenant that will abide for all time. However, it will be not David but his seed who will build the house for Jehovah's name. In addition, Jehovah makes the loving promise: "And your house and your kingdom will certainly be steadfast to time indefinite before you; your very throne will become one firmly established to time indefinite."—7:16.

---

6. How does David react on hearing news of the death of Saul and of Jonathan?
7. What other events mark the early part of David's reign?
8. How does Jehovah prosper David's reign over all Israel?

---

* *Insight on the Scriptures,* Vol. 2, pages 373-4.

9. Describe the events connected with bringing the Ark up to Jerusalem.
10. What covenant and promise of Jehovah next come to our attention?

[11] Overcome by Jehovah's goodness, as expressed through this Kingdom covenant, David pours out his thankfulness for all of God's loving-kindness: "What one nation in the earth is like your people Israel, whom God went to redeem to himself as a people and to assign himself a name and to do for them great and fear-inspiring things? . . . And you yourself, O Jehovah, have become their God." (7:23, 24) Fervently he prays for the sanctification of Jehovah's name and for the house of David to become firmly established before Him.

[12] **David extends Israel's dominion** (8:1–10:19). However, David is not left to rule in peace. Wars are yet to be fought. David proceeds to strike down the Philistines, the Moabites, the Zobahites, the Syrians, and the Edomites, extending Israel's boundary to its God-ordained limits. (2 Sam. 8:1-5, 13-15; Deut. 11:24) He then turns his attention to the house of Saul in order that for the sake of Jonathan, he might express loving-kindness toward any remaining. Ziba, a servant of Saul, calls to his attention a son of Jonathan, Mephibosheth, who is lame in the feet. Immediately, David requires that all of Saul's goods be turned over to Mephibosheth and that his land be cultivated by Ziba and his servants to provide food for Mephibosheth's house. Mephibosheth himself, however, is to eat at the table of David.

[13] When the king of Ammon dies, David sends ambassadors to Hanun his son with expressions of loving-kindness. Hanun's counselors, however, accuse David of sending them to spy out the land, and so they humiliate them and send them back half-naked. Angered by this affront, David sends Joab with his army to avenge the wrong. Dividing his forces, he easily routs the Ammonites and the Syrians who had come up to help them. The Syrians regroup their forces, only to be defeated once again by the armies of Jehovah under the command of David and suffer the loss of 700 charioteers and 40,000 horsemen. Here is further evidence of Jehovah's favor and blessing on David.

[14] **David sins against Jehovah** (11:1–12:31). The following spring David again sends Joab into Ammon to lay siege to Rabbah, while he himself remains in Jerusalem. One evening from his rooftop, he happens to observe the beautiful Bath-sheba, wife of Uriah the Hittite, as she is bathing. Bringing her to his house, he has relations with her, and she becomes pregnant. David tries to cover up by bringing Uriah back from the fighting

at Rabbah and sending him down to his house to refresh himself. However, Uriah refuses to please himself and have relations with his wife while the Ark and the army are "dwelling in booths." In desperation David sends Uriah back to Joab with a letter saying: "Put Uriah in front of the heaviest battle charges, and you men must retreat from behind him, and he must be struck down and die." (11:11, 15) In this way Uriah dies. After Bath-sheba's period of mourning is passed, David immediately takes her to his house, where she becomes his wife, and their child, a son, is born.

[15] This is bad in Jehovah's eyes. He sends the prophet Nathan to David with a message of judgment. Nathan tells David of a rich man and a poor man. The one had many flocks, but the other had one female lamb, which was a pet in the family and "as a daughter to him." However, when it came to making a feast, the rich man took, not a sheep from his own flocks, but the female lamb of the poor man. Incensed at hearing this, David exclaims: "As Jehovah is living, the man doing this deserves to die!" Back come Nathan's words: "You yourself are the man!" (12:3, 5, 7) He then pronounces prophetic judgment that David's wives will be violated publicly by another man, that his house will be plagued by internal warfare, and that his child by Bath-sheba will die.

[16] In sincere sorrow and repentance, David openly acknowledges: "I have sinned against Jehovah." (12:13) True to Jehovah's word, the offspring of the adulterous union dies after seven days' illness. (Later, David has another son by Bath-sheba; this one they call Solomon, which name comes from a root meaning "peace." However, Jehovah sends through Nathan to call him also Jedidiah, meaning "Beloved of Jah.") Following his soul-shaking experience, David is called by Joab to come to Rabbah, where the final assault is being made ready. Having captured the city's water supply, Joab respectfully leaves to the king the honor of capturing the city itself.

[17] **David's domestic difficulties** (13:1–18:33). David's household troubles get started when Amnon, one of David's sons, falls passionately in love with Tamar, the sister of his half brother Absalom. Amnon feigns illness and asks that the beautiful Tamar be sent to care for him. He violates her and then comes to hate her intensely, so that he sends her away in humiliation. Absalom plans vengeance, biding his time. About two years later, he

---

11. With what prayer does David express thankfulness?
12. What wars does David fight, and what kindness does he show to Saul's house?
13. By what further victories does Jehovah show that he is with David?
14. What sins does David commit over Bath-sheba?

---

15. How does Nathan pronounce prophetic judgment on David?
16. (a) What meanings attach to the names of David's second son by Bath-sheba? (b) What is the final outcome of the assault on Rabbah?
17. What internal troubles start to afflict David's household?

prepares a feast to which Amnon and all the other sons of the king are invited. When Amnon's heart becomes merry with wine, he is caught off guard and put to death at Absalom's order.

[18] Fearing the king's displeasure, Absalom flees to Geshur, where he lives in semiexile for three years. Meanwhile, Joab, the chief of David's army, schemes to bring about a reconciliation between David and Absalom. He arranges for a wise woman of Tekoa to pose a fictitious situation before the king concerning retribution, banishment, and punishment. When the king passes judgment, the woman reveals the true reason for her presence, in that the king's own son Absalom is in banishment in Geshur. David recognizes that Joab has planned this but gives permission for his son to return to Jerusalem. It is another two years before the king consents to see Absalom face-to-face.

[19] Despite David's loving-kindness, Absalom soon works up a conspiracy to seize the throne from his father. Absalom is outstandingly handsome among all the valiant men of Israel, and this adds to his ambition and pride. Each year the shearings of his luxuriant head of hair weigh about five pounds. (2 Sam. 14:26, footnote) By various crafty maneuvers, Absalom begins to steal the hearts of the men of Israel. Finally, the conspiracy comes out into the open. Gaining his father's permission to go to Hebron, Absalom there announces his rebellious purpose and calls for the support of all Israel in his uprising against David. As great numbers flock to the side of his rebel son, David flees from Jerusalem with a few loyal supporters, typical of whom is Ittai the Gittite, who declares: "As Jehovah is living and as my lord the king is living, in the place where my lord the king may come to be, whether for death or for life, there is where your servant will come to be!"—15:21.

[20] While in flight from Jerusalem, David learns of the treachery of one of his most trusted counselors, Ahithophel. He prays: "Turn, please, the counsel of Ahithophel into foolishness, O Jehovah!" (15:31) Zadok and Abiathar, priests loyal to David, and Hushai the Archite are sent back to Jerusalem to watch and report on Absalom's activities. Meanwhile, in the wilderness, David meets Ziba, the attendant of Mephibosheth, who reports that his master is now expecting the kingdom to revert to the house of Saul. As David passes on, Shimei, of Saul's house, curses him and hurls stones at him, but David restrains his men from taking vengeance.

[21] Back in Jerusalem, at Ahithophel's suggestion, the usurper Absalom has relations with his father's concubines "under the eyes of all Israel." This is in fulfillment of Nathan's prophetic judgment. (16:22; 12:11) Also, Ahithophel counsels Absalom to take a force of 12,000 men and hunt David down in the wilderness. However, Hushai, who has won his way into Absalom's confidence, recommends a different course. And just as David has prayed, the counsel of Ahithophel is frustrated. Judaslike, the frustrated Ahithophel goes home and strangles himself. Hushai secretly reports Absalom's plans to the priests Zadok and Abiathar, who, in turn, have the message relayed to David in the wilderness.

[22] This enables David to cross the Jordan and to choose the site of battle in the forest at Mahanaim. There he deploys his forces and commands them to treat Absalom gently. The rebels suffer a crushing defeat. As Absalom flees on a mule through the heavily wooded forest, his head gets caught in the lower branches of a massive tree, and there he hangs suspended in midair. Finding him in this predicament, Joab kills him, in utter disregard for the king's command. David's deep grief on hearing of the death of his son is reflected in his lament: "My son Absalom, my son, my son Absalom! O that I might have died, I myself, instead of you, Absalom my son, my son!"—18:33.

[23] **Closing events of David's reign** (19:1–24:25). David continues to mourn bitterly until Joab urges him to resume his rightful position as king. He now appoints Amasa as head over the army in place of Joab. As he returns, he is welcomed by the people, including Shimei, whose life David spares. Mephibosheth also comes to plead his case, and David gives him an equal inheritance with Ziba. Once again, all Israel and Judah are united under David.

[24] However, there are more troubles in store. Sheba, a Benjaminite, declares himself king and turns many aside from David. Amasa, ordered by David to gather men to put down the rebellion, is met by Joab and treacherously murdered. Joab then takes over the army and follows Sheba to the city of Abel of Beth-maacah and lays siege to it. Heeding the advice of a wise woman of the city, the inhabitants execute Sheba, and Joab withdraws. Because Saul had slain Gibeonites and the bloodguilt was still unavenged, there comes to be a

---

18. By what subterfuge is Absalom restored from exile?
19. What conspiracy now comes into the open, and with what result to David?
20, 21. (a) What events occur during David's flight, and how is Nathan's prophecy fulfilled? (b) How does treacherous Ahithophel come to his end?

22. With what sorrow is David's victory tempered?
23. What arrangements mark David's return as king?
24. What further developments take place that involve the tribe of Benjamin?

three-year famine in Israel. To remove the blood-guilt, seven sons of Saul's household are executed. Later, in battle with the Philistines again, David's life is barely saved by Abishai his nephew. His men swear that he must no more go out to battle with them "that you may not extinguish the lamp of Israel!" (21:17) Three of his mighty men then perform notably in striking down Philistine giants.

²⁵ At this point, the writer breaks into the account with a song of David to Jehovah, paralleling Psalm 18 and expressing thanks for deliverance "out of the palm of all his enemies and out of Saul's palm." Joyfully he declares: "Jehovah is my crag and my stronghold and the Provider of escape for me. The One doing great acts of salvation for his king and exercising loving-kindness to his anointed one, to David and to his seed for time indefinite." (22:1, 2, 51) There follows the last song of David, in which he acknowledges, "The spirit of Jehovah it was that spoke by me, and his word was upon my tongue."—23:2.

²⁶ Coming back to the historical record, we find listed the mighty men who belong to David, three of whom are outstanding. These are involved in an incident occurring when an outpost of the Philistines has been established in Bethlehem, David's hometown. David expresses the desire: "O that I might have a drink of the water from the cistern of Bethlehem that is at the gate!" (23:15) At that, the three mighty men force their way into the Philistine camp, draw water from the cistern, and carry it back to David. But David refuses to drink it. Instead, he pours it out on the ground, saying: "It is unthinkable on my part, O Jehovah, that I should do this! Shall I drink the blood of the men going at the risk of their souls?" (23:17) To him the water is the equivalent of the lifeblood they have risked for it. The 30 mightiest men of his army and their exploits are next listed.

²⁷ Finally, David sins in numbering the people. Pleading with God for mercy, he is given the choice between three punishments: seven years of famine, three months of military defeats, or three days of pestilence in the land. David replies: "Let us fall, please, into the hand of Jehovah, for many are his mercies; but into the hand of man do not let me fall." (24:14) The nationwide pestilence kills 70,000 persons, being stopped only when David, acting on Jehovah's instructions through Gad, purchases the threshing floor of Araunah, where he offers up burnt sacrifices and communion sacrifices to Jehovah.

WHY BENEFICIAL

²⁸ There is much to be found in Second Samuel that is beneficial for the modern reader! Almost every human emotion is painted here in colors of the fullest intensity, those of real life. Thus, we are warned in striking terms of the disastrous results of ambition and revenge (3:27-30), of wrongful lust for another's marriage mate (11:2-4, 15-17; 12:9, 10), of traitorous action (15:12, 31; 17:23), of love based only on passion (13:10-15, 28, 29), of hasty judgment (16:3, 4; 19:25-30), and of disrespect for another's acts of devotion.—6:20-23.

²⁹ However, by far the greatest benefit from Second Samuel is to be found on the positive side, by heeding its many excellent examples of right conduct and action. David is a model in his exclusive devotion to God (7:22), his humility before God (7:18), his exalting of Jehovah's name (7:23, 26), his proper viewpoint in adversity (15:25), his sincere repentance of sin (12:13), his faithfulness to his promise (9:1, 7), his keeping balance under trial (16:11, 12), his consistent reliance on Jehovah (5:12, 20), and his deep respect for Jehovah's arrangements and appointments (1:11, 12). No wonder that David was called "a man agreeable to [Jehovah's] heart"!—1 Sam. 13:14.

³⁰ The application of many Bible principles is also to be found in Second Samuel. Among these are the principles of community responsibility (2 Sam. 3:29; 24:11-15), that good intentions do not alter God's requirements (6:6, 7), that headship in Jehovah's theocratic arrangement should be respected (12:28), that blood is to be regarded as sacred (23:17), that atonement is required for bloodguilt (21:1-6, 9, 14), that a wise one can avert disaster for many (2 Sam. 20:21, 22; Eccl. 9:15), and that loyalty to Jehovah's organization and its representatives must be maintained "whether for death or for life."—2 Sam. 15:18-22.

³¹ Most important of all, Second Samuel points forward to and gives brilliant foregleams of God's Kingdom, which he establishes in the hands of the "son of David," Jesus Christ. (Matt. 1:1) The oath that Jehovah made to David concerning the permanence of his kingdom (2 Sam. 7:16) is cited at Acts 2:29-36 with reference to Jesus. That the

---

25. What is expressed in the songs of David next recorded?
26. What is stated concerning David's mighty men, and how does he show respect for their lifeblood?
27. What final sin does David commit? How is the resulting plague stopped?

---

28. What striking warnings are contained in Second Samuel?
29. What excellent examples of right conduct and action are to be found in Second Samuel?
30. What principles are applied and illustrated in Second Samuel?
31. How does Second Samuel provide foregleams of God's Kingdom, as attested to in the Christian Greek Scriptures?

prophecy, "I myself shall become his father, and he himself will become my son" (2 Sam. 7:14), really pointed forward to Jesus is shown by Hebrews 1:5. This was also testified to by Jehovah's voice speaking from heaven: "This is my Son, the beloved, whom I have approved." (Matt. 3:17; 17:5) Finally, the Kingdom covenant with David is referred to by Gabriel in his words to Mary concerning Jesus:

"This one will be great and will be called Son of the Most High; and Jehovah God will give him the throne of David his father, and he will rule as king over the house of Jacob forever, and there will be no end of his kingdom." (Luke 1:32, 33) How thrilling the promise of the Kingdom Seed appears as each step in its development unfolds before our eyes!

Bible Book Number **11**

1 Kings

Writer: **Jeremiah**
Place Written: **Jerusalem and Judah**
Writing Completed: **580 B.C.E.**
Time Covered: **c. 1040–911 B.C.E.**

THE conquests by David had extended Israel's domain to its God-given boundaries, from the river Euphrates in the north to the river of Egypt in the south. (2 Sam. 8:3; 1 Ki. 4:21) By the time David had died and his son Solomon was ruling in his stead, "Judah and Israel were many, like the grains of sand that are by the sea for multitude, eating and drinking and rejoicing." (1 Ki. 4:20) Solomon ruled with great wisdom, a wisdom that far surpassed that of the ancient Greeks. He built a magnificent temple to Jehovah. However, even Solomon fell away to the worship of false gods. At his death the kingdom was ripped in two, and a succession of wicked kings in the rival kingdoms of Israel and Judah acted ruinously, bringing distress to the people, just as Samuel had predicted. (1 Sam. 8:10-18) Of the 14 kings who ruled in Judah and in Israel after Solomon's death and as reviewed in the book of First Kings, only 2 succeeded in doing right in Jehovah's eyes. Is this record, then, "inspired and beneficial"? Most certainly it is, as we shall see from its admonitions, its prophecies and types, and its relation to the dominant Kingdom theme of "all Scripture."

² The book of Kings was originally one roll, or volume, and was called *Mela·khim´* (Kings) in Hebrew. The translators of the *Septuagint* called it *Ba·si·lei´on,* "Kingdoms," and were the first to divide it into two scrolls for convenience' sake. They were later called Third and Fourth Kings, which

designation continues in Catholic Bibles to this day. However, they are now generally known as First and Second Kings. They differ from First and Second Samuel in naming previous records as source material for the compiler. The one compiler, in the course of the two books, refers 15 times to "the book of the affairs of the days of the kings of Judah," 18 times to "the book of the affairs of the days of the kings of Israel," and also to "the book of the affairs of Solomon." (1 Ki. 15:7; 14:19; 11:41) Though these other ancient records have been completely lost, the inspired compilation remains —the beneficial account of First and Second Kings.

³ Who wrote the books of Kings? Their emphasis on the work of the prophets, especially Elijah and Elisha, indicates a prophet of Jehovah. Similarities of language, composition, and style suggest the same writer as for the book of Jeremiah. Many Hebrew words and expressions appear only in Kings and Jeremiah, and in no other Bible book. However, if Jeremiah wrote the books of Kings, why is he not mentioned therein? It was not necessary, for his work had already been covered in the book bearing his name. Moreover, Kings was written to magnify Jehovah and His worship, not to add to Jeremiah's reputation. Actually, Kings and Jeremiah are complementary for the most part, each filling in what the other omits. In addition, there are parallel accounts, as, for example, 2 Kings 24:18–25:30 and Jeremiah 39:1-10; 40:7–41:10; 52:1-34. Jewish tradition confirms that Jeremiah was the writer of First and Second Kings. No doubt he began the compilation of both

---

1. (a) How did Israel's radiant prosperity degenerate into ruin? (b) Yet why may First Kings be described as "inspired and beneficial"?
2. How did the record of First and Second Kings come to be in two scrolls, and how were they compiled?

3. (a) Who undoubtedly wrote the books of Kings, and why do you so answer? (b) When was the writing completed, and what period is covered by First Kings?

books in Jerusalem, and it appears that the second book was completed in Egypt about 580 B.C.E., since he refers to events of that year in the conclusion of his record. (2 Ki. 25:27) First Kings takes up the history of Israel from the end of Second Samuel and carries it through to 911 B.C.E., when Jehoshaphat died.—1 Ki. 22:50.

⁴ First Kings takes its rightful place in the canon of the Holy Scriptures, being accepted by all authorities. Moreover, events in First Kings are confirmed by the secular histories of Egypt and Assyria. Archaeology too supports many of the statements in the book. For example, at 1 Kings 7: 45, 46 we read that it was "in the District of the Jordan . . . between Succoth and Zarethan" that Hiram cast the copper utensils for Solomon's temple. Archaeologists digging on the site of ancient Succoth have unearthed evidence of smelting activities there.* In addition, a relief on a temple wall at Karnak (ancient Thebes) boasts of the Egyptian king Sheshonk's (Shishak's) invasion of Judah, referred to at 1 Kings 14:25, 26.#

⁵ References by other Bible writers and fulfillments of prophecies support the authenticity of First Kings. Jesus spoke of the events surrounding Elijah and the widow of Zarephath as historical realities. (Luke 4:24-26) Speaking of John the Baptizer, Jesus said: "He himself is 'Elijah who is destined to come.'" (Matt. 11:13, 14) Here Jesus was referring to the prophecy of Malachi, who spoke also of a future day: "Look! I am sending to you people Elijah the prophet before the coming of the great and fear-inspiring day of Jehovah." (Mal. 4:5) Jesus further vouched for the canonicity of First Kings by referring to what is written in that book regarding Solomon as well as the queen of the south.—Matt. 6:29; 12:42; compare 1 Kings 10: 1-9.

CONTENTS OF FIRST KINGS

⁶ **Solomon becomes king** (1:1–2:46). The record of First Kings opens with David near death as he draws close to the conclusion of his reign of 40 years. His son Adonijah, with the help of Joab the army chief and Abiathar the priest, conspires to take over the kingship. The prophet Nathan informs David of this and indirectly reminds him that he has already designated Solomon to be king

---

* *The International Standard Bible Encyclopedia,* Vol. 4, 1988, edited by G. W. Bromiley, page 648.
# *Insight on the Scriptures,* Vol. 1, pages 149, 952.

---

4. How do secular history and archaeology confirm First Kings?
5. What inspired testimony proves the authenticity of First Kings?
6. Under what circumstances does Solomon ascend the throne, and how does he become firmly established in the kingdom?

at his death. David therefore has Zadok the priest anoint Solomon as king, even while the conspirators are celebrating Adonijah's succession. David now charges Solomon to be strong and prove himself a man and to walk in the ways of Jehovah his God, after which David dies and is buried in "the City of David." (2:10) In time Solomon banishes Abiathar and executes the troublemakers Adonijah and Joab. Later, Shimei is executed when he does not show respect for the merciful provision made to spare his life. The kingdom is now firmly established in the hands of Solomon.

⁷ **Solomon's wise rule** (3:1–4:34). Solomon forms a marriage alliance with Egypt by marrying Pharaoh's daughter. He prays to Jehovah for an obedient heart in order to judge Jehovah's people with discernment. Because he does not request long life or riches, Jehovah promises to give him a wise and discerning heart and also riches and glory. Early in his reign, Solomon shows his wisdom when two women appear before him claiming the same child. Solomon orders his men to "sever the living child in two" and to give a half to each woman. (3:25) At this the real mother pleads for the child's life, saying the other woman should have it. Solomon thus identifies the rightful mother, and she gets the child. Because of Solomon's God-given wisdom, all Israel prospers and is happy and secure. People from many lands come to hear his wise sayings.

⁸ **Solomon's temple** (5:1–10:29). Solomon recalls Jehovah's words to his father, David: "Your son whom I shall put upon your throne in place of you, he is the one that will build the house to my name." (5:5) Solomon therefore makes preparation for this. Hiram the king of Tyre assists by sending cedar and juniper logs from Lebanon and by providing skilled workers. These, together with Solomon's conscripted workers, start work on the house of Jehovah in the fourth year of Solomon's reign, in the 480th year after the Israelites left Egypt. (6:1) No hammers, axes, or any tools of iron are used at the building site, as all the stones are prepared and fitted at the quarry before being brought to the temple site for assembly. The entire interior of the temple, first covered with cedar on the walls and juniper wood on the floor, is then beautifully overlaid with gold. Two figures of cherubs are made of oil-tree wood, each ten cubits (14.6 ft) high and ten cubits from wingtip to wingtip, and these are placed in the innermost room. Other cherubs, along with palm-tree figures

---

7. What prayer of Solomon does Jehovah answer, and with what result to Israel?
8. (a) How does Solomon go about building the temple? Describe some of its features. (b) What further building program does he carry out?

and blossoms, are engraved on the temple walls. At last, after more than seven years of work, the magnificent temple is completed. Solomon continues his building program: a house for himself, the House of the Forest of Lebanon, the Porch of Pillars, the Porch of the Throne, and a house for Pharaoh's daughter. He also makes two great copper pillars for the porch of Jehovah's house, the molten sea for the court, and the copper carriages, as well as copper basins and golden utensils.*

⁹ Now the time comes for the priests to bring up the ark of Jehovah's covenant and to place it in the innermost room, the Most Holy, under the wings of the cherubs. As the priests come out, 'the glory of Jehovah fills the house of Jehovah,' so that the priests can no longer stand and minister. (8:11) Solomon blesses the congregation of Israel, and he blesses and praises Jehovah. On bended knees and with his palms spread out to the heavens, he prayerfully acknowledges that the heaven of the heavens cannot contain Jehovah, much less this earthly house he has built. He prays that Jehovah will hear all those fearing Him as they pray toward this house, yes, even the foreigner from a distant land, "in order that all the peoples of the earth may get to know your name so as to fear you the same as your people Israel do."—8:43.

¹⁰ During the 14-day feast that follows, Solomon sacrifices 22,000 cattle and 120,000 sheep. Jehovah tells Solomon that He has heard his prayer and that He has sanctified the temple by putting His "name there to time indefinite." Now, if Solomon will walk in uprightness before Jehovah, the throne of his kingdom will continue. However, if Solomon and his sons after him leave Jehovah's worship and serve other gods, then, says Jehovah, "I will also cut Israel off from upon the surface of the ground that I have given to them; and the house that I have sanctified to my name I shall throw away from before me, and Israel will indeed become a proverbial saying and a taunt among all the peoples. And this house itself will become heaps of ruins."—9:3, 7, 8.

¹¹ It has taken Solomon 20 years to complete the two houses, the house of Jehovah and the house of the king. Now he proceeds to build many cities throughout his domain, as well as ships for use in trading with distant lands. The queen of Sheba thus hears of the great wisdom that Jehovah has given Solomon, and she comes to test him with perplexing questions. After hearing him and seeing the prosperity and happiness of his people, she exclaims: "I had not been told the half." (10:7) As Jehovah continues to show love to Israel, Solomon becomes "greater in riches and wisdom than all the other kings of the earth."—10:23.

¹² **Solomon's unfaithfulness and death** (11: 1-43). Contrary to Jehovah's command, Solomon takes many wives from other nations—700 wives and 300 concubines. (Deut. 17:17) His heart is drawn away to serve other gods. Jehovah tells him that the kingdom will be ripped away from him, not in his day, but in the day of his son. Nevertheless, a part of the kingdom, one tribe in addition to Judah, will be ruled over by Solomon's sons. God begins to raise up resisters to Solomon in nearby nations, and Jeroboam of the tribe of Ephraim also lifts himself up against the king. Ahijah the prophet tells Jeroboam that he will become king over ten tribes of Israel, and Jeroboam flees for his life to Egypt. Solomon dies after reigning for 40 years, and his son Rehoboam becomes king in the year 997 B.C.E.

¹³ **The kingdom divided** (12:1–14:20). Jeroboam returns from Egypt and goes up with the people to ask Rehoboam for relief from all the burdens that Solomon had placed upon them. Listening to young men instead of to the wise counsel of the elders in Israel, Rehoboam increases the hardships. Israel rises in revolt and makes Jeroboam king over the northern ten tribes. Rehoboam, left with only Judah and Benjamin, gathers an army to fight the rebels, but at Jehovah's command he turns back. Jeroboam builds Shechem as his capital, but he still feels insecure. He fears that the people will return to Jerusalem to worship Jehovah and that they will come under Rehoboam again. To prevent this, he sets up two golden calves, one in Dan and one in Bethel, and to direct the worship, he selects priests, not from the tribe of Levi, but from among the people in general.*

¹⁴ While Jeroboam is sacrificing at the altar in Bethel, Jehovah sends a prophet to warn him that He will raise up a king from David's line, named Josiah, who will take strong action against this altar of false worship. As a portent, the altar is then and there ripped apart. The prophet himself is later killed by a lion for disobeying Jehovah's

---

* *Insight on the Scriptures,* Vol. 1, pages 750-1.

---

* *Insight on the Scriptures,* Vol. 1, pages 947-8.

---

9. What manifestation of Jehovah and what prayer by Solomon mark the bringing in of the ark of the covenant?
10. With what promise and prophetic warning does Jehovah answer Solomon's prayer?
11. How extensive do Solomon's riches and wisdom become?

12. (a) In what does Solomon fail, and what seeds of revolt begin to appear? (b) What does Ahijah prophesy?
13. How does division occur in the kingdom as Rehoboam begins his reign, and how does Jeroboam try to make his kingship secure?
14. What prophetic warning is sounded against Jeroboam's house, and what adversities begin?

instruction not to eat or drink while on his mission. Adversity now begins to plague Jeroboam's house. His child dies as a judgment from Jehovah, and God's prophet Ahijah foretells that Jeroboam's house will be cut off completely because of his great sin in setting up false gods in Israel. After reigning 22 years, Jeroboam dies and his son Nadab becomes king in his place.

¹⁵ **In Judah: Rehoboam, Abijam, and Asa** (14:21–15:24). Meanwhile, under Rehoboam, Judah is also doing what is bad in Jehovah's eyes, practicing idol worship. The king of Egypt invades and carries off many of the temple treasures. After ruling 17 years, Rehoboam dies, and his son Abijam becomes king. He also keeps sinning against Jehovah, and he dies after a three-year reign. Asa his son now rules and, in contrast, serves Jehovah with a complete heart and removes the dungy idols out of the land. There is constant warfare between Israel and Judah. Asa obtains help from Syria, and Israel is forced to withdraw. Asa rules for 41 years and is succeeded by his son Jehoshaphat.

¹⁶ **In Israel: Nadab, Baasha, Elah, Zimri, Tibni, Omri, and Ahab** (15:25–16:34). What a wicked crowd! Baasha assassinates Nadab after he has reigned only two years and follows through by annihilating the entire house of Jeroboam. He continues in false worship and in fighting with Judah. Jehovah foretells that He will make a clean sweep of Baasha's house, as he has done with Jeroboam's. After Baasha's 24-year reign, he is succeeded by his son Elah, who is assassinated two years later by his servant Zimri. As soon as he takes the throne, Zimri strikes down all the house of Baasha. When the people hear of it, they make Omri, the chief of the army, king and come up against Tirzah, Zimri's capital. When he sees that all is lost, Zimri burns the king's house over himself, so that he dies. Now Tibni tries to reign as a rival king, but after a time the followers of Omri overpower him and kill him.

¹⁷ Omri buys the mountain of Samaria and builds there the city of Samaria. He goes walking in all the ways of Jeroboam, offending Jehovah with idol worship. In fact, he is worse than all the others before him. After reigning 12 years, he dies and Ahab his son becomes king. Ahab marries Jezebel, the daughter of the king of Sidon, and then sets up an altar to Baal in Samaria. He exceeds in wickedness all those who have preceded him. It is at this time that Hiel the Bethelite rebuilds the city of Jericho at the cost of the life of his firstborn

son and his youngest son. True worship is at its lowest ebb.

¹⁸ **Elijah's prophetic work in Israel** (17:1–22:40). Suddenly a messenger from Jehovah appears on the scene. It is Elijah the Tishbite.* Startling indeed is his opening pronouncement to King Ahab: "As Jehovah the God of Israel before whom I do stand is living, there will occur during these years neither dew nor rain, except at the order of my word!" (17:1) Just as suddenly, Elijah retires at Jehovah's direction to a valley east of the Jordan. There is drought in Israel, but ravens bring food to Elijah. When the valley stream dries up, Jehovah sends his prophet to dwell in Zarephath in Sidon. Because of a widow's kindness to Elijah, Jehovah miraculously maintains her small supply of flour and oil so that she and her son do not die of hunger. Later the son becomes sick and dies, but at Elijah's plea Jehovah restores the child's life. Then, in the third year of the drought, Jehovah sends Elijah to Ahab again. Ahab accuses Elijah of bringing ostracism on Israel, but Elijah boldly tells Ahab: "You and the house of your father have" because of following the Baals.—18:18.

¹⁹ Elijah calls on Ahab to assemble all the prophets of Baal at Mount Carmel. No longer will it be possible to limp upon two opinions. The issue is drawn: Jehovah versus Baal! Before all the people, the 450 priests of Baal prepare a bull, set it on wood on the altar, and pray for fire to come down and consume the offering. From morning to noon, they call in vain on Baal, amid taunts from Elijah. They scream and cut themselves, but no answer! Next, the lone prophet, Elijah, builds an altar in the name of Jehovah and prepares the wood and bull for sacrifice. He has the people soak the offering and the wood three times with water, and then he prays to Jehovah: "Answer me, O Jehovah, answer me, that this people may know that you, Jehovah, are the true God." At that, fire flashes from heaven, consuming the offering, the wood, the altar stones, the dust, and the water. When all the people see it, they immediately fall upon their faces and say: "Jehovah is the true God! Jehovah is the true God!" (18:37, 39) Death to the prophets of Baal! Elijah personally takes care of the slaying, so that not one escapes. Then Jehovah gives rain, ending the drought in Israel.

²⁰ When the news of Baal's humiliation reaches

---

* *Insight on the Scriptures,* Vol. 1, pages 949-50.

---

15. What events take place during the reigns of the next three kings in Judah?

16. What turbulent events now occur in Israel, and why?

17. (a) For what is Omri's reign noted? (b) Why does true worship fall to its lowest ebb during Ahab's reign?

18. With what pronouncement does Elijah begin his prophetic work in Israel, and how does he pinpoint the real reason for Israel's troubles?

19. How is the issue of godship drawn, and how is Jehovah's supremacy proved?

20. (a) How does Jehovah appear to Elijah in Horeb, and what instruction and comfort does He provide? (b) What sin and crime are committed by Ahab?

Jezebel, she seeks to have Elijah killed. Out of fear, he flees with his attendant to the wilderness, and Jehovah directs him to Horeb. Jehovah there appears to him—no, not spectacularly in a wind or a quaking or a fire, but with "a calm, low voice." (19: 11, 12) Jehovah tells him to anoint Hazael as king of Syria, Jehu as king over Israel, and Elisha as prophet in his place. He comforts Elijah with the news that 7,000 in Israel have not bent down to Baal. Elijah proceeds straightaway to anoint Elisha by throwing his official garment upon him. Ahab now wins two victories over the Syrians but is rebuked by Jehovah for making a covenant with their king instead of killing him. Then comes the affair of Naboth, whose vineyard Ahab covets. Jezebel has Naboth framed by false witnesses and put to death so that Ahab can take the vineyard. What an unforgivable crime!

[21] Again Elijah appears. He tells Ahab that where Naboth has died, dogs will lick up his blood also, and that his house will be exterminated as completely as those of Jeroboam and Baasha. Dogs will eat up Jezebel in the plot of land of Jezreel. "Without exception no one has proved to be like Ahab, who sold himself to do what was bad in the eyes of Jehovah, whom Jezebel his wife egged on." (21:25) However, because Ahab humbles himself on hearing Elijah's words, Jehovah says that the calamity will not come in his days but in the days of his son. Ahab now teams up with Jehoshaphat, the king of Judah, in the fight against Syria, and contrary to the advice of Jehovah's prophet Micaiah, they go out to battle. Ahab dies of wounds received in battle. As his chariot is washed down at the pool of Samaria, dogs lick up his blood, just as Elijah prophesied. Ahaziah his son becomes king of Israel in his place.

[22] **Jehoshaphat reigns in Judah** (22:41-53). Jehoshaphat, who accompanied Ahab to the battle with Syria, is faithful to Jehovah like Asa his father, but he fails to clear out entirely the high places of false worship. After ruling for 25 years, he dies, and Jehoram his son becomes king. To the north, in Israel, Ahaziah follows in his father's footsteps, offending Jehovah by his Baal worship.

WHY BENEFICIAL

[23] Great benefit is to be derived from the divine instruction in First Kings. Consider, first, the matter of prayer, which so often comes to the fore in this book. Solomon, when faced with the tremen-

dous responsibility of kingship in Israel, prayed humbly to Jehovah in the manner of a child. He asked merely for discernment and an obedient heart, but in addition to wisdom in overflowing measure, Jehovah gave him also riches and glory. (3:7-9, 12-14) May we have assurance today that our humble prayers for wisdom and direction in Jehovah's service will not go unanswered! (Jas. 1:5) May we always pray fervently from the heart, with deep appreciation for all of Jehovah's goodness, as Solomon did at the temple dedication! (1 Ki. 8:22-53) May our prayers always bear the stamp of implicit trust and confidence in Jehovah, as did the prayers of Elijah in time of trial and when face-to-face with a demon-worshiping nation! Jehovah provides wonderfully for those who seek him in prayer.—1 Ki. 17:20-22; 18:36-40; 1 John 5:14.

[24] Further, we should be warned by the examples of those who did not humble themselves before Jehovah. How 'God opposes such haughty ones'! (1 Pet. 5:5) There was Adonijah, who thought he could bypass Jehovah's theocratic appointment (1 Ki 1:5; 2:24, 25); Shimei, who thought he could step out of bounds and back again (2:37, 41-46); Solomon in his later years, whose disobedience brought resisters from Jehovah (11: 9-14, 23-26); and the kings of Israel, whose false religion proved disastrous (13:33, 34; 14:7-11; 16: 1-4). Moreover, there was the wickedly covetous Jezebel, the power behind Ahab's throne, whose notorious example was used a thousand years later in a warning to the congregation in Thyatira: "Nevertheless, I do hold this against you, that you tolerate that woman Jezebel, who calls herself a prophetess, and she teaches and misleads my slaves to commit fornication and to eat things sacrificed to idols." (Rev. 2:20) Overseers must keep congregations clean and free of all Jezebel-like influences!—Compare Acts 20:28-30.

[25] Jehovah's power of prophecy is clearly shown in the fulfillment of many prophecies given in First Kings. For example, there is the remarkable forecast, made more than 300 years in advance, that Josiah would be the one to rip apart Jeroboam's altar at Bethel. Josiah did it! (1 Ki. 13:1-3; 2 Ki. 23:15) However, most outstanding are the prophecies relating to the house of Jehovah, built by Solomon. Jehovah told Solomon that falling away to false gods would result in Jehovah's cutting Israel off from the surface of the ground and in His throwing away before Him the house that He had

---

21. (a) What doom does Elijah pronounce on Ahab and his house, and on Jezebel? (b) What prophecy is fulfilled at Ahab's death?
22. What characterizes the reigns of Jehoshaphat in Judah and Ahaziah in Israel?
23. What assurance and encouragement does First Kings provide with regard to prayer?

---

24. What warning examples are set forth in First Kings, and why, particularly, should overseers take note?
25. What prophecies of First Kings have had remarkable fulfillment, and how can remembrance of these aid us today?

sanctified to his name. (1 Ki. 9:7, 8) At 2 Chronicles 36:17-21 we read how utterly true this prophecy proved to be. Moreover, Jesus showed that the later temple built by Herod the Great on the same site would suffer the same fate and for the same reason. (Luke 21:6) How true this also proved to be! We should remember these catastrophes and the reason for them, and they should remind us always to walk in the ways of the true God.

²⁶ The queen of Sheba came from her far country to marvel at Solomon's wisdom, the prosperity of his people, and the glory of his kingdom, including the magnificent house of Jehovah. However, even Solomon confessed to Jehovah: "The heavens, yes, the heaven of the heavens, themselves cannot

contain you; how much less, then, this house that I have built!" (1 Ki. 8:27; 10:4-9) But centuries later Christ Jesus came to carry out a spiritual building work especially related to the restoration of true worship at Jehovah's great spiritual temple. (Heb. 8:1-5; 9:2-10, 23) To this one, greater than Solomon, Jehovah's promise holds true: "I also shall indeed establish the throne of your kingdom over Israel to time indefinite." (1 Ki. 9:5; Matt. 1:1, 6, 7, 16; 12:42; Luke 1:32) First Kings provides a stimulating forevision of the glory of Jehovah's spiritual temple and of the prosperity, rejoicing, and delightsome happiness of all who come to live under the wise rule of Jehovah's Kingdom by Christ Jesus. Our appreciation of the importance of true worship and of Jehovah's wonderful provision of his Kingdom by the Seed continues to grow!

---

26. What stimulating forevision of Jehovah's temple and Kingdom is provided in First Kings?

Bible Book Number	**12** **2 Kings**	Writer: **Jeremiah** Places Written: **Jerusalem and Egypt** Writing Completed: **580 B.C.E.** Time Covered: **c. 920–580 B.C.E.**

THE book of Second Kings continues to trace the turbulent course of the kingdoms of Israel and Judah. Elisha took up the mantle of Elijah and was blessed with two parts of Elijah's spirit, performing 16 miracles, compared with the 8 of Elijah. He continued to prophesy doom for apostate Israel, where only Jehu provided a brief flash of zeal for Jehovah. More and more, Israel's kings became bogged down in wickedness, until the northern kingdom finally crumbled before Assyria in 740 B.C.E. In the southern kingdom of Judah, a few outstanding kings, notably Jehoshaphat, Jehoash, Hezekiah, and Josiah, swept back the tide of apostasy for a time, but Nebuchadnezzar at last executed Jehovah's judgment by devastating Jerusalem, its temple, and the land of Judah in 607 B.C.E. Thus Jehovah's prophecies were fulfilled, and his word was vindicated!

² Since Second Kings was originally part of the same roll as First Kings, what has already been said concerning Jeremiah's writership applies equally here, as do the proofs of the book's canonicity and authenticity. It was completed about

580 B.C.E. and covers the period beginning with the reign of Ahaziah of Israel in about 920 B.C.E. and ending in the 37th year of Jehoiachin's exile, 580 B.C.E.—1:1; 25:27.

³ Archaeological finds supporting the record of Second Kings give further evidence of its genuineness. For example, there is the famous Moabite Stone, whose inscription gives Moabite king Mesha's version of the warfare between Moab and Israel. (3:4, 5) There is also the black basalt obelisk of the Assyrian Shalmaneser III, now on display in the British Museum, London, which mentions Israel's king Jehu by name. There are the inscriptions of Assyrian king Tiglath-pileser III (Pul), which name several kings of Israel and Judah, including Menahem, Ahaz, and Pekah.—15:19, 20; 16:5-8.*

⁴ A clear proof of the authenticity of the book is to be found in the utmost candor with which it describes the execution of Jehovah's judgments

---

* *Insight on the Scriptures,* Vol. 1, pages 152, 325; Vol. 2, pages 908, 1101.

---

1. What histories are related in Second Kings, and in vindication of what?
2. What may be said as to the writership and canonicity of Second Kings, and what period is covered by it?

3. What remarkable archaeological finds support Second Kings?
4. What proves that Second Kings is an integral part of the inspired Scriptures?

upon his own people. As first the kingdom of Israel and then the kingdom of Judah go crashing into ruin, the telling force of Jehovah's prophetic judgment in Deuteronomy 28:15–29:28 is brought home to us. In the destruction of those kingdoms, "Jehovah's anger blazed against that land by bringing upon it the whole malediction written in this book." (Deut. 29:27; 2 Ki. 17:18; 25:1, 9-11) Other events recorded in Second Kings are elucidated elsewhere in the Scriptures. At Luke 4: 24-27, after Jesus refers to Elijah and the widow of Zarephath, he speaks of Elisha and Naaman in showing why he himself was not accepted as a prophet in his home territory. Thus, both First and Second Kings are seen to be an integral part of the Holy Scriptures.

CONTENTS OF SECOND KINGS

[5] **Ahaziah, king of Israel** (1:1-18). Suffering a fall in his home, this son of Ahab gets sick. He sends to ask Baal-zebub, the god of Ekron, whether he is to recover. Elijah intercepts the messengers and sends them back to the king, reproving him for not inquiring of the true God and telling him that because he did not turn to the God of Israel, he will positively die. When the king sends out a chief with 50 men to take Elijah and bring him to the king, Elijah calls down fire from heaven to devour them. The same thing happens to a second chief with his 50. A third chief and 50 are sent, and this time Elijah spares their lives by virtue of the chief's respectful plea. Elijah goes with them to the king and again pronounces sentence of death on Ahaziah. The king dies just as Elijah said he would. Then Jehoram the brother of Ahaziah becomes king over Israel, for Ahaziah has no son to take his place.

[6] **Elisha succeeds Elijah** (2:1-25). The time comes for Elijah to be taken away. Elisha sticks with him on his journey from Gilgal to Bethel, to Jericho, and finally across the Jordan. Elijah parts the waters of the Jordan by striking them with his official garment. As he sees a fiery war chariot and fiery horses come between himself and Elijah and he sees Elijah go up in a windstorm, Elisha receives the promised two parts in Elijah's spirit. He soon shows that "the spirit of Elijah" has settled down upon him. (2:15) Taking up Elijah's fallen garment, he uses it to divide the waters again. He then heals the bad water at Jericho. On the way to Bethel, small boys begin to jeer at him: "Go up, you baldhead! Go up, you baldhead!" (2:23) Elisha calls on Jehovah, and two she-bears come out of the woods and kill 42 of these juvenile delinquents.

[7] **Jehoram, king of Israel** (3:1-27). This king keeps on doing what is bad in Jehovah's eyes, sticking to the sins of Jeroboam. The king of Moab has been paying tribute to Israel but now revolts, and Jehoram obtains the help of King Jehoshaphat of Judah and the king of Edom in going against Moab. On the way to the attack, their armies come to waterless terrain and are about to perish. The three kings go down to Elisha to inquire of Jehovah his God. Because of faithful Jehoshaphat, Jehovah rescues them and gives them the victory over Moab.

[8] **Elisha's further miracles** (4:1–8:15). As her creditors are about to take her two sons into slavery, the widow of one of the sons of the prophets seeks help from Elisha. He miraculously multiplies the small supply of oil in her house so that she is able to sell enough to pay her debts. A Shunammite woman recognizes Elisha as a prophet of the true God, and she and her husband prepare a room for his use when he is in Shunem. Because of her kindness, Jehovah blesses her with a son. Some years later, the child becomes sick and dies. The woman immediately seeks out Elisha. He accompanies her to her home, and by Jehovah's power he raises the child to life. Returning to the sons of the prophets at Gilgal, Elisha miraculously removes "death in the pot" by rendering poisonous gourds harmless. He then feeds a hundred men with 20 barley loaves, and yet they have "leftovers." —4:40, 44.

[9] Naaman, the chief of the Syrian army, is a leper. A captive Israelite girl tells Naaman's wife that there is a prophet in Samaria who can cure him. Naaman journeys to Elisha, but instead of attending to him personally, Elisha merely sends word for him to go and wash himself seven times in the Jordan River. Naaman is indignant at this apparent lack of respect. Are not the rivers of Damascus better than the waters of Israel? But he is prevailed upon to obey Elisha, and he is cured. Elisha refuses to accept a gift as a reward, but later his attendant Gehazi runs after Naaman and asks for a gift in Elisha's name. When he returns and tries to deceive Elisha, Gehazi is struck with leprosy. Still another miracle is performed when Elisha makes an axhead float.

[10] When Elisha warns the king of Israel of a Syrian plot to kill him, the king of Syria sends a military force to Dothan to capture Elisha. Seeing

---

5. What reproof and sentence does Elijah pass on Ahaziah, and why?
6. Under what circumstances does Elijah part from Elisha, and how is it soon shown that "the spirit of Elijah" has settled on Elisha?

7. Because of what does Jehovah rescue Jehoshaphat and Jehoram?
8. What further miracles does Elisha perform?
9. What miracles are performed in connection with Naaman, and with the axhead?
10. How are the superior forces of Jehovah shown, and how does Elisha turn back the Syrians?

the city surrounded by the armies of Syria, Elisha's attendant becomes fearful. Elisha assures him: "Do not be afraid, for there are more who are with us than those who are with them." Then he prays to Jehovah to let his attendant see the great force that is with Elisha. 'And, look! The mountainous region is full of horses and war chariots of fire all around Elisha.' (6:16, 17) When the Syrians attack, the prophet again prays to Jehovah, and the Syrians are struck with mental blindness and led to the king of Israel. Instead of their being put to death, however, Elisha tells the king to spread a feast for them and send them home.

¹¹ Later on, King Ben-hadad of Syria besieges Samaria, and there is a great famine. The king of Israel blames Elisha, but the prophet predicts an abundance of food for the following day. In the night, Jehovah causes the Syrians to hear the sound of a great army, so that they flee, leaving all their provisions for the Israelites. After some time Ben-hadad becomes sick. On hearing a report that Elisha has come to Damascus, he sends Hazael to inquire if he will recover. Elisha's answer indicates that the king will die and that Hazael will become king in his place. Hazael makes sure of this by himself killing the king and taking over the kingship.

¹² **Jehoram, king of Judah** (8:16-29). Meanwhile, in Judah, Jehoshaphat's son Jehoram is now king. He proves to be no better than the kings of Israel, doing bad in Jehovah's eyes. His wife is Ahab's daughter Athaliah, whose brother, also named Jehoram, is reigning in Israel. At the death of Jehoram of Judah, his son Ahaziah becomes king in Jerusalem.

¹³ **Jehu, king of Israel** (9:1–10:36). Elisha sends one of the sons of the prophets to anoint Jehu to be king over Israel and to commission him to strike down the entire house of Ahab. Jehu loses no time. He sets out after Jehoram, king of Israel, who is at Jezreel recuperating from war wounds. The watchman sees the heaving mass of men approaching, and at last he reports to the king: "The driving is like the driving of Jehu the grandson of Nimshi, for it is with madness that he drives." (9:20) Jehoram of Israel and Ahaziah of Judah inquire as to Jehu's intent. Jehu replies by asking: "What peace could there be as long as there are the fornications of Jezebel your mother and her many sorceries?" (9:22) As Jehoram turns to flee, Jehu shoots an arrow through his heart. His body is

thrown there into the field of Naboth, as further repayment for the innocent blood shed by Ahab. Later Jehu and his men pursue Ahaziah, striking him down so that he dies at Megiddo. Two kings die in Jehu's first lightning campaign.

¹⁴ Now it is Jezebel's turn! As Jehu triumphantly rides into Jezreel, Jezebel appears at her window in her most glamorous makeup. Jehu is unimpressed. "Let her drop!" he calls to some attendants. Down she goes, her blood spattering on the wall and on the horses that trample on her. When they go to bury her, they can find only her skull, her feet, and the palms of her hands. This is in fulfillment of Elijah's prophecy, 'dogs have eaten her, and she has become as manure in the tract of land of Jezreel.'—2 Ki. 9:33, 36, 37; 1 Ki. 21:23.

¹⁵ Next, Jehu orders the slaughter of the 70 sons of Ahab, and he stacks their heads at the gate of Jezreel. All of Ahab's yes-men in Jezreel are struck down. Now, on to Israel's capital, Samaria! On the way he meets the 42 brothers of Ahaziah, who are traveling to Jezreel, unaware of what is happening. They are taken and slain. But now there is a different kind of encounter. Jehonadab the son of Rechab comes out to meet Jehu. To Jehu's question, "Is your heart upright with me, just as my own heart is with your heart?" Jehonadab replies, "It is." Jehu then makes him go along with him in his chariot to see firsthand his "toleration of no rivalry toward Jehovah."—2 Ki. 10:15, 16.

¹⁶ On arrival in Samaria, Jehu annihilates everything left over of Ahab's, according to Jehovah's word to Elijah. (1 Ki. 21:21, 22) However, what of the detestable religion of Baal? Jehu declares, "Ahab, on the one hand, worshiped Baal a little. Jehu, on the other hand, will worship him a great deal." (2 Ki. 10:18) Calling all these demon worshipers to the house of Baal, he has them put on their garments of identification and makes sure there is no worshiper of Jehovah among them. Then he sends his men in to strike them down, not letting a single one escape. Baal's house is demolished, and the place is turned into privies, which remain till Jeremiah's day. 'Thus Jehu annihilates Baal out of Israel.'—10:28.

¹⁷ However, even the zealous Jehu fails. In what? In that he continues to follow the golden calves that Jeroboam set up in Bethel and Dan. He does not "take care to walk in the law of Jehovah the God of Israel with all his heart." (10:31) But

---

11. How are Elisha's prophecies concerning the Syrians and Ben-hadad fulfilled?
12. What kind of king does Jehoshaphat's son Jehoram prove to be?
13. With what lightning campaign does Jehu follow up his anointing?

14. How is Elijah's prophecy concerning Jezebel fulfilled?
15. What different kinds of encounters does Jehu have on the way to Samaria?
16. How thorough is Jehu's action against Ahab's house and against Baal?
17. In what does Jehu fail, and how does Jehovah start to bring punishment on Israel?

because of his action against the house of Ahab, Jehovah promises that his descendants will reign over Israel to the fourth generation. In his days, Jehovah starts to cut off the eastern part of the kingdom, bringing Hazael of Syria against Israel. After reigning 28 years, Jehu dies and is succeeded by his son Jehoahaz.

[18] **Jehoash, king of Judah** (11:1–12:21). The queen mother, Athaliah, is daughter to Jezebel in flesh and in spirit. Hearing of the death of her son Ahaziah, she orders the execution of the entire royal family and takes over the throne. Only Ahaziah's baby son Jehoash escapes death when he is hidden away. In the seventh year of Athaliah's reign, Jehoiada the priest has Jehoash anointed as king and has Athaliah put to death. Jehoiada directs the people in the worship of Jehovah, instructs the youthful king in his duties before God, and arranges for repairing the house of Jehovah. By means of gifts, Jehoash turns back an attack by Hazael the king of Syria. After he has ruled for 40 years in Jerusalem, Jehoash is assassinated by his servants, and Amaziah his son begins to rule as king in place of him.

[19] **Jehoahaz and Jehoash, kings of Israel** (13:1-25). Jehu's son Jehoahaz continues in idol worship, and Israel comes under the power of Syria, although Jehoahaz is not dethroned. Jehovah frees the Israelites in time, but they continue in Jeroboam's calf worship. At Jehoahaz' death, his son Jehoash takes his place as king in Israel, even while the other Jehoash is reigning in Judah. Jehoash of Israel continues in the idol worship of his father. At his death his son Jeroboam becomes king. It is during the reign of Jehoash that Elisha falls sick and dies, after making his final prophecy that Jehoash will strike down Syria three times, which is duly fulfilled. The final miracle accredited to Elisha takes place after his death, when a dead man is thrown into the same burial place, only to stand up alive as soon as he touches Elisha's bones.

[20] **Amaziah, king of Judah** (14:1-22). Amaziah does what is upright in Jehovah's eyes, but he fails to destroy the high places used for worship. He is defeated in war by Jehoash of Israel. After a 29-year reign, he is killed in a conspiracy. Azariah his son is made king in his place.

[21] **Jeroboam II, king of Israel** (14:23-29). The second Jeroboam to be king in Israel continues in the false worship of his forefather. He reigns in

Samaria for 41 years and is successful in winning back Israel's lost territories. Zechariah his son becomes his successor on the throne.

[22] **Azariah (Uzziah), king of Judah** (15:1-7). Azariah rules for 52 years. He is upright before Jehovah but fails to destroy the high places. Later, Jehovah plagues him with leprosy, and his son Jotham takes care of the royal duties, becoming king on Azariah's death.

[23] **Zechariah, Shallum, Menahem, Pekahiah, and Pekah, kings of Israel** (15:8-31). According to Jehovah's promise, the throne of Israel remains in the house of Jehu to the fourth generation, Zechariah. (10:30) Accordingly, he becomes king in Samaria, and six months later an assassin strikes him down. Shallum, the usurper, lasts only one month. False worship, assassination, and intrigue continue to plague Israel as kings Menahem, Pekahiah, and Pekah pass in procession. During Pekah's reign Assyria closes in for the kill. Hoshea assassinates Pekah, to become Israel's last king.

[24] **Jotham and Ahaz, kings of Judah** (15:32–16:20). Jotham practices pure worship but lets the high places continue. Ahaz his son imitates the kings of neighboring Israel by practicing what is bad in Jehovah's eyes. Under attack by the kings of Israel and Syria, he appeals to the king of Assyria for help. The Assyrians come to his aid, capturing Damascus, and Ahaz goes there to meet the king of Assyria. Seeing the altar of worship there, Ahaz has one erected in Jerusalem according to the same pattern, and he begins sacrificing on it instead of on the copper altar at Jehovah's temple. His son Hezekiah becomes king of Judah as his successor.

[25] **Hoshea, last king of Israel** (17:1-41). Israel now comes under the power of Assyria. Hoshea rebels and seeks help from Egypt, but in the ninth year of his reign, Israel is conquered by Assyria and is carried into captivity. Thus ends the ten-tribe kingdom of Israel. Why? "Because the sons of Israel had sinned against Jehovah their God . . . And they continued to serve dungy idols, concerning which Jehovah had said to them: 'You must not do this thing'; therefore Jehovah got very incensed against Israel, so that he removed them from his sight." (17:7, 12, 18) The Assyrians bring in people from the east to settle the land, and these become 'fearers of Jehovah,' though they continue to worship their own gods.—17:33.

18. How is Athaliah's conspiracy in Judah thwarted, and what is noteworthy about the reign of Jehoash?
19. (a) What false worship continues during the reigns of Jehoahaz and Jehoash in Israel? (b) How does Elisha end his course as Jehovah's prophet?
20. Describe Amaziah's reign in Judah.
21. What occurs during the reign of Jeroboam II in Israel?

22. What is related concerning Azariah's reign in Judah?
23. With what evils is Israel plagued as the Assyrian menace arises?
24. After Jotham, how does Ahaz of Judah sin as to worship?
25. How does Israel go into captivity, and why?

²⁶ **Hezekiah, king of Judah** (18:1–20:21). Hezekiah does what is right in Jehovah's eyes, according to all that David his forefather had done. He roots out false worship and tears down the high places, and because the people now worship it, he even destroys the copper serpent Moses made. Sennacherib, king of Assyria, now invades Judah and captures many fortified cities. Hezekiah tries to buy him off with a heavy tribute, but Sennacherib sends his messenger Rabshakeh, who comes up to the walls of Jerusalem and demands surrender and mocks Jehovah within the hearing of all the people. The prophet Isaiah reassures faithful Hezekiah with a message of doom against Sennacherib. "This is what Jehovah has said: 'Do not be afraid.'" (19:6) As Sennacherib continues to threaten, Hezekiah implores Jehovah: "And now, O Jehovah our God, save us, please, out of his hand, that all the kingdoms of the earth may know that you, O Jehovah, are God alone."—19:19.

²⁷ Does Jehovah answer this unselfish prayer? First, through Isaiah, he sends the message that "the very zeal of Jehovah of armies" will turn back the enemy. (19:31) Then, that same night, he sends his angel to strike down 185,000 in the camp of the Assyrians. In the morning 'all of them are dead carcasses.' (19:35) Sennacherib returns in defeat and takes up dwelling in Nineveh. There his god Nisroch fails him once more, for it is while he is bowed in worship that his own sons kill him, in fulfillment of Isaiah's prophecy.—19:7, 37.

²⁸ Hezekiah becomes deathly ill, but Jehovah again heeds his prayer and prolongs his life an additional 15 years. The king of Babylon sends messengers with gifts, and Hezekiah presumes to show them all his treasure house. Isaiah then prophesies that everything in his house will one day be carried to Babylon. Hezekiah then dies, renowned for his mightiness and for the tunnel that he built to bring Jerusalem's water supply into the city.

²⁹ **Manasseh, Amon, and Josiah, kings of Judah** (21:1–23:30). Manasseh succeeds his father, Hezekiah, and reigns 55 years, doing bad in Jehovah's eyes on a large scale. He restores the high places of false worship, sets up altars to Baal, makes a sacred pole as Ahab did, and makes Jehovah's house a place of idolatry. Jehovah foretells that he will bring calamity on Jerusalem as he has done on

Samaria, "wiping it clean and turning it upside down." Manasseh also sheds innocent blood "in very great quantity." (21:13, 16) He is succeeded by his son Amon, who continues to do bad for two years, until struck down by assassins.

³⁰ The people now make Amon's son Josiah king. During his 31-year reign, he briefly reverses Judah's plunge toward destruction 'by walking in all the way of David his forefather.' (22:2) He begins repairs on the house of Jehovah, and there the high priest finds the book of the Law. This confirms that destruction will come on the nation for its disobedience to Jehovah, but Josiah is assured that because of his faithfulness, it will not come in his day. He purges the house of Jehovah and the entire land of demon worship and extends his idol-smashing activity to Bethel, where he destroys Jeroboam's altar in fulfillment of the prophecy at 1 Kings 13:1, 2. He reinstitutes the Passover to Jehovah. "Like him there did not prove to be a king prior to him who returned to Jehovah with all his heart and with all his soul and with all his vital force, according to all the law of Moses." (23:25) Nevertheless, Jehovah's anger still burns because of Manasseh's offenses. Josiah dies in an encounter with the king of Egypt at Megiddo.

³¹ **Jehoahaz, Jehoiakim, and Jehoiachin, kings of Judah** (23:31–24:17). After a three-month reign, Josiah's son Jehoahaz is taken captive by the king of Egypt, and his brother Eliakim, whose name is changed to Jehoiakim, is placed on the throne. He follows in the wrong course of his forefathers and becomes subject to Nebuchadnezzar, king of Babylon, but rebels against him after three years. At Jehoiakim's death his son Jehoiachin begins to reign. Nebuchadnezzar besieges Jerusalem, captures it, and carries the treasures of the house of Jehovah to Babylon, "just as Jehovah had spoken" by Isaiah. (24:13; 20:17) Jehoiachin and thousands of his subjects are carried into exile in Babylon.

³² **Zedekiah, last king of Judah** (24:18–25:30). Nebuchadnezzar makes Jehoiachin's uncle Mattaniah king and changes his name to Zedekiah. He reigns 11 years in Jerusalem and continues to do bad in Jehovah's eyes. He rebels against Babylon, so in Zedekiah's ninth year, Nebuchadnezzar and his entire army come up and build a siege wall all around Jerusalem. After 18 months the city is ravaged by famine. The walls are then breached, and Zedekiah is captured while trying to flee. His

---

26, 27. (a) How does Hezekiah of Judah do right in Jehovah's eyes? (b) How does Jehovah answer Hezekiah's prayer in turning back the Assyrians? (c) What further fulfillment does Isaiah's prophecy have?
28. For what is Hezekiah renowned, but in what does he sin?
29. What idolatry does Manasseh institute, what calamity does Jehovah foretell, and what further sin does Manasseh commit?

---

30. Why and how does Josiah return to Jehovah with all his heart?
31. What setbacks befall Judah following Josiah's death?
32. What dramatic events lead up to the desolation of Jerusalem and of the land?

sons are slaughtered before him, and he is blinded. In the next month, all the principal houses of the city, including the house of Jehovah and the king's house, are burned and the city walls demolished. Most of the survivors are carried off captive to Babylon. Gedaliah is appointed governor over the few lowly ones who remain in the countryside of Judah. However, he is assassinated, and the people flee to Egypt. Thus, from the seventh month of 607 B.C.E., the land lies utterly desolate. The final words of Second Kings tell of the favor the king of Babylon shows to Jehoiachin in the 37th year of his captivity.

WHY BENEFICIAL

33 Though it covers the fatal decline of the kingdoms of Israel and Judah, Second Kings sparkles with many examples of Jehovah's blessing on individuals who showed love for him and his right principles. Like the widow of Zarephath before her, the Shunammite woman received an abundant blessing for her hospitality shown to God's prophet. (4:8-17, 32-37) Jehovah's ability always to provide was shown when Elisha fed a hundred men from 20 loaves, even as Jesus was to perform similar miracles later. (2 Ki. 4:42-44; Matt. 14: 16-21; Mark 8:1-9) Note how Jehonadab received a blessing in being invited to go along in Jehu's chariot to see the destruction of the Baal worshipers. And why? Because he took positive action in coming out to greet the zealous Jehu. (2 Ki. 10: 15, 16) Finally, there are the splendid examples of Hezekiah and Josiah, in their humility and proper respect for Jehovah's name and Law. (19:14-19; 22:11-13) These are splendid examples for us to follow.

34 Jehovah tolerates no disrespect for his official servants. When the delinquents mocked Elisha as the prophet of Jehovah, He brought swift recompense. (2:23, 24) Moreover, Jehovah respects the blood of the innocent. His judgment rested heavily on Ahab's house not only because of Baal worship but also because of the bloodshed that accompanied it. Thus, Jehu was anointed to avenge "the blood of all the servants of Jehovah at the hand of Jezebel." When judgment was executed against Jehoram, Jehu remembered Jehovah's pronouncement that it was on account of "the blood of Naboth and the blood of his sons." (9:7, 26) Likewise, it was Manasseh's bloodguilt that finally sealed Judah's doom. Adding to his sin of false worship, Manasseh 'filled Jerusalem with blood from end to

end.' Even though Manasseh later repented of his bad course, bloodguilt remained. (2 Chron. 33: 12, 13) Not even the good reign of Josiah, and his putting away of all idolatry, could wipe out the community bloodguilt carrying over from Manasseh's reign. Years later, when Jehovah began to bring his executioners up against Jerusalem, he declared that it was because Manasseh had "filled Jerusalem with innocent blood, and Jehovah did not consent to grant forgiveness." (2 Ki. 21:16; 24:4) Likewise, Jesus declared that the Jerusalem of the first century C.E. had to perish because its priests were the sons of those who shed the blood of the prophets, 'that there may come upon them all the righteous blood spilled on earth.' (Matt. 23: 29-36) God warns the world that he will avenge the innocent blood that has been shed, especially the blood "of those slaughtered because of the word of God."—Rev. 6:9, 10.

35 The unerring sureness with which Jehovah brings his prophetic judgments to fulfillment is also shown in Second Kings. Three leading prophets are brought to our attention, Elijah, Elisha, and Isaiah. The prophecies of each one are shown to have striking fulfillments. (2 Ki. 9:36, 37; 10: 10, 17; 3:14, 18, 24; 13:18, 19, 25; 19:20, 32-36; 20:16, 17; 24:13) Elijah is also confirmed as a true prophet in his appearing with the prophet Moses and the Great Prophet, Jesus Christ, in the transfiguration on the mountain. (Matt. 17:1-5) Referring to the magnificence of that occasion, Peter said: "Consequently we have the prophetic word made more sure; and you are doing well in paying attention to it as to a lamp shining in a dark place, until day dawns and a daystar rises, in your hearts."—2 Pet. 1:19.

36 The events recorded in Second Kings clearly reveal that Jehovah's judgment against all practicers of false religion and all willful shedders of innocent blood is extermination. Yet, Jehovah showed favor and mercy to his people "for the sake of his covenant with Abraham, Isaac and Jacob." (2 Ki. 13:23) He preserved them "for the sake of David his servant." (8:19) He will show like mercy to those who turn to him in this day. As we review the Bible record and promises, with what deepening confidence we look forward to the Kingdom of the "son of David," Jesus Christ the promised Seed, in which bloodshed and wickedness will be no more!—Matt. 1:1; Isa. 2:4; Ps. 145:20.

---

33. What fine examples are provided in Second Kings for us to follow?
34. What does Second Kings teach us regarding respect for official servants and regarding bloodguilt?

---

35. (a) How are Elijah, Elisha, and Isaiah confirmed to be true prophets? (b) In connection with Elijah, what does Peter say as to prophecy?
36. Why did Jehovah show his people mercy, and how is our confidence in the Kingdom of the Seed deepened?

Writer: **Ezra**
Place Written: **Jerusalem (?)**
Time of Writing: **c. 460 B.C.E.**
Time Covered: **After 1 Chronicles 9:44: 1077–1037 B.C.E.**

IS First Chronicles just a dry list of genealogies? Is it merely a repetition of the books of Samuel and Kings? Far from it! Here is an illuminating and essential part of the divine record—essential in the day of its writing in reorganizing the nation and its worship, and essential and beneficial in showing a pattern of divine worship for later days, including this present day. First Chronicles contains some of the most beautiful expressions of praise to Jehovah to be found in all Scripture. It provides wonderful foregleams of Jehovah's Kingdom of righteousness, and it is to be studied with profit by all who hope in that Kingdom. The two books of Chronicles have been treasured by Jews and Christians alike through the ages. The Bible translator Jerome had such an exalted opinion of First and Second Chronicles that he considered them an "epitome of the Old Testament" and asserted that "they are of such high moment and importance, that he who supposes himself to be acquainted with the sacred writings, and does not know *them,* only deceives himself."*

² The two books of Chronicles apparently were originally one book, or roll, which was later divided for convenience. Why was Chronicles written? Consider the setting. The exile in Babylon had ended about 77 years before. The Jews were resettled in their land. However, there was a dangerous trend away from Jehovah's worship at the rebuilt temple in Jerusalem. Ezra had been authorized by the king of Persia to appoint judges and teachers of the law of God (as well as that of the king) and to beautify the house of Jehovah. Accurate genealogical lists were necessary to assure that only authorized persons served in the priesthood and also to confirm the tribal inheritances, from which the priesthood gained its support. In view of Jehovah's prophecies regarding the Kingdom, it was also vital to have a clear and dependable record of the lineage of Judah and of David.

* Clarke's *Commentary,* Vol. II, page 574.

1. In what ways is First Chronicles an essential and beneficial part of the divine record?
2. Why was Chronicles written?

³ Ezra was earnestly desirous of arousing the restored Jews from their apathy and of infusing in them the realization that they were indeed the inheritors of Jehovah's covenanted lovingkindness. In the Chronicles, therefore, he set before them a full account of the nation's history and of the origins of mankind, going back as far as the first man, Adam. Since the kingdom of David was the focal point, he highlighted the history of Judah, omitting almost entirely the absolutely unredeeming record of the ten-tribe kingdom. He depicted Judah's greatest kings as engaged in building or restoring the temple and zealously leading in the worship of God. He pointed out the religious sins that led to the kingdom's overthrow, while emphasizing also God's promises of restoration. He stressed the importance of pure worship by focusing attention on the many details pertaining to the temple, its priests, the Levites, the masters of song, and so on. It must have been very encouraging for the Israelites to have a historical record that focused on the reason for their return from exile—the restoration of Jehovah's worship at Jerusalem.

⁴ What is the evidence that Ezra wrote Chronicles? The closing two verses of Second Chronicles are the same as the opening two verses of Ezra, and Second Chronicles ends in the middle of a sentence that is finished in Ezra 1:3. The writer of Chronicles must therefore have been the writer also of Ezra. This is further borne out in that the style, language, wording, and spelling of Chronicles and Ezra are the same. Some of the expressions in these two books are found in no other Bible books. Ezra, who wrote the book of Ezra, must also have written Chronicles. Jewish tradition supports this conclusion.

⁵ No one was better qualified than Ezra to compile this authentic and accurate history. "For Ezra himself had prepared his heart to consult the law

3. (a) What was Ezra desirous of infusing in the Jews? (b) Why did he highlight the history of Judah, and how did he stress the importance of pure worship?
4. What evidence favors Ezra as the writer of Chronicles?
5. What were Ezra's spiritual and secular qualifications?

of Jehovah and to do it and to teach in Israel regulation and justice." (Ezra 7:10) Jehovah aided him by holy spirit. The Persian world-ruler recognized the wisdom of God in Ezra and commissioned him with wide civil powers in the jurisdictional district of Judah. (Ezra 7:12-26) Thus equipped with divine and imperial authority, Ezra could compile his account from the best available documents.

⁶ Ezra was an extraordinary researcher. He searched through older records of Jewish history that had been compiled by reliable prophets contemporary with the times as well as those compiled by official recorders and keepers of public records. Some of the writings he consulted may have been documents of state from both Israel and Judah, genealogical records, historical works written by prophets, and documents possessed by tribal or family heads. Ezra cites at least 20 such sources of information.* By these explicit citations, Ezra honestly gave his contemporaries the opportunity to check his sources if they wished to do so, and this adds considerable weight to the argument for the credibility and authenticity of his word. We today can have confidence in the correctness of the books of Chronicles for the same reason that the Jews of Ezra's time had such confidence.

⁷ Since Ezra "went up from Babylon" in the seventh year of the Persian king Artaxerxes Longimanus, which was 468 B.C.E., and Ezra makes no record of Nehemiah's significant arrival in 455 B.C.E., Chronicles must have been completed between these dates, probably about the year 460 B.C.E., in Jerusalem. (Ezra 7:1-7; Neh. 2:1-18) The Jews of Ezra's day accepted Chronicles as a genuine part of 'all Scripture that is inspired of God and beneficial.' They called it *Div·reh′ Hai·ya·mim′*, which means "The Affairs of the Days," that is, history of the days or times. Some 200 years later, the translators of the Greek *Septuagint* also included Chronicles as canonical. They divided the book into two parts and, supposing it to be supplementary to Samuel and Kings or to the entire Bible of that time, called it *Pa·ra·lei·po·me′non,* meaning "Things Passed Over (Left Untold; Omitted)." Though the name is not particularly appropriate, still their action shows that they regarded Chronicles as authentic, inspired Scripture. In preparing the Latin *Vulgate,* Jerome suggested: "We may more significantly call [them] the *Khro·ni·kon′* of the whole divine history." It is from this that the

title "Chronicles" appears to have been derived. A chronicle is a record of happenings in the order in which they occurred. After listing its genealogies, First Chronicles is concerned mainly with the time of King David, from 1077 B.C.E. down to his death.

CONTENTS OF FIRST CHRONICLES

⁸ This book of First Chronicles divides naturally into two sections: the first 9 chapters, which deal primarily with genealogies, and the last 20 chapters, which cover events during the 40 years from the death of Saul to the end of David's reign.

⁹ **The genealogies** (1:1–9:44). These chapters list the genealogy from Adam down to the line of Zerubbabel. (1:1; 3:19-24) The renderings of many translations take the line of Zerubbabel to the tenth generation. Since he returned to Jerusalem in 537 B.C.E., there would not have been enough time for so many generations to have been born by 460 B.C.E., when Ezra evidently completed the writing. However, the Hebrew text is incomplete in this section, and it cannot be determined how most of the men listed were related to Zerubbabel. Hence, there is no reason to favor a later date for the writing of Chronicles, as some do.

¹⁰ First there are supplied the ten generations from Adam to Noah, and then the ten generations down to Abraham. Abraham's sons and their offspring; the posterity of Esau and of Seir, who lived in the mountainous region of Seir; and early kings of Edom are listed. From the second chapter, however, the record is concerned with the descendants of Israel, or Jacob, from whom the genealogy is first traced through Judah and then ten generations to David. (2:1-14) The listing is also made for the other tribes, with particular reference to the tribe of Levi and the high priests, and ending with a genealogy of the tribe of Benjamin by way of introduction to King Saul, a Benjamite, with whom the historical narrative in a strict sense then opens. Sometimes there may appear to be contradictions between Ezra's genealogies and other Bible passages. However, it must be kept in mind that certain persons were also known by other names and that language changes and the passing of time could change the spelling of some names. Careful study removes most of the difficulties.

¹¹ Ezra intersperses his genealogies here and there with bits of historical and geographical in-

---

* *Insight on the Scriptures,* Vol. 1, pages 444-5.

6. Why may we have confidence in the correctness of Chronicles?
7. When was Chronicles written, who have regarded it as authentic, and what time period does it cover?

---

8. Into what two sections does the book of First Chronicles divide?
9. Why is there no reason to favor a later date for the writing of Chronicles?
10. (a) What generations are first given? (b) What genealogy is logically traced at the start of the second chapter? (c) What other listings are made, ending in what?
11. Give examples of other useful information interspersed in the record of genealogies.

formation that serve to clarify and to give important reminders. For example, in listing Reuben's descendants, Ezra adds an important piece of information: "And the sons of Reuben the firstborn of Israel—for he was the firstborn; but for his profaning the lounge of his father his right as firstborn was given to the sons of Joseph the son of Israel, so that he was not to be enrolled genealogically for the right of the firstborn. For Judah himself proved to be superior among his brothers, and the one for leader was from him; but the right as firstborn was Joseph's." (5:1, 2) Much is explained in these few words. Further, it is only in Chronicles that we learn that Joab, Amasa, and Abishai were all nephews of David, which helps us to appreciate the various events surrounding them.—2:16, 17.

¹² **Saul's unfaithfulness results in his death** (10:1-14). The narrative opens with the Philistines pressing the attack in the battle of Mount Gilboa. Three of Saul's sons, including Jonathan, are struck down. Then Saul is wounded. Not wishing to be taken by the enemy, he urges his armorbearer: "Draw your sword and run me through with it, that these uncircumcised men may not come and certainly deal abusively with me." When his armor-bearer refuses, Saul kills himself. Thus Saul dies for acting "faithlessly against Jehovah concerning the word of Jehovah that he had not kept and also for asking of a spirit medium to make inquiry. And he did not inquire of Jehovah." (10:4, 13, 14) Jehovah gives the kingdom to David.

¹³ **David confirmed in the kingdom** (11:1–12: 40). In time the 12 tribes assemble to David at Hebron and anoint him as king over all Israel. He captures Zion and goes on 'getting greater and greater, for Jehovah of armies is with him.' (11:9) Mighty men are put in charge of the army, and by means of them, Jehovah saves "with a great salvation." (11:14) David receives united support as the men of war flock together with one complete heart to make him king. There is feasting and rejoicing in Israel.

¹⁴ **David and the ark of Jehovah** (13:1–16:36). David consults the national leaders, and they agree to move the Ark to Jerusalem from Kiriath-jearim, where it has been for about 70 years. On the way, Uzzah dies for irreverently ignoring God's instructions, and the Ark is left for a time at the home of Obed-edom. (Num. 4:15) The Philistines resume their raids, but David crushingly defeats them twice, at Baal-perazim and at Gibeon. Instructed

by David, the Levites now follow theocratic procedure in moving the Ark safely to Jerusalem, where it is put in a tent that David has pitched for it, amid dancing and rejoicing. There is an offering of sacrifice and singing, David himself contributing a song of thanks to Jehovah for the occasion. Its grand climax is reached in the theme: "Let the heavens rejoice, and let the earth be joyful, and let them say among the nations, 'Jehovah himself has become king!'" (1 Chron. 16:31) What a stirring, faith-inspiring occasion! Later, this song of David is adapted as the basis for new songs, one of which is Psalm 96. Another is recorded in the first 15 verses of Psalm 105.

¹⁵ **David and Jehovah's house** (16:37-17:27). An unusual arrangement now obtains in Israel. The ark of the covenant resides in a tent in Jerusalem where Asaph and his brothers are in attendance, while a few miles northwest of Jerusalem at Gibeon, Zadok the high priest and his brothers carry on the prescribed sacrifices at the tabernacle. Always mindful of exalting and unifying Jehovah's worship, David indicates his desire to build a house for Jehovah's ark of the covenant. But Jehovah states that not David but his son will build a house for Him and that He will "certainly establish his throne firmly to time indefinite," showing loving-kindness as from a father to a son. (17: 11-13) This marvelous promise by Jehovah—this covenant for an everlasting kingdom—moves David to the heart. His thankfulness overflows in petitioning that Jehovah's name "prove faithful and become great to time indefinite" and that His blessing be upon David's house.—17:24.

¹⁶ **David's conquests** (18:1–21:17). Through David, Jehovah now carries out His promise to give the entire Promised Land to Abraham's seed. (18:3) In a rapid series of campaigns, Jehovah gives "salvation to David" wherever he goes. (18:6) In smashing military victories, David subdues the Philistines, strikes down the Moabites, defeats the Zobahites, forces the Syrians to pay tribute, and conquers Edom and Ammon as well as Amalek. However, Satan incites David to number Israel and thereby to sin. Jehovah sends a pestilence in punishment but mercifully brings an end to the calamity at Ornan's threshing floor, after 70,000 have been executed.

¹⁷ **David's preparation for the temple** (21: 18–22:19). David receives angelic notice through Gad "to erect an altar to Jehovah on the threshing

---

12. What are the circumstances of Saul's death?
13. How does David prosper in the kingdom?
14. How does David fare in battle with the Philistines, and what faith-inspiring occasion gives rise to joyful song?

---

15. With what marvelous promise does Jehovah answer David's desire to build a house for unified worship?
16. What promise does Jehovah carry out through David, but how does David sin?
17. What preparation does David make for building Jehovah's house, and how does he encourage Solomon?

floor of Ornan the Jebusite." (21:18) After purchasing the location from Ornan, David obediently offers sacrifices there and calls upon Jehovah, who answers him "with fire from the heavens upon the altar of burnt offering." (21:26) David concludes that Jehovah wants his house built there, and he sets to work in shaping the materials and assembling them, saying: "Solomon my son is young and delicate, and the house to be built to Jehovah is to be surpassingly magnificent for beauteous distinction to all the lands. Let me, then, make preparation for him." (22:5) He explains to Solomon that Jehovah has not permitted him to build the house, as he has been a man of wars and blood. He exhorts his son to be courageous and strong in this undertaking, saying: "Rise and act, and may Jehovah prove to be with you."—22:16.

¹⁸ **David organizes for Jehovah's worship** (23: 1–29:30). A census is taken, this time according to God's will, for the reorganizing of the priestly and Levitical services. The Levitical services are described in greater detail here than anywhere else in the Scriptures. The divisions of the king's service are then outlined.

¹⁹ Near the end of his eventful reign, David congregates the representatives of the entire nation, "Jehovah's congregation." (28:8) The king rises to his feet. "Hear me, my brothers and my people." He then speaks to them concerning the desire of his heart, "the house of the true God." In their presence he commissions Solomon: "And you, Solomon my son, know the God of your father and serve him with a complete heart and with a delightful soul; for all hearts Jehovah is searching, and every inclination of the thoughts he is discerning. If you search for him, he will let himself be found by you; but if you leave him, he will cast you off forever. See, now, for Jehovah himself has chosen you to build a house as a sanctuary. Be courageous and act." (28:2, 9, 10, 12) He gives young Solomon the detailed architectural plans received by inspiration from Jehovah and contributes an immense personal fortune to the building project—3,000 talents of gold and 7,000 talents of silver, which he has saved up for this purpose. With such a splendid example before them, the princes and the people respond by donating gold worth 5,000 talents and 10,000 darics and silver worth 10,000 talents, as well as much iron and copper.* (29:3-7) The people give way to rejoicing at this privilege.

---

* *Insight on the Scriptures,* Vol. 2, page 1076.

---

18. For what purpose is a census taken?
19. With what words does David commission Solomon, what plans does he provide, and what splendid example does he set?

²⁰ David then praises Jehovah in prayer, acknowledging that all this abundant offering has actually proceeded from His hand and petitioning His continued blessing on the people and upon Solomon. This final prayer of David reaches sublime heights in exalting Jehovah's kingdom and His glorious name: "Blessed may you be, O Jehovah the God of Israel our father, from time indefinite even to time indefinite. Yours, O Jehovah, are the greatness and the mightiness and the beauty and the excellency and the dignity; for everything in the heavens and in the earth is yours. Yours is the kingdom, O Jehovah, the One also lifting yourself up as head over all. The riches and the glory are on account of you, and you are dominating everything; and in your hand there are power and mightiness, and in your hand is ability to make great and to give strength to all. And now, O our God, we are thanking you and praising your beauteous name."—29:10-13.

²¹ Solomon is anointed a second time and begins to sit on 'the throne of Jehovah' in place of the aging David. After a reign of 40 years, David dies "in a good old age, satisfied with days, riches and glory." (29:23, 28) Ezra then concludes First Chronicles on a lofty note, emphasizing the superiority of David's kingdom over all the kingdoms of the nations.

WHY BENEFICIAL

²² Ezra's fellow Israelites derived much benefit from his book. Having this compact history with its fresh and optimistic viewpoint, they appreciated Jehovah's loving mercies toward them on account of his loyalty to the Kingdom covenant with King David and for his own name's sake. Encouraged, they were able to take up the pure worship of Jehovah with renewed zeal. The genealogies strengthened their confidence in the priesthood officiating at the rebuilt temple.

²³ First Chronicles was also of great benefit to the early Christian congregation. Matthew and Luke could draw on its genealogies in clearly establishing that Jesus Christ was the "son of David" and the Messiah with legal right. (Matt. 1: 1-16; Luke 3:23-38) In concluding his final witness, Stephen spoke of David's request to build a house for Jehovah and of Solomon's doing the building. Then he showed that "the Most High does not dwell in houses made with hands," indicating that the temple of Solomon's day pictured

---

20. What sublime heights are reached in David's final prayer?
21. On what lofty note does First Chronicles end?
22. How were Ezra's fellow Israelites encouraged by First Chronicles?
23. How did Matthew, Luke, and Stephen make good use of First Chronicles?

far more glorious heavenly things.—Acts 7:45-50.

²⁴ What of true Christians today? First Chronicles should build and stimulate our faith. There is much that we can copy in David's glowing example. How unlike the faithless Saul he was, in always inquiring of Jehovah! (1 Chron. 10:13, 14; 14:13, 14; 17:16; 22:17-19) In bringing up the ark of Jehovah to Jerusalem, in his psalms of praise, in his organizing of the Levites for service, and in his request to build a glorious house for Jehovah, David showed that Jehovah and His worship were first in his mind. (16:23-29) He was no complainer. He did not seek special privileges for himself but sought only to do Jehovah's will. Thus, when Jehovah assigned the building of the house to his son, he wholeheartedly instructed his son and gave of his time, his energy, and his wealth in

preparing for the work that would commence after his death. (29:3, 9) A splendid example of devotion indeed!—Heb. 11:32.

²⁵ Then there are the climactic concluding chapters. The magnificent language with which David praised Jehovah and glorified his "beauteous name" should stir in us joyful appreciation of our modern-day privilege of making known the glories of Jehovah and his Kingdom by Christ. (1 Chron. 29:10-13) May our faith and joy ever be like David's as we express thankfulness for Jehovah's everlasting Kingdom by pouring ourselves out in His service. (17:16-27) Truly, First Chronicles makes the Bible theme of Jehovah's Kingdom by his Seed scintillate more beauteously than ever, leaving us expectant of further thrilling disclosures of Jehovah's purposes.

---

24. What in David's glowing example may we copy today?

25. To what appreciation of Jehovah's name and Kingdom should First Chronicles stir us?

Bible Book Number 14
2 Chronicles

Writer: **Ezra**

Place Written: **Jerusalem (?)**

Writing Completed: **c. 460 B.C.E.**

Time Covered: **1037–537 B.C.E.**

SINCE First and Second Chronicles evidently were originally one book, the arguments presented in the previous chapter as to background, writership, time of writing, canonicity, and authenticity apply to both books. According to the evidence presented, Ezra completed Second Chronicles about 460 B.C.E., probably in Jerusalem. It was Ezra's purpose to preserve historical materials that were in danger of being lost. The help of the holy spirit, coupled with his ability as a historian to lay hold of and sort out details, enabled Ezra to make an accurate and permanent record. He saved for the future that which he regarded as historical fact. Ezra's work was most timely, as now it was also necessary to collect together the entire body of sacred Hebrew writings that had been recorded over the centuries.

² The Jews of Ezra's day were benefited greatly by Ezra's inspired chronicle. It was written for their instruction and to encourage endurance. Through the comfort from the Scriptures, they

could have hope. They accepted the book of Chronicles as part of the Bible canon. They knew it was trustworthy. They could check it by other inspired writings and by numerous secular histories cited by Ezra. Whereas they allowed the uninspired secular histories to perish, they carefully preserved Chronicles. The *Septuagint* translators included Chronicles as part of the Hebrew Bible.

³ Jesus Christ and the writers of the Christian Greek Scriptures accepted it as authentic and inspired. Jesus no doubt had in mind such incidents as recorded at 2 Chronicles 24:21 when denouncing Jerusalem as a killer and stoner of Jehovah's prophets and servants. (Matt. 23:35; 5:12; 2 Chron. 36:16) When James referred to Abraham as "Jehovah's friend," he perhaps had reference to Ezra's expression at 2 Chronicles 20:7. (Jas. 2:23) The book also contains prophecies that were unerringly fulfilled.—2 Chron. 20:17, 24; 21:14-19; 34:23-28; 36:17-20.

⁴ Archaeology also testifies to the authenticity

---

1. When did Ezra complete Chronicles, and with what purpose in view?
2. Why is there no reason to doubt the accuracy of Chronicles?

3. How do other scriptures indicate that Chronicles is authentic?
4. What archaeological find testifies to the authenticity of Second Chronicles?

of Second Chronicles. Digging on the site of ancient Babylon has unearthed clay tablets relating to the period of Nebuchadnezzar's reign, one of which names "Yaukin, king of the land of Yahud," that is, "Jehoiachin, the king of the land of Judah."* This fits in well with the Bible account of Jehoiachin's being taken captive to Babylon during the seventh regnal year of Nebuchadnezzar.

5 The record of Second Chronicles traces events in Judah from the reign of Solomon, commencing in 1037 B.C.E., to Cyrus' decree of 537 B.C.E. to rebuild the house of Jehovah in Jerusalem. In this 500-year history, the ten-tribe kingdom is referred to only as it becomes involved in the affairs of Judah, and the destruction of that northern kingdom in 740 B.C.E. is not even mentioned. Why is this so? Because the priest Ezra was concerned primarily with Jehovah's worship at its rightful place, His house in Jerusalem, and with the kingdom of the line of David, with whom Jehovah had made His covenant. Thus, it is on the southern kingdom that Ezra concentrates attention in support of true worship and in expectation of the ruler to come out of Judah.—Gen. 49:10.

6 Ezra takes an uplifting viewpoint. Of the 36 chapters of Second Chronicles, the first 9 are devoted to Solomon's reign, and 6 of these wholly to the preparation and dedication of the house of Jehovah. The record omits mention of Solomon's defection. Of the remaining 27 chapters, 14 deal with the five kings who basically followed David's example of exclusive devotion to Jehovah's worship: Asa, Jehoshaphat, Jotham, Hezekiah, and Josiah. Even in the other 13 chapters, Ezra is careful to highlight the good points of the bad kings. He always emphasizes events relating to restoration and preservation of true worship. How stimulating!

CONTENTS OF SECOND CHRONICLES

7 **The glory of Solomon's reign** (1:1–9:31). As Second Chronicles opens, we see Solomon the son of David growing in strength in the kingship. Jehovah is with him and keeps "making him surpassingly great." When Solomon makes sacrifices at Gibeon, Jehovah appears to him at night, saying: "Ask! What shall I give you?" Solomon asks for knowledge and wisdom in order to govern Jehovah's people properly. Because of this unselfish request, God promises to give Solomon not only

wisdom and knowledge but also wealth and riches and honor "such as no kings that were prior to you happened to have, and such as no one after you will come to have." So great is the wealth flowing into the city that in time Solomon comes "to make the silver and the gold in Jerusalem like the stones."—1:1, 7, 12, 15.

8 Solomon conscripts laborers for the work of building the house of Jehovah, and King Hiram of Tyre cooperates by sending timbers and a gifted workman. "In the fourth year of [Solomon's] reign," the building gets under way, and it is completed seven and a half years later, in 1027 B.C.E. (3:2) The temple itself is fronted by a large porch that towers 120 cubits (175 ft) high. Two immense copper pillars, one named Jachin, meaning "May [Jehovah] Firmly Establish," and the other named Boaz, apparently meaning "In Strength," stand in front of the porch. (3:17) The house itself is comparatively small, being 60 cubits (87.5 ft) long, 30 cubits (43.7 ft) high, and 20 cubits (29.2 ft) broad, but its walls and ceiling are overlaid with gold; its innermost room, the Most Holy, is itself elaborately decorated with gold. It also contains the two golden cherubs, one on each side of the room, whose wings stretch across and meet in the center.

9 In the inner courtyard, there is a huge copper altar 20 cubits square (29.2 ft) and 10 cubits (14.6 ft) high. Another striking object in the courtyard is the molten sea, an immense copper bowl resting on the backs of 12 copper bulls that look outward, three in each direction. This sea is capable of holding "three thousand bath measures" (17,430 gal., U.S.) of water, which is used by the priests to wash themselves. (4:5) Also located in the courtyard are ten small copper bowls resting on ornamented copper carriages, and in this water, things having to do with burnt offerings are rinsed. They are filled from the molten sea and wheeled to wherever the water is needed. In addition, there are the ten golden lampstands and many other utensils, some of gold and some of copper, for the temple worship.*

10 Finally, after seven and a half years of work, the house of Jehovah is completed. (1 Ki. 6:1, 38) The day of its inauguration is the time to bring the symbol of Jehovah's presence into the innermost room of this gorgeous building. The priests bring

---

* *Insight on the Scriptures,* Vol. 1, page 147.

5. What time period is covered in Second Chronicles, and why is the history of Judah featured rather than that of the ten-tribe kingdom?
6. In what respects is Second Chronicles uplifting and stimulating?
7. How does Jehovah make Solomon "surpassingly great"?

---

* *Insight on the Scriptures,* Vol. 1, pages 750-1; Vol. 2, pages 1076-8.

8. How does the work on the temple proceed, and what are some details of its construction?
9. Describe the furnishings and the utensils of the courtyard and the temple.
10. What happens when the Ark is brought into the Most Holy?

"the ark of the covenant of Jehovah into its place, into the innermost room of the house, into the Most Holy, to underneath the wings of the cherubs." Then what happens? As the Levite singers and musicians praise and thank Jehovah in united song, the house is filled with a cloud, and the priests are not able to stand to minister because "the glory of Jehovah" fills the house of the true God. (2 Chron. 5:7, 13, 14) Thus Jehovah shows his approval of the temple and betokens his presence there.

¹¹ A copper platform three cubits (4.4 ft) high has been built for the occasion, and it is set in the inner courtyard near the huge copper altar. In this elevated position, Solomon can be seen by the vast throngs that have assembled for the temple dedication. Following the miraculous manifestation of Jehovah's presence by the glory cloud, Solomon kneels before the crowd and offers a moving prayer of thanksgiving and praise, which includes a series of humble requests for forgiveness and blessing. In conclusion, he pleads: "Now, O my God, please, let your eyes prove to be opened and your ears attentive to the prayer respecting this place. O Jehovah God, do not turn back the face of your anointed one. O do remember the loving-kindnesses to David your servant."—6:40, 42.

¹² Does Jehovah hear this prayer of Solomon? As soon as Solomon finishes praying, fire comes down from the heavens and consumes the burnt offering and the sacrifices, and "Jehovah's glory itself" fills the house. This leads all the people to prostrate themselves and thank Jehovah, "for he is good, for his loving-kindness is to time indefinite." (7:1, 3) A huge sacrifice is then made to Jehovah. A week-long feast of dedication is followed by the week-long Feast of Ingathering and a sabbath of refraining from work. After this happy, spiritually strengthening 15-day celebration, Solomon sends the people away to their homes joyful and feeling good at heart. (7:10) Jehovah too is pleased. He reconfirms the Kingdom covenant to Solomon, warning at the same time of the dire consequences of disobedience.

¹³ Solomon now carries on extensive construction work throughout his dominion, building not only a palace for himself but also fortified cities, storage cities, chariot cities, and cities for horsemen, as well as everything he desires to build. It is a period of glorious prosperity and peace because both the king and the people are mindful of Jeho-

vah's worship. Even the queen of Sheba, from more than 1,200 miles away, hears of the prosperity and wisdom of Solomon and undertakes the long, arduous journey to see for herself. Is she disappointed? Not at all, for she confesses: "I did not put faith in their words until I had come that my own eyes might see; and, look! there has not been told me the half of the abundance of your wisdom. You have surpassed the report that I have heard. Happy are your men, and happy are these servants of yours." (9:6, 7) No other kings of the earth surpass Solomon in riches and wisdom. He reigns for 40 years in Jerusalem.

¹⁴ **The reigns of Rehoboam and Abijah** (10: 1–13:22). The harsh and oppressive rule by Solomon's son Rehoboam provokes the northern ten tribes under Jeroboam to revolt in 997 B.C.E. However, the priests and Levites of both kingdoms take their stand with Rehoboam, putting loyalty to the Kingdom covenant above nationalism. Rehoboam soon forsakes Jehovah's law, and Egypt's King Shishak invades, breaking into Jerusalem and stripping the house of Jehovah of its treasures. How sad that scarcely more than 30 years after their construction, these gorgeously decorated buildings are stripped of their glory! The reason: The nation has "behaved unfaithfully toward Jehovah." Just in time Rehoboam humbles himself, so that Jehovah does not bring the nation to complete ruin.—12:2.

¹⁵ At Rehoboam's death one of his 28 sons, Abijah, is made king. Abijah's three-year reign is marked by bloody war with Israel to the north. Judah is outnumbered two to one, 400,000 troops against the 800,000 under Jeroboam. During the tremendous battles that follow, Israel's warriors are reduced to less than half, and calf worshipers to the number of a half million are destroyed. The sons of Judah prove superior because they lean "upon Jehovah the God of their forefathers."—13:18.

¹⁶ **God-fearing King Asa** (14:1–16:14). Abijah is succeeded by his son Asa. Asa is a champion of true worship. He campaigns to cleanse the land of image worship. But, look! Judah is threatened by an overwhelming military force of one million Ethiopians. Asa prays: "Help us, O Jehovah our God, for upon you we do lean, and in your name we have come against this crowd." Jehovah answers by giving him a smashing victory.—14:11.

¹⁷ The spirit of God comes upon Azariah to tell Asa: "Jehovah is with you as long as you prove to

---

11. What prayer does Solomon offer, and what does he petition?
12. How does Jehovah answer Solomon's prayer, and on what happy note does the 15-day celebration end?
13. (a) What construction work follows that of the temple? (b) How does the queen of Sheba express herself on seeing Solomon's kingdom?

14. Why is Israel so soon stripped of her glory?
15. What battles follow Rehoboam's death, and why does Judah prove superior against Israel?
16. How does Jehovah answer Asa's urgent prayer?
17. How is Asa encouraged to reform worship in Judah, but for what is he rebuked?

be with him; and if you search for him, he will let himself be found by you." (15:2) Greatly encouraged, Asa reforms worship in Judah, and the people make a covenant that anyone that will not search for Jehovah should be put to death. However, when Baasha, king of Israel, erects barriers to stop the flow of Israelites into Judah, Asa commits a grave error by hiring Ben-hadad, king of Syria, to fight against Israel, instead of looking to Jehovah for help. For this Jehovah rebukes him. Despite this, Asa's heart proves "to be complete all his days." (15:17) He dies in the 41st year of his reign.

18 **Jehoshaphat's good reign** (17:1–20:37). Asa's son Jehoshaphat continues the fight against image worship and inaugurates a special educational campaign, with instructors traveling throughout the cities of Judah, teaching the people from the book of Jehovah's Law. A time of great prosperity and peace follows, and Jehoshaphat continues "advancing and growing great to a superior degree." (17:12) But then he makes a marriage alliance with wicked King Ahab of Israel and goes down to help him fight against the growing Syrian power, ignoring Jehovah's prophet Micaiah and barely escaping with his life when Ahab is killed in battle at Ramoth-gilead. Jehovah's prophet Jehu rebukes Jehoshaphat for making common cause with wicked Ahab. Thereafter Jehoshaphat appoints judges throughout the land, and he instructs them to carry out their duties in the fear of God.

19 Now comes the climax of Jehoshaphat's reign. The combined forces of Moab, Ammon, and the mountainous region of Seir move against Judah in overwhelming strength. Up they swarm through the wilderness of En-gedi. Fear strikes the nation. Jehoshaphat and all Judah, with "their little ones, their wives and their sons," stand before Jehovah and seek him in prayer. Jehovah's spirit comes upon Jahaziel the Levite, who calls to the assembled throngs: "Pay attention, all Judah and you inhabitants of Jerusalem and King Jehoshaphat! Here is what Jehovah has said to you, 'Do not you be afraid or be terrified because of this large crowd; for the battle is not yours, but God's. Tomorrow go down against them. . . . Jehovah will be with you.'" Rising early in the morning, Judah marches out with the Levite singers in the lead. Jehoshaphat encourages them: "Put faith in Jehovah . . . Put faith in his prophets and so prove successful." The singers joyfully extol Jehovah, "for to time indefinite is his loving-kindness." (20:

13, 15-17, 20, 21) Jehovah manifests his loving-kindness in a marvelous way, setting an ambush against the invading armies so that they annihilate one another. Coming to the watchtower in the wilderness, the exultant Judeans see only dead carcasses. Truly, the battle is God's! To the end of his 25-year reign, Jehoshaphat keeps walking faithfully before Jehovah.

20 **Bad reigns of Jehoram, Ahaziah, and Athaliah** (21:1–23:21). Jehoshaphat's son Jehoram starts off badly by killing all his brothers. However, Jehovah spares him because of His covenant with David. Edom begins to revolt. From somewhere Elijah sends a letter, warning Jehoram that Jehovah will strike his house a great blow and that he will die horribly. (21:12-15) True to the prophecy, the Philistines and the Arabs invade and loot Jerusalem, and the king dies of a loathsome intestinal disease, after an eight-year reign.

21 Jehoram's sole surviving son, Ahaziah (Jehoahaz), succeeds him, but he is influenced for bad by his mother Athaliah, the daughter of Ahab and Jezebel. His reign is cut short after one year by Jehu's purge of the house of Ahab. At this, Athaliah murders her grandchildren and usurps the throne. However, one of Ahaziah's sons survives. He is the one-year-old Jehoash, who is smuggled into the house of Jehovah by his aunt Jehoshabeath. Athaliah reigns for six years, and then Jehoshabeath's husband, the high priest Jehoiada, courageously takes young Jehoash and has him proclaimed king, as one of "the sons of David." Coming to the house of Jehovah, Athaliah rips her clothing apart and cries, "Conspiracy! Conspiracy!" But to no avail. Jehoiada has her thrown out of the temple and put to death.—23:3, 13-15.

22 **Reigns of Jehoash, Amaziah, and Uzziah start well but end badly** (24:1–26:23). Jehoash reigns for 40 years, and as long as Jehoiada is alive to exercise a good influence, he does right. He even takes an interest in the house of Jehovah and has it renovated. When Jehoiada dies, however, Jehoash is influenced by the princes of Judah to turn from Jehovah's worship to serve the sacred poles and idols. When God's spirit moves Zechariah the son of Jehoiada to rebuke the king, Jehoash has the prophet stoned to death. Soon afterward a small military force of Syrians invades, and the much larger Judean army is unable to turn it back because they have "left Jehovah the God of their forefathers." (24:24) Now Jehoash's own servants rise up and assassinate him.

---

18. (a) How does Jehoshaphat campaign for true worship, and with what results? (b) How does his marriage alliance almost lead to disaster?
19. At the climax of Jehoshaphat's reign, how does the battle prove to be God's?

20. What disasters mark Jehoram's reign?
21. What bad things result from Athaliah's domination in Judah, but how does Jehoiada succeed in restoring the throne of David?
22. How does Jehoash's reign start well but end badly?

23 Amaziah succeeds his father Jehoash. He begins his 29-year reign well but later falls from Jehovah's favor because he sets up and worships the idols of the Edomites. "God has resolved to bring you to ruin," Jehovah's prophet warns him. (25:16) However, Amaziah becomes boastful and challenges Israel to the north. True to God's word, he suffers a humiliating defeat at the hands of the Israelites. After that defeat, conspirators rise up and put him to death.

24 Amaziah's son Uzziah follows in his father's footsteps. He reigns well for the greater part of 52 years, gaining fame as a military genius, as a builder of towers, and as "a lover of agriculture." (26:10) He equips and mechanizes the army. However, his strength becomes his weakness. He becomes haughty and presumes to take over the priestly duty of offering incense in the temple of Jehovah. For this, Jehovah smites him with leprosy. As a result, he has to live apart, away from the house of Jehovah and also from the king's house, where his son Jotham judges the people in his place.

25 **Jotham serves Jehovah** (27:1-9). Unlike his father, Jotham does not "invade the temple of Jehovah." Instead 'he keeps doing what is right in Jehovah's eyes.' (27:2) During his 16-year reign, he does much construction work and successfully puts down a revolt of the Ammonites.

26 **Wicked King Ahaz** (28:1-27). Jotham's son Ahaz proves to be one of the wickedest of the 21 Judean kings. He goes to the extreme in offering his own sons as burnt sacrifices to heathen gods. Consequently Jehovah abandons him, in turn, to the armies of Syria, Israel, Edom, and Philistia. So Jehovah humbles Judah because Ahaz 'lets unrestraint grow in Judah, and there is an acting with great unfaithfulness toward Jehovah.' (28:19) Going from bad to worse, Ahaz sacrifices to the gods of Syria because the Syrians prove superior to him in battle. He closes the doors of the house of Jehovah and replaces the worship of Jehovah with the worship of heathen gods. None too soon, Ahaz' reign ends after 16 years.

27 **Faithful King Hezekiah** (29:1–32:33). Hezekiah, the son of Ahaz, reigns for 29 years in Jerusalem. His first act is to reopen and repair the doors of the house of Jehovah. Then he assembles the priests and Levites and gives them instructions to clean the temple and sanctify it for Jehovah's service. He declares that he wants to conclude a covenant with Jehovah to turn back His burning anger. Jehovah's worship is resumed in a grand way.

28 A tremendous Passover is planned, but since there is no time to prepare it in the first month, a provision of the Law is taken advantage of, and it is celebrated in the second month of the first year of Hezekiah's reign. (2 Chron. 30:2, 3; Num. 9: 10, 11) The king invites not only all Judah to attend but Israel as well, and while some in Ephraim, Manasseh, and Zebulun mock the invitation, others humble themselves and come to Jerusalem along with all Judah. Following the Passover, the Festival of Unfermented Cakes is held. What a joyous seven-day feast it is! So upbuilding, indeed, that all the congregation extends the feast another seven days. There is "great rejoicing in Jerusalem, for from the days of Solomon the son of David the king of Israel there was none like this in Jerusalem." (2 Chron. 30:26) The spiritually restored people follow up with a smashing campaign to rid both Judah and Israel of idolatry, while Hezekiah, on his part, restores the material contributions for the Levites and the temple services.

29 Then Sennacherib the king of Assyria invades Judah and threatens Jerusalem. Hezekiah takes courage, repairs the defenses of the city, and defies the taunts of the enemy. Putting complete trust in Jehovah, he keeps praying for aid. Jehovah dramatically answers this prayer of faith. He proceeds "to send an angel and efface every valiant, mighty man and leader and chief in the camp of the king of Assyria." (32:21) Sennacherib returns home in shame. Even his gods cannot help him save face, for later on he is slain at their altar by his own sons. (2 Ki. 19:7) Jehovah miraculously extends Hezekiah's life, and he comes to have great riches and glory, all Judah honoring him at his death.

30 **Manasseh and Amon reign wickedly** (33: 1-25). Hezekiah's son Manasseh reverts to the wicked course of his grandfather Ahaz, undoing all the good accomplished during Hezekiah's reign. He builds up the high places, sets up the sacred poles, and even sacrifices his sons to false gods. Finally, Jehovah brings the king of Assyria against Judah, and Manasseh is carried away captive to Babylon. There he repents of his wrongdoing. When Jehovah shows mercy by restoring him to his kingship, he endeavors to root out demon

---

23. What pattern of unfaithfulness does Amaziah follow?
24. How does Uzziah's strength become his weakness, and with what result?
25. Why does Jotham succeed?
26. To what unprecedented depths of wickedness does Ahaz descend?
27. How does Hezekiah show zeal for Jehovah's worship?

28. What tremendous feast does Hezekiah hold in Jerusalem, and how do the people express their joy?
29. How does Jehovah reward Hezekiah's implicit trust in Him?
30. (a) To what wickedness does Manasseh revert, but what follows his repentance? (b) What marks Amon's short reign?

worship and restore true religion. However, when Manasseh dies after a long 55-year reign, his son Amon ascends the throne and wickedly champions false worship again. After two years, his own servants put him to death.

31 **Josiah's courageous reign** (34:1–35:27). Youthful Josiah, a son of Amon, makes a courageous attempt to restore true worship. He has the altars of the Baals and the graven images pulled down, and he repairs the house of Jehovah, where "the book of Jehovah's law by the hand of Moses," doubtless the original copy, is found. (34:14) Yet, righteous Josiah is told that calamity will come on the land for the unfaithfulness that has already occurred, but not in his day. In the 18th year of his reign, he arranges an outstanding Passover celebration. After a 31-year reign, Josiah meets his death in a vain attempt to prevent the Egyptian hosts from passing through the land on their way to the Euphrates.

32 **Jehoahaz, Jehoiakim, Jehoiachin, Zedekiah, and Jerusalem's desolation** (36:1-23). The wickedness of the last four Judean kings quickly carries the nation to its disastrous end. Josiah's son Jehoahaz rules only three months, being removed by Pharaoh Necho of Egypt. He is replaced by his brother Eliakim, whose name is changed to Jehoiakim, and during whose reign Judah is subjugated by the new world power, Babylon. (2 Ki. 24:1) When Jehoiakim rebels, Nebuchadnezzar comes up to Jerusalem to punish him in 618 B.C.E., but Jehoiakim dies this same year, after reigning 11 years. He is replaced by his 18-year-old son Jehoiachin. After a reign of scarcely three months, Jehoiachin surrenders to Nebuchadnezzar and is carried away captive to Babylon. Nebuchadnezzar now places a third son of Josiah, Jehoiachin's uncle Zedekiah, on the throne. Zedekiah reigns badly for 11 years, refusing to "humble himself on account of Jeremiah the prophet at the order of Jehovah." (2 Chron. 36:12) In large-scale unfaithfulness, priests and people alike defile the house of Jehovah.

33 Finally, Zedekiah rebels against Babylon's yoke, and this time Nebuchadnezzar shows no mercy. Jehovah's rage is full, and there is no healing. Jerusalem falls, its temple is looted and burned, and the survivors of the 18-month siege are carried as captives to Babylon. Judah is left desolate. Thus, in this very year of 607 B.C.E., begins the desolation "to fulfill Jehovah's word by

the mouth of Jeremiah . . . to fulfill seventy years." (36:21) The chronicler then leaps this gap of nearly 70 years to record in the last two verses the historic decree of Cyrus in 537 B.C.E. The Jewish captives are to be set free! Jerusalem must rise again!

WHY BENEFICIAL

34 Second Chronicles adds its powerful testimony to that of other witnesses concerning this eventful period, 1037-537 B.C.E. Moreover, it gives valuable supplementary information not found in other canonical histories, for example, at 2 Chronicles chapters 19, 20, and 29 through 31. Ezra's selection of material emphasized the fundamental and permanent elements in the history of the nation, such as the priesthood and its service, the temple, and the Kingdom covenant. This was beneficial in holding the nation together in hope of the Messiah and his Kingdom.

35 The closing verses of Second Chronicles (36: 17-23) give conclusive proof of the fulfillment of Jeremiah 25:12 and, in addition, show that a *full* 70 years must be counted from the complete desolation of the land to the restoration of Jehovah's worship at Jerusalem in 537 B.C.E. This desolation therefore begins in 607 B.C.E.*—Jer. 29:10; 2 Ki. 25:1-26; Ezra 3:1-6.

36 Second Chronicles contains powerful admonition for those walking in Christian faith. So many of the kings of Judah started well but then lapsed into wicked ways. How forcefully this historical record illustrates that success depends upon faithfulness to God! We should be warned therefore to be not "the sort that shrink back to destruction, but the sort that have faith to the preserving alive of the soul." (Heb. 10:39) Even faithful King Hezekiah became haughty on recovering from his sickness, and it was only because he quickly humbled himself that he was able to avoid Jehovah's indignation. Second Chronicles magnifies Jehovah's wonderful qualities and extols his name and sovereignty. The entire history is presented from the standpoint of exclusive devotion to Jehovah. As it lays emphasis also upon the royal line of Judah, it strengthens our expectation of seeing pure worship exalted under the everlasting Kingdom of Jesus Christ, the loyal "son of David."—Matt. 1:1; Acts 15:16, 17.

---

* *Insight on the Scriptures,* Vol. 1, page 463; Vol. 2, page 326.

31. What are the highlights of Josiah's courageous reign?
32. How do the last four kings lead Judah to its disastrous end?
33. (a) How does the 70-year desolation begin, "to fulfill Jehovah's word"? (b) What historic decree is recorded in the last two verses of Second Chronicles?

34. What is emphasized in Ezra's selection of material, and how was this beneficial to the nation?
35. What important points are proved in the closing verses of Second Chronicles?
36. (a) What powerful admonition is contained in Second Chronicles? (b) How does it strengthen expectation concerning the Kingdom?

15
Ezra

Writer: **Ezra**

Place Written: **Jerusalem**

Writing Completed: **c. 460 B.C.E.**

Time Covered: **537–c. 467 B.C.E.**

THE end of the prophesied 70 years of Jerusalem's desolation under Babylon was drawing near. True, it was Babylon's reputation that she never released her captives, but Jehovah's word would prove stronger than Babylonian might. Release of Jehovah's people was in sight. Jehovah's temple that had been laid low would be rebuilt, and Jehovah's altar would again receive sacrifices of atonement. Jerusalem would again know the shout and praise of the true worshiper of Jehovah. Jeremiah had prophesied the length of the desolation, and Isaiah had prophesied how the release of captives would come about. Isaiah had even named Cyrus of Persia as 'the shepherd of Jehovah,' who would tumble haughty Babylon from her position as the third world power of Bible history.—Isa. 44:28; 45: 1, 2; Jer. 25:12.

² Disaster befell Babylon on the night of October 5, 539 B.C.E. (Gregorian calendar), as the Babylonian king Belshazzar and his grandees were drinking toasts to their demon gods. Adding to their pagan debauchery, they were using the holy vessels from Jehovah's temple as their cups of drunkenness! How fitting that Cyrus was outside Babylon's walls that night to fulfill the prophecy!

³ This date 539 B.C.E. is a pivotal date, that is, a date that may be harmonized with both secular and Biblical history. During his first year as ruler of Babylon, Cyrus "caused a cry to pass through all his realm," authorizing the Jews to go up to Jerusalem to rebuild the house of Jehovah. This decree was evidently issued late in 538 B.C.E. or early in 537 B.C.E.* A faithful remnant journeyed back to Jerusalem in time to set up the altar and offer the first sacrifices in "the seventh month" (Tishri, corresponding to September-October) of the year 537 B.C.E.—70 years to the month after Judah

and Jerusalem's desolation by Nebuchadnezzar. —Ezra 1:1-3; 3:1-6.

⁴ Restoration! This provides the setting of the book of Ezra. The use of the first person in the narration from chapter 7 verse 27 through chapter 9 clearly shows that the writer was Ezra. As "a skilled copyist in the law of Moses" and a man of practical faith who "prepared his heart to consult the law of Jehovah and to do it and to teach" it, Ezra was well qualified to record this history, even as he had recorded Chronicles. (Ezra 7:6, 10) Since the book of Ezra is a continuation of Chronicles, it is generally believed that it was written at the same time, about 460 B.C.E. It covers 70 years, from the time that the Jews were a broken, scattered nation marked as "the sons of death" to the completion of the second temple and the cleansing of the priesthood after Ezra's return to Jerusalem. —Ezra 1:1; 7:7; 10:17; Ps. 102:20, footnote.

⁵ The Hebrew name Ezra means "Help." The books of Ezra and Nehemiah were originally one scroll. (Neh. 3:32, footnote) Later the Jews divided this scroll and called it First and Second Ezra. Modern Hebrew Bibles call the two books Ezra and Nehemiah, as do other modern Bibles. Part of the book of Ezra (4:8 to 6:18 and 7:12-26) was written in Aramaic and the remainder in Hebrew, Ezra being skilled in both languages.

⁶ Today the majority of scholars accept the accuracy of the book of Ezra. Concerning the canonicity of Ezra, W. F. Albright writes in his treatise *The Bible After Twenty Years of Archaeology:* "Archaeological data have thus demonstrated the substantial originality of the Books of Jeremiah and Ezekiel, of Ezra and Nehemiah beyond doubt; they have confirmed the traditional picture of events, as well as their order."

⁷ Though the book of Ezra may not be quoted or

---

* *Insight on the Scriptures,* Vol. 1, pages 452-4, 458.

1. What prophecies gave assurance of Jerusalem's restoration?
2. When and under what circumstances did Babylon fall?
3. What proclamation by Cyrus made it possible to restore Jehovah's worship exactly 70 years after the desolation of Jerusalem began?

4. (a) What is the setting of the book of Ezra, and who wrote it? (b) When was Ezra written, and what period does it cover?
5. What relation has the book of Ezra to the book of Nehemiah, and in what languages was it written?
6. What testifies to the accuracy of the book of Ezra?
7. How is the book of Ezra shown truly to be a part of the divine record?

referred to directly by the Christian Greek Scripture writers, there is no question about its place in the canon of the Bible. It carries the record of Jehovah's dealings with the Jews down to the time of the assembling of the Hebrew catalog, which work was largely accomplished by Ezra, according to Jewish tradition. Moreover, the book of Ezra vindicates all the prophecies concerning the restoration and so proves that it is indeed an integral part of the divine record, with which it also harmonizes completely. In addition, it honors pure worship and sanctifies the great name of Jehovah God.

CONTENTS OF EZRA

⁸ **A remnant returns** (1:1–3:6). His spirit roused by Jehovah, Cyrus king of Persia issues the decree for the Jews to return and build the house of Jehovah in Jerusalem. He urges those Jews who may remain in Babylon to contribute freely toward the project and arranges for the returning Jews to take back the utensils of the original temple. One who is leader from the royal tribe of Judah and a descendant of King David, Zerubbabel (Sheshbazzar), is assigned as governor to lead the released ones, and Jeshua (Joshua) is the high priest. (Ezra 1:8; 5:2; Zech. 3:1) A remnant that may have numbered 200,000 faithful servants of Jehovah, including men, women, and children, make the long journey. By the seventh month, according to the Jewish calendar, they are settled in their cities, and then they gather at Jerusalem to offer sacrifices at the site of the temple altar and to celebrate the Festival of Booths in the fall of 537 B.C.E. Thus the 70 years' desolation ends exactly on time!*

⁹ **Rebuilding the temple** (3:7–6:22). Materials are assembled, and in the second year of their return, the foundation of the temple of Jehovah is laid amid shouts of joy and amid the weeping of the older men who had seen the former house. The neighboring peoples, adversaries, offer to help with the construction, saying they are seeking the same God, but the Jewish remnant flatly refuse any alliance with them. The adversaries continually try to weaken and dishearten the Jews and to frustrate their work, from the reign of Cyrus down to that of Darius. Finally, in the days of "Artaxerxes" (Bardiya or possibly a Magian known as Gaumata, 522 B.C.E.), they have the work forcibly stopped by royal command. This ban continues "until the second year of the reign of Darius the king of Persia" (520 B.C.E.), which is over 15 years after the laying of the foundation. —4:4-7, 24.

¹⁰ Jehovah now sends his prophets Haggai and Zechariah to arouse Zerubbabel and Jeshua, and the building work is taken up with renewed zeal. Again the adversaries complain to the king, but the work goes on with unabated vigor. Darius I (Hystaspis), after referring to Cyrus' original decree, orders the work to continue without interference and even commands the opposers to supply materials to facilitate construction. With continued encouragement from Jehovah's prophets, the builders complete the temple in less than five years. This is in the month Adar of the sixth year of Darius, or near the spring of 515 B.C.E., and the entire construction has taken just about 20 years. (6:14, 15) The house of God is now inaugurated with great joy and with appropriate sacrifices. Then the people celebrate the Passover and go on to hold "the festival of unfermented cakes seven days with rejoicing." (6:22) Yes, joy and rejoicing mark the dedication of this second temple to Jehovah's praise.

¹¹ **Ezra returns to Jerusalem** (7:1–8:36). Almost 50 years elapse, bringing us down to 468 B.C.E., the seventh year of the Persian king Artaxerxes (known as Longimanus because his right hand was longer than his left). The king grants the skilled copyist Ezra "all his request" with respect to a journey to Jerusalem to render much-needed aid there. (7:6) In authorizing him, the king encourages the Jews to go with him and grants Ezra silver and gold vessels for temple use, as well as provisions of wheat, wine, oil, and salt. He exempts the priests and temple workers from taxation. The king makes Ezra responsible to teach the people and declares it to be a capital offense for anyone not to become a doer of the law of Jehovah and the law of the king. With thankfulness to Jehovah for this expression of his lovingkindness through the king, Ezra acts immediately on the commission.

¹² At this point Ezra commences his eyewitness account, writing in the first person. He assembles the returning Jews at the river Ahava for final instructions, and he adds some Levites to the group of about 1,500 adult males already assembled. Ezra recognizes the dangers of the route to

---

* *Insight on the Scriptures*, Vol. 2, page 332.

8. Describe the chain of events leading to the end of the 70 years' desolation.
9. How does the temple work begin, but what happens in the years that follow?

10. (a) How does encouragement from God's prophets combine with the king's order in getting the work completed? (b) What joy marks the dedication of this second temple?
11. How does the king grant Ezra "all his request," and what is Ezra's response?
12. How does Jehovah prove to be with Ezra's group during the journey?

be taken but does not ask the king for an escort, lest it be construed as showing lack of faith in Jehovah. Instead, he proclaims a fast and leads the camp in making entreaty to God. This prayer is answered, and the hand of Jehovah proves to be over them throughout the long journey. Thus, they are able to bring their treasures (worth more than $43,000,000 at modern values) safely to the house of Jehovah in Jerusalem.—8:26, 27, and footnotes.

¹³ **Cleansing the priesthood** (9:1–10:44). But not all has gone well during the 69 years of dwelling in the restored land. Ezra learns of disturbing conditions, in that the people, the priests, and the Levites have intermarried with the pagan Canaanites. Faithful Ezra is stunned. He lays the matter before Jehovah in prayer. The people confess their wrongdoing and ask Ezra to "be strong and act." (10:4) He has the Jews put away the foreign wives that they have taken in disobedience to God's law, and the uncleanness is cleared out in the space of about three months.—10:10-12, 16, 17.

WHY BENEFICIAL

¹⁴ The book of Ezra is beneficial, in the first place, in showing the unerring accuracy with which Jehovah's prophecies are fulfilled. Jeremiah, who had so accurately foretold Jerusalem's desolation, also foretold its restoration after 70 years. (Jer. 29:10) Right on time, Jehovah showed his loving-kindness in bringing his people, a faithful remnant, back again into the Land of Promise to carry on true worship.

¹⁵ The restored temple again exalted Jehovah's worship among his people, and it stood as a testimony that he wonderfully and mercifully blesses those who turn to him with a desire for true worship. Though it lacked the glory of Solomon's temple, it served its purpose in harmony with the divine will. The material splendor was no longer there. It was also inferior in spiritual treasures, lacking, among other things, the ark of the covenant.* Nor was the inauguration of Zerubbabel's temple comparable with the inauguration of the temple in Solomon's day. The sacrifices of cattle and sheep were not even one percent of the sacri-

---

* *Insight on the Scriptures,* Vol. 2, page 1079.

---

13. How does Ezra act in removing uncleanness from among the Jews?
14. What does the book of Ezra show as to Jehovah's prophecies?
15. (a) How did the restored temple serve Jehovah's purpose? (b) In what respects did it lack the glory of the first temple?

fices at Solomon's temple. No cloudlike glory filled the latter house, as it had the former, nor did fire descend from Jehovah to consume the burnt offerings. Both temples, however, served the important purpose of exalting the worship of Jehovah, the true God.

¹⁶ The temple built by Zerubbabel, the tabernacle constructed by Moses, and the temples built by Solomon and Herod, along with their features, were typical, or pictorial. These represented the "true tent, which Jehovah put up, and not man." (Heb. 8:2) This spiritual temple is the arrangement for approaching Jehovah in worship on the basis of Christ's propitiatory sacrifice. (Heb 9: 2-10, 23) Jehovah's great spiritual temple is superlative in glory and incomparable in beauty and desirableness; its splendor is unfading and above that of any material structure.

¹⁷ The book of Ezra contains lessons that are of highest value for Christians today. In it we read of Jehovah's people making willing offerings for his work. (Ezra 2:68; 2 Cor. 9:7) We are encouraged by learning of Jehovah's unfailing provision for and his blessing upon assemblies for his praise. (Ezra 6:16, 22) We see a fine example in the Nethinim and other believing foreigners as they go up with the remnant to give wholehearted support to Jehovah's worship. (2:43, 55) Consider, too, the humble repentance of the people when advised of their wrong course in intermarrying with pagan neighbors. (10:2-4) Bad associations led to divine disapproval. (9:14, 15) Joyful zeal for his work brought his approval and blessing.—6: 14, 21, 22.

¹⁸ Though a king no longer sat on Jehovah's throne at Jerusalem, the restoration aroused expectation that Jehovah would in due course produce his promised King in the line of David. The restored nation was now in position to guard the sacred pronouncements and worship of God until the time of Messiah's appearing. If this remnant had not responded in faith in returning to their land, to whom would Messiah have come? Truly, the events in the book of Ezra are an important part of the history leading to the appearance of the Messiah and King! It is all most beneficial for our study today.

---

16. But what other temple exceeds earthly temples for glory?
17. What valuable lessons are to be found in the book of Ezra?
18. Why was the restoration of Jehovah's people an important step leading to the appearance of Messiah, the King?

Nehemiah

Writer: **Nehemiah**
Place Written: **Jerusalem**
Writing Completed: **After
443 B.C.E.**
Time Covered: **456–after 443 B.C.E.**

NEHEMIAH, whose name means "Jah Comforts," was a Jewish servant of the Persian king Artaxerxes (Longimanus). He was cupbearer to the king. This was a position of great trust and honor, one to be desired, for it gave access to the king at times when he was in a happy frame of mind and ready to grant favors. However, Nehemiah was one of those faithful exiles who preferred Jerusalem above any personal "cause for rejoicing." (Ps. 137:5, 6) It was not position or material wealth that was uppermost in Nehemiah's thoughts but, rather, the restoration of Jehovah's worship.

² In 456 B.C.E. those "left over from the captivity," the Jewish remnant that had returned to Jerusalem, were not prospering. They were in a lamentable condition. (Neh. 1:3) The wall of the city was rubble, and the people were a reproach in the eyes of their ever-present adversaries. Nehemiah was grieved. However, it was Jehovah's appointed time for something to be done about the wall of Jerusalem. Enemies or no enemies, Jerusalem with its protective wall must be built as a time marker in connection with a prophecy that Jehovah had given Daniel concerning the coming of Messiah. (Dan. 9:24-27) Accordingly, Jehovah directed events, using faithful and zealous Nehemiah to carry out the divine will.

³ Nehemiah is undoubtedly the writer of the book that bears his name. The opening statement, "The words of Nehemiah the son of Hacaliah," and the use of the first person in the writing clearly prove this. (Neh. 1:1) Originally the books of Ezra and Nehemiah were one book, called Ezra. Later, the Jews divided the book into First and Second Ezra, and later still Second Ezra became known as Nehemiah. An interval of about 12 years lies between the closing events of Ezra and the opening events of Nehemiah, whose history then covers the period from the end of 456 B.C.E. till after 443 B.C.E.—1:1; 5:14; 13:6.

⁴ The book of Nehemiah harmonizes with the rest of inspired Scripture, with which it rightfully belongs. It contains numerous allusions to the Law, referring to matters such as marriage alliances with foreigners (Deut. 7:3; Neh. 10:30), loans (Lev. 25:35-38; Deut. 15:7-11; Neh. 5: 2-11), and the Festival of Booths (Deut. 31:10-13; Neh. 8:14-18). Further, the book marks the beginning of the fulfillment of Daniel's prophecy that Jerusalem would be rebuilt but not without opposition, "in the straits of the times."—Dan. 9:25.

⁵ What about the date 455 B.C.E. for Nehemiah's journey to Jerusalem to rebuild the city wall? Reliable historical evidence from Greek, Persian, and Babylonian sources points to 475 B.C.E. as the accession year of Artaxerxes and 474 B.C.E. as his first regnal year.* This would make his 20th year 455 B.C.E. Nehemiah 2:1-8 indicates it was in the spring of that year, in the Jewish month Nisan, that Nehemiah, the royal cupbearer, received from the king permission to restore and rebuild Jerusalem, its wall, and its gates. Daniel's prophecy stated that 69 weeks of years, or 483 years, would stretch "from the going forth of the word to restore and to rebuild Jerusalem until Messiah the Leader"—a prophecy that was remarkably fulfilled at Jesus' anointing in 29 C.E., a date that may be harmonized with both secular and Biblical history.# (Dan. 9:24-27; Luke 3:1-3, 23) Indeed, the books of Nehemiah and Luke tie in remarkably with Daniel's prophecy in showing Jehovah God to be the Author and Fulfiller of true prophecy! Nehemiah is truly a part of the inspired Scriptures.

---

* *Insight on the Scriptures*, Vol. 2, pages 613-16.
# *Insight on the Scriptures*, Vol. 2, pages 899-901.

---

1. What position of trust did Nehemiah hold, and what was uppermost in his mind?
2. What sorry condition grieved Nehemiah, but what appointed time was drawing near?
3. (a) What proves Nehemiah to be the writer, and how did the book come to be called Nehemiah? (b) What interval separates this book from the book of Ezra, and what years does the book of Nehemiah cover?

4. How does the book of Nehemiah harmonize with the rest of the Scriptures?
5. (a) Evidence from what sources pinpoints the accession year of Artaxerxes as 475 B.C.E.? (b) What date marks his 20th year? (c) How do the books of Nehemiah and Luke tie in with the fulfillment of Daniel's prophecy about the Messiah?

CONTENTS OF NEHEMIAH

[6] **Nehemiah sent to Jerusalem** (1:1–2:20). Nehemiah is greatly troubled by a report from Hanani, who has returned to Shushan from Jerusalem bearing tidings of the severe plight of the Jews there and the broken-down state of the wall and gates. He fasts and prays to Jehovah as "the God of the heavens, the God great and fear-inspiring, keeping the covenant and loving-kindness toward those loving him and keeping his commandments." (1:5) He confesses Israel's sins and petitions Jehovah to remember His people because of His name, even as He promised Moses. (Deut. 30:1-10) When the king asks Nehemiah about the reason for his gloomy countenance, Nehemiah tells him of the condition of Jerusalem and requests permission to return and rebuild the city and its wall. His request is granted, and immediately he journeys to Jerusalem. Following a nighttime inspection of the city wall to acquaint himself with the job ahead, he reveals his plan to the Jews, emphasizing God's hand in the matter. At this they say: "Let us get up, and we must build." (Neh. 2:18) When the neighboring Samaritans and others hear that the work has started, they begin to deride and mock.

[7] **The wall rebuilt** (3:1–6:19). Work on the wall begins on the third day of the fifth month, with the priests, the princes, and the people sharing together in the labor. The city gates and the walls between are rapidly repaired. Sanballat the Horonite taunts: "What are the feeble Jews doing? . . . Will they finish up in a day?" To this, Tobiah the Ammonite adds his ridicule: "Even what they are building, if a fox went up against it, he would certainly break down their wall of stones." (4:2, 3) As the wall reaches half its height, the combined adversaries grow angry and conspire to come up and fight against Jerusalem. But Nehemiah exhorts the Jews to keep in mind "Jehovah the great and the fear-inspiring One" and to fight for their families and their homes. (4:14) The work is reorganized to meet the tense situation; some stand guard with lances while others work with their swords on their hips.

[8] However, there are also problems among the Jews themselves. Some of them are exacting usury from their fellow worshipers of Jehovah, contrary to his law. (Ex. 22:25) Nehemiah corrects the situation, counseling against materialism, and

the people willingly comply. Nehemiah himself, during all his 12 years of governorship, from 455 B.C.E. to 443 B.C.E., never demands the bread due the governor because of the heavy service upon the people.

[9] The enemies now try more subtle tactics to stop the building. They invite Nehemiah to come down for a conference, but he replies that he cannot take time off from the great work that he is doing. Sanballat now charges Nehemiah with rebellion and planning to make himself king in Judah, and he secretly hires a Jew to frighten Nehemiah into wrongfully hiding in the temple. Nehemiah refuses to be intimidated, and he calmly and obediently goes about his God-assigned task. The wall is completed "in fifty-two days." —Neh. 6:15.

[10] **Instructing the people** (7:1–12:26). There are but few people and houses within the city, for most of the Israelites are living outside according to their tribal inheritances. God directs Nehemiah to assemble the nobles and all the people to get them enrolled genealogically. In doing this, he consults the record of those who returned from Babylon. An eight-day assembly is next called at the public square by the Water Gate. Ezra opens the program from a wooden podium. He blesses Jehovah and then reads from the book of the Law of Moses from daybreak until midday. He is ably assisted by other Levites, who explain the Law to the people and continue 'reading aloud from the book, from the Law of the true God, it being expounded, and there being a putting of meaning into it; and they continue giving understanding in the reading.' (8:8) Nehemiah urges the people to feast and rejoice and to appreciate the force of the words: "The joy of Jehovah is your stronghold." —8:10.

[11] On the second day of the assembly, the heads of the people have a special meeting with Ezra to gain insight into the Law. They learn of the Festival of Booths that should be celebrated this very seventh month, and they immediately arrange to build booths for this feast to Jehovah. There is "very great rejoicing" as they dwell in booths for the seven days, hearing day by day the reading of the Law. On the eighth day, they hold a solemn assembly, "according to the rule."—Neh. 8:17, 18; Lev. 23:33-36.

---

6. (a) What report causes Nehemiah to pray to Jehovah, and what request does the king grant? (b) How do the Jews respond to Nehemiah's plan?

7. How does the work proceed, and what situation calls for reorganization?

8. How does Nehemiah handle problems among the Jews themselves?

9. (a) How does Nehemiah meet subtle tactics to stop the building? (b) In what time is the wall completed?

10. (a) Where do the people live, and what enrollment is made? (b) What assembly is now called, and what is the first day's program?

11. What special meeting is held on the second day, and how does the assembly proceed with rejoicing?

12 On the 24th day of the same month, the sons of Israel again assemble and proceed to separate themselves from all the foreigners. They listen to a special reading of the Law and then a heart-searching review of God's dealings with Israel, presented by a group of the Levites. This takes as its theme: "Rise, bless Jehovah your God from time indefinite to time indefinite. And let them bless your glorious name, which is exalted above all blessing and praise." (Neh. 9:5) They proceed to confess the sins of their forefathers and humbly to petition Jehovah's blessing. This is in the form of a resolution that is attested to by the seal of the nation's representatives. The entire group agree to keep free from intermarriage with the peoples of the land, to observe the Sabbaths, and to provide for the temple service and workers. One person out of every ten is selected by lot to dwell permanently in Jerusalem, inside the wall.

13 **The wall dedicated** (12:27–13:3). The dedication of the newly built wall is a time of song and happiness. It is the occasion for another assembly. Nehemiah arranges for two large thanksgiving choirs and processions to walk upon the wall in opposite directions, finally joining in sacrifices at the house of Jehovah. Arrangements are made for material contributions to support the priests and the Levites at the temple. A further Bible reading reveals that Ammonites and Moabites should not be permitted to come into the congregation, and hence they begin to separate all the mixed company from Israel.

14 **Clearing out uncleanness** (13:4-31). After spending a period of time in Babylon, Nehemiah returns to Jerusalem and finds that new vices have crept in among the Jews. How quickly things have changed! The high priest Eliashib has even made a dining hall in the courtyard of the temple for the use of Tobiah, an Ammonite, one of the enemies of God. Nehemiah wastes no time. He throws out Tobiah's furniture and has all the dining halls cleansed. He finds, too, that the material contributions of the Levites have been discontinued, so they are going outside Jerusalem to make a living. Commercialism runs rampant in the city. The Sabbath is not observed. Nehemiah tells them: "You are adding to the burning anger against Israel by profaning the sabbath." (13:18)

He shuts up the city gates on the Sabbath to keep out the traders, and he orders them away from the city wall. But there is an evil worse than this, something they had solemnly agreed not to do again. They have brought foreign, pagan wives into the city. Already the offspring of these unions no longer speak the Jewish language. Nehemiah reminds them that Solomon sinned because of foreign wives. On account of this sin, Nehemiah chases out the grandson of Eliashib the high priest.* Then he sets in order the priesthood and the work of the Levites.

15 Nehemiah ends his book with the simple and humble request: "Do remember me, O my God, for good."—13:31.

WHY BENEFICIAL

16 Nehemiah's godly devotion should be an inspiration to all lovers of right worship. He left a favored position to become a humble overseer among Jehovah's people. He even refused the material contribution that was his right, and he roundly condemned materialism as a snare. The zealous pursuit and upkeep of Jehovah's worship was what Nehemiah advocated for the entire nation. (5:14, 15; 13:10-13) Nehemiah was a splendid example to us in being entirely unselfish and discreet, a man of action, fearless for righteousness in the face of danger. (4:14, 19, 20; 6:3, 15) He had the proper fear of God and was interested in building up his fellow servants in the faith. (13:14; 8:9) He vigorously applied the law of Jehovah, especially as it related to true worship and the rejection of foreign influences, such as marriages with pagans.—13:8, 23-29.

17 Throughout the book it is evident that Nehemiah had a good knowledge of Jehovah's law, and he made good use of this. He invoked God's blessing because of Jehovah's promise at Deuteronomy 30:1-4, having full faith that Jehovah would act loyally on his behalf. (Neh. 1:8, 9) He arranged numerous assemblies, principally to acquaint the Jews with the things written aforetime. In their reading of the Law, Nehemiah and Ezra were

---

* Some Jewish historians claim that this grandson of Eliashib was named Manasseh and that, with his father-in-law, Sanballat, he built the temple on Mount Gerizim, which became the center of Samaritan worship and at which he officiated as priest during his lifetime. Gerizim is the mountain referred to by Jesus at John 4:21.—*The Second Temple in Jerusalem*, 1908, W. Shaw Caldecott, pages 252-5; see *The Watchtower*, July 15, 1960, pages 425-6.

---

12. (a) What assembly is held later in the same month, with what theme? (b) What resolution is adopted? (c) What arrangement is made for populating Jerusalem?
13. What assembly program marks the dedication of the wall, and what arrangements result?
14. Describe the vices arising during Nehemiah's absence, and the steps he takes to eliminate them.

15. What humble request does Nehemiah make?
16. In what ways is Nehemiah a splendid example for all lovers of right worship?
17. How is Nehemiah an example also in knowledge and in application of God's law?

diligent to make God's Word plain to the people and to follow through by applying it.—8:8, 13-16; 13:1-3.

[18] Nehemiah's complete reliance on Jehovah and his humble petitions should encourage us to develop a like attitude of prayerful dependence on God. Note how his prayers glorified God, showed recognition of the sins of his people, and petitioned that Jehovah's name be sanctified. (1:4-11; 4:14; 6:14; 13:14, 29, 31) That this zealous overseer was a power for strength among God's people was shown by the readiness with which they followed his wise direction and the joy that they found in doing God's will along with him. An inspiring example indeed! However, in the absence of a wise overseer, how quickly materialism, corruption, and outright apostasy crept in! Surely this should impress on all overseers among God's people today the need to be alive, alert, zealous for

the interests of their Christian brothers, and understanding and firm in leading them in the ways of true worship.

[19] Nehemiah showed strong reliance on God's Word. Not only was he a zealous teacher of the Scriptures but he also used them in establishing the genealogical inheritances and the service of the priests and Levites among God's restored people. (Neh. 1:8; 11:1–12:26; Josh. 14:1–21:45) This must have been of great encouragement to the Jewish remnant. It strengthened their confidence in the grand promises previously given concerning the Seed and the greater restoration to come under His Kingdom. It is hope in the Kingdom restoration that stimulates God's servants to fight courageously for Kingdom interests and to be busy in building true worship throughout the earth.

---

18. What lessons should Nehemiah's prayerful leadership impress on all overseers?

19. (a) How did Nehemiah use God's Word to strengthen confidence in the Kingdom promises? (b) How does Kingdom hope stimulate God's servants today?

Bible Book Number	**17**

Esther

Writer: Mordecai

Places Written: **Shushan, Elam**

Writing Completed: **c. 475 B.C.E.**

Time Covered: **493-c. 475 B.C.E.**

SIMPLY told, here is the story of Ahasuerus, king of Persia, thought by some to be Xerxes I, whose disobedient wife Vashti is replaced by the Jewess Esther, cousin of Mordecai. The Agagite Haman plots the death of Mordecai and all the Jews, but he is hung on his own stake, while Mordecai is advanced to be prime minister and the Jews are delivered.

[2] Of course, there are those who want to say that the book of Esther is neither inspired nor beneficial but is simply a beautiful legend. They base their claim on the absence of God's name. While it is true that God is not directly mentioned, in the Hebrew text there appear to be four separate instances of an acrostic of the Tetragrammaton, the initial letters of four successive words, spelling out YHWH (Hebrew, יהוה), or Jehovah. These initials are made especially prominent in at least three ancient Hebrew manuscripts and are

also marked in the Masora by red letters. Also, at Esther 7:5 there is apparently an acrostic on the divine pronouncement "I shall prove to be."—See footnotes on Esther 1:20; 5:4, 13; 7:7, as well as 7:5.

[3] Throughout the record it is strongly evident that Mordecai both accepted and obeyed the law of Jehovah. He refused to bow down to honor a man who probably was an Amalekite; God had marked the Amalekites for extermination. (Esther 3:1, 5; Deut. 25:19; 1 Sam. 15:3) Mordecai's expression at Esther 4:14 indicates that he expected deliverance from Jehovah and that he had faith in divine direction of the entire course of events. Esther's fasting, together with similar action by the other Jews, for three days before she went in to the king shows reliance on God. (Esther 4:16) God's maneuvering of events is also suggested in Esther's finding favor in the eyes of Hegai, the guardian of the women, and in the king's sleeplessness on the night that he called for the official

---

1. What story unfolds in the book of Esther?
2. (a) Why have some questioned the inspiration of the book of Esther? (b) In what form does God's name appear to be used in the book of Esther?

3. What events indicate faith in and prayer to God, and what events suggest God's maneuvering of matters?

records and found that Mordecai had not been honored for his past good deed. (Esther 2:8, 9; 6:1-3; compare Proverbs 21:1.) There is undoubtedly a reference to prayer in the words, "the matters of the fasts and their cry for aid."—Esther 9:31.

4 Many facts establish the record as authentic and factual. It was accepted by the Jewish people, who called the book simply the *Meghil·lah'*, meaning "roll; scroll." It appears to have been included in the Hebrew canon by Ezra, who would certainly have rejected a fable. To this day, the Jews keep the feast of Purim, or Lots, in celebration of the great deliverance in Esther's time. The book presents Persian manners and customs in a lifelike way and in harmony with the known facts of history and archaeological discoveries. For example, the book of Esther accurately describes the way Persians honored a man. (6:8) Archaeological excavations have revealed that the descriptions of the king's palace as given in the book of Esther are exact to the smallest detail.*—5:1, 2.

5 This exactness is also to be noted in the account itself, in its careful naming of court officials and attendants, giving even the names of Haman's ten sons. The lineage of Mordecai and Esther is traced back to Kish of the tribe of Benjamin. (2:5-7) References are made to the official records of the Persian government. (2:23; 6:1; 10:2) The language of the book is late Hebrew, with many Persian and Aramaic words and expressions added, which style matches that of Chronicles, Ezra, and Nehemiah, thus harmonizing completely with the period in which it was written.

6 It is thought that the events of Esther are set in the days when the mighty Persian empire was at its peak and that they cover about 18 years of the reign of Ahasuerus (Xerxes I). The time period, extending down to about 475 B.C.E., is indicated by testimony from Greek, Persian, and Babylonian sources.# Mordecai, eyewitness and a major character in the account, was most likely the writer of the book; the intimate and detailed account shows that the writer must have lived through these events in Shushan the palace.△ Though he is

---

* *Insight on the Scriptures,* Vol. 1, page 764; Vol. 2, pages 327-31.
# *Insight on the Scriptures,* Vol. 2, pages 613-16.
△ McClintock and Strong's *Cyclopedia,* 1981 reprint, Vol. III, page 310.

4. How is the book of Esther established as authentic and factual?
5. What exactness gives the account of Esther a note of genuineness, and with what period does the language harmonize?
6. (a) What time period is indicated for the book of Esther? (b) What does the evidence suggest as to the writer, as well as the place and the time of writing?

not mentioned in any other Bible book, there is no question that Mordecai was an actual individual of history. Interestingly, an undated cuneiform text has been found that is described by A. Ungnad of Germany as referring to Mardukâ (Mordecai?) as a high official at the court of Susa (Shushan) during the reign of Xerxes I.* It was there at Shushan that Mordecai no doubt completed the record of the events of Esther immediately after they took place, that is, about 475 B.C.E.

CONTENTS OF ESTHER

7 **Queen Vashti deposed** (1:1-22). It is the third year of the reign of Ahasuerus. He holds a mighty banquet for the officials of his empire, showing them the riches and glory of his kingdom for 180 days. Next, there is a grand seven-day feast for all the people in Shushan. At the same time, Vashti the queen holds a banquet for the women. The king boasts of his riches and glory and, merry with wine, calls on Vashti to come and show her loveliness to the people and the princes. Queen Vashti keeps refusing. On the advice of court officials, who point out that this bad example can cause the king to lose face throughout the empire, Ahasuerus removes Vashti as queen and publishes documents calling on all wives to "give honor to their owners" and every husband to "be continually acting as prince in his own house."—1:20, 22.

8 **Esther becomes queen** (2:1-23). Later on, the king appoints commissioners to seek out the most beautiful virgins in all the 127 provinces of the empire and to bring them to Shushan, where they are to be prepared by beauty treatment for presentation to the king. Among the young women selected is Esther. Esther is a Jewish orphan, "pretty in form and beautiful in appearance," who has been reared by her cousin Mordecai, an official in Shushan. (2:7) Esther's Jewish name, Hadassah, means "Myrtle." Hegai, the guardian of the women, is pleased with Esther and gives her special treatment. No one knows that she is a Jewess, for Mordecai has instructed her to keep this a secret. The young women are brought in to the king in turn. He selects Esther as his new queen, and a banquet is held to celebrate her coronation. Shortly afterward, Mordecai hears of a conspiracy to assassinate the king, and he has Esther make it known to him "in Mordecai's

---

* A. Ungnad, "Keilinschriftliche Beiträge zum Buch Esra und Ester," *Zeitschrift für die alttestamentliche Wissenschaft,* LVIII (1940-41), pages 240-4.

7. What crisis develops at Ahasuerus' banquet, and what action does the king take as a result?
8. (a) What events lead up to Esther's becoming queen? (b) What plot does Mordecai uncover, and what record is made thereof?

name." (2:22) The plot is uncovered, the conspirators are hanged, and a record is made in the royal annals.

⁹ **Haman's conspiracy** (3:1–5:14). About four years pass by. Haman, apparently a descendant of the Amalekite king Agag whom Samuel slew, becomes prime minister. (1 Sam. 15:33) The king exalts him and orders all his servants in the king's gate to bow before Haman. These include Mordecai. However, Mordecai refuses to do so, making it known to the king's servants that he is a Jew. (Compare Exodus 17:14, 16.) Haman is filled with rage and, finding out that Mordecai is a Jew, sees in this the grand opportunity to get rid of Mordecai and all the Jews once and for all. The lot (pur) is cast to determine a good day for annihilating the Jews. Using his favor with the king, Haman charges lawlessness against the Jews and asks that their destruction be ordered in writing. Haman offers a contribution of 10,000 silver talents (equivalent to about $66,060,000) toward financing the slaughter. The king consents, and written orders, sealed with the king's ring, are sent throughout the empire, setting Adar the 13th as the day for the genocide of the Jews.

¹⁰ On hearing the law, Mordecai and all the Jews go to mourning in sackcloth and ashes. There is "fasting and weeping and wailing." (Esther 4:3) On being informed by Mordecai of the Jews' plight, Esther at first hesitates to intercede. Death is the penalty for appearing uninvited before the king. However, Mordecai shows his faith in Jehovah's power by declaring that if Esther fails them, she will die anyway and deliverance will "stand up for the Jews from another place." Moreover, may it not be that Esther has become queen "for a time like this"? (4:14) Seeing the issue, she agrees to take her life in her hands, and all the Jews in Shushan fast with her for three days.

¹¹ Then, dressed in her royal best, Esther appears before the king. She gains favor in his eyes, and he holds out to her his golden scepter, sparing her life. She now invites the king and Haman to a banquet. During the feast, the king urges her to make known her petition, assuring that it will be granted, "to the half of the kingship," whereupon she invites the two to a further banquet the following day. (5:6) Haman goes out joyful. But there in the king's gate is Mordecai! Again he refuses to do Haman honor or quake before him. Haman's

joy turns to anger. His wife and friends suggest he build a stake 50 cubits (73 ft) high and get an order from the king to hang Mordecai on it. Haman has the stake built immediately.

¹² **The tables are turned** (6:1–7:10). That night the king cannot sleep. He has the book of the records brought and read to him, and he discovers that he has not rewarded Mordecai for saving his life. Later, the king asks who is in the courtyard. It is Haman, who has come to ask the king's warrant for Mordecai's death. The king asks Haman how one who pleases the king should be honored. Thinking that the king has him in mind, Haman outlines a lavish program of honor. But the king commands him: "Do that way to Mordecai the Jew"! (6:10) Haman has no alternative but to clothe Mordecai in regal splendor, seat him on the king's horse, and lead him round the public square of the city, calling out ahead of him. Humiliated, Haman hurries home mourning. His wife and friends have no comfort to offer. Haman is doomed!

¹³ It is now time for Haman to attend the banquet with the king and Esther. The queen declares that she and her people have been sold, to be destroyed. Who has dared to perpetrate this wickedness? Says Esther: "The man, the adversary and enemy, is this bad Haman." (7:6) The king rises up in a rage and walks out into the garden. Alone with the queen, Haman pleads for his life, and the king, returning, is further infuriated at seeing Haman on the queen's couch. Forthwith he orders that Haman be hung on the very stake Haman had prepared for Mordecai!—Ps. 7:16.

¹⁴ **Mordecai promoted, the Jews delivered** (8:1–10:3). The king gives Esther all of Haman's possessions. Esther makes known to Ahasuerus her relationship to Mordecai, whom the king promotes to Haman's previous position, giving him the royal signet ring. Again, Esther risks her life in going in before the king to request the undoing of the written decree to destroy the Jews. However, "the laws of Persia and Media" cannot be annulled! (1:19) The king therefore gives Esther and Mordecai authority to write a new law and seal it with the king's ring. This written order, sent throughout the empire in the same way as the previous one, grants the Jews the right 'to congregate themselves and stand for their souls, to annihilate and kill and destroy all the force of the people and jurisdictional district that are

---

9. How does Mordecai anger Haman, and what royal decree does the latter obtain against the Jews?
10. How do Mordecai and Esther proceed with faith in Jehovah's power?
11. How does Esther use her favor with the king, but what does Haman plot against Mordecai?

12. What turn in events results in Ahasuerus' honoring Mordecai, to Haman's humiliation?
13. What does Esther reveal at the banquet, leading to what doom for Haman?
14. How does the king reward Esther and Mordecai, and with what written decree does he favor the Jews?

showing hostility to them, little ones and women, and to plunder their spoil,' on the same day that Haman's law goes into effect.—8:11.

[15] When the appointed day, the 13th of Adar, comes, not a man can stand before the Jews. On Esther's petitioning the king, the fighting is continued on the 14th day in Shushan. All together, 75,000 of the Jews' enemies are killed throughout the empire. An additional 810 are killed in Shushan the castle. Among these are Haman's ten sons, who are killed the first day and hanged on stakes the second day. No plunder is taken. On the 15th of Adar, there is rest, and the Jews give way to banqueting and rejoicing. Mordecai now gives written instructions for the Jews to observe this feast of "Pur, that is, the Lot," every year on the 14th and 15th of Adar, and this they do to the present day. (9:24) Mordecai is magnified in the kingdom and uses his position as second to King Ahasuerus "for the good of his people and speaking peace to all their offspring."—10:3.

WHY BENEFICIAL

[16] While no other Bible writer makes any direct quotation from Esther, the book is completely in harmony with the rest of the inspired Scriptures. In fact, it provides some splendid illustrations of Bible principles that are stated later in the Christian Greek Scriptures and that apply to Jehovah's worshipers in all ages. A study of the following passages will not only show this to be so but will be upbuilding to Christian faith: Esther 4:5—Philippians 2:4; Esther 9:22—Galatians 2:10. The charge made against the Jews, that they did not obey the king's laws, is similar to the charge raised against the early Christians. (Esther 3:8, 9; Acts 16:21; 25:7) True servants of Jehovah meet

such charges fearlessly and with prayerful reliance on divine power to deliver, after the splendid pattern of Mordecai, Esther, and their fellow Jews.—Esther 4:16; 5:1, 2; 7:3-6; 8:3-6; 9:1, 2.

[17] As Christians, we should not think that our situation is different from that of Mordecai and Esther. We too live under "the superior authorities" in an alien world. It is our desire to be law-abiding citizens in whatever country we reside, but at the same time, we want to draw the line correctly between 'paying back Caesar's things to Caesar and God's things to God.' (Rom. 13:1; Luke 20:25) Prime Minister Mordecai and Queen Esther set good examples of devotion and obedience in their secular duties. (Esther 2:21-23; 6:2, 3, 10; 8:1, 2; 10:2) However, Mordecai fearlessly drew the line at obeying the royal command to bow low before the despicable Agagite, Haman. Moreover, he saw to it that appeal was made to seek legal redress when Haman conspired to destroy the Jews.—3:1-4; 5:9; 4:6-8.

[18] All the evidence points to the book of Esther as being part of the Holy Bible, "inspired of God and beneficial." Even without directly mentioning God or his name, it provides us sterling examples of faith. Mordecai and Esther were no mere figments of some storyteller's imagination, but they were real servants of Jehovah God, persons who placed implicit confidence in Jehovah's power to save. Though they lived under "superior authorities" in a foreign land, they used every legal means to defend the interests of God's people and their worship. We today can follow their examples in "the defending and legally establishing of the good news" of God's Kingdom of deliverance. —Phil. 1:7.

---

15. (a) What is the outcome of the fighting, and what feast does Mordecai institute? (b) To what position is Mordecai exalted, and to what end does he use this authority?
16. What divine principles and worthy pattern do Christians find in the book of Esther?

17. How did Mordecai and Esther exemplify the proper course in subjecting themselves to God and "the superior authorities"?
18. (a) What proves the book of Esther to be "inspired of God and beneficial"? (b) How does it encourage the defense of God's Kingdom interests?

18

Job

Writer: **Moses**

Place Written: **Wilderness**

Writing Completed: **c. 1473 B.C.E.**

Time Covered: **Over 140 years
between 1657 and 1473 B.C.E.**

ONE of the oldest books of the inspired Scriptures! A book that is held in the highest esteem and that is often quoted, yet one that is little understood by mankind. Why was this book written, and what value does it have for us today? The answer is indicated in the meaning of Job's name: "Object of Hostility." Yes, this book takes up two important questions: Why do the innocent suffer? Why does God permit wickedness in the earth? We have the record of Job's suffering and his great endurance for our consideration in answering these questions. It has all been written down, just as Job requested.—Job 19:23, 24.

² Job has become synonymous with patience and endurance. But was there such a person as Job? In spite of all the efforts of the Devil to remove this sterling example of integrity from the pages of history, the answer is clear. Job was an actual person! Jehovah names him along with His witnesses Noah and Daniel, whose existence was accepted by Jesus Christ. (Ezek. 14:14, 20; compare Matthew 24:15, 37.) The ancient Hebrew nation regarded Job as a real person. The Christian writer James points to Job's example of endurance. (Jas. 5:11) Only a true-life example, not a fictitious one, would carry weight, convincing worshipers of God that integrity can be maintained under all circumstances. Moreover, the intensity and feeling of the speeches recorded in Job testify to the reality of the situation.

³ That the book of Job is authentic and inspired is also proved in that the ancient Hebrews always included it in their Bible canon, a fact remarkable in that Job himself was not an Israelite. In addition to the references by Ezekiel and James, the book is quoted by the apostle Paul. (Job 5:13; 1 Cor. 3:19) Powerful proof of the book's inspiration is given in its amazing harmony with the proved facts of the sciences. How could it be known that Jehovah is "hanging the earth upon

nothing," when the ancients had the most fantastic notions as to how the earth was supported? (Job 26:7) One view held in ancient times was that the earth was supported by elephants standing on a large sea turtle. Why does the book of Job not reflect such nonsense? Obviously because Jehovah the Creator supplied the truth by inspiration. The many other descriptions of the earth and its wonders and of the wild animals and birds in their natural habitats are so accurate that only Jehovah God could be the Author and Inspirer of the book of Job.*

⁴ Job lived in Uz, located, according to some geographers, in northern Arabia near the land occupied by the Edomites and east of the land promised to Abraham's offspring. The Sabeans were on the south, the Chaldeans on the east. (1:1, 3, 15, 17) The time of Job's trial was long after Abraham's day. It was at a time when there was "no one like [Job] in the earth, a man blameless and upright." (1:8) This appears to be the period between the death of Joseph (1657 B.C.E.), a man of outstanding faith, and the time that Moses entered upon his course of integrity. Job excelled in pure worship at this period of Israel's contamination by the demon worship of Egypt. Furthermore, the practices mentioned in the first chapter of Job, and God's acceptance of Job as a true worshiper, point to patriarchal times rather than to the later period from 1513 B.C.E. on, when God dealt exclusively with Israel under the Law. (Amos 3:2; Eph. 2:12) Thus, allowing for Job's long life, it appears that the book covers a period between 1657 B.C.E. and 1473 B.C.E., the year of Moses' death; the book was completed by Moses sometime after Job's death and while the Israelites were in the wilderness.—Job 1:8; 42:16, 17.

⁵ Why do we say Moses was the writer? This is according to the oldest tradition, among both Jewish and early Christian scholars. The vigorous

---

1. What does Job's name mean, and what questions does the book of Job answer?
2. What proves that Job was a real person?
3. What evidence testifies to the inspiration of the book of Job?

---

* *Insight on the Scriptures,* Vol. 1, pages 280-1, 663, 668, 1166; Vol. 2, pages 562-3.

---

4. Where and when was the drama enacted, and by when was the writing of the book of Job completed?
5. What indicates Moses' writership of Job?

authentic style of Hebrew poetry used in the book of Job makes it evident that it was an original composition in Hebrew, the language of Moses. It could not have been a translation from another language such as Arabic. Also, the portions in prose bear stronger resemblance to the Pentateuch than to any other writings in the Bible. The writer must have been an Israelite, as Moses was, because the Jews "were entrusted with the sacred pronouncements of God." (Rom. 3:1, 2) After he had reached maturity, Moses spent 40 years in Midian, not far from Uz, where he could obtain the detailed information recorded in Job. Later, when he passed near Job's homeland during Israel's 40-year wilderness journey, Moses could learn of and record the concluding details in the book.

⁶ According to *The New Encyclopædia Britannica*, the book of Job often is "counted among the masterpieces of world literature."* However, the book is much more than a literary masterpiece. Job is outstanding among the books of the Bible in exalting Jehovah's power, justice, wisdom, and love. It reveals most clearly the primary issue before the universe. It illuminates much that is said in other books of the Bible, especially Genesis, Exodus, Ecclesiastes, Luke, Romans, and Revelation. (Compare Job 1:6-12; 2:1-7 with Genesis 3:15; Exodus 9:16; Luke 22:31, 32; Romans 9: 16-19 and Revelation 12:9; also Job 1:21; 24:15; 21:23-26; 28:28 respectively with Ecclesiastes 5:15; 8:11; 9:2, 3; 12:13.) It provides the answers to many of life's questions. It is certainly an integral part of the inspired Word of God, to which it contributes much in the way of beneficial understanding.

CONTENTS OF JOB

⁷ **Prologue to the book of Job** (1:1-5). This introduces us to Job, a man "blameless and upright, and fearing God and turning aside from bad." Job is happy, having seven sons and three daughters. He is a materially rich landholder with numerous flocks and herds. He has many servants and is "the greatest of all the Orientals." (1:1, 3) However, he is not materialistic, for he does not put his trust in his material possessions. He is also rich spiritually, rich in good works, willing at all times to help someone afflicted or in distress, or to give a garment to anyone needing it. (29:12-16; 31:19, 20) All respect him. Job worships the true God, Jehovah. He refuses to bow down to the sun, moon, and stars as did the pagan nations, but he is

faithful to Jehovah, keeping integrity to his God and enjoying a close relationship with Him. (29:7, 21-25; 31:26, 27; 29:4) Job serves as priest for his family, offering up burnt sacrifices regularly, in case they have sinned.

⁸ **Satan challenges God** (1:6–2:13). Marvelously the curtain of invisibility is drawn back so that we can get a view of heavenly things. Jehovah is seen presiding over an assembly of the sons of God. Satan also appears among them. Jehovah calls attention to his faithful servant Job, but Satan challenges Job's integrity, charging that Job serves God because of material benefits received. If God will allow Satan to take these away, Job will turn away from his integrity. Jehovah accepts the challenge, with the restriction that Satan must not touch Job himself.

⁹ Many calamities start to befall the unsuspecting Job. Raids by Sabeans and Chaldeans remove his great riches. A storm kills his sons and daughters. This severe test fails to make Job curse God or turn away from him. Rather, he says, "Let the name of Jehovah continue to be blessed." (1:21) Satan, defeated and proved a liar on this count, appears again before Jehovah and charges: "Skin in behalf of skin, and everything that a man has he will give in behalf of his soul." (2:4) Satan claims that if he was permitted to touch Job's body, he could make Job curse God to his face. With permission to do everything short of taking Job's life, Satan strikes Job with a dreadful disease. His flesh becomes "clothed with maggots and lumps of dust," and his body and breath become foul-smelling to his wife and relatives. (7:5; 19: 13-20) Indicating that Job has not broken his integrity, his wife urges him: "Are you yet holding fast your integrity? Curse God and die!" Job rebukes her and does not "sin with his lips."—2: 9, 10.

¹⁰ Satan now raises up three companions, who come to "comfort" Job. They are Eliphaz, Bildad, and Zophar. At a distance they do not recognize Job, but then they proceed to raise their voices and weep and toss dust on their heads. Next, they sit before him on the earth without speaking a word. After seven days and nights of this silent "comfort," Job finally breaks silence in opening a lengthy debate with his would-be sympathizers. —2:11.

¹¹ **The debate: round one** (3:1–14:22). From

---

* 1987, Vol. 6, page 562.

---

6. In what respects is the book of Job much more than a literary masterpiece?
7. In what situation do we find Job as the book opens?

8. (a) How does Satan come to challenge Job's integrity? (b) How does Jehovah accept the challenge?
9. (a) What severe tests befall Job? (b) What proves that he keeps integrity?
10. What silent "comfort" does Satan provide?
11-13. How does Job open the debate, what accusation does Eliphaz make, and what is Job's spirited reply?

this point on, the drama unfolds in sublime Hebrew poetry. Job calls down evil on the day of his birth and wonders why God has permitted him to go on living.

[12] In response, Eliphaz accuses Job of lacking integrity. The upright have never perished, he declares. He recalls a night vision in which a voice told him that God has no faith in his servants, especially those of mere clay, the dust of the earth. He indicates that Job's suffering is a discipline from Almighty God.

[13] Job spiritedly replies to Eliphaz. He cries out as any creature would who was undergoing persecution and distress. Death would be a relief. He upbraids his companions for scheming against him and protests: "Instruct me, and I, for my part, shall be silent; and what mistake I have committed make me understand." (6:24) Job contends for his own righteousness before God, "the Observer of mankind."—7:20.

[14] Bildad now voices his argument, implying that Job's sons have sinned and that Job himself is not upright, otherwise he would be heard by God. He instructs Job to look to the former generations and to the things searched out by their forefathers as a guide.

[15] Job replies, maintaining God is not unjust. Neither does God have to account to man, for He is "doing great things unsearchable, and wonderful things without number." (9:10) Job cannot win against Jehovah as his opponent-at-law. He can only implore God's favor. And yet, is there any benefit in seeking to do what is right? "One blameless, also a wicked one, he is bringing to their end." (9:22) There is no righteous judgment in the earth. Job fears he will lose his case even with God. He needs a mediator. He asks why he is being tried and implores God to remember that he is made "out of clay." (10:9) He appreciates God's past kindnesses, but he says God will only be more greatly vexed if he argues, even though he is in the right. Could he but expire!

[16] Zophar now enters the debate. He says, in effect: Are we children, to listen to empty talk? You say you are really clean, but if only God would speak, he would reveal your guilt. He asks Job: "Can you find out the deep things of God?" (11:7) He advises Job to put away hurtful practices, for blessings will come to those who do this, whereas "the very eyes of the wicked will fail."—11:20.

[17] Job cries out with strong sarcasm: "For a fact you men are the people, and with you wisdom will die out!" (12:2) He may be a laughingstock, but he is not inferior. If his companions would look to the creations of God, even these would teach them something. Strength and practical wisdom belong to God, who controls all things, even to "making the nations grow great, that he may destroy them." (12:23) Job finds delight in arguing his case with God, but as for his three "comforters" —"you men are smearers of falsehood; all of you are physicians of no value." (13:4) It would be wisdom on their part to keep silent! He expresses confidence in the justness of his case and calls on God to hear him. He turns to the thought that "man, born of woman, is short-lived and glutted with agitation." (14:1) Man soon passes, as a blossom or a shadow. You cannot produce someone clean out of someone unclean. In praying that God would keep him secret in Sheol until His anger turns back, Job asks: "If an able-bodied man dies can he live again?" In answer he expresses strong hope: "I shall wait, until my relief comes."—14: 13, 14.

[18] **The debate: round two** (15:1–21:34). In opening the second debate, Eliphaz ridicules Job's knowledge, saying he has 'filled his belly with the east wind.' (15:2) Again he disparages Job's claim of integrity, holding that neither mortal man nor the holy ones in the heavens can hold faith in Jehovah's eyes. He indirectly accuses Job of trying to show himself superior to God and of practicing apostasy, bribery, and deceit.

[19] Job retorts that his companions are 'troublesome comforters with windy words.' (16:2, 3) If they were in his place, he would not revile them. He greatly desires to be justified, and he looks to Jehovah, who has his record and who will decide his case. Job finds no wisdom in his companions. They take away all hope. Their "comfort" is like saying night is day. The only hope is to 'go down to Sheol.'—17:15, 16.

[20] The argument is becoming heated. Bildad now is bitter, for he feels Job has compared his friends to beasts with no understanding. He asks Job, 'Will the earth be abandoned for your sake?' (18:4) He warns that Job will fall into a terrible snare, as an example to others. Job will have no progeny to live after him.

[21] Job answers: "How long will you men keep irritating my soul and keep crushing me with words?" (19:2) He has lost family and friends, his

---

14, 15. What is Bildad's argument, and why does Job fear he will lose his case with God?

16, 17. (a) What smug advice does Zophar give? (b) How does Job evaluate his "comforters," and what strong confidence does he express?

18, 19. (a) With what ridicule does Eliphaz open the second round of debate? (b) How does Job regard his companions' "comfort," and for what does he look to Jehovah?

20, 21. What bitterness does Bildad express, what does Job protest, and where does Job show his trust to be?

wife and household have turned away from him, and he himself has only escaped 'with the skin of his teeth.' (19:20) He trusts in the appearance of a redeemer to settle the issue in his behalf, so that he will at last "behold God."—19:25, 26.

²² Zophar, like Bildad, feels hurt at having to listen to Job's "insulting exhortation." (20:3) He repeats that Job's sins have caught up with him. The wicked always receive punishment from God, and they have no rest, says Zophar, even while enjoying prosperity.

²³ Job replies with a withering argument: If God always punishes the wicked thus, why is it that the wicked keep living, grow old, become superior in wealth? They spend their days in good times. How often does disaster come upon them? He shows that rich and poor die alike. In fact, a wicked man often dies "carefree and at ease," while a righteous man may die "with a bitter soul."—21:23, 25.

²⁴ **The debate: round three** (22:1–25:6). Eliphaz returns savagely to the attack, ridiculing Job's claim of blamelessness before the Almighty. He brings lying slander against Job, claiming that he is bad, has exploited the poor, has held back bread from the hungry, and has mistreated widows and fatherless boys. Eliphaz says that Job's private life is not as pure as he claims and that this explains Job's bad condition. But "if you return to the Almighty," intones Eliphaz, "he will hear you." —22:23, 27.

²⁵ Job in reply refutes Eliphaz' outrageous charge, saying that he desires a hearing before God, who is aware of his righteous course. There are those who oppress the fatherless, the widow, and the poor and who commit murder, theft, and adultery. They may seem to prosper for a while, but they will get their reward. They will be brought to nothing. "So really now, who will make me out a liar?" Job challenges.—24:25.

²⁶ Bildad makes a brief retort to this, pressing his argument that no man can be clean before God. Zophar fails to take part in this third round. He has nothing to say.

²⁷ **Job's concluding argument** (26:1–31:40). In a final dissertation, Job completely silences his companions. (32:12, 15, 16) With great sarcasm he says: "O how much help you have been to one without power! . . . How much you have advised

one that is without wisdom!" (26:2, 3) Nothing, however, not even Sheol, can cover up anything from God's sight. Job describes God's wisdom in outer space, the earth, the clouds, the sea, and the wind—all of which man has observed. These are but the fringes of the Almighty's ways. They are hardly a whisper of the Almighty's greatness.

²⁸ Convinced of his innocence, he declares: "Until I expire I shall not take away my integrity from myself!" (27:5) No, Job has not done anything to deserve what has befallen him. Contrary to their charges, God will reward integrity by seeing that the things stored up by the wicked in their prosperity will be inherited by the righteous.

²⁹ Man knows where the treasures of earth (silver, gold, copper) come from, "but wisdom itself —from where does it come?" (28:20) He has sought for it among the living; he has looked into the sea; it cannot be bought with gold or silver. God is the one who understands wisdom. He sees to the ends of the earth and the heavens, apportions out the wind and the waters, and controls the rain and the storm clouds. Job concludes: "Look! The fear of Jehovah—that is wisdom, and to turn away from bad is understanding."—28:28.

³⁰ The afflicted Job next presents the history of his life. He desires to be restored to his former intimate status with God, when he was respected even by the leaders of the town. He was a rescuer of the afflicted and eyes to the blind ones. His counsel was good, and people waited upon his words. But now, instead of having an honorable standing, he is laughed at even by those younger in days, whose fathers were not even fit to be with the dogs of his flock. They spit on him and oppose him. Now, in his greatest affliction, they give him no rest.

³¹ Job describes himself as a dedicated man and asks to be judged by Jehovah. "He will weigh me in accurate scales and God will get to know my integrity." (31:6) Job defends his past actions. He has not been an adulterer, nor a schemer against others. He has not neglected to help the needy. He has not trusted in material wealth, even though he was rich. He has not worshiped the sun, moon, and stars, for "that too would be an error for attention by the justices, for I should have denied the true God above." (31:28) Job invites his opponent-at-law to file charges against the true record of his life.

22, 23. (a) Why does Zophar feel hurt, and what does he say about Job's alleged sins? (b) With what withering argument does Job reply?
24, 25. (a) What lying slander does Eliphaz self-righteously bring against Job? (b) What refutation and challenge does Job make in answer?
26. What more do Bildad and Zophar have to say?
27. How does Job now extol the Almighty's greatness?

---

28. What forthright statement does Job make on integrity?
29. How does Job describe wisdom?
30. What restoration does Job desire, but what is his present status?
31. In whose judgment does Job express confidence, and what does he say as to the true record of his life?

[32] **Elihu speaks** (32:1–37:24). Meanwhile, Elihu, a descendant of Buz, a son of Nahor, and hence a distant relative of Abraham, has been listening to the debate. He has waited because of feeling that those of greater age should have greater knowledge. It is not age, however, but God's spirit that gives understanding. Elihu's anger blazes at Job's "declaring his own soul righteous rather than God," but it gets even hotter at Job's three companions for their deplorable lack of wisdom in pronouncing God wicked. Elihu has "become full of words," and God's spirit compels him to give vent to these but without partiality or 'bestowing titles on earthling man.'—Job 32:2, 3, 18-22; Gen. 22:20, 21.

[33] Elihu speaks in sincerity, acknowledging that God is his Creator. He points out that Job has been more concerned with his own vindication than with God's. It was not necessary for God to answer all of Job's words, as if He had to justify His actions, and yet Job had contended against God. However, as Job's soul draws close to death, God favors him with a messenger, saying: "Let him off from going down into the pit! I have found a ransom! Let his flesh become fresher than in youth; let him return to the days of his youthful vigor." (Job 33:24, 25) The righteous will be restored!

[34] Elihu calls on the wise ones to listen. He reproves Job for saying there is no profit in being an integrity-keeper: "Far be it from the true God to act wickedly, and the Almighty to act unjustly! For according to the way earthling man acts he will reward him." (34:10, 11) He can remove the breath of life, and all flesh will expire. God judges without partiality. Job has been putting his own righteousness too much to the fore. He has been rash, not deliberately so, but "without knowledge"; and God has been long-suffering with him. (34:35) More needs to be said for *God's* vindication. God will not take his eyes away from the righteous, but he will reprove them. "He will not preserve anyone wicked alive, but the judgment of the afflicted ones he will give." (36:6) Since God is the supreme Instructor, Job should magnify His activity.

[35] In the awe-inspiring atmosphere of a gathering storm, Elihu speaks of the great things done by God and of His control of natural forces. To Job he says: "Stand still and show yourself attentive to the wonderful works of God." (37:14) Consider the golden splendor and fear-inspiring dignity of God, far beyond human finding out. "He is exalted in power, and justice and abundance of righteousness he will not belittle." Yes, Jehovah will regard those who fear him, not those "wise in their own heart."—37:23, 24.

[36] **Jehovah answers Job** (38:1–42:6). Job had asked God to speak to him. Now Jehovah majestically answers out of the windstorm. He sets before Job a series of questions that are in themselves an object lesson in man's littleness and God's greatness. "Where did you happen to be when I founded the earth? . . . Who laid its cornerstone, when the morning stars joyfully cried out together, and all the sons of God began shouting in applause?" (38: 4, 6, 7) That was long before Job's time! One after another, questions are raised that Job cannot answer, as Jehovah points to earth's sea, its garment of cloud, the dawn, the gates of death, and light and darkness. "Have you come to know because at that time you were being born, and because in number your days are many?" (38:21) And what about the storehouses of snow and of hail, the storm and the rain and the dewdrops, the ice and the hoarfrost, the mighty heavenly constellations, the lightnings and cloud layers, and the beasts and the birds?

[37] Job humbly admits: "Look! I have become of little account. What shall I reply to you? My hand I have put over my mouth." (40:4) Jehovah commands Job to face the issue. He poses a further series of challenging questions that exalt his dignity, superiority, and strength, as displayed in his natural creations. Even Behemoth and Leviathan are much more powerful than Job! Completely humbled, Job acknowledges his wrong viewpoint, and he admits that he spoke without knowledge. Seeing God now, not by hearsay but with understanding, he makes a retraction and repents "in dust and ashes."—42:6.

[38] **Jehovah's judgment and blessing** (42:7-17). Jehovah next charges Eliphaz and his two companions with not speaking truthful things about Him. They must provide sacrifices and have Job pray for them. After this, Jehovah turns back the captive condition of Job, blessing him in double amount. His brothers, sisters, and former friends

---

32. (a) Who now speaks? (b) Why does Elihu's anger blaze against Job and his companions, and what compels him to speak?
33. Wherein has Job erred, yet what favor will God show him?
34. (a) What further reproofs does Elihu give? (b) Instead of magnifying his own righteousness, what should Job do?
35. (a) To what should Job give attention? (b) To whom will Jehovah show favor?

36. By means of what object lesson and by what series of questions does Jehovah himself now teach Job?
37. What further questions humble Job, and what is he compelled to admit and do?
38. (a) How does Jehovah finish with Eliphaz and his companions? (b) What favor and blessing does he bestow on Job?

return to him with gifts, and he is blessed with twice as many sheep, camels, cattle, and she-asses as previously. He again has ten children, his three daughters being the prettiest women in all the land. His life is miraculously extended by 140 years, so that he comes to see four generations of his offspring. He dies "old and satisfied with days." —42:17.

WHY BENEFICIAL

[39] The book of Job exalts Jehovah and testifies to his unfathomable wisdom and power. (12: 12, 13; 37:23) In this one book, God is referred to as the Almighty 31 times, which is more often than in all the rest of the Scriptures. The account extols his eternity and exalted position (10:5; 36: 4, 22, 26; 40:2; 42:2) as well as his justice, loving-kindness, and mercy (36:5-7; 10:12; 42:12). It stresses Jehovah's vindication above man's salvation. (33:12; 34:10, 12; 35:2; 36:24; 40:8) Jehovah, the God of Israel, is shown to be also the God of Job.

[40] The record in Job magnifies and explains the creative work of God. (38:4–39:30; 40:15, 19; 41:1; 35:10) It harmonizes with the Genesis statement that man is made from the dust and that he returns to it. (Job 10:8, 9; Gen. 2:7; 3:19) It uses the terms "redeemer," "ransom," and "live again," thus giving a foreglimpse of teachings prominent in the Christian Greek Scriptures. (Job 19:25; 33: 24; 14:13, 14) Many of the book's expressions have been drawn on or paralleled by the prophets and by Christian writers. Compare, for example, Job 7:17—Psalm 8:4; Job 9:24—1 John 5:19; Job 10:8—Psalm 119:73; Job 12:25—Deuteronomy 28:29; Job 24:23—Proverbs 15:3; Job 26:8 —Proverbs 30:4; Job 28:12, 13, 15-19—Proverbs 3:13-15; Job 39:30—Matthew 24:28.*

[41] Jehovah's righteous standards for living are set forth in many passages. The book strongly condemns materialism (Job 31:24, 25), idolatry (31:26-28), adultery (31:9-12), gloating (31:29), injustice and partiality (31:13; 32:21), selfishness (31:16-21), and dishonesty and lying (31:5), showing that a person who practices these things cannot gain God's favor and eternal life. Elihu is a

fine example of deep respect and modesty, together with boldness, courage, and exaltation of God. (32:2, 6, 7, 9, 10, 18-20; 33:6, 33) Job's own exercise of headship, consideration of his family, and hospitality also provide a fine lesson. (1:5; 2: 9, 10; 31:32) However, Job is remembered most for his integrity-keeping and patient endurance, setting an example that has proved to be a faith-strengthening bulwark for God's servants throughout the ages and especially in these faith-trying times. "You have heard of the endurance of Job and have seen the outcome Jehovah gave, that Jehovah is very tender in affection and merciful." —Jas. 5:11.

[42] Job was not one of the seed of Abraham to whom the Kingdom promises were given, yet the record concerning his integrity does much to clarify understanding of Jehovah's Kingdom purposes. The book is an essential part of the divine record, for it reveals the fundamental issue between God and Satan, which involves man's integrity to Jehovah as his Sovereign. It shows that the angels, who were created before the earth and man, are also spectators and very much interested in this earth and the outcome of the controversy. (Job 1:6-12; 2:1-5; 38:6, 7) It indicates that the controversy existed before Job's day and that Satan is an actual spirit person. If the book of Job was written by Moses, this is the first appearance of the expression has·Sa·tan´ in the Hebrew text of the Bible, giving further identity to "the original serpent." (Job 1:6, footnote; Rev. 12:9) The book also proves that God is not the cause of mankind's suffering, sickness, and death, and it explains why the righteous are persecuted, while the wicked and wickedness are permitted to continue. It shows that Jehovah is interested in pushing the issue to its final settlement.

[43] Now is the time when all who want to live under God's Kingdom rule must answer Satan, "the accuser," by their course of integrity. (Rev. 12:10, 11) Even in the midst of 'puzzling trials,' integrity-keepers must continue praying for God's name to be sanctified and for his Kingdom to come and stamp out Satan and all his derisive seed. That will be God's "day of fight and war," to be followed by the relief and blessings in which Job hoped to share.—1 Pet. 4:12; Matt. 6:9, 10; Job 38:23; 14: 13-15.

---

* Insight on the Scriptures, Vol. 2, page 83.

39. In what various ways does the book of Job exalt and extol Jehovah?
40. (a) How does the book of Job magnify and explain God's creative works? (b) How does it give a foreglimpse of and harmonize with the teachings of the Christian Greek Scriptures?
41. (a) What theocratic standards are emphasized in Job? (b) In what is God's servant Job preeminently a fine example to us today?

42. What fundamental Kingdom issue is clarified in Job, and what interesting aspects of this issue are explained?
43. In harmony with the divine revelations in the book of Job, what course must now be followed by all who seek God's Kingdom blessings?

19 Psalms

Writers: **David and others**

Place Written: **Undetermined**

Writing Completed: **c. 460 B.C.E.**

THE book of Psalms was the inspired song-book of true worshipers of Jehovah in ancient times, a collection of 150 sacred songs, or psalms, set to music and arranged for the public worship of Jehovah God in his temple at Jerusalem. These psalms are songs of praise to Jehovah, and not only that, they also contain prayers of supplication for mercy and help, as well as expressions of trust and confidence. They abound with thanksgivings and exultations and with exclamations of great, yes, superlative, joy. Some are recapitulations of history, contemplating Jehovah's loving-kindness and his great deeds. They are packed with prophecies, many of which have had remarkable fulfillments. They contain much instruction that is beneficial and upbuilding, all of it clothed in lofty language and imagery that stirs the reader to the very depths. The psalms are a sumptuous spiritual meal, beautifully prepared and spread invitingly before us.

² What is the significance of the book's title, and who wrote the Psalms? In the Hebrew Bible, the book is called *Se′pher Tehil·lim′*, meaning "Book of Praises," or simply *Tehil·lim′*, that is, "Praises." This is the plural form of *Tehil·lah′*, meaning "A Praise" or "Song of Praise," found in the superscription of Psalm 145. The name "Praises" is most appropriate, as the book highlights praise to Jehovah. The title "Psalms" comes from the Greek *Septuagint,* which used the word *Psal·moi′*, denoting songs sung with a musical accompaniment. The word is also found at a number of places in the Christian Greek Scriptures, such as at Luke 20:42 and Acts 1:20. A psalm is a sacred song or poem used in the praise and worship of God.

³ Many of the psalms have headings, or superscriptions, and these often name the writer. Seventy-three headings bear the name of David, "the pleasant one of the melodies of Israel." (2 Sam. 23:1) No doubt Psalms 2, 72, and 95 were also written by David. (See Acts 4:25, Psalm 72:20, and

Hebrews 4:7.) Additionally, Psalms 10 and 71 appear to be a continuation of Psalms 9 and 70 respectively and therefore may be attributed to David. Twelve psalms are ascribed to Asaph, evidently denoting the house of Asaph, as some of these speak of events later than Asaph's day. (Ps. 79; 80; 1 Chron. 16:4, 5, 7; Ezra 2:41) Eleven psalms are directly attributed to the sons of Korah. (1 Chron. 6:31-38) Psalm 43 appears to be a continuation of Psalm 42, and therefore it may also be attributed to the sons of Korah. In addition to mentioning "the sons of Korah," Psalm 88 also accredits Heman in its superscription, and Psalm 89 names Ethan as the writer. Psalm 90 is attributed to Moses, and Psalm 91 is probably Moses' as well. Psalm 127 is Solomon's. Over two thirds of the psalms are thus ascribed to various writers.

⁴ The book of Psalms is the Bible's largest single book. As evidenced by Psalms 90, 126, and 137, it was long in the writing, at least from the time Moses wrote (1513-1473 B.C.E.) until after the restoration from Babylon and probably Ezra's day (537–c. 460 B.C.E.). Thus, the writing is seen to span approximately a thousand years. The time covered by the contents is much greater, though, starting from the time of the creation and epitomizing the history of Jehovah's dealings with his servants down to the time of the composition of the last of the psalms.

⁵ The book of Psalms is one that reflects organization. David himself refers to "the processions of my God, my King, into the holy place. The singers went in front, the players on stringed instruments after them; in between were the maidens beating tambourines. In congregated throngs bless God, Jehovah." (Ps. 68:24-26) This gives the reason for the oft repeated expression "To the director" in the superscriptions, as well as the many poetic and musical terms. Some superscriptions explain the use or purpose of a psalm or provide musical

1. What is the book of Psalms, and what does it contain?
2. (a) What titles have been applied to Psalms, and with what meanings? (b) What is a psalm?
3. What do the superscriptions tell as to the writers?

4. What time period is covered by the writing?
5. (a) How does the book of Psalms reflect organization? (b) What further information is supplied by the superscriptions? (c) Why is it not necessary to pronounce the word *"Se′lah"* in reading the psalms?

instructions. (See the superscriptions of Psalms 6, 30, 38, 60, 88, 102, and 120.) For at least 13 of David's psalms, such as Psalms 18 and 51, the events spurring their composition are briefly related. Thirty-four of the psalms are entirely without superscriptions. The little word *"Se´lah,"* occurring 71 times in the main text, is generally thought to be a technical term for music or recitation, although its exact significance is unknown. It is suggested by some that it indicates a pause for silent meditation in the singing or in both the singing and the instrumental music. Hence, it need not be pronounced in reading.

[6] From ancient times, the book of Psalms has been divided into five separate books, or volumes, as follows: (1) Psalms 1-41; (2) Psalms 42-72; (3) Psalms 73-89; (4) Psalms 90-106; (5) Psalms 107-150. It appears that the first collection of these songs was made by David. Evidently Ezra, the priest and "skilled copyist in the law of Moses," was the one used by Jehovah to arrange the book of Psalms into final form.—Ezra 7:6.

[7] The progressive growth of the collection may explain why some of the psalms are repeated in the different sections, such as Psalms 14 and 53; 40: 13-17 and 70; 57:7-11 and 108:1-5. Each of the five sections closes with a blessing pronounced on Jehovah, or a doxology—the first four of these including responses by the people and the last one being the entire Psalm 150.—Ps. 41:13, footnote.

[8] A very special style of composition is employed in nine psalms; it is called acrostic because of its alphabetic structure. (Psalms 9, 10, 25, 34, 37, 111, 112, 119, and 145) In this structure the first verse or verses of the first stanza begin with the first letter of the Hebrew alphabet, *'a´leph* (א), the next verse(s) with the second letter, *behth* (ב), and so on, through all or nearly all the letters of the Hebrew alphabet. This may have served as a memory aid—just think of the temple singers having to remember songs as long as Psalm 119! Interestingly, an acrostic of Jehovah's name is found at Psalm 96:11. The first half of this verse in Hebrew consists of four words, and the initial letters of these words, when read from right to left, are the four Hebrew consonants of the Tetragrammaton, *YHWH* (יהוה).

[9] These sacred, lyric poems are written in un-rhymed Hebrew verse and display unsurpassed beauty of style and rhythmic flow of thought. They speak directly to the mind and heart. They paint vivid pictures. The wonderful breadth and depth, in both the subject matter and the strong emotions expressed, are due in part to David's extraordinary life experiences, which provide background to many of the psalms. Few men have lived so varied a life—as a shepherd boy, a lone warrior against Goliath, a court musician, an outlaw among loyal friends and among traitors, a king and conqueror, a loving father beset with divisions in his own household, one who twice experienced the bitterness of serious sin and yet was ever an enthusiastic worshiper of Jehovah and lover of His Law. Against such a background, it is little wonder that the book of Psalms runs the entire scale of human emotions! Contributing to its power and beauty are the poetic parallelisms and contrasts so characteristic of Hebrew verse.—Ps. 1:6; 22:20; 42:1; 121:3, 4.

[10] The authenticity of these most ancient songs to Jehovah's praise is amply testified to by their being in complete harmony with the rest of the Scriptures. The book of Psalms is quoted numerous times by the writers of the Christian Greek Scriptures. (Ps. 5:9 [Rom. 3:13]; Ps. 10:7 [Rom. 3:14]; Ps. 24:1 [1 Cor. 10:26]; Ps. 50:14 [Matt. 5:33]; Ps. 78:24 [John 6:31]; Ps. 102:25-27 [Heb. 1:10-12]; Ps. 112:9 [2 Cor. 9:9]) David himself said in his last song: "The spirit of Jehovah it was that spoke by me, and his word was upon my tongue." It was this spirit that had operated upon him from the day of his anointing by Samuel. (2 Sam. 23:2; 1 Sam. 16:13) Additionally, the apostles quoted from the Psalms. Peter referred to "scripture . . . which the holy spirit spoke beforehand by David's mouth," and in a number of quotations from the Psalms, the writer to the Hebrews referred to them either as statements spoken by God or introduced them with the words, "just as the holy spirit says." —Acts 1:16; 4:25; Heb. 1:5-14; 3:7; 5:5, 6.

[11] Coming to the strongest proof of authenticity, we quote Jesus, the risen Lord, saying to the disciples: "These are my words which I spoke to you . . . that all the things written in the law of Moses and in the Prophets and Psalms about me must be fulfilled." Jesus was there grouping the entire Hebrew Scriptures in the way adopted by the Jews and well known to them. His mention of the Psalms included the whole of the third group of Scriptures, called the Hagiographa (or Holy Writings), of which Psalms was the first book. This

---

6. (a) Into what separate volumes has the book of Psalms been divided? (b) Who apparently arranged the book of Psalms into final form?
7. What other features of Psalms are to be noted?
8. Explain and illustrate the acrostic style of composition.
9. (a) Because of what background do many of the psalms make a direct appeal to mind and heart? (b) What else contributes to their power and beauty?

---

10. What testifies to the authenticity of Psalms?
11. How is supporting testimony crowned by Jesus' own statements?

is confirmed by what he said a few hours earlier to the two on their way to Emmaus, when "he interpreted to them things pertaining to himself in *all* the Scriptures."—Luke 24:27, 44.

CONTENTS OF PSALMS

¹² **Book One** (Psalms 1-41). All of these are directly ascribed to David except Psalms 1, 2, 10, and 33. Psalm 1 strikes the keynote at the outset, as it pronounces happy the man delighting in Jehovah's law, contemplating it day and night in order to follow it, in contrast with ungodly sinners. This is the first pronouncement of happiness found in Psalms. Psalm 2 opens with a challenging question and tells of the combined stand of all the kings and high officials of earth "against Jehovah and against his anointed one." Jehovah holds them in derision and then speaks to them in hot anger, saying: "I, even I, have installed my king upon Zion, my holy mountain." He is the one who will break and dash in pieces all opposition. You other kings and rulers, "serve Jehovah with fear" and acknowledge His Son lest you perish! (Vss. 2, 6, 11) Thus the Psalms quickly strike up the Kingdom theme of the Bible.

¹³ In this first collection, prayers, both of petition and of thanksgiving, are prominent. Psalm 8 contrasts Jehovah's greatness with man's smallness, and Psalm 14 exposes the folly of people who refuse to submit to God's authority. Psalm 19 shows how the wonderful creation of Jehovah God declares his glory, and verses 7-14 extol the rewarding benefits of keeping God's perfect law, which is later reflected on a grander scale in Psalm 119. Psalm 23 is universally accepted as one of the masterpieces of all literature, but it is even more magnificent in the beautiful simplicity of its expression of loyal trust in Jehovah. Oh, that we may all 'dwell in the house of Jehovah, the Great Shepherd, to the length of days'! (23:1, 6) Psalm 37 gives good counsel to God-fearing people who live among evildoers, and Psalm 40 expresses the delight of doing God's will, even as David did it.

¹⁴ **Book Two** (Psalms 42-72). This section starts with eight Korahite psalms. Psalms 42 and 43 are both attributed to the sons of Korah, since together they are in reality one poem in three stanzas, linked together by a recurring verse. (42:5, 11; 43:5) Psalm 49 emphasizes the impossibility of man's providing his own ransomer, and it points to God as the one strong enough to redeem man "from the hand of Sheol." (Vs. 15) Psalm 51 is a prayer of David, uttered after his terrible sin with Bath-sheba, the wife of Uriah the Hittite, and shows his genuine repentance. (2 Sam. 11:1–12: 24) This section closes with a psalm "regarding Solomon," a prayer for his peaceful reign and for Jehovah's blessing to go with him.—Ps. 72.

¹⁵ **Book Three** (Psalms 73-89). At least two of these, Psalms 74 and 79, were composed following the destruction of Jerusalem in 607 B.C.E. They lament this great catastrophe and implore Jehovah to help his people 'for the sake of the glory of his name.' (79:9) Psalm 78 recounts the history of Israel from the time of Moses until when David "began to shepherd them according to the integrity of his heart" (vs. 72), and Psalm 80 points to Jehovah as the real "Shepherd of Israel." (Vs. 1) Psalms 82 and 83 are strong pleas to Jehovah to execute his judgments against his enemies and the enemies of his people. Far from being vindictive, these petitions are to the end "that people may search for your name, O Jehovah . . . , [and] that people may know that you, whose name is Jehovah, you alone are the Most High over all the earth." (83:16, 18) Last in this section comes Psalm 89, highlighting "Jehovah's expressions of lovingkindness," as shown preeminently in his covenant made with David. This is for an everlasting heir to David's throne, who will rule to time indefinite before Jehovah!—Vss. 1, 34-37.

¹⁶ **Book Four** (Psalms 90-106). Like Book Three, this contains 17 psalms. It begins with the prayer of Moses, setting in sharp relief God's eternal existence and the short life span of mortal man. Psalm 92 extols Jehovah's superior qualities. Then there is that grand group, Psalms 93-100, that commence with the stirring cry, "Jehovah himself has become king!" Hence "all you people of the earth" are called upon to "sing to Jehovah, bless his name . . . , for Jehovah is great and very much to be praised." "Jehovah is great in Zion." (93:1; 96:1, 2, 4; 99:2) Psalms 105 and 106 thank Jehovah for his wondrous deeds in behalf of his people and for his faithfully keeping his covenant with Abraham in giving his seed the land, despite their countless murmurings and backslidings.

¹⁷ Of unusual interest is Psalm 104. This extols Jehovah for the dignity and splendor with which he has clothed himself, and it describes his wisdom as displayed in his many works and productions on earth. Then the theme of the entire book

---

12. How does Psalms quickly strike up a theme of happiness, as well as the Kingdom theme?
13. What else does the first collection of psalms make prominent?
14. What is said about redemption in Book Two of the Psalms, and what prayers of David are featured?

15. What does Book Three state regarding Israel's history, Jehovah's judgments, and his Kingdom covenant?
16. How does Book Four exalt Jehovah's kingship and his keeping covenant?
17. Of what unusual interest is Psalm 104, and what theme is repeated from this point on?

of Psalms is set forth with full force, as the exclamation appears for the first time: "Praise Jah, you people!" (Vs. 35) This call to true worshipers to render Jehovah the praise due his name is, in Hebrew, just one word ha·lelu–Yah´ or "Hallelujah," which latter form is familiar to people all over the earth today. From this verse on, the expression occurs 24 times, a number of psalms both opening and closing with it.

[18] **Book Five** (Psalms 107-150). In Psalm 107 we have a description of Jehovah's deliverances, accompanied by the melodious refrain: "O let people give thanks to Jehovah for his loving-kindness and for his wonderful works to the sons of men." (Vss. 8, 15, 21, 31) Psalms 113 to 118 are the so-called Hallel Psalms. According to the Mishnah, these were sung by the Jews at the Passover and at the festivals of Pentecost, Booths, and Dedication.

[19] Psalm 117 is powerful in its simplicity, being the shortest of all psalms and chapters in the Bible. Psalm 119 is the longest of all psalms and Bible chapters, containing a total of 176 verses in its 22 alphabetic stanzas of 8 verses each. All but two of these verses (90 and 122) refer in some way to the word or law of Jehovah God, repeating several or all of the expressions (law, reminder, orders, commandment, judicial decisions) of Psalm 19:7-14 in each stanza. The word of God is referred to more than 170 times by one or the other of the following 8 expressions: commandment(s), judicial decision(s), law, orders, regulations, reminder(s), saying(s), and word(s).

[20] Next, we find another group of psalms, the 15 Songs of the Ascents, Psalms 120-134. Translators have rendered this expression in various ways because its meaning is not fully understood. Some say it refers to the exalted contents of these psalms, though there does not seem to be clear reason to exalt them above the other inspired psalms. Many commentators suggest that the title derives from the use of these songs by the worshipers traveling up, or "ascending," to Jerusalem for the annual festivals, the trip to the capital being regarded as an ascent because the city was situated high up in the mountains of Judah. (Compare Ezra 7:9.) David especially had a deep appreciation of the need for God's people to unite in worship. He rejoiced to hear the invitation: "To the house of Jehovah let us go"; and the tribes did go up, "to give thanks to the name of Jehovah." On that account he earnestly sought for the peace, security, and prosperity of Jerusalem, praying: "For the sake of the house of Jehovah our God I will keep seeking good for you."—Ps. 122:1, 4, 9.

[21] Psalm 132 tells of David's oath to give himself no rest until he has found an appropriate resting-place for Jehovah, as represented by the ark of the covenant. After the Ark has been set up in Zion, Jehovah is described in beautiful poetic phrase as saying that he has chosen Zion, "my resting-place forever; here I shall dwell, for I have longed for it." He recognized this central place of worship, "for there Jehovah commanded the blessing." "May Jehovah bless you out of Zion."—132:1-6, 13, 14; 133:3; 134:3; see also Psalm 48.

[22] Psalm 135 extols Jehovah as the praiseworthy God who does all his delight, in contrast with the vain and empty idols, whose makers will become just like them. Psalm 136 is for responsive singing, each verse concluding: "For his loving-kindness is to time indefinite." Such responses are shown to have been used on many occasions. (1 Chron. 16:41; 2 Chron. 5:13; 7:6; 20:21; Ezra 3:11) Psalm 137 relates the longing for Zion that dwelt in the hearts of the Jews when exiled in Babylon and also testifies that they did not forget the songs, or psalms, of Zion though they were far from their homeland. Psalm 145 exalts Jehovah's goodness and kingship, showing that he "is guarding all those loving him, but all the wicked ones he will annihilate." (Vs. 20) Then, as a rousing conclusion, Psalms 146-150 strike up again the glorious theme of the book, each one beginning and ending with the words, "Praise Jah, you people!" This melody of praise rises to a grand crescendo in the 150th Psalm, where 13 times in the space of six verses it calls on all creation to praise Jehovah.

WHY BENEFICIAL

[23] Because of their perfection of beauty and style, the psalms of the Bible are to be included among the greatest literature in any language. However, they are much more than literature. They are a living message from the Supreme Sovereign of all the universe, Jehovah God himself. They give deep insight into the fundamental teachings of the Bible, speaking first and foremost of Jehovah, its Author. He is clearly shown to be the Creator of the universe and everything in it. (8:3-9; 90:1, 2; 100:3; 104:1-5, 24; 139:14) The name Jehovah is indeed magnified in the book of Psalms, where it appears about 700 times.

---

18. (a) What refrain highlights Psalm 107? (b) What are the so-called Hallel Psalms?
19. How do Psalms 117 and 119 contrast, and what are some of the features of the latter?
20, 21. (a) What are the Songs of the Ascents? (b) How do they express David's appreciation of the need for united worship?

22. (a) How is Jehovah's praiseworthiness extolled? (b) How does the glorious theme of the book rise to a crescendo in the concluding psalms?
23. (a) What living message is contained in Psalms? (b) How are Jehovah's name and sovereignty exalted?

Additionally, the abbreviated form "Jah" is to be found 43 times, so that all together the divine name is mentioned about 5 times, on the average, in each Psalm. Moreover, Jehovah is spoken of about 350 times as 'Elo·him', or God. Jehovah's supreme rulership is shown in references to him as "Sovereign Lord" in a number of psalms.—68: 20; 69:6; 71:5; 73:28; 140:7; 141:8.

²⁴ In contrast with the eternal God, mortal man is shown to be born in sin and in need of a redeemer, and he is shown as dying and returning to "crushed matter," going down into Sheol, the common grave of mankind. (6:4, 5; 49:7-20; 51:5, 7; 89:48; 90:1-5; 115:17; 146:4) The book of Psalms emphasizes the need for heeding the law of God and trusting in Jehovah. (1:1, 2; 62:8; 65:5; 77:12; 115:11; 118:8; 119:97, 105, 165) It warns against presumptuousness and "concealed sins" (19:12-14; 131:1) and encourages honest and healthful associations. (15:1-5; 26:5; 101:5) It shows that right conduct brings Jehovah's approval. (34:13-15; 97:10) It holds out bright hope in saying that "salvation belongs to Jehovah" and that in the case of those fearing him, he will "deliver their soul from death itself." (3:8; 33:19) This brings us to the prophetic aspect.

²⁵ The book of Psalms is virtually packed with prophecies pointing forward to Jesus Christ, the "son of David," and the role he would play as Jehovah's Anointed One and King.* (Matt. 1:1) As the Christian congregation sprang into life on the day of Pentecost 33 C.E., the holy spirit began to enlighten the apostles as to the fulfillment of these prophecies. On that very day, Peter quoted repeatedly from Psalms in developing the theme of his famous speech. This had to do with an individual: "Jesus the Nazarene." The latter part of his argument is based almost entirely on quotations from the Psalms proving that Christ Jesus is the Greater David and that Jehovah would not leave Jesus' soul in Hades but would raise him from the dead. No, "David did not ascend to the heavens," but as he foretold at Psalm 110:1, his Lord did. Who is David's Lord? Peter reaches his great climax and forcefully answers: "This Jesus whom you impaled"!—Acts 2:14-36; Ps. 16:8-11; 132:11.

²⁶ Was Peter's speech, based on the Psalms, beneficial? The baptism of about 3,000 who were

added to the Christian congregation the same day speaks for itself.—Acts 2:41.

²⁷ Shortly after, at a special gathering, the disciples appealed to Jehovah and quoted Psalm 2: 1, 2. They said that this had been fulfilled in the united opposition of the rulers against God's "holy servant Jesus, whom [God] anointed." And the account goes on to say that they were "all filled with the holy spirit."—Acts 4:23-31.

²⁸ Look, now, at the letter to the Hebrews. In the first two chapters, we find a number of quotations from the Psalms respecting the superiority of Jesus, as God's heavenly enthroned Son, over the angels. Paul shows from Psalm 22:22 and other references that Jesus has a congregation of "brothers," part of Abraham's seed and "partakers of the heavenly calling." (Heb. 2:10-13, 16; 3:1) Then, commencing at Hebrews 6:20 and continuing through chapter 7, the apostle enlarges on the additional office that Jesus occupies as "high priest according to the manner of Melchizedek forever." This refers to God's oath-bound promise at Psalm 110:4, to which Paul makes reference time and again in proving the superiority of Jesus' priesthood over that of Aaron. Paul explains that by Jehovah's oath Jesus Christ is a priest, not on earth, but in heaven and "he remains a priest perpetually"—the benefits of his priestly service will be eternal.—Heb. 7:3, 15-17, 23-28.

²⁹ Further, at Hebrews 10:5-10, we are told of Jesus' fine appreciation for the sacrificial course that was God's will for him and of his determination to carry out that will. This is based on David's words at Psalm 40:6-8. This exemplary spirit of devotion is of the greatest benefit for all of us to consider and to copy so as to win God's approval. —See also Psalm 116:14-19.

³⁰ The course that Jesus took, culminating in that terrible ordeal he endured on the torture stake, was foretold in the Psalms in remarkable detail. This included his being offered vinegar to drink, the casting of lots for his outer garments, the cruel treatment of his hands and feet, the mockery, and the still more bitter mental anguish of that agonizing cry: "My God, my God, why have you forsaken me?" (Matt. 27:34, 35, 43, 46;

---

* *Insight on the Scriptures*, Vol. 2, pages 710-11.

---

24. What is said in Psalms concerning mortal man, and what sound counsel is given?
25. (a) With what is the book of Psalms virtually packed? (b) How did Peter use Psalms in identifying the Greater David?
26. How did Peter's speech prove to be beneficial?

---

27. How did "the holy spirit" interpret Psalm 2?
28. (a) By the use of Psalms, what argument does Paul develop in Hebrews chapters 1 to 3? (b) How does Psalm 110:4 provide a basis for Paul's discussion of the Melchizedekian priesthood?
29. What outstanding example of devotion should we heed, as stated in the Psalms and explained at Hebrews 10:5-10?
30. How did the Psalms foretell Jesus' course in detail, and how must he have drawn comfort from them?

Ps. 22:1, 7, 8, 14-18; 69:20, 21) As indicated by John 19:23-30, even during those hours, Jesus must have drawn much comfort and guidance from the Psalms, knowing that all these scriptures had to be fulfilled down to the last detail. Jesus knew that the Psalms also spoke concerning his resurrection and exaltation. He doubtless had such things in mind when leading in "singing praises," or psalms, with his apostles on the last night before his death.—Matt. 26:30.

³¹ Thus Psalms clearly identifies the "son of David" and Kingdom Seed to be Christ Jesus, who is now exalted as both King and Priest in the heavenly Zion. Space does not permit a description in detail of all the passages from Psalms that are quoted in the Christian Greek Scriptures as fulfilled in this Anointed One of Jehovah, but a few more examples are here listed: Ps. 78:2 —Matt. 13:31-35; Ps. 69:4—John 15:25; Ps. 118:22, 23—Mark 12:10, 11 and Acts 4:11; Ps. 34:20—John 19:33, 36; Ps. 45:6, 7—Heb. 1: 8, 9. Also, Jesus' congregation of true followers is foretold in the Psalms, not as individuals, but as a group taken into God's favor from all nations to share in a work of praise to Jehovah's name.—Ps.

117:1—Rom. 15:11; Ps. 68:18—Eph. 4:8-11; Ps. 95:7-11—Heb. 3:7, 8; 4:7.

³² Our study of the Psalms adds much to our appreciation of the kingship of Jehovah God, which He exercises through the promised Seed and Kingdom Heir, to His glory and vindication. May we ever be among those loyal ones who exult in 'the glorious splendor of Jehovah's dignity' and who are spoken of in Psalm 145, which is referred to as "a praise, of David": "About the glory of your kingship they will talk, and about your mightiness they will speak, to make known to the sons of men his mighty acts and the glory of the splendor of his kingship. Your kingship is a kingship for all times indefinite, and your dominion is throughout all successive generations." (Ps. 145:5, 11-13) True to the prophetic psalm, the splendor of God's established Kingdom by Christ is even now being made known to the sons of men in all nations. How thankful we should be for that Kingdom and its King! Appropriate, indeed, are the closing words of the Psalms: "Every breathing thing—let it praise Jah. Praise Jah, you people!"—150:6.

31. What does the book of Psalms foretell in connection with the Kingdom Seed and Jesus' congregation?

32. (a) What does the study of Psalms reveal as to Jehovah's vindication and Kingdom purposes? (b) In appreciation of his kingship, how should we express loyalty and thankfulness?

Bible Book Number	**20**	Speakers: **Solomon, Agur, Lemuel**
	Proverbs	Place Written: **Jerusalem**
		Writing Completed: **c. 717 B.C.E.**

WHEN Solomon, the son of David, became king of Israel in 1037 B.C.E., he prayed to Jehovah for "wisdom and knowledge" to "judge this great people." In response, Jehovah gave him 'knowledge and wisdom and an understanding heart.' (2 Chron. 1: 10-12; 1 Ki. 3:12; 4:30, 31) As a result, Solomon came to "speak three thousand proverbs." (1 Ki. 4:32) Some of this spoken wisdom was recorded in the Bible book of Proverbs. Since his wisdom was really that which "God had put in his heart," then in studying Proverbs we are in fact studying the wisdom of Jehovah God. (1 Ki. 10:23, 24) These proverbs sum up eternal truths. They are just as up-to-date now as when they were first uttered.

² The reign of Solomon was an appropriate time for providing this divine guidance. Solomon was said to "sit upon Jehovah's throne." The theocratic kingdom of Israel was at its height, and Solomon was favored with surpassing "royal dignity." (1 Chron. 29:23, 25) It was a time of peace and plenty, a time of security. (1 Ki. 4: 20-25) However, even under that theocratic rule, the people still had their personal problems and difficulties due to human imperfections. That the people would look to wise King Solomon to help them solve their problems is understandable. (1 Ki. 3:16-28) In the course of pronouncing judgment in these many cases, he uttered proverbial sayings that fitted the many circumstanc-

1. What wisdom is to be found in the book of Proverbs?

2. Why was Solomon's time an appropriate one in which to provide the divine guidance in Proverbs?

es of life arising from day to day. These brief but impressive sayings were greatly treasured by those who desired to regulate their lives in accordance with the will of God.

³ The record does not say that Solomon *wrote* the Proverbs. However, it says that he *'spoke'* proverbs, also that "he . . . made a thorough search, that he might arrange many proverbs in order," thus showing that he had an interest in preserving proverbs for later use. (1 Ki. 4:32; Eccl. 12:9) In the time of David and Solomon, there were official secretaries in the lists of court officials. (2 Sam. 20:25; 2 Ki. 12:10) Whether these scribes in his court wrote and collected his proverbs, we do not know, but the expressions of any ruler of his caliber would be highly regarded and would normally be recorded. It is generally agreed that the book is a collection compiled from other collections.

⁴ The book of Proverbs may be divided into five sections. These are: (1) Chapters 1-9, opening with the words, "The proverbs of Solomon the son of David"; (2) Chapters 10-24, described as the "Proverbs of Solomon"; (3) Chapters 25-29, which division begins: "These also are the proverbs of Solomon that the men of Hezekiah the king of Judah transcribed"; (4) Chapter 30, introduced as "The words of Agur the son of Jakeh"; and (5) Chapter 31, which comprises "The words of Lemuel the king, the weighty message that his mother gave to him in correction." Solomon was thus the originator of the bulk of the proverbs. As to Agur and Lemuel, nothing definite is known about their identity. Some commentators suggest that Lemuel may have been another name for Solomon.

⁵ When was Proverbs written and compiled? The greater part was no doubt written down during Solomon's reign (1037-998 B.C.E.) before his deflection. Because of uncertainty as to the identity of Agur and Lemuel, it is not possible to date their material. Since one of the collections was made in the reign of Hezekiah (745-717 B.C.E.), it could not have been before his reign that the final collecting was done. Were the last two divisions also collected under King Hezekiah's purview? In answer there is an illuminating footnote to Proverbs 31:31 in the *New World Translation of the Holy Scriptures—With References:* "Some ed[itions] of the Heb[rew] text display the trigrammaton, or three letters, *Chehth, Za'yin, Qohph* (חזק) that stand as King Hezekiah's

signature to the copy-work done by his scribes to signify that the work had been completed."

⁶ In Hebrew Bibles the book was first called by the opening word in the book, *mish·leh´,* meaning "proverbs." *Mish·leh´* is the plural number, construct state, of the Hebrew noun *ma·shal´,* which noun is generally thought to be derived from a root word meaning "be like" or "be comparable." These terms nicely describe the contents of the book, for proverbs are pithy sayings that often employ likenesses or comparisons and that are designed to make the hearer think. The brief form of the proverbs makes them easy to follow and interesting, and in this form they are easily taught, learned, and remembered. The idea sticks.

⁷ The style of expression in the book is also most interesting. It is in Hebrew poetic style. The structure of most of the book is parallel poetry. This does not make the ends of lines or verses rhyme, or sound alike. It consists of making rhythmic lines give parallel thoughts or ideas. Its beauty and power of instruction lie in this thought rhythm. The thoughts may be synonymous or contrasting, but the power of the parallel is there to give extension to the thought, to enlarge upon the idea, and to make sure of conveying the meaning in the thought. Examples of the synonymous parallelism are to be found at Proverbs 11:25; 16:18; and 18:15, and examples of the more abundant contrasting parallelism at Proverbs 10:7, 30; 12:25; 13:25; and 15:8. Another type of structure is found right at the end of the book. (Prov. 31:10-31) The 22 verses there are arranged so that in Hebrew each one begins with the succeeding letter of the Hebrew alphabet, this being the acrostic style that is used also in a number of the psalms. For beauty this style has no parallel in ancient writings.

⁸ The authenticity of Proverbs is also shown in the wide use made of the book by the early Christians in stating rules of conduct. James was apparently very familiar with Proverbs and used its basic principles in the fine counsel he gave for Christian conduct. (Compare Proverbs 14:29; 17:27 with James 1:19, 20; Proverbs 3:34 with James 4:6; Proverbs 27:1 with James 4:13, 14.) Direct quotations from Proverbs are also to be found in the following passages: Romans 12:20 —Proverbs 25:21, 22; Hebrews 12:5, 6—Proverbs 3:11, 12; 2 Peter 2:22—Proverbs 26:11.

---

3. How did Proverbs come to be compiled?
4. (a) How is the book of Proverbs generally divided? (b) Who originated the bulk of the proverbs?
5. When was Proverbs written and compiled?

6. What is a proverb, and why is the Hebrew title of the book fitting?
7. What should be noted about the style of Proverbs?
8. How does the use made of Proverbs by the early Christians testify to its authenticity?

⁹ In addition, Proverbs shows itself to be in harmony with the rest of the Bible, thus proving it to be a part of "all Scripture." It presents striking unity of thought when compared with the Law of Moses, Jesus' teaching, and the writings of Jesus' disciples and apostles. (See Proverbs 10: 16—1 Corinthians 15:58 and Galatians 6:8, 9; Proverbs 12:25—Matthew 6:25; Proverbs 20:20 —Exodus 20:12 and Matthew 15:4.) Even when touching on such points as the readying of the earth for human habitation, there is oneness of thinking with other Bible writers.—Prov. 3: 19, 20; Gen. 1:6, 7; Job 38:4-11; Ps. 104:5-9.

¹⁰ Also testifying to the book's divine inspiration is its scientific accuracy, whether the proverb involves chemical, medical, or health principles. Proverbs 25:20 apparently tells of acid-alkali reactions. Proverbs 31:4, 5 agrees with modern scientific findings that alcohol dulls the thinking processes. Many doctors and nutritionists agree that honey is a healthful food, calling to mind the proverb: "My son, eat honey, for it is good." (Prov. 24:13) Modern observations on psychosomatics are not new to Proverbs. "A heart that is joyful does good as a curer."—17:22; 15:17.

¹¹ Indeed, so completely does the book of Proverbs cover every human need and situation that one authority stated: "There is no relation in life which has not its appropriate instruction, no good or evil tendency without its proper incentive or correction. The human consciousness is everywhere brought into immediate relation with the Divine, . . . and man walks as in the presence of his Maker and Judge . . . Every type of humanity is found in this ancient book; and though sketched three thousand years ago, is still as true to nature as if now drawn from its living representative."—Smith's *Dictionary of the Bible,* 1890, Vol. III, page 2616.

CONTENTS OF PROVERBS

¹² **The First Section** (1:1–9:18). This is a connected poem made up of short discourses as though from a father to a son, dealing with the need for wisdom to guide the heart, or the whole inner person, and to direct desire. It teaches the value of wisdom and its blessings: happiness, pleasantness, peace, and life. (1:33; 3:13-18; 8: 32-35) It contrasts this with the lack of wisdom

and its results: suffering and finally death. (1: 28-32; 7:24-27; 8:36) Considering the infinite situations and possibilities of life, it gives one a basic study in human conduct and the present and future consequences of that conduct. The words at Proverbs 1:7 set the pattern for the entire book: "The fear of Jehovah is the beginning of knowledge." All actions must show that Jehovah is taken into consideration. There is constant repetition of the need not to forget God's laws, to keep close to his commandments and not to forsake them.

¹³ The prominent threads that run through the fabric of this first section are practical wisdom, knowledge, fear of Jehovah, discipline, and discernment. Warnings are given against bad company, rejecting Jehovah's discipline, and improper relations with strange women. (1:10-19; 3:11, 12; 5:3-14; 7:1-27) Twice, wisdom is described as being in public places, thus obtainable, available. (1:20, 21; 8:1-11) It is personified and speaks appealingly to the inexperienced ones, even throwing some light on the creation of the earth. (1:22-33; 8:4-36) What an amazing book this is! This section closes out on its starting theme, that "the fear of Jehovah is the start of wisdom." (9:10) Throughout, it argues that recognition of Jehovah in all our ways, together with our adherence to his righteousness, is the way of life and can guard us against so much that is undesirable.

¹⁴ **The Second Section** (10:1–24:34). Here we find many choice, unconnected maxims that apply wisdom to the complex situations of life. By teaching us the proper applications, it aims to promote greater happiness and pleasant living. Contrasts in the parallelisms make these teachings stand out in our minds. Here is a partial list of the subjects that are considered in just chapters 10, 11, and 12:

> love vs. hatred
> wisdom vs. foolishness
> honesty vs. cheating
> faithfulness vs. slander
> truth vs. falsehood
> generosity vs. holding back
> diligence vs. slackness
> walking in integrity vs. crooked ways
> good counsel vs. no skillful direction
> capable wife vs. shameful wife
> righteousness vs. wickedness
> modesty vs. presumptuousness

Considering this list in relation to daily living must convince us that Proverbs really is a practical book!

---

9. How does Proverbs harmonize with the rest of the Bible?
10, 11. What further testifies to the book's divine inspiration?
12. (a) What connected poem makes up the first section of Proverbs? (b) What does it teach concerning wisdom and human conduct? (c) How does Proverbs 1:7 set the pattern for the entire book?

13. Trace the prominent threads that run through the first section of Proverbs.
14. What contrasting parallelisms make the practical teachings of Proverbs stand out?

¹⁵ The rest of this section (13:1–24:34) continues with its reminders of Jehovah's standards so that we may have insight and discernment. A list of the great variety of human situations dealt with will show what a broad coverage this book gives. It is most beneficial to have this Bible counsel on pretense, presumptuousness, keeping one's word, shrewdness, associations, child correction and training, man's view of what is right, being slow to anger, favor to the afflicted, fraud, prayer, ridicule, contentment with life's necessities, pride, unjust profit, bribery, contention, self-control, isolation, silence, partiality, quarreling, humility, luxury, care of a father and a mother, intoxicating beverages, cheating, qualities of a wife, gifts, borrowing, lending, kindness, confidence, property lines, building up the household, envy, retaliation, vanity, mild answer, meditation, and true companionship. Quite a wealth of counsel to go to for sound guidance on everyday affairs! To some, a number of these items may seem unimportant, but herein we note that the Bible does not neglect our needs even in seemingly small things. In this, Proverbs is of inestimable value.

¹⁶ **The Third Section** (25:1–29:27). Upbuilding counsel is given on such matters as honor, patience, enemies, dealing with stupid persons, having fun, flattery, jealousy, hurt caused by a friend, hunger, slander, attention to responsibility, interest, confession, results of wicked rule, arrogance, the blessings of righteous rule, child delinquency, treatment of servants, insight, and vision.

¹⁷ **The Fourth Section** (30:1-33). This is "the weighty message" attributed to Agur. After a humble admission of his own unimportance, the writer makes reference to the inability of man to create the earth and the things in it. He calls God's Word refined and a shield. He asks that the lying word be put far away from him and that he be given neither riches nor poverty. He describes an impure, proud, and greedy generation that calls down evil upon its parents. Four things that have not said "Enough!" are identified, along with four things that are too difficult to comprehend. (30: 15, 16) An adulterous woman's brazen self-acquittal is given. Then there are described four things under which the earth cannot endure, four small things instinctively wise, and four things that excel in their moving along. By apt comparisons, the writer warns that "the squeezing out of anger is what brings forth quarreling."—30:33.

¹⁸ **The Fifth Section** (31:1-31). Here is another "weighty message," that of Lemuel the king. This is in two styles of writing. The first part discusses the ruin to which one can come through a bad woman, warns how intoxicating liquor can pervert judgment, and calls for righteous judgment. The acrostic in the latter part is devoted to a classic description of a capable wife. In some detail it considers her value, pointing out that she is trusted and rewarding to her owner. Her qualities include being industrious, an early riser, a careful buyer, kind to the poor, as well as exercising foresight and speaking with wisdom. She is also alert, respected by her children, and praised by her husband. Above all, she fears Jehovah.

WHY BENEFICIAL

¹⁹ The beneficial purpose of Proverbs is stated in the opening verses: "For one to know wisdom and discipline, to discern the sayings of understanding, to receive the discipline that gives insight, righteousness and judgment and uprightness, to give to the inexperienced ones shrewdness, to a young man knowledge and thinking ability." (1:2-4) In harmony with that stated purpose, the book highlights knowledge, wisdom, and understanding, each of which is beneficial in its particular way.

²⁰ (1) *Knowledge* is man's great need, for it is not good for man to fall into ignorance. One can never acquire accurate knowledge without the fear of Jehovah, for knowledge starts with that fear. Knowledge is to be preferred rather than choice gold. Why? Through knowledge the righteous are rescued; it holds us back from hastening into sin. How we need to search for it, to take it in! Precious it is. So "incline your ear and hear the words of the wise ones, that you may apply your very heart to my knowledge."—22:17; 1:7; 8:10; 11:9; 18:15; 19:2; 20:15.

²¹ (2) *Wisdom,* the ability to use knowledge aright to the praise of Jehovah, "is the prime thing." Acquire it. Its Source is Jehovah. Lifegiving wisdom has its start in knowing and fearing Jehovah God—that is the great secret of wisdom. So fear God, not man. Wisdom personified issues a proclamation, urging all to mend their ways. Wisdom cries aloud in the very streets. Jehovah calls out to all those inexperienced ones and those in want of heart to turn aside and feed themselves with wisdom's bread. Then, with the

---

15. Give some examples of the variety of the human situations dealt with in Proverbs.
16. What upbuilding counsel is given in the third section of Proverbs?
17. (a) What "weighty message" does Agur convey? (b) What different sets of four things does he describe?

---

18. What does King Lemuel have to say about (a) a bad woman and (b) a capable wife?
19. How does Proverbs itself make known its beneficial purpose?
20. What does Proverbs say about knowledge?
21. What is the divine teaching concerning wisdom?

fear of Jehovah, they will be happy even if they have little. Many are the blessings of wisdom; greatly beneficial are its effects. Wisdom and knowledge—these are preliminary fundamentals for thinking ability, the kind that will safeguard us. As honey is beneficial and pleasant, so is wisdom. It is of more value than gold; it is a tree of life. People perish without wisdom, for wisdom preserves life; it means life.—4:7; 1:7, 20-23; 2:6, 7, 10, 11; 3:13-18, 21-26; 8:1-36; 9:1-6, 10; 10:8; 13:14; 15:16, 24; 16:16, 20-24; 24:13, 14.

22 (3) Besides knowledge and wisdom, *understanding* is vital; hence, "with all that you acquire, acquire understanding." Understanding is the ability to see a thing in its connected parts; it means discernment, always with God in mind, for man cannot lean upon his own understanding. How utterly impossible to have understanding or discernment if one works in opposition to Jehovah! To make it our own, we must keenly seek understanding as a hidden treasure. To understand, we must have knowledge. The search that the understanding one makes for knowledge is rewarded, and wisdom is in front of him. He is safeguarded from this world's innumerable pitfalls, such as from the countless bad people who might try to ensnare one to walk with them in the way of darkness. Thanks be to Jehovah God—the Source of life-giving knowledge, wisdom, and understanding!—4:7; 2:3, 4; 3:5; 15:14; 17:24; 19:8; 21:30.

23 In harmony with the beneficial purpose of Proverbs, the book presents an abundance of wise, inspired counsel to help us acquire understanding and safeguard the heart, "for out of it are the sources of life." (4:23) Following is a selection of the wise counsel stressed throughout the book.

24 *The wicked and the righteous contrasted:* The wicked one will be caught in his crooked ways, and his treasures will not save him in the day of fury. The righteous one is in line for life and will be rewarded by Jehovah.—2:21, 22; 10: 6, 7, 9, 24, 25, 27-32; 11:3-7, 18-21, 23, 30, 31; 12:2, 3, 7, 28; 13:6, 9; 14:2, 11; 15:3, 8, 29; 29:16.

25 *The need for clean morals:* Solomon warns continually against immorality. Adulterous persons will receive a plague as well as dishonor, and their reproach will not be wiped out. "Stolen waters" may seem sweet to a youth, but the prostitute descends to death and takes her inexperi-

enced victims with her. Those who fall into the deep pit of immorality are denounced by Jehovah. —2:16-19; 5:1-23; 6:20-35; 7:4-27; 9:13-18; 22: 14; 23:27, 28.

26 *The need for self-control:* Drunkenness and gluttony are condemned. All who will have God's approval must practice moderation in eating and drinking. (20:1; 21:17; 23:21, 29-35; 25:16; 31: 4, 5) Those who are slow to anger are abundant in discernment and greater than a mighty man that captures a city. (14:17, 29; 15:1, 18; 16:32; 19: 11; 25:15, 28; 29:11, 22) Self-control is also needed to avoid envy and jealousy, which is rottenness in one's bones.—14:30; 24:1; 27:4; 28:22.

27 *Wise and unwise use of speech:* Crooked speech, the slanderer, the false witness, and the falsifier will be uncovered, for they are detestable to Jehovah. (4:24; 6:16-19; 11:13; 12:17, 22; 14: 5, 25; 17:4; 19:5, 9; 20:17; 24:28; 25:18) If one's mouth speaks good things, it is a source of life; but the mouth of the foolish person precipitates his ruin. "Death and life are in the power of the tongue, and he that is loving it will eat its fruitage." (18:21) Slander, deceitful speech, flattery, and hasty words are condemned. It is the course of wisdom to speak truth, to honor God.—10:11, 13, 14; 12:13, 14, 18, 19; 13:3; 14:3; 16:27-30; 17:27, 28; 18:6-8, 20; 26:28; 29:20; 31:26.

28 *The folly of pride and the need for humility:* The proud person elevates himself to a height that he really does not have, so that he crashes. The proud in heart are detestable to Jehovah, but he gives humble ones wisdom, glory, riches, and life. —3:7; 11:2; 12:9; 13:10; 15:33; 16:5, 18, 19; 18:12; 21:4; 22:4; 26:12; 28:25, 26; 29:23.

29 *Diligence, not slothfulness:* Many are the descriptions of a lazy person. He should go to the ant for a lesson and become wise. Ah, but the diligent one—he will prosper!—1:32; 6:6-11; 10:4, 5, 26; 12:24; 13:4; 15:19; 18:9; 19:15, 24; 20:4, 13; 21: 25, 26; 22:13; 24:30-34; 26:13-16; 31:24, 25.

30 *Right association:* It is folly to associate with those who do not fear Jehovah, with wicked or stupid ones, with hot-tempered people, with talebearers, or with gluttons. Rather, associate with wise persons, and you will become still wiser.—1: 10-19; 4:14-19; 13:20; 14:7; 20:19; 22:24, 25; 28:7.

---

22. What safeguard is to be found in understanding?
23. What kind of wise counsel will next be discussed?
24. What is stated concerning the wicked and the righteous?
25. How does Proverbs warn against immorality?

26. What is said concerning self-control?
27. (a) What is unwise use of speech? (b) Why is the wise use of our lips and tongue so vital?
28. What harm does pride bring, but what benefits result from humility?
29. How is laziness to be regarded, and of what value is diligence?
30. How does Proverbs stress right association?

³¹ *Need for reproof and correction:* "The one whom Jehovah loves he reproves," and those who pay heed to this discipline are on the way to glory and life. He who hates reproof will come to dishonor.—3:11, 12; 10:17; 12:1; 13:18; 15:5, 31-33; 17:10; 19:25; 29:1.

³² *Counsel on being a good wife:* Repeatedly the Proverbs warn against a wife's being contentious and acting shamefully. The discreet, capable God-fearing wife has the law of loving-kindness on her tongue; whoever finds such a wife gets goodwill from Jehovah.—12:4; 18:22; 19:13, 14; 21:9, 19; 27:15, 16; 31:10-31.

³³ *The rearing of children:* Teach them God's commandments regularly so that they "do not forget." Bring them up from infancy in the instruction of Jehovah. Do not spare the rod when it is needed; as an expression of love, the rod and reproof give a boy wisdom. Those who rear children God's way will have wise children who will bring rejoicing and much pleasure to father and mother.—4:1-9; 13:24; 17:21; 22:6, 15; 23:13, 14, 22, 24, 25; 29:15, 17.

³⁴ *Responsibility to help others:* This is often stressed in the Proverbs. The wise one must spread knowledge about for the benefit of others. A person must also be generous in showing favor to those of little means, and in doing so, he is really lending to Jehovah, who guarantees repayment.—11:24-26; 15:7; 19:17; 24:11, 12; 28:27.

³⁵ *Reliance upon Jehovah:* Proverbs gets to the heart of our problems in counseling that we put complete trust in God. We must take notice of Jehovah in all our ways. A man may plan his course, but Jehovah must direct his steps. The name of Jehovah is a strong tower, into which the righteous run and gain protection. Hope in Jehovah and go to his Word for guidance.—3:1, 5, 6; 16:1-9; 18:10; 20:22; 28:25, 26; 30:5, 6.

³⁶ How beneficial for teaching and disciplining ourselves and others is the book of Proverbs! No phase of human relationship seems to be overlooked. Is there a person who isolates himself from his fellow worshipers of God? (18:1) Is one in a high position coming to conclusions before hearing both sides of a matter? (18:17) Is one a dangerous practical joker? (26:18, 19) Does one tend to be partial? (28:21) The tradesman in his store, the farmer in his field, the husband and wife and child—all receive wholesome instruction. Parents are helped so they can expose the many snares lurking in the path of youth. Wise ones can teach the inexperienced ones. The proverbs are practical wherever we live; the book's instruction and counsel never go out of date: "The book of Proverbs," once said American educator William Lyon Phelps, "is more up to date than this morning's newspaper."* Up-to-date, practical, and beneficial for teaching is the book of Proverbs because it is inspired of God.

³⁷ Being beneficial for setting things straight, the book of Proverbs, spoken largely by Solomon, turns men to Almighty God. So, too, did Jesus Christ, the one referred to at Matthew 12:42 as "something more than Solomon."

³⁸ How thankful we can be that this preeminently wise One is Jehovah's choice as the Kingdom Seed! His throne it is that "will be firmly established by righteousness itself," for a peaceful reign far more glorious than even that of King Solomon. Concerning that Kingdom rule, it will be said, "Loving-kindness and trueness—they safeguard the king; and by loving-kindness he has sustained his throne." That will open up an eternity of righteous government for mankind, concerning which the Proverbs also say: "Where a king is judging the lowly ones in trueness, his throne will be firmly established for all time." Thus, we come to appreciate with joy that the Proverbs not only light our pathway to knowledge, wisdom, and understanding, as well as to everlasting life, but, more important, they magnify Jehovah as the Source of true wisdom, which he dispenses through Christ Jesus, the Kingdom Heir. Proverbs adds much to our appreciation of God's Kingdom and the righteous principles by which it now governs.—Prov. 25:5; 16:12; 20:28; 29:14.

---

31. What is the wise counsel concerning reproof?
32. What fine admonition is provided on being a good wife?
33. What beneficial advice is presented on child training?
34. Of what advantage is it to take responsibility in helping others?
35. Getting to the very heart of our problems, what counsel does Proverbs give?
36. From what viewpoints may Proverbs be described as up-to-date, practical, and beneficial?

---

* *Treasury of the Christian Faith,* 1949, edited by Stuber and Clark, page 48.

---

37. How does Proverbs harmonize with the teachings of the Greater Solomon?
38. How does Proverbs add to our appreciation of God's Kingdom and its righteous principles?

Ecclesiastes

Writer: **Solomon**

Place Written: **Jerusalem**

Writing Completed: **Before 1000 B.C.E.**

HE book of Ecclesiastes was written for a lofty purpose. Solomon, as leader of a people dedicated to Jehovah, had the responsibility to hold them together in faithfulness to their dedication. He sought to fulfill this responsibility by means of the wise counsel of Ecclesiastes.

2 In Ecclesiastes 1:1 he refers to himself as "the congregator." The word in the Hebrew language is *Qo·he′leth,* and in the Hebrew Bible, the book is given that name. The Greek *Septuagint* gives the title as *Ek·kle·si·a·stes′,* meaning "a member of an ecclesia (congregation; assembly)," from which is derived the English name Ecclesiastes. However, *Qo·he′leth* is more aptly translated "The Congregator," and this is also a more fitting designation for Solomon. It conveys Solomon's purpose in writing the book.

3 In what sense was King Solomon a congregator, and to what did he do congregating? He was a congregator of his people, the Israelites, and of their companions, the temporary residents. He congregated all of these to the worship of his God, Jehovah. Previously he had built Jehovah's temple in Jerusalem, and at its dedication he had called together, or congregated, all of them to the worship of God. (1 Ki. 8:1) Now, by means of Ecclesiastes, he sought to congregate his people to worthwhile works and away from the vain, fruitless works of this world.—Eccl. 12:8-10.

4 Though Solomon is not specifically named, several passages are quite conclusive in establishing him as the writer. The congregator introduces himself as "the son of David" who "happened to be king over Israel in Jerusalem." This could apply only to King Solomon, for his successors in Jerusalem were kings over Judah only. Moreover, as the congregator writes: "I myself have greatly increased in wisdom more than anyone that happened to be before me in Jerusalem, and my own heart saw a great deal of wisdom and knowledge." (1:1, 12, 16) This fits Solomon. Ecclesiastes 12:9 tells us that "he pondered and made a thorough search, that he might arrange many proverbs in order." King Solomon spoke 3,000 proverbs. (1 Ki. 4:32) Ecclesiastes 2:4-9 tells of the writer's building program; vineyards, gardens and parks; irrigation system; arrangement of menservants and maidservants; accumulation of silver and gold; and other accomplishments. All of this was true of Solomon. When the queen of Sheba saw Solomon's wisdom and prosperity, she said: "I had not been told the half."—1 Ki. 10:7.

5 The book identifies Jerusalem as the place of writing in saying that the congregator was king "in Jerusalem." The time must have been before the year 1000 B.C.E., well along in Solomon's 40-year reign, after he had engaged in the numerous pursuits referred to in the book but before his fall into idolatry. By then he would have gained extensive knowledge of this world's occupations and its striving after material gains. At the time he would still have been in God's favor and under His inspiration.

6 How can we be sure that Ecclesiastes is "inspired of God"? Some may query its inspiration in that it does not once mention the divine name, Jehovah. However, it certainly advocates the true worship of God, and it repeatedly uses the expression *ha·′Elo·him′,* "the true God." Another objection may be raised because there are no direct quotations from Ecclesiastes in the other Bible books. However, the teachings presented and the principles laid down in the book are entirely in harmony with the remainder of the Scriptures. Clarke's *Commentary,* Volume III, page 799, states: "The book, entitled *Koheleth,* or *Ecclesiastes,* has ever been received, both by the Jewish and Christian Church, as written under the *inspiration* of the Almighty; and was held to be properly a part of the sacred canon."

---

1. For what lofty purpose was Ecclesiastes written?
2. How is this purpose expressed in Ecclesiastes' Hebrew name, thus making this more appropriate than the Greek and English names?
3. In what sense was Solomon a congregator?
4. How is Solomon established as the writer?

5. Where and when must Ecclesiastes have been written?
6. What objections have been raised as to Ecclesiastes' inspiration, but how may these be refuted?

[7] Worldly-wise "higher critics" have claimed that Ecclesiastes is not Solomon's writing or a genuine part of "all Scripture," saying that its language and its philosophy are of a later date. They ignore the fund of information that Solomon would have accumulated through his progressive development of international trade and industry, as well as from traveling dignitaries and other contacts with the outside world. (1 Ki. 4:30, 34; 9: 26-28; 10:1, 23, 24) As F. C. Cook in his *Bible Commentary,* Volume IV, page 622, writes: "The daily occupations and chosen pursuits of the great Hebrew king must have carried him far out of the sphere of ordinary Hebrew life, thought and language."

[8] However, are outside sources really needed to argue the canonicity of Ecclesiastes? An examination of the book itself will reveal not only its inward harmony but also its harmony with the rest of the Scriptures, of which it is indeed a part.

CONTENTS OF ECCLESIASTES

[9] **The vanity of man's way of life** (1:1–3:22). The opening words sound the theme of the book: "'The greatest vanity!' the congregator has said, 'the greatest vanity! Everything is vanity!'" What profit is there in mankind's toil and labor? Generations come and go, the natural cycles repeat on earth, and "there is nothing new under the sun." (1:2, 3, 9) The congregator has set his heart to seek and explore wisdom with regard to the calamitous occupations of the sons of men, but he finds that in wisdom and in folly, in exploits and in hard work, in eating and in drinking, everything is "vanity and a striving after wind." He comes to 'hate life,' a life of calamity and materialistic pursuits. —1:14; 2:11, 17.

[10] For everything there is an appointed time —yes, God has 'made everything pretty in its time.' He wants his creatures to enjoy life on earth. "I have come to know that there is nothing better for them than to rejoice and to do good during one's life; and also that every man should eat and indeed drink and see good for all his hard work. It is the gift of God." But, alas! For sinful mankind there is the same eventuality as for the beasts: "As the one dies, so the other dies; and they all have but one spirit, so that there is no superiority of the man over the beast, for everything is vanity."—3: 1, 11-13, 19.

[11] **Wise counsel for those who fear God** (4:1–7: 29). Solomon congratulates the dead, for they are free of "all the acts of oppression that are being done under the sun." Then he continues to describe vain and calamitous works. He also wisely counsels that "two are better than one" and that "a threefold cord cannot quickly be torn in two." (4:1, 2, 9, 12) He gives fine advice on the congregating of God's people: "Guard your feet whenever you go to the house of the true God; and let there be a drawing near to hear." Do not be hasty in speaking before God; let 'your words prove to be few,' and pay what you vow to God. "Fear the true God himself." When the poor are oppressed, remember that "one that is higher than the high one is watching, and there are those who are high above them." The mere servant, he observes, will have sweet sleep, but the rich man is too worried to sleep. Yet, he has come naked into the world, and for all his hard work, he can carry nothing out of the world.—5:1, 2, 4, 7, 8, 12, 15.

[12] A man may receive riches and glory, but what is the use of living "a thousand years twice over" if he has not seen what is good? It is better to take to heart the serious issues of life and death than to associate with the stupid "in the house of rejoicing"; yes, better to receive the rebuke of the wise one, for as the crackling "sound of thorns under the pot, so is the laughter of the stupid one." Wisdom is advantageous. "For wisdom is for a protection the same as money is for a protection; but the advantage of knowledge is that wisdom itself preserves alive its owners." Why, then, has the way of mankind become calamitous? "The true God made mankind upright, but they themselves have sought out many plans."—6:6; 7:4, 6, 12, 29.

[13] **The one eventuality to all** (8:1–9:12). "Keep the very order of the king," advises the congregator; but he observes that it is because sentence against bad work has not been executed speedily that "the heart of the sons of men has become fully set in them to do bad." (8:2, 11) He himself commends rejoicing, but there is another calamitous thing! All kinds of men go the same way—to death! The consciousness of the living is that they will die, "but as for the dead, they are conscious of nothing at all . . . All that your hand finds to do, do with your very power, for there is no work nor devising nor knowledge nor wisdom in Sheol, the place to which you are going."—9:5, 10.

---

7. What in Solomon's background made him eminently qualified to write the book of Ecclesiastes?
8. What is the strongest argument for the canonicity of Ecclesiastes?
9. What does the congregator find as to the occupations of the sons of men?
10. What is God's gift, but what eventuality befalls sinful man?

---

11. What wise counsel does the congregator give the God-fearing man?
12. What advice is given on the serious issues of life, and on the advantage of wisdom over money?
13. What does the congregator advise and commend, and what does he say concerning the place where man is going?

¹⁴ **Practical wisdom and man's obligation** (9:13–12:14). The congregator speaks of other calamities, such as "foolishness . . . in many high positions." He also sets forth many proverbs of practical wisdom, and he declares that even "youth and the prime of life are vanity"—unless true wisdom is heeded. He states: "Remember, now, your grand Creator in the days of your young manhood." Otherwise, old age will merely return one to the dust of the earth, to the accompaniment of the congregator's words: "The greatest vanity! . . . Everything is vanity." He himself has taught the people knowledge continually, for "the words of the wise ones are like oxgoads," spurring on to right works, but regarding worldly wisdom he warns: "To the making of many books there is no end, and much devotion to them is wearisome to the flesh." Then the congregator brings the book to its grand climax, summing up all that he has discussed on vanity and wisdom: "The conclusion of the matter, everything having been heard, is: Fear the true God and keep his commandments. For this is the whole obligation of man. For the true God himself will bring every sort of work into the judgment in relation to every hidden thing, as to whether it is good or bad."—10:6; 11:1, 10; 12: 1, 8-14.

WHY BENEFICIAL

¹⁵ Far from being a book of pessimism, Ecclesiastes is studded with bright gems of divine wisdom. When enumerating the many accomplishments that he labels vanity, Solomon does not include the building of Jehovah's temple on Mount Moriah in Jerusalem, nor the pure worship of Jehovah. He does not describe God's gift of life as vanity, but he shows that it was for the purpose of man's rejoicing and doing good. (3:12, 13; 5: 18-20; 8:15) The calamitous occupations are those that ignore God. A father may lay up wealth for his son, but a disaster destroys all and nothing remains for him. Far better it would be to provide an enduring inheritance of spiritual riches. It is calamitous to possess an abundance and not be able to enjoy it. Calamity overtakes all the worldly rich when they "go away" in death, with nothing in their hand.—5:13-15; 6:1, 2.

¹⁶ At Matthew 12:42, Christ Jesus referred to himself as "something more than Solomon." Since Solomon pictured Jesus, do we find the words of Solomon in the book *Qo·heʹleth* to be in harmony

with the teachings of Jesus? We find many parallels! For example, Jesus underlined the extensive scope of the work of God in saying, "My Father has kept working until now, and I keep working." (John 5:17) Solomon also refers to God's works: "And I saw all the work of the true God, how mankind are not able to find out the work that has been done under the sun; however much mankind keep working hard to seek, yet they do not find out. And even if they should say they are wise enough to know, they would be unable to find out." —Eccl. 8:17.

¹⁷ Both Jesus and Solomon encouraged true worshipers to congregate. (Matt. 18:20; Eccl. 4: 9-12; 5:1) Jesus' comments on "the conclusion of the system of things" and "the appointed times of the nations" are in harmony with the statement by Solomon that "for everything there is an appointed time, even a time for every affair under the heavens."—Matt. 24:3; Luke 21:24; Eccl. 3:1.

¹⁸ Above all, Jesus and his disciples join with Solomon in warning of the pitfalls of materialism. Wisdom is the true protection, for it "preserves alive its owners," says Solomon. "Keep on, then, seeking first the kingdom and his righteousness, and all these other things will be added to you," says Jesus. (Eccl. 7:12; Matt. 6:33) At Ecclesiastes 5:10 it is written: "A mere lover of silver will not be satisfied with silver, neither any lover of wealth with income. This too is vanity." Very similar is the counsel that Paul gives at 1 Timothy 6:6-19 that "the love of money is a root of all sorts of injurious things." There are similar parallel passages on other points of Bible instruction.—Eccl. 3:17—Acts 17:31; Eccl. 4:1—Jas. 5:4; Eccl. 5: 1, 2—Jas. 1:19; Eccl. 6:12—Jas. 4:14; Eccl. 7:20 —Rom. 3:23; Eccl. 8:17—Rom. 11:33.

¹⁹ The Kingdom rule of God's beloved Son, Jesus Christ, who in the flesh was a descendant of wise King Solomon, will establish a new earthly society. (Rev. 21:1-5) What Solomon wrote for the guidance of his subjects in his typical kingdom is of vital interest to all who now put their hope in God's Kingdom under Christ Jesus. Under its rule mankind will live by the same wise principles that the congregator set forth and will rejoice eternally in God's gift of happy life. Now is the time to be congregated in Jehovah's worship, in order to realize to the full the joys of life under his Kingdom. —Eccl. 3:12, 13; 12:13, 14.

---

14. (a) What practical wisdom does the congregator stress? (b) What is the conclusion of the matter?
15. How does Solomon distinguish between calamitous occupations and worthwhile works?
16. How does *Qo·heʹleth,* or Ecclesiastes, harmonize with the teachings of Jesus?

17. What other parallels are to be found in Jesus' and Solomon's words?
18. In giving what warnings do Jesus and his disciples join with Solomon?
19. With what happy prospect may we congregate in Jehovah's worship today?

The Song of Solomon

Writer: Solomon

Place Written: Jerusalem

Writing Completed: **c. 1020 B.C.E.**

"THE whole world was not worthy of the day in which this sublime Song was given to Israel." Thus the Jewish "rabbi" Akiba, who lived in the first century of the Common Era, expressed his appreciation for The Song of Solomon.* The book's title is a contraction of the opening words, "The superlative song, which is Solomon's." According to the Hebrew word-for-word text, it is the "Song of the songs," denoting superlative excellence, similar to the expression "heavens of the heavens," for the highest heavens. (Deut. 10:14) It is not a collection of songs but one song, "a song of the utmost perfection, one of the best that existed, or had ever been penned."#

2 King Solomon of Jerusalem was the writer of this song, as is borne out by its introduction. He was highly qualified to write this supremely beautiful example of Hebrew poetry. (1 Ki. 4:32) It is an idyllic poem loaded with meaning and most colorful in its description of beauty. The reader who can visualize the Oriental setting will appreciate this still more. (Song of Sol. 4:11, 13; 5:11; 7:4) The occasion for its writing was a unique one. The great king Solomon, glorious in wisdom, mighty in power, and dazzling in the luster of his material wealth, which evoked the admiration even of the queen of Sheba, could not impress a simple country girl with whom he fell in love. Because of the constancy of her love for a shepherd boy, the king lost out. The book, therefore, could rightly be called The Song of Solomon's Frustrated Love. Jehovah God inspired him to compose this song for the benefit of Bible readers of the ages to follow. He wrote it in Jerusalem. Perhaps this was about 1020 B.C.E., some years after the temple had been completed. By the time he wrote the song, Solomon had "sixty queens and eighty concubines," compared with "seven hundred wives, princesses, and three hundred concubines" at the end of his reign.—Song of Sol. 6:8; 1 Ki. 11:3.

3 The canonicity of The Song of Solomon was wholly unchallenged in early times. It was regarded as an integral and inspired portion of the Hebrew canon long before the Common Era. It was embodied in the Greek *Septuagint.* Josephus inserted it in his catalog of the sacred books. Therefore, it has the same evidence for its canonicity as is commonly adduced for any other book of the Hebrew Scriptures.

4 Some, however, have questioned the book's canonicity on the ground that there is no reference to God in it. The absence of any mention of God would not disqualify the book any more than the mere presence of the word "God" would make it canonical. The divine name does appear in its abbreviated form at chapter 8, verse 6, where love is said to be "the flame of Jah." The book unquestionably forms a part of those writings to which Jesus Christ referred with approval when he said: "You are searching the Scriptures, because you think that by means of them you will have everlasting life." (John 5:39) Moreover, its powerful portrayal of the exquisite quality of mutual love, such as exists, in a spiritual sense, between Christ and his "bride," marks The Song of Solomon for its unique place in the Bible canon.—Rev. 19:7, 8; 21:9.

CONTENTS OF THE SONG OF SOLOMON

5 The material in the book is presented through a series of conversations. There is a constant change of speakers. The persons with speaking parts are Solomon the king of Jerusalem, a shepherd, his beloved Shulammite, her brothers, court

---

* The Jewish Mishnah (*Yadayim* 3:5).
# Clarke's *Commentary,* Vol. III, page 841.

---

1. In what respect is this the "Song of the songs"?
2. (a) Who was the writer of The Song of Solomon, what were his qualifications, and why could the book be called a song of frustrated love? (b) Where was the book written, and when?

---

3. What evidence is there for the Song of Solomon's canonicity?
4. (a) Does the absence of the word "God" argue against the canonicity of The Song of Solomon? (b) What marks it for its unique place in the Bible canon?
5. (a) How are the characters in the drama identified? (b) What touching theme is expressed?

ladies ("daughters of Jerusalem"), and women of Jerusalem ("daughters of Zion"). (Song of Sol. 1: 5-7; 3:5, 11) They are identified by what they say of themselves or by what is said to them. The drama unfolds near Shunem, or Shulem, where Solomon is camped with his court entourage. It expresses a touching theme—the love of a country girl of the village of Shunem for her shepherd companion.

6 **The Shulammite maiden in Solomon's camp** (1:1-14). The maiden appears in the royal tents into which the king has brought her, but she is anxious only to see her shepherd lover. With longing for her loved one, she speaks out as if he were present. The ladies of the court who wait on the king, the "daughters of Jerusalem," look curiously at the Shulammite because of her swarthy complexion. She explains that she is sunburned from caring for her brothers' vineyards. She then speaks to her lover as though she were free and asks where she might find him. The court ladies bid her to go out and pasture her flock by the tents of the shepherds.

7 Solomon comes forward. He is unwilling to let her go. He praises her beauty and promises to adorn her with "circlets of gold" and "studs of silver." The Shulammite resists his advances and lets him know that the only love she can feel is for her beloved.—1:11.

8 **The shepherd lover appears** (1:15–2:2). The Shulammite's lover makes his way into Solomon's camp and encourages her. He assures her of his love. The Shulammite yearns for the nearness of her dear one and the simple pleasure of dwelling at one with him out in the fields and woods.

9 The Shulammite is a modest girl. "A mere saffron of the coastal plain I am," she says. Her shepherd lover thinks her to be without compare, saying: "Like a lily among thorny weeds, so is my girl companion among the daughters."—2:1, 2.

10 **The maiden longs for her shepherd** (2:3–3:5). Separated again from her lover, the Shulammite shows how she esteems him above all others, and she tells the daughters of Jerusalem that they are under oath not to try to arouse in her unwanted love for another. The Shulammite remembers the time when her shepherd answered her call and invited her to the hills in springtime. She sees

him climbing upon the mountains, leaping with joy. She hears him cry out to her: "Rise up, come, O girl companion of mine, my beautiful one, and come away." However, her brothers, who were not sure of her steadiness, got angry and set her to work in guarding the vineyards. She declares, "My dear one is mine and I am his," and she pleads for him to hurry to her side.—2:13, 16.

11 The Shulammite describes her detainment in Solomon's camp. At night in bed, she longs for her shepherd. Again she reminds the daughters of Jerusalem that they are under oath not to awaken unwanted love in her.

12 **The Shulammite in Jerusalem** (3:6–5:1). Solomon returns to Jerusalem in regal splendor, and the people admire his cortege. In this critical hour, the shepherd lover does not fail the Shulammite. He follows his girl companion, who is veiled, and gets in touch with her. He strengthens his beloved with warm expressions of endearment. She tells him she wants to get free and leave the city, and then he bursts into an ecstasy of love: "You are altogether beautiful, O girl companion of mine." (4:7) A mere glimpse of her makes his heart beat faster. Her expressions of endearment are better than wine, her fragrance is like that of Lebanon, and her skin is like a paradise of pomegranates. The maiden invites her dear one to come into "his garden," and he accepts. Friendly women of Jerusalem encourage them: "Eat, O companions! Drink and become drunk with expressions of endearment!"—4:16; 5:1.

13 **The maiden's dream** (5:2–6:3). The Shulammite tells the court ladies of a dream, in which she hears a knock. Her dear one is outside, pleading for her to let him in. But she is in bed. When she finally gets up to open the door, he has disappeared into the night. She goes out after him, but he cannot be found. The watchmen mistreat her. She tells the court ladies that if they see her lover, they are under obligation to tell him that she is lovesick. They ask her what makes him so outstanding. She launches into an exquisite description of him, saying he is "dazzling and ruddy, the most conspicuous of ten thousand." (5:10) The court women ask her of his whereabouts. She says he has gone to shepherd among the gardens.

14 **Solomon's final advances** (6:4–8:4). King Solomon approaches the Shulammite. Again he tells

---

6. What conversation takes place between the maiden and the court ladies of Solomon's camp?
7. What advances does Solomon make, but with what result?
8. How does the maiden's lover encourage her? For what does she yearn?
9. How do the girl and her lover appraise her beauty?
10. What does the maiden recall concerning her love?

11. Of what oath does the Shulammite again remind the daughters of Jerusalem?
12. What further encouragement does her lover give when the maiden is taken by Solomon to Jerusalem?
13. What dream does the maiden have, and how does she describe her lover to the court ladies?
14. Despite all his arts, how does Solomon lose out in his quest?

her how beautiful she is, more lovely than "sixty queens and eighty concubines," but she rejects him. (6:8) She is here only because an errand of service had brought her near his camp. 'What do you see in me?' she asks. Solomon takes advantage of her innocent question to tell her of her beauty, from the soles of her feet to the crown of her head, but the maiden resists all his arts. Courageously she declares her devotion to her shepherd, crying out for him. For the third time, she reminds the daughters of Jerusalem that they are under oath not to awaken love in her against her will. Solomon lets her go home. He has lost out in his quest for the Shulammite's love.

[15] **The Shulammite returns** (8:5-14). Her brothers see her approaching, but she is not alone. She is "leaning upon her dear one." She calls to mind having met her lover under an apple tree and declares the unbreakableness of her love for him. Some of her brothers' earlier comments about their concern over her when "a little sister" are mentioned, but she declares she has proved herself a mature and stable woman. (8:8) Let her brothers now consent to her marriage. King Solomon can have his wealth! She is content with her one vineyard, for she loves one who is exclusively dear to her. In her case this love is as strong as death and its blazings as "the flame of Jah." Insistence on exclusive devotion "as unyielding as Sheol" has triumphed and has led to the glorious heights of union with her shepherd lover.—8:5, 6.

WHY BENEFICIAL

[16] What lessons are taught in this song of love that the man of God might find beneficial today? Faithfulness, loyalty, and integrity to godly principles are clearly shown. The song teaches the beauty of virtue and innocence in a true lover. It teaches that genuine love remains unconquerable, inextinguishable, unpurchasable. Young Christian men and women as well as husbands and wives can benefit from this fitting example of integrity when temptations arise and allurements present themselves.

---

15. (a) With what request does the maiden return to her brothers? (b) How has exclusive devotion triumphed?
16. What valuable lessons are taught in this song?

[17] But this inspired song is also most beneficial for the Christian congregation as a whole. It was recognized as part of the inspired Scriptures by the Christians of the first century, one of whom wrote: "All the things that were written aforetime were written for our instruction, that through our endurance and through the comfort from the Scriptures we might have hope." (Rom. 15:4) This same inspired writer, Paul, could well have had in mind the Shulammite girl's exclusive love for her shepherd when he wrote to the Christian congregation: "For I am jealous over you with a godly jealousy, for I personally promised you in marriage to one husband that I might present you as a chaste virgin to the Christ." Paul also wrote of the love of Christ for the congregation as that of a husband for a wife. (2 Cor. 11:2; Eph. 5:23-27) Not only is Jesus Christ the Fine Shepherd for them but he is also their King who holds out to his anointed followers the indescribable joy of "marriage" with him in the heavens.—Rev. 19:9; John 10:11.

[18] Certainly these anointed followers of Christ Jesus can benefit much from the example of the Shulammite girl. They also must be loyal in their love, unenticed by the materialistic glitter of the world, keeping balance in their integrity clear through to the attainment of the reward. They have their minds set on the things above and 'seek first the Kingdom.' They welcome the loving endearments of their Shepherd, Jesus Christ. They are overjoyed in knowing that this dear one, though unseen, is close beside them, calling on them to take courage and conquer the world. Having that unquenchable love, as strong as "the flame of Jah," for their Shepherd King, they will indeed overcome and be united with him as fellow heirs in the glorious Kingdom of the heavens. Thus will Jah's name be sanctified!—Matt. 6:33; John 16:33.

---

17. (a) How does Paul show this song to have been written for the instruction of the Christian congregation? (b) Why may Paul well have had it in mind in writing to the Corinthians and the Ephesians? (c) What interesting comparisons may be made with inspired writings of John?
18. In what way may the anointed followers of Christ Jesus benefit from the example of the Shulammite girl?

Isaiah

Writer: **Isaiah**
Place Written: **Jerusalem**
Writing Completed: **After 732 B.C.E.**
Time Covered:
c. 778–after 732 B.C.E.

THE menacing shadow of the cruel Assyrian monarch hung heavy over the other empires and lesser kingdoms of the Middle East. The whole area was alive with talk of conspiracy and confederation. (Isa. 8:9-13) Apostate Israel to the north would soon fall victim to this international intrigue, while Judah's kings to the south were reigning precariously. (2 Ki., chaps. 15-21) New weapons of war were being developed and put into action, adding to the terror of the times. (2 Chron. 26:14, 15) Where could anyone look for protection and salvation? Although the name of Jehovah was on the lips of the people and the priests in the little kingdom of Judah, their hearts turned far off in other directions, first to Assyria and then down to Egypt. (2 Ki. 16:7; 18:21) Faith in Jehovah's power waned. Where it was not outright idolatry, there prevailed a hypocritical way of worship, based on formalism and not the true fear of God.

² Who, then, would speak for Jehovah? Who would declare his saving power? "Here I am! Send me," came the ready response. The speaker was Isaiah, who had already been prophesying before this. It was the year that leprous King Uzziah died, about 778 B.C.E. (Isa. 6:1, 8) The name Isaiah means "Salvation of Jehovah," which is the same meaning, though written in the reverse order, of the name Jesus ("Jehovah Is Salvation"). From start to finish, Isaiah's prophecy highlights this fact, that Jehovah is salvation.

³ Isaiah was the son of Amoz (not to be confused with Amos, another prophet from Judah). (1:1) The Scriptures are silent as to his birth and death, though Jewish tradition has him sawn asunder by wicked King Manasseh. (Compare Hebrews 11: 37.) His writings show him stationed in Jerusalem with his prophetess wife and at least two sons with prophetic names. (Isa. 7:3; 8:1, 3) He served during the time of at least four kings of Judah: Uzziah, Jotham, Ahaz, and Hezekiah; evidently beginning about 778 B.C.E. (when Uzziah died, or possibly earlier) and continuing at least till after 732 B.C.E. (Hezekiah's 14th year), or no less than 46 years. No doubt he had also committed his prophecy to writing by this latter date. (1:1; 6:1; 36:1) Other prophets of his day were Micah in Judah and, to the north, Hosea and Oded.—Mic. 1:1; Hos. 1:1; 2 Chron. 28:6-9.

⁴ That Jehovah commanded Isaiah to write down prophetic judgments is established by Isaiah 30:8: "Now come, write it upon a tablet with them, and inscribe it even in a book, that it may serve for a future day, for a witness to time indefinite." The ancient Jewish rabbis recognized Isaiah as the writer and included the book as the first book of the major prophets (Isaiah, Jeremiah, and Ezekiel).

⁵ Though some have pointed to the book's change of style from chapter 40 onward as indicating a different writer, or "Second Isaiah," the change in subject matter should be sufficient to explain this. There is much evidence that Isaiah wrote the entire book that bears his name. For example, the oneness of the book is indicated by the expression, "the Holy One of Israel," which appears 12 times in chapters 1 to 39, and 13 times in chapters 40 to 66, a total of 25 times; whereas it appears only 6 times throughout the rest of the Hebrew Scriptures. The apostle Paul also testifies to the unity of the book by quoting from all parts of the prophecy and crediting the whole work to one writer, Isaiah.—Compare Romans 10:16, 20; 15:12 with Isaiah 53:1; 65:1; 11:1.

⁶ Interestingly, starting in the year 1947, some ancient documents were brought out of the darkness of caves not far from Khirbet Qumran, near the northwest shore of the Dead Sea. These were

1. What was the situation in the Middle East, and particularly in Israel and Judah, in the eighth century B.C.E.?
2. (a) Who answered the call to speak for Jehovah, and when? (b) What is significant about this prophet's name?
3. (a) What is known concerning Isaiah? (b) Throughout what period did he prophesy, and who were other prophets of his day?

4. What indicates that Isaiah was the writer of the book?
5. What testifies to the unity of the book of Isaiah?
6. How does the Dead Sea Scroll of Isaiah give convincing proof (a) that our Bibles today represent the original inspired writing and (b) that the entire book was written by the one Isaiah?

the Dead Sea Scrolls, which included the prophecy of Isaiah. This is beautifully written in well-preserved pre-Masoretic Hebrew and is some 2,000 years old, from the end of the second century B.C.E. Its text is thus about a thousand years older than the oldest existing manuscript of the Masoretic text, on which modern translations of the Hebrew Scriptures are based. There are some minor variations of spelling and some differences in grammatical construction, but it does not vary doctrinally from the Masoretic text. Here is convincing proof that our Bibles today contain the original inspired message of Isaiah. Moreover, these ancient scrolls refute the critics' claims of two "Isaiahs," since chapter 40 begins on the last line of the column of writing containing chapter 39, the opening sentence being completed in the next column. Thus, the copyist was obviously unaware of any supposed change in writer or of any division in the book at this point.*

⁷ There is abundant proof of the authenticity of Isaiah's book. Aside from Moses, no other prophet is more often quoted by the Christian Bible writers. There is likewise a wealth of historical and archaeological evidence that proves it genuine, such as the historical records of the Assyrian monarchs, including Sennacherib's hexagonal prism on which he gives his own account of the siege of Jerusalem.# (Isa., chaps. 36, 37) The heap of ruins that was once Babylon still bears witness to the fulfillment of Isaiah 13:17-22.△ There was a living testimony in each one of the thousands of Jews that marched back from Babylon, freed by a king whose name, Cyrus, had been penned by Isaiah nearly 200 years earlier. It may well be that Cyrus was later shown this prophetic writing, for, on freeing the Jewish remnant, he spoke of being commissioned by Jehovah to do so.—Isa. 44:28; 45:1; Ezra 1:1-3.

⁸ Outstanding in the book of Isaiah are the Messianic prophecies. Isaiah has been called "the Evangelist prophet," so numerous are the predictions fulfilled in the events of Jesus' life. Chapter 53, for long a "mystery chapter," not only to the Ethiopian eunuch referred to in Acts chapter 8 but to the Jewish people as a whole, foretells so vividly the treatment accorded Jesus that it is like an eyewitness account. The Christian Greek Scriptures record the prophetic fulfillments of this re-markable chapter of Isaiah, as the following comparisons show: vs. 1—John 12:37, 38; vs. 2 —John 19:5-7; vs. 3—Mark 9:12; vs. 4—Matthew 8:16, 17; vs. 5—1 Peter 2:24; vs. 6—1 Peter 2:25; vs. 7—Acts 8:32, 35; vs. 8—Acts 8:33; vs. 9 —Matthew 27:57-60; vs. 10—Hebrews 7:27; vs. 11—Romans 5:18; vs. 12—Luke 22:37. Who but God could be the source of such accurate forecasting?

CONTENTS OF ISAIAH

⁹ The first six chapters give the setting in Judah and Jerusalem and relate Judah's guilt before Jehovah and Isaiah's commissioning. Chapters 7 to 12 deal with threatened enemy invasions and the promise of relief by the Prince of Peace commissioned by Jehovah. Chapters 13 to 35 contain a series of pronouncements against many nations and a forecast of salvation to be provided by Jehovah. Historic events of Hezekiah's reign are described in chapters 36 to 39. The remaining chapters, 40 to 66, have as their theme the release from Babylon, the return of the Jewish remnant, and the restoration of Zion.

¹⁰ **Isaiah's message "concerning Judah and Jerusalem"** (1:1–6:13). See him there in sackcloth and sandals as he stands in Jerusalem and cries out: Dictators! People! Listen! Your nation is sick from head to toe, and you have wearied Jehovah with your bloodstained hands upraised in prayer. Come, set matters straight with him, that scarlet sins may be made white like snow. In the final part of the days, the mountain of Jehovah's house will be lifted up, and all nations will stream to it for instruction. No more will they learn war. Jehovah will be raised on high and sanctified. But at present Israel and Judah, though planted a choice vine, produce grapes of lawlessness. They make good bad and bad good, for they are wise in their own eyes.

¹¹ "I, however, got to see Jehovah, sitting on a throne lofty and lifted up," says Isaiah. Along with the vision comes Jehovah's commission: "Go, and you must say to this people, 'Hear again and again.'" For how long? "Until the cities actually crash in ruins."—6:1, 9, 11.

¹² **Threatened enemy invasions and promise of relief** (7:1–12:6). Jehovah uses Isaiah and his sons as prophetic 'signs and miracles' to show that

---

* Insight on the Scriptures, Vol. 1, pages 1221-3.
# Insight on the Scriptures, Vol. 1, page 957; Vol. 2, pages 894-5.
△ Insight on the Scriptures, Vol. 2, page 324.

---

7. What abundant proof is there concerning Isaiah's authenticity?
8. How is inspiration proved by fulfillment of the Messianic prophecies?

9. Into what divisions do the contents of Isaiah fall?
10. (a) Why does Isaiah call on the nation to set matters straight? (b) What does he prophesy for the final part of the days?
11. Along with what vision does Isaiah receive his commission?
12. (a) How are Isaiah and his sons used as prophetic signs? (b) What outstanding promise is given in Isaiah chapter 9?

first the combine of Syria and Israel against Judah will fail but in time Judah will go into captivity with only a remnant returning. A maiden will become pregnant and bear a son. His name? Immanuel (meaning, "With Us Is God"). Let the combined enemies against Judah take note! "Gird yourselves, and be shattered to pieces!" There will be hard times, but then a great light will shine upon God's people. For a child has been born to us, "and his name will be called Wonderful Counselor, Mighty God, Eternal Father, Prince of Peace." —7:14; 8:9, 18; 9:6.

¹³ "Aha, the Assyrian," Jehovah cries, "the rod for my anger." After using that rod against "an apostate nation," God will cut down the insolent Assyrian himself. Later, "a mere remnant will return." (10:5, 6, 21) See now a sprout, a twig from the stump of Jesse (David's father)! This "twig" will rule in righteousness, and by him there will be enjoyment for all creation, with no harm or ruin, "because the earth will certainly be filled with the knowledge of Jehovah as the waters are covering the very sea." (11:1, 9) With this one as signal for the nations, a highway goes out from Assyria for the returning remnant. There will be exultation in drawing water from the springs of salvation and making melody to Jehovah.

¹⁴ **Pronouncing Babylon's doom** (13:1–14:27). Isaiah now looks past the Assyrian's day into the time of Babylon's zenith. Listen! The sound of numerous people, the uproar of kingdoms, of nations gathered together! Jehovah is mustering the army of war! It is a dark day for Babylon. Amazed faces flame, and hearts melt. The pitiless Medes will tumble Babylon, "the decoration of kingdoms." She is to become an uninhabited desolation and a haunt of wild creatures "for generation after generation." (13:19, 20) The dead in Sheol are stirred to receive the king of Babylon. Maggots become his couch and worms his covering. What a comedown for this 'shining one, the son of the dawn'! (14:12) He aspired to elevate his throne but has become a carcass thrown out, as Jehovah sweeps Babylon with the broom of annihilation. No name, no remnant, no progeny, no posterity, are to remain!

¹⁵ **International desolations** (14:28–23:18). Isaiah now points back to Philistia along the Mediterranean Sea and then to Moab, southeast of the Dead Sea. He directs his prophecy up beyond Israel's northern boundary to Syrian Damascus, dips

deep south into Ethiopia, and moves up the Nile into Egypt, with God's judgments producing desolation all along the way. He tells of the Assyrian king Sargon, the predecessor of Sennacherib, sending commander Tartan against the Philistine city of Ashdod, west of Jerusalem. At this time Isaiah is told to strip and go naked and barefoot for three years. Thus he vividly portrays the futility of trusting in Egypt and Ethiopia, who, with "buttocks stripped," will be led captive by the Assyrian.—20:4.

¹⁶ A lookout upon his watchtower sees the fall of Babylon and her gods, and he sees adversities for Edom. Jehovah himself addresses Jerusalem's boisterous people who are saying, "Let there be eating and drinking, for tomorrow we shall die." 'Die you shall,' says Jehovah. (22:13, 14) The ships of Tarshish too are to howl, and Sidon is to be ashamed, for Jehovah has given counsel against Tyre, to "treat with contempt all the honorable ones of the earth."—23:9.

¹⁷ **Jehovah's judgment and salvation** (24:1–27: 13). But look now at Judah! Jehovah is emptying the land. People and priest, servant and master, buyer and seller—all must go, for they have bypassed God's laws and broken the indefinitely lasting covenant. But in time he will turn his attention to the prisoners and gather them. He is a stronghold and refuge. He will set a banquet in his mountain and swallow up death forever, wiping tears from off all faces. "This is our God" will be said. "This is Jehovah." (25:9) Judah has a city with salvation for walls. Continuous peace is for those trusting in Jehovah, "for in Jah Jehovah is the Rock of times indefinite." But the wicked "simply will not learn righteousness." (26:4, 10) Jehovah will slay his adversaries, but he will restore Jacob.

¹⁸ **God's indignation and blessings** (28:1–35: 10). Woe to Ephraim's drunkards, whose "decoration of beauty" must fade! But Jehovah is to "become as a crown of decoration and as a garland of beauty" to the remnant of his people. (28:1, 5) However, the braggarts of Jerusalem look to a lie for refuge, rather than to the tried and precious foundation stone in Zion. A flash flood will wash them all away. Jerusalem's prophets are asleep, and God's book is sealed to them. Lips draw close, but hearts are far away. Yet the day will come

---

13. (a) What outcome awaits the insolent Assyrian? (b) What will result from the rule of the "twig" from Jesse?
14. What comedown is foretold for Babylon?
15. Concerning what international desolations does Isaiah prophesy?

16. What calamities are seen for Babylon, Edom, and Jerusalem's boisterous ones, as well as for Sidon and Tyre?
17. What judgment and what restoration are foretold for Judah?
18, 19. (a) What contrasting woes and joys are proclaimed for Ephraim and Zion? (b) In what capacities is Jehovah to save and govern his people?

when the deaf will hear the words of the book. The blind will see and the meek rejoice.

[19] Woe to those who go down to Egypt for refuge! This stubborn people want smooth, deceptive visions. They will be cut off, but Jehovah will restore a remnant. These will see their Grand Instructor, and they will scatter their images, calling them "mere dirt!" (30:22) Jehovah is Jerusalem's true Defender. A king will rule in righteousness, together with his princes. He will bring in peace, quietness, and security to time indefinite. Treachery will cause the messengers of peace to weep bitterly, but to his own people the Majestic One, Jehovah, is Judge, Statute-Giver, and King, and he himself will save them. No resident will then say: "I am sick."—33:24.

[20] Jehovah's indignation must break out against the nations. Carcasses will stink, and mountains will melt with blood. Edom must be desolated. But for Jehovah's repurchased ones, the desert plain will blossom, and "the glory of Jehovah, the splendor of our God," will appear. (35:2) The blind, the deaf, and the speechless will be healed, and the Way of Holiness will be opened for the redeemed of Jehovah as they return to Zion with rejoicing.

[21] **Jehovah turns back Assyria in Hezekiah's day** (36:1–39:8). Is Isaiah's exhortation to rely on Jehovah practical? Can it stand the test? In the 14th year of Hezekiah's reign, Sennacherib of Assyria makes a scythelike sweep through Palestine and diverts some of his troops to try to intimidate Jerusalem. His Hebrew-speaking spokesman, Rabshakeh, hurls taunting questions at the people lining the city's walls: 'What is your confidence? Egypt? A crushed reed! Jehovah? There is no god that can deliver from the king of Assyria!' (36:4, 6, 18, 20) In obedience to the king, the people give no answer.

[22] Hezekiah prays to Jehovah for salvation for His name's sake, and through Isaiah, Jehovah answers that He will put his hook in the Assyrian's nose and lead him back the way he has come. An angel strikes 185,000 Assyrians dead, and Sennacherib scurries back home, where his own sons later murder him in his pagan temple.

[23] Hezekiah becomes deathly ill. However, Jehovah miraculously causes the shadow produced by the sun to retreat, as a sign that Hezekiah will be healed, and 15 years are added to Hezekiah's life. In thankfulness he composes a beautiful psalm of praise to Jehovah. When the king of Babylon sends messengers, hypocritically congratulating him on his recovery, Hezekiah indiscreetly shows them the royal treasures. As a result, Isaiah prophesies that everything in Hezekiah's house will one day be carried to Babylon.

[24] **Jehovah comforts his witnesses** (40:1–44:28). The opening word of chapter 40, "Comfort," well describes the rest of Isaiah. A voice in the wilderness cries out: "Clear up the way of Jehovah, you people!" (40:1, 3) There is good news for Zion. Jehovah shepherds his flock, carrying young lambs in his bosom. From lofty heavens he looks down on earth's circle. To what can he be compared for greatness? He gives full power and dynamic energy to the tired and weary ones who hope in him. He declares the molten images of the nations to be wind and unreality. His chosen one will be as a covenant for the peoples and a light of the nations to open blind eyes. Jehovah says to Jacob, "I myself have loved you," and he calls to sunrising, sunset, north, and south: 'Give up! Bring back my sons and my daughters.' (43:4, 6) With court in session, he challenges the gods of the nations to produce witnesses to prove their godship. Israel's people are Jehovah's witnesses, his servant, testifying that he is God and Deliverer. To Jeshurun ("Upright One," Israel) he promises his spirit and then casts shame on the makers of see-nothing, know-nothing images. Jehovah is the Repurchaser of his people; Jerusalem will again be inhabited and its temple rebuilt.

[25] **Vengeance upon Babylon** (45:1–48:22). For the sake of Israel, Jehovah names Cyrus to vanquish Babylon. Men will be made to know that Jehovah alone is God, the Creator of the heavens, the earth, and man upon it. He mocks Babylon's gods Bel and Nebo, for only He can tell the finale from the beginning. The virgin daughter of Babylon is to sit in the dust, dethroned and naked, and the multitude of her counselors will be burned up like stubble. Jehovah tells the 'iron-necked, copper-headed' Israelite idol worshipers that they could have peace, righteousness, and prosperity by listening to him, but 'there is no peace for the wicked ones.'—48:4, 22.

[26] **Zion comforted** (49:1–59:21). Giving his servant as a light of the nations, Jehovah cries to

---

20. What indignation is to break out against the nations, but what blessing awaits the restored remnant?
21. The Assyrian hurls what taunts at Jerusalem?
22. How does Jehovah answer Hezekiah's prayer, and how does He fulfill Isaiah's prophecy?
23. (a) What occasions Hezekiah's composing a psalm to Jehovah? (b) What indiscretion does he commit, resulting in what prophecy by Isaiah?

---

24. (a) What news of comfort does Jehovah proclaim? (b) Can the gods of the nations compare with Jehovah for greatness, and what witness does he call for?
25. What are men to come to know by Jehovah's judgments on Babylon and her false gods?
26. How will Zion be comforted?

those in darkness: "Come out!" (49:9) Zion will be comforted, and her wilderness will become like Eden, the garden of Jehovah, overflowing with exultation, rejoicing, thanksgiving, and the voice of melody. Jehovah will make the heavens go up in smoke, the earth wear out like a garment, and its inhabitants die like a mere gnat. So why fear the reproach of mortal men? The bitter goblet that Jerusalem has drunk must now pass to the nations that have trampled on her.

27 'Wake up, O Zion, and rise from the dust!' See the messenger, bounding over the mountains with good news and calling to Zion, "Your God has become king!" (52:1, 2, 7) Get out of the unclean place and keep yourselves clean, you in Jehovah's service. The prophet now describes 'Jehovah's servant.' (53:11) He is a man despised, avoided, carrying our pains and yet accounted as stricken by God. He was pierced for our transgressions, but he healed us by his wounds. Like a sheep brought to the slaughter, he did no violence and he spoke no deception. He gave his soul as a guilt offering to bear the errors of many people.

28 As husbandly owner, Jehovah tells Zion to cry out joyfully because of her coming fruitfulness. Though afflicted and tempest-tossed, she will become a city of sapphire foundations, ruby battlements, and gates of fiery glowing stones. Her sons, taught by Jehovah, will enjoy abundant peace, and no weapon formed against them will be successful. "Hey there, all you thirsty ones!" cries Jehovah. If they come, he will conclude with them his "covenant respecting the loving-kindnesses to David"; he will give a leader and commander as a witness to the national groups. (55:1-4) God's thoughts are infinitely higher than man's, and his word will have certain success. Eunuchs keeping his law, no matter of what nationality, will receive a name better than sons and daughters. Jehovah's house will be called a house of prayer for all the peoples.

29 As the High and Lofty One, whose name is holy, Jehovah tells the sex-crazy idolaters that he will not contend with Israel to time indefinite. Their pious fasts are cover-ups for wickedness. The hand of Jehovah is not too short to save, nor his ear too heavy to hear, but it is 'the very errors of you people that have become the things causing division between you and your God,' says Isaiah. (59:2) That is why they hope for light but grope in darkness. On the other hand, Jehovah's spirit upon his faithful covenant people guarantees that his word will remain in their mouth to all future generations, irremovably.

30 **Jehovah beautifies Zion** (60:1-64:12). "Arise, O woman, shed forth light, for . . . the very glory of Jehovah has shone forth." In contrast, thick gloom envelops the earth. (60:1, 2) At that time Zion will lift her eyes and become radiant, and her heart will quiver as she sees the resources of the nations coming to her on a heaving mass of camels. Like clouds of flying doves, they will flock to her. Foreigners will build her walls, kings will minister to her, and her gates will never close. Her God must become her beauty, and he will swiftly multiply one into a thousand and a small one into a mighty nation. God's servant exclaims that Jehovah's spirit is upon him, anointing him to tell this good news. Zion gets a new name, My Delight Is in Her (Hephzibah), and her land is called Owned as a Wife (Beulah). (62:4, footnote) The order goes out to bank up the highway back from Babylon and to raise a signal in Zion.

31 Out of Bozrah in Edom comes one in bloodred garments. In his anger he has stamped down people in a wine trough, causing them to spurt blood. Jehovah's people feel keenly their unclean condition and offer a poignant prayer, saying, 'O Jehovah, you are our Father. We are the clay, and you are our Potter. Do not be indignant, O Jehovah, to the extreme. We are all your people.'—64:8, 9.

32 **"New heavens and a new earth"!** (65:1-66:24). The people who have abandoned Jehovah for gods of "Good Luck" and "Destiny" will starve and suffer shame. (65:11) God's own servants will rejoice in abundance. Look! Jehovah is creating new heavens and a new earth. What joyfulness and exultation are to be found in Jerusalem and her people! Houses will be built and vineyards planted, while wolf and lamb feed as one. There will be no harm or ruin.

33 The heavens are his throne and the earth is his footstool, so what house can men build for Jehovah? A nation is to be born in one day, and all lovers of Jerusalem are invited to rejoice as Jehovah extends to her peace just like a river. Against his enemies he will come as a very fire—storm-wind chariots paying back his anger against all disobedient flesh, with sheer rage and flames of

---

27. What good news is proclaimed to Zion, and what is prophesied concerning 'Jehovah's servant'?
28. How is the coming blessedness of Zion described, and in connection with what covenant?
29. What does Jehovah tell the idolaters, but what assurance does he give his people?

---

30. How does Jehovah beautify Zion, as illustrated by what new names?
31. Who comes from Edom, and what prayer do God's people utter?
32. In contrast with those who abandon Jehovah, at what may Jehovah's own people exult?
33. What rejoicing, glory, and permanence are foretold for lovers of Jerusalem?

fire. Messengers will go out among all nations and to faraway islands to tell of his glory. His new heavens and earth are to be permanent. Similarly, those serving him and their offspring will keep standing. It is either this or everlasting death.

WHY BENEFICIAL

[34] Viewed from every angle, the prophetic book of Isaiah is a most beneficial gift from Jehovah God. It beams forth the lofty thoughts of God. (Isa. 55:8-11) Public speakers of Bible truths can draw on Isaiah as a treasure-house of vivid illustrations that strike home with forcefulness like that of Jesus' parables. Isaiah powerfully impresses us with the foolishness of the man who uses the same tree both for fuel and for making an idol of worship. He makes us feel the discomfort of the man on a couch that is too short with a sheet that is too narrow, and he makes us hear the heavy slumbering of the prophets who are like dumb dogs, too lazy to bark. If we ourselves, as Isaiah exhorts, 'search in the book of Jehovah and read out loud,' we can appreciate the powerful message that Isaiah has for this day.—44:14-20; 28:20; 56:10-12; 34:16.

[35] The prophecy focuses particularly on God's Kingdom by Messiah. Jehovah himself is the supreme King, and he it is that saves us. (33:22) But what of Messiah himself? The angel's announcement to Mary concerning the child that would be born showed that Isaiah 9:6, 7 was to be fulfilled in his receiving the throne of David; "and he will rule as king over the house of Jacob forever, and there will be no end of his kingdom." (Luke 1: 32, 33) Matthew 1:22, 23 shows that Jesus' birth by a virgin was a fulfillment of Isaiah 7:14 and identifies him as "Immanuel." Some 30 years later, John the Baptizer came preaching that "the kingdom of the heavens has drawn near." All four Gospel writers quote Isaiah 40:3 to show that this John was the one 'calling out in the wilderness.' (Matt. 3:1-3; Mark 1:2-4; Luke 3:3-6; John 1:23) At his baptism Jesus became the Messiah—the Anointed of Jehovah, the twig or root of Jesse—to rule the nations. On him they must rest their hope, in fulfillment of Isaiah 11:1, 10.—Rom. 15: 8, 12.

[36] See how Isaiah continues to identify Messiah the King! Jesus read his commission from an Isaiah scroll to show that he was Jehovah's Anointed, and then he proceeded to "declare the good news

of the kingdom of God, because," as he said, "for this I was sent forth." (Luke 4:17-19, 43; Isa. 61: 1, 2) The four Gospel accounts are full of details as to Jesus' earthly ministry and his manner of death as foretold in Isaiah chapter 53. Though they heard the good news of the Kingdom and saw Jesus' marvelous works, the Jews did not get the meaning because of their unbelieving hearts, in fulfillment of Isaiah 6:9, 10; 29:13; and 53:1. (Matt. 13:14, 15; John 12:38-40; Acts 28:24-27; Rom. 10:16; Matt. 15:7-9; Mark 7:6, 7) Jesus was a stone of stumbling to them, but he became the foundation cornerstone that Jehovah laid in Zion and upon which He builds his spiritual house in fulfillment of Isaiah 8:14 and 28:16.—Luke 20: 17; Rom. 9:32, 33; 10:11; 1 Pet. 2:4-10.

[37] The apostles of Jesus Christ continued to make good use of Isaiah's prophecy, applying it to the ministry. For example, in showing that preachers are needed in order to build faith, Paul quotes Isaiah in saying: "How comely are the feet of those who declare good news of good things!" (Rom. 10:15; Isa. 52:7; see also Romans 10:11, 16, 20, 21.) Peter too quotes Isaiah in showing the permanence of the good news: "For 'all flesh is like grass, and all its glory is like a blossom of grass; the grass becomes withered, and the flower falls off, but the saying of Jehovah endures forever.' Well, this is the 'saying,' this which has been declared to you as good news."—1 Pet. 1:24, 25; Isa. 40:6-8.

[38] Gloriously does Isaiah paint the Kingdom hope for the future! Look! It is the "new heavens and a new earth," wherein "a king will reign for righteousness itself" and princes will rule for justice. What cause for joyfulness and exultation! (65: 17, 18; 32:1, 2) Again, Peter takes up the glad message of Isaiah: "But there are new heavens and a new earth that we are awaiting according to [God's] promise, and in these righteousness is to dwell." (2 Pet. 3:13) This wondrous Kingdom theme comes to full glory in the closing chapters of Revelation.—Isa. 66:22, 23; 25:8; Rev. 21:1-5.

[39] Thus, the book of Isaiah, while containing scathing denunciations of Jehovah's enemies and of those hypocritically professing to be his servants, points in exalted tones to the magnificent hope of Messiah's Kingdom whereby Jehovah's great name will be sanctified. It does much to explain the wondrous truths of Jehovah's Kingdom and to warm our hearts in joyful expectation of "salvation by him."—Isa. 25:9; 40:28-31.

---

34. What are some of the vivid illustrations that add power to Isaiah's message?
35. How does Isaiah focus attention on the Kingdom by Messiah, and on the forerunner, John the Baptizer?
36. What rich prophetic fulfillments clearly identify Messiah the King?

---

37. How did Jesus' apostles quote and apply Isaiah?
38. What glorious Kingdom theme is painted in Isaiah, to be taken up later by other Bible writers?
39. To what magnificent hope does Isaiah point?

24
Jeremiah

Writer: **Jeremiah**

Places Written: **Judah and Egypt**

Writing Completed: **580 B.C.E.**

Time Covered: **647–580 B.C.E.**

THE prophet Jeremiah lived during dangerous and turbulent times. He was commissioned by Jehovah in the year 647 B.C.E., the 13th year of the reign of God-fearing King Josiah of Judah. During repairs on the house of Jehovah, the book of the Law of Jehovah was found and was read to the king. He worked hard at enforcing this, but he could at most only temporarily turn back the falling away to idolatry. Josiah's grandfather Manasseh, who had reigned for 55 years, and his father Amon, who had been assassinated after a reign of just 2 years, had both done wickedly. They had encouraged the people in impure orgies and gruesome rites, so that they had become accustomed to offering incense to the "queen of the heavens" and human sacrifices to demon gods. Manasseh had filled Jerusalem with innocent blood.—Jer. 1:2; 44:19; 2 Ki. 21:6, 16, 19-23; 23:26, 27.

² Jeremiah's task was no easy one. He had to serve as Jehovah's prophet in foretelling the desolation of Judah and Jerusalem, the burning of the magnificent temple of Jehovah, and the captivity of his people—catastrophes almost unbelievable! His prophesying in Jerusalem had to continue 40 years, through the reigns of bad Kings Jehoahaz, Jehoiakim, Jehoiachin (Coniah), and Zedekiah. (Jer. 1:2, 3) Later, in Egypt, he had to prophesy concerning the idolatries of the Jewish refugees there. His book was completed in 580 B.C.E. The time covered by Jeremiah is thus an eventful period of 67 years.—52:31.

³ In Hebrew the name of the prophet and of his book is *Yir·meyah'* or *Yir·meya'hu,* meaning, possibly, "Jehovah Exalts; or, Jehovah Loosens [likely from the womb]." The book occurs in all the catalogs of the Hebrew Scriptures, and its canonicity is generally accepted. The dramatic fulfillment of a number of the prophecies during Jeremiah's own lifetime attests fully to its authenticity. Moreover,

Jeremiah is referred to several times by name in the Christian Greek Scriptures. (Matt. 2:17, 18; 16:14; 27:9) That Jesus had studied the book of Jeremiah is evident from his combining the language of Jeremiah 7:11 with that of Isaiah 56:7 when he cleansed the temple. (Mark 11:17; Luke 19:46) Because of Jesus' boldness and courage, some people even thought him to be Jeremiah. (Matt. 16:13, 14) Jeremiah's prophecy of a new covenant (Jer. 31:31-34) is referred to by Paul at Hebrews 8:8-12 and 10:16, 17. Paul quotes Jeremiah 9:24 in saying: "He that boasts, let him boast in Jehovah." (1 Cor. 1:31) At Revelation 18:21 there is an even more forceful application of Jeremiah's illustration (Jer. 51:63, 64) of Babylon's downfall.

⁴ Archaeological findings also give support to the record in Jeremiah. For example, a Babylonian chronicle tells of Nebuchadnezzar's (Nebuchadrezzar) capture of Jerusalem in 617 B.C.E., when he seized the king (Jehoiachin) and appointed one of his own choice (Zedekiah).—24:1; 29:1, 2; 37:1.*

⁵ We possess a more complete biography of Jeremiah than of any of the other ancient prophets with the exception of Moses. Jeremiah reveals much about himself, his feelings, and his emotions, indicating an intrepid boldness and courage, mingled with humility and tenderness of heart. He was not only a prophet but also a priest, a compiler of Scripture, and an accurate historian. By birth he was the son of priest Hilkiah of Anathoth, a priest's city in the country to the north of Jerusalem, "in the land of Benjamin." (1:1) Jeremiah's style of writing is clear, direct, and easily understood. Illustrations and pictorial imagery abound, and the book consists of both prose and poetry.

CONTENTS OF JEREMIAH

⁶ The material is arranged not chronologically

---

1. When and by whom was Jeremiah commissioned?
2. What was Jeremiah's task, and what eventful years did his prophesying cover?
3. (a) How were the canonicity and authenticity of the book of Jeremiah established in Hebrew times? (b) What further testimony on this is to be found in the Christian Greek Scriptures?

---

* *Insight on the Scriptures,* Vol. 2, pages 326, 480.

---

4. How does archaeology support the record?
5. (a) What is known concerning Jeremiah himself? (b) What may be said as to his style of writing?
6. How is the subject matter of the prophecy arranged?

but according to subject matter. Thus, the account makes many changes as to time and surrounding circumstances. Finally, the desolation of Jerusalem and Judah is described in stark detail in chapter 52. This not only shows the fulfillment of much of the prophecy but also provides the setting for the book of Lamentations, which follows.

[7] **Jehovah commissions Jeremiah** (1:1-19). Is it because Jeremiah wanted to be a prophet or because he came from a priestly family that he is commissioned? Jehovah himself explains: "Before I was forming you in the belly I knew you, and before you proceeded to come forth from the womb I sanctified you. Prophet to the nations I made you." It is an assignment from Jehovah. Is Jeremiah willing to go? In humility he offers the excuse, "I am but a boy." Jehovah reassures him: "Here I have put my words in your mouth. See, I have commissioned you this day to be over the nations and over the kingdoms, in order to uproot and to pull down and to destroy and to tear down, to build and to plant." Jeremiah must not be afraid. "They will be certain to fight against you, but they will not prevail against you, for 'I am with you,' is the utterance of Jehovah, 'to deliver you.'"—1:5, 6, 9, 10, 19.

[8] **Jerusalem, an unfaithful wife** (2:1-6:30). What message does the word of Jehovah bring to Jeremiah? Jerusalem has forgotten her first love. She has left Jehovah, the Source of living waters, and prostituted herself with strange gods. From a choice red vine, she has been changed into "the degenerate shoots of a foreign vine." (2:21) Her skirts have been bloodied with the souls of the poor innocent ones. Even prostitute Israel has proved more righteous than Judah. God calls on these renegade sons to return because he is their husbandly owner. But they have been as a treacherous wife. They may return if they will take away their disgusting things and circumcise their hearts. "Raise a signal toward Zion," for Jehovah will bring a calamity from the north. (4:6) Crash upon crash! As a lion out of his thicket, as a searing wind through the wilderness, with chariots like a storm wind, so will Jehovah's executioner come.

[9] Go roving through Jerusalem. What do you see? Only transgressions and unfaithfulness! The people have denied Jehovah, and His word in Jeremiah's mouth must become a fire to devour them like pieces of wood. Just as they have left

Jehovah to serve a foreign god, so He will make them serve strangers in a foreign land. Stubborn ones! They have eyes but cannot see, and ears but cannot hear. How horrible! Prophets and priests actually prophesy in falsehood, "and my own people have loved it that way," says Jehovah. (5:31) Calamity approaches from the north, yet "from the least one of them even to the greatest one of them, every one is making for himself unjust gain." They are saying, "'There is peace! There is peace!' when there is no peace." (6:13, 14) But suddenly the despoiler will come. Jehovah has made Jeremiah a metal tester among them, but there is nothing but dross and rejected silver. They are entirely bad.

[10] **Warning that temple is no protection** (7:1-10:25). The word of Jehovah comes to Jeremiah, and he is to make proclamation at the temple gate. Hear him as he cries out to those entering in: 'You are bragging about the temple of Jehovah, but what are you doing? Oppressing the fatherless and widow, shedding innocent blood, walking after other gods, stealing, murdering, committing adultery, swearing falsely, and making sacrifices to Baal! Hypocrites! You have made Jehovah's house "a mere cave of robbers." Recall what Jehovah did to Shiloh. He will do the same to your house, O Judah, and he will throw you out, just as he threw out Ephraim (Israel) to the north.'—Jer. 7:4-11; 1 Sam. 2:12-14; 3:11-14; 4:12-22.

[11] Judah is past praying for. Why, the people are even making cakes to sacrifice to the "queen of the heavens"! Truly, "this is the nation whose people have not obeyed the voice of Jehovah its God, and have not taken discipline. Faithfulness has perished." (Jer. 7:18, 28) Judah has set disgusting things in Jehovah's house and has burned her sons and daughters on the high places of Topheth in the valley of Hinnom. Look! It will be called "the valley of the killing," and their dead bodies will become food for fowl and beast. (7:32) Rejoicing and exultation must cease out of Judah and Jerusalem.

[12] They were hoping for peace and healing, but look, terror! Scattering, extermination, and lamentation will result from their stubbornness. 'Jehovah is the living God and the King to time indefinite.' As for the gods that did not make the heavens and the earth, there is no spirit in them. They are a vanity and a work of mockery, and they will perish. (10:10-15) Jehovah will sling out the inhabitants of the earth. Listen! A great pounding from the land of the north that is to

---

7. How did Jeremiah become a prophet, and how does Jehovah reassure him?
8. (a) In what has Jerusalem been unfaithful? (b) How will Jehovah bring calamity?
9. (a) What word does Jeremiah have for stubborn Jerusalem? (b) Of what use are their cries of peace?

10. Why must Jerusalem meet up with the same fate as Shiloh and Ephraim?
11. Why is Judah past praying for?
12. Instead of peace, what is to overtake Judah and her adopted gods?

desolate the cities of Judah. The prophet acknowledges: 'It is not in earthling man to direct his course,' and he prays for correction that he may not be reduced to nothing.—10:23.

¹³ **The covenant breakers cursed** (11:1–12:17). Judah has disobeyed the words of its covenant with Jehovah. It is useless for the people to call for aid. Jeremiah must not pray for Judah, for Jehovah "has set a fire blazing" against this once luxuriant olive tree. (11:16) As Jeremiah's fellow citizens of Anathoth conspire to destroy him, the prophet turns to Jehovah for strength and help. Jehovah promises vengeance on Anathoth. Jeremiah asks, 'Why is it that the way of the wicked has succeeded?' Jehovah assures him: 'I will uproot and destroy the disobedient nation.'—12: 1, 17.

¹⁴ **Jerusalem irreformable and doomed** (13: 1–15:21). Jeremiah recounts how Jehovah commanded him to put a linen belt on his hips and then to hide it in a crag by the Euphrates. When Jeremiah came to dig it up, it had been ruined. "It was not fit for anything." Thus Jehovah illustrated his determination to bring to ruin "the pride of Judah and the abundant pride of Jerusalem." (13: 7, 9) He will dash them together in their drunkenness, like large jars filled with wine. "Can a Cushite change his skin? or a leopard its spots?" (13: 23) Just so, Jerusalem is irreformable. Jeremiah must not pray for these people. Even if Moses and Samuel came before Jehovah to intercede for them, he would not listen, for he has determined to devote Jerusalem to destruction. Jehovah strengthens Jeremiah against his reproachers. Jeremiah finds and eats Jehovah's words, resulting in 'exultation and rejoicing of heart.' (15:16) It is a time, not for idle joking, but for trusting in Jehovah, who has promised to make Jeremiah a fortified copper wall against the people.

¹⁵ **Jehovah will send fishers and hunters** (16: 1–17:27). In view of the impending desolation, Jehovah commands Jeremiah: "You must not take for yourself a wife, and you must not come to have sons and daughters in this place." (16:2) It is time neither to mourn nor to banquet with the people, for Jehovah is about to hurl them out of the land.

Then Jehovah also promises to send 'fishers to fish them and hunters to hunt them,' and by his accomplishing all of this, "they will have to know that [his] name is Jehovah." (16:16, 21) The sin of Judah is engraved on the hearts of the people with an iron stylus, yes, with a diamond point. "The heart is more treacherous than anything else and is desperate," but Jehovah can search the heart. None can deceive him. Those apostatizing "have left the source of living water, Jehovah." (17: 9, 13) If Judah will not sanctify the Sabbath day, Jehovah will devour her gates and towers with fire.

¹⁶ **The potter and the clay** (18:1–19:15). Jehovah commands Jeremiah to go down to the potter's house. There he observes how the potter turns back a spoiled vessel of clay, making it into another vessel as he pleases. Jehovah then declares himself to be the Potter to the house of Israel, with power to pull down or to build up. Next, he tells Jeremiah to take a potter's flask to the Valley of Hinnom and there pronounce calamity from Jehovah because the people have filled the place with innocent blood, burning their sons in the fire as whole burnt offerings to the Baal. Jeremiah must then break the flask in symbol of Jehovah's breaking Jerusalem and the people of Judah.

¹⁷ **No quitting under persecution** (20:1–18). Irritated by Jeremiah's bold preaching, the temple commissioner Pashhur puts Jeremiah in stocks for a night. On his release, Jeremiah foretells Pashhur's captivity and death in Babylon. Grieved by the derision and reproach leveled against him, Jeremiah contemplates quitting. However, he cannot keep silent. The word of Jehovah comes to be 'in his heart like a burning fire shut up in his bones,' so that he is compelled to speak. Though cursing the day of his birth, he cries out: "Sing to Jehovah, you people! Praise Jehovah! For he has delivered the soul of the poor one out of the hand of evildoers."—20:9, 13.

¹⁸ **Jehovah's indignation against the rulers** (21:1–22:30). In answer to an inquiry from Zedekiah, Jeremiah notifies him of Jehovah's rage against the city: The king of Babylon will lay siege against it, and it will be destroyed by pestilence, sword, famine, and fire. Shallum (Jehoahaz) will die in exile, Jehoiakim will have the burial of a he-ass, and his son Coniah (Jehoiachin) will be hurled out of Judah to die in Babylon.

---

13. Why is Jeremiah forbidden to pray for Judah, and how does Jehovah strengthen Jeremiah in an hour of danger?
14. (a) By what illustrations does Jehovah make known that Jerusalem is irreformable and that the judgment against her is irreversible? (b) What results to Jeremiah from eating Jehovah's words?
15. (a) How serious are the times, and by what command does Jehovah give this emphasis? (b) How will the people come to know Jehovah's name, and why does their sin not deceive him?

---

16. What does Jehovah illustrate by the potter and his clay vessels?
17. What hard experience does Jeremiah have, but does this silence him?
18. Of what does Jeremiah notify Zedekiah?

[19] **Hope in "a righteous sprout"** (23:1–24:10). Jehovah promises real shepherds to replace the false shepherds and "a righteous sprout" out of the stock of David, a king who "will certainly reign and act with discretion and execute justice and righteousness in the land." His name? "He will be called, Jehovah Is Our Righteousness." He will gather the dispersed remnant. (23:5, 6) If the prophets had stood in Jehovah's intimate group, they would have caused the people to hear and turn back from their bad way. Instead, says Jehovah, they "cause my people to wander about because of their falsehoods." (23:22, 32) "Look! Two baskets of figs." Jeremiah uses the good and the bad figs to illustrate a faithful remnant returning to their land in God's favor and another class coming to a calamitous finish.—24:1, 5, 8-10.

[20] **Jehovah's controversy with the nations** (25: 1-38). This chapter is a summary of judgments that appear in greater detail in chapters 45-49. By three parallel prophecies, Jehovah now pronounces calamity for all the nations on earth. First, Nebuchadrezzar is identified as Jehovah's servant to devastate Judah and the surrounding nations, "and these nations will have to serve the king of Babylon seventy years." Then it will be Babylon's turn, and she will become "desolate wastes to time indefinite."—25:1-14.

[21] The second prophecy is the vision of the cup of wine of Jehovah's rage. Jeremiah must take this cup to the nations, and "they must drink and shake back and forth and act like crazed men" because of Jehovah's destruction coming against them. First, to Jerusalem and Judah! Then, on to Egypt, back to Philistia, across to Edom, up to Tyre, to lands near and far, and to "all the other kingdoms of the earth that are on the surface of the ground; and the king of Sheshach himself will drink after them." They shall 'drink and puke and fall.' None will be spared.—25:15-29.

[22] In the third prophecy, Jeremiah rises to magnificent poetic heights. "From on high Jehovah himself will roar . . . against all the inhabitants of the earth." A noise, a calamity, a great tempest! "And those slain by Jehovah will certainly come to be in that day from one end of the earth clear to the other end of the earth." No lamenting, no funerals. They will be as manure on the ground. The false shepherds will be slaughtered, along with the majestic ones of their flock. There is no escape for them. Listen to their howling! Jehovah himself "is despoiling their pasturage . . . because of his burning anger."—25:30-38.

[23] **Jeremiah vindicated** (26:1–28:17). The rulers and people conspire to put Jeremiah to death. Jeremiah makes his defense. It is the word of Jehovah that he has spoken. If they kill him, they will kill an innocent man. The verdict: not guilty. The older men introduce the precedents of the prophets Micah and Urijah in discussing Jeremiah's case. Jehovah next commands Jeremiah to make bands and yokes, put them upon his neck, and then send them to the nations round about as symbols that they must serve the king of Babylon for three generations of rulers. Hananiah, one of the false prophets, opposes Jeremiah. He declares that the yoke of Babylon will be broken within two years and pictures this by breaking the wooden yoke. Jehovah underlines his prophecy by having Jeremiah make iron yokes and foretell that Hananiah must die that year. Hananiah dies.

[24] **Comfort for the exiles in Babylon** (29:1–31: 40). Jeremiah writes to the exiles taken to Babylon with Jeconiah (Jehoiachin): Settle down there, for before Jehovah brings you back, there is coming a period of 70 years of exile. Jehovah commands Jeremiah to write of their return in a book: Jehovah will break their yoke, and "they will certainly serve Jehovah their God and David their king, whom I [Jehovah] shall raise up for them." (30:9) Rachel must hold her voice back from weeping, for her sons "will certainly return from the land of the enemy." (31:16) And now, a reassuring declaration by Jehovah! He will conclude with the houses of Judah and Israel a new covenant. Far grander this than the covenant they have broken! Jehovah will write his law deep down inside, on their hearts. "And I will become their God, and they themselves will become my people." From the least to the greatest, all will know Jehovah, and he will forgive their error. (31:31-34) Their city will be rebuilt as something holy to Jehovah.

[25] **Jehovah's covenant with David sure** (32: 1–34:22). During Nebuchadrezzar's final siege of Jerusalem, Jeremiah is under restraint. However, as a sign that Jehovah will certainly restore Israel,

---

19. What does Jeremiah prophesy concerning "a righteous sprout," and what is illustrated by the two baskets of figs?

20. How does Jehovah use Babylon as his servant, but what, in turn, will be her fate?

21. Who must drink of the cup of Jehovah's rage? With what result?

22. In what great calamity will Jehovah's burning anger be expressed?

23. (a) What conspiracy is formed against Jeremiah, what is his defense, and what precedents are referred to in acquitting him? (b) How does Jeremiah enact the coming Babylonian bondage, and what prophecy concerning Hananiah comes true?

24. (a) What message does Jeremiah send to the exiles in Babylon? (b) With whom will Jehovah conclude a new covenant, and how will this prove to be grander than the former covenant?

25. How is the certainty of Israel's restoration emphasized, and what news does the word of Jehovah bring?

Jeremiah buys a field in Anathoth and puts the deeds aside in an earthenware vessel. The word of Jehovah now brings good news: Judah and Jerusalem will rejoice again, and Jehovah will fulfill his covenant with David. But you, O Zedekiah, be warned that the king of Babylon will burn this city with fire and you yourself will go in captivity to Babylon. Woe to the slave owners who agreed to free their slaves but who have violated their covenant!

26 Jehovah's promise to Rechab (35:1-19). In the days of King Jehoiakim, Jehovah sends Jeremiah to the Rechabites. These took refuge in Jerusalem at the first approach of the Babylonians. Jeremiah offers them wine to drink. They refuse it because of the command of their forefather Jonadab, given over 250 years earlier. A striking contrast, indeed, to the unfaithful course of Judah! Jehovah promises them: "There will not be cut off from Jonadab the son of Rechab a man to stand before me always."—35:19.

27 Jeremiah rewrites the book (36:1-32). Jehovah orders Jeremiah to write down all the words of his prophecies to date. Jeremiah dictates these to Baruch, who then reads them aloud in the house of Jehovah on a fast day. King Jehoiakim sends for the roll and, on hearing a part, angrily tears it up and pitches it into the fire. He commands the arrest of Jeremiah and Baruch, but Jehovah conceals them and tells Jeremiah to write a duplicate roll.

28 Jerusalem's last days (37:1-39:18). The record returns to the reign of Zedekiah. The king asks Jeremiah to pray to Jehovah on Judah's behalf. The prophet refuses, saying Jerusalem's doom is certain. Jeremiah attempts to go to Anathoth but is seized as a deserter, beaten, and imprisoned many days. Zedekiah then sends for him. Is there word from Jehovah? To be sure there is! "Into the hand of the king of Babylon you will be given!" (37:17) Angered by Jeremiah's persistent prophecies of doom, the princes throw him into a miry cistern. Ebed-melech the Ethiopian, a eunuch in the king's house, kindly intercedes for him, so that Jeremiah is rescued from a lingering death, but he remains in detention in the Courtyard of the Guard. Again Zedekiah calls Jeremiah before him, only to be told: 'Surrender to the king of Babylon or face captivity and the destruction of Jerusalem!' —38:17, 18.

29 The siege of Jerusalem lasts 18 months, and then the city is broken through in the 11th year of Zedekiah. The king flees with his army but is overtaken. His sons and the nobles are slain before his eyes, and he is blinded and carried to Babylon in fetters. The city is burned and laid in ruins, and all except a few poor people are taken into exile to Babylon. By Nebuchadrezzar's order, Jeremiah is released from the courtyard. Before his release he tells Ebed-melech of Jehovah's promise to deliver him, 'because he trusted in Jehovah.'—39:18.

30 Final events at Mizpah and in Egypt (40: 1–44:30). Jeremiah remains at Mizpah with Gedaliah, whom the Babylonians make governor over the remaining people. After two months Gedaliah is murdered. The people seek Jeremiah's advice, and he relays God's word to them: 'Jehovah will not uproot you from this land. Do not be afraid because of the king of Babylon. If, however, you go down to Egypt, you will die!' Down to Egypt they go, taking Jeremiah and Baruch with them. At Tahpanhes in Egypt, Jeremiah makes known Jehovah's judgment of doom: The king of Babylon will set his throne in Egypt. It is useless for Israel to worship the gods of Egypt and to resume sacrifice to the "queen of the heavens." Have they forgotten how Jehovah desolated Jerusalem for its idolatry? Jehovah will bring calamity on them in the land of Egypt, and they will not return to Judah. As a sign, Jehovah is giving Pharaoh Hophra himself into the hand of his enemies.

31 Baruch's lot (45:1-5). Baruch is distressed at hearing Jeremiah's repeated prophecies of doom. He is told to think first of Jehovah's work of building up and tearing down instead of "seeking great things" for himself. (45:5) He will be saved through all the calamity.

32 Jehovah's sword against the nations (46: 1–49:39). Jeremiah tells of Babylon's victories over Egypt at Carchemish and elsewhere. Though the nations are exterminated, Jacob will remain but will not go unpunished. "The sword of Jehovah" will come against the Philistines, against proud Moab and bragging Ammon, against Edom and Damascus, Kedar and Hazor. (47:6) The bow of Elam will be broken.

33 Jehovah's sword against Babylon (50:1–51: 64). Jehovah speaks concerning Babylon: Tell it

---

26. What promise does Jehovah make to the Rechabites, and why?
27. What makes necessary the rewriting of the prophecies of Jeremiah?
28. (a) What persistent prophecies does Jeremiah make? (b) How does Ebed-melech's course contrast with that of the princes?

29. What calamity now befalls Jerusalem, but how do Jeremiah and Ebed-melech fare?
30. How do the remaining people fail to heed Jeremiah's advice, and what judgment of doom does Jeremiah make known in Egypt?
31. What assurance is given Baruch?
32. Against whom will "the sword of Jehovah" come?
33. (a) What will happen to the golden cup, Babylon? (b) How, therefore, must God's people act?

among the nations. Hide nothing. Babylon has been captured and her gods shamed. Flee out of her. This forge hammer that has smashed the nations of all the earth has herself been broken. "O Presumptuousness," the oppressor of captive Israel and Judah, know that Jehovah of armies is their Repurchaser. Babylon will become a haunt of howling animals. "Just as with God's overthrow of Sodom and of Gomorrah . . . , no man will dwell there." (50:31, 40) Babylon has been a golden cup in Jehovah's hand to make the nations drunk, but suddenly she has fallen, so that she herself is broken. Howl over her, you people. Jehovah has aroused the spirit of the kings of the Medes to bring her to ruin. The mighty men of Babylon have ceased to fight. They have become like women. The daughter of Babylon will be trodden down solid like a threshing floor. "They must sleep an indefinitely lasting sleep, from which they will not wake up." The sea has come up and covered Babylon with a multitude of waves. "Get out of the midst of her, O my people, and provide each one his soul with escape from the burning anger of Jehovah." (51:39, 45) Listen to the outcry, to the great crash from Babylon! Babylon's weapons of war must be shattered, for Jehovah is a God of recompense. Without fail he will repay.

³⁴ Jeremiah commands Seraiah: 'Go to Babylon and read aloud these words of the prophecy against Babylon. Then tie a stone to the book and pitch it into the midst of the Euphrates. "And you must say, 'This is how Babylon will sink down and never rise up because of the calamity that I am bringing in upon her.'"'—51:61-64.

³⁵ **Record of Jerusalem's fall** (52:1-34). This account is almost identical with that previously covered at 2 Kings 24:18-20; 25:1-21, 27-30.

WHY BENEFICIAL

³⁶ This inspired prophecy is altogether upbuilding and beneficial. Look at the courageous example of the prophet himself. He was fearless in proclaiming an unpopular message to a godless people. He spurned fellowship with the wicked. He appreciated the urgency of Jehovah's message, giving himself wholeheartedly to Jehovah's work and never quitting. He found God's word to be like a fire in his bones, and it was the exultation and rejoicing of his heart. (Jer. 15:16-20; 20:8-13) May we ever be as zealous for the word of Jehovah! May we also give loyal support to God's servants, as Baruch did to Jeremiah. The sincere

obedience of the Rechabites is also a splendid example to us, and so is Ebed-melech's kindly consideration for the persecuted prophet.—36: 8-19, 32; 35:1-19; 38:7-13; 39:15-18.

³⁷ The word of Jehovah that came to Jeremiah was fulfilled with astounding accuracy. This certainly strengthens faith in Jehovah's power of prophecy. Take, for example, the prophecy fulfillments that Jeremiah himself survived to see, such as the captivity of Zedekiah and the destruction of Jerusalem (21:3-10; 39:6-9), the dethronement and the death in captivity of King Shallum (Jehoahaz) (Jer. 22:11, 12; 2 Ki. 23:30-34; 2 Chron. 36: 1-4), the taking captive of King Coniah (Jehoiachin) to Babylon (Jer. 22:24-27; 2 Ki. 24:15, 16), and the death within one year of the false prophet Hananiah (Jer. 28:16, 17). All these prophecies, and more, were fulfilled just as Jehovah had foretold. Later prophets and servants of Jehovah also found Jeremiah's prophecy authoritative and beneficial. For example, Daniel discerned from the writings of Jeremiah that Jerusalem's desolation must be 70 years, and Ezra drew attention to the fulfillment of Jeremiah's words at the end of the 70 years.—Dan. 9:2; 2 Chron. 36:20, 21; Ezra 1:1; Jer. 25:11, 12; 29:10.

³⁸ On the occasion when he established the celebration of the Lord's Evening Meal with his disciples, Jesus indicated the fulfillment of Jeremiah's prophecy concerning the new covenant. Thus, he referred to "the new covenant by virtue of my blood," whereby their sins were forgiven and they were gathered as Jehovah's spiritual nation. (Luke 22:20; Jer. 31:31-34) The spirit-begotten ones brought into the new covenant are the ones whom Christ takes into a covenant for the Kingdom, to rule with him in the heavens. (Luke 22:29; Rev. 5: 9, 10; 20:6) Reference is made to this Kingdom a number of times in Jeremiah's prophecy. Amid all the denunciations of faithless Jerusalem, Jeremiah pointed out this ray of hope: "'Look! There are days coming,' is the utterance of Jehovah, 'and I will raise up to David a righteous sprout. And a king will certainly reign and act with discretion and execute justice and righteousness in the land.'" Yes, a king called "Jehovah Is Our Righteousness."—Jer. 23:5, 6.

³⁹ Again Jeremiah speaks of a restoration: "And they will certainly serve Jehovah their God and David their king, whom I shall raise up for them."

---

34. What sign illustrates Babylon's fall?
35. What record now follows?
36. (a) What example of courageous zeal do we find in Jeremiah? (b) In what respects are Baruch, the Rechabites, and Ebed-melech also fine examples for us?

37. How does a consideration of Jeremiah strengthen faith in Jehovah's power of prophecy?
38. (a) What covenant, referred to also by Jesus, is highlighted in Jeremiah's prophecy? (b) What Kingdom hope is proclaimed?
39. The return of a remnant from Babylon, as foretold by Jeremiah, gives assurance of what?

(30:9) Finally, he tells of the good word that Jehovah has spoken concerning Israel and Judah, to the effect that "in those days and at that time [Jehovah will] make sprout for David a righteous sprout," so as to multiply his seed and so that there will be "a son ruling as king upon his throne." (33: 15, 21) As surely as a remnant returned from Babylon, so will the Kingdom of this righteous "sprout" execute justice and righteousness in all the earth.—Luke 1:32.

Bible Book Number 25

Lamentations

Writer: **Jeremiah**

Place Written: **Near Jerusalem**

Writing Completed: **607 B.C.E.**

THIS book of the inspired Scriptures is certainly well named. It is a lament expressing deep sorrow over that calamitous happening in the history of God's chosen people, the destruction of Jerusalem in 607 B.C.E. by Nebuchadnezzar, king of Babylon. In Hebrew this book is named by its first word, 'Eh·khah'!, meaning "How!" The translators of the Greek *Septuagint* called the book *Thre'noi,* which means "Dirges; Laments." The Babylonian Talmud uses the term *Qi·nohth',* which means "Dirges; Elegies." It was Jerome, writing in Latin, who named it *Lamentationes,* from which the English title comes.

² In English versions of the Bible, Lamentations is placed after Jeremiah, but in the Hebrew canon, it is usually found in the Hagiographa, or Writings, along with The Song of Solomon, Ruth, Ecclesiastes, and Esther—a small group collectively known as the five *Meghil·lohth'* (Rolls). In some modern Hebrew Bibles, it is placed between Ruth or Esther and Ecclesiastes, but in ancient copies it is said to have followed Jeremiah, as it does in our Bible today.

³ The book does not name the writer. Yet, there is little doubt it was Jeremiah. In the Greek *Septuagint,* the book carries this preface: "And it occurred that, after Israel had been taken captive and Jerusalem had been desolated, Jeremiah sat down weeping and lamented with this lamentation over Jerusalem and said." Jerome considered these words spurious and omitted them from his version. However, the ascribing of Lamentations to Jeremiah is the accepted tradition of the Jews and is confirmed by the Syriac version, the Latin *Vulgate,* the Targum of Jonathan, and the Babylonian Talmud, among others.

⁴ Some critics have tried to prove that Jeremiah did not write Lamentations. However, *A Commentary on the Holy Bible* cites as evidence of Jeremiah's writership "the vivid descriptions of Jerusalem in chs. 2 and 4, which are evidently the pen-pictures of an eyewitness; likewise the strongly sympathetic temper and prophetic spirit of the poems throughout, as well as their style, phraseology, and thought, which are all so characteristic of Jeremiah."* There are many parallel expressions in Lamentations and Jeremiah, such as that of the extreme sorrow of 'eyes running down with waters (tears)' (Lam. 1:16; 2:11; 3: 48, 49; Jer. 9:1; 13:17; 14:17) and those of disgust at the prophets and priests because of their corruption. (Lam. 2:14; 4:13, 14; Jer. 2:34; 5:30, 31; 14: 13, 14) The passages at Jeremiah 8:18-22 and 14: 17, 18 show that Jeremiah was quite capable of the mournful style of Lamentations.

⁵ The time of writing is generally agreed to have been soon after the fall of Jerusalem in 607 B.C.E. The horror of both the siege and the burning of the city was still fresh in Jeremiah's mind, and his anguish is vividly expressed. One commentator remarks that no single facet of sorrow is fully exploited in any given place, but each returns again and again in the several poems. Then he says: "This tumult of thought . . . is one of the very strongest evidences that the book stands close to the events and emotions it purports to communicate."#

⁶ The construction of Lamentations is of great interest to the Bible scholar. There are five chap-

---

* 1952, edited by J. R. Dummelow, page 483.
# *Studies in the Book of Lamentations,* 1954, Norman K. Gottwald, page 31.

---

1. Why is the book of Lamentations well named?
2. How has Lamentations been grouped and placed in the Bible?
3, 4. What evidence is there for Jeremiah's writership?

5. By what reasoning do we arrive at the time of writing?
6. What is interesting in the style and construction of Lamentations?

ters, that is, five lyric poems. The first four are acrostic, with each verse beginning successively with one of the 22 letters of the Hebrew alphabet. On the other hand, the third chapter has 66 verses, so that 3 successive verses begin with the same letter before passing on to the next letter. The fifth poem is not acrostic, though it does have 22 verses.

⁷ Lamentations expresses overwhelming grief at the siege, capture, and destruction of Jerusalem by Nebuchadnezzar, and it is unsurpassed in any literature for its vividness and pathos. The writer expresses deep sorrow over the desolation, misery, and confusion that he views. Famine, sword, and other horrors have brought dreadful suffering to the city—all as a direct penalty from God, on account of the sins of the people, the prophets, and the priests. However, hope and faith in Jehovah remain, and to him go the prayers for restoration.

CONTENTS OF LAMENTATIONS

⁸ "O how she has come to sit solitary, the city that was abundant with people!" Thus **the first poem** opens its lament. The daughter of Zion was a princess, but her lovers have abandoned her and her people have gone into exile. Her gates are laid desolate. Jehovah has punished her for the abundance of her transgressions. She has lost her splendor. Her adversaries have laughed over her collapse. She has gone down in a wondrous manner and has no comforter, and her remaining people are hungry. She (Jerusalem personified) asks: "Does there exist any pain like my pain?" She stretches out her hands and says: "Jehovah is righteous, for it is against his mouth that I have rebelled." (1:1, 12, 18) She calls on Jehovah to bring calamity on her exulting enemies, even as he has done on her.

⁹ "O how Jehovah in his anger beclouds the daughter of Zion!" (2:1) **The second poem** shows that it is Jehovah himself who has thrown down to earth the beauty of Israel. He has caused festival and Sabbath to be forgotten, and he has cast off his altar and sanctuary. Oh, the pathetic sights in Jerusalem! Jeremiah exclaims: "My eyes have come to their end in sheer tears. My intestines are in a ferment. My liver has been poured out to the very earth, on account of the crash of the daughter of my people." (2:11) To what shall he liken the daughter of Jerusalem? How shall he comfort the daughter of Zion? Her own prophets proved worthless and unsatisfying. Now passersby laugh scornfully at her: "Is this the city of which they used to say, 'It is the perfection of prettiness, an exultation for all the earth'?" (2:15) Her enemies have opened their mouth and whistled and ground their teeth, saying, 'This is the day we have hoped for to swallow her down.' Her children faint for famine, and women eat their own offspring. Corpses litter the streets. "In the day of the wrath of Jehovah there proved to be no escapee or survivor."—2:16, 22.

¹⁰ **The third poem,** of 66 verses, stresses Zion's hope in God's mercy. By many metaphors the prophet shows that it is Jehovah who has brought the captivity and desolation. In the bitterness of the situation, the writer asks God to remember his affliction and expresses faith in the lovingkindness and mercies of Jehovah. Three successive verses begin with "Good" and show the propriety of waiting for salvation from Jehovah. (3:25-27) Jehovah has caused grief, but he will also show mercy. But for now, despite confession of rebellion, Jehovah has not forgiven; he has blocked the prayers of his people and made them "mere offscouring and refuse." (3:45) With bitter tears the prophet recalls that his enemies hunted for him as for a bird. However, Jehovah drew near to him in the pit and said: "Do not be afraid." He calls on Jehovah to answer the reproach of the enemy: "You will pursue in anger and annihilate them from under the heavens of Jehovah."—3:57, 66.

¹¹ "O how the gold that shines becomes dim, the good gold!" (4:1) **The fourth poem** bemoans the faded glory of Jehovah's temple, whose stones are poured out in the streets. The precious sons of Zion have become of little value, like jars of earthenware. There is neither water nor bread, and those raised in luxury "have had to embrace ash heaps." (4:5) The punishment is even greater than that for the sin of Sodom. The Nazirites, once 'purer than snow and whiter than milk,' have become "darker than blackness itself" and are all shriveled up. (4:7, 8) Better to have been slain by the sword than die by the famine, at a time when women have boiled their own children! Jehovah has poured out his burning anger. The unbelievable has happened —the adversary has come into the gates of Jerusalem! And why? "Because of the sins of her prophets, the errors of her priests," who poured out righteous blood. (4:13) The face of Jehovah is not toward them. However, the error of the daughter of Zion has come to its finish, and she will not again be carried into exile. Now it is your turn, O daughter of Edom, to drink the bitter cup of Jehovah!

¹² **The fifth poem** opens with an appeal to

---

7. What grief does Jeremiah express, but what hope remains?
8. What desolation is described in the first poem, but how does Jerusalem personified express herself?
9. (a) From whom has calamity come on Jerusalem? (b) How does Jeremiah speak of the scorn heaped on her and of the terrible conditions in the city?

---

10. As a basis for hope, what qualities of God does Jeremiah mention?
11. In what ways has Jehovah's burning anger been poured out on Zion, and why?
12. What humble appeal is made in the fifth poem?

Jehovah to remember his orphaned people. The inhabitants of Jerusalem are pictured as speaking. It is their forefathers that have sinned, and it is their error the people must now bear. Mere servants rule over them, and they are tortured by pangs of hunger. The exultation of their heart has ceased, and their dancing has been changed into mourning. They are sick at heart. Humbly they acknowledge Jehovah: "As for you, O Jehovah, to time indefinite you will sit. Your throne is for generation after generation." They cry out: "Bring us back, O Jehovah, to yourself, and we shall readily come back. Bring new days for us as in the long ago. However, you have positively rejected us. You have been indignant toward us very much."—5:19-22.

WHY BENEFICIAL

13 The book of Lamentations expresses Jeremiah's complete confidence in God. In the very depths of sorrow and crushing defeat, with absolutely no hope of comfort from any human source, the prophet looks forward to salvation by the hand of the great God of the universe, Jehovah. Lamentations should inspire obedience and integrity in all true worshipers, while at the same time providing a fearsome warning concerning those who disregard the greatest name and what it stands for. History does not show another ruined city lamented in such pathetic and touching language. It is certainly of benefit in describing the severity

---

13. What confidence does Lamentations express, yet why is it beneficial in showing the severity of God?

of God toward those who continue to be rebellious, stiff-necked, and unrepentant.

14 Lamentations is also beneficial in showing the fulfillment of a number of divine warnings and prophecies. (Lam. 1:2—Jer. 30:14; Lam. 2:15—Jer. 18:16; Lam. 2:17—Lev. 26:17; Lam. 2:20—Deut. 28:53) Also note that Lamentations provides vivid testimony to the fulfillment of Deuteronomy 28:63-65. Moreover, the book contains a number of references to other parts of the sacred Scriptures. (Lam. 2:15—Ps. 48:2; Lam. 3:24—Ps. 119:57) Daniel 9:5-14 corroborates Lamentations 1:5 and 3:42 in showing that the calamity came on account of the people's own transgressions.

15 Heartrending indeed is the tragic plight of Jerusalem! Amid all of this, Lamentations voices confidence that Jehovah will show loving-kindness and mercy and that he will remember Zion and bring her back. (Lam. 3:31, 32; 4:22) It expresses hope in "new days" like the days of long ago when Kings David and Solomon reigned in Jerusalem. There is still Jehovah's covenant with David for an everlasting kingdom! "His mercies will certainly not come to an end. They are new each morning." And they will continue toward those who love Jehovah until, under his righteous Kingdom rule, every creature that lives will exclaim in thankfulness: "Jehovah is my share." —5:21; 3:22-24.

---

14. What divine warnings and prophecies are shown by Lamentations to be fulfilled, and how does the book tie in with other inspired writings?
15. To what "new days" does Lamentations point forward?

Bible Book Number	**26**	
	Ezekiel	

Writer: **Ezekiel**

Place Written: **Babylon**

Writing Completed: **c. 591 B.C.E.**

Time Covered: **613–c. 591 B.C.E.**

IN THE year 617 B.C.E., Jehoiachin, king of Judah, surrendered Jerusalem to Nebuchadnezzar, who took the foremost people of the land and the treasures of the house of Jehovah and of the king's house to Babylon. Among the captives were the king's family and the princes; the valiant, mighty men; the craftsmen and builders; and Ezekiel the son of Buzi the priest. (2 Ki. 24:11-17; Ezek. 1:1-3) With heavy hearts, these exiled Israelites had completed their weary journey from a land of hills, springs, and valleys to one of vast level plains. Now they lived by the river Chebar in the midst of a mighty empire, surrounded by a people of strange customs and of pagan worship. Nebuchadnezzar permitted the Israelites to have their own houses, keep servants, and engage in business. (Ezek. 8:1; Jer. 29:5-7; Ezra 2:65) If industrious, they could become prosperous. Would they fall into the traps of Babylonian religion and materialism? Would they continue to rebel against

---

1. What were the circumstances of the exiles in Babylon, and what new tests did they face?

Jehovah? Would they accept their exile as discipline from him? They would meet new tests in the land of their exile.

[2] During these critical years leading down to the destruction of Jerusalem, Jehovah did not deprive himself or the Israelites of the services of a prophet. Jeremiah was stationed in Jerusalem itself, Daniel was in the court of Babylon, and Ezekiel was the prophet to the Jewish exiles in Babylonia. Ezekiel was both priest and prophet, a distinction likewise enjoyed by Jeremiah and later by Zechariah. (Ezek. 1:3) Throughout his book he is addressed over 90 times as "son of man," a point of significance when studying his prophecy because, in the Christian Greek Scriptures, Jesus is similarly referred to as "Son of man" nearly 80 times. (Ezek. 2:1; Matt. 8:20) His name Ezekiel (Hebrew, *Yechez·qe'l'*) means "God Strengthens." It was in the fifth year of Jehoiachin's exile, 613 B.C.E., that Ezekiel was commissioned by Jehovah as prophet. We read of him still at his work in the 27th year of the exile, 22 years later. (Ezek. 1:1, 2; 29:17) He was married, but his wife died on the day that Nebuchadnezzar began his final siege of Jerusalem. (24:2, 18) The date and manner of his own death are unknown.

[3] That Ezekiel actually wrote the book that bears his name and that it has a rightful place in the canon of Scripture is not in dispute. It was included in the canon in Ezra's day and appears in the catalogs of early Christian times, notably in the canon of Origen. Its authenticity is also testified to by the striking similarity between its symbolisms and those of Jeremiah and the Revelation.—Ezek. 24:2-12—Jer. 1:13-15; Ezek. 23:1-49—Jer. 3: 6-11; Ezek. 18:2-4—Jer. 31:29, 30; Ezek. 1:5, 10 —Rev. 4:6, 7; Ezek. 5:17—Rev. 6:8; Ezek. 9:4 —Rev. 7:3; Ezek. 2:9; 3:1—Rev. 10:2, 8-10; Ezek. 23:22, 25, 26—Rev. 17:16; 18:8; Ezek. 27:30, 36 —Rev. 18:9, 17-19; Ezek. 37:27—Rev. 21:3; Ezek. 48:30-34—Rev. 21:12, 13; Ezek. 47:1, 7, 12 —Rev. 22:1, 2.

[4] Further proof of authenticity is to be found in the dramatic fulfillment of Ezekiel's prophecies against neighboring nations, such as Tyre, Egypt, and Edom. For example, Ezekiel prophesied that Tyre would be devastated, and this was partly fulfilled when Nebuchadnezzar took the city after

a siege of 13 years. (Ezek. 26:2-21) This conflict did not mean the complete end for Tyre. However, Jehovah's judgment was that it should be *totally* destroyed. He had foretold through Ezekiel: "I will scrape her dust away from her and make her a shining, bare surface of a crag. . . . Your stones and your woodwork and your dust they will place in the very midst of the water." (26:4, 12) This was all fulfilled more than 250 years later when Alexander the Great moved against the island city of Tyre. Alexander's soldiers scraped up all the debris of the ruined mainland city and threw it into the sea, making a half-mile causeway out to the island city. Then, with an intricate siegework, they scaled the 150-foot-high walls to take the city in 332 B.C.E. Thousands were killed, and many more were sold into slavery. As Ezekiel had also predicted, Tyre became the 'bare surface of a crag and a drying yard for dragnets.' (26:14)[*] On the other side of the Promised Land, the treacherous Edomites were also annihilated, in fulfillment of Ezekiel's prophecy. (25:12, 13; 35:2-9)[#] And, of course, Ezekiel's prophecies about the destruction of Jerusalem and Israel's restoration also proved to be accurate.—17:12-21; 36:7-14.

[5] In the early years of his prophetic career, Ezekiel proclaimed God's certain judgments against unfaithful Jerusalem and warned the exiles against idolatry. (14:1-8; 17:12-21) The captive Jews were showing no real signs of repentance. Their responsible men made a practice of consulting Ezekiel, but they paid no attention to the messages from Jehovah that Ezekiel conveyed to them. They went right ahead with their idolatry and materialistic practices. The loss of their temple, their holy city, and their dynasty of kings came as a terrific shock, but it awakened only a few to humility and repentance.—Ps. 137:1-9.

[6] Ezekiel's prophecies in the later years emphasized the hope of restoration. They also took Judah's neighbor nations to task for exulting over her downfall. Their own humiliation, together with Israel's restoration, would sanctify Jehovah before their eyes. In summary, the purpose of the captivity and of the restoration was: 'You people, both of the Jews and of the nations, will have to know that I am Jehovah.' (Ezek. 39:7, 22) This sanctification of Jehovah's name is highlighted throughout the book, there being more than 60 occurrences of the expression: "You [or, they] will have to know that I am Jehovah."—6:7, footnote.

---

2. (a) Which three prophets were outstanding during the critical years before Jerusalem's destruction? (b) Significantly, how is Ezekiel addressed, and what does his name mean? (c) During what years did Ezekiel prophesy, and what is known of his life and his death?
3. What can be said about Ezekiel's writership, as well as the canonicity and authenticity of the book of Ezekiel?
4. What dramatic fulfillments have Ezekiel's prophecies seen?

---

[*] *Insight on the Scriptures*, Vol. 2, pages 531, 1136.
[#] *Insight on the Scriptures*, Vol. 1, pages 681-2.

---

5. How did the Jews react to Ezekiel's early prophecies?
6. What do Ezekiel's later prophecies emphasize, and how is the sanctification of Jehovah's name highlighted?

CONTENTS OF EZEKIEL

7 The book falls naturally into three sections. The first, chapters 1 to 24, contains warnings of the certain destruction of Jerusalem. The second section, chapters 25 to 32, contains prophecies of doom to several pagan nations. The last section, chapters 33 to 48, consists of prophecies of the restoration, culminating in the vision of a new temple and holy city. For the most part, the prophecies are arranged chronologically as well as topically.

8 **Jehovah commissions Ezekiel as watchman** (1:1–3:27). In his initial vision, in 613 B.C.E., Ezekiel sees a violent wind from the north, together with a cloud mass and quivering fire. Out of it come four winged living creatures, with faces of a man, a lion, a bull, and an eagle. They have the appearance of burning coals, and each is accompanied, as it were, by a wheel in the midst of a wheel of fearful height, with rims full of eyes. They move in any direction in constant unity. Above the heads of the living creatures is the likeness of an expanse, and above the expanse is a throne on which is "the appearance of the likeness of the glory of Jehovah."—1:28.

9 Jehovah calls on the prostrate Ezekiel: "Son of man, stand up." He then commissions him as prophet to Israel and to the rebellious nations round about. Whether they heed or not is beside the point. At least they will know that a prophet of the Lord Jehovah has been in their midst. Jehovah makes Ezekiel eat the roll of a book, which becomes like honey for sweetness in his mouth. He tells him: "Son of man, a watchman is what I have made you to the house of Israel." (2:1; 3:17) Ezekiel must faithfully give the warning, or he will die.

10 **Enacting the siege of Jerusalem** (4:1–7:27). Jehovah tells Ezekiel to engrave a sketch of Jerusalem on a brick. He must stage a mock siege against it as a sign to Israel. To impress the point, he is to lie before the brick 390 days on his left side and 40 days on his right side, while subsisting on a very meager diet. That Ezekiel actually acts out the scene is indicated by his plaintive appeal to Jehovah for a change of cooking fuel.—4:9-15.

11 Jehovah has Ezekiel portray the calamitous end of the siege by shaving off his hair and his beard. A third of this he must burn, a third hack with a sword, and a third scatter to the wind. Thus,

at the end of the siege, some of Jerusalem's inhabitants will die by famine, pestilence, and the sword, and the rest will be scattered among the nations. Jehovah will make her a devastation. Why? Because of the offensiveness of her depraved and detestable idolatry. Wealth will buy no relief. In the day of Jehovah's fury, the people of Jerusalem will throw their silver in the streets, "and they will have to know that I am Jehovah."—7:27.

12 **Ezekiel's vision of apostate Jerusalem** (8:1–11:25). It is now 612 B.C.E. In a vision Ezekiel is transported to faraway Jerusalem, where he sees the detestable things that are happening in Jehovah's temple. In the courtyard, there is a disgusting symbol inciting Jehovah to jealousy. Boring through the wall, Ezekiel finds 70 of the elderly men worshiping before wall carvings of loathsome beasts and dungy idols. They excuse themselves by saying: "Jehovah is not seeing us. Jehovah has left the land." (8:12) At the north gate, women are weeping over the pagan god Tammuz. But that is not all! Right in the entrance of the temple itself, there are 25 men, with their backs to the temple, worshiping the sun. They are profaning Jehovah to his face, and he will surely act in his rage!

13 Now look! Six men appear with smashing weapons in their hands. Among them is a seventh clothed with linen, with a secretary's inkhorn. Jehovah tells this man in linen to pass through the midst of the city and put a mark on the foreheads of the men sighing and groaning over the detestable things being done in its midst. Next, he tells the six men to move in and kill off everyone, "old man, young man and virgin and little child and women," on whom there is no mark. This they do, starting with the old men before the house. The man in linen reports: "I have done just as you have commanded me."—9:6, 11.

14 Ezekiel again sees the glory of Jehovah, rising above the cherubs. A cherub thrusts out fiery coals from between the wheelwork, and the man in linen takes them and scatters them over the city. As for the scattered ones of Israel, Jehovah promises to regather them and give them a new spirit. But what of these wicked false worshipers in Jerusalem? "Upon their head I shall certainly bring their own way," says Jehovah. (11:21) The glory of Jehovah is seen ascending from over the city, and Ezekiel proceeds to tell the vision to the exiled people.

7. Into what three sections does the book of Ezekiel naturally fall?
8. What does Ezekiel see in his initial vision?
9. What is involved in Ezekiel's commission?
10. What sign to Israel does Ezekiel enact?
11. (a) How does Ezekiel portray the calamitous end of the siege? (b) Why will there be no relief?

12. What detestable things are seen by Ezekiel in his vision of apostate Jerusalem?
13. What orders do the man in linen and the six men with weapons carry out?
14. What does the vision finally show as to Jehovah's glory and his judgments?

[15] **Further prophecies in Babylon concerning Jerusalem** (12:1–19:14). Ezekiel becomes the actor in another symbolic scene. During the daytime, he brings out of his house his luggage for exile, and then at night he goes through a hole in the wall of the city with his face covered. He explains this to be a portent: "Into exile, into captivity they will go." (12:11) Those stupid prophets who walk after their own spirit! They are crying, "There is peace!" when there is no peace. (13:10) Even if Noah, Daniel, and Job were in Jerusalem, they could not deliver a soul but themselves.

[16] The city is like a worthless vine. The wood is no good for making poles, not even pegs! It is burned at both ends and scorched in the middle —useless. How faithless and worthless has Jerusalem become! Born from the land of the Canaanites, she was picked up by Jehovah as an abandoned infant. He reared her and entered into a marriage covenant with her. He made her beautiful, "fit for royal position." (16:13) But she has become a prostitute, turning to the nations as they pass by. She has worshiped their images and burned her sons in the fire. Her end will be destruction at the hands of these same nations, her paramours. She is worse than her sisters Sodom and Samaria. Even so, Jehovah, the merciful God, will make atonement for her and restore her according to his covenant.

[17] Jehovah gives the prophet a riddle and then relates the interpretation. It illustrates the futility of Jerusalem's turning to Egypt for help. A great eagle (Nebuchadnezzar) comes and plucks the top (Jehoiachin) of a lofty cedar, brings him to Babylon, and plants in his place a vine (Zedekiah). The vine turns its branches toward another eagle (Egypt), but is it successful? It is torn out by the roots! Jehovah himself will take a tender twig from the lofty treetop of the cedar and transplant it upon a high and lofty mountain. There it will grow into a majestic cedar as a residing place for "all the birds of every wing." All will have to know that Jehovah has done it.—17:23, 24.

[18] Jehovah reproves the Jewish exiles for their proverbial saying: "Fathers are the ones that eat unripe grapes, but it is the teeth of the sons that get set on edge." No, "the soul that is sinning—it itself will die." (18:2, 4) The righteous one will keep living. Jehovah takes no delight in the death of the wicked. His delight is to see the wicked turn from his evil ways and live. As for the kings of Judah, like young lions they have been snared by Egypt and by Babylon. Their voice will "no more be heard on the mountains of Israel."—19:9.

[19] **Denunciations against Jerusalem** (20:1–23:49). Time has moved on to 611 B.C.E. Again the elders among the exiles come to Ezekiel to inquire of Jehovah. What they hear is a recital of Israel's long history of rebellion and depraved idolatry and a warning that Jehovah has called for a sword to execute judgment against her. He will make Jerusalem "a ruin, a ruin, a ruin." But, glorious hope! Jehovah will hold the kingship ("the crown") for the one who comes with "the legal right" and will give it to him. (21:26, 27) Ezekiel reviews the detestable things done in Jerusalem, "the bloodguilty city." The house of Israel has become like "scummy dross" and is to be gathered into Jerusalem and liquefied there as in a furnace. (22:2, 18) The unfaithfulness of Samaria (Israel) and of Judah is illustrated by two sisters. Samaria as Oholah prostitutes herself to the Assyrians and is destroyed by her lovers. Judah as Oholibah does not learn a lesson but does even worse, prostituting herself first to Assyria and then to Babylon. She will be utterly destroyed, "and you people will have to know that I am the Sovereign Lord Jehovah."—23:49.

[20] **The final siege of Jerusalem commences** (24:1-27). It is 609 B.C.E. Jehovah announces to Ezekiel that the king of Babylon has besieged Jerusalem on this tenth day of the tenth month. He compares the walled city to a widemouthed cooking pot, with its choice inhabitants as the flesh therein. Heat it up! Boil out all the uncleanness of Jerusalem's abominable idolatry! On that same day, Ezekiel's wife dies, but in obedience to Jehovah, the prophet does not mourn. This is a sign that the people must not mourn at Jerusalem's destruction, for it is a judgment from Jehovah, in order that they may know who he is. Jehovah will send an escapee to advise of the destruction of "the beautiful object of their exultation," and until he arrives, Ezekiel must speak no more to the exiles. —24:25.

[21] **Prophecies against the nations** (25:1–32:32). Jehovah foresees that the surrounding nations will rejoice at Jerusalem's downfall and use it as an occasion for casting reproach on the God of Judah. They shall not go unpunished! Ammon will be

---

15. By what further illustration does Ezekiel show the certainty of Jerusalem's inhabitants going into captivity?
16. How is the worthlessness of Jerusalem pictured, but why will there be a restoration?
17. What does Jehovah show by the riddle of the eagle and the vine?
18. (a) What principles does Jehovah state in reproving the Jewish exiles? (b) What judgment awaits the kings of Judah?

---

19. (a) Against the background of ruin, what hope does Ezekiel make known? (b) How does he illustrate the unfaithfulness of Israel and Judah and its result?
20. To what is besieged Jerusalem likened, and what powerful sign does Jehovah give with regard to his judgment on her?
21. How will the nations have to know Jehovah and his vengeance?

given to the Orientals, and Moab will also. Edom will be made a devastated place, and great acts of vengeance will be executed against the Philistines. All of them, Jehovah says, "will have to know that I am Jehovah when I bring my vengeance on them."—25:17.

²² Tyre receives special mention. Proud of her thriving commerce, she is like a pretty ship in the midst of the seas, but soon she will lie broken in the depths of the waters. "I am god," boasts her leader. (28:9) Jehovah has his prophet deliver a dirge concerning the king of Tyre: As a beauteous anointed cherub, he has been in Eden, the garden of God; but Jehovah will put him out of His mountain as profane, and he will be devoured by a fire from within. Jehovah says He will also be sanctified by bringing destruction on scornful Sidon.

²³ Jehovah now tells Ezekiel to set his face against Egypt and its Pharaoh and to prophesy against them. "My Nile River belongs to me, and I—I have made it for myself," brags Pharaoh. (29:3) Pharaoh, and the Egyptians who believe in him, will also have to know that Jehovah is God, and the lesson will be administered by a 40-year desolation. Ezekiel here inserts some information actually revealed to him later, in 591 B.C.E. Jehovah will give Egypt to Nebuchadnezzar as compensation for his service in wearing down Tyre. (Nebuchadnezzar took very little spoil at Tyre, since the Tyrians escaped with most of their wealth to their island city.) In a dirge, Ezekiel makes known that Nebuchadnezzar will despoil the pride of Egypt, and "they will also have to know that I am Jehovah."—32:15.

²⁴ **Watchman to the exiles; restoration foretold** (33:1–37:28). Jehovah reviews with Ezekiel his responsibility as watchman. The people are saying, "The way of Jehovah is not adjusted right." So Ezekiel must make it clear to them how wrong they are. (33:17) But now it is 607 B.C.E., the fifth day of the tenth month.* An escapee arrives from Jerusalem to tell the prophet: "The city has been struck down!" (33:21) Ezekiel, now free again to speak to the exiles, tells them that any thoughts they have of rescuing Judah are futile. Though they come to Ezekiel to hear Jehovah's word, he is to them just like a singer of love songs, like one

with a pretty voice playing well on a stringed instrument. They pay no attention. However, when it comes true, they will know that a prophet has been in their midst. Ezekiel rebukes the false shepherds who have forsaken the flock to feed themselves. Jehovah, the Perfect Shepherd, will gather the scattered sheep and bring them to a fat pasturage on the mountains of Israel. There he will raise up over them one shepherd, 'even his servant David.' (34:23) Jehovah himself will become their God. He will make a covenant of peace and pour upon them rains of blessing.

²⁵ Ezekiel again prophesies desolation for Mount Seir (Edom). However, the devastated places of Israel will be rebuilt, for Jehovah will have compassion for his holy name, to sanctify it before the nations. He will give his people a new heart and a new spirit, and their land will again become "like the garden of Eden." (36:35) Ezekiel now sees a vision of Israel represented as a valley of dry bones. Ezekiel prophesies over the bones. Miraculously they begin to have flesh, breath, and life again. Just so will Jehovah open the burial places of captivity in Babylon and restore Israel to its land again. Ezekiel takes two sticks representing the two houses of Israel, Judah and Ephraim. In his hand they become one stick. Thus, when Jehovah restores Israel, they will be united in a covenant of peace under his servant "David."—37:24.

²⁶ **The attack by Gog of Magog on restored Israel** (38:1–39:29). Then will come invasion from a new quarter! Drawn out to the attack by the tantalizing peace and prosperity of Jehovah's restored people, Gog of Magog will make his frenzied attack. He will rush in to engulf them. At this, Jehovah will rise in the fire of his fury. He will set each one's sword against his brother and bring on them pestilence and blood and a flooding downpour of hailstones, fire, and sulfur. They will go down knowing that Jehovah is "the Holy One in Israel." (39:7) His people will then light fires with the enemies' shattered war equipment and bury the bones in "the Valley of Gog's Crowd." (39:11) Carrion birds and beasts will eat the flesh of those slain and drink their blood. Henceforth Israel will dwell in security, with no one to make them tremble, and Jehovah will pour out his spirit on them.

²⁷ **Ezekiel's vision of the temple** (40:1–48:35). We come to the year 593 B.C.E. It is the 14th year since the destruction of Solomon's temple, and the repentant ones among the exiles are in need of encouragement and hope. Jehovah transports Eze-

---

* While the Masoretic text says that the escapee arrived from Jerusalem in the 12th year, other manuscripts read "eleventh year," and the text is so rendered by Lamsa and Moffatt as well as *An American Translation.*

---

22. What special mention does Tyre receive, and how will Jehovah be sanctified in connection with Sidon?
23. What will Egypt have to know, and how will this come about?
24. (a) What is Ezekiel's responsibility as watchman? (b) At news of Jerusalem's fall, what message does Ezekiel proclaim to the exiles? (c) What promise of blessing is highlighted in chapter 34?

25. (a) Why and how will Jehovah make the land like Eden? (b) What is illustrated by the vision of the dry bones? by that of the two sticks?
26. Why does Gog of Magog attack, and with what result?
27. What does Ezekiel see in a visionary visit to the land of Israel, and how does God's glory appear?

kiel in a vision to the land of Israel and sets him down on a very high mountain. Here, in vision, he sees a temple and "the structure of a city to the south." An angel instructs him: "Tell everything that you are seeing to the house of Israel." (40:2, 4) Then he shows Ezekiel all the details of the temple and its courtyards, measuring the walls, the gates, the guard chambers, the dining rooms, and the temple itself, with its Holy and Most Holy. He takes Ezekiel to the east gate. "And, look! the glory of the God of Israel was coming from the direction of the east, and his voice was like the voice of vast waters; and the earth itself shone because of his glory." (43:2) The angel fully instructs Ezekiel concerning the House (or temple); the altar and its sacrifices; the rights and duties of the priests, the Levites, and the chieftain; and the apportioning of the land.

²⁸ The angel brings Ezekiel back to the entrance of the House, where the prophet sees water going forth from the threshold of the House toward the east, by the south side of the altar. It starts as a trickle but gets bigger and bigger until it becomes a torrent. Then it flows into the Dead Sea, where fish come to life and a fishing industry springs up. On either side of the torrent, trees provide food and healing for the people. The vision then gives the inheritances of the 12 tribes, not overlooking the alien resident and the chieftain, and describes the holy city to the south, with its 12 gates named after the tribes. The city is to be called by a most glorious name: "Jehovah Himself Is There." —48:35.

WHY BENEFICIAL

²⁹ The pronouncements, the visions, and the promises that Jehovah gave to Ezekiel were all faithfully related to the Jews in exile. While many scoffed at and ridiculed the prophet, some did believe. These benefited greatly. They were strengthened by the promises of restoration. Unlike other nations taken into captivity, they preserved their national identity, and Jehovah restored a remnant, as he foretold, in 537 B.C.E. (Ezek. 28:25, 26; 39:21-28; Ezra 2:1; 3:1) They rebuilt the house of Jehovah and renewed true worship there.

³⁰ The principles set out in Ezekiel are also invaluable to us today. Apostasy and idolatry, coupled with rebellion, can only lead to Jehovah's disfavor. (Ezek. 6:1-7; 12:2-4, 11-16) Each one will answer for his own sin, but Jehovah will forgive the one who turns back from his wrong course. That one will be granted mercy and will keep living. (18:20-22) God's servants must be faithful watchmen like Ezekiel, even in difficult assignments and under ridicule and reproach. We must not let the wicked die unwarned, with their blood upon our heads. (3:17; 33:1-9) Shepherds of God's people bear a heavy responsibility to care for the flock.—34:2-10.

³¹ Outstanding in the book of Ezekiel are the prophecies concerning the Messiah. He is referred to as the one "who has the legal right" to the throne of David and to whom it must be given. In two places he is spoken of as "my servant David," also as "shepherd," "king," and "chieftain." (21:27; 34: 23, 24; 37:24, 25) Since David had long since died, Ezekiel was speaking of the One who was to be both David's Son and Lord. (Ps. 110:1; Matt. 22: 42-45) Ezekiel, like Isaiah, speaks of the planting of a tender twig that will be put on high by Jehovah.—Ezek. 17:22-24; Isa. 11:1-3.

³² It is of interest to compare Ezekiel's temple vision with the Revelation vision of "the holy city Jerusalem." (Rev. 21:10) There are differences to be noted; for example, Ezekiel's temple is separate and to the north of the city, while Jehovah himself is the temple of the city of Revelation. In each case, however, there is the flowing forth of the river of life, there are the trees bearing monthly crops of fruit and leaves for healing, and there is the presence of the glory of Jehovah. Each vision makes its contribution toward appreciation for Jehovah's kingship and his provision of salvation for those who render him sacred service.—Ezek. 43:4, 5 —Rev. 21:11; Ezek. 47:1, 8, 9, 12—Rev. 22:1-3.

³³ The book of Ezekiel emphasizes that Jehovah is holy. It makes known that the sanctification of Jehovah's name is more important than anything else. "'I shall certainly sanctify my great name, . . . and the nations will have to know that I am Jehovah,' is the utterance of the Sovereign Lord Jehovah." As the prophecy shows, he will sanctify his name by destroying all profaners of that name, including Gog of Magog. Wise are all those who now sanctify Jehovah in their lives by meeting his requirements for acceptable worship. These will find healing and eternal life by the river that flows from his temple. Transcendent in glory and exquisite in beauty is the city that is called "Jehovah Himself Is There"!—Ezek. 36:23; 38:16; 48:35.

---

28. What does Ezekiel's vision show concerning the stream that proceeds forth from the House, and what is revealed as to the city and its name?
29. In what way did the Jewish exiles benefit from Ezekiel's prophecy?
30. What principles set out in Ezekiel are valuable to us today?

---

31. What prophecies of Ezekiel foretell the coming of the Messiah?
32. How does Ezekiel's temple vision compare with the Revelation vision of "the holy city"?
33. What does Ezekiel emphasize, and what will result to those who now sanctify Jehovah in their lives?

27
Daniel

Writer: **Daniel**

Place Written: **Babylon**

Writing Completed: **c. 536 B.C.E.**

Time Covered: **618–c. 536 B.C.E.**

IN THIS day when all nations of earth stand on the brink of disaster, the book of Daniel brings to attention prophetic messages of momentous import. Whereas the Bible books of Samuel, Kings, and Chronicles are based on eyewitness records of the history of God's typical kingdom (the Davidic dynasty), Daniel focuses on the nations of the world and gives forevisions of the power struggle of the great dynasties from Daniel's time down till "the time of the end." This is world history written in advance. It leads up to an absorbing climax in showing what comes to pass "in the final part of the days." Like Nebuchadnezzar, the nations have to learn the hard way "that the Most High is Ruler in the kingdom of mankind" and that finally he gives it to one "like a son of man," the Messiah and Leader, Christ Jesus. (Dan. 12:4; 10:14; 4:25; 7:13, 14; 9:25; John 3:13-16) By paying close attention to the prophetic fulfillments of the inspired book of Daniel, we will appreciate more fully Jehovah's power of prophecy and his assurances of protection and blessing for his people.—2 Pet. 1:19.

² The book is named after its writer. "Daniel" (Hebrew, Da·ni·ye'l') means "My Judge Is God." Ezekiel, who lived at the same time, confirms that Daniel was an actual person, naming him along with Noah and Job. (Ezek. 14:14, 20; 28:3) Daniel dates the beginning of his book as "the third year of the kingship of Jehoiakim the king of Judah." This was 618 B.C.E., Jehoiakim's third year as *tributary king* to Nebuchadnezzar.* Daniel's prophetic visions continued down to Cyrus' third year, about 536 B.C.E. (Dan. 1:1; 2:1; 10:1, 4) What eventful years were covered by Daniel's life span! His early days were spent under God's kingdom in Judah. Then, as a teenage prince, along with his noble Judean companions, he was taken to Babylon to live through the rise and fall of that third world power of Bible history. Daniel survived to serve as government official in the fourth world

power, Medo-Persia. Daniel must have lived nearly one hundred years.

³ The book of Daniel has always been included in the Jewish catalog of inspired Scriptures. Fragments of Daniel have been found among those of the other canonical books in the Dead Sea Scrolls, some of which date from the first half of the first century B.C.E. However, an even more important proof of the book's authenticity is to be found in the references to it in the Christian Greek Scriptures. Jesus specifically names Daniel in his prophecy on "the conclusion of the system of things," wherein he makes several quotations from the book.—Matt 24:3; see also Dan. 9:27; 11:31; and 12:11—Matt. 24:15 and Mark 13:14; Dan. 12:1—Matt. 24:21; Dan. 7:13, 14—Matt. 24:30.

⁴ Though higher critics of the Bible have called in question the historicalness of Daniel's book, archaeological finds over the years have completely routed their assertions. For example, these critics leveled scorn at Daniel's statement that Belshazzar was king in Babylon at the time that Nabonidus was reputed to be ruler. (Dan. 5:1) Archaeology has now established beyond question that Belshazzar was an actual person and that he was a coregent of Nabonidus in the last years of the Babylonian Empire. For example, an ancient cuneiform text described as the "Verse Account of Nabonidus" clearly confirms that Belshazzar exercised kingly authority at Babylon and explains the manner of his becoming coruler with Nabonidus.* Other cuneiform evidence supports the view that Belshazzar exercised regal functions. A tablet, dated in the 12th year of Nabonidus, contains an oath made in the name of Nabonidus, the king, and Belshazzar, the king's son, thus showing that Belshazzar ranked with his father.# This is also of interest in explaining why Belshazzar offered to make Daniel "the third one in the kingdom" if he

---

* *Insight on the Scriptures*, Vol. 1, page 1269.

---

* *Insight on the Scriptures*, Vol. 1, page 283.
# *Archaeology and the Bible*, 1949, George A. Barton, page 483.

1. What kind of history is contained in Daniel, and what does it highlight?
2. What confirms that Daniel was an actual person, and during what eventful period did he prophesy?

3. What proves the canonicity and authenticity of the book of Daniel?
4, 5. How has archaeology routed the assertions of higher critics regarding Daniel?

could interpret the handwriting on the wall. Nabonidus would be considered the first, Belshazzar would be the second, and Daniel would be heralded as the third ruler. (5:16, 29) One researcher says: "Cuneiform allusions to Belshazzar have thrown so much light upon the role which he played that his place in history stands clearly revealed. There are many texts which indicate that Belshazzar almost equaled Nabonidus in position and prestige. Dual rulership during most of the last Neo-Babylonian reign is an established fact. Nabonidus exercised supreme authority from his court in Tema in Arabia, while Belshazzar acted as coregent in the homeland with Babylon as his center of influence. It is evident that Belshazzar was not a feeble viceroy; he was entrusted with 'the kingship.'"*

5 Some have tried to discredit Daniel's account of the fiery furnace (chap. 3), saying that it is a legendary invention. An Old-Babylonian letter reads, in part: "Thus says Rîm-Sin your lord: Because he has cast the slave-lad into the oven, do you cast the slave into the furnace." Interestingly, referring to it, G. R. Driver stated that this punishment "appears in the story of the Three Holy Men (Dan. III 6, 15, 19-27)."#

6 The Jews included the book of Daniel, not with the Prophets, but with the Writings. On the other hand, the English Bible follows the catalog order of the Greek *Septuagint* and the Latin *Vulgate* by placing Daniel between the major and the minor prophets. There are actually two parts to the book. The first of these, chapters 1 to 6, gives in chronological order the experiences of Daniel and his companions in government service from 617 B.C.E. to 538 B.C.E. (Dan. 1:1, 21) The second part, comprising chapters 7 to 12, is written in the first person by Daniel himself as recorder and describes private visions and angelic interviews that Daniel had from about 553 B.C.E.△ to about 536 B.C.E. (7:2, 28; 8:2; 9:2; 12:5, 7, 8) The two parts together make up the one harmonious book of Daniel.

CONTENTS OF DANIEL

7 **Preparation for State service** (1:1-21). In

---

* *The Yale Oriental Series · Researches*, Vol. XV, 1929.
# *Archiv für Orientforschung*, Vol. 18, 1957-58, page 129.
△ Belshazzar evidently began to reign as coregent from Nabonidus' third year on. Since Nabonidus is believed to have begun his rule in 556 B.C.E., the third year of his rule and "the first year of Belshazzar" was evidently 553 B.C.E.—Daniel 7:1; see *Insight on the Scriptures*, Vol. 1, page 283; Vol. 2, page 457.

6. What two parts make up the book of Daniel?
7. What leads to Daniel and his companions' entering Babylonian government service?

---

617 B.C.E. Daniel comes to Babylon with the captive Jews. The sacred utensils from Jerusalem's temple come also, to be stored in a pagan treasurehouse. Daniel and his three Hebrew companions are among the royal Judean youths chosen for a three-year course of training in the king's palace. Resolved in his heart not to pollute himself with the king's pagan delicacies and wine, Daniel proposes a ten-day test of a vegetable diet. The test turns out in favor of Daniel and his companions, and God gives them knowledge and wisdom. Nebuchadnezzar appoints the four to stand before him as counselors. The last verse of chapter 1, which may have been added long after the preceding portion was written, indicates that Daniel was still in royal service some 80 years after his going into exile, which would be in about 538 B.C.E.

8 **Dream of the dreadful image** (2:1-49). In the second year of his kingship (probably dating from Jerusalem's destruction in 607 B.C.E.), Nebuchadnezzar is agitated by a dream. His magic-practicing priests are unable to reveal the dream and its interpretation. He offers them great gifts, but they protest that no one but the gods can show the king the thing that he is asking. The king becomes furious and orders that the wise men be put to death. Since the four Hebrews are included in this decree, Daniel asks for time to reveal the dream. Daniel and his companions pray to Jehovah for guidance. Jehovah reveals the dream and its meaning to Daniel, who then goes before the king and says: "There exists a God in the heavens who is a Revealer of secrets, and he has made known to King Nebuchadnezzar what is to occur in the final part of the days." (2:28) Daniel describes the dream. It is about an immense image. The head of the image is of gold, its breasts and arms of silver, its belly and thighs of copper, and its legs of iron, with feet partly iron and partly clay. A stone strikes and crushes the image and becomes a large mountain to fill the whole earth. What does this mean? Daniel makes known that the king of Babylon is the head of gold. After his kingdom there will follow a second, a third, and a fourth. Finally, "the God of heaven will set up a kingdom that will never be brought to ruin. . . . It will crush and put an end to all these kingdoms, and it itself will stand to times indefinite." (2:44) In gratitude and appreciation, the king extols Daniel's God as "a God of gods" and makes Daniel "ruler over all the jurisdictional district of Babylon and the chief prefect over all the wise men of Babylon." Daniel's three companions are made administrators in the kingdom.—2:47, 48.

---

8. What dream and interpretation does God reveal to Daniel, and how does Nebuchadnezzar show his appreciation?

⁹ **Three Hebrews survive the fiery furnace** (3: 1-30). Nebuchadnezzar erects a mighty image of gold, 60 cubits (88 ft) high, and orders the rulers of the empire to assemble for its dedication. At the sound of special music, all are to fall down and worship the image. Any who fail to do so are to be thrown into the burning fiery furnace. It is reported that Daniel's three companions, Shadrach, Meshach, and Abednego, have failed to comply. They are brought before the enraged king, where they boldly testify: "Our God whom we are serving is able to rescue us. . . . The image of gold that you have set up we will not worship." (3:17, 18) Filled with fury, the king orders that the furnace be heated seven times more than customary and that the three Hebrews be bound and thrown in. As they do this, the would-be executioners are killed by the fiery flame. Nebuchadnezzar becomes frightened. What is this he sees in the furnace? Four men are walking about unharmed in the midst of the fire, and "the fourth one is resembling a son of the gods." (3:25) The king calls on the three Hebrews to step out of the fire. Out they come, unsinged, without even the smell of fire itself upon them! As a result of their courageous stand for true worship, Nebuchadnezzar proclaims freedom of worship for the Jews throughout the empire.

¹⁰ **Dream of the "seven times"** (4:1-37). This dream appears in the record as Daniel's transcription of a state document of Babylon. It was written by the humbled Nebuchadnezzar. Nebuchadnezzar first acknowledges the might and kingdom of the Most High God. Then he relates a frightening dream and how it was fulfilled upon him. He saw a tree that reached to heaven and provided shelter and food for all flesh. A watcher called out: 'Chop the tree down. Band its stump with iron and copper. Let seven times pass over it, so that it will be known that the Most High is Ruler in the kingdom of mankind and sets up over it the lowliest one of mankind.' (4:14-17) Daniel interpreted the dream, making known that the tree represented Nebuchadnezzar. A fulfillment of this prophetic dream soon followed. At a time of expressing great pride, the king was afflicted with madness; and he lived as a beast in the field for seven years. After that, his sanity was restored, and he acknowledged Jehovah's supremacy.

¹¹ **Belshazzar's feast: handwriting interpreted** (5:1-31). It is the fateful night of October 5, 539 B.C.E. King Belshazzar, son of Nabonidus, as coregent of Babylon, makes a big feast for a thousand of his grandees. The king, under the influence of wine, calls for the sacred gold and silver vessels from Jehovah's temple, and from these Belshazzar and his guests drink, in their debauchery, while praising their pagan gods. Immediately a hand appears and writes a cryptic message on the wall. The king is terrified. His wise men cannot interpret the writing. Finally Daniel is brought in. The king offers to make him the third one in the kingdom if he can read and interpret the writing, but Daniel tells him to keep his gifts to himself. Then he goes on to make known the writing and its meaning: "MENE, MENE, TEKEL and PARSIN. . . . God has numbered the days of your kingdom and has finished it. . . . You have been weighed in the balances and have been found deficient. . . . Your kingdom has been divided and given to the Medes and the Persians." (5:25-28) That very night Belshazzar is killed, and Darius the Mede receives the kingdom.

¹² **Daniel in the lions' pit** (6:1-28). High officials in Darius' government frame mischief against Daniel by having the king pass a law that places a 30-day prohibition on making a petition to any god or man other than the king. Anyone disobeying it is to be thrown to the lions. Daniel refuses to obey this law affecting his worship and turns to Jehovah in prayer. He is thrown into the lions' pit. Miraculously, Jehovah's angel shuts the mouths of the lions, and next morning King Darius is glad to find Daniel unharmed. The enemies are now fed to the lions, and the king issues a decree to fear the God of Daniel, as "he is the living God." (6:26) Daniel prospers in government service on into the reign of Cyrus.

¹³ **Visions of the beasts** (7:1–8:27). We return to "the first year of Belshazzar," whose reign evidently began in 553 B.C.E. Daniel receives a private dream, which he records in Aramaic.* He sees four huge and fearsome beasts appear each in its turn. The fourth is unusually strong, and a small horn comes up among its other horns "speaking grandiose things." (7:8) The Ancient of Days appears and takes his seat. "A thousand thousands" minister to him. "Someone like a son of man" comes before him and is "given rulership and dignity and kingdom, that the peoples, national groups and languages should all serve even him." (7:10, 13, 14)

---

* Daniel 2:4b–7:28 was written in Aramaic, while the rest of the book was written in Hebrew.

---

9. What results from the three Hebrews' bold stand against image worship?
10. What frightening dream involving "seven times" did Nebuchadnezzar have, and was it fulfilled upon him?
11. During what debauchery does Belshazzar see the fateful handwriting, how does Daniel interpret it, and how is it fulfilled?

12. How is a plot against Daniel thwarted, and what decree does Darius then issue?
13. In a private dream, what vision does Daniel have concerning four beasts and the rulership of the Kingdom?

Daniel then receives the interpretation of the vision of the four beasts. They represent four kings, or kingdoms. From among ten horns on the fourth beast, a small horn arises. It becomes mighty and makes war on the holy ones. However, the heavenly Court steps in to give "the kingdom and the rulership and the grandeur of the kingdoms under all the heavens . . . to the people who are the holy ones of the Supreme One."—7:27.

[14] Two years later, long before Babylon's fall, Daniel sees another vision, which he records in Hebrew. A he-goat with a conspicuous horn between its eyes struggles with, and overcomes, a proud ram that has two horns. The he-goat's great horn is broken, and four lesser horns come forth. Out of one of these comes a little horn that becomes great, even to defying the army of the heavens. A period of 2,300 days is foretold until the holy place is to be brought into its "right condition." (8:14) Gabriel explains the vision to Daniel. The ram stands for the kings of Media and Persia. The he-goat is the king of Greece, whose kingdom will be broken into four. Later, a king of fierce countenance will stand up "against the Prince of princes." Since the vision "is yet for many days," Daniel must keep it secret for the present.—8:25, 26.

[15] **Messiah the Leader foretold** (9:1-27). "The first year of Darius . . . of the Medes" finds Daniel examining Jeremiah's prophecy. Realizing that the foretold 70-year desolation of Jerusalem is nearing its close, Daniel prays to Jehovah in confession of his own sins and those of Israel. (Dan. 9:1-4; Jer. 29:10) Gabriel appears in order to make known that there will be "seventy weeks . . . to terminate the transgression, and to finish off sin, and to make atonement for error." Messiah the Leader will come at the end of 69 weeks, after which he will be cut off. The covenant will be kept in force for the many till the end of the 70th week, and finally, there will be desolation and an extermination. —Dan. 9:24-27.

[16] **North versus south, Michael stands up** (10: 1–12:13). It is "the third year of Cyrus," and hence about 536 B.C.E., not long after the Jews' return to Jerusalem. After a three-week fast, Daniel is by the bank of the river Hiddekel. (Dan. 10:1, 4; Gen. 2:14) An angel appears to him and explains that 'the prince of Persia' opposed his coming to Daniel but that "Michael, one of the foremost princes," helped him. He now relates to Daniel a vision that is for "the final part of the days."—Dan. 10:13, 14.

[17] As it opens, this enthralling vision speaks of the Persian dynasty and a coming struggle with Greece. A mighty king will stand up with extensive dominion, but his kingdom will be broken into four parts. Eventually there will be two long lines of kings, the king of the south as opposed to the king of the north. The power struggle will surge back and forth. These incorrigibly bad kings will keep speaking a lie at one table. "At the time appointed," the warfare will flare up again. There is to be a profaning of God's sanctuary, and "the disgusting thing that is causing desolation" is to be set in place. (11:29-31) The king of the north will speak marvelous things against the God of gods and give glory to the god of fortresses. When "in the time of the end" the king of the south engages with the king of the north in a pushing, the king of the north will flood over into many lands, entering also "into the land of the Decoration." Disturbed by reports out of the east and north, he will rage forth and plant "his palatial tents between the grand sea and the holy mountain of Decoration." So "he will have to come all the way to his end, and there will be no helper for him."—11:40, 41, 45.

[18] The grand vision continues: Michael is seen standing 'in behalf of the sons of God's people.' There is to be "a time of distress" unprecedented in human history, but those found written in the book will escape. Many will awake from the dust to everlasting life, "and the ones having insight will shine like the brightness of the expanse." They will bring many to righteousness. Daniel is to seal up the book "until the time of the end." "How long will it be to the end of the wonderful things?" The angel mentions time periods of three and a half times, 1,290 days, and 1,335 days and says that only "the ones having insight will understand." Happy are such ones! Finally, the angel holds out to Daniel the reassuring promise that he will rest and then stand up for his lot "at the end of the days."—12:1, 3, 4, 6, 10, 13.

WHY BENEFICIAL

[19] All who are determined to maintain integrity in an alien world do well to consider the fine example of Daniel and his three companions. No matter how vicious the threat, these continued to live by divine principles. When their lives were in peril, Daniel acted "with counsel and sensibleness" and with respect for the king's superior authority.

---

14. What vision does Daniel have featuring a he-goat and a two-horned ram? How does Gabriel explain it?
15. What causes Daniel to pray to Jehovah, and what does Gabriel now make known concerning "seventy weeks"?
16. Under what circumstances does an angel again appear to Daniel?

---

17. What prophetic history of the king of the north and the king of the south does Daniel now record?
18. What things occur during Michael's standing 'in behalf of the sons of God's people'?
19. What fine examples of integrity and prayerful reliance on Jehovah are to be found in the book of Daniel?

(2:14-16) When the issue was forced, the three Hebrews preferred the burning fiery furnace to an act of idolatry, and Daniel preferred the lions' den to forgoing his privilege of prayer to Jehovah. In each instance Jehovah granted protection. (3:4-6, 16-18, 27; 6:10, 11, 23) Daniel himself provides a splendid example of prayerful reliance on Jehovah God.—2:19-23; 9:3-23; 10:12.

20 Daniel's visions are thrilling and faith-strengthening to review. First, consider the four visions concerning the world powers: (1) There is the vision of the dreadful image, whose head of gold represents the dynasty of Babylonian kings starting with Nebuchadnezzar, after which three other kingdoms rise, as pictured by the other parts of the image. These are the kingdoms that are crushed by the "stone," which in its turn becomes "a kingdom that will never be brought to ruin," God's Kingdom. (2:31-45) (2) There follow Daniel's private visions, the first being that of the four beasts, representing "four kings." These are like a lion, a bear, a leopard with four heads, and a beast that has big teeth of iron, ten horns, and later a small horn. (7:1-8, 17-28) (3) Next, there is the vision of the ram (Medo-Persia), the he-goat (Greece), and the small horn. (8:1-27) (4) Finally, we have the vision of the king of the south and the king of the north. Daniel 11:5-19 accurately describes the rivalry between the Egyptian and Seleucid offshoots of Alexander's Grecian Empire following Alexander's death in 323 B.C.E. From verse 20 the prophecy continues to trace the course of successor nations of the south and north. Jesus' reference to "the disgusting thing that is causing desolation" (11:31), in his prophecy about the sign of his presence, shows that this power struggle of the two kings continues right down to "the conclusion of the system of things." (Matt. 24:3) How comforting the prophecy's assurance that in the "time of distress such as has not been made to occur since there came to be a nation until that time," Michael himself will stand up to remove ungodly nations and bring peace to obedient mankind!—Dan. 11:20–12:1

21 Then, there is Daniel's prophecy of the "seventy weeks." After 69 weeks "Messiah the Leader" was to appear. Remarkably, 483 years (69 times 7 years) after "the going forth of the word" to rebuild Jerusalem, as authorized by Artaxerxes in his 20th year and put into effect by Nehemiah in Jerusalem, Jesus of Nazareth was baptized in the

Jordan River and anointed with holy spirit, becoming Christ, or Messiah (that is, Anointed One).* That was in the year 29 C.E. Thereafter, as Daniel also foretold, there came "an extermination" when Jerusalem was desolated in 70 C.E.—Dan. 9:24-27; Luke 3:21-23; 21:20.

22 In Nebuchadnezzar's dream concerning the chopped-down tree, as recorded by Daniel in chapter 4, it is related that the king, who boasted of his own achievements and had confidence in his own might, was humbled by Jehovah God. He was made to live as a beast of the field until he recognized "that the Most High is Ruler in the kingdom of mankind, and that to the one whom he wants to he gives it." (Dan. 4:32) Are we today going to be like Nebuchadnezzar, boasting in our achievements and placing our confidence in the might of men, so that God has to mete out punishment to us, or will we wisely acknowledge that He is the Ruler in the kingdom of mankind and place our confidence in his Kingdom?

23 The Kingdom hope is emphasized throughout the book of Daniel in a faith-inspiring way! Jehovah God is shown as the Supreme Sovereign who sets up a Kingdom that will never be brought to ruin and that will crush all other kingdoms. (2:19-23, 44; 4:25) Even the pagan kings Nebuchadnezzar and Darius were compelled to acknowledge Jehovah's supremacy. (3:28, 29; 4:2, 3, 37; 6:25-27) Jehovah is exalted and glorified as the Ancient of Days who judges the Kingdom issue and gives to "someone like a son of man" the everlasting "rulership and dignity and kingdom, that the peoples, national groups and languages should all serve even him." It is "the holy ones of the Supreme One" that share with Christ Jesus, "the Son of man," in the Kingdom. (Dan. 7:13, 14, 18, 22; Matt. 24:30; Rev. 14:14) He is Michael, the great prince, who exercises his Kingdom power to crush and put an end to all the kingdoms of this old world. (Dan. 12:1; 2:44; Matt. 24:3, 21; Rev. 12:7-10) The understanding of these prophecies and visions should encourage lovers of righteousness to bestir themselves and rove through the pages of God's Word to find the truly "wonderful things" of God's Kingdom purposes that are revealed to us through the inspired and beneficial book of Daniel.—Dan. 12:2, 3, 6.

* Nehemiah 2:1-8; see also Insight on the Scriptures, Vol. 2, pages 899-901.

20. What four visions are recorded concerning the world powers, and why is it faith-strengthening to consider these today?
21. How did Daniel's prophecy of the "seventy weeks" have a remarkable fulfillment?

22. What lesson do we learn from the humbling of Nebuchadnezzar?
23. (a) How is the Kingdom hope emphasized throughout Daniel? (b) What should this book of prophecy encourage us to do?

28

Hosea

Writer: **Hosea**
Place Written: **Samaria (District)**
Writing Completed: **After
745 B.C.E.**
Time Covered: **Before 804–after
745 B.C.E.**

THE last 12 books of the Hebrew Scriptures are commonly referred to as "the minor prophets." The expression in common use in Germany, "the little prophets," would seem to be more appropriate, for these books are certainly not minor in importance, although their combined length is still less than that of Isaiah or Jeremiah. In the Hebrew Bible, they were considered as one volume and called "The Twelve." Their collection together in this manner was probably for the purpose of preservation, since a single small roll might have been easily lost. As with each of these 12 books, the first one is named after its writer, Hosea, whose name is a shortened form of Hoshaiah, meaning "Saved by Jah; Jah Has Saved."

² In the book bearing his name, little is revealed concerning Hosea except that he was the son of Beeri. His prophecies concern Israel almost exclusively, Judah being mentioned only in passing; and while Jerusalem is not mentioned by Hosea, Israel's dominant tribe, Ephraim, is spoken of by name 37 times and Israel's capital, Samaria, 6 times.

³ The first verse of the book tells us that Hosea served as Jehovah's prophet for an unusually long time, from near the end of the reign of Israel's King Jeroboam II on into the reign of Hezekiah of Judah. That is from no later than 804 B.C.E. until after 745 B.C.E., no less than 59 years. His time of prophetic service no doubt spread over some years into the reigns of Jeroboam II and Hezekiah. During this time Amos, Isaiah, Micah, and Oded were other faithful prophets of Jehovah.—Amos 1:1; Isa. 1:1; Mic. 1:1; 2 Chron. 28:9.

⁴ The authenticity of the prophecy is confirmed by its being quoted a number of times in the Christian Greek Scriptures. Jesus himself quoted Hosea 10:8 in pronouncing judgment on Jerusalem: "Then they will start to say to the mountains,

'Fall over us!' and to the hills, 'Cover us over!'" (Luke 23:30) This same passage is partially quoted at Revelation 6:16. Matthew quotes Hosea 11:1 in showing the fulfillment of the prophecy: "Out of Egypt I called my son." (Matt. 2:15) Hosea's prophecy of the restoration of *all* Israel was fulfilled in that many from the ten-tribe kingdom joined with Judah before its captivity and their descendants were among those who returned after the exile. (Hos. 1:11; 2 Chron. 11:13-17; 30: 6-12, 18, 25; Ezra 2:70) From the time of Ezra, the book has occupied its rightful place in the Hebrew canon as "the word of Jehovah by Hosea." —Hos. 1:2.

⁵ Why did Jehovah send Hosea as his prophet to Israel? It was because of Israel's unfaithfulness and contamination with Baal worship, in violation of Jehovah's covenant. In the Promised Land, Israel had become an agricultural people, but in doing so they adopted not only the Canaanites' way of life but also their religion with its worship of Baal, a god symbolic of the reproductive forces of nature. In Hosea's day Israel had turned completely from the worship of Jehovah to a riotous, drunken ceremonial that included immoral relations with temple prostitutes. Israel attributed prosperity to Baal. She was disloyal to Jehovah, unworthy of him, and therefore had to be disciplined. Jehovah was going to show her that her material possessions were not from Baal, and so he sent Hosea to warn Israel what failure to repent would mean. After Jeroboam II died, Israel faced her most terrible period. A reign of terror, with a number of rulers being assassinated, continued down until the Assyrian captivity in 740 B.C.E. During this time, two factions fought each other, one wanting to form an alliance with Egypt, and the other, with Assyria. Neither group trusted in Jehovah.

⁶ Hosea's style of writing is revealing. He is often tender and sensitive in his wording and repeatedly emphasizes Jehovah's loving-kindness and mercy. He dwells on each small sign of repentance that he sees. His language is at other times

---

1, 2. (a) What are the last 12 books of the Hebrew Scriptures sometimes called? (b) What is known about Hosea, and whom does his prophecy concern?
3. For how long did Hosea prophesy, and who were other prophets of this period?
4. What quotations and prophetic fulfillments confirm the authenticity of Hosea?

---

5. Because of what unfaithfulness did Jehovah punish Israel?
6. What is revealing about Hosea's style of writing?

abrupt and impulsive. What he lacks in rhythm, he makes up for in force and power. He expresses very strong feeling, and he changes thought rapidly.

7 At the outset of his prophetic career, Hosea was commanded to take "a wife of fornication." (1:2) Certainly Jehovah had a purpose in this. Israel had been to Jehovah like a wife who had become unfaithful, committing fornication. Yet he would show his love for her and try to recover her. Hosea's wife, Gomer, could accurately illustrate this. It is understood that after the birth of the first child, she became unfaithful and apparently bore the other children in adultery. (2:5-7) This is indicated by the record's stating she "bore to *him* [Hosea] a son" but omitting any reference to the prophet in connection with the birth of the other two children. (1:3, 6, 8) Chapter 3, verses 1-3, seems to speak of Hosea's taking back Gomer, purchasing her as though a slave, and this ties in with Jehovah's taking back his people after they repented of their adulterous course.

8 The ten-tribe northern kingdom of Israel, to whom the words of Hosea's prophecy are principally directed, was also known as Ephraim, after the name of the dominant tribe in the kingdom. These names, Israel and Ephraim, are used interchangeably in the book.

CONTENTS OF HOSEA

9 **Israel's adulterous course illustrated** (1:1–3:5). Hosea's "wife of fornication" bears the prophet a son, Jezreel. Later she has two other children, a daughter, Lo-ruhamah, meaning "[She Was] Not Shown Mercy," and a son, Lo-ammi, meaning "Not My People." These two names Jehovah gave to indicate that he would "no more show mercy again to the house of Israel" and to emphasize his rejection of them as a whole as his people. (1:2, 6, 9) Yet, the sons of Judah and Israel, as "sons of the living God," are to be gathered in unity under one head, "because great will be the day of Jezreel." (1:10, 11) Cleansed of adulterous Baal worship, God's people will return to Jehovah and accept him as their husband. (2:16) Jehovah will give security to Israel and will engage her to him for time indefinite in righteousness, in justice, in loving-kindness, in mercies, and in faithfulness. In harmony with the name Jezreel (meaning "God Will Sow Seed"), Jehovah promises: "I shall certainly sow her like seed for me in the earth, . . . and I will say to those not my people: 'You are my

people'; and they, for their part, will say: 'You are my God.'" (2:23) Like a wife repentant of her adultery, "Israel will come back and certainly look for Jehovah their God, and for David their king." —3:5.

10 **Prophetic judgments against Ephraim (and Judah)** (4:1–14:9). The first verse of chapter 4 gives the setting for the prophetic warnings that follow: "Jehovah has a legal case with the inhabitants of the land, for there is no truth nor loving-kindness nor knowledge of God in the land." What will result from this condition? "Because the knowledge is what you yourself have rejected, I shall also reject you from serving as a priest to me; and because you keep forgetting the law of your God, I shall forget your sons, even I," says Jehovah. (4:1, 6) The very spirit of fornication has caused Israel to wander away. There will be an accounting for harlotlike Israel and Judah, but they will seek Jehovah when they find themselves "in sore straits."—5:15.

11 Hosea pleads with the people: "Let us return to Jehovah, for . . . he will heal us." Jehovah delights in loving-kindness and divine knowledge rather than in sacrifices and burnt offerings, but the loving-kindness of Ephraim and Judah is "like the dew that early goes away." (6:1, 4) Ephraim is "like a simpleminded dove without heart." The people go to Egypt and to Assyria for aid rather than to Jehovah. (7:11) It is woe to them. Why? They are loafing about, scheming bad things, overstepping Jehovah's covenant, and transgressing his law. "For it is wind that they keep sowing, and a storm wind is what they will reap." (8:7) Jehovah will remember their error and give attention to their sins. "They will become fugitives among the nations." (9:17) Israel is a degenerating vine whose heart has become hypocritical. Instead of sowing seed in righteousness and reaping in accord with loving-kindness, Israel has plowed wickedness and reaped unrighteousness. "Out of Egypt I called my son," reminds Jehovah. (11:1) Yes, He loved Israel from his boyhood, but Israel has surrounded Him with lying and deception. Jehovah counsels: "To your God you should return, keeping loving-kindness and justice; and let there be a hoping in your God constantly."—12:6.

12 In the 13th chapter, Hosea sums up all that has gone before regarding Israel's early promise and Jehovah's tender care, as well as Israel's forgetfulness and the nation's finally turning against

---

7. What is illustrated in Gomer's unfaithfulness and her later recovery?
8. What names are used interchangeably in the book?
9. What do the names of Gomer's children indicate as to how Jehovah would deal with Israel?

10. What is to result from the nation's rejection of knowledge?
11. How does Hosea plead with the people, but why is it woe to them?
12. (a) What does Hosea sum up in the 13th chapter? (b) What restoration is promised?

Jehovah. Jehovah declares: "I proceeded to give you a king in my anger, and I shall take him away in my fury." (13:11) But, then, there will be restoration: "From the hand of Sheol I shall redeem them; from death I shall recover them. Where are your stings, O Death? Where is your destructiveness, O Sheol?" (13:14) However, horrible indeed will be the fate of rebellious Samaria.

¹³ The book concludes with the heartrending plea: 'Do come back, O Israel, to Jehovah your God, for you have stumbled in your error. Seek pardon, and offer in return the young bulls of your lips. Jehovah will show you mercy and love. He will become like refreshing dew to you, and you will blossom as the lily and the olive tree.' The wise and discreet will understand these things: "For the ways of Jehovah are upright, and the righteous are the ones who will walk in them; but the transgressors are the ones who will stumble in them."—14:1-6, 9.

WHY BENEFICIAL

¹⁴ The book of Hosea strengthens faith in Jehovah's inspired prophecies. Everything that Hosea prophesied concerning Israel and Judah came true. Israel was deserted by her lovers among the idolatrous neighbor nations and reaped the whirlwind of destruction from Assyria in 740 B.C.E. (Hos. 8:7-10; 2 Ki. 15:20; 17:3-6, 18) However, Hosea had foretold that Jehovah would show mercy to Judah and save her, but not by military might. This was fulfilled when Jehovah's angel slew 185,000 of the Assyrians threatening Jerusalem. (Hos. 1:7; 2 Ki. 19:34, 35) Nevertheless, Judah was included in the judgment of Hosea 8:14: "And I shall certainly send fire into his cities and it must devour the dwelling towers of each one," a forecast that had terrible fulfillment when Nebuchadnezzar laid waste Judah and Jerusalem, 609-607 B.C.E. (Jer. 34:6, 7; 2 Chron. 36:19) Hosea's many prophecies of restoration were fulfilled when Jehovah collected together Judah and Israel, and 'they went up out of the land' of their exile in 537 B.C.E.—Hos. 1:10, 11; 2:14-23; 3:5; 11:8-11; 13:14; 14:1-9; Ezra 2:1; 3:1-3.

¹⁵ References to Hosea's prophecy by the writ-

ers of the Christian Greek Scriptures are also most beneficial for our consideration today. For example, Paul makes a powerful application of Hosea 13:14 in discussing the resurrection: "Death, where is your victory? Death, where is your sting?" (1 Cor. 15:55) In emphasizing Jehovah's undeserved kindness as expressed toward vessels of mercy, Paul quotes from Hosea 1:10 and 2:23: "It is as he says also in Hosea: 'Those not my people I will call "my people," and her who was not beloved "beloved"; and in the place where it was said to them, "You are not my people," there they will be called "sons of the living God."'" (Rom. 9:25, 26) Peter paraphrases these same passages from Hosea in saying: "For you were once not a people, but are now God's people; you were those who had not been shown mercy, but are now those who have been shown mercy."—1 Pet. 2:10.

¹⁶ Thus, Hosea's prophecy is seen to have been fulfilled not only in the return of a remnant in Zerubbabel's day but also in Jehovah's merciful gathering of a spiritual remnant who become 'beloved sons of the living God.' By inspiration Hosea saw the requirements for these. It is not an appearance of worship with formal ceremony, but in the words of Hosea 6:6 (which Jesus repeated at Matthew 9:13 and 12:7): "In loving-kindness I have taken delight, and not in sacrifice; and in the knowledge of God rather than in whole burnt offerings."

¹⁷ The illustration of the adulterous wife that was so vividly acted out in Hosea's own life shows that Jehovah abhors those who turn from him into ways of idolatry and false worship, thus committing spiritual adultery. Any who have stumbled in error must come back to Jehovah in true repentance and 'offer in return the young bulls of their lips.' (Hos. 14:2; Heb. 13:15) These may rejoice with the remnant of the spiritual sons of Israel in the fulfillment of the Kingdom promise of Hosea 3:5: "Afterwards the sons of Israel will come back and certainly look for Jehovah their God, and for David their king; and they will certainly come quivering to Jehovah and to his goodness in the final part of the days."

---

13. What plea ends the book of Hosea, and who will walk in Jehovah's ways?
14. What accurate fulfillments of Hosea's prophecy are to be noted?
15. How do writers of the Christian Greek Scriptures apply quotations from the book of Hosea?

16. What words of Hosea did Jesus repeat as showing Jehovah's requirements for worship?
17. (a) What is necessary for any who stumble into spiritual adultery? (b) What joyful Kingdom promise is contained in Hosea?

29

Joel

Writer: **Joel**

Place Written: **Judah**

Writing Completed:
c. 820 B.C.E. (?)

WAVE upon wave, a horde of insects desolates the land. Fire ahead of them and flame behind complete the devastation. Everywhere there is famine. The sun turns into darkness and the moon into blood, for the great and fear-inspiring day of Jehovah is at hand. He gives the command to thrust in the sickle and gather the nations for destruction. However, some "will get away safe." (Joel 2:32) The consideration of these dramatic events makes Joel's prophecy both intensely interesting and of great benefit to us.

² The book is introduced as "the word of Jehovah that occurred to Joel the son of Pethuel." The Bible tells us nothing more than this about Joel himself. It is the prophetic message that is emphasized and not its writer. The name "Joel" (Hebrew, Yoh·ʹel) is understood to mean "Jehovah Is God." Joel's firsthand familiarity with Jerusalem, its temple, and the details of temple service may indicate that he wrote his book in Jerusalem or Judah.—Joel 1:1, 9, 13, 14; 2:1, 15, 16, 32.

³ When was the book of Joel written? This cannot be stated with certainty. Scholars variously assign dates ranging from before 800 B.C.E. to about 400 B.C.E. The description of Jehovah's judgment of the nations in the plain of Jehoshaphat suggests that Joel wrote his prophecy sometime after Jehovah's great victory on behalf of King Jehoshaphat of Judah, and hence after Jehoshaphat became king in 936 B.C.E. (Joel 3:2, 12; 2 Chron. 20:22-26) The prophet Amos may have quoted from the text of Joel. This, then, would mean that Joel's prophecy was written before that of Amos, who began prophesying sometime between 829 and 804 B.C.E. (Joel 3:16; Amos 1:2) An early date may also be indicated by the book's position in the Hebrew canon between Hosea and Amos. Hence a date of approximately 820 B.C.E. is suggested for Joel's prophecy.

⁴ The authenticity of the prophecy is proved by quotations and references to it in the Christian Greek Scriptures. On the day of Pentecost, Peter spoke of "the prophet Joel" and applied one of his prophecies. Paul quoted the same prophecy and showed its fulfillment toward both Jew and non-Jew. (Joel 2:28-32; Acts 2:16-21; Rom. 10:13) Joel's prophecies against neighbor nations were all fulfilled. The great city of Tyre was besieged by Nebuchadnezzar, and later the island city was brought to ruin by Alexander the Great. Philistia likewise perished. Edom became a wilderness. (Joel 3:4, 19) The Jews never questioned the canonicity of Joel, and they placed the book second among the so-called minor prophets.

⁵ The style of Joel is both vivid and expressive. He repeats for emphasis and uses striking similes. Locusts are called a nation, a people, and an army. Their teeth are like those of lions, their appearance like horses, and their sound like chariots of an army drawn up for battle. *The Interpreter's Bible* quotes an authority on locust control as saying: "Joel's description of a locust invasion has never been surpassed for its dramatic accuracy of detail."* Listen now as Joel prophesies of the fear-inspiring day of Jehovah.

CONTENTS OF JOEL

⁶ **Insect invasion strips the land; day of Jehovah near** (1:1–2:11). What a terrible vision of calamity Joel sees! A devastating onslaught by the caterpillar, the locust, the creeping unwinged locust, and the cockroach. Vines and fig trees have been stripped bare, and starvation stalks the land. There are no grain or drink offerings for the house of Jehovah. Joel warns the priests and ministers of God to repent. "Alas for the day," he cries out, "because the day of Jehovah is near, and like a despoiling from the Almighty One it will come!" (1:15) Animals wander in confusion. Flames have

* 1956, Vol. VI, page 733.

---

1. What dramatic events highlight Joel's prophecy?
2. What do we know of Joel and the circumstances of his prophesying?
3. For what reasons is a date of about 820 B.C.E. suggested for Joel's prophecy?

4. What proofs are there of the authenticity of Joel?
5. In what way is the prophecy of Joel strikingly expressive?
6. What terrible vision does Joel first see?

scorched the pastureland and trees, and the wilderness has been seared by fire.

[7] Sound the alert! "Blow a horn in Zion, O men, and shout a war cry in my holy mountain." (2:1) The day of Jehovah is near, a day of darkness and thick gloom. Look! A people numerous and mighty. They turn the Edenlike land into a desolate wilderness. Nothing escapes. Like horses and with a sound like chariots on the mountaintops they run. Like a people in battle order they rush into the city, climbing on walls and houses and through windows. The land is agitated and the heavens rock. Jehovah is in command of this numerous military force. "The day of Jehovah is great and very fear-inspiring, and who can hold up under it?"—2:11.

[8] **Turn to Jehovah; spirit to be poured out** (2:12-32). But something can be done to stem the invasion. Jehovah counsels: "Come back to me with all your hearts, . . . rip apart your hearts, and not your garments; and come back to Jehovah your God." (2:12, 13) A horn blast summons the people to solemn assembly. If they return to him, "Jehovah will be zealous for his land and will show compassion upon his people." (2:18) There will be blessings and forgiveness, and the invader will be turned back. Rather than a time for fear, it is a time to be joyful and rejoice, for there will be fruit and grain and new wine and oil. Jehovah will compensate for the years that his great military force of locusts has eaten. His promise is: "You will certainly eat, eating and becoming satisfied, and you will be bound to praise the name of Jehovah your God, who has done with you so wonderfully." (2:26) They will learn that Jehovah alone is their God in the midst of Israel.

[9] "And after that it must occur that I shall pour out my spirit on every sort of flesh," says Jehovah, "and your sons and your daughters will certainly prophesy. As for your old men, dreams they will dream. As for your young men, visions they will see. And even on the menservants and on the maidservants in those days I shall pour out my spirit." There will be terrifying portents in sun and moon before the coming of the day of Jehovah. Yet some will survive. "It must occur that everyone who calls on the name of Jehovah will get away safe."—2:28-32.

[10] **Nations to be judged in "plain of Jehoshaphat"** (3:1-21). Jehovah will bring back the captives of Judah and Jerusalem. The nations will be gathered; Tyre, Sidon, and Philistia will pay dearly for reproaching and enslaving Jehovah's people. Listen to Jehovah as he challenges the nations: "Sanctify war! Arouse the powerful men! Let them draw near! Let them come up, all the men of war!" (3:9) Let them beat plowshares into swords and come up to the low plain of Jehoshaphat (meaning "Jehovah Is Judge"). Jehovah's command rings out: "Thrust in a sickle, for harvest has grown ripe. . . . The press vats actually overflow; for their badness has become abundant. Crowds, crowds are in the low plain of the decision, for the day of Jehovah is near." (3:13, 14) Sun and moon become dark. Jehovah roars out of Zion, causing heaven and earth to rock, but he proves to be a refuge and fortress for his own people. They will have to know that he is Jehovah their God.

[11] What paradisaic plenty will be seen "in that day"! (3:18) The mountains will drip wine, the hills will flow with milk, and the streambeds will course with abundant water. A refreshing spring will go forth from the house of Jehovah. Egypt and Edom, who have shed innocent blood in Judah, will become desolate wastes, but Judah and Jerusalem will be inhabited to time indefinite, "and Jehovah will be residing in Zion."—3:21.

WHY BENEFICIAL

[12] Some commentators have described Joel as a prophet of gloom. However, from the point of view of God's own people, he appears as the proclaimer of glorious tidings of deliverance. The apostle Paul emphasizes this thought at Romans 10:13, saying: "For 'everyone who calls on the name of Jehovah will be saved.'" (Joel 2:32) There was a striking fulfillment of Joel's prophecy on the day of Pentecost 33 C.E. On that occasion Peter was inspired to explain that the outpouring of God's spirit upon Christ's disciples was a fulfillment of Joel's prophecy. (Acts 2:1-21; Joel 2:28, 29, 32) Peter laid great stress on the prophetic import of Joel's words: "And everyone who calls on the name of Jehovah will be saved."—Acts 2:21, 39, 40.

[13] Striking similarities can be seen between the locust plague described by Joel and the plague prophesied in Revelation chapter 9. Again the sun is darkened. The locusts resemble horses prepared for battle, they make a sound like that of chariots, and they have teeth like those of lions. (Joel 2:4,

---

7. How is Jehovah's invading military force described?
8. (a) How only may the insect invasion be stemmed? (b) What compensation does Jehovah promise?
9. What heart-stirring prophecy follows?
10. What is to take place in the low plain of Jehoshaphat?

11. How does Joel then describe the blessings from Jehovah that are to follow?
12. What prophetic import of Joel did Peter stress at Pentecost?
13. (a) What striking similarities can be seen between Joel and Revelation? (b) What parallels to Joel are to be found with other prophecies?

5, 10; 1:6; Rev. 9:2, 7-9) Joel's prophecy at Joel 2: 31, which tells of the sun turning into darkness, is paralleled as an event by the words at Isaiah 13: 9, 10 and Revelation 6:12-17, and also at Matthew 24:29, 30, where Jesus shows the prophecy to apply at the time he comes as the Son of man with power and great glory. The words of Joel 2:11, "the day of Jehovah is great and very fear-inspiring," are apparently referred to at Malachi 4:5. Parallel descriptions of this 'day of darkness and thick gloom' are also to be found at Joel 2:2 and Zephaniah 1:14, 15.

[14] The prophecy of Revelation looks forward to "the great day" of divine wrath. (Rev. 6:17) Joel also prophesies of that time, showing that when

the great "day of Jehovah" comes upon the nations, those who call on him for protection and deliverance "will get away safe." "Jehovah will be a refuge for his people." Edenic prosperity will be restored: "And it must occur in that day that the mountains will drip with sweet wine, and the very hills will flow with milk, and the very streambeds of Judah will all flow with water. And out of the house of Jehovah there will go forth a spring." In presenting these bright promises of restoration, Joel also magnifies the sovereignty of Jehovah God and appeals to those of sincere heart on the basis of His great mercy: "Come back to Jehovah your God, for he is gracious and merciful, slow to anger and abundant in loving-kindness." All who heed this inspired appeal will reap eternal bene-fits.—Joel 2:1, 32; 3:16, 18; 2:13.

---

14. What passages in Joel magnify Jehovah's sovereign-ty and his loving-kindness?

Bible
Book
Number **30**

Amos

Writer: **Amos**

Place Written: **Judah**

Writing Completed: **c. 804 B.C.E.**

NOT a prophet nor the son of a prophet but a raiser of sheep and a nipper of figs of sycamore trees—this was Amos when Je-hovah called him and sent him to prophesy not only to his own nation of Judah but particularly to the northern kingdom of Israel. He was one of the prophets referred to at 2 Kings 17:13, 22, 23. He came from Tekoa in Judah, about ten miles south of Jerusalem and about a day's journey from the southern border of the ten-tribe kingdom of Isra-el.—Amos 1:1; 7:14, 15.

[2] The opening verse of his prophecy states that it was during the days of Uzziah the king of Judah and of Jeroboam II the son of Joash, the king of Israel, that he began his career as prophet, two years before an earthquake of unusual note. This places the prophecy within the 26-year period from 829 to about 804 B.C.E., during which the reigns of these two kings overlapped. The prophet Zechariah mentions the disastrous earthquake in the days of Uzziah, at which time the people fled in fear. (Zech. 14:5) The Jewish historian Jose-phus states that an earthquake occurred at the time Uzziah presumptuously attempted to offer up

incense in the temple. However, it seems that the earthquake that Amos mentioned occurred earlier in Uzziah's reign.

[3] The name Amos means "Being a Load" or "Carrying a Load." While he carried messages bur-dened with woe to Israel and Judah (and also to numerous heathen nations), he also bore a mes-sage of comfort concerning the restoration of Je-hovah's people. There was every reason for pro-nouncing a burden of woe in Israel. Prosperity, luxurious living, and licentiousness were the or-der of the day. The people had forgotten the Law of Jehovah. Their apparent prosperity blinded them to the fact that like overripe fruit, they were already in the process of decay leading to destruc-tion. Amos prophesied that in just a few short years, the ten-tribe kingdom would go into exile beyond Damascus. In this he magnified the righ-teousness and sovereignty of Jehovah, whom he refers to 21 times as the "Sovereign Lord."—Amos 1:8.

[4] The fulfillment of this and other prophecies

---

1. Who was Amos?
2. How may the time of Amos' prophecy be determined?

3. (a) Why was Amos' message of woe timely? (b) How did he magnify Jehovah's sovereignty?
4. The fulfillment of what prophecies testifies to the authenticity of Amos?

attests to the authenticity of Amos. The prophet also foretold that the enemy nations round about Israel—the Syrians, the Philistines, the Tyrians, the Edomites, the Ammonites, and the Moabites—would all be devoured by the fire of destruction. It is a matter of history that each of these enemy strongholds was in time broken. The ways of Judah and Israel were even more reprehensible because they left Jehovah for the practice of false worship. The last stronghold of Israel, the fortified city of Samaria, after being besieged by the Assyrian army under Shalmaneser V, fell in the year 740 B.C.E. (2 Ki. 17:1-6) Judah did not learn from what happened to her sister nation, and thus she was destroyed in 607 B.C.E.

⁵ Amos condemned Israel for its luxurious living, for the rich were defrauding the poor to build their "houses of ivory," in which they wined and dined sumptuously. (Amos 3:15; 5:11, 12; 6:4-7) Archaeologists have uncovered the evidence of this prosperity. Numerous ivory objects were found in the excavation of Samaria. The *Encyclopedia of Archaeological Excavations in the Holy Land* states: "Two main groups can be distinguished: 1. Plaques carved in high relief, . . . 2. Plaques carved in low relief, and decorated with insets of precious stones, colored glass, gold foil, etc. . . . The ivories are considered as products of Phoenician art, and they were probably used as inlays in the palace furniture of the Israelite kings. The Bible mentions the 'ivory house' which Ahab built (1 Kings 22:39) and the 'beds of ivory,' symbolizing the life of luxury led in Samaria in the words of reproof of Amos (6:4)."*

⁶ That the book of Amos belongs in the Bible canon there can be no doubt. Clinching its authenticity are Stephen's paraphrase of three verses at Acts 7:42, 43 and James' quotation from the book at Acts 15:15-18.—Amos 5:25-27; 9:11, 12.

CONTENTS OF AMOS

⁷ **Judgments against the nations** (1:1–2:3). "Jehovah—out of Zion he will roar." (1:2) Amos proceeds to warn of His fiery judgments against the nations. Damascus (Syria) has threshed Gilead with iron threshing instruments. Gaza (Philistia) and Tyre have handed over Israelite captives to Edom. In Edom itself mercy and brotherly love have been lacking. Ammon has invaded Gilead. Moab has burned the bones of the king of Edom for lime. Jehovah's hand is against all these na-

tions, and he says: "I shall not turn it back."—1:3, 6, 8, 9, 11, 13; 2:1.

⁸ **Judgment against Judah and Israel** (2:4-16). Nor will Jehovah turn his anger back from Judah. They have transgressed by "rejecting the law of Jehovah." (2:4) And Israel? Jehovah annihilated the formidable Amorites for them and gave them the good land. He raised up Nazirites and prophets among them, but they made the Nazirites break their vow and commanded the prophets: "You must not prophesy." (2:12) Therefore Jehovah is making their foundations sway like a wagon loaded with newly cut grain. As for their mighty men, they will flee naked.

⁹ **The accounting with Israel** (3:1–6:14). By his use of striking illustrations, Amos emphasizes that the fact of his prophesying, in itself, proves that Jehovah has spoken. "For the Sovereign Lord Jehovah will not do a thing unless he has revealed his confidential matter to his servants the prophets. . . . The Sovereign Lord Jehovah himself has spoken! Who will not prophesy?" (3:7, 8) Amos *does* specially prophesy against the luxury-loving despoilers dwelling in Samaria. Jehovah will snatch them off their splendid couches, and their houses of ivory will perish.

¹⁰ Jehovah recounts his chastisements and corrections of Israel. Five times he reminds them: "You did not come back to me." Therefore, O Israel, "get ready to meet your God." (4:6-12) Amos takes up a prophetic dirge: "The virgin, Israel, has fallen; she cannot get up again. She has been forsaken upon her own ground; there is no one raising her up." (5:2) However, Jehovah, the Maker of wonderful things in heaven and earth, keeps calling Israel to search for him and keep living. Yes, "search for what is good, and not what is bad, to the end that you people may keep living." (5:4, 6, 14) But what will the day of Jehovah mean to them? It will be a day of woe. Like a torrent it will sweep them into exile beyond Damascus, and the ivory-decked houses of their sprawling feasts will be turned to rubble and debris.

¹¹ **Amos prophesies in spite of opposition** (7:1-17). Jehovah shows his prophet a plummet set in the midst of Israel. There will be no further excusing. He will devastate the sanctuaries of Israel and rise up against the house of Jeroboam II with a sword. Amaziah the priest of Bethel sends

---

* 1978, Jerusalem, page 1046.

---

5. How does archaeology confirm the record in Amos?
6. What clinches the authenticity of Amos?
7. Amos warns of Jehovah's judgments against what nations?

---

8. Why is Jehovah's judgment also proclaimed against Judah and Israel?
9. What proves that Jehovah has spoken, and against whom does Amos specially prophesy?
10. Of what does Jehovah remind Israel, and what day of woe is due to come?
11. By what authority does Amos insist on prophesying against Israel?

to Jeroboam, saying: "Amos has conspired against you." (7:10) Amaziah tells Amos to go to Judah to do his prophesying. Amos makes clear his authority, saying: "Jehovah proceeded to take me from following the flock, and Jehovah went on to say to me, 'Go, prophesy to my people Israel.'" (7:15) Amos then foretells calamity for Amaziah and his household.

[12] **Oppression, punishment, and restoration** (8:1–9:15). Jehovah shows Amos a basket of summer fruit. He condemns Israel's oppression of the poor and swears "by the Superiority of Jacob" that they will have to mourn on account of their bad works. "'Look! There are days coming,' is the utterance of the Sovereign Lord Jehovah, 'and I will send a famine into the land, a famine, not for bread, and a thirst, not for water, but for hearing the words of Jehovah.'" (8:7, 11) They will fall to rise up no more. Whether they dig down into Sheol or climb up to the heavens, Jehovah's own hand will take them. The sinners of his people will die by the sword. Then, a glorious promise! "In that day I shall raise up the booth of David that is fallen, and I shall certainly repair their breaches. . . . I shall certainly build it up as in the days of long ago." (9:11) So prosperous will the regathered captives become that the plowman will overtake the harvester before he can gather in his bumper crops. Permanent will be these blessings from Jehovah!

WHY BENEFICIAL

[13] Bible readers today can benefit by noting the reason for the warnings that Amos proclaimed to Israel, Judah, and their near neighbors. Those who reject the law of Jehovah, defraud and oppress the poor, are greedy and immoral, and practice idolatry cannot have Jehovah's approval. But Jehovah forgives those who turn away from such things and repent, and to them he shows mercy. We are wise if we separate from corrupting associations in this evil world and heed Jehovah's admonition: "Search for me, and keep living."—5: 4, 6, 14.

[14] At the time of his martyrdom, Stephen cited Amos. He reminded the Jews that it had been Israel's idolatry with foreign gods, such as Moloch and Rephan, that had brought on the captivity.

Did those Jews benefit by hearing Amos' words repeated? No! Enraged, they stoned Stephen to death and so placed themselves in line for further calamity at the destruction of Jerusalem, 70 C.E. —Amos 5:25-27; Acts 7:42, 43.

[15] It is beneficial to consider the fulfillment of the many prophecies of Amos, not only those that were fulfilled in the punishment of Israel, Judah, and the other nations but also the prophecies of restoration. True to Jehovah's word through Amos, the captives of Israel returned in 537 B.C.E. to build and inhabit their desolated cities and plant their vineyards and gardens.—Amos 9:14; Ezra 3:1.

[16] However, there was a glorious and upbuilding fulfillment of Amos' prophecy in the days of the apostles. In discussing the gathering of non-Israelites into the Christian congregation, James, under inspiration, makes clear that this was foretold in the prophecy at Amos 9:11, 12. He indicates that the 'rebuilding of the booth of David that had fallen down' finds fulfillment in connection with the Christian congregation, "in order that those who remain of the men may earnestly seek Jehovah, together with people of all the nations, people who are called by my name, says Jehovah." Here, indeed, was the Scriptural support for the new development, as related by Simon Peter—that God was taking out of the nations "a people for his name."—Acts 15:13-19.

[17] Jesus Christ, the Head of this Christian congregation, is elsewhere identified as the "son of David" who inherits "the throne of David his father" and rules forever. (Luke 1:32, 33; 3:31) Thus the prophecy of Amos points forward to the fulfillment of the covenant with David for a kingdom. Not only do the concluding words of Amos give a marvelous vision of overflowing prosperity at the time of raising up "the booth of David" but they also underline the permanence of God's Kingdom: "'And I shall certainly plant them upon their ground, and they will no more be uprooted from their ground that I have given them,' Jehovah your God has said." Earth will abound with everlasting blessings as Jehovah fully restores "the booth of David"!—Amos 9:13-15.

---

12. What famine is foretold for Israel, but with what glorious promise does the prophecy end?
13. How may we today benefit from Amos' warnings?
14. Did the Jews of Stephen's time benefit from Amos' reminders?

---

15. What prophecies of restoration are beneficial to consider?
16. How did James indicate a fulfillment of Amos 9: 11, 12 in connection with the Christian congregation?
17. What prosperity and permanence does Amos foretell in connection with God's Kingdom?

Obadiah

Writer: **Obadiah**

Writing Completed: **c. 607 B.C.E.**

IN JUST 21 verses, Obadiah, the shortest book of the Hebrew Scriptures, proclaims a judgment of God that resulted in the end of a nation, while foretelling the eventual triumph of the Kingdom of God. The introductory words simply state: "The vision of Obadiah." When and where he was born, of what tribe, the details of his life—none of this is told. Clearly, the identity of the prophet is not the important thing; the message is, and rightly so, because as Obadiah himself declared, it is 'a report from Jehovah.'

[2] The report focuses its chief attention on Edom. Extending south from the Dead Sea along the Arabah, the land of Edom, also known as Mount Seir, is a rugged country of lofty mountains and deep ravines. At some points, the mountainous range to the east of the Arabah reaches an altitude of 5,600 feet. The district of Teman was renowned for the wisdom and courage of its people. The very geography of the land of Edom, with its natural defenses, made its inhabitants feel secure and proud.*

[3] The Edomites were descendants of Esau, the brother of Jacob. Jacob's name was changed to Israel, and so the Edomites were closely related to the Israelites; so much so that they were viewed as 'brothers.' (Deut. 23:7) Yet Edom's conduct had been anything but brotherly. Shortly before the Israelites entered the Promised Land, Moses sent to the king of Edom requesting permission to pass peaceably through his land, but in a display of hostility, the Edomites coldly refused and backed up their refusal with a display of force. (Num. 20: 14-21) Though subjugated by David, they later conspired with Ammon and Moab against Judah in the days of Jehoshaphat, revolted against Jehoshaphat's son King Jehoram, took charge of Israelite captives from Gaza and Tyre, and raided Judah in the days of King Ahaz to take even more captives.

—2 Chron. 20:1, 2, 22, 23; 2 Ki. 8:20-22; Amos 1: 6, 9; 2 Chron. 28:17.

[4] This hostility reached a peak in 607 B.C.E. when Jerusalem was desolated by the Babylonian hordes. Not only did the Edomites watch approvingly but they urged on the conquerors to make the desolation complete. "Lay it bare! Lay it bare to the foundation within it!" they shouted. (Ps. 137:7) When lots were cast over the booty, they were among those to share the loot; and when escapees of the Jews tried to flee out of the land, they blocked the roads and handed them over to the enemy. It is this violence at the time of Jerusalem's destruction that evidently is the basis for the denunciation recorded by Obadiah, and it was no doubt written while Edom's despicable act was still fresh in mind. (Obad. 11, 14) Since Edom itself was apparently captured and plundered by Nebuchadnezzar within five years after Jerusalem's destruction, the book must have been written before then; 607 B.C.E. is suggested as the most likely date.

[5] Obadiah's prophecy against Edom was fulfilled —all of it! In reaching its climax, the prophecy states: "The house of Esau [must become] as stubble; and they must set them ablaze and devour them. And there will prove to be no survivor to the house of Esau; for Jehovah himself has spoken it." (Vs. 18) Edom lived by the sword and died by the sword, and no trace of her descendants remains. Thus the record is proved to be authentic and true. Obadiah had all the credentials of a true prophet: He spoke in the name of Jehovah, his prophecy honored Jehovah, and it came true as subsequent history proved. His name appropriately means "Servant of Jehovah."

CONTENTS OF OBADIAH

[6] **Judgment upon Edom** (Vss. 1-16). At the

---

* *Insight on the Scriptures,* Vol. 1, page 679.

1. What shows the message, rather than the messenger, to be important?
2. On what country does the prophecy of Obadiah focus, and what made its inhabitants feel secure?
3. Had the Edomites acted as brothers to Israel?

4. (a) What despicable action evidently provided the basis for Obadiah's denunciation of Edom? (b) What evidence suggests 607 B.C.E. as the most likely date of writing?
5. (a) What proves the record of Obadiah to be authentic and true? (b) How did Obadiah fulfill the requirements of a true prophet, and why is his name appropriate?
6. How does Jehovah speak of Edom, and from where will he bring her down?

command of Jehovah, Obadiah makes known his vision. The nations are summoned to join in war against Edom. "Rise up, you people, and let us rise up against her in battle," God commands. Then, directing his remarks to Edom itself, he assesses her position. Edom is just a small one among the nations and is despised, yet she is presumptuous. She feels safe lodged in among the lofty crags, sure that no one can bring her down. Nevertheless, Jehovah declares that even if her dwelling were as high as the eagle's, even if she were to nest among the stars themselves, from there he would bring her down. She is due for punishment.—Vs. 1.

[7] What is going to happen to her? If thieves were to despoil Edom, they would take only what they wanted. Even grape gatherers would leave some gleanings. But what lies ahead for the sons of Esau is worse than this. Their treasures will be completely ransacked. The very allies of Edom will be the ones to turn on her. Those who have been her close friends will catch her in a net as one without discernment. Her men known for wisdom and her warriors known for valor will be no help in the time of her calamity.

[8] But why this severe punishment? It is because of the violence that the sons of Edom did to the sons of Jacob, their brothers! They rejoiced at the fall of Jerusalem and even joined with the invaders in dividing up the plunder. In strong denunciation, as if Obadiah is witnessing the vile deeds, Edom is told: You ought not to rejoice at your brother's distress. You ought not to hinder the flight of his escapees and hand them over to the enemy. The day of Jehovah's reckoning is near, and you will be called to account. The way you have done is the way it will be done to you.

[9] **Restoration for the house of Jacob** (Vss. 17-21). In contrast, the house of Jacob is due for restoration. Men will return to Mount Zion. They will devour the house of Esau as fire does stubble. They will take hold of the land to the south, the Negeb, as well as the mountainous region of Esau and the Shephelah; to the north they will possess the land of Ephraim and Samaria, and the region as far as Zarephath; to the east they will get the territory of Gilead. Proud Edom must cease to be, Jacob must be restored, and "the kingship must become Jehovah's."—Vs. 21.

WHY BENEFICIAL

[10] Attesting to the sureness of the fulfillment of

this message of judgment against Edom, Jehovah had similar pronouncements made by others of his prophets. Outstanding among them are the ones recorded at Joel 3:19; Amos 1:11, 12; Isaiah 34:5-7; Jeremiah 49:7-22; Ezekiel 25:12-14; 35:2-15. The earlier pronouncements obviously make reference to acts of hostility in times past, while the ones of later date evidently are indictments of Edom for her unpardonable conduct, referred to by Obadiah, at the time the Babylonians seized Jerusalem. It will strengthen faith in Jehovah's power of prophecy if we examine how the foretold calamities befell Edom. Moreover, it will build confidence in Jehovah as the God who always brings to pass his stated purpose.—Isa. 46:9-11.

[11] Obadiah had foretold that "the very men in covenant with" Edom, those "at peace with" her, would be the ones to prevail against her. (Obad. 7) Babylon's peace with Edom did not last. During the sixth century B.C.E., Babylonian forces under King Nabonidus conquered Edom.[*] Nevertheless, a century after Nabonidus' invasion of the land, confident Edom still hoped to make a comeback, and concerning it, Malachi 1:4 reports: "Because Edom keeps saying, 'We have been shattered, but we shall return and build the devastated places,' this is what Jehovah of armies has said, 'They, for their part, will build; but I, for my part, shall tear down.'" Despite Edom's efforts at recovery, by the fourth century B.C.E. the Nabataeans were firmly established in the land. Having been pushed out of their land, the Edomites dwelt in the southern part of Judea, which came to be called Idumea. They never succeeded in reconquering the land of Seir.

[12] According to Josephus, in the second century B.C.E. the remaining Edomites were subjugated by the Jewish king John Hyrcanus I, were forced to submit to circumcision, and were gradually absorbed into the Jewish domain under a Jewish governor. Following the Roman destruction of Jerusalem in 70 C.E., their name disappeared from history.[#] It was as Obadiah had foretold: "You will have to be cut off to time indefinite. . . . And there will prove to be no survivor to the house of Esau." —Obad. 10, 18.

[13] In contrast with Edom's desolation, the Jews were restored to their homeland in 537 B.C.E.

[*] *Insight on the Scriptures,* Vol. 1, page 682.
[#] *Jewish Antiquities,* XIII, 257, 258 (ix, 1); XV, 253, 254 (vii, 9).

---

7. To what extent is Edom to be despoiled?
8. Why is Edom's punishment so severe?
9. What restoration is foretold?
10. What other prophecies foretold Edom's doom, and why will it be beneficial to consider these along with Obadiah?

11, 12. (a) How did those "at peace with" Edom come to prevail against her? (b) By what stages did Edom come to be "cut off to time indefinite"?
13. What happened to the Jews, in contrast to the Edomites?

under the governorship of Zerubbabel, where they rebuilt the temple in Jerusalem and became firmly established in the land.

¹⁴ How evident it is that pride and presumptuousness lead to calamity! Let all who proudly exalt

---

14. (a) What warning is to be found in Edom's fate? (b) What should all acknowledge, as did Obadiah, and why?

themselves and cruelly gloat over the hardship that comes upon the servants of God take warning from the fate of Edom. Let them acknowledge, as did Obadiah, that "the kingship must become Jehovah's." Those who fight against Jehovah and his people will be completely cut off to time indefinite, but Jehovah's majestic Kingdom and eternal kingship will stand vindicated forever!—Vs. 21.

Bible Book Number *32*

Jonah

Writer: Jonah

Writing Completed: **c. 844 B.C.E.**

JONAH—foreign missionary of the ninth century B.C.E.! How did he view his assignment from Jehovah? What new experiences did this open up for him? Did he find the people in his assignment receptive? How successful was his preaching? The dramatic record of the book of Jonah answers these questions. Written at a time when Jehovah's chosen nation had broken covenant with him and fallen into pagan idolatry, the prophetic record shows that God's mercy is not limited to any one nation, not even to Israel. Moreover, it exalts Jehovah's great mercy and loving-kindness, in contrast with the lack of mercy, patience, and faith so often observed in imperfect man.

² The name Jonah (Hebrew, *Yoh·nah´*) means "Dove." He was the son of the prophet Amittai of Gath-hepher in Galilee in the territory of Zebulun. At 2 Kings 14:23-25 we read that Jeroboam the king of Israel extended the boundary of the nation according to the word that Jehovah spoke through Jonah. This would place the time of Jonah's prophesying at about 844 B.C.E., the year of the accession of Jeroboam II of Israel and many years before Assyria, with its capital at Nineveh, began to dominate Israel.

³ There is no question that the entire account of Jonah is authentic. The "Perfecter of our faith, Jesus," referred to Jonah as an actual person and gave the inspired interpretation of two of the

prophetic happenings in Jonah, thus showing the book to contain true prophecy. (Heb. 12:2; Matt. 12:39-41; 16:4; Luke 11:29-32) Jonah has always been placed by the Jews among their canonical books and is regarded by them as historical. Jonah's own candor in describing his mistakes and weaknesses, without any attempt to gloss over them, also marks the record as genuine.

⁴ What about the "great fish" that swallowed Jonah? There has been considerable speculation as to what kind of fish this may have been. The sperm whale is fully capable of swallowing a man whole. So is the great white shark. The Bible, though, simply states: "Jehovah appointed a great fish to swallow Jonah." (Jonah 1:17) The kind of fish is not specified. It cannot be determined with certainty whether it was a sperm whale, a great white shark, or some other unidentified sea creature.* The Bible record that it was "a great fish" is sufficient for our information.

CONTENTS OF JONAH

⁵ **Jonah assigned to Nineveh but runs away** (1:1-16). "And the word of Jehovah began to occur to Jonah the son of Amittai, saying: 'Get up, go to Nineveh the great city, and proclaim against her that their badness has come up before me.'" (1:1, 2) Does Jonah relish this

---

* *Insight on the Scriptures*, Vol. 2, pages 99-100.

---

1. What questions are answered in the book of Jonah, and what does it show as to Jehovah's mercy?
2. What is known concerning Jonah, and about what year did he prophesy?
3. What proves the account of Jonah to be authentic?

4. What kind of fish may have swallowed Jonah? Yet, what is sufficient for our information?
5. How does Jonah react to his assignment, and with what result?

assignment? Not one bit! He runs away in the opposite direction, taking a ship for Tarshish, possibly identified with Spain. Jonah's ship meets up with a great storm. In fear the mariners call for aid, "each one to his god," while Jonah sleeps in the ship's hold. (1:5) After arousing Jonah, they cast lots in an attempt to discover who is responsible for their plight. The lot falls upon Jonah. It is now that he makes known to them that he is a Hebrew, a worshiper of Jehovah, and that he is running away from his God-given task. He invites them to hurl him into the sea. After making further efforts to bring the ship through, they at last pitch Jonah overboard. The sea stops its raging.

⁶ **Swallowed by "a great fish"** (1:17–2:10). "Now Jehovah appointed a great fish to swallow Jonah, so that Jonah came to be in the inward parts of the fish three days and three nights." (1:17) He prays fervently to Jehovah from inside the fish. "Out of the belly of Sheol" he cries for help and declares that he will pay what he has vowed, for "salvation belongs to Jehovah." (2: 2, 9) At Jehovah's command, the fish vomits Jonah onto the dry land.

⁷ **Preaching in Nineveh** (3:1–4:11). Jehovah renews his command to Jonah. No longer does Jonah evade his assignment, but he goes to Nineveh. There he marches through the city streets and cries: "Only forty days more, and Nineveh will be overthrown." (3:4) His preaching is effective. A wave of repentance sweeps through Nineveh, and its people begin to put faith in God. The king proclaims that man and beast must fast and be clothed in sackcloth. Jehovah mercifully spares the city.

⁸ This is more than Jonah can bear. He tells Jehovah he knew all along that He would show mercy and that is why he ran away to Tarshish. He wishes he could die. Thoroughly disgruntled, Jonah encamps to the east of the city and waits to see what will happen. Jehovah appoints a bottle-gourd plant to come up as shade over his moody prophet. Jonah's rejoicing at this is short-lived. Next morning Jehovah appoints a worm to smite the plant, so that its comforting protection is replaced by exposure to a parching east wind and the broiling sun. Again Jonah wishes he could die. Self-righteously he justifies his anger. Jehovah points out his inconsistency: Jonah felt sorry for one bottle-gourd plant but is angry because

Jehovah now feels sorry for the great city of Nineveh.

WHY BENEFICIAL

⁹ Jonah's course of action and its outcome should stand as a warning to us. He ran away from God-given work; he should have put his hand to the task and trusted in God to uphold him. (Jonah 1:3; Luke 9:62; Prov. 14:26; Isa. 6:8) When he got going in the wrong direction, he showed a negative attitude in failing to identify himself freely to the mariners as a worshiper of "Jehovah the God of the heavens." He had lost his boldness. (Jonah 1:7-9; Eph. 6:19, 20) Jonah's self-centeredness led him to regard Jehovah's mercy toward Nineveh as a personal affront; he tried to save face by telling Jehovah that he had known all along that this would be the outcome —so why send him as prophet? He was reproved for this disrespectful, complaining attitude, so we should benefit from his experience and refrain from finding fault with Jehovah's showing mercy or with his way of doing things.—Jonah 4:1-4, 7-9; Phil. 2:13, 14; 1 Cor. 10:10.

¹⁰ Overshadowing everything else in the book of Jonah is its portrayal of the magnificent qualities of Jehovah's loving-kindness and mercy. Jehovah showed loving-kindness toward Nineveh in sending his prophet to warn of impending destruction, and he was ready to show mercy when the city repented—a mercy that permitted Nineveh to survive more than 200 years until its destruction by the Medes and Babylonians about 632 B.C.E. He showed mercy toward Jonah in delivering him from the storm-tossed sea and in providing the gourd to "deliver him from his calamitous state." By providing the protecting gourd and then taking it away, Jehovah made known to Jonah that He will show mercy and loving-kindness according to His own good pleasure.—Jonah 1:2; 3:2-4, 10; 2:10; 4:6, 10, 11.

¹¹ At Matthew 12:38-41, Jesus told the religious leaders that the only sign that would be given them was "the sign of Jonah." After three days and three nights in "the belly of Sheol," Jonah went and preached to Nineveh, thereby becoming a "sign" to the Ninevites. (Jonah 1:17; 2:2; 3:1-4) Similarly, Jesus spent parts of three days in the grave and was resurrected. When his disciples proclaimed the evidence of that event, Jesus became a sign to that generation. According to the Jewish method of measuring time and the facts in fulfillment of Jesus' case, this period of

---

6. What is Jonah's experience with the "great fish"?
7. How effective is Jonah's preaching in Nineveh?
8. How does Jonah react to Jehovah's expressing mercy on the city, and how does Jehovah expose the prophet's inconsistency?

9. What attitude and course of Jonah should stand as a warning to us?
10. How are Jehovah's loving-kindness and mercy illustrated in the book of Jonah?
11. What is "the sign of Jonah"?

"three days and three nights" allows for less than three full days.*

¹² In this same discussion, Jesus contrasts the repentance of the Ninevites with the hardness of heart and outright rejection he experienced from the Jews during his own ministry, saying: "Men of Nineveh will rise up in the judgment with this generation and will condemn it; because they repented at what Jonah preached, but, look! something more than Jonah is here." (See also Matthew 16:4 and Luke 11:30, 32.) "Something

---

* *Insight on the Scriptures,* Vol. 1, page 593.

---

12. (a) What else does Jesus say concerning the Ninevites and the Jews of his generation? (b) How did "something more than Jonah" appear, having what connection with Jehovah's Kingdom and salvation?

more than Jonah"—what did Jesus mean by these words? He was referring to himself as the greatest prophet of all, the One sent by Jehovah to preach: "Repent, you people, for the kingdom of the heavens has drawn near." (Matt. 4:17) Nevertheless, most of the Jews of that generation rejected "the sign of Jonah." What about today? Although most are not heeding Jehovah's message of warning, many thousands worldwide are having the glorious opportunity of hearing the good news of God's Kingdom that was first preached by Jesus, "the Son of man." Like the repentant Ninevites, who were blessed through the preaching of Jonah, these also may share in Jehovah's abundant and merciful provision for extended life, for truly "salvation belongs to Jehovah."—Jonah 2:9.

<table>
<tr><td>Bible
Book
Number</td><td># 33

Micah</td><td>Writer: **Micah**
Place Written: **Judah**
Writing Completed: **Before
717 B.C.E.**
Time Covered: **c. 777–717 B.C.E.**</td></tr>
</table>

THINK of a man of maturity, one who has spent many years in faithful service to Jehovah. Think of a bold man, one who could tell the rulers of his nation, "You haters of what is good and lovers of badness, . . . you the ones who have also eaten the organism of my people, and have stripped their very skin from off them." Think of a humble man, one giving all credit for his powerful utterances to Jehovah, by whose spirit he spoke. Would you not enjoy the acquaintance of a man like that? What a wealth of information and sound counsel he could impart! The prophet Micah was such a man. We still have access to his choice counsel in the book that bears his name.—Mic. 3:2, 3, 8.

² As is true of many of the prophets, very little is said concerning Micah himself in his book; it was the message that was important. The name Micah is a shortened form of Michael (meaning, "Who Is Like God?") or Micaiah (meaning, "Who Is Like Jehovah?"). He served as prophet during the reigns of Jotham, Ahaz, and Hezekiah (777-717 B.C.E.), which made him a contempo-

rary of the prophets Isaiah and Hosea. (Isa. 1:1; Hos. 1:1) The exact period of his prophesying is uncertain, but at most it was 60 years. His prophecies of Samaria's ruin must have been given before the city's destruction in 740 B.C.E., and the entire writing must have been completed by the end of Hezekiah's reign, 717 B.C.E. (Mic. 1:1) Micah was a rural prophet from the village of Moresheth in the fertile Shephelah, southwest of Jerusalem. His familiarity with rural life is shown in the kind of illustrations he used to drive home the points of his declarations.—2:12; 4:12, 13; 6:15; 7:1, 4, 14.

³ Micah lived in dangerous and significant times. Fast-moving events were foreboding doom for the kingdoms of Israel and Judah. Moral corruption and idolatry had gone to seed in Israel, and this brought the nation destruction from Assyria, evidently during Micah's own lifetime. Judah swung from doing right in the reign of Jotham to duplicating Israel's wickedness in Ahaz' rebellious reign and then to a recovery during the reign of Hezekiah. Jehovah raised up Micah to warn His people strongly of what He was bringing upon them. Micah's prophecies served to

---

1. What kind of man was Micah?
2. What is known concerning Micah and the period of his prophesying?

3. In what significant times did Micah serve, and why did Jehovah commission him as prophet?

corroborate those of Isaiah and Hosea.—2 Ki. 15: 32–20:21; 2 Chron. chaps. 27-32; Isa. 7:17; Hos. 8:8; 2 Cor. 13:1.

⁴ There is an abundance of evidence to show the authenticity of the book of Micah. It has always been accepted by the Jews as part of the Hebrew canon. Jeremiah 26:18, 19 refers directly to Micah's words: "Zion will be plowed up as a mere field, and Jerusalem herself will become mere heaps of ruins." (Mic. 3:12) This prophecy was accurately fulfilled in 607 B.C.E. when the king of Babylon razed Jerusalem, "so as to cause ruin." (2 Chron. 36:19) A similar prophecy about Samaria, that it would become "a heap of ruins of the field," was likewise fulfilled. (Mic. 1:6, 7) Samaria was ruined by the Assyrians in 740 B.C.E. when they took the northern kingdom of Israel into captivity. (2 Ki. 17:5, 6) It was later conquered by Alexander the Great in the fourth century B.C.E. and suffered devastation by the Jews under John Hyrcanus I in the second century B.C.E. Of this last destruction of Samaria, *The New Westminster Dictionary of the Bible,* 1970, page 822, states: "The victor demolished it, attempting to efface all proofs that a fortified city had ever stood on the hill."

⁵ Archaeological evidence also adds its voice in support of the fulfillments of Micah's prophecy. Samaria's destruction by the Assyrians is referred to in Assyrian annals. For example, the Assyrian king Sargon boasted: "I besieged and conquered Samaria (*Sa-me-ri-na*)."* However, it may actually have been Sargon's predecessor, Shalmaneser V, who completed the conquest. Concerning Shalmaneser, a Babylonian chronicle states: "He ravaged Samaria."# The invasion of Judah in Hezekiah's reign, as foretold by Micah, was well chronicled by Sennacherib. (Mic. 1:6, 9; 2 Ki. 18:13) He had a large four-paneled relief made on the wall of his palace at Nineveh depicting the capture of Lachish. On his prism he states: "I laid siege to 46 of his strong cities . . . I drove out (of them) 200,150 people . . . Himself I made a prisoner in Jerusalem, his royal residence, like a bird in a cage." He also lists tribute paid to him by Hezekiah, although he exaggerates the amount. He makes no mention of the calamity that befell his troops.△—2 Ki. 18:14-16; 19:35.

---

* *Ancient Near Eastern Texts,* edited by James B. Pritchard, 1974, page 284.
# *Assyrian and Babylonian Chronicles,* by A. K. Grayson, 1975, page 73.
△ *Ancient Near Eastern Texts,* 1974, page 288; *Insight on the Scriptures,* Vol. 2, pages 894-5.

---

4. What proves the authenticity of the book of Micah?
5. How does archaeology testify to the fulfillment of Micah's prophecies?

⁶ Putting the inspiration of the book beyond all doubt is the outstanding prophecy of Micah 5: 2, which foretells the birthplace of the Messiah. (Matt. 2:4-6) There are also passages that are paralleled by statements in the Christian Greek Scriptures.—Mic. 7:6, 20; Matt. 10:35, 36; Luke 1:72, 73.

⁷ While Micah may have been from the rurals of Judah, he certainly was not lacking in ability to express himself. Some of the finest expressions in God's Word are to be found in his book. Chapter 6 is written in striking dialogue. Abrupt transitions grip the reader's attention as Micah moves swiftly from one point to another, from cursing to blessing and back again. (Mic. 2:10, 12; 3:1, 12; 4:1) Vivid figures of speech abound: At Jehovah's going forth, "the mountains must melt under him, and the low plains themselves will split apart, like wax because of the fire, like waters being poured down a steep place."—1:4; see also 7:17.

⁸ The book may be divided into three sections, each section beginning with "Hear" and containing rebukes, warnings of punishment, and promises of blessing.

CONTENTS OF MICAH

⁹ **Section 1** (1:1–2:13). Jehovah is coming forth from his temple to punish Samaria for her idolatry. He will make her "a heap of ruins" and "pour down into the valley her stones," while crushing to pieces her graven images. There will be no healing for her. Judah too is guilty and will suffer invasion "to the gate of Jerusalem." Those scheming harmful things are condemned and will lament: "We have positively been despoiled!"—1: 6, 12; 2:4.

¹⁰ Abruptly Jehovah's mercy comes into focus as, in Jehovah's name, the prophet declares: "I shall positively gather Jacob . . . In unity I shall set them, like a flock in the pen, like a drove in the midst of its pasture; they will be noisy with men." —2:12.

¹¹ **Section 2** (3:1–5:15). Micah then continues: "Hear, please, you heads of Jacob and you commanders of the house of Israel." A scathing denunciation is leveled against these "haters of what is good and lovers of badness" who oppress the peo-

---

6. What puts the inspiration of Micah beyond all doubt?
7. What may be said of Micah's power of expression?
8. What is contained in each of the three sections of Micah?
9. What punishments are decreed against Samaria and Judah?
10. How does Jehovah's mercy come into focus?
11. (a) What denunciation is now leveled against the rulers of Jacob and Israel? (b) How does Micah acknowledge the source of his courage?

ple. They have "smashed to pieces their very bones." (3:1-3) Included with them are the false prophets who give no true guidance, causing God's people to wander. More than human courage is needed to proclaim this message! But Micah confidently states: "I myself have become full of power, with the spirit of Jehovah, and of justice and mightiness, in order to tell to Jacob his revolt and to Israel his sin." (3:8) His denunciation of the bloodguilty rulers reaches a scathing climax: "Her own head ones judge merely for a bribe, and her own priests instruct just for a price, and her own prophets practice divination simply for money." (3:11) Therefore Zion will be plowed like a field, and Jerusalem will become nothing more than a heap of ruins.

¹² Again in sudden contrast, the prophecy turns to "the final part of the days" to give a grand, moving description of the restoration of Jehovah's worship at his mountain. (4:1) Many nations will go up to learn Jehovah's ways, for his law and word will proceed out of Zion and out of Jerusalem. They will learn war no more, but each one will sit under his vine and fig tree. They will be unafraid. Let the peoples follow each one its god, but true worshipers will walk in the name of Jehovah their God, and he will rule over them as King forever. First, however, Zion must go into exile to Babylon. Only at her restoration will Jehovah pulverize her enemies.

¹³ Micah now foretells that the ruler in Israel "whose origin is from early times" will come out of Bethlehem Ephrathah. He will rule as a 'shepherd in the strength of Jehovah' and be great, not just in Israel, but "as far as the ends of the earth." (5: 2, 4) The invading Assyrian will have but fleeting success, for he will be turned back and his own land laid waste. "The remaining ones of Jacob" will be like "dew from Jehovah" among the people and like a lion for courage among nations. (5:7) Jehovah will root out false worship and execute vengeance upon the disobedient nations.

¹⁴ **Section 3** (6:1–7:20). A striking court scene is now presented in dialogue. Jehovah has "a legal case" with Israel, and he calls on the very hills and mountains as witnesses. (6:1) He challenges Israel to testify against him, and he recounts his righteous acts in their behalf. What does Jehovah require of earthling man? Not a multitude of ani-

mal sacrifices, but, rather, "to exercise justice and to love kindness and to be modest in walking with [his] God." (6:8) This is just what is lacking in Israel. Instead of justice and kindness there are "wicked scales," violence, falsehood, and trickery. (6:11) Instead of walking in a modest way with God, they are walking in the wicked counsels and idol worship of Omri and Ahab, who reigned in Samaria.

¹⁵ The prophet deplores the moral decay of his people. Why, even their "most upright one is worse than a thorn hedge." (7:4) There is treachery among intimate friends and within households. Micah does not lose heart. "It is for Jehovah that I shall keep on the lookout. I will show a waiting attitude for the God of my salvation. My God will hear me." (7:7) He warns others not to rejoice over Jehovah's punishment of His people, for deliverance will come. Jehovah will shepherd and feed his people and show them "wonderful things," making the nations afraid. (7:15) In closing his book, Micah echoes the sense of his name by praising Jehovah for His delightsome lovingkindness. Yes, 'Who is a God like Jehovah?' —7:18.

WHY BENEFICIAL

¹⁶ Almost 2,700 years ago, the prophesying of Micah proved most 'beneficial for reproving,' for King Hezekiah of Judah responded to his message and led the nation to repentance and religious reformation. (Mic. 3:9-12; Jer. 26:18, 19; compare 2 Kings 18:1-4.) Today this inspired prophecy is even more beneficial. Hear, all professing worshipers of God, Micah's plain warnings against false religion, idol worship, lying, and violence! (Mic. 1:2; 3:1; 6:1) Paul corroborates these warnings at 1 Corinthians 6:9-11, where he says that true Christians have been washed clean and that no one who indulges in such practices will inherit God's Kingdom. Simply and clearly, Micah 6:8 states that Jehovah's requirement is for man to walk with Him in justice, kindness, and modesty.

¹⁷ Micah delivered his message among a people so divided that 'a man's enemies were the men of his household.' True Christians often preach in similar circumstances, and some even meet with betrayals and bitter persecution within their own family relationship. Always they need to wait patiently on Jehovah, the 'God of their salvation.'

---

12. What grand prophecy is given for "the final part of the days"?
13. What kind of ruler will come out of Bethlehem, and like what will "the remaining ones of Jacob" become?
14. (a) With the use of what illustration does section 3 of Micah begin? (b) What requirements of Jehovah have the people of Israel failed to meet?

15. (a) What does the prophet deplore? (b) What fitting conclusion does the book of Micah have?
16. (a) How did the prophecy of Micah prove beneficial in Hezekiah's day? (b) What powerful admonitions does it contain for this present day?
17. What encouragement does Micah provide for those who serve God under persecution and difficulty?

(Mic. 7:6, 7; Matt. 10:21, 35-39) In persecution or when faced with a difficult assignment, those who rely courageously on Jehovah will, like Micah, "become full of power, with the spirit of Jehovah," in telling forth His message. Micah prophesied that such courage would be especially evident in "the remaining ones of Jacob." These would be like 'a lion among the nations, in the midst of many peoples,' and at the same time like refreshing dew and showers from Jehovah. These qualities were certainly manifest in the 'remnant of Israel (Jacob)' who became members of the Christian congregation of the first century.—Mic. 3:8; 5:7, 8; Rom. 9:27; 11:5, 26.

18 Jesus' birth at Bethlehem, in fulfillment of Micah's prophecy, not only confirms the divine inspiration of the book but illuminates the context of the verse as prophetic of the coming of the Kingdom of God under Christ Jesus. Jesus is the one who appears out of Bethlehem (House of Bread) with life-giving benefits for all who exercise faith in his sacrifice. He it is that does "shepherding in the strength of Jehovah" and that becomes great and spells peace to the ends of the earth among the restored, unified flock of God. —Mic. 5:2, 4; 2:12; John 6:33-40.

19 Great encouragement is to be found in Micah's prophecy concerning "the final part of the days," when "many nations" seek instruction from Jehovah. "And they will have to beat their swords into plowshares and their spears into pruning shears. They will not lift up sword, nation against nation, neither will they learn war anymore. And they will actually sit, each one under his vine and under his fig tree, and there will be no one making them tremble; for the very mouth of Jehovah of armies has spoken it." Abandoning all false worship, they join with Micah in affirming: "We, for our part, shall walk in the name of Jehovah our God to time indefinite, even forever." Truly Micah's prophecy is faith-inspiring in providing a forevision of these momentous happenings. It is outstanding, too, in exalting Jehovah as the eternal Sovereign and King. How thrilling the words: "Jehovah will actually rule as king over them in Mount Zion, from now on and into time indefinite"!—Mic. 4:1-7; 1 Tim. 1:17.

---

18. What prophecy of Micah ties in with God's Kingdom rule by means of Christ Jesus?

19. (a) What faith-inspiring encouragement is provided for those who live in "the final part of the days"? (b) How does Micah exalt Jehovah's sovereignty?

Bible Book Number 34
Nahum

Writer: **Nahum**

Place Written: **Judah**

Writing Completed: **Before 632 B.C.E.**

"THE pronouncement against Nineveh." (Nah. 1:1) Nahum's prophecy opens with these ominous words. But why did he make this declaration of doom? What is known of ancient Nineveh? Her history is summarized by Nahum in three words: "city of bloodshed." (3:1) Two mounds located on the east bank of the Tigris River opposite the modern city of Mosul, in northern Iraq, mark the site of ancient Nineveh. It was heavily fortified by walls and moats and was the capital of the Assyrian Empire in the latter part of its history. However, the origin of the city goes back to the days of Nimrod, the "'mighty hunter in opposition to Jehovah.' . . . He went forth into Assyria and set himself to building Nineveh." (Gen. 10:9-11) Nineveh thus had a bad beginning. She became specially renowned during the reigns of Sargon, Sennacherib, Esar-haddon, and Ashurbanipal, in the closing period of the Assyrian Empire. By wars and conquests, she enriched herself with loot and became famed on account of the cruel, inhuman treatment that her rulers meted out to the multitude of captives.* Says C. W. Ceram, on page 266 of his book *Gods, Graves and Scholars* (1954): "Nineveh was impressed on the consciousness of mankind by little else than murder, plunder, suppression, and the violation of the weak; by war and all manner of physical violence; by the deeds of a sanguinary dynasty of rulers who held down the

---

1. What is known of ancient Nineveh?

* *Insight on the Scriptures,* Vol. 1, page 201.

people by terror and who often were liquidated by rivals more ferocious than themselves."

² What of Nineveh's religion? She worshiped a great pantheon of gods, many of whom were imported from Babylon. Her rulers invoked these gods as they went out to destroy and exterminate, and her greedy priests egged her campaigns of conquest on, looking forward to rich repayment from the booty. In his book *Ancient Cities* (1886, page 25), W. B. Wright says: "They worshiped strength, and would say their prayers only to colossal idols of stone, lions and bulls whose ponderous limbs, eagle wings, and human heads were symbols of strength, courage, and victory. Fighting was the business of the nation, and the priests were incessant fomenters of war. They were supported largely from the spoils of conquest, of which a fixed percentage was invariably assigned them before others shared, for this race of plunderers was excessively religious."

³ Nahum's prophecy, though short, is packed with interest. All that we know of the prophet himself is contained in the opening verse: "The book of the vision of Nahum the Elkoshite." His name (Hebrew, *Na·chumʹ*) means "Comforter." His message was certainly no comfort to Nineveh, but to God's true people, it spelled sure and lasting relief from an implacable and mighty foe. It is of comfort, too, that Nahum makes no mention of the sins of his own people. Although the site of Elkosh is not definitely known, it seems probable that the prophecy was written in Judah. (Nah. 1:15) The fall of Nineveh, which occurred in 632 B.C.E., was still future when Nahum recorded his prophecy, and he compares this event to the fall of No-amon (Thebes, in Egypt) that took place shortly before this. (3:8) Hence, Nahum must have written his prophecy sometime during this period.

⁴ The style of the book is distinctive. It contains no superfluous words. Its vigor and realism are in keeping with its being part of the inspired writings. Nahum excels in descriptive, emotional, and dramatic language, as well as in dignified expression, clearness of imagery, and graphically striking phraseology. (1:2-8, 12-14; 2:4, 12; 3:1-5, 13-15, 18, 19) Most of the first chapter appears to be in the style of an acrostic poem. (1:8, footnote) Nahum's style is enriched by the singleness of his theme. He has utter abhorrence for Israel's treacherous foe. He sees nothing but the doom of Nineveh.

⁵ The authenticity of Nahum's prophecy is proved by the accuracy of its fulfillment. In Nahum's day, who else but a prophet of Jehovah would have dared to forecast that the proud capital of the Assyrian world power could be breached at the "gates of the rivers," her palace be dissolved, and she herself become "emptiness and voidness, and a city laid waste"? (2:6-10) The events that followed showed that the prophecy was indeed inspired of God. The annals of the Babylonian king Nabopolassar describe the capture of Nineveh by the Medes and the Babylonians: "The city [they turned] into ruin-hills and hea[ps (of debris) . . .]."* So complete was the ruin of Nineveh that even its site was forgotten for many centuries. Some critics came to ridicule the Bible on this point, saying that Nineveh could never have existed.

⁶ However, adding further to the evidence of Nahum's authenticity, the site of Nineveh was discovered, and excavations were begun there in the 19th century. It was estimated that millions of tons of earth would have to be moved to excavate it completely. What has been unearthed in Nineveh? Much that supports the accuracy of Nahum's prophecy! For example, her monuments and inscriptions testify to her cruelties, and there are the remains of colossal statues of winged bulls and lions. No wonder Nahum spoke of her as "the lair of lions"!—2:11.#

⁷ The canonicity of Nahum is shown by the book's being accepted by the Jews as part of the inspired Scriptures. It is completely in harmony with the rest of the Bible. The prophecy is uttered in the name of Jehovah, to whose attributes and supremacy it bears eloquent testimony.

CONTENTS OF NAHUM

⁸ **Pronouncement of Jehovah against Nineveh** (1:1-15). "Jehovah is a God exacting exclusive devotion and taking vengeance." With these words the prophet sets the scene for "the pronouncement against Nineveh." (1:1, 2) Though Jehovah is slow to anger, see him now as he expresses vengeance by wind and storm. Mountains rock, hills melt, and the earth heaves. Who can stand before the heat of his anger?

---

* *Ancient Near Eastern Texts*, edited by J. B. Pritchard, 1974, page 305; brackets and parentheses theirs; *Insight on the Scriptures*, Vol. 1, page 958.
# *Insight on the Scriptures*, Vol. 1, page 955.

---

2. Of what kind was Nineveh's religion?
3. (a) In what way is the meaning of Nahum's name appropriate? (b) To what period does Nahum's prophecy belong?
4. What qualities of writing are apparent in the book of Nahum?

5. What proves the authenticity of Nahum's prophecy?
6. What has been uncovered at the site of ancient Nineveh that vindicates the accuracy of Nahum?
7. What supports the canonicity of the book of Nahum?
8. What doom is pronounced for Nineveh, but what good news for Judah?

Nonetheless, Jehovah is a stronghold for those who seek refuge in him. But Nineveh is doomed. She will be exterminated by a flood, and "distress will not rise up a second time." (1:9) Jehovah will blot out her name and her gods. He will bury her. In refreshing contrast, there is good news for Judah! What is it? A publisher of peace calls on them to celebrate their festivals and pay their vows, for the enemy, the "good-for-nothing person," is doomed. "In his entirety he will certainly be cut off."—1:15.

⁹ **Foreview of Nineveh's destruction** (2:1–3:19). Nahum issues a taunting challenge to Nineveh to reinforce herself against an oncoming scatterer. Jehovah will regather his own, 'the pride of Jacob and of Israel.' See the shield and the crimson garb of his men of vital energy and the fiery iron fittings of his "war chariot in the day of his getting ready"! War chariots "keep driving madly" in the streets, running like lightnings. (2:2-4) Now we get a prophetic view of the battle. The Ninevites stumble and hasten to defend the wall but to no avail. The river gates open, the palace dissolves, and the slave girls moan and beat upon their hearts. The fleeing men are commanded to stand still, but no one turns back. The city is plundered and laid waste. Hearts melt. Where now is this lair of lions? The lion has filled his cave with prey for his whelps, but Jehovah declares: "Look! I am against you." (2:13) Yes, Jehovah will burn up Nineveh's war machine, send a sword to devour her young lions, and cut off her prey from the earth.

¹⁰ "Woe to the city of bloodshed . . . full of deception and of robbery." Hear the lash of the whip and the rattling of the wheel. See the dashing horse, the leaping chariot, the mounted horseman, the flame of the sword, and the lightning of the spear—and then, the heavy mass of carcasses. "There is no end to the dead bodies." (3:1, 3) And why? It is because she has ensnared nations with her prostitutions and families with her sorceries. A second time Jehovah declares: "Look! I am against you." (3:5) Nineveh will be exposed as an adulteress and will be despoiled, her fate being no better than that of No-amon (Thebes), whom Assyria took into captivity. Her fortresses are like ripe figs, "which, if they get wiggled, will certain-ly fall into the mouth of an eater." (3:12) Her warriors are like women. Nothing can save Nineveh from fire and sword. Her guardsmen will flee like a locust swarm on a sunny day, and her people will be scattered. The king of Assyria will know that there is no relief, nor is there healing for this catastrophe. All those hearing the report will clap their hands, for all have suffered from the badness of Assyria.

WHY BENEFICIAL

¹¹ The prophecy of Nahum illustrates some fundamental Bible principles. The opening words of the vision repeat God's reason for giving the second of the Ten Commandments: "Jehovah is a God exacting exclusive devotion." Immediately thereafter he makes known the certainty of his "taking vengeance against his adversaries." Assyria's cruel pride and pagan gods could not save her from the execution of Jehovah's judgment. We can be confident that in due course Jehovah will likewise mete out justice to all the wicked. "Jehovah is slow to anger and great in power, and by no means will Jehovah hold back from punishing." Thus Jehovah's justice and supremacy are exalted against the background of his extermination of mighty Assyria. Nineveh did become "emptiness and voidness, and a city laid waste!"—1:2, 3; 2:10.

¹² In contrast to Nineveh's being 'entirely cut off,' Nahum announces restoration for 'the pride of Jacob and of Israel.' Jehovah also sends happy tidings to his people: "Look! Upon the mountains the feet of one bringing good news, one publishing peace." These tidings of peace have a connection with God's Kingdom. How do we know this? It is apparent because of Isaiah's use of the same expression, but to which he adds the words: "The one bringing good news of something better, the one publishing salvation, the one saying to Zion: 'Your God has become king!'" (Nah. 1:15; 2:2; Isa. 52:7) In turn, the apostle Paul at Romans 10:15 applies the expression to those whom Jehovah sends forth as Christian preachers of good news. These proclaim the "good news of the kingdom." (Matt. 24:14) True to the meaning of his name, Nahum provides much comfort for all who seek the peace and salvation that come with God's Kingdom. All of these will surely realize that 'Jehovah is good, a stronghold in the day of distress for those seeking refuge in him.'—Nah. 1:7.

---

9. What prophetic view do we get of the defeat of Nineveh?
10. As what is Nineveh exposed, and how is her end further described?

11. What fundamental Bible principles are illustrated in Nahum?
12. What restoration does Nahum announce, and how may his prophecy be linked with the Kingdom hope?

35

Habakkuk

Writer: **Habakkuk**

Place Written: **Judah**

Writing Completed:
c. 628 B.C.E.(?)

HABAKKUK is another of the so-called minor prophets of the Hebrew Scriptures. However, his vision and pronouncement inspired by God are by no means minor in significance to God's people. Encouraging as well as strengthening, his prophecy sustains God's servants in time of stress. The book highlights two sublime truths: Jehovah God is the Universal Sovereign, and the righteous live by faith. The writing serves also as a warning to opposers of God's servants and to those who hypocritically profess to be his people. It sets a pattern for strong faith in Jehovah, who is worthy of all songs of praise.

2 The book of Habakkuk opens: "The pronouncement that Habakkuk the prophet visioned." (Hab. 1:1) Who was this prophet Habakkuk (Hebrew, *Chavaq·quqʹ*), whose name means "Ardent Embrace"? No information is provided concerning Habakkuk's parentage, tribe, circumstances in life, or death. Whether he was a Levitical temple musician cannot be stated definitely, although this has been inferred from the subscription at the end of the book: "To the director on my stringed instruments."

3 When did Habakkuk make his prophetic pronouncements? The above-mentioned subscription and the words "Jehovah is in his holy temple" indicate that the temple in Jerusalem was still standing. (2:20) This, together with the message of the prophecy, suggests that it was spoken not long before Jerusalem's destruction in 607 B.C.E. But how many years before? It must have been after the reign of God-fearing King Josiah, 659-629 B.C.E. The prophecy itself provides the clue in foretelling an activity that the people in Judah will not believe even if it is related. What is this? It is the raising up of the Chaldeans (Babylonians) by God to punish faithless Judah. (1:5, 6) This would fit the early part of the reign of idolatrous King Jehoiakim, a time when disbelief and injustice were rampant in Judah. Jehoiakim had

been put on the throne by Pharaoh Necho, and the nation was within Egypt's sphere of influence. Under such circumstances the people would feel they had cause to discredit any possibility of invasion from Babylon. But Nebuchadnezzar defeated Pharaoh Necho in the battle of Carchemish in 625 B.C.E., thus breaking the power of Egypt. The prophecy would therefore have been delivered before that event. So the indications point to the beginning of Jehoiakim's reign (begun in 628 B.C.E.), making Habakkuk a contemporary of Jeremiah.

4 How can we know that the book is inspired of God? Ancient catalogs of the Hebrew Scriptures confirm the canonicity of Habakkuk. While they do not mention the book by name, it was evidently included in their references to the 'twelve Minor Prophets,' for without Habakkuk there would not be 12. The apostle Paul recognized the prophecy as part of the inspired Scriptures and makes a direct quotation of Habakkuk 1:5, referring to it as something "said in the Prophets." (Acts 13:40, 41) He made several references to the book in his letters. Certainly the fulfillment of Habakkuk's utterances against Judah and Babylon marks him as a true prophet of Jehovah, in whose name and for whose glory he spoke.

5 The book of Habakkuk is made up of three chapters. The first two chapters are a dialogue between the writer and Jehovah. They relate the strength of the Chaldeans, as well as the grief awaiting the Babylonian nation that multiplies what is not its own, that makes evil gain for its house, that builds a city by bloodshed, and that worships the carved image. The third chapter deals with the magnificence of Jehovah in the day of battle, and it is unrivaled in the power and vibrancy of its dramatic style. This chapter is a prayer in dirges and has been called "one of the most splendid and magnificent within the whole compass of Hebrew poetry."*

---

* *The Book of the Twelve Minor Prophets,* 1868, E. Henderson, page 285.

---

1. What sublime truths are highlighted in the prophecy of Habakkuk?
2. What information is given about the writer, Habakkuk?
3. What circumstances affecting Judah help to indicate the time of writing of Habakkuk?

4. What proves the book of Habakkuk to be inspired of God?
5. Briefly summarize the contents of Habakkuk.

CONTENTS OF HABAKKUK

[6] **The prophet cries out to Jehovah** (1:1–2:1). Faithlessness in Judah has provoked questions in Habakkuk's mind. "How long, O Jehovah, must I cry for help, and you do not hear?" he asks. "Why are despoiling and violence in front of me?" (1: 2, 3) Law grows numb, the wicked one is surrounding the righteous one, and justice goes forth crooked. Because of this, Jehovah will carry on an activity that will cause amazement, something that the "people will not believe although it is related." He is actually "raising up the Chaldeans"! Frightful indeed is the vision that Jehovah gives of this fierce nation as it comes swiftly. It is devoted to violence, and it gathers up captives "just like the sand." (1:5, 6, 9) Nothing will stand in its way, not even kings and high officials, for it laughs at all of them. It captures every fortified place. All of this is for a judgment and a reproving from Jehovah, the "Holy One." (1:12) Habakkuk waits attentively for God to speak.

[7] **The vision of the five woes** (2:2-20). Jehovah answers: "Write down the vision, and set it out plainly upon tablets." Even if it seems to be delayed, it will without fail come true. Jehovah comforts Habakkuk with the words: "As for the righteous one, by his faithfulness he will keep living." (2:2, 4) The self-assuming foe will not reach his goal, even though he keeps gathering to himself nations and peoples. Why, these are the very ones who will take up against him the proverbial saying of the five woes:

[8] "Woe to him who is multiplying what is not his own." He himself will become something to pillage. He will be despoiled "because of the shedding of blood of mankind and the violence to the earth." (2:6, 8) "Woe to the one that is making evil gain for his house." His cutting off of many peoples will cause the very stones and woodwork of his house to cry out. (2:9) "Woe to the one that is building a city by bloodshed." His peoples will toil only for fire and nothingness, declares Jehovah. "For the earth will be filled with the knowing of the glory of Jehovah as the waters themselves cover over the sea."—2:12, 14.

[9] 'Woe to the one who in anger makes his companion drunk so as to see his parts of shame.' Jehovah will make him drink from the cup of His right hand, bringing him disgrace in place of glory "because of the shedding of blood of mankind and the violence done to the earth." Of what use is a carved image to its maker—are not such valueless gods speechless? (2:15, 17) "Woe to the one saying to the piece of wood: 'O do awake!' to a dumb stone: 'O wake up! It itself will give instruction'!" In contrast with these lifeless gods, "Jehovah is in his holy temple. Keep silence before him, all the earth!"—2:19, 20.

[10] **Jehovah in the day of battle** (3:1-19). In solemn prayer, Habakkuk graphically recalls the fearsome activity of Jehovah. At Jehovah's appearing "his dignity covered the heavens; and with his praise the earth became filled." (3:3) His brightness was like the light, and pestilence kept going before him. He stood still, shaking up the earth, causing the nations to leap and the eternal mountains to be smashed. Jehovah went riding like a mighty warrior with naked bow and with chariots of salvation. Mountains and the watery deep were agitated. Sun and moon stood still, and there were the light of his arrows and the lightning of his spear as he marched through the earth, threshing the nations in anger. He went forth for the salvation of his people and of his anointed one and for the laying bare of the foundation of the wicked one, "clear up to the neck."—3:13.

[11] The prophet is overwhelmed by this vision of the might of Jehovah's former work and of his coming world-shaking activity. "I heard, and my belly began to be agitated; at the sound my lips quivered; rottenness began to enter into my bones; and in my situation I was agitated, that I should quietly wait for the day of distress, for his coming up to the people, that he may raid them." (3:16) However, Habakkuk is determined that regardless of the bad times that must be faced —no blossom on the fig tree, no yield on the vines, no flock in the pen—still he will exult in Jehovah and be joyful in the God of his salvation. He concludes his song of ecstasy with the words: "Jehovah the Sovereign Lord is my vital energy; and he will make my feet like those of the hinds, and upon my high places he will cause me to tread."—3:19.

WHY BENEFICIAL

[12] Recognizing Habakkuk's prophecy as beneficial for teaching, the apostle Paul quoted from chapter 2, verse 4, on three different occasions. When stressing that the good news is God's power for salvation to everyone having faith, Paul wrote the Christians in Rome: "For in it God's righteous-

---

6. What is the condition in Judah, and what amazing activity will Jehovah therefore carry on?
7. How does Jehovah comfort Habakkuk?
8, 9. Against what kinds of persons are the five woes of the vision directed?

10. What fearsome activity accompanies Jehovah's appearing in the day of battle?
11. How does the vision affect Habakkuk, but what is his determination?
12. What beneficial applications of Habakkuk 2:4 did Paul make?

ness is being revealed by reason of faith and toward faith, just as it is written: 'But the righteous one—by means of faith he will live.'" When writing the Galatians, Paul stressed the point that blessing comes through faith: "That by law no one is declared righteous with God is evident, because 'the righteous one will live by reason of faith.'" Paul also wrote in his letter to the Hebrews that Christians must show a live, soul-preserving faith, and he again referred to Jehovah's words to Habakkuk. However, he quotes not only Habakkuk's words, "my righteous one will live by reason of faith," but also his further words according to the Greek *Septuagint:* "If he shrinks back, my soul has no pleasure in him." Then he sums up by saying: We are "the sort that have faith to the preserving alive of the soul."—Rom. 1:17; Gal. 3:11; Heb. 10: 38, 39.

[13] Habakkuk's prophecy is most beneficial today to Christians, who need vital energy. It teaches reliance upon God. It is also beneficial for warning others of God's judgments. The warning lesson is forceful: Do not consider God's judgments as being too delayed; they will "without fail come true." (Hab. 2:3) Without fail the prophecy of Judah's destruction by Babylon came true, and without fail Babylon itself was captured, the Medes and Persians taking the city in 539 B.C.E. What a warning to believe God's words! Thus, the apostle Paul found it beneficial to quote Habakkuk when he warned the Jews of his day not to be faithless: "See to it that what is said in the Prophets does not

come upon you, 'Behold it, you scorners, and wonder at it, and vanish away, because I am working a work in your days, a work that you will by no means believe even if anyone relates it to you in detail.'" (Acts 13:40, 41; Hab. 1:5, *LXX*) The faithless Jews would not heed Paul, even as they had not believed Jesus' warning of Jerusalem's destruction; they suffered the consequences for their faithlessness when Rome's armies devastated Jerusalem in 70 C.E.—Luke 19:41-44.

[14] Likewise, today, Habakkuk's prophecy encourages Christians to hold strong faith, while living in a world filled with violence. It helps them to teach others and to answer the question people all over the world have asked, Will God execute vengeance on the wicked? Note again the words of the prophecy: "Keep in expectation of it; for it will without fail come true. It will not be late." (Hab. 2:3) Whatever the commotions that occur in the earth, the anointed remnant of Kingdom heirs recall Habakkuk's words concerning Jehovah's past acts of vengeance: "You went forth for the salvation of your people, to save your anointed one." (3:13) Jehovah is indeed their "Holy One," from long ago, and the "Rock" who will reprove the unrighteous and give life to those whom he embraces in his love. All who love righteousness may rejoice in his Kingdom and sovereignty, saying: "As for me, I will exult in Jehovah himself; I will be joyful in the God of my salvation. Jehovah the Sovereign Lord is my vital energy."—1:12; 3: 18, 19.

---

13. The accurate fulfillment of Habakkuk's prophecies against Judah and Babylon emphasize what as to God's judgments?

14. (a) How does Habakkuk's prophecy encourage Christians today to hold strong faith? (b) As stated in the prophecy, what joyful confidence may lovers of righteousness now have?

Bible Book Number **36**

Zephaniah

Writer: **Zephaniah**
Place Written: **Judah**
Writing Completed: **Before 648 B.C.E.**

EARLY in the reign of King Josiah of Judah (659-629 B.C.E.), at a time when Baal worship was running rampant and "the foreign-god priests" were taking a lead in this unclean worship, the people of Jerusalem must have been startled by the message proclaimed by

the prophet Zephaniah. Though he was possibly a descendant of King Hezekiah of the royal house of Judah, Zephaniah was highly critical of conditions in the nation. (Zeph. 1:1, 4) His message was one of doom. God's people had become disobedient, and only Jehovah could restore them to pure worship and bless them so that they might serve as "a name and a praise among all the peoples of the earth." (3:20) Zephaniah pointed out that only by

---

1. (a) Why was Zephaniah's message appropriate to his time? (b) How did the meaning of his name fit the situation?

divine intervention might one "be concealed in the day of Jehovah's anger." (2:3) How appropriate his name *Tsephan·yah´* (Hebrew), meaning "Jehovah Has Concealed (Treasured Up)"!

² Zephaniah's efforts bore fruit. King Josiah, who had ascended the throne at the age of eight, started in the 12th year of his reign "to cleanse Judah and Jerusalem." He rooted out false worship, repaired "the house of Jehovah," and reinstituted the celebration of the Passover. (2 Chron., chaps. 34, 35) King Josiah's reforms were only temporary, however, for he was succeeded by three of his sons and one of his grandsons, all of whom did "bad in the eyes of Jehovah." (2 Chron. 36:1-12) This was all in fulfillment of Zephaniah's words: "I will give attention to the princes, and to the sons of the king, and to . . . those who are filling the house of their masters with violence and deception."—Zeph. 1:8, 9.

³ From the above it appears that "the word of Jehovah . . . occurred to Zephaniah" sometime before 648 B.C.E., the 12th year of Josiah. Not only does the first verse identify him as speaking in Judah but the detailed knowledge he shows of the localities and customs of Jerusalem argue for his residence in Judah. The message contained in the book is twofold, being both threatening and consoling. For the most part, it centers around the day of Jehovah, a day of terror that is imminent, but at the same time, it foretells that Jehovah will restore a humble people that "actually take refuge in the name of Jehovah."—1:1, 7-18; 3:12.

⁴ The authenticity of this book of prophecy cannot be successfully disputed. Jerusalem was destroyed in 607 B.C.E., more than 40 years after Zephaniah had foretold it. Not only do we have secular history's word for this but the Bible itself contains internal proof that this happened exactly as Zephaniah had prophesied. Shortly after Jerusalem's destruction, Jeremiah wrote the book of Lamentations, describing the horrors he had witnessed, while they were still vivid in his mind. A comparison of several passages bears out that Zephaniah's message is indeed "inspired of God." Zephaniah warns of the need for repentance *"before* there comes upon you people the burning anger of Jehovah," whereas Jeremiah refers to something that has already happened when he says, "Jehovah . . . *has poured out* his burning anger." (Zeph. 2:2; Lam. 4:11) Zephaniah foretells that Jehovah *"will cause* distress to mankind, and

they *will* certainly *walk* like blind men . . . And their blood *will* actually *be poured out* like dust." (Zeph. 1:17) Jeremiah speaks of this as an accomplished fact: "They *have wandered* about as blind in the streets. They *have become polluted* with blood."—Lam. 4:14; compare also Zephaniah 1:13 —Lamentations 5:2; Zephaniah 2:8, 10—Lamentations 1:9, 16 and 3:61.

⁵ History likewise reports the destruction of the heathen nations, Moab and Ammon as well as Assyria, including its capital Nineveh, just as Zephaniah had foretold at God's direction. Even as the prophet Nahum foretold Nineveh's destruction (Nah. 1:1; 2:10), so Zephaniah declared that Jehovah "will make Nineveh a desolate waste, a waterless region like the wilderness." (Zeph. 2:13) This destruction was so complete that scarcely 200 years later, the historian Herodotus wrote of the Tigris as "the river upon which the town of Nineveh formerly stood."* About 150 C.E. the Greek writer Lucian wrote that "there is not a trace of it left now."# *The New Westminster Dictionary of the Bible* (1970), page 669, states that the invading armies "were greatly aided by a sudden rise of the Tigris, which carried away a great part of the city wall and rendered the place indefensible. . . . So complete was the desolation that in Greek and Roman times Nineveh became almost like a myth. Yet all the while part of the city lay buried under mounds of apparent rubbish." On page 627 the same volume shows that Moab was also destroyed as was prophesied: "Nebuchadnezzar subjugated the Moabites." Josephus also reports the subjugation of Ammon.△ Both the Moabites and the Ammonites eventually ceased to exist as a people.

⁶ The Jews have always given Zephaniah its rightful place in the canon of inspired Scriptures. Its declarations uttered in Jehovah's name have been notably fulfilled, to Jehovah's vindication.

CONTENTS OF ZEPHANIAH

⁷ **Day of Jehovah at hand** (1:1-18). The book opens on a note of doom. "'I shall without fail finish everything off the surface of the ground,' is the utterance of Jehovah." (1:2) Nothing will es-

---

* McClintock and Strong's *Cyclopedia*, 1981 Reprint, Vol. VII, page 112.
# *Lucian,* translated by A. M. Harmon, 1968, Vol. II, p. 443.
△ *Jewish Antiquities,* X, 181, 182 (ix, 7).

---

2. How did Zephaniah's efforts bear fruit, but why was this only temporary?
3. When and where did Zephaniah prophesy, and what twofold message does the book contain?
4. What proves the book of Zephaniah to be authentic and inspired of God?

5. How does history show that the prophecy of Zephaniah was accurately fulfilled?
6. Why, then, does Zephaniah take a rightful place in the Bible canon?
7. What will the great day of Jehovah mean for his enemies?

cape, of man or of beast. Baal worshipers, foreign-god priests, rooftop worshipers of the heavens, those who mix Jehovah's worship with Malcam's, those drawing back from Jehovah, and those not interested in seeking him—all must perish. The prophet commands: "Keep silence before the Sovereign Lord Jehovah; for the day of Jehovah is near." (1:7) Jehovah himself has prepared a sacrifice. Princes, violent ones, deceivers, and the indifferent at heart—all will be sought out. Their wealth and possessions will be brought to nothing. The great day of Jehovah is near! It is "a day of fury, a day of distress and of anguish, a day of storm and of desolation, a day of darkness and of gloominess, a day of clouds and of thick gloom." The blood of those sinning against Jehovah will be poured out like dust. "Neither their silver nor their gold will be able to deliver them in the day of Jehovah's fury." The fire of his zeal will devour the whole earth.—1:15, 18.

8 Seek Jehovah; nations to be destroyed (2:1-15). Before that day passes like the chaff, let the meek "seek Jehovah . . . Seek righteousness, seek meekness," and it may be you will be "concealed in the day of Jehovah's anger." (2:3) The utterance of Jehovah continues, pronouncing woe on the land of the Philistines, which is later to become "a region for the remaining ones of the house of Judah." Proud Moab and Ammon will be desolated like Sodom and Gomorrah "because they reproached and kept putting on great airs against the people of Jehovah of armies." Their gods will perish with them. (2:7, 10) Jehovah's "sword" will also slay the Ethiopians. What of Assyria, with its capital of Nineveh, to the north? It will become a barren wilderness and a dwelling for wild animals, yes, "an object of astonishment," so that "everyone passing along by her will whistle" in amazement.—2:12, 15.

9 Rebellious Jerusalem called to account; humble remnant blessed (3:1-20). It is woe, also, to Jerusalem, the rebellious and oppressive city! Her princes, "roaring lions," and her prophets, "men of treachery," have not trusted in her God, Jehovah. He will call for a full accounting. Will her inhabitants fear Jehovah and accept discipline? No, for they act "promptly in making all their dealings ruinous." (3:3, 4, 7) It is Jehovah's judicial decision to gather the nations and pour out upon them all his burning anger, and all the earth will be devoured by the fire of his zeal. But, there is a wonderful promise! Jehovah will "give to peoples the change to a pure language, in order for them all to call upon the name of Jehovah, in order to serve him shoulder to shoulder." (3:9) The haughtily exultant ones will be removed, and a humble remnant that does righteousness will find refuge in Jehovah's name. Joyful cries, cheers, rejoicing, and exultation break out in Zion, for Jehovah the King of Israel is in their midst. This is no time to be afraid or to let hands drop down, for Jehovah will save and exult over them in his love and joy. "'For I shall make you people to be a name and a praise among all the peoples of the earth, when I gather back your captive ones before your eyes,' Jehovah has said."—3:20.

WHY BENEFICIAL

10 King Josiah, for one, heeded Zephaniah's warning message and benefited from it greatly. He embarked on a great campaign of religious reform. This also brought to light the book of the Law, which had been lost when the house of Jehovah fell into disrepair. Josiah was grief-stricken at hearing the consequences for disobedience read to him from this book, which confirmed at the mouth of another witness, Moses, what Zephaniah had been prophesying all along. Josiah now humbled himself before God, with the result that Jehovah promised him that the foretold destruction would not come in his day. (Deut., chaps. 28-30; 2 Ki. 22:8-20) The land had been spared disaster! But not for long, for Josiah's sons failed to follow the good example he set. However, for Josiah and his people, their paying attention to "the word of Jehovah that occurred to Zephaniah" proved highly beneficial indeed.—Zeph. 1:1.

11 In his famous Sermon on the Mount, Christ Jesus, God's greatest prophet, supported Zephaniah as a true prophet of God by speaking words that are strikingly similar to Zephaniah's counsel at chapter 2, verse 3: "Seek Jehovah, all you meek ones of the earth . . . Seek righteousness, seek meekness." Jesus' admonition was: "Keep on, then, seeking first the kingdom and his righteousness." (Matt. 6:33) Those who seek first God's Kingdom must guard against the indifference that Zephaniah warned about when he spoke of "those who are drawing back from following Jehovah and who have not sought Jehovah and have not inquired of him" and "who are saying in their heart, 'Jehovah will not do good, and he will not do

---

8. (a) How may protection be found? (b) What woes are pronounced against the nations?
9. (a) Why is it woe to Jerusalem, and what is Jehovah's judicial decision upon the nations? (b) On what joyful note does the prophecy end?

10. Of what benefit was the prophecy of Zephaniah in King Josiah's days?
11. (a) How does Zephaniah tie in with the Sermon on the Mount and with Paul's letter to the Hebrews in giving sound admonition? (b) Why does Zephaniah say "probably you may be concealed"?

bad.'" (Zeph. 1:6, 12) In his letter to the Hebrews, Paul likewise tells of a coming day of judgment and warns against shrinking back. He adds: "Now we are not the sort that shrink back to destruction, but the sort that have faith to the preserving alive of the soul." (Heb. 10:30, 37-39) It is not to the quitters or to the unappreciative ones but to those who meekly and earnestly seek Jehovah in faith that the prophet says: "Probably you may be concealed in the day of Jehovah's anger." Why "probably"? Because final salvation depends on the course of the individual. (Matt. 24:13) It is also a reminder that we cannot presume on God's mercy. Zephaniah's prophecy leaves no question as to the suddenness with which that day will break upon the unsuspecting.—Zeph. 2:3; 1:14, 15; 3:8.

[12] Here, then, is a message foreboding destruction for those who sin against Jehovah but providing bright foregleams of blessings for those who repentantly "seek Jehovah." These repentant ones may take courage, for, says Zephaniah, "the king of Israel, Jehovah, is in the midst of you." It is no time for Zion to be afraid or to let hands drop down in inactivity. It is a time to trust in Jehovah. "As a mighty One, he will save. He will exult over you with rejoicing. He will become silent in his love. He will be joyful over you with happy cries." Happy also are those who 'seek first his kingdom,' in anticipation of his loving protection and eternal blessing!—3:15-17.

12. What basis for courage does Zephaniah give for those who "seek Jehovah"?

Bible Book Number	*37* *Haggai*	Writer: **Haggai**

Writer: **Haggai**
Place Written: **Jerusalem**
Writing Completed: **520 B.C.E.**
Time Covered: **112 days (520 B.C.E.)**

HAGGAI was his name; a prophet and "messenger of Jehovah" was his position, but what was his origin? (Hag. 1:13) Who was he? Haggai is the tenth of the so-called minor prophets, and he was the first of the three that served after the Jews returned to their homeland in 537 B.C.E., the other two being Zechariah and Malachi. Haggai's name (Hebrew, *Chag·gai´*) means "[Born on a] Festival." This may indicate he was born on a feast day.

[2] As handed down by Jewish tradition, it is reasonable to conclude that Haggai was born in Babylon and returned to Jerusalem with Zerubbabel and High Priest Joshua. Haggai served side by side with the prophet Zechariah, and at Ezra 5:1 and 6:14, the two are shown encouraging the sons of the exile to resume temple building. He was a prophet of Jehovah in two respects, in that he both exhorted the Jews to fulfill their duties toward God and foretold, among other things, the shaking of all nations.—Hag. 2:6, 7.

[3] Why did Jehovah commission Haggai? For this reason: In 537 B.C.E., Cyrus had issued the decree permitting the Jews to return to their homeland to rebuild the house of Jehovah. But it was now 520 B.C.E., and the temple was far from being completed. All these years the Jews had let enemy opposition along with their own apathy and materialism prevent them from realizing the very purpose of their return.—Ezra 1:1-4; 3: 10-13; 4:1-24; Hag. 1:4.

[4] As the record shows, no sooner had the foundation of the temple been laid (in 536 B.C.E.) than "the people of the land were continually weakening the hands of the people of Judah and disheartening them from building, and hiring counselors against them to frustrate their counsel." (Ezra 4: 4, 5) Finally, in 522 B.C.E., these non-Jewish opposers succeeded in having an official ban placed on the work. It was in the second year of the reign of the Persian king Darius Hystaspis, that is, in 520 B.C.E., that Haggai began to prophesy, and this encouraged the Jews to resume their temple building. At that, a letter was sent to Darius by the neighboring governors asking for a ruling on the matter; Darius revived the decree of Cyrus and supported the Jews against their enemies.

[5] There was never any question among the Jews about Haggai's prophecy belonging in the

---

1, 2. What information is given about the prophet Haggai, and what was his twofold message?
3. What had the Jews failed to realize as to the purpose of their return from exile?

4. What had hindered the temple building, but what developments took place when Haggai started to prophesy?
5. What proves that the book of Haggai belongs in the Bible canon?

Hebrew canon, and this is also supported by the reference to him at Ezra 5:1 as prophesying "in the name of the God of Israel," as well as at Ezra 6:14. That his prophecy is part of 'all Scripture inspired of God' is proved by Paul's quoting it at Hebrews 12:26: "Now he has promised, saying: 'Yet once more I will set in commotion not only the earth but also the heaven.'"—Hag. 2:6.

⁶ Haggai's prophecy consists of four messages given over a period of 112 days. His style is simple and direct, and his emphasis on Jehovah's name is particularly noteworthy. In his 38 verses, he mentions Jehovah's name 35 times, 14 times in the expression "Jehovah of armies." He leaves no doubt that his message is from Jehovah: "Haggai the messenger of Jehovah went on to say to the people according to the messenger's commission from Jehovah, saying: 'I am with you people,' is the utterance of Jehovah."—1:13.

⁷ This was a very important time in the history of God's people, and Haggai's work proved to be most beneficial. He was not the least backward in performing his task as a prophet, and he did not mince words with the Jews. He was straightforward in telling them that it was time to quit procrastinating and to get down to business. It was time to rebuild Jehovah's house and to restore pure worship if they wanted to enjoy any prosperity from the hand of Jehovah. The whole tenor of Haggai's message is that if a person is to enjoy blessings from Jehovah, he must serve the true God and do the work Jehovah commands to be done.

CONTENTS OF HAGGAI

⁸ **The first message** (1:1-15). This is directed to Governor Zerubbabel and High Priest Joshua, but in the hearing of the people. The people have been saying, "The time has not come, the time of the house of Jehovah, for it to be built." Jehovah through Haggai asks a searching question: "Is it the time for you yourselves to dwell in your paneled houses, while this house is waste?" (1:2, 4) They have sown much in a material way, but it has benefited them little in the way of food, drink, and clothing. "Set your heart upon your ways," admonishes Jehovah. (1:7) It is high time to bring in lumber and build the house, that Jehovah may be glorified. The Jews are taking good care of their own houses, but Jehovah's house lies waste. Therefore, Jehovah has withheld the dew of heaven and the increase of the field and his blessing from upon man and his toil.

⁹ Ah, they get the point! Haggai has not prophesied in vain. Rulers and people begin "to listen to the voice of Jehovah their God." Fear of Jehovah replaces fear of man. Jehovah's assurance through his messenger Haggai is: "I am with you people." (1:12, 13) It is Jehovah himself who rouses up the spirit of the governor, the spirit of the high priest, and the spirit of the remnant of His people. They get to work, just 23 days after the start of Haggai's prophesying and despite the official ban of the Persian government.

¹⁰ **The second message** (2:1-9). Less than a month passes after the building activity is revived, and Haggai gives his second inspired message. This is addressed to Zerubbabel, Joshua, and the remaining ones of the people. Evidently some of the Jews who returned from the exile and who had seen the former temple of Solomon felt that this temple would be nothing by comparison. But what is the utterance of Jehovah of armies? 'Be strong and work, for I am with you people.' (2:4) Jehovah reminds them of his covenant with them, and he tells them not to be afraid. He strengthens them with the promise that he will rock all the nations and cause their desirable things to come in and that he will fill his house with glory. The glory of this later house will be even greater than that of the former, and in this place he will give peace.

¹¹ **The third message** (2:10-19). Two months and three days later, Haggai addresses the priests. He uses an allegory to drive home his point. Will a priest's carrying holy flesh make holy any other food he touches? The answer is no. Does the touching of something unclean, such as a dead body, make the one touching it unclean? The answer is yes. Haggai then applies the allegory. The people of the land are unclean by reason of their neglect of pure worship. Whatever they offer appears unclean to Jehovah God. Because of this, Jehovah has not blessed their labors, and in addition he has sent on them scorching heat, mildew, and hail. Let them change their ways. Then Jehovah will bless them.

¹² **The fourth message** (2:20-23). Haggai delivers this message on the same day as the third message, but it is directed to Zerubbabel. Again Jehovah speaks of "rocking the heavens and the earth," but this time he extends this theme to the complete annihilation of the kingdoms of the nations. Many will be brought down, "each one by the sword of his brother." (2:21, 22) Haggai

---

6. Of what does Haggai's prophecy consist, and what emphasis is put on Jehovah's name?
7. What did Haggai encourage the Jews to do, and what was the tenor of his message?
8. Why are the Jews not being blessed materially by Jehovah?

---

9. How does Jehovah rouse up the Jews to get to work?
10. What do some Jews feel about the temple they are building, but what does Jehovah promise?
11. (a) By what allegory does Haggai point out the priests' neglect? (b) What has resulted therefrom?
12. What final message does Haggai direct to Zerubbabel?

concludes his prophecy with an assurance of Jehovah's favor for Zerubbabel.

WHY BENEFICIAL

[13] Jehovah's four messages communicated through Haggai were beneficial to the Jews of that day. They were encouraged to go right to work, and in four and a half years, the temple was completed to advance true worship in Israel. (Ezra 6:14, 15) Jehovah blessed their zealous activity. It was during this time of temple building that Darius the king of Persia examined the state records and reaffirmed the decree of Cyrus. The temple work was thus completed with his official backing. —Ezra 6:1-13.

[14] The prophecy also contains wise counsel for our day. How so? For one thing, it underscores the need for the creature to put the interests of God's worship ahead of his own personal interests. (Hag. 1:2-8; Matt. 6:33) It also drives home the point that selfishness is self-defeating, that it is futile to pursue materialism; it is the peace and blessing of Jehovah that make rich. (Hag. 1:9-11; 2:9; Prov. 10:22) It also stresses that the service of God itself does not make one clean unless it is pure and whole-souled, and that it must not be contaminated by unclean conduct. (Hag. 2:10-14; Col. 3:23; Rom. 6:19) It shows that God's servants must not be pessimistic, looking back to "good old days," but be forward-looking, 'setting their heart upon their ways' and seeking to bring glory to Jehovah. Then Jehovah will be with them.—Hag. 2:3, 4; 1:7, 8, 13; Phil. 3:13, 14; Rom. 8:31.

[15] Once they got busy in the temple work, the

---

13. Of what immediate benefit was Haggai's prophesying?
14. What wise counsel does Haggai provide for our day?
15. What does the book of Haggai show as to the results of zealous obedience?

Jews were favored by Jehovah, and they prospered. Obstacles vanished. The work was accomplished in good time. Fearless, zealous activity for Jehovah will always be rewarded. Difficulties, real or imagined, can be overcome by exercising courageous faith. Obedience to "the word of Jehovah" gets results.—Hag. 1:1.

[16] What of the prophecy that Jehovah will 'rock the heavens and the earth'? The apostle Paul gives the application of Haggai 2:6 in these words: "But now [God] has promised, saying: 'Yet once more I will set in commotion not only the earth but also the heaven.' Now the expression 'Yet once more' signifies the removal of the things being shaken as things that have been made, in order that the things not being shaken may remain. Wherefore, seeing that we are to receive a kingdom that cannot be shaken, let us continue to have undeserved kindness, through which we may acceptably render God sacred service with godly fear and awe. For our God is also a consuming fire." (Heb. 12:26-29) Haggai shows that the rocking is in order to "overthrow the throne of kingdoms and annihilate the strength of the kingdoms of the nations." (Hag. 2:21, 22) In quoting the prophecy, Paul speaks, in contrast, of God's Kingdom "that cannot be shaken." In contemplation of this Kingdom hope, let us, then, 'be strong and work,' rendering God sacred service. Let us be mindful, too, that before Jehovah overthrows the nations of earth, something precious is to be stirred up and is to come out of them, for survival: "'I will rock all the nations, and the desirable things of all the nations must come in; and I will fill this house with glory,' Jehovah of armies has said."—2:4, 7.

---

16. What relation does the prophecy of Haggai have to the Kingdom hope, and to what service should it stir us today?

<table>
<tr><td>Bible Book Number 38

Zechariah</td><td>Writer: Zechariah

Place Written: Jerusalem

Writing Completed: 518 B.C.E.

Time Covered: 520–518 B.C.E.</td></tr>
</table>

AT A standstill! That was the state of the construction work on Jehovah's temple in Jerusalem when Zechariah began to prophesy. Whereas Solomon had built the original

---

1. What was the situation as to the temple in Jerusalem when Zechariah began to prophesy?

temple in 7 1/2 years (1 Ki. 6:37, 38), the repatriated Jews had been back in Jerusalem for 17 years and the building was yet far from completion. The work had finally stopped altogether following the ban by Artaxerxes (either Bardiya or Gaumata). But now, despite this official ban, the work was once more getting under way. Jehovah was using Haggai and Zechariah to stir up the people to renew the construction and to stay with it until completed.—Ezra 4:23, 24; 5:1, 2.

² The task before them looked mountainous. (Zech. 4:6, 7) They were few, the opposers many, and although they had a prince of the Davidic line, Zerubbabel, they had no king and were under foreign domination. How easy to sink into a weak, self-centered attitude, when the time really demanded strong faith and energetic action! Zechariah was used to draw their attention to God's present purposes and even grander future purposes, thus strengthening them for the work to be done. (8:9, 13) It was no time to be like their unappreciative forefathers.—1:5, 6.

³ Who was Zechariah? There are about 30 different persons mentioned in the Bible with the name Zechariah. However, the writer of the book that bears this name is identified as "Zechariah the son of Berechiah the son of Iddo the prophet." (Zech. 1:1; Ezra 5:1; Neh. 12:12, 16) His name (Hebrew, *Zekhar·yah´*) means "Jehovah Has Remembered." The book of Zechariah makes it very plain that "Jehovah of armies" remembers His people, to deal well with them for His own name's sake. (Zech. 1:3) The dates mentioned in the book give it a coverage of at least two years. It was in the "eighth month in the second year of Darius" (October/November 520 B.C.E.) that the temple building was resumed and Zechariah commenced prophesying. (1:1) The book also makes a reference to "the fourth day of the ninth month, that is, Chislev," in "the fourth year of Darius" (about December 1, 518 B.C.E.). (7:1) Hence, Zechariah's prophecy would no doubt be spoken and also recorded during the years 520-518 B.C.E.—Ezra 4:24.

⁴ Students of the book of Zechariah will find ample proof of its authenticity. Take the case of Tyre. It was after a 13-year-long siege that the Babylonian king Nebuchadnezzar ruined Tyre. This, though, did not mean the complete end for Tyre. Zechariah, many years later, foretold the total destruction of Tyre. It was the island city of Tyre that Alexander the Great overthrew at the time of his famous causeway-building feat; he ruthlessly burned her, thus fulfilling Zechariah's prophecy of some two centuries earlier.*—Zech. 9:2-4.

---

* *Insight on the Scriptures,* Vol. 2, pages 531, 1136.

---

2. Why did the task look mountainous, but to what did Zechariah draw their attention?
3. (a) How is Zechariah identified, and why is his name appropriate? (b) When was Zechariah's prophecy spoken and recorded?
4. 5. (a) Why did Zechariah predict Tyre's fall long after the siege of that city by Nebuchadnezzar? (b) The fulfillment of what particular prophecies convincingly proves the book's inspiration?

⁵ The most convincing proof of the book's divine inspiration, however, is to be found in the fulfillment of its prophecies concerning the Messiah, Christ Jesus, as can be seen by comparing Zechariah 9:9 with Matthew 21:4, 5 and John 12:14-16; Zechariah 12:10 with John 19:34-37; and Zechariah 13:7 with Matthew 26:31 and Mark 14:27. Also, there are the similarities to be noted between Zechariah 8:16 and Ephesians 4:25; Zechariah 3:2 and Jude 9; and Zechariah 14:5 and Jude 14. The harmony found in God's Word is truly marvelous!

⁶ There are some Bible critics who say that the change in style of writing from chapter 9 onward indicates that that section could not have been written by Zechariah. The change in style, however, is certainly no greater than the change in subject matter would justify. Whereas the first eight chapters deal with matters of more present importance to the people of Zechariah's day, in chapters 9 to 14 the prophet looks forward into a more distant future. Some have queried why it is that Matthew quotes Zechariah but attributes his words to Jeremiah. (Matt. 27:9; Zech. 11:12) It appears that Jeremiah was at times reckoned as first of the Later Prophets (instead of Isaiah, as in our present Bibles); hence Matthew, in referring to Zechariah as "Jeremiah," could have been following the Jewish practice of including a whole section of Scripture under the name of the first book of the section. Jesus himself used the designation "Psalms" to include all the books known as the Writings.—Luke 24:44.*

⁷ Up to chapter 6, verse 8, the book consists of a series of eight visions, similar in type to those of Daniel and Ezekiel, relating generally to the temple's reconstruction. These are followed by pronouncements and prophecies regarding sincere worship, restoration, and Jehovah's day of war.

CONTENTS OF ZECHARIAH

⁸ **First vision: The four horsemen** (1:1-17). "Return to me, . . . and I shall return to you," says Jehovah, and then he asks, "My words and my regulations that I commanded my servants, the prophets, did they not catch up with your fathers?" (1:3, 6) The people admit they have received their just due. Zechariah's first vision now appears. At night four horsemen stand among trees near Jerusalem, having returned from

---

* *Encyclopaedia Judaica,* 1973, Vol. 4, col. 828; *Insight on the Scriptures,* Vol. 1, pages 1080-1.

---

6. (a) What accounts for the change of style from chapter 9 of Zechariah onward? (b) What may be the reason for Matthew's referring to Zechariah as "Jeremiah"?
7. How is the book of Zechariah arranged?
8. What does the vision of the four horsemen show concerning Jerusalem and the nations?

inspecting the whole earth, which they found undisturbed and at ease. But Jehovah's angel, who interviews them, *is* disturbed over Jerusalem's condition. Jehovah himself declares his great indignation against the nations that helped toward Zion's calamity, and he says that he will "certainly return to Jerusalem with mercies." His own house will be built in her, and his cities "will yet overflow with goodness."—1:16, 17.

⁹ **Second vision: The horns and craftsmen** (1: 18-21). Zechariah sees the four horns that dispersed Judah, Israel, and Jerusalem. Then Jehovah shows him four craftsmen, explaining that these will come to cast down the horns of the nations that oppose Judah.

¹⁰ **Third vision: Jerusalem's prosperity** (2: 1-13). A man is seen measuring Jerusalem. The city will be blessed with expansion, and Jehovah will be a wall of fire all around her and a glory in the midst of her. He calls out, "Hey there, Zion! Make your escape," and adds the warning, "He that is touching you is touching my eyeball." (2: 7, 8) With Jehovah residing in her, Zion will rejoice, and many nations will join themselves to Jehovah. All flesh is commanded to keep silence before Jehovah, "for he has aroused himself from his holy dwelling."—2:13.

¹¹ **Fourth vision: Joshua's deliverance** (3: 1-10). High Priest Joshua is shown on trial, with Satan opposing him and Jehovah's angel rebuking Satan. Is not Joshua "a log snatched out of the fire"? (3:2) Joshua is declared cleansed, and his befouled garments are exchanged for clean "robes of state." He is urged to walk in the ways of Jehovah, who is 'bringing in his servant Sprout' and who puts before Joshua a stone upon which there are seven eyes.—3:4, 8.

¹² **Fifth vision: The lampstand and olive trees** (4:1-14). The angel awakens Zechariah to see a gold lampstand of seven lamps, flanked by two olive trees. He hears this word of Jehovah to Zerubbabel: 'Not by military force, nor by power, but by God's spirit.' A "great mountain" will be leveled before Zerubbabel, and the temple headstone will be brought forth to the cry: "How charming! How charming!" Zerubbabel has laid the temple foundations, and Zerubbabel will finish the work. The seven lamps are Jehovah's eyes that "are roving about in all the earth." (4:6, 7, 10) The two olive trees are Jehovah's two anointed ones.

¹³ **Sixth vision: The flying scroll** (5:1-4). Zechariah sees a flying scroll, about 30 feet long and 15 feet wide. The angel explains that this is the curse that is going forth because of all those stealing and swearing falsely in Jehovah's name.

¹⁴ **Seventh vision: The ephah measure** (5: 5-11). The lid is lifted from an ephah measure (about 20 dry qt, U.S.), revealing a woman named "Wickedness." She is thrust back into the ephah, which is then lifted toward heaven by two winged women, to be carried to Shinar (Babylon) and "deposited there upon her proper place."—5:8, 11.

¹⁵ **Eighth vision: The four chariots** (6:1-8). Look! From between two copper mountains, four chariots appear, with horses of different colors. They are the four spirits of the heavens. At the angel's command, they go walking about in the earth.

¹⁶ **The Sprout; insincere fasting** (6:9–7:14). Jehovah now instructs Zechariah to place a grand crown on High Priest Joshua's head. He speaks prophetically of the "Sprout," who will build Jehovah's temple and rule as a priest on his throne. —6:12.

¹⁷ Two years after Zechariah started prophesying, a delegation arrives from Bethel to ask the temple priests whether certain periods of weeping and fasting should continue to be observed. Through Zechariah, Jehovah asks the people and the priests whether they are really sincere in their fasting. What Jehovah desires is 'obedience, true justice, loving-kindness, and mercies.' (7: 7, 9) Because they resist his prophetic words with stubborn shoulders and emery-stone hearts, he will hurl them tempestuously throughout all the nations.

¹⁸ **Restoration; "ten men"** (8:1-23). Jehovah declares he will return to Zion and reside in Jerusalem, which will be called "the city of trueness." Old people will sit in her public squares, and children will play there. This is not too difficult for Jehovah, the true and righteous God! Jehovah promises the seed of peace to the remnant of his people, saying: "Do not be afraid. May your hands be strong." (8:3, 13) These things they should do: Speak truthfully with one another and judge with truth, keeping hearts free from calamitous schemes and false oaths. Why, the time will come when the people of many cities will certainly invite one another to go up earnestly to seek Jehovah, and "ten men" out of all the languages

---

9. How does Jehovah explain the vision of the horns and craftsmen?
10. How is Jehovah associated with Jerusalem's prosperity?
11. How is High Priest Joshua vindicated, and what course is urged upon him?
12. What encouragement and assurance are given concerning the temple building?

13-15. What is seen in the visions of the flying scroll, the ephah measure, and the four chariots?
16. What is prophesied concerning the "Sprout"?
17. As to worship, what does Jehovah desire, and what is to result to those resisting his words?
18. What glorious promises of restoration does Jehovah make?

will "take hold of the skirt of a man who is a Jew" and go along with God's people.—8:23.

[19] **Pronouncements against nations, false shepherds** (9:1–11:17). In the book's second section, chapters 9 to 14, Zechariah turns from the allegorical visions to the more customary prophetic style. He begins with a severe pronouncement against various cities, including the rocky island-city of Tyre. Jerusalem is told to shout in joyful triumph, for, "Look! Your king himself comes to you. He is righteous, yes, saved; humble, and riding upon an ass." (9:9) Cutting off war chariots and bow, this one will speak peace to the nations and will rule to the ends of the earth. Jehovah will fight for his people against Greece, and he will save them. "For O how great his goodness is, and how great his handsomeness is!" (9:17) Jehovah, the Rain-Giver, condemns the diviners and false shepherds. He will make the house of Judah superior and those of Ephraim like a mighty man. As for the redeemed ones, "their heart will be joyful in Jehovah . . . and in his name they will walk about."—10:7, 12.

[20] Zechariah is now assigned to shepherd the flock, which has been sold into slaughter by compassionless shepherds who say: "May Jehovah be blessed, while I shall gain riches." (11:5) The prophet takes two staffs and names them "Pleasantness" and "Union." (11:7) Breaking "Pleasantness," he symbolizes a covenant broken. Then he calls for his wages, and they weigh him out 30 pieces of silver. Jehovah orders Zechariah to throw it into the treasury and, with superlative sarcasm, says, "the majestic value with which I have been valued." (11:13) Now staff "Union" is cut up, breaking the brotherhood of Judah and Israel. A sword will come upon the false shepherds who have neglected Jehovah's sheep.

[21] **Jehovah wars, becomes king** (12:1–14:21). Another pronouncement begins. Jehovah will make Jerusalem a bowl that causes peoples to reel and a burdensome stone that scratches those lifting it. He will annihilate all nations that come against Jerusalem. Upon the house of David, Jehovah will pour out the spirit of favor and entreaties, and the people will look upon the one they pierced through, wailing over him "as in the wailing over an only son." (12:10) Jehovah of armies declares a cutting off of all idols and false prophets; the very parents of such a one must wound him so that in shame he removes his prophet's garb. Jehovah's

associate shepherd is to be struck and the flock scattered, but Jehovah will refine a "third part" to call upon his name. Jehovah will say: "It is my people," and it will answer: "Jehovah is my God." —13:9.

[22] "Look! There is a day coming, belonging to Jehovah." All nations will attack Jerusalem, and half the city will go into exile, leaving behind a remnant. Then Jehovah will go forth and war against those nations, "as in the day of his warring, in the day of fight." (14:1, 3) The mountain of olive trees, on the east of Jerusalem, will split from east to west, making a valley for refuge. In that day living waters will flow east and west from Jerusalem, in summer and in winter, and "Jehovah must become king over all the earth." (14:9) While Jerusalem enjoys security, Jehovah will scourge those warring against her. As they stand, their flesh, eyes, and tongues will rot away. Confusion will hit them. The hand of each one will turn against his neighbor's. Those left alive of all the nations will have to "go up from year to year to bow down to the King, Jehovah of armies." —14:16.

WHY BENEFICIAL

[23] All who study and meditate on the prophecy of Zechariah will be benefited in gaining faith-strengthening knowledge. More than 50 times Zechariah draws attention to "Jehovah of armies" as the One who fights for and protects His people, filling them with power according to their need. When mountainlike opposition threatened the completion of the temple building, Zechariah declared: "This is the word of Jehovah to Zerubbabel, saying, '"Not by a military force, nor by power, but by my spirit," Jehovah of armies has said. Who are you, O great mountain? Before Zerubbabel you will become a level land.'" The temple was completed with the help of Jehovah's spirit. Likewise today, obstacles will melt if tackled with faith in Jehovah. It is just as Jesus told his disciples: "If you have faith the size of a mustard grain, you will say to this mountain, 'Transfer from here to there,' and it will transfer, and nothing will be impossible for you."—Zech. 4: 6, 7; Matt. 17:20.

[24] In chapter 13, verses 2 to 6, Zechariah illustrates the loyalty that to this day marks Jehovah's organization. This must transcend every human relationship, such as that of close flesh-and-blood relatives. If a close relative should prophesy

---

19. What severe pronouncements follow, but what is said concerning Jerusalem's king?
20. What symbols are enacted with the staffs "Pleasantness" and "Union"?
21. (a) What is Jehovah's judgment on those who fight against Jerusalem? (b) What scattering and refining are foretold?

22. What is to happen to the nations and to Jerusalem in 'the day belonging to Jehovah'?
23. How is the record of Zechariah strengthening to faith?
24. What illustration of loyalty is given in chapter 13 of Zechariah?

falsehood in the name of Jehovah, that is, speak contrary to the Kingdom message and try wrongly to influence others in the congregation of God's people, the family members of that one must loyally support any judicial action taken by the congregation. The same position must be held with regard to any intimate associate who prophesies falsely, so that he may become ashamed and wounded at heart because of his wrong action.

²⁵ As our introductory paragraphs showed, Jesus' entry into Jerusalem as king, "humble, and riding upon an ass," his betrayal for "thirty pieces of silver," the scattering of his disciples at that time, and his being pierced on the stake by the soldier's spear were all foretold by Zechariah in exact detail. (Zech. 9:9; 11:12; 13:7; 12:10) The prophecy also names the "Sprout" as the builder of the temple of Jehovah. A comparison of Isaiah 11:1-10; Jeremiah 23:5; and Luke 1:32, 33 shows this one to be Jesus Christ, who "will rule as king over the house of Jacob forever." Zechariah describes the "Sprout" as "a priest upon his throne," which ties in with the apostle Paul's words: "Jesus . . . has become a high priest according to the manner of Melchizedek forever," also, "He has sat down at the right hand of the throne of the Majesty in the heavens." (Zech. 6:12, 13; Heb. 6:20; 8:1) Thus the prophecy points to the "Sprout" as High Priest and King at God's right hand in the heavens, while at the same time it proclaims Jehovah as Sovereign Ruler over all: "And Jehovah must become king over all the earth. In that day Jehovah will prove to be one, and his name one."—Zech. 14:9.

25. How does the prophecy of Zechariah link with other scriptures in identifying Messiah, the "Sprout," and his office as High Priest and King under Jehovah?

²⁶ Referring to that time, the prophet repeats the phrase "in that day" some 20 times, and it even concludes his prophecy. An examination of its many occurrences shows it to be the day when Jehovah cuts off the names of the idols and removes the false prophets. (13:2, 4) It is the day when Jehovah wars on the aggressor nations and spreads confusion in their ranks as he annihilates them and provides 'the valley of his mountains' as a refuge for his own people. (14:1-5, 13; 12:8, 9) Yes, "Jehovah their God will certainly save them in that day like the flock of his people," and they will call one to the other from under the vine and fig tree. (Zech. 9:16; 3:10; Mic. 4:4) It is the glorious day when Jehovah of armies "will reside in the midst" of his people and when "living waters will go forth from Jerusalem." These words of Zechariah identify events "in that day" as harbingers of "a new heaven and a new earth" of Kingdom promise. —Zech. 2:11; 14:8; Rev. 21:1-3; 22:1.

²⁷ "Who has despised the day of small things?" asks Jehovah. Look! This prosperity is to embrace the entire earth: 'Many peoples and mighty nations will actually come to seek Jehovah of armies in Jerusalem, and ten men out of all the languages of the nations will take hold of the skirt of a man who is a Jew, saying: "We will go with you people, for we have heard that God is with you people."' "In that day" even the bells of the horse will bear the words "Holiness belongs to Jehovah!" These heartwarming prophecies are most beneficial to consider, for they show that Jehovah's name will indeed be sanctified through his Kingdom Seed! —Zech. 4:10; 8:22, 23; 14:20.

26. To what glorious "day" does Zechariah repeatedly refer?
27. How does the prophecy of Zechariah focus attention on the sanctification of Jehovah's name?

| Bible Book Number | **39** Malachi | Writer: **Malachi**
Place Written: **Jerusalem**
Writing Completed: **After 443 B.C.E.** |

WHO was Malachi? There is not a single fact recorded regarding his ancestry or personal history. However, from the tenor of his prophecy, it is quite evident that he was most zealous in his devotion to Jehovah God, upholding His name and pure worship, and that he felt strong indignation toward those who profess to serve God but who serve only themselves. The name of Jehovah is mentioned 48 times in the four chapters of his prophecy.

² His name in Hebrew is *Mal·'a·khi'*, which possibly means "My Messenger." The Hebrew Scriptures, the *Septuagint,* and the chronological

1. What indicates Malachi's zeal for Jehovah?

2. What does Malachi's name possibly mean, and when, apparently, did he live?

order of the books all place Malachi last among the 12 so-called minor prophets. According to the tradition of the Great Synagogue, he lived after the prophets Haggai and Zechariah and was a contemporary of Nehemiah.

³ When was the prophecy written? It was during the administration of a governor, which places it in the time of the restoration of Jerusalem following the 70 years' desolation of Judah. (Mal. 1:8) But which governor? Since the temple service is mentioned but without reference to building the temple, it must have been after the time of Governor Zerubbabel, during whose tenure of office the temple was completed. There is only one other governor of this period mentioned in the Scriptures, and he is Nehemiah. Does the prophecy fit Nehemiah's time? Nothing is stated in Malachi concerning the rebuilding of Jerusalem and its wall, which eliminates the early part of Nehemiah's governorship. However, much is said concerning the abuses by the priesthood, tying Malachi in with the situation that existed when Nehemiah came a second time to Jerusalem, following his recall to Babylon by Artaxerxes in 443 B.C.E., the 32nd year of the king's reign. (Mal. 2:1; Neh. 13:6) Similar passages in Malachi and Nehemiah indicate that the prophecy applies to this particular time.—Mal. 2:4-8, 11, 12 —Neh. 13:11, 15, 23-26; Mal. 3:8-10—Neh. 13: 10-12.

⁴ The book of Malachi has always been accepted by the Jews as authentic. Quotations from it in the Christian Greek Scriptures, a number of which show fulfillments of its prophecy, prove that Malachi was inspired and part of the canon of Hebrew Scriptures that was recognized by the Christian congregation.—Mal. 1:2, 3—Rom. 9:13; Mal. 3:1—Matt. 11:10 and Luke 1:76 and 7:27; Mal. 4:5, 6—Matt. 11:14 and 17:10-13, Mark 9:11-13 and Luke 1:17.

⁵ Malachi's prophecy indicates that the religious zeal and enthusiasm aroused by the prophets Haggai and Zechariah at the time of rebuilding the temple had passed away. Priests had become careless, proud, and self-righteous. Temple services had become a mockery. Tithes and offerings had lapsed because of a feeling that God was not interested in Israel. The hopes centered in Zerubbabel had not been realized, and contrary to some expectations, Messiah had not come. The Jews' spiritual state was at a very low ebb. What

ground was there for encouragement and hope? How could the people be made aware of their true state and be awakened to return to righteousness? The prophecy of Malachi supplied the answer.

⁶ Malachi's style of writing is direct and forceful. He first states the proposition and then answers the objections of those whom he addresses. Finally, he reasserts his original proposition. This adds strength and vividness to his argument. Instead of soaring to heights of eloquence, he uses an abrupt, strongly argumentative style.

CONTENTS OF MALACHI
⁷ **Jehovah's commandment to the priests** (1:1–2:17). Jehovah first expresses his love for his people. He has loved Jacob and hated Esau. Let Edom try to build its devastated places; Jehovah will tear them down and they will be called "the territory of wickedness," the people denounced by Jehovah, for Jehovah will "be magnified over the territory of Israel."—1:4, 5.

⁸ Now Jehovah addresses directly the 'priests who are despising his name.' As they try to justify themselves, Jehovah points to their blind, lame, and sick sacrifices, and he asks, Will even the governor approve such offerings? Jehovah himself has no delight in them. His name must be exalted among the nations, but these men are profaning him by saying: "The table of Jehovah is something polluted." A curse will come on them because they have cunningly sidestepped their vows by offering worthless sacrifices. "'For I am a great King,' Jehovah of armies has said, 'and my name will be fear-inspiring among the nations.'" —1:6, 12, 14.

⁹ Jehovah now gives a commandment to the priests, saying that if they do not take this counsel to heart, he will send a curse upon them and upon their blessings. He will scatter the dung of their festivals upon their faces because of their failure to keep the covenant of Levi. "For the lips of a priest are the ones that should keep knowledge, and the law is what people should seek from his mouth; for he is the messenger of Jehovah of armies." (2:7) Malachi confesses the great sin of Israel and Judah. They have dealt treacherously with one another and have profaned the holiness of Jehovah, their Father and Creator, by taking the daughter of a foreign god as bride. They have gone to the extreme in wearying

---

3. What indicates that the prophecy of Malachi was written after 443 B.C.E.?
4. What proves the book of Malachi to be authentic and inspired?
5. What low spiritual condition prompted Malachi's prophecy?

6. What is Malachi's style of writing?
7. What love and hatred does Jehovah express?
8. How have the priests polluted Jehovah's table, and why will a curse come on them?
9. In what have the priests failed, and how have they profaned Jehovah's holiness?

Jehovah. They have even asked, "Where is the God of justice?"—2:17.

¹⁰ **The true Lord and the messenger** (3:1-18). The prophecy now reaches a climax in the words of "Jehovah of armies": "Look! I am sending my messenger, and he must clear up a way before me. And suddenly there will come to His temple the true Lord, whom you people are seeking, and the messenger of the covenant in whom you are delighting. Look! He will certainly come." (3:1) As a refiner, He will cleanse the sons of Levi and will become a speedy witness against the wicked who have not feared Him. Jehovah does not change, and because they are sons of Jacob, he will mercifully return to them if they return to him.

¹¹ They have been robbing God, but now let them test him by bringing their tithes into the storehouse that there may be food in his house, confident that he will pour forth from the floodgates of the heavens the very fullness of his blessing. They will become a land of delight pronounced happy by all nations. Those in fear of Jehovah have been speaking to one another, and Jehovah has been paying attention and listening. "And a book of remembrance began to be written up before him for those in fear of Jehovah and for those thinking upon his name." (3:16) They will certainly become Jehovah's in the day of his producing a special property.

¹² **The great and fear-inspiring day of Jehovah** (4:1-6). This is the coming day that will devour the wicked, leaving neither root nor bough. But the sun of righteousness will shine forth to those who fear Jehovah's name, and they will be healed. Jehovah admonishes them to remember the Law of Moses. Before his great and fear-inspiring day, Jehovah promises to send Elijah the prophet. "And he must turn the heart of fathers back toward sons, and the heart of sons back toward fathers; in order that I may not come and actually strike the earth with a devoting of it to destruction."—4:6.

WHY BENEFICIAL

¹³ The book of Malachi helps in understanding the unchanging principles and merciful love of Jehovah God. At the outset, it emphasizes Jehovah's great love for his people "Jacob." He de-

clared to the sons of Jacob: "I am Jehovah; I have not changed." Despite their great wickedness, he was ready to return to his people if they would return to him. A merciful God indeed! (Mal. 1:2; 3:6, 7; Rom. 11:28; Ex. 34:6, 7) Through Malachi, Jehovah stressed that a priest's lips "should keep knowledge." All who are entrusted with the teaching of God's Word should pay heed to this point, making sure that it is accurate knowledge that they impart. (Mal. 2:7; Phil. 1:9-11; compare James 3:1.) Jehovah does not tolerate hypocrites, those who try to make out that "doing bad is good in the eyes of Jehovah." No one should think that he can deceive Jehovah by making the mere pretense of an offering to this great King. (Mal. 2:17; 1:14; Col. 3:23, 24) Jehovah will be a speedy witness against all who violate his righteous laws and principles; no one may expect to act wickedly and get away with it. Jehovah will judge them. (Mal. 3:5; Heb. 10:30, 31) The righteous may have full assurance that Jehovah will remember their deeds and reward them. They should pay attention to the Law of Moses, even as Jesus did, for it contains many things that are fulfilled in him.—Mal. 3:16; 4:4; Luke 24:44, 45.

¹⁴ As the last book of the inspired Hebrew Scriptures, Malachi points forward to events surrounding the coming of the Messiah, whose appearance more than four centuries later provided the reason for the writing of the Christian Greek Scriptures. As recorded at Malachi 3:1, Jehovah of armies said: "Look! I am sending my messenger, and he must clear up a way before me." Speaking under inspiration, the aged Zechariah showed that this had a fulfillment in his son, John the Baptizer. (Luke 1:76) Jesus Christ confirmed this, stating at the same time: "There has not been raised up a greater than John the Baptist; but a person that is a lesser one in the kingdom of the heavens is greater than he is." John had been sent, as Malachi foretold, to 'prepare the way,' so that he was not among those with whom Jesus later made a covenant for a Kingdom.—Matt. 11: 7-12; Luke 7:27, 28; 22:28-30.

¹⁵ Then, at Malachi 4:5, 6, Jehovah promised: "Look! I am sending to you people Elijah the prophet." Who is this "Elijah"? Both Jesus and the angel who appeared to Zechariah apply these words to John the Baptizer, showing that he was the one to "restore all things" and "to get ready for Jehovah a prepared people" to receive the Messiah. However, Malachi says also that "Elijah" is the forerunner of "the great and fear-inspiring day of Jehovah," thus indicating a still future

---

10. For what work of judgment does the Lord come to his temple?
11. How should they now test God, and what blessings will follow?
12. What is promised concerning Jehovah's fear-inspiring day?
13. What does Malachi have to say as to (a) Jehovah's mercy and love? (b) the responsibility of teachers of God's Word? (c) those who violate God's laws and principles?

---

14. (a) To what, particularly, does Malachi point forward? (b) How was Malachi 3:1 fulfilled in the first century C.E.?
15. Who is the "Elijah" of Malachi's prophecy?

fulfillment in a day of judgment.—Matt. 17:11; Luke 1:17; Matt. 11:14; Mark 9:12.

¹⁶ Looking forward to that day, Jehovah of armies says: "From the sun's rising even to its setting my name will be great among the nations. . . . For I am a great King, . . . and my name will be fear-inspiring among the nations." Fear-inspiring indeed! For 'the day will burn like the furnace, and all the presumptuous ones and all those doing wickedness must become as stubble.' Yet, happy are those who fear Jehovah's name, for to them "the sun of righteousness will certainly shine forth, with healing in its wings." This focuses on the happy time when obedient ones of the human family will be completely healed—spiritually, emotionally, mentally, and physically. (Rev.

21:3, 4) In pointing forward to that glorious and blessed day, Malachi encourages us to be wholehearted in bringing our offering into Jehovah's house: "'Test me out, please, in this respect,' Jehovah of armies has said, 'whether I shall not open to you people the floodgates of the heavens and actually empty out upon you a blessing until there is no more want.'"—Mal. 1:11, 14; 4:1, 2; 3:10.

¹⁷ While continuing to warn of 'a devoting of the earth to destruction,' this last book of the Prophets calls for optimism and rejoicing in line with Jehovah's words to his people: "All the nations will have to pronounce you happy, for you yourselves will become a land of delight."—4:6; 3:12.

---

16. To what blessed day does Malachi point forward, and what warm encouragement does he give?

17. Malachi's warnings are tempered with what call for optimism?

Bible Book Number 40

Matthew

Writer: Matthew

Place Written: **Palestine**

Writing Completed: **c. 41 C.E.**

Time Covered: **2 B.C.E.–33 C.E.**

FROM the time of the rebellion in Eden, Jehovah has held before mankind the comforting promise that he will provide deliverance for all lovers of righteousness through the Seed of his "woman." This Seed, or Messiah, he purposed to bring forth from the nation of Israel. As the centuries passed, he caused to be recorded scores of prophecies through the inspired Hebrew writers, showing that the Seed would be Ruler in the Kingdom of God and that he would act for the sanctification of Jehovah's name, clearing it forever of the reproach that has been heaped upon it. Many details were provided through these prophets concerning this one who would be Jehovah's vindicator and who would bring about deliverance from fear, oppression, sin, and death. With the completion of the Hebrew Scriptures, the hope in the Messiah was firmly established among the Jews.

² In the meantime the world scene had been changing. God had maneuvered the nations in

preparation for Messiah's appearance, and the circumstances were ideal for spreading the news of that event far and wide. The fifth world power, Greece, had provided a common language, a universal means of communication among the nations. Rome, the sixth world power, had welded its subject nations into one world empire and had provided roads to make all parts of the empire accessible. Many Jews had been scattered throughout this empire, so that others had learned of the Jews' expectation of a coming Messiah. And now, more than 4,000 years after the Edenic promise, the Messiah had appeared! The long-awaited promised Seed had come! The most important events thus far in the history of mankind unfolded as the Messiah faithfully carried out here on earth the will of his Father.

³ It was again time for inspired writings to be made to record these momentous happenings. The spirit of Jehovah inspired four faithful men to write independent accounts, thus providing a

---

1. (a) What promise has Jehovah held before mankind from Eden onward? (b) How did the hope in the Messiah become firmly established among the Jews?

2. At Messiah's appearance, how were circumstances ideal for spreading the good news?

3. (a) What provision did Jehovah make for recording the details of Jesus' life? (b) What is distinctive about each of the Gospels, and why are all four of them necessary?

fourfold witness that Jesus was the Messiah, the promised Seed and King, and giving the details of his life, his ministry, his death, and his resurrection. These accounts are called Gospels, the word "gospel" meaning "good news." While the four are parallel and often cover the same incidents, they are by no means mere copies of one another. The first three Gospels are often called synoptic, meaning "like view," since they take a similar approach in recounting Jesus' life on earth. But each one of the four writers—Matthew, Mark, Luke, and John—tells his own story of the Christ. Each one has his own particular theme and objective, reflects his own personality, and keeps in mind his immediate readers. The more we search their writings, the more we appreciate the distinctive features of each and that these four inspired Bible books form independent, complementary, and harmonious accounts of the life of Jesus Christ.

⁴ The first to put the good news about the Christ into writing was Matthew. His name is probably a shortened form of the Hebrew "Mattithiah," meaning "Gift of Jehovah." He was one of the 12 apostles chosen by Jesus. During the time the Master traveled throughout the land of Palestine preaching and teaching about God's Kingdom, Matthew had a close, intimate relationship with him. Before becoming a disciple of Jesus, Matthew was a tax collector, an occupation the Jews thoroughly loathed, since it was a constant reminder to them that they were not free but under the domination of imperial Rome. Matthew was otherwise known as Levi and was the son of Alphaeus. He readily responded to Jesus' invitation to follow him.—Matt. 9:9; Mark 2:14; Luke 5:27-32.

⁵ While the Gospel credited to Matthew does not name him as the writer, the overwhelming testimony of early church historians stamps him as such. Perhaps no ancient book has its writer more clearly and unanimously established than the book of Matthew. From as far back as Papias of Hierapolis (early second century C.E.) onward, we have a line of early witnesses to the fact that Matthew wrote this Gospel and that it is an authentic part of the Word of God. McClintock and Strong's *Cyclopedia* states: "Passages from Matthew are quoted by Justin Martyr, by the author of the letter to Diognetus (see in Otto's *Justin Martyr,* vol. ii), by Hegesippus, Irenæus, Tatian, Athenagoras, Theophilus, Clement, Tertullian, and Origen. It is not merely from the matter, but the manner of the quotations, from the calm

appeal as to a settled authority, from the absence of all hints of doubt, that we regard it as proved that the book we possess had not been the subject of any sudden change."* The fact that Matthew was an apostle and, as such, had God's spirit upon him assures that what he wrote would be a faithful record.

⁶ Matthew wrote his account in Palestine. The exact year is not known, but subscriptions at the end of some manuscripts (all later than the tenth century C.E.) say that it was 41 C.E. There is evidence to indicate that Matthew originally wrote his Gospel in the popular Hebrew of the time and later translated it into Greek. In his work *De viris inlustribus* (Concerning Illustrious Men), chapter III, Jerome says: "Matthew, who is also Levi, and who from a publican came to be an apostle, first of all composed a Gospel of Christ in Judaea in the Hebrew language and characters for the benefit of those of the circumcision who had believed."# Jerome adds that the Hebrew text of this Gospel was preserved in his day (fourth and fifth centuries C.E.) in the library that Pamphilus had collected in Caesarea.

⁷ Early in the third century, Origen, in discussing the Gospels, is quoted by Eusebius as saying that the "first was written . . . according to Matthew, . . . who published it for those who from Judaism came to believe, composed as it was in the Hebrew language."△ That it was written primarily with the Jews in mind is indicated by its genealogy, which shows Jesus' legal descent starting from Abraham, and by its many references to the Hebrew Scriptures, showing that they pointed forward to the coming Messiah. It is reasonable to believe that Matthew used the divine name Jehovah in the form of the Tetragrammaton when he quoted from parts of the Hebrew Scriptures that contained the name. That is why the book of Matthew in the *New World Translation* contains the name Jehovah 18 times, as does the Hebrew version of Matthew originally produced by F. Delitzsch in the 19th century. Matthew would have had the same attitude as Jesus toward the divine name and would not have been restrained by a prevailing Jewish superstition about not using that name.—Matt. 6:9; John 17:6, 26.

---

* 1981 Reprint, Vol. V, page 895.
# Translation from the Latin text edited by E. C. Richardson and published in the series "Texte und Untersuchungen zur Geschichte der altchristlichen Literatur," Leipzig, 1896, Vol. 14, pages 8, 9.
△ *The Ecclesiastical History,* VI, xxv, 3-6.

6, 7. (a) When and in what language was Matthew's Gospel first written? (b) What indicates it was written primarily for the Jews? (c) How many times does the *New World Translation* contain the name Jehovah in this Gospel, and why?

---

4. What is known of the writer of the first Gospel?
5. How is Matthew established as the writer of the first Gospel?

⁸ Since Matthew had been a tax collector, it was natural that he would be explicit in his mention of money, figures, and values. (Matt. 17:27; 26:15; 27:3) He keenly appreciated God's mercy in allowing him, a despised tax collector, to become a minister of the good news and an intimate associate of Jesus. Therefore, we find Matthew alone of the Gospel writers giving us Jesus' repeated insistence that mercy is required in addition to sacrifice. (9:9-13; 12:7; 18:21-35) Matthew was greatly encouraged by Jehovah's undeserved kindness and appropriately records some of the most comforting words Jesus uttered: "Come to me, all you who are toiling and loaded down, and I will refresh you. Take my yoke upon you and learn from me, for I am mild-tempered and lowly in heart, and you will find refreshment for your souls. For my yoke is kindly and my load is light." (11:28-30) How refreshing were these tender words for this former tax collector, toward whom, no doubt, his fellow countrymen had directed little but insults!

⁹ Matthew particularly stressed that the theme of Jesus' teaching was "the kingdom of the heavens." (4:17) To him, Jesus was the Preacher-King. He used the term "kingdom" so frequently (more than 50 times) that his Gospel might be called the Kingdom Gospel. Matthew was concerned more with a logical presentation of Jesus' public discourses and sermons than with a strict chronological sequence. For the first 18 chapters, Matthew's highlighting of the Kingdom theme led him to depart from a chronological arrangement. However, the last ten chapters (19 to 28) generally follow a chronological sequence as well as continue to stress the Kingdom.

¹⁰ Forty-two percent of Matthew's Gospel account is not to be found in any of the other three Gospels.* This includes at least ten parables, or illustrations: The weeds in the field (13:24-30), the hidden treasure (13:44), the pearl of high value (13:45, 46), the dragnet (13:47-50), the unmerciful slave (18:23-35), the workers and the denarius (20:1-16), the father and two children (21:28-32), the marriage of the king's son (22:1-14), the ten virgins (25:1-13), and the talents (25:14-30). In all, the book gives the account from the birth of Jesus, 2 B.C.E., until his meeting with his disciples just prior to his ascension, 33 C.E.

---

* *Introduction to the Study of the Gospels,* 1896, B. F. Westcott, page 201.

---

8. How is the fact that Matthew had been a tax collector reflected in the contents of his Gospel?
9. What theme and style of presentation characterize Matthew?
10. How much of the contents is to be found only in Matthew, and what period does the Gospel cover?

CONTENTS OF MATTHEW

¹¹ **Introducing Jesus and news of "the kingdom of the heavens"** (1:1–4:25). Logically, Matthew begins with Jesus' genealogy, proving Jesus' legal right as heir of Abraham and David. Thus, the attention of the Jewish reader is arrested. Then we read the account of Jesus' miraculous conception, his birth in Bethlehem, the visit of the astrologers, Herod's angry slaying of all the boys in Bethlehem under two years old, Joseph and Mary's flight into Egypt with the young child, and their subsequent return to dwell in Nazareth. Matthew is careful to draw attention to the fulfillments of prophecy to establish Jesus as the foretold Messiah.—Matt. 1:23—Isa. 7:14; Matt. 2:1-6 —Mic. 5:2; Matt. 2:13-18—Hos. 11:1 and Jer. 31:15; Matt. 2:23—Isa. 11:1, footnote.

¹² Matthew's account now skips down through nearly 30 years. John the Baptizer is preaching in the wilderness of Judea: "Repent, for the kingdom of the heavens has drawn near." (Matt. 3:2) He is baptizing the repentant Jews in the river Jordan and warning the Pharisees and Sadducees of wrath to come. Jesus comes from Galilee and is baptized. Immediately God's spirit descends on him, and a voice from the heavens says: "This is my Son, the beloved, whom I have approved." (3:17) Jesus is then led into the wilderness, where, after fasting 40 days, he is tempted by Satan the Devil. Three times he turns Satan back by quotations from God's Word, saying finally: "Go away, Satan! For it is written, 'It is Jehovah your God you must worship, and it is to him alone you must render sacred service.'"—4:10.

¹³ "Repent, you people, for the kingdom of the heavens has drawn near." These electrifying words are now proclaimed in Galilee by the anointed Jesus. He calls four fishermen from their nets to follow him and become "fishers of men," and he travels with them "throughout the whole of Galilee, teaching in their synagogues and preaching the good news of the kingdom and curing every sort of disease and every sort of infirmity among the people."—4:17, 19, 23.

¹⁴ **The Sermon on the Mount** (5:1–7:29). As crowds begin to follow him, Jesus goes up into the mountain, sits down, and begins teaching his

---

11. (a) How does the Gospel logically open, and what early events are related? (b) What are some of the prophetic fulfillments that Matthew draws to our attention?
12. What occurs at Jesus' baptism and immediately thereafter?
13. What electrifying campaign now gets under way in Galilee?
14. In his Sermon on the Mount, of what happinesses does Jesus speak, and what does he say about righteousness?

disciples. He opens this thrilling discourse with nine 'happinesses': Happy are those who are conscious of their spiritual need, those who mourn, the mild-tempered, those who hunger and thirst for righteousness, the merciful, the pure in heart, the peaceable, those persecuted for righteousness' sake, and those reproached and lyingly spoken against. "Rejoice and leap for joy, since your reward is great in the heavens." He calls his disciples "the salt of the earth" and "the light of the world" and explains the righteousness, so different from the formalism of the scribes and Pharisees, that is required for entering the Kingdom of the heavens. "You must accordingly be perfect, as your heavenly Father is perfect."—5:12-14, 48.

[15] Jesus warns against hypocritical gifts and prayers. He teaches his disciples to pray for the sanctification of the Father's name, for His Kingdom to come, and for their daily sustenance. Throughout the sermon Jesus holds the Kingdom to the fore. He cautions those who follow him not to worry about or work merely for material riches, for the Father knows their actual needs. "Keep on, then," he says, "seeking first the kingdom and his righteousness, and all these other things will be added to you."—6:33.

[16] The Master counsels on relations with others, saying: "All things, therefore, that you want men to do to you, you also must likewise do to them." The few that find the road to life will be those who are doing the will of his Father. The workers of lawlessness will be known by their fruits and will be rejected. Jesus likens the one who obeys his sayings to the "discreet man, who built his house upon the rock-mass." What effect does this discourse have on the crowds who are listening? They are "astounded at his way of teaching," for he teaches "as a person having authority, and not as their scribes."—7:12, 24-29.

[17] **Kingdom preaching expanded** (8:1–11:30). Jesus performs many miracles—healing lepers, paralytics, and the demon-possessed. He even demonstrates authority over the wind and waves by calming a storm, and he raises a girl from the dead. What compassion Jesus feels for the crowds as he sees how skinned and thrown about they are, "like sheep without a shepherd"! As he says to his disciples, "the harvest is great, but the workers are few. Therefore, beg the Master of the harvest to send out workers into his harvest."—9:36-38.

[18] Jesus selects and commissions the 12 apostles. He gives them definite instructions on how to do their work and emphasizes the central doctrine of their teaching: "As you go, preach, saying, 'The kingdom of the heavens has drawn near.'" He gives them wise and loving admonition: "You received free, give free." "Prove yourselves cautious as serpents and yet innocent as doves." They will be hated and persecuted, even by close relatives, but Jesus reminds them: "He that finds his soul will lose it, and he that loses his soul for my sake will find it." (10:7, 8, 16, 39) On their way they go, to teach and preach in their assigned cities! Jesus identifies John the Baptizer as the messenger sent forth before him, the promised "Elijah," but "this generation" accept neither John nor him, the Son of man. (11:14, 16) So woe to this generation and the cities that have not repented at seeing his powerful works! But those who become his disciples will find refreshment for their souls.

[19] **Pharisees refuted and denounced** (12:1-50). The Pharisees try to find fault with Jesus on the Sabbath issue, but he refutes their charges and launches into a scathing condemnation of their hypocrisy. He tells them: "Offspring of vipers, how can you speak good things, when you are wicked? For out of the abundance of the heart the mouth speaks." (12:34) No sign will be given them except that of Jonah the prophet: The Son of man will be three days and nights in the heart of the earth.

[20] **Seven Kingdom illustrations** (13:1-58). Why does Jesus speak in illustrations? To his disciples he explains: "To you it is granted to understand the sacred secrets of the kingdom of the heavens, but to those people it is not granted." He pronounces his disciples happy because they see and hear. What refreshing instruction he now provides for them! After he explains the illustration of the sower, Jesus gives the illustrations of the weeds in the field, the mustard grain, the leaven, the hidden treasure, the pearl of high value, and the dragnet—all portraying something in connection with "the kingdom of the heavens." However, the people stumble at him, and Jesus tells them: "A prophet is not unhonored except in his home territory and in his own house."—13:11, 57.

[21] **Further ministry and miracles of "the Christ"** (14:1–17:27). Jesus is deeply affected by

---

15. What does Jesus have to say about prayer and about the Kingdom?
16. (a) What is Jesus' counsel on relations with others, and what does he say concerning those who obey God's will and those who do not? (b) What effect does his sermon have?
17. How does Jesus show his authority as Messiah, and what loving concern does he express?

18. (a) What instruction and admonition does Jesus give his apostles? (b) Why is it woe to "this generation"?
19. When the Pharisees question his conduct on the Sabbath, how does Jesus denounce them?
20. (a) Why does Jesus speak in illustrations? (b) What Kingdom illustrations does he now give?
21. (a) What miracles does Jesus perform, and as what do they identify him? (b) What vision is given concerning the Son of man's coming in his Kingdom?

the report of the beheading of John the Baptizer at the order of spineless Herod Antipas. He miraculously feeds a crowd of 5,000 and more; walks on the sea; turns back further criticism from the Pharisees, who, he says, are 'overstepping the commandment of God because of their tradition'; heals the demon-possessed, the "lame, maimed, blind, dumb, and many otherwise"; and again feeds more than 4,000, from seven loaves and a few little fishes. (15:3, 30) Responding to a question by Jesus, Peter identifies him, saying: "You are the Christ, the Son of the living God." Jesus commends Peter and declares: "On this rock-mass I will build my congregation." (16:16, 18) Jesus now begins to speak of his approaching death and of his resurrection on the third day. But he also promises that some of his disciples "will not taste death at all until first they see the Son of man coming in his kingdom." (16:28) Six days later, Jesus takes Peter, James, and John up into a lofty mountain to see him transfigured in glory. In a vision, they behold Moses and Elijah conversing with him, and they hear a voice from heaven saying: "This is my Son, the beloved, whom I have approved; listen to him." After coming down from the mountain, Jesus tells them that the promised "Elijah" has already come, and they perceive that he is speaking about John the Baptizer.—17:5, 12.

²² **Jesus counsels his disciples** (18:1-35). While at Capernaum Jesus talks to the disciples about humility, the great joy of recovering a stray sheep, and settling offenses between brothers. Peter asks: 'How many times must I forgive my brother?' and Jesus answers: "I say to you, not, Up to seven times, but, Up to seventy-seven times." To add force to this, Jesus gives the illustration of the slave whose master forgave him a debt of 60 million denarii. This slave later had a fellow slave imprisoned because of a debt of only 100 denarii, and as a result, the merciless slave was likewise handed over to the jailers.* Jesus makes the point: "In like manner my heavenly Father will also deal with you if you do not forgive each one his brother from your hearts."—18:21, 22, 35.

²³ **Closing days of Jesus' ministry** (19:1-22: 46). The tempo of events quickens and tension mounts as the scribes and Pharisees become more incensed at Jesus' ministry. They come to trip him up on a matter of divorce but fail; Jesus shows

that the only Scriptural ground for divorce is fornication. A rich young man comes to Jesus, asking the way to everlasting life, but goes away grieved when he finds he must sell all he has and be a follower of Jesus. After giving the illustration of the workers and the denarius, Jesus speaks again of his death and resurrection, and he says: "The Son of man came, not to be ministered to, but to minister and to give his soul a ransom in exchange for many."—20:28.

²⁴ Jesus now enters the last week of his human life. He makes his triumphal entry into Jerusalem as 'King, mounted upon the colt of an ass.' (21:4, 5) He cleanses the temple of the money changers and other profiteers, and the hatred of his foes mounts as he tells them: "The tax collectors and the harlots are going ahead of you into the kingdom of God." (21:31) His pointed illustrations of the vineyard and of the marriage feast hit home. He skillfully answers the Pharisees' tax question by telling them to pay back "Caesar's things to Caesar, but God's things to God." (22:21) Likewise he turns back a catch question by the Sadducees and upholds the resurrection hope. Again the Pharisees come to him with a question on the Law, and Jesus tells them that the greatest commandment is to love Jehovah completely, and the second is to love one's neighbor as oneself. Jesus then asks them, 'How can the Christ be both David's son and his Lord?' Nobody can answer, and thereafter no one dares to question him.—22:45, 46.

²⁵ **'Woe to you, hypocrites'** (23:1-24:2). Speaking to the crowds at the temple, Jesus delivers another scathing denunciation of the scribes and Pharisees. Not only have they disqualified themselves from entering into the Kingdom but they exert all their wiles to prevent others from entering. Just like whitewashed graves, they appear beautiful on the outside, but inside they are full of corruption and decay. Jesus concludes with this judgment against Jerusalem: "Your house is abandoned to you." (23:38) As he leaves the temple, Jesus prophesies its destruction.

²⁶ **Jesus gives 'sign of his presence'** (24:3-25: 46). On the Mount of Olives, his disciples question him about 'the sign of his presence and the conclusion of the system of things.' In answer Jesus points forward to a time of wars, 'nation against nation and kingdom against kingdom,' food shortages, earthquakes, an increasing of lawlessness, the earth-wide preaching of "this good news of the

---

* In Jesus' day, a denarius equaled a day's wage; so 100 denarii equaled about one third of a year's wages. Sixty million denarii equaled wages that would require thousands of lifetimes to accumulate.—*Insight on the Scriptures,* Vol. 1, page 614.

22. What does Jesus counsel on forgiveness?
23. What does Jesus explain concerning divorce and concerning the way to life?

24. As Jesus enters the last week of his human life, what encounters does he have with religious opposers, and how does he deal with their questions?
25. How does Jesus forcefully denounce the scribes and Pharisees?
26. What prophetic sign does Jesus provide concerning his presence in kingly glory?

kingdom," the appointment of "the faithful and discreet slave . . . over all his belongings," and many other features of the composite sign that is to mark 'the arrival of the Son of man in his glory to sit down on his glorious throne.' (24:3, 7, 14, 45-47; 25:31) Jesus concludes this important prophecy with the illustrations of the ten virgins and of the talents, which hold forth joyful rewards to the alert and faithful, and the illustration of the sheep and the goats, which shows goatish people departing "into everlasting cutting-off, but the righteous ones into everlasting life."—25:46.

27 Events of Jesus' final day (26:1–27:66). After celebrating the Passover, Jesus institutes something new with his faithful apostles, inviting them to partake of unleavened bread and wine as symbols of his body and his blood. Then they go to Gethsemane, where Jesus prays. There Judas comes with an armed crowd and betrays Jesus with a hypocritical kiss. Jesus is taken to the high priest, and the chief priests and the entire Sanhedrin look for false witnesses against Jesus. True to Jesus' prophecy, Peter disowns him when put to the test. Judas, feeling remorse, throws his betrayal money into the temple and goes off and hangs himself. In the morning Jesus is led before the Roman governor Pilate, who hands him over to be impaled under pressure from the priest-incited mob who cry: "His blood come upon us and upon our children." The governor's soldiers make fun of his kingship and then lead him out to Golgotha, where he is staked between two robbers, with a sign over his head reading, "This is Jesus the King of the Jews." (27:25, 37) After hours of torture, Jesus finally dies at about three in the afternoon and is then laid in the new memorial tomb belonging to Joseph of Arimathea. It has been the most eventful day in all history!

28 Jesus' resurrection and final instructions (28:1-20). Matthew now climaxes his account with the very best of news. The dead Jesus is resurrected—he lives again! Early on the first day of the week, Mary Magdalene and "the other Mary" come to the tomb and hear the angel's announcement of this joyful fact. (28:1) To confirm it, Jesus himself appears to them. The enemies even try to fight the fact of his resurrection, bribing the soldiers who had been on guard at the tomb to say, "His disciples came in the night and stole him while we were sleeping." Later, in Galilee, Jesus has another meeting with his disciples. What is his departing instruction for them? This: "Go . . . make disciples of people of all the nations, baptizing them in the name of the Father and of

the Son and of the holy spirit." Would they have guidance in this preaching work? The last utterance of Jesus that Matthew records gives this assurance: "Look! I am with you all the days until the conclusion of the system of things."—28:13, 19, 20.

WHY BENEFICIAL

29 The book of Matthew, first of the four Gospels, truly provides an excellent bridge from the Hebrew Scriptures into the Christian Greek Scriptures. Unmistakably, it identifies the Messiah and King of God's promised Kingdom, makes known the requirements for becoming his followers, and sets out the work that lies ahead for these on earth. First John the Baptizer, then Jesus, and finally his disciples went preaching, "The kingdom of the heavens has drawn near." Moreover, Jesus' command reaches right down to the conclusion of the system of things: "And this good news of the kingdom will be preached in all the inhabited earth for a witness to all the nations; and then the end will come." Truly it was, and still is, a grand and wonderful privilege to share in this Kingdom work, including 'making disciples of people of all the nations,' working after the pattern of the Master.—3:2; 4:17; 10:7; 24:14; 28:19.

30 Matthew's Gospel is indeed "good news." Its inspired message was "good news" to those who heeded it in the first century of the Common Era, and Jehovah God has seen to it that it has been preserved as "good news" until this day. Even non-Christians have been compelled to acknowledge the power of this Gospel, as, for example, the Hindu leader Mohandas (Mahatma) Gandhi, who is reported to have said to Lord Irwin, a former viceroy of India: "When your country and mine shall get together on the teachings laid down by Christ in this Sermon on the Mount, we shall have solved the problems not only of our countries but those of the whole world."* On another occasion Gandhi said: "By all means drink deep of the fountains that are given to you in the Sermon on the Mount . . . For the teaching of the Sermon was meant for each and every one of us."#

31 However, the whole world, including that

---

* *Treasury of the Christian Faith,* 1949, edited by S. I. Stuber and T. C. Clark, page 43.
# *Mahatma Gandhi's Ideas,* 1930, by C. F. Andrews, page 96.

29. (a) How does Matthew bridge over from the Hebrew to the Greek Scriptures? (b) What privilege enjoyed by Jesus is still open to Christians today?
30. What particular portion of Matthew has gained recognition for its practical value?
31. Who have shown real appreciation for the counsel in Matthew, and why is it profitable to study this Gospel again and again?

---

27. What events mark Jesus' final day on earth?
28. With what best of news does Matthew climax his account, and with what commission does he conclude?

part claiming to be Christian, continues with its problems. It has been left to a small minority of true Christians to treasure, study, and apply the Sermon on the Mount and all the other sound counsel of the good news according to Matthew and thereby derive inestimable benefits. It is profitable to study again and again Jesus' fine admonitions on finding the real happiness, as well as on morals and marriage, the power of love, acceptable prayer, spiritual versus material values, seeking the Kingdom first, having respect for holy things, and being watchful and obedient. Matthew chapter 10 gives Jesus' service instructions to those who take up preaching the good news of "the kingdom of the heavens." The many parables of Jesus carry vital lessons for all who 'have ears to hear.' Moreover, Jesus' prophecies, such as his detailed foretelling of 'the sign of his presence,' build strong hope and confidence in the future. —5:1–7:29; 10:5-42; 13:1-58; 18:1–20:16; 21: 28–22:40; 24:3–25:46.

[32] Matthew's Gospel abounds with fulfilled prophecies. Many of his quotations from the inspired Hebrew Scriptures were for the purpose of showing these fulfillments. They provide indisputable evidence that Jesus is the Messiah, for it

would have been utterly impossible to prearrange all these details. Compare, for example, Matthew 13:14, 15 with Isaiah 6:9, 10; Matthew 21:42 with Psalm 118:22, 23; and Matthew 26:31, 56 with Zechariah 13:7. Such fulfillments give us strong assurance, too, that all the prophetic forecasts of Jesus himself, recorded by Matthew, would in due course come true while Jehovah's glorious purposes with regard to "the kingdom of the heavens" reach fruition.

[33] How exact God was in foretelling the life of the King of the Kingdom, even to minute details! How exact was the inspired Matthew in faithfully recording the fulfillment of these prophecies! As they reflect on all the prophetic fulfillments and promises recorded in the book of Matthew, lovers of righteousness can indeed exult in the knowledge and hope of "the kingdom of the heavens" as Jehovah's instrument for sanctifying his name. It is this Kingdom by Jesus Christ that brings untold blessings of life and happiness to the mild-tempered and spiritually hungry ones "in the re-creation, when the Son of man sits down upon his glorious throne." (Matt. 19:28) All of this is contained in the stimulating good news "according to Matthew."

---

32. (a) Illustrate how fulfilled prophecy proves Jesus' Messiahship. (b) What strong assurance do these fulfillments give us today?

---

33. In what knowledge and hope can lovers of righteousness now exult?

Bible Book Number **41** *Mark*	Writer: **Mark** Place Written: **Rome** Writing Completed: 　c. **60–65 C.E.** Time Covered: **29–33 C.E.**

WHEN Jesus was arrested at Gethsemane and the apostles fled, he was followed by "a certain young man wearing a fine linen garment over his naked body." When the crowd tried to seize him too, "he left his linen garment behind and got away naked." This young man is generally believed to be Mark. He is described in Acts as "John who was surnamed Mark" and may have come from a comfortably situated family in Jerusalem, for they had their own house and servants. His mother, Mary, was also a Christian, and the early congregation used her home as a meeting place. On the occasion when he was

delivered by the angel from prison, Peter went to this house and found the brothers assembled there.—Mark 14:51, 52; Acts 12:12, 13.

[2] The missionary Barnabas, a Levite from Cyprus, was the cousin of Mark. (Acts 4:36; Col. 4:10) When Barnabas came with Paul to Jerusalem in connection with famine relief, Mark also got to know Paul. These associations in the congregation and with zealous visiting ministers no doubt instilled in Mark the desire to enter missionary service. So we find him as companion and attendant to Paul and Barnabas on their first

---

1. What is known concerning Mark and his family?

2, 3. (a) What no doubt stirred Mark to enter missionary service? (b) What association did he have with other missionaries, particularly with Peter and Paul?

missionary journey. For some reason, however, Mark left them in Perga, Pamphylia, and returned to Jerusalem. (Acts 11:29, 30; 12:25; 13:5, 13) Because of this, Paul refused to take Mark along on the second missionary tour, and this resulted in a break between Paul and Barnabas. Paul took Silas, while Barnabas took his cousin Mark and sailed with him to Cyprus.—Acts 15:36-41.

3 Mark proved himself in the ministry and became a valuable help not only to Barnabas but later also to the apostles Peter and Paul. Mark was with Paul (c. 60-61 C.E.) during his first imprisonment in Rome. (Philem. 1, 24) Then we find Mark with Peter in Babylon between the years 62 and 64 C.E. (1 Pet. 5:13) Paul is again a prisoner in Rome probably in the year 65 C.E., and in a letter he asks Timothy to bring Mark with him, saying, "for he is useful to me for ministering." (2 Tim. 1:8; 4:11) This is the latest mention of Mark in the Bible record.

4 The composition of this shortest of the Gospels is credited to this Mark. He was a coworker with Jesus' apostles and one who placed his own life in the service of the good news. But Mark was not one of the 12 apostles, and he was not an immediate companion of Jesus. Where did he get the intimate details that make his account of Jesus' ministry really live from beginning to end? According to the earliest tradition of Papias, Origen, and Tertullian, this source was Peter, with whom Mark was closely associated.* Did not Peter call him "my son"? (1 Pet. 5:13) Peter was an eyewitness of practically all that Mark recorded, so he could have learned from Peter many descriptive points that are lacking in the other Gospels. For example, Mark speaks of "the hired men" that worked for Zebedee, the leper entreating Jesus "on bended knee," the demonized man "slashing himself with stones," and Jesus' giving his prophecy about the 'coming of the Son of man with great power and glory' while he was sitting on the Mount of Olives "with the temple in view."—Mark 1:20, 40; 5:5; 13:3, 26.

5 Peter himself was a man of deep emotions and so could appreciate and describe to Mark the feelings and emotions of Jesus. So it is that Mark frequently records how Jesus felt and reacted; for example, that he looked "around upon them with indignation, being thoroughly grieved," that he "sighed deeply," and that he "groaned deeply with

his spirit." (3:5; 7:34; 8:12) It is Mark who tells us of Jesus' sentiments toward the rich young ruler, saying that he "felt love for him." (10:21) And what warmth we find in the account that Jesus not only stood a young child in the midst of his disciples but also "put his arms around it," and that on another occasion "he took the children into his arms"!—9:36; 10:13-16.

6 Some of Peter's characteristics are to be seen in Mark's style, which is impulsive, living, vigorous, vital, and descriptive. It seems he can hardly relate events fast enough. For example, the word "immediately" occurs again and again, carrying the story along in dramatic style.

7 Although Mark had access to the Gospel of Matthew and his record contains only 7 percent that is not contained in the other Gospels, it would be a mistake to believe that Mark simply condensed Matthew's Gospel and added a few special details. Whereas Matthew had portrayed Jesus as the promised Messiah and King, Mark now considers his life and works from another angle. He portrays Jesus as the miracle-working Son of God, the conquering Savior. Mark puts stress on the activities of Christ rather than on his sermons and teachings. Only a small proportion of the parables and one of Jesus' longer discourses are reported, and the Sermon on the Mount is omitted. It is for this reason that Mark's Gospel is shorter, though it contains just as much action as the others. At least 19 miracles are specifically referred to.

8 While Matthew wrote his Gospel for the Jews, Mark evidently wrote primarily for the Romans. How do we know this? The Law of Moses is mentioned only when reporting conversation that referred to it, and the genealogy of Jesus is left out. The gospel of Christ is represented as of universal importance. He makes explanatory comments on Jewish customs and teachings with which non-Jewish readers might be unfamiliar. (2:18; 7:3, 4; 14:12; 15:42) Aramaic expressions are translated. (3:17; 5:41; 7:11, 34; 14:36; 15: 22, 34) He qualifies Palestinian geographic names and plant life with explanations. (1:5, 13; 11:13; 13:3) The value of Jewish coins is given in Roman money. (12:42, footnote) He uses more Latin words than the other Gospel writers, examples being *speculator* (body guardsman), *praetorium* (governor's palace), and *centurio* (army officer). —6:27; 15:16, 39.

9 Since Mark evidently wrote primarily for the

---

* *Insight on the Scriptures,* Vol. 2, page 337.

4-6. (a) How was Mark able to get the intimate details for his Gospel? (b) What indicates his close association with Peter? (c) Give examples of Peter's characteristics in the Gospel.

7. What distinguishes Mark's Gospel from that of Matthew?

8. What features indicate Mark's Gospel was evidently written for the Romans?

9. Where and when was the book of Mark written, and what confirms its authenticity?

Romans, he most likely did his writing in Rome. Both earliest tradition and the contents of the book allow for the conclusion that it was composed in Rome during either the first or the second imprisonment of the apostle Paul, and hence during the years 60-65 C.E. In those years Mark was in Rome at least once, and likely twice. All the leading authorities of the second and third centuries confirm that Mark was the writer. The Gospel was already in circulation among Christians by the middle of the second century. Its appearance in all the early catalogs of the Christian Greek Scriptures confirms the authenticity of Mark's Gospel.

[10] However, the long and short conclusions that are sometimes added after chapter 16, verse 8, are not to be regarded as authentic. They are missing in most of the ancient manuscripts, such as the Sinaitic and the Vatican No. 1209. The fourth-century scholars Eusebius and Jerome are in agreement that the authentic record closes with the words "they were in fear." The other conclusions were probably added with a view to smoothing over the abruptness with which the Gospel ends.

[11] That Mark's account is accurate is to be seen from the full harmony of his Gospel not only with the other Gospels but also with all the Holy Scriptures from Genesis to Revelation. Moreover, Jesus is shown again and again as one having authority not only in his spoken word but over the forces of nature, over Satan and the demons, over sickness and disease, yes, over death itself. So Mark opens his narrative with the impressive introduction: "The beginning of the good news about Jesus Christ." His coming and ministry meant "good news," and hence the study of Mark's Gospel must be beneficial to all readers. The events described by Mark cover the period from spring 29 C.E. to spring 33 C.E.

CONTENTS OF MARK

[12] **Baptism and temptation of Jesus** (1:1-13). Mark begins the good news by identifying John the Baptizer. He is the foretold messenger, sent to proclaim: "Prepare the way of Jehovah, you people, make his roads straight." Of the One soon to come, the baptizer says, 'He is stronger than I.' Yes, he will baptize, not with water, but with holy spirit. Jesus now comes from Nazareth of Galilee, and John baptizes him. The spirit descends on

Jesus like a dove, and a voice is heard out of the heavens: "You are my Son, the beloved; I have approved you." (1:3, 7, 11) Jesus is tempted by Satan in the wilderness, and angels minister to him. All these dramatic events are packed into Mark's first 13 verses.

[13] **Jesus begins ministry in Galilee** (1:14–6:6). After John is arrested, Jesus goes preaching the good news of God in Galilee. What a startling message he has! "The kingdom of God has drawn near. Be repentant, you people, and have faith in the good news." (1:15) He calls Simon and Andrew and James and John from their fishing nets to be his disciples. On the Sabbath he begins to teach in the synagogue at Capernaum. The people are astounded, for he teaches "as one having authority, and not as the scribes." He demonstrates his authority as "the Holy One of God" by driving an unclean spirit out of a possessed man and by healing Simon's mother-in-law, who was sick with a fever. The news spreads like wildfire, and by nighttime "the whole city" has gathered outside Simon's house. Jesus cures many that are sick and expels many demons.—1:22, 24, 33.

[14] Jesus declares his mission: "That I may preach." (1:38) Throughout the whole of Galilee he preaches. Wherever he goes, he expels demons and heals the sick, including a leper and a paralytic to whom he says: "Your sins are forgiven." Some of the scribes reason in their hearts, 'This is blasphemy. Who can forgive sins but God?' Discerning their thoughts, Jesus proves that "the Son of man has authority to forgive sins" by telling the paralytic to get up and go home. The people glorify God. When the tax collector Levi (Matthew) becomes his follower, Jesus tells the scribes: "I came to call, not righteous people, but sinners." He shows himself to be "Lord even of the sabbath." —2:5, 7, 10, 17, 28.

[15] Jesus now forms the group of 12 apostles. His relatives manifest some opposition, and then some scribes from Jerusalem accuse him of expelling demons by means of the ruler of the demons. Jesus asks them, "How can Satan expel Satan?" and warns them: "Whoever blasphemes against the holy spirit has no forgiveness forever, but is guilty of everlasting sin." During the discussion, his mother and brothers come seeking him, and Jesus is moved to declare: "Whoever does the will of God, this one is my brother and sister and mother."—3:23, 29, 35.

---

10. How are the long and short conclusions of Mark to be regarded, and why?
11. (a) What proves Mark's Gospel to be accurate, and what authority is emphasized? (b) Why is this "good news," and what period does Mark's Gospel cover?
12. What is packed into the first 13 verses of Mark?

13. In what ways does Jesus early demonstrate his authority as "the Holy One of God"?
14. How does Jesus give proof of his authority to forgive sins?
15. What does Jesus declare about those who deny his miracles, and what does he say about family ties?

[16] Jesus starts teaching "the sacred secret of the kingdom of God" by illustrations. He speaks of the man who sows seed that falls on various kinds of soil (illustrating the different kinds of hearers of the word) and of the lamp shining from its lampstand. In another illustration, Jesus says that the Kingdom of God is as when a man casts the seed upon the ground: "Of its own self the ground bears fruit gradually, first the grass-blade, then the stalk head, finally the full grain in the head." (4:11, 28) He also gives the illustration of a mustard grain, which, though the tiniest of all seeds, grows large with great branches for shelter.

[17] As they cross the Sea of Galilee, Jesus miraculously causes a violent wind to abate, and the stormy sea becomes calm at his command: "Hush! Be quiet!" (4:39) Over in the country of the Gerasenes, Jesus expels a "Legion" of demons from one man and permits them to enter into a herd of about 2,000 swine, which, in turn, rush over a precipice and are drowned in the sea. (5:8-13) After this, Jesus crosses back to the opposite shore. A woman is healed of a flow of blood, incurable for 12 years, merely by touching Jesus' outer garment, as he is on the way to raise the 12-year-old daughter of Jairus to life again. Truly, the Son of man has authority over both life and death! However, the people in Jesus' home territory dispute his authority. He wonders at their lack of faith but continues "round about to the villages in a circuit, teaching."—6:6.

[18] **Galilean ministry expanded** (6:7–9:50). The 12 are sent out 2 by 2 with instructions and authority to preach and teach, to cure people, and to expel demons. The name of Jesus is becoming well-known, some thinking it is John the Baptizer raised from the dead. This possibility worries Herod, during whose birthday party John had been beheaded. The apostles return from their preaching tour and make a report of their activity to Jesus. A great crowd of people follow Jesus around Galilee, and he is 'moved with pity for them, because they are as sheep without a shepherd.' So he starts to teach them many things. (6:34) He lovingly provides material food too, feeding 5,000 men with five loaves of bread and two fishes. Shortly after, when the disciples in their boat are hard put battling against a windstorm as they make for Bethsaida, he comes walking to them on the sea and calms the wind. No wonder that even his disciples are "much amazed"!—6:51.

[19] In the district of Gennesaret, Jesus gets into a discussion with the scribes and Pharisees from Jerusalem about eating with unwashed hands, and he rebukes them for 'letting go the commandment of God and holding fast the tradition of men.' He says it is not what enters from outside that defiles a man, but it is what issues from inside, out of the heart, namely, "injurious reasonings." (7:8, 21) Going north into the regions of Tyre and Sidon, he performs a miracle for a Gentile, expelling a demon from the daughter of a Syrophoenician woman.

[20] Back in Galilee, Jesus again feels pity for the crowd following him and feeds 4,000 men with seven loaves and a few little fishes. He warns his disciples of the leaven of the Pharisees and the leaven of Herod, but at the time they fail to get the point. Then, another miracle—the healing of a blind man at Bethsaida. In a discussion on the way to the villages in Caesarea Philippi, Peter convincingly identifies Jesus as "the Christ" but then objects strongly when Jesus speaks of the approaching sufferings and death of the Son of man. For this, Jesus reproves him: "Get behind me, Satan, because you think, not God's thoughts, but those of men." (8:29, 33) Jesus exhorts his disciples to follow him continually for the sake of the good news; if they become ashamed of him, he will be ashamed of them when he arrives in the glory of his Father.

[21] Six days later, when up on a lofty mountain, Peter, James, and John are privileged to see "the kingdom of God already come in power" as they behold Jesus transfigured in glory. (9:1) Jesus again demonstrates his authority by expelling a speechless spirit from a boy, and a second time he speaks of his coming suffering and death. He counsels his disciples not to allow anything to hinder them from entering into life. Does your hand make you stumble? Cut it off! Your foot? Cut it off! Your eye? Throw it away! It is far better to enter into the Kingdom of God maimed than to be pitched whole into Gehenna.

[22] **Ministry in Perea** (10:1-52). Jesus comes to the frontiers of Judea and "across the Jordan" (into Perea). Pharisees now question him about divorce, and he uses the opportunity to state godly principles for marriage. A rich young man questions him about inheriting everlasting life but is grieved at hearing that to have treasure in heav-

---

16. By illustrations, what does Jesus teach about "the kingdom of God"?
17. How do Jesus' miracles demonstrate the extent of his authority?
18. (a) How is Jesus' ministry expanded? (b) What moves Jesus to teach and to perform miracles?

19, 20. (a) How does Jesus give reproof to the scribes and Pharisees? (b) What circumstances lead to Peter's also being reproved?
21. (a) Who see "the kingdom of God already come in power," and how? (b) How does Jesus emphasize putting the Kingdom first?
22. What counsel highlights Jesus' ministry in Perea?

en, he must sell his possessions and become Jesus' follower. Jesus tells his disciples: "It is easier for a camel to go through a needle's eye than for a rich man to enter into the kingdom of God." He encourages those who have forsaken all on account of the good news, promising them "a hundredfold now . . . with persecutions, and in the coming system of things everlasting life."—10:1, 25, 30.

²³ Jesus and the 12 now set out on the way to Jerusalem. Jesus tells them a third time about the suffering before him and also of his resurrection. He asks them if they are able to drink the same cup that he is drinking, and he tells them: "Whoever wants to be first among you must be the slave of all." On their way out of Jericho, a blind beggar calls from the roadside: "Son of David, Jesus, have mercy on me!" Jesus makes the blind man see —his last miraculous healing as recorded by Mark.—10:44, 47, 48.

²⁴ **Jesus in and around Jerusalem** (11:1–15:47). The account moves quickly! Jesus rides upon a colt into the city, and the people acclaim him as King. The next day he cleanses the temple. The chief priests and the scribes become fearful of him and seek his death. "By what authority do you do these things?" they ask. (11:28) Jesus skillfully turns the question back on them and tells the illustration of the cultivators who killed the heir of the vineyard. They see the point and leave him.

²⁵ Next they send some of the Pharisees to catch him on the tax question. Calling for a denarius, he asks: "Whose image and inscription is this?" They reply: "Caesar's." Jesus then says: "Pay back Caesar's things to Caesar, but God's things to God." No wonder they marvel at him! (12:16, 17) Now the Sadducees, who do not believe in the resurrection, try to catch him with the question: 'If a woman had seven husbands in succession, whose wife will she be in the resurrection?' Jesus promptly replies that those who rise from the dead will be "as angels in the heavens," for they will not marry. (12:19-23, 25) "Which commandment is first of all?" asks one of the scribes. Jesus answers: "The first is, 'Hear, O Israel, Jehovah our God is one Jehovah, and you must love Jehovah your God with your whole heart and with your whole soul and with your whole mind and with your whole strength.' The second is this, 'You must love your neighbor as yourself.'" (12:28-31) After this, nobody dares to question him. Jesus' authority as the perfect teacher is upheld. The great crowd listen

with pleasure, and Jesus warns them against the pompous scribes. Then he commends to his disciples the poor widow who put more into the temple treasury chest than all the others, for her two small coins were "all of what she had, her whole living."—12:44.

²⁶ Seated on the Mount of Olives with the temple in view, Jesus tells four of his disciples privately of "the sign" of the conclusion of these things. (This is the only long discourse recorded by Mark, and it parallels that of Matthew chapters 24 and 25.) It closes with Jesus' admonition: "Concerning that day or the hour nobody knows, neither the angels in heaven nor the Son, but the Father. But what I say to you I say to all, Keep on the watch."—13:4, 32, 37.

²⁷ At nearby Bethany a woman anoints Jesus with costly perfumed oil. Some protest this as a waste, but Jesus says it is a fine deed, a preparation for his burial. At the appointed time, Jesus and the 12 assemble in the city for the Passover. He identifies his betrayer and institutes the memorial supper with his faithful disciples, and they depart for the Mount of Olives. On the way Jesus tells them that they will all be stumbled. "I will not be," exclaims Peter. But Jesus says to him: "This night, before a cock crows twice, even you will disown me three times." On reaching the spot named Gethsemane, Jesus withdraws to pray, asking his disciples to keep on the watch. His prayer is climaxed with the words: "*Abba*, Father, all things are possible to you; remove this cup from me. Yet not what I want, but what you want." Three times Jesus returns to his disciples, and three times he finds them sleeping, even "at such a time as this"! (14:29, 30, 36, 41) But the hour has come! Look!—the betrayer!

²⁸ Judas draws close and kisses Jesus. This is the sign for the chief priests' armed men to arrest him. They bring him to the court of the high priest, where many bear false witness against him, but their testimonies are not in agreement. Jesus himself keeps silent. Finally, the high priest questions him: "Are you the Christ the Son of the Blessed One?" Jesus replies, "I am." The high priest cries, 'Blasphemy!' and they all condemn him to be liable to death. (14:61-64) In the courtyard below, Peter has denied Jesus three times. A cock crows a second time, and Peter, recalling Jesus' words, breaks down and weeps.

---

23. What conversation and miracle ensue on the way to Jerusalem?
24, 25. (a) By what actions does Jesus testify to his authority? (b) With what arguments does he answer his opponents? (c) What warning does Jesus give the crowd, and what does he commend to his disciples?

26. What is the only long discourse recorded by Mark, and with what admonition does it end?
27. Describe the events leading up to Jesus' betrayal in Gethsemane.
28. What are the circumstances of Jesus' arrest and appearance before the high priest?

²⁹ Immediately at dawn the Sanhedrin consults and sends Jesus bound to Pilate. He quickly recognizes that Jesus is no criminal and tries to release him. However, at the insistence of the mob incited by the chief priests, he finally hands Jesus over to be impaled. Jesus is brought to Golgotha (meaning, "Skull Place") and is impaled, with the charge against him written above: "The King of the Jews." Passersby reproach him: "Others he saved; himself he cannot save!" At noon (the sixth hour) a darkness falls over the whole land until three o'clock. Then Jesus cries out with a loud voice, "My God, my God, why have you forsaken me?" and expires. At seeing these things, an army officer remarks: "Certainly this man was God's Son." Joseph of Arimathea, one of the Sanhedrin but a believer in the Kingdom of God, asks Pilate for Jesus' body and lays it in a tomb quarried out of rock.—15:22, 26, 31, 34, 39.

³⁰ **Events after Jesus' death** (16:1-8). Very early on the first day of the week, three women go out to the tomb. To their surprise they find that the large stone at the entrance has been rolled away. "A young man" who is sitting inside tells them that Jesus is raised up. (16:5) He is no longer there but is going ahead of them into Galilee. They flee from the tomb, trembling and in fear.

WHY BENEFICIAL

³¹ Through this vivid pen picture of Jesus Christ, all readers of Mark, from early Christian times until now, have been able to identify the fulfillment of many prophecies of the Hebrew Scriptures concerning the Messiah. From the opening quotation, "Look! I am sending forth my messenger before your face," to Jesus' agonized words on the stake, "My God, my God, why have you forsaken me?" the entire account of his zealous ministry, as recorded by Mark, is in accord with what the Hebrew Scriptures foretold. (Mark 1:2; 15:34; Mal. 3:1; Ps. 22:1) Moreover, his miracles and marvelous works, his healthful teaching, his flawless refutations, his utter dependence on Jehovah's Word and spirit, and his tender shepherding of the sheep—all these things mark him as the One who came with authority as the Son of God. He taught "as one having authority," authority received from Jehovah, and he emphasized

"preaching the good news of God," namely, that "the kingdom of God has drawn near," as his primary work here on earth. His teaching has proved to be of inestimable benefit to all who have paid heed to it.—Mark 1:22, 14, 15.

³² Jesus said to his disciples: "To you the sacred secret of the kingdom of God has been given." Mark uses this expression "kingdom of God" 14 times and sets out many guiding principles for those who would gain life through the Kingdom. Jesus stated: "Whoever loses his soul for the sake of me and the good news will save it." Every hindrance to gaining life must be removed: "It is finer for you to enter one-eyed into the kingdom of God than with two eyes to be pitched into Gehenna." Jesus further declared: "Whoever does not receive the kingdom of God like a young child will by no means enter into it," and, "How difficult a thing it will be for those with money to enter into the kingdom of God!" He said that the one who discerns that keeping the two great commandments is worth far more than all the whole burnt offerings and sacrifices is "not far from the kingdom of God." These and other Kingdom teachings of Mark's Gospel contain much good admonition that we can apply in our daily lives.—4:11; 8:35; 9:43-48; 10:13-15, 23-25; 12:28-34.

³³ The good news "according to Mark" can perhaps be read through entirely in one or two hours, giving the reader a thrilling, quick, and dynamic review of Jesus' ministry. Such straight reading of this inspired account, as well as closer study and meditation on it, will always prove beneficial. Mark's Gospel is of benefit to persecuted Christians today in the same way as in the first century, for true Christians now face "critical times hard to deal with" and have need for such inspired guidance as is found in this record concerning our Exemplar, Jesus Christ. Read it, thrill to its dramatic action, and draw encouragement to follow in the steps of the Chief Agent and Perfecter of our faith, Jesus, with the same invincible joy that he showed. (2 Tim. 3:1; Heb. 12:2) Yes, see him as a man of action, be imbued with his zeal, and copy his uncompromising integrity and courage amid trial and opposition. Gain comfort from this rich portion of the inspired Scriptures. Let it benefit you in your pursuit of everlasting life!

---

29. What record does Mark make of Jesus' final trial and execution, and how is the Kingdom shown to be at issue?
30. On the first day of the week, what happens at the tomb?
31. (a) How does Mark testify to Jesus' being the Messiah? (b) What proves Jesus' authority as the Son of God, and what did he emphasize?

32. How many times does Mark use the expression "kingdom of God," and what are some of the guiding principles he sets out for gaining life through the Kingdom?
33. (a) How may we gain benefit from Mark's Gospel? (b) To what course should Mark encourage us, and why?

42

Luke

Writer: **Luke**
Place Written: **Caesarea**
Writing Completed:
c. 56–58 C.E.
Time Covered: **3 B.C.E.–33 C.E.**

THE Gospel of Luke was written by a man with a keen mind and a kind heart, and this fine blend of qualities, with the guidance of God's spirit, has resulted in an account that is both accurate and full of warmth and feeling. In the opening verses, he says, "I resolved also, because I have traced all things from the start with accuracy, to write them in logical order to you." His detailed, meticulous presentation fully bears out this claim.—Luke 1:3.

² Although Luke is nowhere named in the account, ancient authorities are agreed that he was the writer. The Gospel is attributed to Luke in the Muratorian Fragment (c. 170 C.E.) and was accepted by such second-century writers as Irenaeus and Clement of Alexandria. Internal evidence also points strongly to Luke. Paul speaks of him at Colossians 4:14 as "Luke the beloved physician," and his work is of the scholarly order one would expect from a well-educated man, such as a doctor. His fine choice of language and his extensive vocabulary, larger than that of the other three Gospel writers combined, make possible a most careful and comprehensive treatment of his vital subject. His account of the prodigal son is regarded by some as the best short story ever written.

³ Luke uses more than 300 medical terms or words to which he gives a medical meaning that are not used in the same way (if they are used at all) by the other writers of the Christian Greek Scriptures.* For example, when speaking of leprosy, Luke does not always use the same term as the others. To them leprosy is leprosy, but to the physician, there are different stages of leprosy, as when Luke speaks of "a man full of leprosy." Lazarus, he says, was "full of ulcers." No other Gospel writer says that Peter's mother-in-law had "a *high* fever." (5:12; 16:20; 4:38) Although the other three tell us of Peter's cutting off the ear of the slave of the high priest, only Luke mentions

that Jesus healed him. (22:51) It is like a doctor to say of a woman that she had "a spirit of weakness for eighteen years, and she was bent double and was unable to raise herself up at all." And who but "Luke the beloved physician" would have recorded in such detail the first aid rendered to a man by the Samaritan who "bound up his wounds, pouring oil and wine upon them"?—13:11; 10:34.

⁴ When did Luke write his Gospel? Acts 1:1 indicates that the writer of Acts (who was also Luke) had earlier composed "the first account," the Gospel. Acts was most probably completed about 61 C.E. while Luke was in Rome with Paul, who was awaiting his appeal to Caesar. So the Gospel account was probably written by Luke in Caesarea about 56-58 C.E., after he returned with Paul from Philippi at the end of Paul's third missionary journey and while Paul was waiting two years in prison at Caesarea before being taken to Rome for his appeal. Since Luke was there in Palestine, during this time he was well situated to 'trace all things from the start with accuracy' concerning the life and ministry of Jesus. Thus, Luke's account appears to have preceded Mark's Gospel.

⁵ Luke was not, of course, an eyewitness of all the events he records in his Gospel, not being one of the 12 and probably not even a believer until after Jesus' death. However, he was very closely associated with Paul in the missionary field. (2 Tim. 4:11; Philem. 24) So, as might be expected, his writing shows evidence of Paul's influence, as can be seen by comparing their two accounts of the Lord's Evening Meal, at Luke 22:19, 20 and 1 Corinthians 11:23-25. As a further source of material, Luke could have referred to Matthew's Gospel. In 'tracing all things with accuracy,' he would be able personally to interview many eyewitnesses of the events of Jesus' life, such as the surviving disciples and possibly Jesus' mother, Mary. We can be sure that he left no stone unturned in assembling the reliable details.

---

* The Medical Language of Luke, 1954, W. K. Hobart, pages xi-xxviii.

---

1. What kind of Gospel did Luke write?
2, 3. What external and internal evidence points to the physician Luke as writer of this Gospel?

4. When, probably, was Luke written, and what circumstances support this view?
5. From what sources may Luke have 'traced with accuracy' the events of Jesus' life?

⁶ It becomes clear on examining the four Gospel accounts that the writers do not simply repeat one another's narratives, nor do they write solely to provide several witnesses for this most vital Bible record. Luke's account is most individualistic in its treatment. In all, 59 percent of his Gospel is unique with him. He records at least six specific miracles and more than twice that number of illustrations that are not mentioned in the other Gospel accounts, devoting one third of his Gospel to narrative and two thirds to the spoken word; his Gospel is the longest of the four. Matthew wrote primarily for the Jews, and Mark for non-Jewish readers, especially the Romans. Luke's Gospel was addressed to the "most excellent Theophilus" and through him to other persons, both Jews and non-Jews. (Luke 1:3, 4) In giving his account a universal appeal, he traces the genealogy of Jesus back to "Adam, son of God," and not just to Abraham, as does Matthew in writing specially for the Jews. He particularly notes the prophetic words of Simeon that Jesus would be the means of "removing the veil from the nations," and tells that "all flesh will see the saving means of God."—3:38; 2:29-32; 3:6.

⁷ Throughout his writing, Luke proves to be an outstanding narrator, his accounts being well arranged and accurate. These qualities of accuracy and fidelity in Luke's writings are strong proof of their authenticity. A legal writer once observed: "While romances, legends and false testimony are careful to place events related in some distant place and some indefinite time, thereby violating the first rules we lawyers learn of good pleading, that 'the declaration must give time and place,' the Bible narratives give us the date and place of the things related with the utmost precision."* In proof he cited Luke 3:1, 2: "In the fifteenth year of the reign of Tiberius Caesar, when Pontius Pilate was governor of Judea, and Herod was district ruler of Galilee, but Philip his brother was district ruler of the country of Ituraea and Trachonitis, and Lysanias was district ruler of Abilene, in the days of chief priest Annas and of Caiaphas, God's declaration came to John the son of Zechariah in the wilderness." There is no indefiniteness here as to time or place, but Luke names no less than seven public officials so that we can establish the time of the beginning of John's ministry and that of Jesus.

⁸ Luke also gives us two pointers for fixing the time of Jesus' birth when he says, at Luke 2:1, 2: "Now in those days a decree went forth from Caesar Augustus for all the inhabited earth to be registered; (this first registration took place when Quirinius was governor of Syria)." This was when Joseph and Mary went up to Bethlehem to be registered, and Jesus was born while they were there.* We cannot but agree with the commentator who says: "It is one of the most searching tests of Luke's historical sense that he always manages to achieve perfect accuracy."# We must acknowledge as valid Luke's claim to have "traced all things from the start with accuracy."

⁹ Luke also points out how the prophecies of the Hebrew Scriptures were accurately fulfilled in Jesus Christ. He quotes Jesus' inspired testimony on this. (24:27, 44) Further, he accurately records Jesus' own prophecies concerning future events, and many of these have already had remarkable fulfillments in all their foretold detail. For example, Jerusalem was surrounded by siegeworks of pointed stakes and perished in a frightful holocaust in 70 C.E., just as Jesus foretold. (Luke 19: 43, 44; 21:20-24; Matt. 24:2) The secular historian Flavius Josephus, who was an eyewitness with the Roman army, testifies that the countryside was denuded of trees to a distance of about ten miles to provide stakes, that the siege wall was four and a half miles long, that many women and children died from famine, and that more than 1,000,000 Jews lost their lives and 97,000 were taken captive. To this day, the Arch of Titus in Rome portrays the Roman victory procession with spoils of war from Jerusalem's temple.△ We can be sure that other inspired prophecies recorded by Luke will be just as accurately fulfilled.

CONTENTS OF LUKE

¹⁰ **Luke's introduction** (1:1-4). Luke records that he has traced all things from the start with accuracy and that he has resolved to write them in logical order so that the "most excellent Theophilus . . . may know fully the certainty" of these things.—1:3, 4.

¹¹ **The early years of Jesus' life** (1:5–2:52). An

---

* *A Lawyer Examines the Bible*, 1943, I. H. Linton, page 38.

---

* *Insight on the Scriptures*, Vol. 2, pages 766-7.
# *Modern Discovery and the Bible*, 1955, A. Rendle Short, page 211.
△ *The Jewish War*, V, 491-515, 523 (xii, 1-4); VI, 420 (ix, 3); see also *Insight on the Scriptures*, Vol. 2, pages 751-2.

---

6. How much of Luke's Gospel is unique with him, and for whom did he write? Why do you so answer?
7. What testifies strongly to the authenticity of Luke's Gospel?

8. How does Luke indicate the time of Jesus' birth "with accuracy"?
9. What prophecy of Jesus, recorded by Luke, had a remarkable fulfillment in 70 C.E.?
10. What did Luke set out to do?
11. What joyful events are related in the first chapter of Luke?

angel appears to the aged priest Zechariah with the joyful news that he will have a son whom he is to call John. But until the boy is born, Zechariah will not be able to speak. As promised, his wife, Elizabeth, becomes pregnant, though also "well along in years." About six months later, the angel Gabriel appears to Mary and tells her that she will conceive by "power of the Most High" and bear a son who is to be called Jesus. Mary visits Elizabeth and, after a happy greeting, declares exultantly: "My soul magnifies Jehovah, and my spirit cannot keep from being overjoyed at God my Savior." She speaks of Jehovah's holy name and of his great mercy toward those who fear him. At John's birth, Zechariah's tongue is loosed to declare also God's mercy and that John will be a prophet who will make Jehovah's way ready.—1:7, 35, 46, 47.

[12] In due course, Jesus is born at Bethlehem, and an angel announces this "good news of a great joy" to shepherds watching their flocks at night. Circumcision is carried out according to the Law, and then, when Jesus' parents "present him to Jehovah" at the temple, the aged Simeon and the prophetess Anna speak concerning the child. Back in Nazareth, he 'continues growing and getting strong, being filled with wisdom, and God's favor continues with him.' (2:10, 22, 40) At the age of 12, on a visit from Nazareth to Jerusalem, Jesus amazes the teachers with his understanding and his answers.

[13] **Preparation for the ministry** (3:1–4:13). In the 15th year of the reign of Tiberius Caesar, God's declaration comes to John the son of Zechariah, and he goes "preaching baptism in symbol of repentance for forgiveness of sins," that all flesh may "see the saving means of God." (3:3, 6) When all the people are baptized at the Jordan, Jesus is also baptized, and as he prays, the holy spirit descends on him, and his Father expresses approval from heaven. Jesus Christ is now about 30 years of age. (Luke supplies his genealogy.) Following his baptism, the spirit leads Jesus about in the wilderness for 40 days. Here the Devil tempts him without success and then retires "until another convenient time."—4:13.

[14] **Jesus' early ministry, largely in Galilee** (4:14–9:62). In the synagogue of his hometown of Nazareth, Jesus makes clear his commission, reading and applying to himself the prophecy of Isaiah 61:1, 2: "Jehovah's spirit is upon me, because he anointed me to declare good news to the poor, he

sent me forth to preach a release to the captives and a recovery of sight to the blind, to send the crushed ones away with a release, to preach Jehovah's acceptable year." (4:18, 19) The people's initial pleasure at his words turns to anger as he continues his discourse, and they attempt to do away with him. So he moves down to Capernaum, where he heals many people. Crowds follow him and try to detain him, but he tells them: "Also to other cities I must declare the good news of the kingdom of God, because for this I was sent forth." (4:43) He goes on to preach in the synagogues of Judea.

[15] In Galilee, Jesus provides Simon (also called Peter), James, and John with a miraculous catch of fish. He tells Simon: "From now on you will be catching men alive." So they abandon everything and follow him. Jesus continues in prayer and in teaching, and 'Jehovah's power is there for him to do healing.' (5:10, 17) He calls Levi (Matthew), a despised tax collector, who honors Jesus with a big feast, attended also by "a great crowd of tax collectors." (5:29) This results in the first of a number of encounters with the Pharisees that leave them maddened and conspiring to do him harm.

[16] After a whole night of prayer to God, Jesus chooses 12 apostles from among his disciples. Further works of healing follow. Then he gives the sermon recorded at Luke 6:20-49, paralleling in shorter form the Sermon on the Mount at Matthew chapters 5 to 7. Jesus draws the contrast: "Happy are you poor, because yours is the kingdom of God. But woe to you rich persons, because you are having your consolation in full." (6:20, 24) He admonishes his hearers to love their enemies, to be merciful, to practice giving, and to bring forth good out of the good treasure of the heart.

[17] Returning to Capernaum, Jesus receives a request from an army officer to cure an ailing slave. He feels unworthy to have Jesus under his roof and asks Jesus to "say the word" from where he is. Accordingly, the slave is healed, and Jesus is moved to comment: "I tell you, Not even in Israel have I found so great a faith." (7:7, 9) For the first time, Jesus raises a dead person, the only son of a widow of Nain, for whom he "was moved with pity." (7:13) As the news concerning Jesus spreads through Judea, John the Baptizer sends to

---

12. What is stated concerning Jesus' birth and childhood?
13. What does John preach, and what occurs at Jesus' baptism and immediately thereafter?
14. Where does Jesus make clear his commission, what is it, and how do his hearers respond?

15. Describe the calling of Peter, James, and John, as well as that of Matthew.
16. (a) Following what does Jesus choose the 12 apostles? (b) What points are highlighted by Luke in giving a parallel version of the Sermon on the Mount?
17. (a) What miracles does Jesus next perform? (b) How does Jesus answer the messengers of John the Baptizer concerning whether Jesus is the Messiah?

him from prison to ask, "Are you the Coming One?" In answer Jesus tells the messengers: "Go your way, report to John what you saw and heard: the blind are receiving sight, the lame are walking, the lepers are being cleansed and the deaf are hearing, the dead are being raised up, the poor are being told the good news. And happy is he who has not stumbled over me."—7:19, 22, 23.

¹⁸ Accompanied by the 12, Jesus goes "from city to city and from village to village, preaching and declaring the good news of the kingdom of God." He gives the illustration of the sower, and he rounds out the discussion by saying: "Therefore, pay attention to how you listen; for whoever has, more will be given him, but whoever does not have, even what he imagines he has will be taken away from him." (8:1, 18) Jesus continues to perform wonderful works and miracles. He also gives the 12 authority over the demons and the power to cure sicknesses and sends them forth "to preach the kingdom of God and to heal." Five thousand are miraculously fed. Jesus is transfigured on the mountain and the following day heals a demon-possessed boy whom the disciples could not cure. He cautions those who want to follow him: "Foxes have dens and birds of heaven have roosts, but the Son of man has nowhere to lay down his head." To be fit for the Kingdom of God, a person must set his hand to the plow and not look back.—9:2, 58.

¹⁹ **Jesus' later Judean ministry** (10:1–13:21). Jesus sends out 70 others into "the harvest," and they are filled with joy at the success of their ministry. As he is preaching, a man, wanting to prove himself righteous, asks Jesus: "Who really is my neighbor?" In answer, Jesus gives the illustration of the neighborly Samaritan. A man, lying on the roadside half-dead from a beating by robbers, is ignored by a passing priest and by a Levite. It is a despised Samaritan who stops, tenderly cares for his wounds, lifts him up on his own beast, brings him to an inn, and pays for him to be taken care of. Yes, it is "the one that acted mercifully toward him" who made himself neighbor.—10:2, 29, 37.

²⁰ In Martha's house, Jesus mildly rebukes her for becoming overly anxious about her household chores, and he commends Mary for choosing the better part, sitting down and listening to his word. To his disciples he teaches the model prayer and also the need for persistence in prayer, saying: "Keep on asking, and it will be given you; keep on seeking, and you will find." Later he expels demons and declares happy "those hearing the word

of God and keeping it." While at a meal, he clashes with the Pharisees over the Law and pronounces woes upon them for taking away "the key of knowledge."—11:9, 28, 52.

²¹ As he is again with the crowds, a certain one urges Jesus: "Tell my brother to divide the inheritance with me." Jesus goes to the heart of the problem in replying: "Keep your eyes open and guard against every sort of covetousness, because even when a person has an abundance his life does not result from the things he possesses." Then he gives the illustration of the wealthy man who tore down his storehouses to build bigger ones, only to die that very night and leave his wealth to others. Jesus concisely makes the point: "So it goes with the man that lays up treasure for himself but is not rich toward God." After urging his disciples to seek first God's Kingdom, Jesus tells them: "Have no fear, little flock, because your Father has approved of giving you the kingdom." His healing on the Sabbath of a woman who has been sick for 18 years leads to a further clash with his opposers, who are put to shame.—12:13, 15, 21, 32.

²² **Jesus' later ministry, largely in Perea** (13:22–19:27). Jesus uses colorful word illustrations in pointing his hearers to the Kingdom of God. He shows that those who seek prominence and honor will be abased. Let the one who spreads a feast invite the poor, who cannot repay; he will be happy and be "repaid in the resurrection of the righteous ones." Next, there is the illustration of the man spreading a grand evening meal. One after another the invited ones make excuses: One has bought a field, another has purchased some oxen, and another has just married a wife. In anger the householder sends out to bring in "the poor and crippled and blind and lame," and he declares that none of those first invited will have so much as "a taste" of his meal. (14:14, 21, 24) He gives the illustration of the lost sheep that is found, saying, "I tell you that thus there will be more joy in heaven over one sinner that repents than over ninety-nine righteous ones who have no need of repentance." (15:7) The illustration of the woman who sweeps her house to recover one drachma coin makes a similar point.*

²³ Jesus then tells of the prodigal son who asked his father for his share in the property and then

---

* A drachma was a Greek silver coin weighing about 0.109 oz. troy.

---

18. With what illustrations, works, and words of counsel does the Kingdom preaching continue?
19. How does Jesus illustrate true love of neighbor?
20. (a) What point does Jesus make with Martha and Mary? (b) What stress does he lay on prayer?

21. What warning does Jesus give against covetousness, and what does he urge his disciples to do?
22. By what pointed illustrations does Jesus instruct concerning the Kingdom?
23. What is illustrated in the account of the prodigal son?

squandered it "by living a debauched life." Falling into dire need, the son came to his senses and returned home to throw himself upon his father's mercy. His father, moved with pity, "ran and fell upon his neck and tenderly kissed him." Fine clothing was provided, a big feast was prepared, and "they started to enjoy themselves." But the elder brother objected. In kindness his father set him straight: "Child, you have always been with me, and all the things that are mine are yours; but we just had to enjoy ourselves and rejoice, because this your brother was dead and came to life, and he was lost and was found."—15:13, 20, 24, 31, 32.

[24] On hearing the illustration of the unrighteous steward, the money-loving Pharisees sneer at Jesus' teaching, but he tells them: "You are those who declare yourselves righteous before men, but God knows your hearts; because what is lofty among men is a disgusting thing in God's sight." (16:15) By the illustration of the rich man and Lazarus, he shows how great is the chasm that is fixed between those favored and those disapproved by God. Jesus warns the disciples that there will be causes for stumbling, but "woe to the one through whom they come!" He speaks of difficulties to appear "when the Son of man is to be revealed." "Remember the wife of Lot," he tells them. (17:1, 30, 32) By an illustration, he gives assurance that God will certainly act in behalf of those who "cry out to him day and night." (18:7) Then, by another illustration, he reproves the self-righteous: A Pharisee, praying in the temple, thanks God that he is not like other men. A tax collector, standing at a distance and not willing even to raise his eyes to heaven, prays: "O God, be gracious to me a sinner." How does Jesus evaluate this? He declares the tax collector to be more righteous than the Pharisee, "because everyone that exalts himself will be humiliated, but he that humbles himself will be exalted." (18:13, 14) Jesus is entertained at Jericho by the tax collector Zacchaeus and gives the illustration of the ten minas, contrasting the result of faithfully using entrusted interests with that of hiding them away.

[25] **Final public ministry in and around Jerusalem** (19:28–23:25). As Jesus rides into Jerusalem on a colt and is hailed by the multitude of the disciples as "the One coming as the King in Jehovah's name," the Pharisees call on him to rebuke his disciples. Jesus replies: "If these remained si-

lent, the stones would cry out." (19:38, 40) He gives his memorable prophecy of Jerusalem's destruction, saying that she will be surrounded with pointed stakes, distressed, and dashed to the ground with her children and that not one stone will be left on another. Jesus teaches the people in the temple, declaring the good news and answering the subtle questions of the chief priests, the scribes, and the Sadducees by skillful illustrations and argumentation. Jesus gives a powerful portrayal of the great sign of the end, mentioning again the surrounding of Jerusalem by encamped armies. Men will become faint out of fear at the things coming to pass, but when these things occur, his followers are to 'raise themselves erect and lift their heads up, because their deliverance is getting near.' They are to keep awake to succeed in escaping what is destined to occur.—21:28.

[26] It is now Nisan 14, 33 C.E. Jesus holds the Passover and then introduces "the new covenant" to his faithful apostles, associating this with the symbolic meal that he commands them to observe in remembrance of him. He also tells them: "I make a covenant with you, just as my Father has made a covenant with me, for a kingdom." (22: 20, 29) That same night, as Jesus prays at the Mount of Olives, 'an angel from heaven appears to him and strengthens him. But getting into an agony, he continues praying more earnestly; and his sweat becomes as drops of blood falling to the ground.' The atmosphere grows tense as Judas the betrayer leads in the mob to arrest Jesus. The disciples cry: "Lord, shall we strike with the sword?" One of them does lop off the ear of the high priest's slave, but Jesus rebukes them and heals the wounded man.—22:43, 44, 49.

[27] Jesus is hustled along to the high priest's house for questioning, and in the chill of the night, Peter mingles with the crowd around a fire. On three occasions he is accused of being a follower of Jesus, and three times he denies it. Then the cock crows. The Lord turns and looks upon Peter, and Peter, recalling how Jesus had foretold this very thing, goes out and weeps bitterly. After being haled into the Sanhedrin hall, Jesus is now led before Pilate and accused of subverting the nation, forbidding payment of taxes, and "saying he himself is Christ a king." Learning that Jesus is a Galilean, Pilate sends him to Herod, who happens to be in Jerusalem at the time. Herod and his

---

24. What truths does Jesus emphasize in the illustrations of the rich man and Lazarus as well as of the Pharisee and the tax collector?
25. How does Jesus enter upon the final stage of his ministry, and what prophetic warnings does he give?

26. (a) What covenants does Jesus introduce, and with what does he associate them? (b) How is Jesus strengthened under trial, and what rebuke does he give at the time of his arrest?
27. (a) Wherein does Peter fail? (b) What charges are brought against Jesus, and under what circumstances is he tried and sentenced?

guards make fun of Jesus and send him back for trial before a frenzied mob. Pilate 'surrenders Jesus to their will.'—23:2, 25.

28 Jesus' death, resurrection, and ascension (23:26–24:53). Jesus is impaled between two evildoers. One taunts him, but the other manifests faith and asks to be remembered in Jesus' Kingdom. Jesus promises: "Truly I tell you today, You will be with me in Paradise." (23:43) Then an unusual darkness falls, the curtain of the sanctuary is rent down the middle, and Jesus cries out: "Father, into your hands I entrust my spirit." At this he expires, and his body is taken down and laid in a tomb carved in the rock. On the first day of the week, the women who have come with him from Galilee go to the tomb but cannot find Jesus' body. Just as he himself foretold, he has risen on the third day!—23:46.

29 Appearing unidentified to two of his disciples on the road to Emmaus, Jesus speaks of his sufferings and interprets the Scriptures to them. Suddenly they recognize him, but he disappears. Now they comment: "Were not our hearts burning as he was speaking to us on the road, as he was fully opening up the Scriptures to us?" They hurry back to Jerusalem to tell the other disciples. Even while they are speaking these things, Jesus appears in their midst. They cannot believe it for sheer joy and wonderment. Then he 'opens up their minds fully to grasp' from the Scriptures the meaning of all that has happened. Luke concludes his Gospel account with a description of the ascension of Jesus to heaven.—24:32, 45.

WHY BENEFICIAL

30 The good news "according to Luke" builds a person's confidence in the Word of God and strengthens his faith so he can stand against the buffetings of an alien world. Luke supplies many examples of accurate fulfillments of the Hebrew Scriptures. Jesus is shown drawing his commission in specific terms from the book of Isaiah, and Luke seems to use this as a theme throughout the book. (Luke 4:17-19; Isa. 61:1, 2) This was one of the occasions of Jesus' quoting from the Prophets. He also quoted from the Law, as when rejecting the Devil's three temptations, and from the Psalms, as when asking his adversaries, "How is it they say that the Christ is David's son?" Luke's account contains many other quotations from the

Hebrew Scriptures.—Luke 4:4, 8, 12; 20:41-44; Deut. 8:3; 6:13, 16; Ps. 110:1.

31 When Jesus rode into Jerusalem on a colt as foretold at Zechariah 9:9, the multitudes hailed him joyously, applying to him the scripture at Psalm 118:26. (Luke 19:35-38) In one place two verses of Luke are sufficient to cover six points that the Hebrew Scriptures prophesied concerning Jesus' reproachful death and his resurrection. (Luke 18:32, 33; Ps. 22:7; Isa. 50:6; 53:5-7; Jonah 1:17) Finally, after his resurrection, Jesus forcefully brought home to the disciples the importance of the entire Hebrew Scriptures. "He now said to them: 'These are my words which I spoke to you while I was yet with you, that all the things written in the law of Moses and in the Prophets and Psalms about me must be fulfilled.' Then he opened up their minds fully to grasp the meaning of the Scriptures." (Luke 24:44, 45) Like those first disciples of Jesus Christ, we too can be enlightened and gain strong faith by paying attention to the fulfillments of the Hebrew Scriptures, so accurately explained by Luke and the other writers of the Christian Greek Scriptures.

32 Throughout his account, Luke continually points his reader to the Kingdom of God. From the beginning of the book, where the angel promises Mary that the child she will bear "will rule as king over the house of Jacob forever, and there will be no end of his kingdom," to the closing chapters, where Jesus speaks of taking the apostles into the covenant for the Kingdom, Luke highlights the Kingdom hope. (1:33; 22:28, 29) He shows Jesus taking the lead in Kingdom preaching and sending out the 12 apostles, and later the 70, to do this very work. (4:43; 9:1, 2; 10:1, 8, 9) The single-minded devotion needed in order to enter the Kingdom is underlined by Jesus' pointed words: "Let the dead bury their dead, but you go away and declare abroad the kingdom of God," and, "No man that has put his hand to a plow and looks at the things behind is well fitted for the kingdom of God."—9:60, 62.

33 Luke emphasizes the matter of prayer. His Gospel is outstanding in this. It tells of the multitude praying while Zechariah was in the temple, of John the Baptizer being born in answer to prayers for a child, and of Anna the prophetess praying night and day. It describes Jesus' praying at the time of his baptism, his spending the whole night in prayer before choosing the 12, and his praying during the transfiguration. Jesus admon-

---

28. (a) What does Jesus promise to the thief who shows faith in him? (b) What does Luke record concerning Jesus' death, burial, and resurrection?
29. With what joyful account does Luke's Gospel conclude?
30, 31. (a) How does Luke build confidence that the Hebrew Scriptures are inspired of God? (b) What words of Jesus does Luke quote to support this?

---

32. How does Luke's account highlight the Kingdom and what our attitude should be toward the Kingdom?
33. Give examples of Luke's emphasis on prayer. What lesson can we draw from this?

ishes his disciples "always to pray and not to give up," illustrating this by a persistent widow who continually petitioned a judge until he gave her justice. Only Luke tells of the disciples' request for Jesus to teach them to pray and of the angel's strengthening Jesus as he prayed on the Mount of Olives; and he alone records the words of Jesus' final prayer: "Father, into your hands I entrust my spirit." (1:10, 13; 2:37; 3:21; 6:12; 9:28, 29; 18: 1-8; 11:1; 22:39-46; 23:46) As in the day when Luke recorded his Gospel, so today prayer is a vital provision for strengthening all who are doing the divine will.

34 With his keenly observant mind and his fluent, descriptive pen, Luke gives warmth and vibrant life to Jesus' teaching. The love, kindness, mercy, and compassion of Jesus toward the weak, oppressed, and downtrodden show up in sharp contrast to the cold, formal, narrow, hypocritical

religion of the scribes and Pharisees. (4:18; 18:9) Jesus gives constant encouragement and help to the poor, the captives, the blind, and the crushed ones, thus providing splendid precedents for those who are seeking to "follow his steps closely." —1 Pet. 2:21.

35 Just as Jesus, the perfect, wonder-working Son of God, manifested loving concern for his disciples and all men of honest heart, we also should strive to carry out our ministry in love, yes, "because of the tender compassion of our God." (Luke 1:78) To this end the good news "according to Luke" is indeed most beneficial and helpful. We can be truly grateful to Jehovah for inspiring Luke, "the beloved physician," to write this accurate, upbuilding, and encouraging account, pointing as it does to salvation through the Kingdom by Jesus Christ, "the saving means of God."—Col. 4:14; Luke 3:6.

---

34. What qualities of Jesus does Luke stress as fine precedents for Christians?

35. Why can we be truly grateful to Jehovah for his provision of Luke's Gospel?

Bible Book Number **43**	
# John	**Writer: Apostle John** *Place Written:* **Ephesus or near** *Writing Completed:* **c. 98 C.E.** *Time Covered:* **After prologue, 29–33 C.E.**

THE Gospel records of Matthew, Mark, and Luke had been circulating for over 30 years and had come to be treasured by first-century Christians as the works of men inspired by holy spirit. Now, as the close of the century neared and the number of those who had been with Jesus dwindled, the question may well have arisen, Was there still something to be told? Was there still someone who could, from personal memories, fill in precious details of the ministry of Jesus? Yes, there was. The aged John had been singularly blessed in his association with Jesus. He was apparently among the first of John the Baptizer's disciples to be introduced to the Lamb of God and one of the first four to be invited by the Lord to join him full-time in the ministry. (John 1: 35-39; Mark 1:16-20) He continued in intimate association with Jesus throughout his ministry and was the disciple "Jesus loved" who reclined in front of Jesus' bosom at the last Passover. (John

13:23; Matt. 17:1; Mark 5:37; 14:33) He was present at the heartbreaking scene of execution, where Jesus entrusted to him the care of His fleshly mother, and it was he that outran Peter as they sped to the tomb to investigate the report that Jesus had risen.—John 19:26, 27; 20:2-4.

2 Mellowed by almost 70 years in the active ministry and charged with the visions and meditations of his recent lonely imprisonment on the isle of Patmos, John was well equipped to write of things he had long treasured in his heart. Holy spirit now energized his mind to recall and set down in writing many of those precious, life-giving sayings so that each one reading 'might believe that Jesus is the Christ, the Son of God, and that, because of believing, he might have life by means of Jesus' name.'—20:31.

3 Christians of the early second century accepted John as the writer of this account and also

---

1. What do the Scriptures show as to the closeness of John's association with Jesus?

2. How was John equipped and energized to write his Gospel, and for what purpose?

3, 4. What is the external and internal evidence for (a) the Gospel's canonicity, and (b) John's writership?

treated this writing as an unquestioned part of the canon of the inspired Scriptures. Clement of Alexandria, Irenaeus, Tertullian, and Origen, all of whom were of the late second and early third centuries, testify to John's writership. Moreover, much internal evidence that John was the writer is to be found in the book itself. Obviously the writer was a Jew and was well acquainted with the Jews' customs and their land. (2:6; 4:5; 5:2; 10:22, 23) The very intimacy of the account indicates that he was not only an apostle but one of the inner circle of three—Peter, James, and John —who accompanied Jesus on special occasions. (Matt. 17:1; Mark 5:37; 14:33) Of these, James (the son of Zebedee) is eliminated because he was martyred by Herod Agrippa I about 44 C.E., long before this book was written. (Acts 12:2) Peter is eliminated because he is mentioned along with the writer at John 21:20-24.

4 In these closing verses, the writer is referred to as the disciple "Jesus used to love," this and similar expressions being used several times in the record, though the name of the apostle John is never mentioned. Jesus is here quoted as saying about him: "If it is my will for him to remain until I come, of what concern is that to you?" (John 21: 20, 22) This suggests that the disciple referred to would long survive Peter and the other apostles. All of this fits the apostle John. It is of interest that John, after being given the Revelation vision of Jesus' coming, concludes that remarkable prophecy with the words: "Amen! Come, Lord Jesus."—Rev. 22:20.

5 Although John's writings themselves give no definite information on the matter, it is generally believed that John wrote his Gospel after his return from exile on the island of Patmos. (Rev. 1:9) The Roman emperor Nerva, 96-98 C.E., recalled many who had been exiled at the close of the reign of his predecessor, Domitian. After writing his Gospel, about 98 C.E., John is believed to have died peacefully at Ephesus in the third year of Emperor Trajan, 100 C.E.

6 As to Ephesus or its vicinity as the place of writing, the historian Eusebius (c. 260-342 C.E.) quotes Irenaeus as saying: "John, the disciple of the Lord, who had even rested on his breast, himself also gave forth the gospel, while he was living at Ephesus in Asia."* That the book was written outside Palestine is supported by its many references to Jesus' opponents by the general

term, "the Jews," rather than "Pharisees," "chief priests," and so forth. (John 1:19; 12:9) Also, the Sea of Galilee is explained by its Roman name, Sea of Tiberias. (6:1; 21:1) For the sake of the non-Jews, John gives helpful explanations of the Jewish festivals. (6:4; 7:2; 11:55) The place of his exile, Patmos, was near Ephesus, and his acquaintance with Ephesus, as well as with the other congregations of Asia Minor, is indicated by Revelation chapters 2 and 3.

7 Bearing on the authenticity of John's Gospel are important manuscript finds of the 20th century. One of these is a fragment of John's Gospel found in Egypt, now known as the Papyrus Rylands 457 (P^{52}), containing John 18:31-33, 37, 38, and preserved at the John Rylands Library, Manchester, England.* As to its bearing on the tradition of John's writership at the end of the first century, the late Sir Frederic Kenyon said in his book *The Bible and Modern Scholarship,* 1949, page 21: "Small therefore as it is, it suffices to prove that a manuscript of this Gospel was circulating, presumably in provincial Egypt where it was found, about the period A.D. 130-150. Allowing even a minimum time for the circulation of the work from its place of origin, this would throw back the date of composition so near to the traditional date in the last decade of the first century that there is no longer any reason to question the validity of the tradition."

8 John's Gospel is remarkable for its introduction, which reveals the Word, who was "in the beginning with God," as the One through whom all things came into existence. (1:2) After making known the precious relationship between Father and Son, John launches into a masterly portrayal of Jesus' works and discourses, especially from the viewpoint of the intimate love that binds in union everything in God's great arrangement. This account of Jesus' life on earth covers the period 29-33 C.E., and it is careful to make mention of the four Passovers that Jesus attended during his ministry, thus providing one of the lines of proof that his ministry was three and a half years in duration. Three of these Passovers are mentioned as such. (2:13; 6:4; 12:1; 13:1) One of them is referred to as "a festival of the Jews," but the context places it shortly after Jesus said there were "yet four months before the harvest," thus indicating the festival to be the Passover, which

---

* *The Ecclesiastical History,* Eusebius, V, VIII, 4.

* *Insight on the Scriptures,* Vol. 1, page 323.

---

5. When is John believed to have written his Gospel?
6. What evidence indicates that the Gospel of John was written outside Palestine, at or near Ephesus?

7. Of what importance is the Papyrus Rylands 457?
8. (a) What is remarkable about the introduction of John's Gospel? (b) What proof does it supply that Jesus' ministry was three and a half years in duration?

took place about the beginning of the harvest. —4:35; 5:1.*

[9] The good news "according to John" is largely supplementary; 92 percent is new material not covered in the other three Gospels. Even so, John concludes with the words: "There are, in fact, many other things also which Jesus did, which, if ever they were written in full detail, I suppose, the world itself could not contain the scrolls written."—21:25.

CONTENTS OF JOHN

[10] **Prologue: Introducing "the Word"** (1:1-18). With beauteous simplicity, John states that in the beginning "the Word was with God," that life itself was by means of him, that he became "the light of men," and that John (the Baptizer) bore witness about him. (1:1, 4) The light was in the world, but the world did not know him. Those who did receive him became God's children, being born from God. Just as the Law was given through Moses, so "the undeserved kindness and the truth came to be through Jesus Christ."—1:17.

[11] **Presenting "the Lamb of God" to men** (1:19-51). John the Baptizer confesses *he* is not the Christ but says there is one coming behind him, and the lace of that one's sandal he is not worthy to untie. The next day, as Jesus comes toward him, John identifies him as "the Lamb of God that takes away the sin of the world." (1:27, 29) Next, he introduces two of his disciples to Jesus, and one of these, Andrew, brings his brother Peter to Jesus. Philip and Nathanael also accept Jesus as 'the Son of God, the King of Israel.'—1:49.

[12] **Jesus' miracles prove he is "the Holy One of God"** (2:1-6:71). Jesus performs his first miracle in Cana of Galilee, turning water into the best of wine at a wedding feast. This is "the beginning of his signs, . . . and his disciples put their faith in him." (2:11) Jesus goes up to Jerusalem for the Passover. Finding peddlers and money changers in the temple, he takes a whip and drives them out with such vigor that his disciples recognize the fulfillment of the prophecy: "The zeal for your house will eat me up." (John 2:17; Ps. 69:9) He predicts that the temple of his own body will be broken down and raised up again in three days.

[13] The fearful Nicodemus comes to Jesus at night. He confesses that Jesus is sent from God, and Jesus tells him that one must be born from water and spirit to enter the Kingdom of God. Believing in the Son of man from heaven is necessary for life. "For God loved the world so much that he gave his only-begotten Son, in order that everyone exercising faith in him might not be destroyed but have everlasting life." (John 3:16) The light that has come into the world is in conflict with darkness, "but he that does what is true comes to the light," concludes Jesus. John the Baptizer then learns of Jesus' activity in Judea and declares that while he himself is not the Christ, yet "the friend of the bridegroom . . . has a great deal of joy on account of the voice of the bridegroom." (3:21, 29) Jesus must now increase, and John decrease.

[14] Jesus sets out again for Galilee. On the way, dust-laden and "tired out from the journey," he sits down to rest at Jacob's fountain in Sychar, while his disciples are off buying food in the city. (4:6) It is midday, the sixth hour. A Samaritan woman approaches to draw water, and Jesus asks for a drink. Then, weary though he is, he begins to speak to her about the real "water" that truly refreshes, imparting everlasting life to those who worship God "with spirit and truth." The disciples return and urge him to eat, and he declares: "My food is for me to do the will of him that sent me and to finish his work." He spends two more days in the area, so that many of the Samaritans come to believe that "this man is for a certainty the savior of the world." (4:24, 34, 42) On reaching Cana of Galilee, Jesus heals a nobleman's son without even going near his bedside.

[15] Jesus goes up again to Jerusalem for the Jews' festival. He heals a sick man on the Sabbath, and this raises a great storm of criticism. Jesus counters: "My Father has kept working until now, and I keep working." (5:17) The Jewish leaders now claim that Jesus has added blasphemy, that of making himself equal to God, to the crime of Sabbath-breaking. Jesus answers that the Son cannot do a single thing of his own initiative but is entirely dependent on the Father. He makes the marvelous statement that "all those in the memorial tombs will hear his voice and come out" to a resurrection. But to his faithless audience, Jesus says: "How can you believe, when you are accepting glory from one another and you are not seeking the glory that is from the only God?"—5:28, 29, 44.

---

* *Insight on the Scriptures*, Vol. 2, pages 57-8.

9. What shows John's Gospel to be supplementary, and yet does it fill out all the details of Jesus' ministry?
10. What does John say about "the Word"?
11. As what does John the Baptizer identify Jesus, and as what do John's disciples accept Jesus?
12. (a) What is Jesus' first miracle? (b) What does he do when up at Jerusalem for the first Passover during his ministry?
13. (a) What does Jesus show to be necessary for gaining life? (b) How does John the Baptizer speak of himself in relation to Jesus?

14. What does Jesus explain to the Samaritan woman at Sychar, and what results from his preaching there?
15. What charges are made against Jesus in Jerusalem, but how does he answer his critics?

[16] When Jesus miraculously feeds 5,000 men with five loaves and two small fishes, the crowd consider seizing him and making him king, but he withdraws into a mountain. Later, he reproves them for going after "the food that perishes." Rather, they should work "for the food that remains for life everlasting." He points out that exercising faith in him as the Son is the partaking of the bread of life, and he adds: "Unless you eat the flesh of the Son of man and drink his blood, you have no life in yourselves." Many of his disciples are offended at this and leave him. Jesus asks the 12: "You do not want to go also, do you?" and Peter replies: "Lord, whom shall we go away to? You have sayings of everlasting life; and we have believed and come to know that you are the Holy One of God." (6:27, 53, 67-69) However, Jesus, knowing that Judas will betray him, says that one of them is a slanderer.

[17] **"The light" conflicts with darkness** (7:1–12:50). Jesus goes up secretly to Jerusalem and appears halfway through the Festival of Tabernacles, teaching openly in the temple. The people argue about whether he is really the Christ. Jesus tells them: "I have not come of my own initiative, but he that sent me is real, . . . and that One sent me forth." On another occasion he cries out to the crowd: "If anyone is thirsty, let him come to me and drink." Officers who are sent to arrest Jesus return empty-handed and report to the priests: "Never has another man spoken like this." Infuriated, the Pharisees answer that none of the rulers have believed, nor is any prophet to be raised up out of Galilee.—7:28, 29, 37, 46.

[18] In a further speech, Jesus says: "I am the light of the world." To the malicious charges that he is a false witness, that he has been born out of wedlock, and that he is a Samaritan and demon-possessed, Jesus forcefully replies: "If I glorify myself, my glory is nothing. It is my Father that glorifies me." When he declares, "Before Abraham came into existence, I have been," the Jews make another abortive attempt on his life. (8:12, 54, 58) Frustrated, they later question a man whose sight Jesus has miraculously restored, and they throw the man out.

[19] Again Jesus speaks to the Jews, this time concerning the fine shepherd, who calls his sheep by name and who surrenders his soul in behalf of the sheep 'that they might have life in abundance.' He says: "I have other sheep, which are not of this fold; those also I must bring, and they will listen to my voice, and they will become one flock, one shepherd." (10:10, 16) He tells the Jews that no one can snatch the sheep out of the hand of his Father, and he says that he and his Father are one. Again they seek to stone him to death. In answer to their charge of blasphemy, he reminds them that in the book of Psalms, certain mighty ones of earth are referred to as "gods," whereas he has referred to himself as God's Son. (Ps. 82:6) He urges them at least to believe his works.—John 10:34.

[20] From Bethany near Jerusalem comes news that Lazarus, brother of Mary and Martha, is ill. By the time Jesus arrives there, Lazarus is dead and already four days in the tomb. Jesus performs the stupendous miracle of recalling Lazarus to life, causing many to put faith in Jesus. This precipitates a special meeting of the Sanhedrin, where the high priest, Caiaphas, is compelled to prophesy that Jesus is destined to die for the nation. As the chief priests and Pharisees take counsel to kill him, Jesus retires temporarily from the public scene.

[21] Six days before the Passover, Jesus comes again to Bethany on his way to Jerusalem, and he is entertained by Lazarus' household. Then, the day after the Sabbath, on Nisan 9, seated upon a young ass, he makes an entry into Jerusalem amid the acclamations of a great crowd; and the Pharisees say to one another: "You are getting absolutely nowhere. See! The world has gone after him." By the illustration of a grain of wheat, Jesus intimates that he must be planted in death in order for fruitage to be produced for everlasting life. He calls on his Father to glorify His name, and a voice is heard from heaven: "I both glorified it and will glorify it again." Jesus urges his hearers to avoid the darkness and to walk in the light, yes, to become "sons of light." As the forces of darkness close in on him, he makes a strong public appeal for the people to put faith in him 'as a light that has come into the world.'—12:19, 28, 36, 46.

[22] **Jesus' parting counsel to the faithful apostles** (13:1–16:33). While the evening meal of the Passover with the 12 is in progress, Jesus rises

---

16. (a) What does Jesus teach concerning food and life? (b) How does Peter express the conviction of the apostles?

17. What effect does Jesus' teaching in the temple at the Festival of Tabernacles have?

18. What opposition do the Jews bring against Jesus, and how does he reply?

19. (a) How does Jesus speak of his relationship with his Father and his care for his sheep? (b) How does he answer the Jews when they threaten him?

20. (a) What outstanding miracle does Jesus next perform? (b) To what does this lead?

21. (a) How do the people and the Pharisees respond to Jesus' entry into Jerusalem? (b) What illustration does Jesus give regarding his death and its purpose, and what does he urge upon his hearers?

22. What pattern does Jesus provide at the Passover meal, and what new commandment does he give?

and, removing his outer garments, takes a towel and foot basin and proceeds to wash the feet of his disciples. Peter protests, but Jesus tells him he too must have his feet washed. Jesus admonishes the disciples to follow his pattern of humility, for "a slave is not greater than his master." He speaks of the betrayer and then dismisses Judas. After Judas goes out, Jesus begins to speak intimately with the others. "I am giving you a new commandment, that you love one another; just as I have loved you, that you also love one another. By this all will know that you are my disciples, if you have love among yourselves."—13:16, 34, 35.

[23] Jesus speaks wonderful words of comfort for his followers in this critical hour. They must exercise faith in God and also in him. In his Father's house, there are many abodes, and he will come again and receive them home to himself. "I am the way and the truth and the life," says Jesus. "No one comes to the Father except through me." Comfortingly he tells his followers that by exercising faith, they will do greater works than he and that he will grant whatever they ask in his name, in order that his Father may be glorified. He promises them another helper, "the spirit of the truth," which will teach them all things and bring back to their minds all that he has told them. They should rejoice that he is going away to his Father, for, says Jesus, "the Father is greater than I am."—14:6, 17, 28.

[24] Jesus speaks of himself as the true vine and his Father as the cultivator. He urges them to remain in union with him, saying: "My Father is glorified in this, that you keep bearing much fruit and prove yourselves my disciples." (15:8) And how may their joy become full? By loving one another just as he has loved them. He calls them friends. What a precious relationship! The world will hate them as it has hated him, and it will persecute them, but Jesus will send the helper to bear witness about him and to guide his disciples into all truth. Their present grief will give way to rejoicing when he sees them again, and no one will take their joy from them. Consoling are his words: "The Father himself has affection for you, because you have had affection for me and have believed that I came out as the Father's representative." Yes, they will be scattered, but, says Jesus, "I have said these things to you that by means of me you may have peace. In the world you will have tribulation, but take courage! I have conquered the world."—16:27, 33.

[25] **Jesus' prayer in behalf of his disciples** (17: 1-26). In prayer Jesus acknowledges to his Father: "This means everlasting life, their taking in knowledge of you, the only true God, and of the one whom you sent forth, Jesus Christ." Having finished his assigned work on earth, Jesus now asks to be glorified alongside his Father with the glory he had before the world was. He has made the Father's name manifest to his disciples and asks the Father to watch over them 'on account of His own name.' He requests the Father, not that they be taken out of the world, but to keep them from the wicked one and to sanctify them by His word of truth. Jesus broadens out his prayer to embrace all those who will yet exercise faith through hearing the word of these disciples, "in order that they may all be one, just as you, Father, are in union with me and I am in union with you, that they also may be in union with us, in order that the world may believe that you sent me forth." He asks that these also may share with him in his heavenly glory, for he has made the Father's name known to them, that His love may abide in them.—17:3, 11, 21.

[26] **Christ tried and impaled** (18:1–19:42). Jesus and his disciples go now to a garden across the Kidron Valley. It is here that Judas appears with a soldier band and betrays Jesus, who mildly submits. However, Peter defends him with a sword and is reproved: "The cup that the Father has given me, should I not by all means drink it?" (18:11) Jesus is then led away bound to Annas, the father-in-law of Caiaphas, the high priest. John and Peter follow closely, and John gets them access to the courtyard of the high priest, where Peter three times denies knowing Christ. Jesus is first questioned by Annas and then brought before Caiaphas. Afterward, Jesus is brought before Roman governor Pilate, with the Jews clamoring for the death sentence.

[27] To Pilate's question, "Are you a king?" Jesus replies: "You yourself are saying that I am a king. For this I have been born, and for this I have come into the world, that I should bear witness to the truth." (18:37) Pilate, finding no real evidence against Jesus, offers to release him, as it was the custom to free some prisoner at the Passover, but the Jews call for the robber Barabbas instead. Pilate has Jesus scourged, and again he tries to

---

23. As comfort, what hope and what promised helper does Jesus discuss?
24. How does Jesus discuss the relationship of the apostles with himself and the Father, with what blessings for them?

25. (a) What does Jesus acknowledge in prayer to his Father? (b) What does he request with regard to himself, his disciples, and those who will exercise faith through their word?
26. What does the account say concerning Jesus' arrest and trial?
27. (a) What questions as to kingship and authority are raised by Pilate, and how does Jesus comment? (b) What stand on kingship do the Jews take?

release him, but the Jews cry: "Impale him! Impale him! . . . because he made himself God's son." When Pilate tells Jesus he has authority to impale him, Jesus answers: "You would have no authority at all against me unless it had been granted to you from above." Again the Jews cry out: "Take him away! Take him away! Impale him! . . . We have no king but Caesar." At this, Pilate hands him over to be impaled.—19:6, 7, 11, 15.

[28] Jesus is taken away "to the so-called Skull Place, which is called *Golgotha* in Hebrew," and is impaled between two others. Above him Pilate fastens the title "Jesus the Nazarene the King of the Jews," written in Hebrew, Latin, and Greek, for all to see and understand. (19:17, 19) Jesus entrusts his mother to the care of John and, after receiving some sour wine, exclaims: "It has been accomplished!" Then he bows his head and expires. (19:30) In fulfillment of the prophecies, the executional squad casts lots for his garments, refrains from breaking his legs, and jabs his side with a spear. (John 19:24, 32-37; Ps. 22:18; 34:20; 22:17; Zech. 12:10) Afterward, Joseph of Arimathea and Nicodemus prepare the body for burial and place it in a new memorial tomb located nearby.

[29] **Appearances of the resurrected Christ** (20:1–21:25). John's array of evidence as to the Christ concludes on the happy note of the resurrection. Mary Magdalene finds the tomb empty, and Peter and another disciple (John) run there but see only the bandages and headcloth remaining. Mary, who has remained near the tomb, speaks with two angels and finally, as she thinks, with the gardener. When he answers, "Mary!" she immediately recognizes him to be Jesus. Next, Jesus manifests himself to his disciples behind locked doors, and he tells them of the power they will receive through holy spirit. Afterward, Thomas, who was not present, refuses to believe, but eight days later Jesus again appears and gives him the proof, at which Thomas exclaims: "My Lord and my God!" (20:16, 28) Days later Jesus again meets his disciples, at the Sea of Tiberias; he provides them a miraculous catch of fish and then breakfasts with them. Three times he asks Peter whether he loves him. As Peter insists he does, Jesus says pointedly: "Feed my lambs," "Shepherd my little sheep," "Feed my little sheep." Then he foretells by what sort of death Peter will glorify God. Peter asks about John, and Jesus says: "If it is my will for him to remain until I come, of what concern is that to you?"—21:15-17, 22.

---

28. What takes place at Golgotha, and what prophecies are there fulfilled?
29. (a) What appearances does the resurrected Jesus make to his disciples? (b) What points does Jesus make in his final remarks to Peter?

WHY BENEFICIAL

[30] Powerful in its directness and convincing in its intimate, heartwarming portrayal of the Word, who became Christ, the good news "according to John" gives us a close-up view of this anointed Son of God in word and in action. Though John's style and vocabulary are simple, marking him as an "unlettered and ordinary" man, there is tremendous power in his expression. (Acts 4:13) His Gospel soars to its greatest heights in making known the intimate love between Father and Son, as well as the blessed, loving relationship to be found by being in union with them. John uses the words "love" and "loved" more often than the other three Gospels combined.

[31] In the beginning what a glorious relationship existed between the Word and God the Father! In God's providence "the Word became flesh and resided among us, and we had a view of his glory, a glory such as belongs to an only-begotten son from a father; and he was full of undeserved kindness and truth." (John 1:14) Then, throughout John's account, Jesus emphasizes his relationship to be one of subjection in unquestioning obedience to the will of the Father. (4:34; 5:19, 30; 7:16; 10:29, 30; 11:41, 42; 12:27, 49, 50; 14:10) His expression of this intimate relationship reaches its glorious climax in the moving prayer recorded in John chapter 17, where Jesus reports to his Father that he has finished the work He gave him to do in the earth and adds: "So now you, Father, glorify me alongside yourself with the glory that I had alongside you before the world was."—17:5.

[32] What of Jesus' relationship with his disciples? Jesus' role as the sole channel through which God's blessings are extended to these and to all mankind is continually kept to the fore. (14:13, 14; 15:16; 16:23, 24) He is referred to as "the Lamb of God," "the bread of life," "the light of the world," "the fine shepherd," "the resurrection and the life," "the way and the truth and the life," and "the true vine." (1:29; 6:35; 8:12; 10:11; 11:25; 14:6; 15:1) It is under this illustration of "the true vine" that Jesus makes known the marvelous unity that exists not only between his true followers and himself but also with the Father. By bearing much fruit, they will glorify his Father. "Just as the Father has loved me and I have loved you, remain in my love," counsels Jesus.—15:9.

---

30. How does John give special emphasis to the quality of love?
31. What relationship is stressed throughout the Gospel of John, and how does it reach its climactic expression?
32. By what expressions does Jesus show his own relationship with his disciples and that he is the sole channel through which blessings of life come to mankind?

³³ Then how fervently he prays to Jehovah that all these loved ones, and also 'those putting faith in him through their word,' may be one with his Father and himself, sanctified by the word of truth! Indeed, the entire purpose of Jesus' ministry is wonderfully expressed in the final words of his prayer to his Father: "I have made your name known to them and will make it known, in order that the love with which you loved me may be in them and I in union with them."—17:20, 26.

³⁴ Though Jesus was leaving his disciples in the world, he was not going to leave them without a helper, "the spirit of the truth." Moreover, he gave them timely counsel on their relationship with the world, showing them how to overcome as "sons of light." (14:16, 17; 3:19-21; 12:36) "If you remain in my word, you are really my disciples," said Jesus, "and you will know the truth, and the truth will set you free." In contrast, he said to the sons of darkness: "You are from your father the Devil, and you wish to do the desires of your father. . . . He did not stand fast in the truth, because truth is not in him." Let us be determined, then, always to stand fast in the truth, yes, to "worship the Father with spirit and truth," and to draw strength from Jesus' words: "Take courage! I have conquered the world."—8:31, 32, 44; 4:23; 16:33.

³⁵ All of this has a relation, also, to God's Kingdom. Jesus testified when on trial: "My kingdom is no part of this world. If my kingdom were part of this world, my attendants would have fought that I should not be delivered up to the Jews. But, as it is, my kingdom is not from this source." Then, in answer to Pilate's question, he said: "You yourself are saying that I am a king. For this I have been born, and for this I have come into the world, that I should bear witness to the truth. Everyone that is on the side of the truth listens to my voice." (18: 36, 37) Happy indeed are those who listen and who are "born again" to "enter into the kingdom of God" in union with the King. Happy are the "other sheep" who listen to the voice of this Shepherd-King and gain life. There is, indeed, cause for gratitude for the provision of John's Gospel, for it was written "that you may believe that Jesus is the Christ the Son of God, and that, because of believing, you may have life by means of his name."—3:3, 5; 10:16; 20:31.

---

33. What purpose of his ministry does Jesus express in prayer?
34. What beneficial counsel did Jesus give on how to overcome the world?

35. (a) What testimony does Jesus give concerning God's Kingdom? (b) Why does John's Gospel give cause for happiness and gratitude?

Bible Book Number	**44** Acts	Writer: **Luke** Place Written: **Rome** Writing Completed: **c. 61 C.E.** Time Covered: **33–c. 61 C.E.**

IN THE 42nd book of the inspired Scriptures, Luke gives an account covering the life, activity, and ministry of Jesus and his followers up to the time of Jesus' ascension. The historical record of the 44th book of the Scriptures, Acts of Apostles, continues the history of early Christianity by describing the founding of the congregation as a result of the operation of the holy spirit. It also describes the expansion of the witness, first among the Jews and then to people of all the nations. The greater part of the material in the first 12 chapters covers the activities of Peter, and the remaining 16 chapters, the activities of Paul. Luke had an intimate association with Paul, accompanying him on many of his travels.

² The book is addressed to Theophilus. Since he is referred to as "most excellent," it is possible that he occupied some official position, or it may simply be an expression of high esteem. (Luke 1:3) The account provides an accurate historical record of the establishment and growth of the Christian congregation. It commences with Jesus' appearances to his disciples following his resurrection and then records important events of the period from 33 to about 61 C.E., covering approximately 28 years in all.

³ From ancient times the writer of the Gospel of Luke has been credited with the writing of Acts.

1, 2. (a) What historical events and activities are described in Acts? (b) What time period does the book cover?

3. Who wrote the book of Acts, and when was the writing completed?

Both books are addressed to Theophilus. By repeating the closing events of his Gospel in the opening verses of Acts, Luke binds the two accounts together as the work of the same author. It appears that Luke completed Acts about 61 C.E., probably toward the close of a two-year stay in Rome while in the company of the apostle Paul. Since it records events down to that year, it could not have been completed earlier, and its leaving Paul's appeal to Caesar undecided indicates that it was completed by that year.

[4] From the most ancient times, Acts has been accepted by Bible scholars as canonical. Parts of the book are to be found among some of the oldest extant papyrus manuscripts of the Greek Scriptures, notably the Michigan No. 1571 (P^{38}) of the third or fourth century C.E. and Chester Beatty No. 1 (P^{45}) of the third century. Both of these indicate that Acts was circulating with other books of the inspired Scriptures and hence was part of the catalog at an early date. Luke's writing in the book of Acts reflects the same remarkable accuracy as we have already noted marks his Gospel. Sir William M. Ramsay rates the writer of Acts "among the historians of the first rank," and he explains what this means by saying: "The first and the essential quality of the great historian is truth. What he says must be trustworthy."[*]

[5] Illustrating the accurate reporting that so characterizes Luke's writings, we quote Edwin Smith, commander of a flotilla of British warships in the Mediterranean during World War I, writing in the magazine *The Rudder,* March 1947: "The ancient vessels were not steered as those in modern times by a single rudder hinged to the stern post, but by two great oars or paddles, one on each side of the stern; hence the mention of them in the plural number by St. Luke. [Acts 27:40] . . . We have seen in our examination that every statement as to the movements of this ship, from the time when she left Fair Havens until she was beached at Malta, as set forth by St. Luke has been verified by external and independent evidence of the most exact and satisfying nature; and that his statements as to the time the ship remained at sea correspond with the distance covered; and finally that his description of the place arrived at is in conformity with the place as it is. All of which goes to show that Luke actually made the voyage as described, and has moreover shown himself to be a man whose observations and statements may be taken as reliable and trustworthy in the highest degree."[#]

[6] Archaeological findings also confirm the accuracy of Luke's account. For example, excavations at Ephesus have unearthed the temple of Artemis as well as the ancient theater where the Ephesians rioted against the apostle Paul. (Acts 19:27-41) Inscriptions have been discovered that confirm the correctness of Luke's use of the title "city rulers" as applying to the officials of Thessalonica. (17:6, 8) Two Maltese inscriptions show that Luke was also correct in referring to Publius as "the principal man" of Malta.—28:7.[*]

[7] Further, the various speeches made by Peter, Stephen, Cornelius, Tertullus, Paul, and others, as recorded by Luke, are all different in style and composition. Even the speeches of Paul, spoken before different audiences, changed in style to suit the occasion. This indicates that Luke recorded only what he himself heard or what other eyewitnesses reported to him. Luke was no fiction writer.

[8] Very little is known of the personal life of Luke. Luke himself was not an apostle but was associated with those who were. (Luke 1:1-4) In three instances the apostle Paul mentions Luke by name. (Col. 4:10, 14; 2 Tim. 4:11; Philem. 24) For some years he was the constant companion of Paul, who called him "the beloved physician." There is a shifting back and forth in the account between "they" and "we," indicating that Luke was with Paul at Troas during Paul's second missionary tour, that he may have remained behind at Philippi until Paul returned some years later, and that he then rejoined Paul and accompanied him on his trip to Rome for trial.—Acts 16:8, 10; 17:1; 20:4-6; 28:16.

CONTENTS OF ACTS

[9] **Events till Pentecost** (1:1-26). As Luke opens this second account, the resurrected Jesus tells his eager disciples that they will be baptized in holy spirit. Will the Kingdom be restored at this time? No. But they will receive power and become witnesses "to the most distant part of the earth." As Jesus is lifted up out of their sight, two men in white tell them: "This Jesus who was received up from you into the sky will come thus in the same manner."—1:8, 11.

---

[*] *Insight on the Scriptures,* Vol. 1, pages 153-4, 734-5; Vol. 2, page 748.

---

6. What examples show how archaeological findings confirm the accuracy of Acts?
7. How do the speeches recorded show the record of Acts to be factual?
8. What do the Scriptures tell us of Luke and his association with Paul?
9. What things are the disciples told at the time of Jesus' ascension?

---

[*] *St. Paul the Traveller,* 1895, page 4.
[#] Quoted in *Awake!* of July 22, 1947, pages 22-3; see also *Awake!* of April 8, 1971, pages 27-8.

---

4. What proves that Acts is canonical and authentic?
5. Illustrate Luke's accurate reporting.

¹⁰ **The memorable day of Pentecost** (2:1-42). The disciples are all assembled in Jerusalem. Suddenly a noise like a rushing wind fills the house. Tongues as if of fire rest on those present. They are filled with holy spirit and begin speaking in different languages about "the magnificent things of God." (2:11) Onlookers are perplexed. Now Peter stands up and speaks. He explains that this outpouring of the spirit is in fulfillment of the prophecy of Joel (2:28-32) and that Jesus Christ, now resurrected and exalted to God's right hand, 'has poured out this which they see and hear.' Stabbed to the heart, about 3,000 embrace the word and are baptized.—2:33.

¹¹ **The witness expands** (2:43–5:42). Daily, Jehovah continues to join to them those being saved. Outside the temple Peter and John come upon a crippled man who has never walked in his life. "In the name of Jesus Christ the Nazarene, walk!" commands Peter. Immediately the man begins "walking and leaping and praising God." Peter then appeals to the people to repent and turn around, "that seasons of refreshing may come from the person of Jehovah." Annoyed that Peter and John are teaching Jesus' resurrection, the religious leaders arrest them, but the ranks of the believers swell to about 5,000 men.—3:6, 8, 19.

¹² The next day, Peter and John are taken before the Jewish rulers for questioning. Peter testifies outspokenly that salvation is only through Jesus Christ, and when commanded to stop their preaching work, both Peter and John reply: "Whether it is righteous in the sight of God to listen to you rather than to God, judge for yourselves. But as for us, we cannot stop speaking about the things we have seen and heard." (4: 19, 20) They are released, and all the disciples continue to speak the word of God with boldness. Because of the circumstances, they pool their material possessions and make distributions according to the need. However, a certain Ananias and his wife, Sapphira, sell some property and secretly keep back part of the price while giving the appearance of turning in the entire sum. Peter exposes them, and they drop dead because they have played false to God and the holy spirit.

¹³ Again the outraged religious leaders throw the apostles into jail, but this time Jehovah's angel releases them. The next day they are again brought before the Sanhedrin and charged with 'filling Jerusalem with their teaching.' They reply: "We must obey God as ruler rather than men." Though flogged and threatened, they still refuse to stop, and 'every day in the temple and from house to house they continue without letup teaching and declaring the good news about the Christ, Jesus.'—5:28, 29, 42.

¹⁴ **Stephen's martyrdom** (6:1–8:1a). Stephen is one of seven appointed by holy spirit to distribute food to tables. He also witnesses powerfully to the truth, and so zealous is his support of the faith that his enraged opponents have him brought before the Sanhedrin on the charge of blasphemy. In making his defense, Stephen tells first of Jehovah's long-suffering toward Israel. Then, in fearless eloquence, he comes to the point: 'Obstinate men, you are always resisting the holy spirit, you who received the Law as transmitted by angels but have not kept it.' (7:51-53) This is too much for them. They rush upon him, throw him outside the city, and stone him to death. Saul looks on in approval.

¹⁵ **Persecutions, Saul's conversion** (8:1b–9: 30). The persecution that begins that day against the congregation in Jerusalem scatters all except the apostles throughout the land. Philip goes to Samaria, where many accept the word of God. Peter and John are sent there from Jerusalem so that these believers may receive holy spirit "through the laying on of the hands of the apostles." (8:18) An angel then directs Philip south to the Jerusalem-Gaza road, where he finds a eunuch of the royal court of Ethiopia riding in his chariot and reading the book of Isaiah. Philip enlightens him as to the meaning of the prophecy and baptizes him.

¹⁶ Meanwhile, Saul, "still breathing threat and murder against the disciples of the Lord," sets out to arrest those 'belonging to The Way' in Damascus. Suddenly a light from heaven flashes around him, and he falls to the ground blinded. A voice from heaven tells him: "I am Jesus, whom you are persecuting." After three days in Damascus, a disciple named Ananias ministers to him. Saul recovers his sight, gets baptized, and becomes filled with holy spirit, so that he becomes a zealous and able preacher of the good news. (9:1, 2, 5) In this amazing turn of events, the persecutor becomes the persecuted and has to flee for his life, first from Damascus and then from Jerusalem.

¹⁷ **The good news goes to uncircumcised Gentiles** (9:31–12:25). The congregation now 'enters

---

10. (a) What memorable things happen on the day of Pentecost? (b) What explanation does Peter give, and what results from it?
11. How does Jehovah prosper the preaching work?
12. (a) What answer do the disciples give when commanded to stop preaching? (b) For what are Ananias and Sapphira punished?
13. With what are the apostles charged, how do they reply, and what do they continue to do?

---

14. How does Stephen meet martyrdom?
15. What results from persecution, and what preaching experiences does Philip have?
16. How does the conversion of Saul come about?
17. How does the good news go to uncircumcised Gentiles?

into a period of peace, being built up; and as it walks in the fear of Jehovah and in the comfort of the holy spirit, it keeps on multiplying.' (9:31) At Joppa, Peter raises the beloved Tabitha (Dorcas) from the dead, and it is from here that he receives the call to go to Caesarea, where an army officer named Cornelius awaits him. He preaches to Cornelius and his household and they believe, and the holy spirit is poured out upon them. Having perceived "that God is not partial, but in every nation the man that fears him and works righteousness is acceptable to him," Peter baptizes them—the first uncircumcised Gentile converts. Peter later explains this new development to the brothers in Jerusalem, at which they glorify God.—10:34, 35.

¹⁸ As the good news continues to spread rapidly, Barnabas and Saul teach quite a crowd in Antioch, 'and it is first in Antioch that the disciples are by divine providence called Christians.' (11:26) Once again persecution breaks out. Herod Agrippa I has James the brother of John killed with the sword. He also throws Peter into prison, but once again Jehovah's angel sets Peter free. Too bad for the wicked Herod! Because he fails to give glory to God, he is eaten up with worms and dies. On the other hand, 'the word of Jehovah goes on growing and spreading.'—12:24.

¹⁹ **Paul's first missionary trip, with Barnabas** (13:1–14:28).* Barnabas and "Saul, who is also Paul," are set apart and sent forth from Antioch by holy spirit. (13:9) On the island of Cyprus, many become believers, including the proconsul Sergius Paulus. On the mainland of Asia Minor, they make a circuit of six or more cities, and everywhere it is the same story: A clear division appears between those who gladly accept the good news and the stiff-necked opponents who incite rock-throwing mobs against Jehovah's messengers. After making appointments of older men in the newly formed congregations, Paul and Barnabas return to Syrian Antioch.

²⁰ **Settling the circumcision issue** (15:1-35). With the great influx of non-Jews, the question arises whether these should be circumcised. Paul and Barnabas take the issue to the apostles and the older men in Jerusalem, where the disciple James presides and arranges to send out the unanimous decision by formal letter: "The holy spirit and we ourselves have favored adding no further burden to you, except these necessary things, to keep abstaining from things sacrificed to idols and from blood and from things strangled and from fornica-

tion." (15:28, 29) The encouragement of this letter causes the brothers in Antioch to rejoice.

²¹ **Ministry expands with Paul's second trip** (15:36–18:22).* "After some days" Barnabas and Mark sail for Cyprus, while Paul and Silas set out through Syria and Asia Minor. (15:36) The young man Timothy joins Paul at Lystra, and they journey on to Troas on the Aegean seacoast. Here in a vision Paul sees a man entreating him: "Step over into Macedonia and help us." (16:9) Luke joins Paul, and they take a ship to Philippi, the principal city of Macedonia, where Paul and Silas are thrown into prison. This results in the jailer's becoming a believer and getting baptized. After their release, they push on to Thessalonica, and there the jealous Jews incite a mob against them. So by night the brothers send Paul and Silas out to Beroea. Here the Jews show noble-mindedness by receiving the word "with the greatest eagerness of mind, carefully examining the Scriptures daily" in search of confirmation of the things learned. (17:11) Leaving Silas and Timothy with this new congregation, as he had left Luke in Philippi, Paul continues on south to Athens.

²² In this city of idols, high-minded Epicurean and Stoic philosophers deride Paul as a "chatterer" and "a publisher of foreign deities," and they take him up to the Areopagus, or Mars' Hill. With skillful oratory Paul argues in favor of seeking the true God, the "Lord of heaven and earth," who guarantees a righteous judgment by the one whom He has resurrected from the dead. Mention of the resurrection divides his audience, but some become believers.—17:18, 24.

²³ Next, in Corinth, Paul stays with Aquila and Priscilla, joining with them in the trade of tentmaking. Opposition to his preaching compels him to move out of the synagogue and to hold his meetings next door, in the home of Titius Justus. Crispus, the presiding officer of the synagogue, becomes a believer. After a stay of 18 months in Corinth, Paul departs with Aquila and Priscilla for Ephesus, where he leaves them and continues on to Antioch in Syria, thus completing his second missionary tour.

²⁴ **Paul revisits congregations, third tour** (18: 23–21:26).# A Jew named Apollos comes to Ephe-

---

* Insight on the Scriptures, Vol. 2, page 747.

18. (a) What next occurs in Antioch? (b) What persecution breaks out, but does it achieve its object?
19. How extensive is Paul's first missionary journey, and what is accomplished?
20. By what decision is the circumcision issue settled?

---

* Insight on the Scriptures, Vol. 2, page 747.
# Insight on the Scriptures, Vol. 2, page 747.

21. (a) Who are associated with Paul on his second missionary trip? (b) What events mark the visit to Macedonia?
22. What results from Paul's skillful speech on the Areopagus?
23. What is accomplished in Corinth?
24, 25. (a) At the time of Paul's starting his third journey, what takes place in Ephesus? (b) What commotion marks the conclusion of Paul's three-year stay?

sus from Alexandria, Egypt, speaking boldly in the synagogue about Jesus, but Aquila and Priscilla find it necessary to correct his teaching before he goes on to Corinth. Paul is now on his third journey and in due course comes to Ephesus. Learning that the believers here have been baptized with John's baptism, Paul explains baptism in Jesus' name. He then baptizes about 12 men; and when he lays his hands upon them, they receive the holy spirit.

25 During Paul's three-year stay in Ephesus, 'the word of Jehovah keeps growing and prevailing in a mighty way,' and many give up their worship of the city's patron goddess, Artemis. (19:20) Angered at the prospective loss of business, the makers of silver shrines throw the city into such an uproar that it takes hours to disperse the mob. Soon afterward Paul leaves for Macedonia and Greece, visiting the believers along the way.

26 Paul stays three months in Greece before returning by way of Macedonia, where Luke rejoins him. They cross over to Troas, and here, as Paul is discoursing into the night, a young man falls asleep and tumbles out of a third-story window. He is picked up dead, but Paul restores him to life. The next day Paul and his party leave for Miletus, where Paul stops over en route to Jerusalem, to have a meeting with the older men from Ephesus. He informs them they will see his face no more. How urgent, then, it is for them to take the lead and shepherd the flock of God, 'among which the holy spirit has appointed them overseers'! He recalls the example he has set among them, and he admonishes them to keep awake, not sparing themselves in giving in behalf of the brothers. (20:28) Though warned against setting foot in Jerusalem, Paul does not turn back. His companions acquiesce, saying: "Let the will of Jehovah take place." (21:14) There is great rejoicing when Paul reports to James and the older men concerning God's blessing on his ministry among the nations.

27 **Paul arrested and tried** (21:27–26:32). When Paul appears in the temple in Jerusalem, he is given a hostile reception. Jews from Asia stir up the whole city against him, and Roman soldiers rescue him just in the nick of time.

28 What is all the uproar about? Who is this Paul? What is his crime? The puzzled military commander wants to know the answers. Because of his Roman citizenship, Paul escapes the whip-

ping rack and is brought before the Sanhedrin. Ah, a divided court of Pharisees and Sadducees! Paul therefore raises the question of the resurrection, setting them one against another. As the dissension becomes violent, the Roman soldiers have to snatch Paul from the midst of the Sanhedrin before he is pulled to pieces. He is sent secretly by night to Governor Felix in Caesarea with heavy soldier escort.

29 Charged with sedition by his accusers, Paul ably defends himself before Felix. But Felix holds out in hopes of getting bribe money for Paul's release. Two years pass. Porcius Festus succeeds Felix as governor, and a new trial is ordered. Again, serious charges are made, and again Paul declares his innocence. But Festus, to gain favor with the Jews, suggests a further trial before him in Jerusalem. Paul therefore declares: "I appeal to Caesar!" (25:11) More time passes. Finally, King Herod Agrippa II pays a courtesy visit to Festus, and Paul is again brought into the judgment hall. So forceful and convincing is his testimony that Agrippa is moved to say to him: "In a short time you would persuade me to become a Christian." (26:28) Agrippa likewise recognizes Paul's innocence and that he could be released if he had not appealed to Caesar.

30 **Paul goes to Rome** (27:1–28:31).* The prisoner Paul and others are taken on a boat for the first stage of the journey to Rome. The winds being contrary, progress is slow. At the port of Myra, they change ships. On reaching Fair Havens, in Crete, Paul recommends wintering there, but the majority advise setting sail. They have hardly put to sea when a tempestuous wind seizes them and drives them along unmercifully. After two weeks their vessel is finally pounded to pieces on a shoal off the coast of Malta. True to Paul's previous assurance, not one of the 276 aboard loses his life! The inhabitants of Malta show extraordinary human kindness, and during that winter, Paul cures many of them by the miraculous power of God's spirit.

31 The next spring Paul reaches Rome, and the brothers come out on the roadway to meet him. The sight of them causes Paul to 'thank God and take courage.' Though still a prisoner, Paul is permitted to stay in his own hired house with a soldier guard. Luke ends his account, describing Paul's kindly receiving all those who came in to

---

* *Insight on the Scriptures,* Vol. 2, page 750.

---

26. (a) What miracle does Paul perform at Troas? (b) What counsel does he give the overseers from Ephesus?
27. What reception does Paul receive at the temple?
28. (a) What question does Paul raise before the Sanhedrin, and with what result? (b) Where is he then sent?

29. Charged with sedition, what series of trials or hearings does Paul have, and what appeal does he make?
30. What experiences attend Paul's voyage as far as Malta?
31. How is Paul greeted on arrival at Rome, and in what does he busy himself there?

him and "preaching the kingdom of God to them and teaching the things concerning the Lord Jesus Christ with the greatest freeness of speech, without hindrance."—28:15, 31.

WHY BENEFICIAL

[32] The book of Acts adds testimony to that of the Gospel accounts in confirming the authenticity and inspiration of the Hebrew Scriptures. As Pentecost approached, Peter cited the fulfillment of two prophecies that "the holy spirit spoke beforehand by David's mouth about Judas." (Acts 1: 16, 20; Ps. 69:25; 109:8) Peter also told the astonished Pentecost crowd that they were actually witnessing fulfillment of prophecy: "This is what was said through the prophet Joel."—Acts 2: 16-21; Joel 2:28-32; compare also Acts 2:25-28, 34, 35 with Psalm 16:8-11 and 110:1.

[33] To convince another crowd outside the temple, Peter again called upon the Hebrew Scriptures, first quoting Moses and then saying: "And all the prophets, in fact, from Samuel on and those in succession, just as many as have spoken, have also plainly declared these days." Later, before the Sanhedrin, Peter quoted Psalm 118:22 in showing that Christ, the stone that they rejected, had become "the head of the corner." (Acts 3:22-24; 4:11) Philip explained to the Ethiopian eunuch how the prophecy of Isaiah 53:7, 8 had been fulfilled, and on being enlightened, this one humbly requested baptism. (Acts 8:28-35) Likewise, speaking to Cornelius concerning Jesus, Peter testified: "To him all the prophets bear witness." (10:43) When the matter of circumcision was being debated, James backed up his decision by saying: "With this the words of the Prophets agree, just as it is written." (15:15-18) The apostle Paul relied on the same authorities. (26:22; 28:23, 25-27) The evident ready acceptance by the disciples and their hearers of the Hebrew Scriptures as part of God's Word sets the seal of inspired approval on those writings.

[34] Acts is most beneficial in showing how the Christian congregation was founded and how it grew under power of holy spirit. Throughout this dramatic account, we observe God's blessings of expansion, the boldness and joy of the early Christians, their uncompromising stand in the face of persecution, and their willingness to serve, as exemplified in Paul's answering the calls to enter foreign service and to go into Macedonia. (4: 13, 31; 15:3; 5:28, 29; 8:4; 13:2-4; 16:9, 10) The

Christian congregation today is no different, for it is bound together in love, unity, and common interest as it speaks "the magnificent things of God" under guidance of holy spirit.—2:11, 17, 45; 4:34, 35; 11:27-30; 12:25.

[35] The book of Acts shows just how the Christian activity of proclaiming God's Kingdom should be carried out. Paul himself was an example, saying: "I did not hold back from telling you any of the things that were profitable nor from teaching you publicly and from house to house." Then he goes on to say: "I *thoroughly* bore witness." This theme of 'thorough witnessing' strikes our attention throughout the book, and it comes impressively to the fore in the closing paragraphs, where Paul's wholehearted devotion to his preaching and teaching, even under prison bonds, is borne out in the words: "And he explained the matter to them by bearing thorough witness concerning the kingdom of God and by using persuasion with them concerning Jesus from both the law of Moses and the Prophets, from morning till evening." May we ever be as singlehearted in our Kingdom activity! —20:20, 21; 28:23; 2:40; 5:42; 26:22.

[36] Paul's discourse to the overseers from Ephesus contains much practical counsel for overseers today. Since these have been appointed by holy spirit, it is most important that they 'pay attention to themselves and to all the flock,' shepherding them tenderly and guarding them against oppressive wolves that seek their destruction. No light responsibility this! Overseers have need to keep awake and build themselves up on the word of God's undeserved kindness. As they labor to assist those who are weak, they "must bear in mind the words of the Lord Jesus, when he himself said, 'There is more happiness in giving than there is in receiving.'"—20:17-35.

[37] The other discourses of Paul also sparkle with clear exposition of Bible principles. For example, there is the classic argumentation of his talk to the Stoics and Epicureans on the Areopagus. First he quotes the altar inscription, "To an Unknown God," and uses this as his reason for explaining that the one true God, the Lord of heaven and earth, who made out of one man every nation of men, "is not far off from each one of us." Then he quotes the words of their poets, "For we are also his progeny," in showing how ridiculous it is to suppose that they sprang from lifeless idols of gold, silver, or stone. Thus Paul tactfully estab-

---

32. Before and at Pentecost, how did Peter testify to the authenticity of the Hebrew Scriptures?
33. How did Peter, Philip, James, and Paul all show the Hebrew Scriptures to be inspired?
34. What does Acts reveal concerning the Christian congregation, and is this any different today?

35. How does Acts show how the witness was to be given, and what quality in the ministry is emphasized?
36. What practical counsel by Paul applies forcefully to overseers today?
37. By what tactful argumentation did Paul get across his point on the Areopagus?

lishes the sovereignty of the living God. It is only in his concluding words that he raises the issue of the resurrection, and even then he does not mention Christ by name. He got across his point of the supreme sovereignty of the one true God, and some became believers as a result.—17:22-34.

[38] The book of Acts encourages continuous, diligent study of "all Scripture." When Paul first preached in Beroea, the Jews there, because "they received the word with the greatest eagerness of mind, carefully examining the Scriptures daily as to whether these things were so," were commended as being "noble-minded." (17:11) Today, as then, this eager searching of the Scriptures in association with Jehovah's spirit-filled congregation will result in the blessings of conviction and strong faith. It is by such study that one may come to a clear appreciation of the divine principles. A fine statement of some of these principles is recorded at Acts 15:29. Here the governing body of apostles and older brothers in Jerusalem made known that while circumcision was not a requirement for spiritual Israel, there were definite prohibitions on idolatry, blood, and fornication.

[39] Those early disciples really studied the inspired Scriptures and could quote and apply them as needed. They were strengthened through accurate knowledge and by God's spirit to meet fierce persecutions. Peter and John set the pattern for all faithful Christians when they boldly told the opposing rulers: "Whether it is righteous in the sight of God to listen to you rather than to God, judge for yourselves. But as for us, we cannot stop speaking about the things we have seen and heard." And

---

38. What blessings will result from the kind of study encouraged in Acts?
39. (a) How were the disciples strengthened to meet persecutions? (b) What bold testimony did they give? Was it effective?

when brought again before the Sanhedrin, which had "positively ordered" them not to keep teaching on the basis of Jesus' name, they said unequivocally: "We must obey God as ruler rather than men." This fearless testimony resulted in a fine witness to the rulers, and it led the famous Law teacher Gamaliel to make his well-known statement in favor of freedom of worship, which led to the apostles' release.—4:19, 20; 5:28, 29, 34, 35, 38, 39.

[40] Jehovah's glorious purpose concerning his Kingdom, which runs like a golden thread throughout the entire Bible, stands out very prominently in the book of Acts. At the outset Jesus is shown during the 40 days prior to his ascension "telling the things about the kingdom of God." It was in answer to the disciples' question about the restoration of the Kingdom that Jesus told them that they must first be his witnesses to the most distant part of the earth. (1:3, 6, 8) Starting in Jerusalem, the disciples preached the Kingdom with unflinching boldness. Persecutions brought the stoning of Stephen and scattered many of the disciples into new territories. (7:59, 60) It is recorded that Philip declared "the good news of the kingdom of God" with much success in Samaria and that Paul and his associates proclaimed "the kingdom" in Asia, Corinth, Ephesus, and Rome. All these early Christians set sterling examples of unswerving reliance on Jehovah and his sustaining spirit. (8:5, 12; 14:5-7, 21, 22; 18:1, 4; 19:1, 8; 20:25; 28:30, 31) Viewing their indomitable zeal and courage and noting how abundantly Jehovah blessed their efforts, we also have wonderful incentive to be faithful in "bearing thorough witness concerning the kingdom of God."—28:23.

---

40. What incentive does Acts give us to bear thorough witness to the Kingdom?

Bible Book Number 45

Romans

Writer: **Paul**	
Place Written: **Corinth**	
Writing Completed: **c. 56 C.E.**	

I N Acts we watched Paul, formerly a violent persecutor of Jewish Christians, become Christ's zealous apostle to the non-Jewish nations. With Romans we begin the 14 books of the

---

1. What does Paul discuss in his letter to the Romans?

Bible that the holy spirit inspired this former Pharisee, now a faithful servant of God, to write. By the time he wrote Romans, Paul had already completed two long preaching tours and was well along on the third. He had written five other inspired letters: First and Second Thessalonians,

Galatians, and First and Second Corinthians. Yet it seems appropriate that in our modern Bibles, Romans precedes the others, since it discusses at length the new equality between Jews and non-Jews, the two classes to whom Paul preached. It explains a turning point in God's dealings with his people and shows that the inspired Hebrew Scriptures had long foretold that the good news would be proclaimed also to the non-Jews.

[2] Paul, using Tertius as secretary, laces rapid argument and an astounding number of Hebrew Scripture quotations into one of the most forceful books of the Christian Greek Scriptures. With remarkable beauty of language, he discusses the problems that arose when first-century Christian congregations were composed of both Jews and Greeks. Did Jews have priority because of being Abraham's descendants? Did mature Christians, exercising their liberty from the Mosaic Law, have the right to stumble weaker Jewish brothers who still held to ancient customs? In this letter Paul firmly established that Jews and non-Jews are equal before God and that men are declared righteous, not through the Mosaic Law, but through faith in Jesus Christ and by God's undeserved kindness. At the same time, God requires Christians to show proper subjection to the various authorities under which they find themselves.

[3] How did the Roman congregation get started? There had been a sizable Jewish community in Rome at least since the time of Pompey's capturing Jerusalem in 63 B.C.E. At Acts 2:10 it is specifically stated that some of those Jews were in Jerusalem at Pentecost 33 C.E., where they heard the good news preached. The converted sojourners stayed in Jerusalem to learn from the apostles, and later the ones from Rome no doubt returned there, some probably at the time when persecution broke out in Jerusalem. (Acts 2:41-47; 8:1, 4) Further, the people of that day were great travelers, and this may explain Paul's intimate acquaintance with so many members of the Roman congregation, some of whom may have heard the good news in Greece or Asia as a result of Paul's preaching.

[4] The first reliable information about this congregation is found in Paul's letter. It is clear from this that the congregation was made up of both Jewish and non-Jewish Christians and that their

zeal was praiseworthy. He tells them: "Your faith is talked about throughout the whole world," and, "Your obedience has come to the notice of all." (Rom. 1:8; 16:19) Suetonius, writing in the second century, reports that during the rule of Claudius (41-54 C.E.), the Jews were banished from Rome. They later returned, however, as is shown by the presence of Aquila and Priscilla in Rome. They were Jews whom Paul met in Corinth and who had left Rome at the time of Claudius' decree but who were back in Rome at the time Paul wrote to the congregation there.—Acts 18:2; Rom. 16:3.

[5] The letter's authenticity is firmly established. It is, as its introduction says, from "Paul, a slave of Jesus Christ and called to be an apostle, . . . to all those who are in Rome as God's beloved ones, called to be holy ones." (Rom. 1:1, 7) Its outside documentation is among the earliest to be found for the Christian Greek Scriptures. Peter uses so many similar expressions in his first letter, written probably six to eight years later, that many scholars think he must have already seen a copy of Romans. Romans was clearly regarded as a part of Paul's writings and was cited as such by Clement of Rome, Polycarp of Smyrna, and Ignatius of Antioch, all of whom lived in the late first and early second centuries C.E.

[6] The book of Romans is found, together with eight others of Paul's letters, in a codex called Chester Beatty Papyrus No. 2 (P^{46}). Regarding this early codex, Sir Frederic Kenyon wrote: "Here, then, we have a nearly complete manuscript of the Pauline Epistles, written apparently about the beginning of the third century."* The Chester Beatty Greek Biblical papyri are older than the well-known Sinaitic Manuscript and Vatican Manuscript No. 1209, both of the fourth century C.E. These too contain the book of Romans.

[7] When and from where was Romans written? There is no disagreement among Bible commentators that this letter was written from Greece, most probably from Corinth, when Paul visited there for some months toward the end of his third missionary journey. The internal evidence points to Corinth. Paul wrote the letter from the home of Gaius, who was a member of the congregation there, and recommends Phoebe of the nearby congregation of Cenchreae, Corinth's seaport. Appar-

---

* *Our Bible and the Ancient Manuscripts,* 1958, page 188.

---

2. (a) What problems does Paul discuss in Romans? (b) What is firmly established by this letter?

3. How did the congregation in Rome get started, and what may account for Paul's knowing so many there?

4. (a) What information does Romans provide concerning the congregation in that city? (b) What is indicated by the presence of Aquila and Priscilla in Rome?

5. What facts establish the authenticity of Romans?

6. How does an ancient papyrus testify to the canonicity of Romans?

7. What evidence is there as to place and time of writing of Romans?

ently it was Phoebe who carried this letter to Rome. (Rom. 16:1, 23; 1 Cor. 1:14) At Romans 15:23 Paul wrote: "I no longer have untouched territory in these regions," and he indicates in the following verse that he intends to extend his missionary work west, toward Spain. He could well write this way toward the end of his third tour, at the beginning of 56 C.E.

CONTENTS OF ROMANS

⁸ **God's impartiality toward Jew and Gentile** (1:1–2:29). What does the inspired Paul tell the Romans? In his opening words, he identifies himself as an apostle chosen by Christ to teach 'obedience by faith' among the nations. He expresses his fervent desire to visit the holy ones in Rome, to enjoy "an interchange of encouragement" with them, and to declare among them the good news that is "God's power for salvation to everyone having faith." As had long ago been written, the righteous one will live "by means of faith." (1:5, 12, 16, 17) Both Jews and Greeks, he shows, merit God's wrath. Man's ungodliness is inexcusable because God's "invisible qualities are clearly seen from the world's creation onward." (1:20) Yet, the nations foolishly make gods of created things. However, the Jews should not judge the nations harshly, since they also are guilty of sins. Both classes will be judged according to their deeds, for God is not partial. Fleshly circumcision is not the determining factor; "he is a Jew who is one on the inside, and his circumcision is that of the heart." —2:29.

⁹ **By faith all are declared righteous** (3:1–4: 25). "What, then, is the superiority of the Jew?" It is great, for the Jews were entrusted with God's sacred pronouncements. Yet, "Jews as well as Greeks are all under sin," and no one is "righteous" in God's sight. Seven quotations are made from the Hebrew Scriptures to prove this point. (Rom. 3:1, 9-18; Ps. 14:1-3; 5:9; 140:3; 10:7; Prov. 1:16; Isa. 59:7, 8; Ps. 36:1) The Law shows up man's sinfulness, so "by works of law no flesh will be declared righteous." However, through God's undeserved kindness and the release by ransom, both Jews and Greeks are being declared righteous "by faith apart from works of law." (Rom. 3: 20, 28) Paul supports this argument by citing the example of Abraham, who was counted righteous, not because of works or circumcision, but because of his exemplary faith. Thus Abraham became the

father not only of the Jews but of "all those having faith."—4:11.

¹⁰ **No longer slaves to sin but to righteousness through Christ** (5:1–6:23). Through the one man, Adam, sin entered into the world, and sin brought death, "and thus death spread to all men because they had all sinned." (5:12) Death ruled as king from Adam down to Moses. When the Law was given through Moses, sin abounded, and death continued to reign. But God's undeserved kindness now abounds even more, and through Christ's obedience many are declared righteous for everlasting life. Yet this is no license for living in sin. Persons baptized into Christ must be dead to sin. Their old personality is impaled, and they live with reference to God. Sin no longer rules over them, but they become slaves to righteousness, with holiness in view. "The wages sin pays is death, but the gift God gives is everlasting life by Christ Jesus our Lord."—6:23.

¹¹ **Dead to the Law, alive by spirit in union with Christ** (7:1–8:39). Paul uses the example of a wife, who is bound to her husband as long as he lives but who is free to marry another if he dies, to show how through Christ's sacrifice Christian Jews were made dead to the Law and were free to become Christ's and bear fruit to God. The holy Law made sin more evident, and sin brought death. Sin, dwelling in our fleshly bodies, wars against our good intentions. As Paul says: "For the good that I wish I do not do, but the bad that I do not wish is what I practice." Thus, "the one working it out is no longer I, but the sin dwelling in me."—7:19, 20.

¹² What can save man from this miserable state? God can make those who belong to Christ alive through His spirit! They are adopted as sons, are declared righteous, become heirs of God and joint heirs with Christ, and are glorified. To them Paul says: "If God is for us, who will be against us? Who will separate us from the love of the Christ?" No one! Triumphantly he declares: "We are coming off completely victorious through him that loved us. For I am convinced that neither death nor life nor angels nor governments nor things now here nor things to come nor powers nor height nor depth nor any other creation will be able to separate us from God's love that is in Christ Jesus our Lord."—8:31, 35, 37-39.

---

8. (a) What does Paul say about his mission? (b) How does he show that both Jews and Greeks merit God's wrath?

9. (a) In what are the Jews superior, and yet what scriptures does Paul quote to show that all are under sin? (b) How, then, will a man be declared righteous, and what example supports this argument?

10. (a) How did death come to rule as king? (b) What has resulted through Christ's obedience, but what warning is sounded with regard to sin?

11. (a) How does Paul illustrate the release of Christian Jews from the Law? (b) What did the Law make evident, and so what things are at war in the Christian?

12. How do some become joint heirs with Christ, and in what are these completely victorious?

[13] **"Israel" saved through faith and by God's mercy** (9:1–10:21). Paul expresses "great grief" for his fellow Israelites, but he recognizes that not all fleshly Israel is really "Israel," since God has the authority to choose as sons whomever he wishes. As is shown by God's dealings with Pharaoh and by the illustration of the potter, "it depends, not upon the one wishing nor upon the one running, but upon God, who has mercy." (9:2, 6, 16) He calls sons "not only from among Jews but also from among nations," as Hosea long before foretold. (Hos. 2:23) Israel fell short because of seeking to gain God's favor, "not by faith, but as by works," and because of stumbling over Christ, the "rock-mass of offense." (Rom. 9:24, 32, 33) They had "a zeal for God" but not "according to accurate knowledge." Christ is the end of the Law for those exercising faith for righteousness, and to gain salvation one must publicly declare "that Jesus is Lord" and exercise faith "that God raised him up from the dead." (10:2, 9) Preachers are sent forth to enable people of all nations to hear, to have faith, and to call upon the name of Jehovah in order to be saved.

[14] **Illustration of the olive tree** (11:1-36). Because of undeserved kindness, a remnant of natural Israel has been chosen, but because the majority stumbled, "there is salvation to people of the nations." (11:11) Using the illustration of an olive tree, Paul shows how, because of the lack of faith of fleshly Israel, non-Jews were grafted in. Nevertheless, non-Jews should not rejoice over the rejection of Israel, since if God did not spare the unfaithful natural branches, neither will he spare the wild olive branches grafted in from among the nations.

[15] **Making over the mind; the superior authorities** (12:1–13:14). Present your bodies as living sacrifices to God, Paul counsels. No longer be "fashioned after this system of things," but be "transformed by making your mind over." Do not be haughty. The body of Christ, like a human body, has many members, which have different functions, but they work together in unity. Return evil for evil to no one. Leave vengeance to Jehovah. Conquer "the evil with the good."—12:2, 21.

[16] Be in subjection to superior authorities; it is the arrangement of God. Keep doing good and do not be owing anyone a single thing except to love one another. Salvation approaches, so "put off the works belonging to darkness" and "put on the weapons of the light." (13:12) Walk in good behavior, not according to the desires of the flesh.

[17] **Welcome all impartially without judging** (14:1–15:33). Put up with those who, because their faith is weak, abstain from certain foods or observe feast days. Neither judge your brother nor stumble him by your own eating and drinking, since God judges everyone. Pursue peace and upbuilding things, and bear the weaknesses of others.

[18] The apostle writes: "All the things that were written aforetime were written for our instruction," and he gives four more Hebrew Scripture quotations as final proof that the inspired prophets had long before foretold that God's promises would extend to the non-Jewish nations. (Rom. 15:4, 9-12; Ps. 18:49; Deut. 32:43; Ps. 117:1; Isa. 11:1, 10) "Therefore," Paul admonishes, "welcome one another, just as the Christ also welcomed us, with glory to God in view." (Rom. 15:7) Paul expresses appreciation for the undeserved kindness given to him by God to be a public servant to the nations, "engaging in the holy work of the good news of God." He is always seeking to open up new territories instead of "building on another man's foundation." And he is not yet finished, for he plans, after taking contributions to Jerusalem, an even greater preaching tour to distant Spain and, on his way there, to bring "a full measure of blessing from Christ" to his spiritual brothers in Rome.—15:16, 20, 29.

[19] **Concluding salutations** (16:1-27). Paul sends personal greetings to 26 members of the Roman congregation by name, as well as to others, and exhorts them to avoid persons who cause divisions and to "be wise as to what is good, but innocent as to what is evil." All is for God's glory "through Jesus Christ forever. Amen."—16:19, 27.

WHY BENEFICIAL

[20] The book of Romans presents a logical basis for belief in God, stating that "his invisible qualities are clearly seen from the world's creation onward, because they are perceived by the things

---

13. (a) According to prophecy, who are included in the real Israel of God, and this is according to what divine principle? (b) Why did fleshly Israel fall short, but what is necessary for salvation?
14. What does Paul illustrate by the olive tree?
15. What is involved in presenting living sacrifices to God?
16. How must Christians walk before authorities and others?

17. What is counseled concerning judging and building up the weak?
18. (a) What further quotations does Paul make in showing God's acceptance of the non-Jews? (b) How does Paul himself take advantage of God's undeserved kindness?
19. What salutations and exhortation conclude the letter?
20. (a) What logical reason does Romans give for belief in God? (b) How are God's righteousness and mercy illustrated, and what does this lead Paul to exclaim?

made, even his eternal power and Godship." But more than this, it goes on to exalt his righteousness and to make known his great mercy and undeserved kindness. This is beautifully brought to our attention through the illustration of the olive tree, in which the wild branches are grafted in when the natural branches are lopped off. In contemplation of this severity and kindness of God, Paul exclaims: "O the depth of God's riches and wisdom and knowledge! How unsearchable his judgments are and past tracing out his ways are!"—1:20; 11:33.

²¹ It is in this connection that the book of Romans explains the further development of God's sacred secret. In the Christian congregation, there is no longer a distinction between Jew and Gentile, but persons of all nations may share in Jehovah's undeserved kindness through Jesus Christ. "There is no partiality with God." "He is a Jew who is one on the inside, and his circumcision is that of the heart by spirit, and not by a written code." "There is no distinction between Jew and Greek, for there is the same Lord over all, who is rich to all those calling upon him." For all of these it is faith, and not works, that is counted to them as righteousness.—2:11, 29; 10:12; 3:28.

²² The practical counsel contained in this letter to the Christians in Rome is equally beneficial to Christians today, who have to meet similar problems in an alien world. The Christian is exhorted to "be peaceable with all men," including those outside the congregation. Every soul must "be in subjection to the superior authorities," for these constitute an arrangement of God and are an object of fear, not to the law-abiding, but to those who do bad deeds. Christians are to be in law-abiding subjection not only on account of the fear of punishment but on account of Christian conscience, therefore paying their taxes, rendering their dues, meeting their obligations, owing no one anything, "except to love one another." Love fulfills the Law.—12:17-21; 13:1-10.

²³ Paul emphasizes the matter of public testimony. While it is with the heart that one exercises faith for righteousness, it is with the mouth that one makes public declaration for salvation. "Everyone who calls on the name of Jehovah will be saved." But in order for this to take place, it is necessary for preachers to go forth and "declare

good news of good things." Happy is our portion if we are among these preachers whose sound has now gone out "to the extremities of the inhabited earth"! (10:13, 15, 18) And in preparation for this preaching work, may we try to become as familiar with the inspired Scriptures as was Paul, for in this one passage (10:11-21) he makes quotation upon quotation from the Hebrew Scriptures. (Isa. 28:16; Joel 2:32; Isa. 52:7; 53:1; Ps. 19:4; Deut. 32:21; Isa. 65:1, 2) He could well say: "All the things that were written aforetime were written for our instruction, that through our endurance and through the comfort from the Scriptures we might have hope."—Rom. 15:4.

²⁴ Wonderfully practical advice is given on relations within the Christian congregation. Whatever their previous national, racial, or social background, all must make over their minds to render God sacred service according to his "good and acceptable and perfect will." (11:17-22; 12:1, 2) What practical reasonableness breathes through all of Paul's counsel at Romans 12:3-16! Here indeed is excellent admonition for building zeal, humility, and tender affection among all in the Christian congregation. In the closing chapters, Paul gives strong admonition on watching and avoiding those who cause divisions, but he also speaks of the mutual joy and refreshment that come from clean associations in the congregation. —16:17-19; 15:7, 32.

²⁵ As Christians, we must continue to watch our relations with one another. "For the kingdom of God does not mean eating and drinking, but means righteousness and peace and joy with holy spirit." (14:17) This righteousness, peace, and joy is especially the portion of the "joint heirs with Christ," who are to be "glorified together" with him in the heavenly Kingdom. Note, too, how Romans points to a further step in the fulfillment of the Kingdom promise given in Eden, saying: "The God who gives peace will crush Satan under your feet shortly." (Rom. 8:17; 16:20; Gen. 3:15) Believing these great truths, may we continue to be filled with all joy and peace and abound in hope. Let our determination be to come off victorious with the Kingdom Seed, for we are convinced that nothing in heaven above or in earth below "nor any other creation will be able to separate us from God's love that is in Christ Jesus our Lord." —Rom. 8:39; 15:13.

---

21. How does Romans show the further development of God's sacred secret?
22. What practical counsel does Romans give concerning relations with those outside the congregation?
23. How does Paul emphasize the importance of public declaration, and what example does he give as to preparation for the ministry?

---

24. What advice does Paul give with a view to building zeal and happy relations within the congregation?
25. (a) What proper view and further understanding does Romans give concerning God's Kingdom? (b) In what ways should the study of Romans benefit us?

1 Corinthians

Writer: **Paul**

Place Written: **Ephesus**

Writing Completed: **c. 55 C.E.**

CORINTH was "a renowned and voluptuous city, where the vices of East and West met."* Situated on the narrow isthmus between the Peloponnesus and continental Greece, Corinth commanded the land route to the mainland. In the days of the apostle Paul, its population of about 400,000 was exceeded only by Rome, Alexandria, and Syrian Antioch. To the east of Corinth lay the Aegean Sea, and to the west, the Gulf of Corinth and the Ionian Sea. So Corinth, the capital of the province of Achaia, with its two ports of Cenchreae and Lechaeum, held a position of strategic importance commercially. It was also a center of Greek learning. "Its wealth," it has been said, "was so celebrated as to be proverbial; so were the vice and profligacy of its inhabitants."# Among its pagan religious practices was the worship of Aphrodite (counterpart of the Roman Venus). Sensuality was a product of Corinthian worship.

2 It was to this thriving but morally decadent metropolis of the Roman world that the apostle Paul traveled in about 50 C.E. During his stay of 18 months, a Christian congregation was established there. (Acts 18:1-11) What love Paul felt toward these believers to whom he had first carried the good news about Christ! By letter he reminded them of the spiritual bond that existed, saying: "Though you may have ten thousand tutors in Christ, you certainly do not have many fathers; for in Christ Jesus I have become your father through the good news."—1 Cor. 4:15.

3 Deep concern for their spiritual welfare moved Paul to write his first letter to the Corinthian Christians while in the course of his third missionary tour. A few years had passed since he had resided in Corinth. It was now about 55 C.E., and Paul was in Ephesus. Apparently he had received a letter from the relatively new congrega-

tion in Corinth, and it required a reply. Furthermore, disturbing reports had reached Paul. (7:1; 1:11; 5:1; 11:18) So distressing were these that the apostle did not even refer to their letter of inquiry until the opening verse of chapter 7 of his letter. Especially because of the reports he had received did Paul feel compelled to write to his fellow Christians in Corinth.

4 But how do we know Paul wrote First Corinthians from Ephesus? For one thing, in concluding the letter with greetings, the apostle includes those of Aquila and Prisca (Priscilla). (16:19) Acts 18:18, 19 shows that they had transferred from Corinth to Ephesus. Since Aquila and Priscilla were residing there and Paul included them in the closing greetings of First Corinthians, he must have been in Ephesus when he wrote the letter. A point that leaves no uncertainty, however, is Paul's statement at 1 Corinthians 16:8: "But I am *remaining* in Ephesus until the festival of Pentecost." So First Corinthians was written by Paul at Ephesus, apparently near the end of his stay there.

5 The authenticity of First Corinthians, and also of Second Corinthians, is unquestionable. These letters were ascribed to Paul and accepted as canonical by the early Christians, who included them in their collections. In fact, it is said that First Corinthians is alluded to and quoted at least six times in a letter from Rome to Corinth dated about 95 C.E. and called First Clement. With apparent reference to First Corinthians, the writer urged the recipients of this letter to "take up the epistle of the blessed Paul the apostle."* First Corinthians is also directly quoted by Justin Martyr, Athenagoras, Irenaeus, and Tertullian. There is strong evidence that a corpus, or collection, of Paul's letters, including First and Second Corinthians, "was formed and published in the last decade of the first century."#

---

* *Halley's Bible Handbook,* 1988, H. H. Halley, page 593.
\# Smith's *Dictionary of the Bible,* 1863, Vol. 1, page 353.

1. What kind of city was Corinth in the days of Paul?
2. How was the Corinthian congregation established, and hence what bond did it have with Paul?
3. What moved Paul to write his first letter to the Corinthians?

---

* *The Interpreter's Bible,* Vol. 10, 1953, page 13.
\# *The Interpreter's Bible,* Vol. 9, 1954, page 356.

4. What proves that Paul wrote First Corinthians from Ephesus?
5. What establishes the authenticity of the letters to the Corinthians?

⁶ Paul's first letter to the Corinthians gives us an opportunity to look inside the Corinthian congregation itself. These Christians had problems to face, and they had questions to be resolved. There were factions within the congregation, for some were following men. A shocking case of sexual immorality had arisen. Some were living in religiously divided households. Should they remain with their unbelieving mates or separate? And what of eating meat sacrificed to idols? Should they partake of it? The Corinthians needed advice regarding the conducting of their meetings, including the celebration of the Lord's Evening Meal. What should be the position of women in the congregation? Then, too, there were those in their midst who denied the resurrection. Problems were many. Particularly, though, was the apostle interested in bringing about a spiritual restoration of the Corinthians.

⁷ Because conditions inside the congregation and the environment outside in ancient Corinth, with its prosperity and licentiousness, have modern parallels, Paul's sterling counsel penned under divine inspiration commands our attention. What Paul said is so full of meaning for our own day that thoughtful consideration of his first letter to his beloved Corinthian brothers and sisters will prove beneficial indeed. Recall now the spirit of the time and place. Think searchingly, as the Corinthian Christians must have done, while we review the penetrating, stirring, inspired words of Paul to his fellow believers in Corinth of old.

CONTENTS OF FIRST CORINTHIANS

⁸ **Paul exposes sectarianism, exhorts unity** (1:1–4:21). Paul has good wishes for the Corinthians. But what of the factions, the dissensions, among them? "The Christ exists divided." (1:13) The apostle is thankful that he has baptized so few of them, so they cannot say they have been baptized in his name. Paul preaches Christ impaled. This is a cause of stumbling to the Jews and foolishness to the nations. But God chose the foolish and weak things of the world to put to shame the wise and strong. So Paul does not use extravagant speech but lets the brothers see the spirit and power of God through his words, that their faith may not be in men's wisdom but in God's power. We speak the things revealed by God's spirit, says Paul, "for the spirit searches into all things, even the deep things of God." These cannot be understood by the physical man but only by the spiritual man.—2:10.

⁹ They are following men—some Apollos, some Paul. But who are these? Only ministers through whom the Corinthians became believers. The ones planting and watering are not anything, for "God kept making it grow," and they are his "fellow workers." The test of fire will prove whose works are durable. Paul tells them, "You people are God's temple," in whom His spirit dwells. "The wisdom of this world is foolishness with God." Hence, let no one boast in men, for indeed all things belong to God.—3:6, 9, 16, 19.

¹⁰ Paul and Apollos are humble stewards of God's sacred secrets, and stewards should be found faithful. Who are the brothers at Corinth to boast, and what do they have that they did not receive? Have they become rich, begun ruling as kings, and become so discreet and strong, while the apostles, who have become a theatrical spectacle to both angels and to men, are yet foolish and weak, the offscouring of all things? Paul is sending Timothy to help them remember his methods in connection with Christ and become his imitators. If Jehovah wills, Paul himself will come shortly and get to know, not just the speech of those who are puffed up, but their power.

¹¹ **On keeping the congregation clean** (5:1–6:20). A shocking case of immorality has been reported among the Corinthians! A man has taken his father's wife. He must be handed over to Satan because a little leaven ferments the whole lump. They must quit mixing in company with anyone called a brother who is wicked.

¹² Why, the Corinthians have even been taking one another to court! Would it not be better to let themselves be defrauded? Since they are going to judge the world and angels, can they not find someone among them to judge between brothers? More than that, they should be clean, for fornicators, idolaters, and the like will not inherit God's Kingdom. That is what some of them were, but they have been washed clean and sanctified. "Flee from fornication," says Paul. "For you were bought with a price. By all means, glorify God in the body of you people."—6:18, 20.

¹³ **Counsel on singleness and marriage** (7:1-40). Paul answers a question about marriage. Because of the prevalence of fornication, it may be advisable for a man or a woman to be married, and

---

6. What problems existed in the Corinthian congregation, and in what was Paul especially interested?
7. With what attitude of mind should we consider First Corinthians, and why?
8. (a) How does Paul expose the folly of sectarianism in the congregation? (b) What does Paul show is necessary in order to understand the things of God?

---

9. By what argument does Paul show that no one should boast in men?
10. Why is the boasting of the Corinthians out of place, and what steps is Paul taking to remedy the situation?
11. What immorality has arisen among them, what must be done about it, and why?
12. (a) What does Paul argue about taking one another to court? (b) Why does Paul say, "Flee from fornication"?
13. (a) Why does Paul counsel some to marry? But once married, what should they do? (b) How does the single person "do better"?

those who are married should not be depriving each other of conjugal dues. It is well for the unmarried and the widows to remain single, like Paul; but if they do not have self-control, let them marry. Once they marry, they should remain together. Even if one's mate is an unbeliever, the believer should not depart, for in that way the believer may save the unbelieving mate. As to circumcision and slavery, let each one be content to remain in the state in which he was called. With regard to the married person, he is divided because he wants to gain the approval of his mate, whereas the single person is anxious only for the things of the Lord. Those who marry do not sin, but those who do not marry "do better."—7:38.

¹⁴ Doing all things for the sake of the good news (8:1–9:27). What about food offered to idols? An idol is nothing! There are many "gods" and "lords" in the world, but for the Christian there is only "one God the Father" and "one Lord, Jesus Christ." (8:5, 6) Yet someone may be offended if he observes you eating meat sacrificed to an idol. Under these circumstances, Paul advises, refrain from it so as not to cause your brother to stumble.

¹⁵ Paul denies himself many things for the sake of the ministry. As an apostle, he has a right "to live by means of the good news," but he has refrained from doing so. However, necessity is laid upon him to preach; in fact, he says, "Woe is me if I did not declare the good news!" So he has made himself a slave to all, becoming "all things to people of all sorts" that he "might by all means save some," doing all things "for the sake of the good news." To win the contest and the incorruptible crown, he browbeats his body so that after preaching to others, he himself "should not become disapproved somehow."—9:14, 16, 19, 22, 23, 27.

¹⁶ Warning against injurious things (10:1–33). What of the "forefathers"? These were under the cloud and were baptized into Moses. Most of them did not gain God's approval but were laid low in the wilderness. Why? They desired injurious things. Christians should take warning from this and refrain from idolatry and fornication, from putting Jehovah to the test, and from murmuring. The one who thinks he is standing should be careful that he does not fall. Temptation will come, but God will not let his servants be tempted beyond what they can bear; he will provide a way out so they can endure it. "Therefore,"

writes Paul, "flee from idolatry." (10:1, 14) We cannot be partakers of the table of Jehovah and the table of demons. However, should you be eating in a home, do not inquire regarding the source of the meat. If someone advises you that it has been sacrificed to idols, though, refrain from eating on account of that one's conscience. "Do all things for God's glory," writes Paul.—10:31.

¹⁷ Headship; the Lord's Evening Meal (11:1–34). "Become imitators of me, even as I am of Christ," Paul declares, and then he proceeds to set out the divine principle of headship: The head of the woman is the man, the head of the man is Christ, the head of Christ is God. Therefore, the woman should have "a sign of authority" upon her head when she prays or prophesies in the congregation. Paul cannot commend the Corinthians, for divisions exist among them when they meet together. In this condition, how can they properly partake of the Lord's Evening Meal? He reviews what occurred when Jesus instituted the Memorial of his death. Each must scrutinize himself before partaking, lest he bring judgment against himself for failure to discern "the body."—11:1, 10, 29.

¹⁸ Spiritual gifts; love and its pursuit (12:1–14:40). There are varieties of spiritual gifts, yet the same spirit; varieties of ministries and operations, yet the same Lord and the same God. Likewise there are many members in the one united body of Christ, each member needing the other, as in the human body. God has set every member in the body as He pleases, and each has his work to do, so "there should be no division in the body." (12:25) Users of spiritual gifts are nothing without love. Love is long-suffering and kind, not jealous, not puffed up. It rejoices only with the truth. "Love never fails." (13:8) Spiritual gifts, such as prophesying and tongues, will be done away with, but faith, hope, and love remain. Of these, the greatest is love.

¹⁹ "Pursue love," Paul admonishes. Spiritual gifts are to be used in love for the upbuilding of the congregation. For this reason, prophesying is to be preferred over speaking in tongues. He would rather speak five words with understanding to teach others than ten thousand in an unknown language. Tongues are for a sign to unbelievers, but prophesying is for the believers. They should not be "young children" in their under-

---

14. What does Paul say about "gods" and "lords," yet when is it wise to refrain from food offered to idols?
15. How does Paul conduct himself in the ministry?
16. (a) What warning should Christians take from the "forefathers"? (b) As to idolatry, how may Christians do all things for God's glory?

---

17. (a) What principle does Paul set out concerning headship? (b) How does he tie in the question of division in the congregation with a discussion of the Lord's Evening Meal?
18. (a) While there are varieties of gifts and ministries, why should there be no division in the body? (b) Why is love preeminent?
19. What counsel does Paul give for building up the congregation and for the orderly arrangement of things?

standing of these matters. As for women, they should be in subjection in the congregation. "Let all things take place decently and by arrangement."—14:1, 20, 40.

²⁰ **The certainty of the resurrection hope** (15: 1–16:24). The resurrected Christ appeared to Cephas, to the 12, to upward of 500 brothers at one time, to James, to all the apostles, and last of all to Paul. 'If Christ has not been raised up,' writes Paul, 'our preaching and faith are in vain.' (15:14) Each one is raised in his own order, Christ the firstfruits, then afterward those who belong to him during his presence. Finally he hands over the Kingdom to his Father after all enemies have been put under his feet. Even death, the last enemy, is to be brought to nothing. Of what use is it for Paul to face perils of death continually if there is no resurrection?

²¹ But how are the dead to be raised? In order for the body of a plant to develop, the sown grain must die. It is similar with the resurrection of the dead. "It is sown a physical body, it is raised up a spiritual body. . . . Flesh and blood cannot inherit God's kingdom." (15:44, 50) Paul tells a sacred secret: Not all will fall asleep in death, but during the last trumpet, they will be changed in the twinkling of an eye. When this that is mortal puts on immortality, death will be swallowed up forever. "Death, where is your victory? Death, where is your sting?" From the heart Paul exclaims: "But thanks to God, for he gives us the victory through our Lord Jesus Christ!"—15:55, 57.

²² In conclusion Paul counsels on orderliness in collecting the contributions for sending to Jerusalem to aid needy brothers. He tells of his coming visit via Macedonia and indicates that Timothy and Apollos may also visit. "Stay awake," Paul exhorts. "Stand firm in the faith, carry on as men, grow mighty. Let all your affairs take place with love." (16:13, 14) Paul sends greetings from the congregations in Asia, and then he writes a final greeting in his own hand, conveying his love.

WHY BENEFICIAL

²³ This letter of the apostle Paul is most beneficial in enlarging our understanding of the Hebrew Scriptures, from which it makes many quotations.

In the tenth chapter, Paul points out that the Israelites under Moses drank from a spiritual rock-mass, which meant the Christ. (1 Cor. 10:4; Num. 20:11) Then he goes on to refer to the disastrous consequences of desiring injurious things, as exemplified by the Israelites under Moses, and adds: "Now these things went on befalling them as examples, and they were written for a warning to us upon whom the ends of the systems of things have arrived." Never let us become self-reliant, thinking that we cannot fall! (1 Cor. 10: 11, 12; Num. 14:2; 21:5; 25:9) Again, he draws an illustration from the Law. He refers to the communion sacrifices in Israel to show how partakers of the Lord's Evening Meal should partake worthily of the table of Jehovah. Then, to back up his argument that it is proper to eat everything sold in the meat market, he quotes from Psalm 24:1, saying, "To Jehovah belong the earth and that which fills it."—1 Cor. 10:18, 21, 26; Ex. 32:6; Lev. 7:11-15.

²⁴ In showing the superiority of "the things that God has prepared for those who love him" and the futility of "the reasonings of the wise men" of this world, Paul again draws on the Hebrew Scriptures. (1 Cor. 2:9; 3:20; Isa. 64:4; Ps. 94:11) As authority for his instructions in chapter 5 on disfellowshipping the wrongdoer, he quotes Jehovah's law to 'clear what is bad from your midst.' (Deut. 17:7) In discussing his right to live by the ministry, Paul again refers to the Law of Moses, which said that working animals must not be muzzled to prevent their eating and that the Levites in temple service were to receive their portion from the altar.—1 Cor. 9:8-14; Deut. 25:4; 18:1.

²⁵ What benefits of inspired instruction we have received from Paul's first letter to Corinthian Christians! Meditate upon the counsel given against divisions and following men. (Chapters 1-4) Recall the case of immorality and how Paul emphasized the need for virtue and cleanliness within the congregation. (Chapters 5, 6) Consider his inspired advice relative to singleness, marriage, and separation. (Chapter 7) Think of the apostle's discussion of foods offered to idols as well as of how the necessity of guarding against stumbling others and falling into idolatry was so forcefully brought to the fore. (Chapters 8-10) Admonition concerning proper subjection, a consideration of spiritual gifts, that most practical discussion on the excellence of the enduring, unfailing quality of love—these things too have passed in review.

---

20. (a) What evidence does Paul give as to Christ's resurrection? (b) What is the order of the resurrection, and what enemies are to be put down?
21. (a) How are those who are to inherit God's Kingdom raised? (b) What sacred secret does Paul reveal, and what does he say about victory over death?
22. What closing counsel and exhortation does Paul give?
23. (a) How does Paul illustrate the disastrous consequences of wrong desire and self-reliance? (b) To what authority does Paul refer in counseling on the Lord's Evening Meal and proper foods?

24. What other references does Paul make to the Hebrew Scriptures in support of his arguments?
25. What are some of the outstanding points of beneficial instruction contained in First Corinthians?

And how well the apostle accentuated the need for orderliness in Christian meetings! (Chapters 11-14) What a marvelous defense of the resurrection he penned under inspiration! (Chapter 15) All of this and more has moved before the mind's eye —and it is so valuable to Christians in our day!

[26] This letter adds notably to our understanding of the glorious Bible theme of the Kingdom of God. It gives a stern warning that unrighteous persons will not enter the Kingdom, and it lists many of the vices that would disqualify a person. (1 Cor. 6: 9, 10) But most important, it explains the relation between the resurrection and God's Kingdom. It shows that Christ, "the firstfruits" of the resurrec-

tion, must "rule as king until God has put all enemies under his feet." Then, when he has put down all enemies, including death, "he hands over the kingdom to his God and Father, . . . that God may be all things to everyone." Finally, in fulfillment of the Kingdom promise made in Eden, the complete bruising of the Serpent's head is accomplished by Christ, along with His resurrected spiritual brothers. Grand, indeed, is the resurrection prospect of those who are to share incorruptibility with Christ Jesus in the heavenly Kingdom. It is on the basis of the resurrection hope that Paul admonishes: "Consequently, my beloved brothers, become steadfast, unmovable, always having plenty to do in the work of the Lord, knowing that your labor is not in vain in connection with the Lord."—1 Cor. 15:20-28, 58; Gen. 3:15; Rom. 16:20.

---

26. (a) What long-foretold work does the resurrected Christ accomplish when he rules as King? (b) On the basis of the resurrection hope, what powerful encouragement does Paul give?

<table>
<tr><td>Bible Book Number 47</td><td>Writer: Paul</td></tr>
<tr><td></td><td>Place Written: Macedonia</td></tr>
<tr><td># 2 Corinthians</td><td>Writing Completed: c. 55 C.E.</td></tr>
</table>

IT WAS now probably late summer or early fall of 55 C.E. There were still some matters in the Christian congregation at Corinth that were causing concern to the apostle Paul. Not many months had passed since the writing of his first letter to the Corinthians. Since then Titus had been dispatched to Corinth to assist in the collection being undertaken there for the holy ones in Judea and possibly also to observe the reaction of the Corinthians to the first letter. (2 Cor. 8:1-6; 2:13) How had they taken it? What comfort it brought Paul to know that it had moved them to sorrow and repentance! Titus had returned to Paul in Macedonia with this good report, and now the apostle's heart was filled to overflowing with love for his beloved Corinthian fellow believers.—7: 5-7; 6:11.

[2] So Paul wrote again to the Corinthians. This heartwarming and forceful second letter was written from Macedonia and was delivered apparently by Titus. (9:2, 4; 8:16-18, 22-24) One of the matters of concern that moved Paul to write was the presence among the Corinthians of "superfine

apostles," whom he also described as "false apostles, deceitful workers." (11:5, 13, 14) The spiritual welfare of the comparatively young congregation was in jeopardy, and Paul's authority as an apostle was under attack. His second letter to Corinth thus filled a great need.

[3] It may be noted that Paul said: "This is the third time I am ready to come to you." (2 Cor. 12:14; 13:1) He had planned to visit them a second time when he wrote his first letter, but though he got ready, this "second occasion for joy" did not materialize. (1 Cor. 16:5; 2 Cor. 1:15) Actually, then, Paul had been there only once before, for 18 months in 50-52 C.E., when the Christian congregation was founded in Corinth. (Acts 18:1-18) However, Paul later realized the fulfillment of his wish to visit Corinth once more. While in Greece for three months, probably in 56 C.E., he spent at least part of the time in Corinth, and it was from there that he wrote his letter to the Romans. —Rom. 16:1, 23; 1 Cor. 1:14.

[4] Second Corinthians has always been reckoned along with First Corinthians and the other Pauline epistles as an authentic part of the Bible canon.

1, 2. (a) What led to Paul's writing his second letter to the Corinthians? (b) From where did Paul write, and about what was he concerned?

3, 4. (a) What visits did Paul himself make to Corinth? (b) How does Second Corinthians benefit us now?

Again we are enabled to look inside the congregation at Corinth and derive benefit from Paul's inspired words given to admonish them as well as us.

CONTENTS OF SECOND CORINTHIANS

[5] **Help from "the God of all comfort"** (1:1–2:11). Paul includes Timothy in the opening salutation. "Blessed," says Paul, is "the Father of tender mercies and the God of all comfort, who comforts us in all our tribulation," that we, in turn, may be able to comfort others. Though Paul and his companions have been under extreme pressure and their lives were in danger, God has rescued them. The Corinthians can help, too, with prayers on their behalf. It is with confidence in his sincerity and in God's undeserved kindness that he is writing to them. God's promises have become "Yes" by means of Jesus, and He has anointed those who belong to Christ and given them "the token of what is to come, that is, the spirit" in their hearts. —1:3, 4, 20, 22.

[6] It appears that the man who was the object of Paul's comments in the fifth chapter of his first letter was ousted from the congregation. He has repented and is showing sorrow. Paul therefore tells the Corinthians to extend genuine forgiveness and to confirm their love for the penitent one.

[7] **Qualified as ministers of the new covenant** (2:12–6:10). Paul presents himself and the Corinthian Christians as being in a triumphal procession with Christ. (The Corinthians were familiar with the odor of sweet incense that was burned along the route of the processions of victorious armies in that day.) There is a strong contrast between the "odor" of the Christian to those who will gain life and the "odor" to those who are perishing. "We are not peddlers of the word of God," affirms Paul.—2:16, 17.

[8] Paul and his fellow workers need no documents, written letters of recommendation, to or from the Corinthians. The Corinthian believers themselves are letters of recommendation, written "by us as ministers" and inscribed, not on tablets of stone, but "on fleshly tablets, on hearts," declares Paul. God has adequately qualified the ministers of the new covenant. The written code was an administration of death, with fading glory, and it was temporary. The administration of the spirit, however, leads to life, is lasting, and is of abounding glory. When "Moses is read," a veil rests upon the hearts of the sons of Israel, but when there is a turning to Jehovah, the veil is removed, and they are "transformed into the same image from glory to glory."—3:3, 15, 18.

[9] Then Paul continues: 'We have this ministry due to the mercy that was shown to us. We have renounced underhanded things and have not adulterated God's word, but we have recommended ourselves by making the truth manifest. If the message of good news is veiled, it is because the god of this world has blinded the minds of unbelievers. Our hearts, however, are illuminated with the glorious knowledge of God by the face of Christ. How great this treasure that we have! It is in earthen vessels so that the power beyond what is normal may be God's. Under persecution and stress, yes, in the face of death itself, we exercise faith and do not give up, for the momentary tribulation works out for us a glory that is of more and more surpassing weight and is everlasting. So we keep our eyes on the things unseen.'—4:1-18.

[10] 'We know,' writes Paul, 'that our earthly house will give way to an everlasting one in the heavens. In the meantime we press on in faith and are of good courage. Though absent from Christ, we seek to be acceptable to him.' (5:1, 7-9) Those in union with Christ are "a new creation" and have a ministry of reconciliation. They are "ambassadors substituting for Christ." (5:17, 20) In every way Paul recommends himself as a minister of God. How? 'By the endurance of much in the way of tribulations, beatings, labors, sleepless nights; by purity, by knowledge, by long-suffering, by kindness, by holy spirit, by love free from hypocrisy, by truthful speech, by God's power, as poor but making many rich, as having nothing and yet possessing all things.'—6:4-10.

[11] **"Perfecting holiness in God's fear"** (6:11–7:16). Paul tells the Corinthians: 'Our heart has widened out to receive you.' They too should widen out their tender affections. But now comes a warning! "Do not become unevenly yoked with unbelievers." (6:11, 14) What fellowship does light have with darkness, or Christ with Belial? As a temple of a living God, they must separate themselves and quit touching the unclean thing. Says Paul: "Let us cleanse ourselves of every defilement of flesh and spirit, perfecting holiness in God's fear."—7:1.

---

5. (a) What does Paul write concerning comfort? (b) What has come about through Christ that is of further assurance?
6. What does Paul counsel should be done for the disfellowshipped wrongdoer who is now repentant?
7. How does Paul present himself and the Corinthians, and what does he affirm?
8. (a) What credentials did Paul and his fellow workers have as ministers? (b) How is the ministry of the new covenant superior?

---

9. How does Paul describe the treasure of the ministry?
10. (a) What does Paul say of those in union with Christ? (b) How does Paul recommend himself as a minister of God?
11. What counsel and warning does Paul give?

[12] Paul states further: "I am filled with comfort, I am overflowing with joy in all our affliction." (7:4) Why? Not only because of the presence of Titus but also because of the good report from Corinth, that of their longing, their mourning, and their zeal for Paul. He realizes that his first letter caused temporary sadness, but he rejoices that the Corinthians were saddened for repentance to salvation. He commends them for cooperating with Titus.

[13] **Generosity will be rewarded** (8:1–9:15). In connection with contributions for the needy "holy ones," Paul cites the example of the Macedonians, whose generosity despite deep poverty was really beyond their ability; and he now hopes to see the same kind of giving on the part of the Corinthians as a demonstration of the genuineness of their love for the Lord Jesus Christ, who became poor that they might be rich. This giving according to what they have will result in an equalizing, so that the one with much will not have too much, and the one with little, not too little. Titus and others are being sent to them in connection with this kind gift. Paul has been boasting about the generosity and readiness of the Corinthians, and he does not want them put to shame by any failure to complete the bountiful gift. Yes, "he that sows bountifully will also reap bountifully." Let it be from the heart, for "God loves a cheerful giver." He is also able to make his undeserved kindness abound toward them and to enrich them for every sort of generosity. "Thanks be to God for his indescribable free gift."—9:1, 6, 7, 15.

[14] **Paul argues his apostleship** (10:1–13:14). Paul acknowledges that he is lowly in appearance. But Christians do not war according to the flesh; their weapons are spiritual, "powerful by God" for overturning reasonings contrary to the knowledge of God. (10:4) Some, seeing things just at their face value, say that the apostle's letters are weighty but his speech contemptible. Let them know that Paul's actions will be just the same as his word by letter. The Corinthians should realize that Paul is not boasting about accomplishments in someone else's territory. He has personally carried the good news to them. Furthermore, if there is to be any boasting, let it be in Jehovah.

[15] Paul feels his responsibility to present the Corinthian congregation to the Christ as a chaste virgin. Just as Eve was seduced by the Serpent's cunning, so there is danger that their minds may be corrupted. With force, therefore, Paul speaks out against the "superfine apostles" of the Corinthian congregation. (11:5) They are false apostles. Satan himself keeps transforming himself into an angel of light, so it is no wonder that his ministers do the same. But as to being ministers of Christ, how do they compare with Paul's record? He has endured much: imprisonment, beatings, shipwreck three times, many dangers, going often without sleep or food. Yet through it all he never lost sight of the needs of the congregations and always felt incensed when someone was stumbled.

[16] So if anyone has reason to boast, it is Paul. Could the other so-called apostles at Corinth tell about being caught away into paradise, to hear unutterable things? Yet Paul speaks about his weaknesses. That he might not feel overly exalted, he was given "a thorn in the flesh." Paul entreated that it be removed but was told: "My undeserved kindness is sufficient for you." Paul would rather boast in his weaknesses, that "the power of the Christ" may remain over him like a tent. (12:7, 9) No, Paul has not proved inferior to the "superfine apostles," and the Corinthians have seen the proofs of apostleship that he produced among them "by all endurance, and by signs and portents and powerful works." He is not seeking their possessions, just as Titus and his other fellow workers whom he sent did not take advantage of them.—12:11, 12.

[17] All things are for their upbuilding. However, Paul expresses fear that when he arrives in Corinth, he will find some who have not repented of works of the flesh. He warns the sinners in advance that he will take appropriate action and spare none, and he advises all in the congregation to keep testing whether they are in the faith in union with Jesus Christ. Paul and Timothy will pray to God for them. He bids them rejoice and be restored to unity, in order that the God of love and peace will be with them, and concludes by sending greetings from the holy ones and his own best wishes for their spiritual blessing.

WHY BENEFICIAL

[18] How stimulating and encouraging is Paul's appreciation for the Christian ministry as expressed in Second Corinthians! Let us view it as he did. The Christian minister who has been adequately qualified by God is no peddler of the Word

---

12. Why did Paul rejoice at the report from Corinth?
13. (a) What examples of generosity does Paul cite? (b) What principles does Paul discuss in connection with giving?
14. What points does Paul make in support of his apostleship?
15. (a) With what illustrations does Paul speak out against the false apostles? (b) What is Paul's own record?

---

16. (a) Of what might Paul boast, but why would he rather speak of his weaknesses? (b) How has Paul produced proofs of his apostleship?
17. What final admonition does Paul give the Corinthians?
18. What right view should Christians take of the ministry?

but serves out of sincerity. What recommends him is, not some written document, but the fruitage he bears in the ministry. However, while the ministry is indeed glorious, this is no cause for his becoming puffed up. God's servants as imperfect humans have this treasure of service in frail earthen vessels, that the power may plainly be seen to be God's. So this calls for humility in accepting the glorious privilege of being God's ministers, and what an undeserved kindness from God it is to serve as "ambassadors substituting for Christ"! How appropriate, then, was Paul's exhortation "not to accept the undeserved kindness of God and miss its purpose"!—2:14-17; 3:1-5; 4:7; 5:18-20; 6:1.

[19] Paul certainly provided a splendid example for Christian ministers to copy. For one thing, he valued and studied the inspired Hebrew Scriptures, repeatedly quoting from, alluding to, and applying them. (2 Cor. 6:2, 16-18; 7:1; 8:15; 9:9; 13:1; Isa. 49:8; Lev. 26:12; Isa. 52:11; Ezek. 20:41; 2 Sam. 7:14; Hos. 1:10) Moreover, as an overseer, he displayed deep concern for the flock, saying: "For my part I will most gladly spend and be completely spent for your souls." He gave himself entirely in behalf of the brothers, as the record clearly shows. (2 Cor. 12:15; 6:3-10) He was untiring in his labors as he taught, exhorted, and set things straight in the Corinthian congregation. He warned plainly against fellowship with darkness, telling the Corinthians: "Do not become unevenly yoked with unbelievers." Because of his loving concern for them, he did not want to see their minds become corrupted, "as the serpent seduced Eve by its cunning," and so he heartily admonished them: "Keep testing whether you are in the faith, keep proving what you yourselves are." He stirred them to Christian generosity, showing them that "God loves a cheerful giver," and he himself expressed the most appreciative thanks to God for His indescribable free gift. Truly his brothers at Corinth were inscribed in love on the fleshly tablet of Paul's heart, and his unstinted service in their interests was everything that should mark a zealous, wide-awake overseer. What an outstanding model for us today!—6:14; 11:3; 13:5; 9:7, 15; 3:2.

[20] The apostle Paul sets our minds in the right direction in pointing to "the Father of tender mercies and the God of all comfort" as the real source of strength in time of trial. He it is that "comforts us in all our tribulation" in order that we may endure for salvation into his new world. Paul points also to the glorious hope of "a building from God, a house not made with hands, everlasting in the heavens," and says: "Consequently if anyone is in union with Christ, he is a new creation; the old things passed away, look! new things have come into existence." Second Corinthians does indeed contain wonderful words of assurance for those who, like Paul, will inherit the heavenly Kingdom. —1:3, 4; 5:1, 17.

---

19. In what various ways did Paul provide an outstanding model for Christian ministers today, especially for overseers?

20. (a) How does Paul set our minds in the right direction? (b) To what glorious hope does Second Corinthians point?

Bible Book Number 48

Galatians

Writer: **Paul**

Place Written: **Corinth or Syrian Antioch**

Writing Completed: **c. 50–52 C.E.**

THE congregations of Galatia addressed by Paul at Galatians 1:2 apparently included Pisidian Antioch, Iconium, Lystra, and Derbe—places in different districts but all within this Roman province. Acts chapters 13 and 14 tells of the first missionary journey of Paul with Barnabas through this area, which led to the organizing of the Galatian congregations. These were made up of a mixture of Jews and non-Jews, no doubt including Celts, or Gauls. This was shortly after Paul's visit to Jerusalem about 46 C.E.—Acts 12:25.

[2] In the year 49 C.E., Paul and Silas started out on Paul's second missionary tour into the Galatian territory, which resulted in 'the congregations

---

1. Which congregations are addressed in Galatians, and how and when were they organized?

2. (a) What resulted from Paul's second tour in Galatia, but what followed thereafter? (b) In the meantime, how did Paul proceed with his journey?

being made firm in the faith and increasing in number day by day.' (Acts 16:5; 15:40, 41; 16: 1, 2) However, hot on their heels came false teachers, Judaizers, who persuaded some in the Galatian congregations to believe that circumcision and observance of the Law of Moses were essential parts of true Christianity. In the meantime Paul had journeyed on past Mysia into Macedonia and Greece, eventually arriving in Corinth, where he spent more than 18 months with the brothers. Then, in 52 C.E., he departed by way of Ephesus for Syrian Antioch, his home base, arriving there in the same year.—Acts 16:8, 11, 12; 17:15; 18:1, 11, 18-22.

[3] Where and when did Paul write the letter to the Galatians? No doubt he wrote it as soon as word reached him concerning the activity of the Judaizers. This could have been in Corinth, Ephesus, or Syrian Antioch. It could well have been during his 18-month stay in Corinth, 50-52 C.E., as information would have had time to reach him there from Galatia. Ephesus is unlikely, as he stayed there only briefly on his return journey. However, he then "passed some time" at his home base of Syrian Antioch, apparently in the summer of 52 C.E., and since there was ready communication between this city and Asia Minor, it is possible that he received the report concerning the Judaizers and wrote his letter to the Galatians from Syrian Antioch at this time.—Acts 18:23.

[4] The letter describes Paul as "an apostle, neither from men nor through a man, but through Jesus Christ and God the Father." It also discloses many facts about Paul's life and apostleship, proving that, as an apostle, he worked in harmony with the apostles in Jerusalem and that he even exercised his authority in correcting another apostle, Peter.—Gal. 1:1, 13-24; 2:1-14.

[5] What facts argue for the authenticity and canonicity of Galatians? It is referred to by name in the writings of Irenaeus, Clement of Alexandria, Tertullian, and Origen. Moreover, it is included in the following important Bible manuscripts of rank: Sinaitic, Alexandrine, Vatican No. 1209, Codex Ephraemi Syri rescriptus, Codex Bezae, and Chester Beatty Papyrus No. 2 (P[46]). Moreover, it is entirely in harmony with the other Greek Scripture writings and also with the Hebrew Scriptures, to which it frequently refers.

[6] In Paul's powerful and hard-hitting letter "to the congregations of Galatia," he proves (1) that he is a true apostle (a fact that the Judaizers had sought to discredit) and (2) that justification is by faith in Christ Jesus, not by the works of the Law, and that therefore circumcision is unnecessary for Christians. Though it was Paul's custom to have a secretary write down his epistles, he himself wrote Galatians in 'large letters with his own hand.' (6:11) The contents of the book were of the greatest importance, both to Paul and to the Galatians. The book emphasizes appreciation for the freedom that true Christians have through Jesus Christ.

CONTENTS OF GALATIANS

[7] **Paul defends his apostleship** (1:1–2:14). After greeting the congregations in Galatia, Paul marvels that they are being so quickly removed to another sort of good news, and he firmly declares: "Even if we or an angel out of heaven were to declare to you as good news something beyond what we declared to you as good news, let him be accursed." The good news that he has declared is not something human, neither was he taught it, "except through revelation by Jesus Christ." Previously, as a zealous exponent of Judaism, Paul had persecuted the congregation of God, but then God called him through His undeserved kindness to declare the good news about his Son to the nations. It was not until three years after his conversion that he went up to Jerusalem, and then, of the apostles, he saw only Peter, as well as James the brother of the Lord. He was unknown in person to the congregations of Judea, though they used to hear of him and "began glorifying God" because of him.—1:8, 12, 24.

[8] After 14 years Paul went up to Jerusalem again and explained privately the good news that he was preaching. His companion Titus, though a Greek, was not even required to be circumcised. When James and Cephas and John saw that Paul had entrusted to him the good news for those who are uncircumcised, just as Peter had the good news for those who are circumcised, they gave Paul and Barnabas the right hand of sharing together to go to the nations, while they themselves went to the circumcised. When Cephas came to Antioch and failed to walk straight "according to the truth of the good news" for fear of the circumcised class, Paul rebuked him before them all. —2:14.

[9] **Declared righteous by faith, not by law** (2:15–3:29). We Jews know, argues Paul, "that a

---

3. From where and when may Galatians have been written?
4. What does Galatians disclose as to Paul's apostleship?
5. What facts argue for the authenticity and canonicity of Galatians?
6. (a) What two points does the letter of Galatians establish? (b) What was unusual about the writing of this letter, and what does it emphasize?

7, 8. (a) What does Paul argue concerning the good news? (b) How was Paul confirmed as apostle to the uncircumcised, and how did he demonstrate his authority in connection with Cephas?
9. On the basis of what is the Christian declared righteous?

man is declared righteous, not due to works of law, but only through faith toward Christ Jesus." He now lives in union with Christ and is alive by faith to do the will of God. "If righteousness is through law, Christ actually died for nothing." —2:16, 21.

[10] Are the Galatians so senseless as to believe that having started by receiving the spirit due to faith, they can finish serving God by works of Law? It is the hearing by faith that counts, as with Abraham, who "put faith in Jehovah, and it was counted to him as righteousness." Now, according to God's promise, "those who adhere to faith are being blessed together with faithful Abraham." They have been released from the curse of the Law by Christ's death on the stake. Christ is the Seed of Abraham, and the Law made 430 years later does not abolish the promise concerning that Seed. What, then, was the purpose of the Law? It was "our tutor leading to Christ, that we might be declared righteous due to faith." Now we are no longer under the tutor, nor is there now any distinction between Jew and Greek, for all are one in union with Christ Jesus and "are really Abraham's seed, heirs with reference to a promise." —3:6, 9, 24, 29.

[11] **Stand fast in Christian freedom** (4:1–6:18). God sent forth his Son to release those under Law, that they "might receive the adoption as sons." (4:5) So why turn back to the slavery of the weak and beggarly elementary things? Since the Galatians are now observing days and months and seasons and years, Paul is afraid his work in their behalf has been wasted. On his first visit to them, they received Paul like an angel of God. Has he now become their enemy because he tells them the truth? Let those who want to be under Law hear what the Law says: Abraham acquired two sons by two women. The one woman, the servant girl, Hagar, corresponds to the nation of fleshly Israel, bound to Jehovah by the Mosaic Law covenant, which covenant brings forth children for slavery. The free woman, though, Sarah, corresponds to the Jerusalem above, who, Paul says, "is free, and she is our mother." "What," asks Paul, "does the Scripture say?" This: "By no means shall the son of the servant girl be an heir with the son of the free woman." And we are children, not of a servant girl, "but of the free woman."—4:30, 31.

[12] Circumcision or lack of it means nothing, explains Paul, but it is faith operating through love that counts. The entire Law is fulfilled in the saying: "You must love your neighbor as yourself." Keep walking by the spirit, for "if you are being led by spirit, you are not under law." As to the works of the flesh, Paul forewarns "that those who practice such things will not inherit God's kingdom." In glowing contrast, he describes the fruitage of the spirit, against which there is no law, and adds: "If we are living by spirit, let us go on walking orderly also by spirit" and put away egotism and envy.—5:14, 18, 21, 25.

[13] If a man takes some false step before he is aware of it, those spiritually qualified must try to restore him "in a spirit of mildness." Christians fulfill the law of the Christ by carrying the burdens of one another, but each one should carry his own load in proving what his own work is. A person will reap according to what he sows, either corruption from the flesh or everlasting life from the spirit. Those who want the Galatians to be circumcised are only out to please men and avoid persecution. The thing of vital concern is, not circumcision or uncircumcision, but a new creation. Peace and mercy will be upon those who walk orderly according to this rule of conduct, even upon "the Israel of God."—6:1, 16.

WHY BENEFICIAL

[14] The letter to the Galatians reveals Paul as the devastating persecutor who became the alert apostle to the nations, always ready to contend in behalf of the interests of his brothers. (1:13-16, 23; 5:7-12) Paul showed by example that an overseer should move quickly to handle problems, quashing false reasonings by logic and Scripture.—1:6-9; 3:1-6.

[15] The letter was beneficial to the congregations in Galatia in clearly establishing their freedom in Christ and discrediting the perverters of the good news. It made plain that it is by faith that one is declared righteous and that circumcision is no longer necessary in order for one to gain salvation. (2:16; 3:8; 5:6) By setting aside such fleshly distinctions, it served to unify Jew and Gentile in the one congregation. The freedom from the Law was not to serve as an inducement for the desires of the flesh, for the principle still held: "You must love your neighbor as yourself." It continues to hold as a guidepost to Christians today.—5:14.

[16] Paul's letter helped the Galatians on many

---

10. What is it that counts for God's blessing, and so what was the purpose of the Law?
11. (a) What release are the Galatians ignoring? (b) How does Paul illustrate the Christian's freedom?
12. (a) By what must the Galatians now walk? (b) What important contrast does Paul make?

13. How is the law of the Christ fulfilled, and what is of vital concern?
14. What example does Paul set for overseers?
15. How was the letter beneficial to the Galatian congregations, and what guidepost does it provide for Christians today?
16. What faith-building explanations of the Hebrew Scriptures are to be found in Galatians?

points of doctrine, drawing on the Hebrew Scriptures for powerful illustrations. It gave the inspired interpretation of Isaiah 54:1-6, identifying Jehovah's woman as "the Jerusalem above." It explained the "symbolic drama" of Hagar and Sarah, showing that the heirs of God's promises are those made free by Christ and not those remaining in bondage to the Law. (Gal. 4:21-26; Gen. 16: 1-4, 15; 21:1-3, 8-13) It clearly explained that the Law covenant did not negate the Abrahamic covenant but was added to it. It also pointed out that the time interval between the making of the two covenants was 430 years, which is important in Bible chronology. (Gal. 3:17, 18, 23, 24) The record of these things has been preserved for building up Christian faith today.

¹⁷ Most important, Galatians unmistakably identifies the Kingdom Seed, to which all the prophets looked forward. "Now the promises were spoken to Abraham and to his seed . . . who is

Christ." Those who become sons of God through faith in Christ Jesus are shown to be adopted into this seed. "If you belong to Christ, you are really Abraham's seed, heirs with reference to a promise." (3:16, 29) The fine admonition given in Galatians should be heeded by these Kingdom heirs and those who labor with them: 'Stand fast in the freedom for which Christ has set you free!' 'Do not give up in doing what is fine, for in due season we shall reap if we do not tire out.' 'Work what is good, especially toward those related to us in the faith.'—5:1; 6:9, 10.

¹⁸ Finally, there is the powerful warning that those who practice the works of the flesh "will not inherit God's kingdom." Let all, then, turn completely from worldly filth and strife and set their hearts entirely upon bringing forth the fruitage of the spirit, which is "love, joy, peace, long-suffering, kindness, goodness, faith, mildness, self-control."—5:19-23.

17. (a) What important identification does Galatians make? (b) What fine admonition is given to the Kingdom heirs and their colaborers?

18. What final powerful warning and admonition are given in Galatians?

Bible Book Number 49

Ephesians

Writer: **Paul**

Place Written: **Rome**

Writing Completed: **c. 60–61 C.E.**

IMAGINE that you are in prison. You are there because of being persecuted for your zealous activity as a Christian missionary. Now that you can no longer travel and visit the congregations to strengthen them, what are you going to do? Can you not write letters to those who have become Christians through your preaching work? Are they not probably wondering how you are, and are they not perhaps in need of encouragement? Of course they are! So you begin to write. You are now doing exactly what the apostle Paul did when he was imprisoned in Rome the first time, about 59-61 C.E. He had appealed to Caesar, and although awaiting trial and under guard, he had freedom for some activity. Paul wrote his letter "To the Ephesians" from Rome, probably 60 or 61 C.E., and sent it by Tychicus, who was accompanied by Onesimus.—Eph. 6:21; Col. 4: 7-9.

² Paul identifies himself as the writer in the very first word and four times refers or alludes to himself as "the prisoner in the Lord." (Eph. 1:1; 3: 1, 13; 4:1; 6:20) Arguments against Paul's writership have come to nothing. The Chester Beatty Papyrus No. 2 (P⁴⁶), believed to be from about 200 C.E., has 86 leaves out of a codex containing Paul's epistles. Among them is the epistle to the Ephesians, thus showing that it was grouped among his letters at that time.

³ Early ecclesiastical writers confirm that Paul wrote the letter and that it was "To the Ephesians." For example, Irenaeus, of the second century C.E., quoted Ephesians 5:30 as follows: "As the blessed Paul says in the epistle to the Ephesians, that we are members of his body." Clement of Alexandria, of the same period, quoted Ephesians 5:21 in reporting: "Wherefore, also, in the epistle to the Ephesians he writes, Be subject

1. When and under what circumstances did Paul write the letter to the Ephesians?

2, 3. What conclusively proves Paul's writership and, at the same time, the canonicity of Ephesians?

one to another in the fear of God." Origen, writing in the first half of the third century C.E., quoted Ephesians 1:4 in saying: "But also the apostle in the epistle to the Ephesians, uses the same language when he says, Who chose us before the foundation of the world."* Eusebius, another authority on early Christian history (c. 260-342 C.E.), includes Ephesians in the Bible canon, and most other early ecclesiastical writers make references to Ephesians as part of the inspired Scriptures.#

⁴ The Chester Beatty Papyrus, the Vatican Manuscript No. 1209, and the Sinaitic Manuscript omit the words "in Ephesus" in chapter 1, verse 1, and thus do not indicate the destination of the letter. This fact, together with the absence of greetings to individuals in Ephesus (though Paul had labored there for three years), has led some to surmise that the letter may have been addressed elsewhere or at least that it may have been a circular letter to the congregations in Asia Minor, including Ephesus. However, most other manuscripts include the words "in Ephesus," and as we have noted above, the early ecclesiastical writers accepted it as a letter to the Ephesians.

⁵ Some background information will help us to understand the purpose of this letter. In the first century of the Common Era, Ephesus was noted for its sorcery, magic, astrology, and worship of the fertility goddess Artemis.△ Around the statue of the goddess, there had been erected a magnificent temple that was regarded as one of the seven wonders of the ancient world. According to excavations of the site in the 19th century, the temple was built on a platform that measured about 240 feet wide and 418 feet long. The temple itself was about 164 feet wide and 343 feet long. It contained 100 marble columns, each about 55 feet in height. The roof was covered with large white marble tiles. Gold is said to have been used instead of mortar between the joints of the marble blocks. The temple attracted tourists from all over the earth, and visitors numbering hundreds of thousands would throng into the city during festivals. The silversmiths of Ephesus carried on a lucrative business selling small silver shrines of Artemis to pilgrims as souvenirs.

⁶ Paul had stopped in Ephesus on his second

---

* *Origin and History of the Books of the Bible,* 1868, C. E. Stowe, page 357.
# *New Bible Dictionary,* second edition, 1986, edited by J. D. Douglas, page 175.
△ *Insight on the Scriptures,* Vol. 1, page 182.

---

4. What has led some to surmise that Ephesians was addressed elsewhere, but what evidence supports Ephesus as its destination?
5. What was noteworthy about the Ephesus of Paul's day?
6. What was the extent of Paul's activity in Ephesus?

missionary journey for a short visit of preaching and then left Aquila and Priscilla there to continue the work. (Acts 18:18-21) He returned on his third missionary journey and stayed for about three years, preaching and teaching "The Way" to many. (Acts 19:8-10; 20:31) Paul worked hard while in Ephesus. In his book *Daily Life in Bible Times,* A. E. Bailey writes: "Paul's general practice was to work at his trade from sunrise till 11 a.m. (Acts 20:34, 35) at which hour Tyrannus had finished his teaching; then from 11 a.m. to 4 p.m. to preach in the hall, hold conferences with helpers, . . . then lastly to make a house-to-house evangelistic canvass that lasted from 4 p.m. till far into the night. (Acts 20:20, 21, 31) One wonders when he found time to eat and sleep."—1943, page 308.

⁷ In the course of this zealous preaching, Paul exposed the use of images in worship. This stirred up the wrath of those making and selling them, such as the silversmith Demetrius, and in the uproar Paul finally had to leave the city.—Acts 19:23–20:1.

⁸ Now, while in prison, Paul is thinking of the problems faced by the Ephesian congregation, surrounded by pagan worshipers and in the shadow of the awe-inspiring temple of Artemis. These anointed Christians no doubt needed the fitting illustration Paul now gives them, showing that they constitute "a holy temple," in which Jehovah dwells by his spirit. (Eph. 2:21) "The sacred secret" being revealed to the Ephesians, concerning God's administration (his way of managing his household affairs) by which he would restore unity and peace through Jesus Christ, was unquestionably a great inspiration and comfort to them. (1:9, 10) Paul emphasizes the union of Jew and Gentile in Christ. He exhorts to oneness, to unity. Thus, we can now appreciate the purpose, value, and obvious inspiration of this book.

CONTENTS OF EPHESIANS

⁹ **God's purpose to bring about unity by means of Christ** (1:1–2:22). Paul the apostle sends greetings. God is to be blessed for his glorious undeserved kindness. This has to do with His choosing of them to be in union with Jesus Christ, by means of whom they have the release by ransom through his blood. Furthermore, God has made his love abound toward them by making known the sacred secret of his will. For he has purposed an administration, "to gather all things together again in the Christ," in union with whom they were also assigned as heirs. (1:10) As a token

---

7. What resulted from Paul's zealous preaching?
8. In what points was Paul's letter to the Ephesians most timely?
9. How has God made his love abound, and what is Paul's prayer?

of this in advance, they have been sealed by holy spirit. Paul's prayer is that they will be firmly convinced of the hope to which they have been called and realize that God will use the same power toward them that He did in resurrecting Christ and in placing him far above every government and authority and making him Head over all things to the congregation.

¹⁰ God, out of the richness of his mercy and his great love, has made them alive, though they were dead in their trespasses and sins, and has seated them together "in the heavenly places in union with Christ Jesus." (2:6) This is all due to undeserved kindness and faith and is not a result of any works of their own. Christ is their peace who has broken down the wall, the Law of commandments, that had fenced off Gentiles from Jews. Now both peoples have the approach to the Father through Christ. Therefore the Ephesians are no longer aliens, but they are "fellow citizens of the holy ones" and are growing into a holy temple for Jehovah to inhabit by spirit.—2:19.

¹¹ **"The sacred secret of the Christ"** (3:1-21). God has now revealed to his holy apostles and prophets "the sacred secret of the Christ . . . that people of the nations should be joint heirs and fellow members of the body and partakers with us of the promise in union with Christ Jesus through the good news." (3:4, 6) By God's undeserved kindness, Paul has become a minister of this, to declare the unfathomable riches of the Christ and make men see how the sacred secret is administered. It is through the congregation that the greatly diversified wisdom of God is made known. Because of this, Paul prays that they will be made mighty with power through God's spirit in order that they may fully know the love of Christ, which surpasses knowledge, and realize that God can "do more than superabundantly beyond all the things we ask or conceive."—3:20.

¹² **Putting on "the new personality"** (4:1–5:20). Christians should walk worthily of their calling, in lowliness of mind, in long-suffering and love, and in the uniting bond of peace. For there is but one spirit, one hope, one faith, and "one God and Father of all persons, who is over all and through all and in all." (4:6) Therefore Christ, the "one Lord," has given prophets, evangelizers, shepherds, and teachers, "with a view to the readjustment of the holy ones, for ministerial work, for the building up of the body of the Christ." So, writes Paul, "speaking the truth, let us by love

grow up in all things into him who is the head, Christ," as a body harmoniously joined together with every member cooperating. (4:5, 12, 15) The immoral, unprofitable, and ignorant ways of the old personality are to be put away; each person should be made new in the force actuating his mind and "put on the new personality which was created according to God's will in true righteousness and loyalty." Because all belong to one another, they are to speak the truth and put away wrath, stealing, rotten sayings, malicious bitterness—not grieving God's holy spirit. Instead, let them 'become kind to one another, tenderly compassionate, freely forgiving one another, just as God also by Christ freely forgave them.'—4: 24, 32.

¹³ All should become imitators of God. Fornication, uncleanness, and greediness should not even be mentioned among them, for those who practice such things have no inheritance in the Kingdom. Paul admonishes the Ephesians: "Go on walking as children of light." "Keep strict watch" on how you walk, buying out the opportune time, "because the days are wicked." Yes, they must "go on perceiving what the will of Jehovah is" and speak about the praises of God in a thankful way.—5:8, 15-17.

¹⁴ **Proper subjection; Christian warfare** (5:21–6:24). Wives should be in subjection to husbands, even as the congregation is in subjection to the Christ, and husbands should continue loving their wives, "just as the Christ also loved the congregation." Likewise, "the wife should have deep respect for her husband."—5:25, 33.

¹⁵ Children should live at unity with parents, in obedience and responding to godly discipline. Slaves and masters also should conduct themselves so as to be pleasing to God, for the Master of all "is in the heavens, and there is no partiality with him." Finally, let all "go on acquiring power in the Lord and in the mightiness of his strength," putting on the complete suit of armor from God so as to be able to stand firm against the Devil. "Above all things, take up the large shield of faith," also "the sword of the spirit, that is, God's word." Carry on prayer, and keep awake. Paul asks that they pray also for him, that he may with all freeness of speech "make known the sacred secret of the good news."—6:9, 10, 16, 17, 19.

WHY BENEFICIAL

¹⁶ The epistle to the Ephesians touches almost

---

10. How have the Ephesians become "fellow citizens of the holy ones"?
11. What is "the sacred secret," and for what does Paul pray in behalf of the Ephesians?
12. (a) How should Christians walk, and why? (b) What gifts has Christ given, and for what purpose? (c) What is involved in putting on "the new personality"?

13. To become an imitator of God, what must one do?
14. What are the mutual responsibilities of husbands and wives?
15. What does Paul counsel with regard to children and parents, slaves and masters, and the Christian's armor?
16. What questions find a practical answer in Ephesians, and what is said about the personality that is pleasing to God?

every aspect of the Christian's life. In view of the present-day upsurge of distressing problems and delinquency in the world, Paul's sound, practical advice is of real benefit to those who desire to live godly lives. How should children conduct themselves toward parents, and parents toward children? What are the responsibilities of a husband toward his wife, and of a wife toward her husband? What must the individuals in the congregation do in order to maintain unity in love and Christian purity in the midst of a wicked world? Paul's counsel covers all these questions, and he goes on to show what is involved in putting on the new Christian personality. Through the study of Ephesians, all will be able to gain real appreciation for the kind of personality that is pleasing to God and that is "created according to God's will in true righteousness and loyalty."—4:24-32; 6:1-4; 5:3-5, 15-20, 22-33.

¹⁷ The letter also shows the purpose of appointments and assignments in the congregation. This is "with a view to the readjustment of the holy ones, for ministerial work, for the building up of the body of the Christ," with maturity in view. By cooperating fully in these congregational arrangements, the Christian can "by love grow up in all things into him who is the head, Christ."—4:12, 15.

¹⁸ The letter to the Ephesians greatly benefited the early congregation in sharpening their understanding of "the sacred secret of the Christ." Here it was made plain that along with believing Jews, "people of the nations" were being called to be "joint heirs and fellow members of the body and partakers . . . of the promise in union with Christ Jesus through the good news." The wall of partition, "the Law of commandments," that had fenced off Gentile from Jew had been abolished, and now by the blood of the Christ, all had become fellow citizens of the holy ones and members of the household of God. In striking contrast to the pagan temple of Artemis, these were being built up together in union with Christ Jesus into a place for God to inhabit by spirit—"a holy temple for Jehovah."—3:4, 6; 2:15, 21.

¹⁹ With regard to "the sacred secret," Paul also spoke of "an administration . . . to gather all things together again in the Christ, the things in the heavens [those chosen to be in the heavenly Kingdom] and the things on the earth [those who would live on earth in the realm of the Kingdom]." Thus God's grand purpose to restore peace and unity is brought to the fore. In this connection Paul prayed in behalf of the Ephesians, the eyes of whose hearts had been enlightened, that they might fully grasp the hope to which God had called them and see "what the glorious riches are which he holds as an inheritance for the holy ones." These words must have greatly encouraged them in their hope. And the inspired letter to the Ephesians continues to be upbuilding to the congregation in this day, that 'in everything we may be filled with all the fullness that God gives.'—1:9-11, 18; 3:19.

17. What does Ephesians show as to cooperation with arrangements in the congregation?
18. What is made plain with regard to "the sacred secret" and a spiritual temple?
19. What hope and encouragement does Ephesians continue to hold forth to this day?

Bible Book Number 50
Philippians

Writer: **Paul**

Place Written: **Rome**

Writing Completed: **c. 60–61 C.E.**

WHEN the apostle Paul received the call in a vision to carry the good news into Macedonia, he and his companions, Luke, Silas, and young Timothy, were quick to obey. From Troas in Asia Minor, they traveled by ship to Neapolis and set out at once for Philippi, about 9.5 miles inland over a mountain pass. The city is described by Luke as "the principal city of the district of Macedonia." (Acts 16:12) It was named Philippi after the Macedonian king Philip II (father of Alexander the Great), who captured the city in 356 B.C.E. Later it was taken by the Romans. It was the site of decisive battles in 42 B.C.E. that helped to strengthen the position of Octavian, who later became Caesar Augustus. In commemoration of the victory, he made Philippi a Roman colony.

1. (a) How did the Philippians come to hear the good news? (b) What historical background is of interest about the city of Philippi?

² It was Paul's custom on arrival in a new city to preach first to the Jews. However, on his first arrival in Philippi about 50 C.E., he found these few in number and apparently without a synagogue, for they used to meet for prayer on a riverbank outside the town. Paul's preaching quickly bore fruit, one of the first converts being Lydia, a businesswoman and Jewish proselyte, who readily embraced the truth about the Christ and insisted that the travelers stay at her house. "She just made us come," writes Luke. Opposition was soon encountered, however, and Paul and Silas were beaten with rods and then imprisoned. While they were in the prison, an earthquake occurred, and the jailer and his family, listening to Paul and Silas, became believers. The next day Paul and Silas were released from prison, and they visited the brothers at the home of Lydia and encouraged them before leaving the city. Paul carried with him vivid memories of the tribulations surrounding the birth of the new congregation in Philippi.—Acts 16:9-40.

³ A few years later, during his third missionary tour, Paul was again able to visit the Philippian congregation. Then, about ten years after first establishing the congregation, a touching expression of the love of the brothers in Philippi moved Paul to write them the inspired letter that has been preserved in the Holy Scriptures under the name of that beloved congregation.

⁴ That Paul did write the letter, as stated in its first verse, is generally accepted by Bible commentators, and with good reason. Polycarp (69?-155? C.E.) in his own letter to the Philippians mentions that Paul had written to them. The letter is quoted as from Paul by such early Bible commentators as Ignatius, Irenaeus, Tertullian, and Clement of Alexandria. It is cited in the Muratorian Fragment of the second century C.E. and in all other early canons, and it appears side by side with eight other letters of Paul in the Chester Beatty Papyrus No. 2 (P⁴⁶), believed to be from about 200 C.E.

⁵ The place and date of writing can be established with reasonable certainty. At the time of writing, Paul was a prisoner in the custody of the Roman emperor's bodyguard, and there was a great deal of Christian activity going on around him. He closed his letter with greetings from the faithful ones in Caesar's household. These facts combine to point to Rome as the place from which the letter was sent.—Phil. 1:7, 13, 14; 4:22; Acts 28:30, 31.

⁶ But when was the letter written? It seems that Paul had already been in Rome long enough for the news of and reasons for his imprisonment as a Christian to have spread right through the emperor's Praetorian Guard and to many others. Also, there had been time for Epaphroditus to come from Philippi (some 600 miles distant) with a gift for Paul, for news of Epaphroditus' illness in Rome to get back to Philippi again, and for expressions of sorrow at this to come from Philippi to Rome. (Phil. 2:25-30; 4:18) Since Paul's first imprisonment in Rome took place about 59-61 C.E., he very likely wrote this letter about 60 or 61 C.E., a year or more after his first arrival in Rome.

⁷ The birth pangs experienced in begetting these children at Philippi through the word of truth, the Philippians' affection and generosity with gifts of needed things that followed Paul through many of his travels and hardships, and Jehovah's signal blessings of the initial missionary labors in Macedonia all combined to forge a strong bond of mutual love between Paul and the Philippian brothers. Now their kind gift, followed by their anxious inquiry about Epaphroditus and the progress of the good news in Rome, stirred Paul to write them a warm and affectionate letter of upbuilding encouragement.

CONTENTS OF PHILIPPIANS

⁸ **Defense and advancement of the good news** (1:1-30). Paul and Timothy send greetings, and Paul thanks God for the contribution the Philippians have made to the good news "from the first day until this moment." He is confident they will carry their good work to a completion, for they are sharers with him in the undeserved kindness, including "the defending and legally establishing of the good news." He yearns for all of them in tender affection and says: "This is what I continue praying, that your love may abound yet more and more . . . that you may make sure of the more important things." (1:5, 7, 9, 10) Paul wants them to know that his "affairs have turned out for the advancement of the good news," in that his prison bonds have become public knowledge and the brothers have been encouraged to speak the word of God fearlessly. While there is gain for Paul to

2. What progress did Paul make with his preaching in Philippi, and what events attended the birth of the congregation there?
3. What later contacts did Paul have with the Philippian congregation?
4. What identifies the writer of Philippians, and what proves the authenticity of the letter?
5. What points to Rome as the place of writing?

6. What evidence is there for the time of the writing of Philippians?
7. (a) What bond existed between Paul and the Philippians, and what stirred him to write? (b) What kind of letter is Philippians?
8. (a) How does Paul express his confidence in and affection for the Philippian brothers? (b) What does Paul say about his prison bonds, and what counsel does he give?

die now, yet he knows that for the sake of their advancement and joy, it is more necessary for him to remain. He counsels them to behave in a manner worthy of the good news, for whether he comes to them or not, he wants to hear that they are fighting on in unity and are 'in no respect being frightened by their opponents.'—1:12, 28.

⁹ **Keeping the same mental attitude as Christ** (2:1-30). Paul encourages the Philippians to lowliness of mind, 'keeping an eye, not in personal interest upon just their own matters, but also in personal interest upon those of the others.' They should be of the same mental attitude as Christ Jesus, who, though existing in God's form, emptied himself to become a man and humbled himself in obedience as far as death, so that God has exalted him and given him a name above every other name. Paul exhorts them: "Keep working out your own salvation with fear and trembling." "Keep doing all things free from murmurings and arguments," and keep "a tight grip on the word of life." (2:4, 12, 14, 16) He hopes to send Timothy to them and is confident that he himself will also come shortly. For the present, that they may rejoice again, he is sending them Epaphroditus, who has recovered from his sickness.

¹⁰ **"Pursuing down toward the goal"** (3:1–4: 23). 'We of the real circumcision,' says Paul, 'must look out for the dogs, for those who mutilate the flesh.' If anyone has grounds for confidence in the flesh, Paul has more so, and his record as a circumcised Jew and a Pharisee proves it. Yet all of this he has considered loss 'on account of the excelling value of the knowledge of Christ Jesus his Lord.' Through the righteousness that is by faith, he hopes to "attain to the earlier resurrection from the dead." (3:2, 3, 8, 11) Therefore, says Paul, "forgetting the things behind and stretching forward to the things ahead, I am pursuing down toward the goal for the prize of the upward call of God by means of Christ Jesus." Let as many as are mature have the same mental attitude. There are those whose god is their belly, who have their minds upon things on the earth, and whose end is destruction, but "as for us," Paul affirms, "our citizenship exists in the heavens."—3:13, 14, 20.

¹¹ 'Rejoice in the Lord,' Paul exhorts, 'and let your reasonableness become known to all men. Continue considering the things that are true and of serious concern, things that are righteous, chaste, lovable, well spoken of, virtuous, and praiseworthy. Practice what you learned and accepted and heard and saw in connection with me, and the God of peace will be with you.' (4:4-9) Paul rejoices greatly in the Philippians' generous thoughts toward him, though he has the strength for all things "by virtue of him who imparts power." He thanks them warmly for their gift. From the start of his declaring the good news in Macedonia, they have excelled in giving. In turn, God will fully supply all their "need to the extent of his riches in glory by means of Christ Jesus." (4: 13, 19) He sends greetings from all the holy ones, including those of the household of Caesar.

WHY BENEFICIAL

¹² How beneficial the book of Philippians is for us! We certainly desire Jehovah's approval and the same kind of commendation from our Christian overseers that the congregation at Philippi received from Paul. This can be ours if we follow the fine example of the Philippians and the loving counsel of Paul. Like the Philippians, we should manifest generosity, be concerned to aid our brothers when they are in difficulty, and share in the defending and legally establishing of the good news. (1:3-7) We should continue "standing firm in one spirit, with one soul striving side by side for the faith of the good news," shining as "illuminators" in among a crooked and twisted generation. As we do these things and continue considering the things of serious concern, we may become a joy to our brothers in the same way that the Philippians became a crowning joy to the apostle Paul.—1:27; 2:15; 4:1, 8.

¹³ "Unitedly become imitators of me," says Paul. Imitate him in what way? One way is to be self-sufficient under all circumstances. Whether Paul had an abundance or was in want, he learned to adjust himself uncomplainingly to the circumstances, so as to continue zealously and with rejoicing in God's ministry. All should be like Paul, too, in showing tender affection for faithful brothers. With what affectionate joy he spoke of the ministry of Timothy and Epaphroditus! And how close he felt to his Philippian brothers, whom he addressed as "beloved and longed for, my joy and crown"!—3:17; 4:1, 11, 12; 2:19-30.

¹⁴ How else may Paul be imitated? By "pursuing down toward the goal"! All who have set their minds on the 'things of serious concern' are vitally interested in Jehovah's marvelous arrangement in heaven and earth, wherein 'every tongue will

---

9. How may the Philippians keep Christ's mental attitude?
10. How has Paul pursued toward the goal, and what does he admonish for others?
11. (a) What are the things to be considered and practiced? (b) What expression does Paul make with regard to the Philippians' generosity?

---

12. How may we today, like the brothers at Philippi, gain God's approval and become a joy to our brothers?
13. In what ways may we unitedly imitate Paul?
14. What fine counsel does the letter to the Philippians give with regard to the goal of life and the Kingdom, and to whom especially is the letter addressed?

openly acknowledge that Jesus Christ is Lord to the glory of God the Father.' The fine counsel in Philippians encourages all who hope for eternal life in connection with God's Kingdom to pursue that goal. The letter to the Philippians, however, is addressed primarily to those whose "citizenship exists in the heavens" and who eagerly await being "conformed to [Christ's] glorious body." "Forgetting the things behind and stretching forward to the things ahead," let all of these imitate the apostle Paul in "pursuing down toward the goal for the prize of the upward call," their glorious inheritance in the Kingdom of the heavens! —4:8; 2:10, 11; 3:13, 14, 20, 21.

Bible Book Number 51

Colossians

Writer: Paul

Place Written: Rome

Writing Completed: c. 60–61 C.E.

LEAVING Ephesus behind them, two men traveled east through Asia Minor along the Maeander (Menderes) River. On reaching the tributary called Lycus, in the country of Phrygia, they swung southeast to follow the river up through the mountain-enclosed valley. Before them was a beautiful sight: fertile green pastures with large flocks of sheep. (Wool products were a principal source of income for the region.*) Proceeding up the valley, the travelers passed, on the right, the wealthy city of Laodicea, center of Roman administration for the district. To their left, across the river, they could see Hierapolis, famous for its temples and hot springs. There were Christian congregations in both these cities and also in the small town of Colossae, about ten miles farther up the valley.

2 Colossae was the destination of the travelers. They were both Christians. One of them, at least, knew the region well, as he was from Colossae. His name was Onesimus, and he was a slave returning to his master, who was a member of the congregation there. Onesimus' companion was Tychicus, a freeman, and both were envoys from the apostle Paul, carrying a letter from him addressed to the "faithful brothers in union with Christ at Colossae." As far as we know, Paul never visited Colossae. The congregation, which consisted mainly of non-Jews, was probably founded by Epaphras, who had labored among them and who was now with Paul in Rome.—Col. 1:2, 7; 4:12.

3 The apostle Paul was the writer of this letter, as he states in its opening and closing words. (1:1; 4:18) His conclusion states also that he wrote it from prison. This would be the time of his first imprisonment in Rome, 59-61 C.E., when he wrote a number of letters of encouragement, the letter to the Colossians being dispatched along with the one to Philemon. (Col. 4:7-9; Philem. 10, 23) It appears it was written about the same time as the letter to the Ephesians, as many ideas and phrases are the same.

4 There are no grounds for doubting the authenticity of the letter to the Colossians. Its presence with other Pauline epistles in the Chester Beatty Papyrus No. 2 (P[46]) of about 200 C.E. shows that it was accepted by the early Christians as one of Paul's letters. Its genuineness is testified to by the same early authorities who testify to the authenticity of Paul's other letters.

5 What prompted Paul to write a letter to the Colossians? For one thing, Onesimus was going back to Colossae. Epaphras had recently joined Paul, and no doubt his report on conditions at Colossae provided a further reason for the letter. (Col. 1:7, 8; 4:12) A certain danger threatened the Christian congregation there. The religions of the day were in the process of dissolution, and new religions were constantly being formed by fusing parts of old ones. There were heathen philosophies involving asceticism, spiritism, and idolatrous superstition, and these, combined with Jewish abstinence from foods and observance of days, may have influenced some in the congregation.

---

* *The New Westminster Dictionary of the Bible,* 1970, page 181.

---

1. Where was the town of Colossae located?
2. (a) Who were the two envoys sent by Paul to Colossae? (b) What is known concerning the Colossian congregation?

3. What does the letter of Colossians itself reveal regarding the writer, as well as the time and place of writing?
4. What testifies to the genuineness of Colossians?
5. (a) What prompted Paul's writing to the Colossians? (b) What does the letter emphasize?

Whatever the problem, it appears to have been sufficient reason for Epaphras to make the long journey to Rome to see Paul. However, that the congregation as a whole was not in immediate danger is indicated by Epaphras' encouraging report on their love and steadfastness. On hearing the report, Paul came strongly to the defense of accurate knowledge and clean worship by writing this letter to the Colossian congregation. It emphasized the God-given superiority of Christ in the face of heathen philosophy, worship of angels, and Jewish traditions.

CONTENTS OF COLOSSIANS

⁶ **Have faith in Christ, the head of the congregation** (1:1–2:12). After the opening greetings from Timothy and himself, Paul gives thanks for the Colossians' faith in Christ and for their love. They have learned of the undeserved kindness of God as a result of Epaphras' preaching the good news among them. Since hearing the report concerning them, Paul has not ceased praying that they may be filled with "the accurate knowledge of his will in all wisdom and spiritual comprehension, in order to walk worthily of Jehovah" and "to endure fully and be long-suffering with joy." (1: 9-11) The Father has delivered them into "the kingdom of the Son of his love," who is the image of the invisible God, and through whom and for whom all things have been created. He is the Head of the congregation and the firstborn from the dead. Through Jesus' blood, God saw good to reconcile all things again to himself, yes, including the once alienated Colossians, 'provided, of course, that they continue in the faith.'—1:13, 23.

⁷ Paul rejoices in filling up the sufferings of the Christ in behalf of the congregation, whose minister he became. This was in order to preach fully in their interest the word of God concerning 'the sacred secret, the glorious riches of which God has now been pleased to make known to his holy ones.' 'It is Christ we are publicizing,' says Paul, 'admonishing and teaching in all wisdom, that we may present every man complete in union with Christ.' —1:26-28.

⁸ Paul's struggle in behalf of the Colossians, the Laodiceans, and others is in order that they may be comforted and harmoniously joined together in love, with a view to their gaining 'an accurate knowledge of the sacred secret of God, namely, Christ, in whom are carefully concealed all the treasures of wisdom and of knowledge.' He does not want to see them deluded by persuasive arguments, but, rather, they should go on walking in

union with Christ, "rooted and being built up in him and being stabilized in the faith." Paul now sounds a warning. "Look out: perhaps there may be someone who will carry you off as his prey through the philosophy and empty deception according to the tradition of men."—2:2, 3, 7, 8.

⁹ **Become dead to works of the flesh but alive to Christ** (2:13–3:17). Though they were dead in their trespasses and uncircumcision, God has made them alive together with Christ, blotting out the handwritten document of the Law, which was against the Jews. "Therefore let no man judge" them with respect to the Law or its observances, which are but a shadow of the reality, Christ. Also, if they have died together with Christ toward the elementary things of the world, why do they subject themselves to the decrees: "Do not handle, nor taste, nor touch," according to the commands and teachings of men? A showy self-imposed form of worship, mock humility, severe treatment of the body—these are of no value in combating desires of the flesh.—2:16, 21.

¹⁰ Rather, Paul counsels: "Go on seeking the things above, where the Christ is seated at the right hand of God. Keep your minds fixed on the things above, not on the things upon the earth." This can be done by stripping off the old personality and putting on the new personality, which through accurate knowledge makes no fleshly distinction between Jew and Greek, for "Christ is all things and in all." It means becoming clothed "as God's chosen ones" with the tender affections of compassion, kindness, lowliness of mind, mildness, and long-suffering. Says the apostle: "As Jehovah freely forgave you, so do you also. But, besides all these things, clothe yourselves with love, for it is a perfect bond of union." In word or in work, everything should be done "in the name of the Lord Jesus, thanking God the Father through him."—3:1, 2, 11-14, 17.

¹¹ **Relationships with others** (3:18–4:18). As to family relationships, let wives be subject to husbands and let husbands love their wives, let children obey parents and let not fathers exasperate their children. Slaves are to be obedient to their masters in fear of Jehovah, and masters are to deal righteously with their slaves. Let all persevere in prayer and go on walking in wisdom toward those on the outside. Tychicus and Onesimus will relate to them personally the things concerning Paul and his fellow workers for the

---

6. (a) What prayer does Paul make in the Colossians' behalf? (b) What does Paul discuss as to Jesus' position and ministry in connection with the congregation?
7. What is Paul preaching, and for what purpose?
8. Why does Paul struggle in behalf of his brothers?

9. Against what kind of worship does Paul warn, and why should the Colossians not subject themselves to the Law?
10. How may one keep seeking the things above and be clothed with the new personality?
11. (a) What counsel is given concerning family and other relations? (b) What greetings are conveyed in conclusion?

Kingdom of God. They send greetings to Colossae, and Paul also greets the brothers at Laodicea, asking that they exchange the letters he is sending. Paul writes a concluding greeting in his own hand: "Continue bearing my prison bonds in mind. The undeserved kindness be with you."—4:18.

WHY BENEFICIAL

¹² We can imagine how quickly the news of the arrival of the two brothers from Rome circulated among the brothers at Colossae. With keen anticipation they would assemble, possibly at Philemon's house, to hear the reading of Paul's letter. (Philem. 2) What refreshing truths it provided on the exact position of Christ and the need for accurate knowledge! How clearly were philosophies of men and Jewish traditions put in their place, and the peace and the word of the Christ exalted! Here was nourishment for mind and heart for all in the congregation—overseers, husbands, wives, fathers, children, masters, slaves. Certainly there was good advice for Philemon and Onesimus as they entered once again into the relation of master and slave. What a fine lead was given to the overseers in restoring the flock to right doctrine! How Paul's words sharpened the Colossians' appreciation for their privilege of working wholesouled as to Jehovah! And the upbuilding counsel to the Colossians on getting free from the enslaving thoughts and practices of the world remains as a living message for the congregation today. —Col. 1:9-11, 17, 18; 2:8; 3:15, 16, 18-25; 4:1.

¹³ Excellent advice for the Christian minister is set out at Colossians 4:6: "Let your utterance be always with graciousness, seasoned with salt, so

---

12. What refreshing truths did Paul's letter to the Colossians provide, and with what benefit to the congregation?
13. What does Paul admonish with regard to gracious words, prayer, and Christian association?

as to know how you ought to give an answer to each one." Gracious words of truth will prove appetizing to honesthearted persons and will work to their permanent benefit. Also, the wideawake prayer of the Christian, expressed from an appreciative heart, will bring rich blessings from Jehovah: "Be persevering in prayer, remaining awake in it with thanksgiving." And what joy and upbuilding refreshment is to be found in Christian association! "Keep on teaching and admonishing one another," says Paul, "singing in your hearts to Jehovah." (4:2; 3:16) You will find many other gems of sound, practical instruction as you search through the letter to the Colossians.

¹⁴ Concerning the observances of the Law, the letter says: "Those things are a shadow of the things to come, but the reality belongs to the Christ." (2:17) It is this reality of the Christ that is highlighted in Colossians. The letter refers frequently to the glorious hope reserved in the heavens for those in union with Christ. (1:5, 27; 3:4) Such ones can be most thankful that the Father has already delivered them from the authority of the darkness and transplanted them "into the kingdom of the Son of his love." Thus they have become subject to the One who is "the image of the invisible God, the firstborn of all creation; because by means of him all other things were created in the heavens and upon the earth, the things visible and the things invisible, no matter whether they are thrones or lordships or governments or authorities." This One is eminently qualified to rule in righteousness in the Kingdom of God. Thus, it is that Paul admonishes the anointed Christians: "If, however, you were raised up with the Christ, go on seeking the things above, where the Christ is seated at the right hand of God."—1: 12-16; 3:1.

---

14. (a) What reality is highlighted in Colossians?
(b) How is the Kingdom hope emphasized?

1 Thessalonians

I T WAS about the year 50 C.E. that the apostle Paul, during his second preaching tour, visited the Macedonian city of Thessalonica and there established a Christian congregation. Within a year, while in Corinth accompanied by Silvanus (Silas of the book of Acts) and Timothy, Paul was moved to write his first letter to the Thessalonians to comfort them and build them up in the faith. It was likely late 50 C.E. This letter apparently enjoys the distinction of being the first of Paul's writings to become part of the Bible canon and, with the probable exception of Matthew's Gospel, the first book of the Christian Greek Scriptures to be put into writing.

² The evidence supporting the authenticity and integrity of the letter is overwhelming. Paul identifies himself by name as the writer, and the book is internally harmonious with the rest of the inspired Word. (1 Thess. 1:1; 2:18) The epistle is mentioned by name in many of the earliest catalogs of the inspired Scriptures, including the Muratorian Fragment.* First Thessalonians is either quoted or alluded to by many of the early ecclesiastical writers, including Irenaeus (second century C.E.), who mentions it by name. The Chester Beatty Papyrus No. 2 (P⁴⁶), of about 200 C.E., contains First Thessalonians, and another papyrus of the third century (P³⁰), now in Ghent, Belgium, contains fragments of both First and Second Thessalonians.#

³ A glance at the brief history of the congregation at Thessalonica, prior to the writing of this letter, establishes the background for Paul's deep concern for the brothers in that city. From the very beginning, the congregation underwent se-

vere persecution and opposition. In Acts chapter 17, Luke reports the arrival of Paul and Silas at Thessalonica, "where there was a synagogue of the Jews." For three Sabbaths, Paul preached to them, reasoning with them from the Scriptures, and there are indications that he stayed there even longer than this, for he had time to set himself up in his trade and, above all, to establish and organize a congregation.—Acts 17:1; 1 Thess. 2:9; 1:6, 7.

⁴ The record at Acts 17:4-7 graphically relates the effect of the apostle's preaching in Thessalonica. Jealous about the success of Paul's Christian ministry, the Jews organized a mob and threw the city into an uproar. They assaulted Jason's house and dragged him and other brothers to the city rulers, crying out: "These men that have overturned the inhabited earth are present here also, and Jason has received them with hospitality. And all these men act in opposition to the decrees of Caesar, saying there is another king, Jesus." Jason and the others were compelled to provide bond before they were released. For the sake of the brothers in the congregation, as well as for their own personal safety, Paul and Silas were dispatched by night to Beroea. But the congregation at Thessalonica was now established.

⁵ Fiery opposition from the Jews pursued Paul to Beroea and threatened to stop his preaching there. He then moved on to Athens, in Greece. Still he longed to know how his brothers in Thessalonica were faring under tribulation. Twice he attempted to return to them, but each time 'Satan cut across his path.' (1 Thess. 2:17, 18) Filled with concern for the young congregation and painfully aware of the tribulation they were undergoing, Paul sent Timothy back to Thessalonica to comfort the brothers and make them more firm in the faith. When Timothy returned with his heartwarming report, Paul was overjoyed with the news of their stalwart integrity amid violent persecution. Their record by now had become an example to believers throughout all Macedonia

---

* See chart "Outstanding Early Catalogs of the Christian Greek Scriptures," page 303.
# *The Text of the New Testament,* by Kurt and Barbara Aland, translated by E. F. Rhodes, 1987, pages 97, 99.

---

1. (a) How did First Thessalonians come to be written? (b) When was this, and what distinction does the letter thus enjoy?
2. What evidence is there for the writership and authenticity of First Thessalonians?
3, 4. What resulted from the early success of Paul's ministry at Thessalonica?

5. How did Paul show his concern for and loving interest in the Thessalonian congregation?

and Achaia. (1:6-8; 3:1-7) Paul was thankful to Jehovah God for their faithful endurance, but he also realized that as they continued to grow to maturity, they would need further guidance and counsel. Therefore, while in Corinth in the company of Timothy and Silvanus, Paul wrote his first letter to the Thessalonians.

CONTENTS OF
FIRST THESSALONIANS

⁶ **Thessalonians an example to other believers** (1:1-10). Paul begins his letter to the Thessalonians with warm commendation for their faithful work, loving labor, and endurance in hope. The good news preached among them had not been with speech alone but 'also with power and strong conviction.' Imitating the example given them, the Thessalonians had accepted the word "with joy of holy spirit" and had themselves become an example to all the believers in Macedonia, Achaia, and even beyond. They had turned completely from their idols, "to slave for a living and true God, and to wait for his Son from the heavens."—1:5, 6, 9, 10.

⁷ **Paul's loving concern for the Thessalonians** (2:1–3:13). After receiving insolent treatment in Philippi, Paul and his companions mustered up boldness to preach to the Thessalonians. This they did not as men pleasers or as flatterers or as seeking glory from men. On the contrary, says Paul, "we became gentle in the midst of you, as when a nursing mother cherishes her own children. So, having a tender affection for you, we were well pleased to impart to you, not only the good news of God, but also our own souls, because you became beloved to us." (2:7, 8) They kept exhorting the Thessalonians, as a father does his children, to go on walking worthily of God, who was calling them to his Kingdom and glory.

⁸ Paul commends them for their ready acceptance of the good news for what it is, "the word of God." They are not alone in being persecuted by their own countrymen, for the first believers in Judea suffered similar persecutions at the hands of the Jews. Anxious about their welfare, Paul, on two occasions, wanted to come to them in person but was thwarted by Satan. To Paul and his coworkers, the Thessalonian brothers are a crown of exultation, their "glory and joy." (2:13, 20) When he could no longer bear the lack of news concerning them, Paul sent Timothy to Thessalo-

nica to make firm their faith and to comfort them. Now Timothy has just returned with the good news of their spiritual prosperity and love, and this has brought comfort and joy to the apostle. Paul gives thanks to God and prays that the Lord may give them increase, that they may abound in love to one another, and that their hearts may be "unblamable in holiness" before God the Father at the presence of the Lord Jesus.—3:13.

⁹ **Serving in sanctification and honor** (4:1-12). Paul commends the Thessalonians for walking so as to please God, and he exhorts them to keep on doing it more fully. Each one "should know how to get possession of his own vessel in sanctification and honor, not in covetous sexual appetite." In this, no one should encroach upon his brother's rights. For God called them, "not with allowance for uncleanness, but in connection with sanctification. So, then, the man that shows disregard is disregarding, not man, but God." (4:4, 5, 7, 8) Paul commends the Thessalonians because they are showing love one to another, and he exhorts them to keep doing this in fuller measure, making it their aim to live quietly and to mind their own business and to work with their hands. For they must walk decently "as regards people outside." —4:12.

¹⁰ **The resurrection hope** (4:13-18). With regard to those sleeping in death, the brothers must not sorrow as do those who have no hope. If their faith is that Jesus died and rose again, so, too, God through Jesus will raise others who have fallen asleep in death. At the presence of the Lord, he will descend from heaven with a commanding call, "and those who are dead in union with Christ will rise first." Afterward, those surviving will "be caught away in clouds to meet the Lord in the air," to be always with the Lord.—4:16, 17.

¹¹ **Keeping awake as Jehovah's day approaches** (5:1-28). "Jehovah's day is coming exactly as a thief in the night." It is when people are saying "Peace and security!" that sudden destruction will be instantly upon them. Let the Thessalonians, therefore, stay awake as "sons of light and sons of day," keeping their senses and having "on the breastplate of faith and love and as a helmet the hope of salvation." (5:2, 3, 5, 8) This is a time for them to keep comforting and building one another up. Let all give "more than extraordinary consideration in love" to those working hard and presiding among them. On the other hand, the disorder-

---

6. For what does Paul commend the Thessalonians?
7. What attitude had Paul and his companions displayed while among the Thessalonians, and what had they exhorted them to do?
8. How have the Thessalonians become an exultation to Paul, and what does he pray on their behalf?

9. What does Paul exhort concerning sanctification and love one to another?
10. What attitude should the brothers have with regard to those who have fallen asleep in death?
11. Why should the Thessalonians stay awake, and what should they keep doing?

ly must be admonished, the weak built up, and all must be shown long-suffering. Yes, writes Paul, "always pursue what is good toward one another and to all others."—5:13, 15.

[12] Finally, Paul counsels on a number of vital matters: 'Always be rejoicing. Pray incessantly, giving thanks for everything. Maintain the fire of the spirit. Have respect for prophesyings. Make sure of all things and hold fast to what is fine. Abstain from every form of wickedness.' (5: 16-22) Then he prays for the very God of peace to sanctify them completely and that they may remain blameless in spirit, soul, and body at the presence of the Lord Jesus Christ. He closes the letter with warm words of encouragement and with solemn instruction that the letter be read to all the brothers.

WHY BENEFICIAL

[13] In this letter Paul demonstrated a spirit of loving concern for his brothers. He and his fellow ministers had set a noble example of tender affection, imparting not only the good news of God but even their own souls in behalf of their beloved brothers in Thessalonica. Let all overseers endeavor to forge such ties of love with their congregations! Such expression of love will incite all to show love for one another, even as Paul said: "Moreover, may the Lord cause you to increase, yes, make you abound, in love to one another and to all, even as we also do to you." This love expressed willingly among all of God's people is most upbuilding. It makes hearts "firm, unblamable in holiness before our God and Father at the presence of our Lord Jesus with all his holy ones." It sets Christians apart from a corrupt and immoral world so they can walk in holiness and sanctification and thus please God.—3:12, 13; 2:8; 4:1-8.

[14] This letter provides an excellent model of tactful, loving counsel in the Christian congregation. Though the Thessalonian brothers were zealous and faithful, there were points of correction to be made. In each case, however, Paul commends the brothers on their good qualities. For example, in warning against moral uncleanness, he first commends them on walking so as to please God and then urges them to do it "more fully," each one keeping his vessel in sanctification and honor. Then, after commending them on their brotherly love, he exhorts them to continue in this way "in fuller measure," minding their own business and living decent lives before those on the outside. Tactfully Paul directs his brothers to "pursue what is good toward one another and to all others."—4: 1-7, 9-12; 5:15.

[15] On four occasions Paul makes mention of the "presence" of Jesus Christ. Apparently the newly converted Christians at Thessalonica were very much interested in this teaching. While in their city, Paul had no doubt preached boldly concerning God's Kingdom in the hands of Christ, as is indicated by the accusation brought against him and his companions: "All these men act in opposition to the decrees of Caesar, saying there is another king, Jesus." (Acts 17:7; 1 Thess. 2:19; 3:13; 4:15; 5:23) The Thessalonian brothers had set their hope on the Kingdom and, having faith toward God, were waiting "for his Son from the heavens, whom he raised up from the dead, namely, Jesus," to deliver them from the wrath to come. Likewise, all who hope in God's Kingdom today need to heed the fine counsel of First Thessalonians to abound in love, with hearts firm and unblamable, so that they may 'go on walking worthily of God who is calling them to his kingdom and glory.'—1 Thess. 1:8, 10; 3:12, 13; 2:12.

---

12. On what vital matters does Paul finally give counsel, and how does he close his letter to the Thessalonians?
13. In what were Paul and his companions a noble example, and what effect does the willing expression of love have in the congregation?

14. In what way is First Thessalonians an excellent example of tactful, loving counsel?
15. What indicates that Paul zealously preached the Kingdom hope while at Thessalonica, and what fine counsel did he give in this connection?

2 Thessalonians

Writer: **Paul**

Place Written: **Corinth**

Writing Completed: **c. 51 C.E.**

THE apostle Paul's second letter to the Thessalonians closely followed the first one. We know that it was written shortly after the first letter, and also from the same city of Corinth, for the same brothers, Silvanus and Timothy, again join with Paul in greeting the congregation at Thessalonica. They were all traveling servants of the early Christian congregation, and there is no record that all three came together again after this association in Corinth. (2 Thess. 1:1; Acts 18:5, 18) The subject matter and nature of the discussion indicate that Paul felt an urgent need to correct the congregation promptly with regard to an error into which it had fallen.

² The letter's authenticity is just as well attested as the authenticity of First Thessalonians. It also is quoted by Irenaeus (second century C.E.) as well as by other early writers, including Justin Martyr (also of the second century), who apparently refers to 2 Thessalonians 2:3 when writing of "the man of lawlessness [sin]." It appears in the same early catalogs as First Thessalonians. Though it is now missing from the Chester Beatty Papyrus No. 2 (P⁴⁶), it was almost certainly contained in the first two of seven leaves that are missing after First Thessalonians.

³ What was the purpose of this letter? From the counsel that Paul offered the Thessalonians, we learn that some in the congregation were contending that the presence of the Lord was imminent, that these speculators were actively preaching this theory of theirs, and that they were creating no little stir in the congregation. It appears that some were even using this as an excuse for not working to provide for themselves. (2 Thess. 3:11) In his first letter, Paul had made references to the presence of the Lord, and no doubt when these speculators heard the letter read, they were quick to twist Paul's words and read into them meanings that were never intended. It is also possible that a letter wrongly attributed to Paul was interpreted as indicating that "the day of Jehovah is here."—2: 1, 2.

⁴ It seems that Paul had received a report on this condition, probably from the person who delivered his first letter to the congregation, and he would therefore be very anxious to correct the thinking of his brothers for whom he had such great affection. So in the year 51 C.E., Paul, in association with his two companions, sent a letter from Corinth to the congregation in Thessalonica. In addition to correcting the wrong viewpoint on Christ's presence, Paul gives warm encouragement to stand firm in the truth.

CONTENTS OF
SECOND THESSALONIANS

⁵ **The revelation of the Lord Jesus** (1:1-12). Paul and his companions thank God on account of the fine growth of the Thessalonians' faith and their love toward one another. Their endurance and faith under persecutions are proof of God's righteous judgment that they are counted worthy of the Kingdom. God will repay tribulation to those who make it for the congregation, and he will give relief to those who suffer. This will be "at the revelation of the Lord Jesus from heaven with his powerful angels . . . at the time he comes to be glorified in connection with his holy ones." (1: 7, 10) Paul and his companions always pray for the Thessalonians, that God may count them worthy of His calling and that the name of the Lord Jesus may be glorified in them and they in union with him.

⁶ **Apostasy to come before Jesus' presence** (2: 1-12). The brothers should not become excited by any message that the day of Jehovah is here. "It will not come unless the apostasy comes first and the man of lawlessness gets revealed, the son of destruction." They know now "the thing that acts as a restraint," but the mystery of this lawlessness

---

1. What indicates the time and place of writing, and what prompted the second letter to the Thessalonians?
2. What attests the authenticity of Second Thessalonians?
3, 4. (a) What problem had arisen in the Thessalonian congregation? (b) When and where was the letter written, and what did Paul seek to accomplish by it?

5. For what do Paul and his companions thank God, what assurance do they give, and what do they pray?
6. What must come before the day of Jehovah, and how?

is already at work. When this restraint is removed, "then, indeed, the lawless one will be revealed, whom the Lord Jesus will do away with by the spirit of his mouth and bring to nothing by the manifestation of his presence." The lawless one's presence is according to the operation of Satan with powerful works and deception, and God is permitting an operation of error to go to those who did not accept the love of the truth that they may get to believe the lie.—2:3, 6, 8.

⁷ **Stand firm in faith** (2:13–3:18). Paul continues: "We are obligated to thank God always for you, brothers loved by Jehovah, because God selected you from the beginning for salvation by sanctifying you with spirit and by your faith in the truth." To this end the good news was declared to them. The brothers should therefore stand firm and maintain their hold on the traditions they were taught, that Jesus Christ and the Father, who lovingly gave everlasting comfort and hope, may make them "firm in every good deed and word." (2:13, 17) Paul asks for their prayers, "that the word of Jehovah may keep moving speedily and being glorified." (3:1) The Lord, who is faithful, will make them firm and keep them from the wicked one, and it is Paul's prayer that the Lord continue directing their hearts successfully into love of God and into endurance for the Christ.

⁸ Strong admonition follows: "Now we are giving you orders, brothers, in the name of the Lord Jesus Christ, to withdraw from every brother walking disorderly and not according to the tradition you received from us." (3:6) The apostle reminds them of the example his missionary group gave, laboring night and day so as not to become an expense to them, so that they were able to give the order: "If anyone does not want to work, neither let him eat." But now they hear that certain disorderly ones are not working and are meddlers. These should get to earning their own food. —2 Thess. 3:10; 1 Thess. 4:11.

⁹ The brothers should not give up in doing right. But if one of them is not obedient to Paul's letter, the congregation should shame him by marking

him and no longer associating with him, at the same time admonishing him as a brother. Paul expresses the prayer that the Lord of peace may give them "peace constantly in every way," and he concludes his letter with greetings in his own hand.—2 Thess. 3:16.

WHY BENEFICIAL

¹⁰ This short inspired letter to the Thessalonians touches on a vast array of Christian truth, all of which is beneficial for consideration. Consider the following basic teachings and principles that are covered: Jehovah is the God of salvation, and he sanctifies by spirit and faith in the truth (2:13); the Christian must endure suffering to be counted worthy of the Kingdom of God (1:4, 5); Christians are to be gathered together to the Lord Jesus Christ at his presence (2:1); Jehovah will bring righteous judgment on those who disobey the good news (1:5-8); those called will be glorified in union with Christ Jesus, in accordance with God's undeserved kindness (1:12); they are called through the preaching of the good news (2:14); faith is a vital requirement (1:3, 4, 10, 11; 2:13; 3:2); it is proper to work in order to provide for oneself in the ministry; if a person does not work, he may become lazy and start to meddle in things that do not concern him (3:8-12); the love of God is associated with endurance (3:5). What a treasure of upbuilding information can be found in one short inspired letter!

¹¹ In this letter Paul showed deep concern for the spiritual welfare of his brothers in Thessalonica and for the unity and prosperity of the congregation. He set them right on the timing of the day of Jehovah, showing that "the man of lawlessness" must first appear, to sit down in "the temple of The God, publicly showing himself to be a god." However, those "counted worthy of the kingdom of God" may have absolute assurance that the Lord Jesus will in due course be revealed from heaven, taking vengeance in flaming fire "at the time he comes to be glorified in connection with his holy ones and to be regarded in that day with wonder in connection with all those who exercised faith." —2:3, 4; 1:5, 10.

---

7. How may the brothers stand firm and find protection from the wicked one?
8. What strong admonition is given, and wherein have Paul and his group set the example?
9. What does Paul say about doing right and shaming the disobedient, and how does he end his letter?

---

10. What are some of the basic teachings and principles covered in Second Thessalonians?
11. What important information and assurance are presented in connection with the Kingdom?

54
1 Timothy

Writer: **Paul**

Place Written: **Macedonia**

Writing Completed:
c. 61–64 C.E.

LUKE'S account of Paul's life in the book of Acts ends with Paul in Rome awaiting the outcome of his appeal to Caesar. Paul is shown as dwelling in his own hired house, preaching the Kingdom of God to all who came to him, and doing so "with the greatest freeness of speech, without hindrance." (Acts 28:30, 31) But in his second letter to Timothy, Paul writes: "I am suffering evil to the point of prison bonds as an evildoer," and he speaks of his death as imminent. (2 Tim. 2:9; 4: 6-8) What a change! In the first instance, he was treated as an honorable prisoner, in the second, as a felon. What had happened between the time of Luke's comment on Paul's situation in 61 C.E., at the end of two years in Rome, and Paul's own writing of his condition to Timothy, which appears to have been written shortly before his death?

2 The difficulty of fitting the writing of Paul's letters to Timothy and Titus into the period covered by the book of Acts has led some Bible commentators to the conclusion that Paul was successful in his appeal to Caesar and was released about 61 C.E. Says *The New Westminster Dictionary of the Bible:* "The closing verse of The Acts accords better with this view [that Paul was released after two years' confinement] than with the supposition that the imprisonment which has been described ended in the apostle's condemnation and death. Luke emphasizes the fact that no one hindered his work, thus certainly giving the impression that the end of his activity was not near."* It is, then, to the period between his release from his first imprisonment in Rome and his final imprisonment there, or about 61-64 C.E., that the writing of First Timothy belongs.

3 On his release from prison, Paul evidently resumed his missionary activity in association with Timothy and Titus. Whether Paul ever reached Spain, as some suppose, is not certain. Clement of Rome wrote (c. 95 C.E.) that Paul came "to the extreme limit of the W[est]," which could have included Spain.*

4 From where did Paul write his first letter to Timothy? First Timothy 1:3 indicates that Paul arranged for Timothy to attend to certain congregation matters in Ephesus while he himself went his way to Macedonia. From here, it appears, he wrote the letter back to Timothy in Ephesus.

5 The two letters to Timothy have been accepted from the earliest times as written by Paul and as being part of the inspired Scriptures. The early Christian writers, including Polycarp, Ignatius, and Clement of Rome, all agree on this, and the letters are included in the catalogs of the first few centuries as Paul's writings. One authority writes: "There are few N[ew] T[estament] writings which have stronger attestation . . . Objections to authenticity must therefore be regarded as modern innovations contrary to the strong evidence from the early church."#

6 Paul wrote this first letter to Timothy to set out clearly certain organizational procedures in the congregation. There was also a need for him to warn Timothy to be on guard against false teachings and to strengthen the brothers to resist such 'false knowledge.' (1 Tim. 6:20) The commercial city of Ephesus would also provide the temptations of materialism and "love of money," and so it would be timely to give some advice on this also. (6:10) Timothy certainly had a fine background of experience and training to be used for this work. He was born of a Greek father and a God-fearing Jewish mother. It is not known exactly when

---

* 1970, edited by H. S. Gehman, page 721.

1, 2. (a) What contrast is seen between the descriptions of Paul's imprisonment in Acts and Second Timothy? (b) When does it appear that First Timothy was written, and why?
3, 4. (a) On his release from prison, what did Paul evidently do? (b) From where did he write First Timothy?

---

* *The Ante-Nicene Fathers,* Vol. I, page 6, "The First Epistle of Clement to the Corinthians," chap. V.
# *New Bible Dictionary,* second edition, 1986, edited by J. D. Douglas, page 1203.

5. What testimony is there to the authenticity of the letters to Timothy?
6. (a) For what several reasons did Paul write First Timothy? (b) What was Timothy's background, and what indicates that he was a mature worker?

Timothy had his first contact with Christianity. When Paul visited Lystra on his second missionary tour, likely in late 49 C.E. or early 50 C.E., Timothy (perhaps in his late teens or early 20's) was already "well reported on by the brothers in Lystra and Iconium." So Paul arranged for Timothy to travel with Silas and himself. (Acts 16:1-3) Timothy is mentioned by name in 11 of Paul's 14 letters as well as in the book of Acts. Paul always took a fatherly interest in him and on several occasions assigned him to visit and serve different congregations—an evidence Timothy had done good work in the missionary field and was qualified to handle weighty responsibilities.—1 Tim. 1:2; 5:23; 1 Thess. 3:2; Phil. 2:19.

CONTENTS OF FIRST TIMOTHY

[7] **Exhortation to faith with a good conscience** (1:1-20). After greeting Timothy as "a genuine child in the faith," Paul encourages him to remain in Ephesus. He is to correct those teaching a "different doctrine," which is leading to useless questions rather than to a dispensing of faith. Paul says the objective of this mandate is "love out of a clean heart and out of a good conscience and out of faith without hypocrisy." He adds: "By deviating from these things certain ones have been turned aside into idle talk."—1:2, 3, 5, 6.

[8] Though Paul was formerly a blasphemer and a persecutor, nevertheless, the undeserved kindness of the Lord "abounded exceedingly along with faith and love that is in connection with Christ Jesus," so that he was shown mercy. He had been the foremost of sinners; and thus he became a demonstration of the long-suffering of Christ Jesus, who "came into the world to save sinners." How worthy is the King of eternity to receive honor and glory forever! Paul charges Timothy to wage a fine warfare, "holding faith and a good conscience." He must not be like those who have "experienced shipwreck concerning their faith," such as Hymenaeus and Alexander, whom Paul has disciplined on account of blasphemy.—1:14, 15, 19.

[9] **Instructions regarding worship and organization in the congregation** (2:1–6:2). Prayers are to be made concerning all sorts of men, including those in high station, to the end that Christians may live peaceably in godly devotion. It is the will of God, the Savior, that "all sorts of men should be saved and come to an accurate knowledge of truth. For there is one God, and one mediator between God and men, a man, Christ Jesus, who gave

himself a corresponding ransom for all." (2:4-6) Paul was appointed an apostle and teacher of these things. So he calls on the men to pray in loyalty and the women to dress modestly and sensibly, as befits those who reverence God. A woman must learn in silence and not exercise authority over a man, "for Adam was formed first, then Eve." —2:13.

[10] The man who reaches out to be an overseer is desirous of a fine work. Paul then lists the qualifications for overseers and ministerial servants. An overseer must be "irreprehensible, a husband of one wife, moderate in habits, sound in mind, orderly, hospitable, qualified to teach, not a drunken brawler, not a smiter, but reasonable, not belligerent, not a lover of money, a man presiding over his own household in a fine manner, having children in subjection with all seriousness . . . , not a newly converted man . . . He should also have a fine testimony from people on the outside." (3:2-7) There are similar requirements for ministerial servants, and they should be tested as to fitness before serving. Paul writes these things in order that Timothy may know how he ought to conduct himself in the congregation of God, which is "a pillar and support of the truth."—3:15.

[11] In later times some will fall away from the faith through the teachings of demons. Hypocritical men speaking lies will forbid marriage and command to abstain from foods that God created to be partaken of with thanksgiving. As a fine minister, Timothy must turn down false stories and 'old women's tales.' On the other hand, he should be training himself with godly devotion as his aim. "To this end we are working hard and exerting ourselves," says Paul, "because we have rested our hope on a living God, who is a Savior of all sorts of men, especially of faithful ones." Therefore Timothy must keep on giving these commands and teaching them. He is to let no man look down on his youth but, on the contrary, become an example in conduct and godly service. He is to be absorbed in these things and to pay constant attention to himself and to his teaching, for in staying by these things, he will 'save both himself and those listening to him.'—4:7, 10, 16.

[12] Paul counsels Timothy on how to deal with individuals: older men as fathers, younger men as brothers, older women as mothers, younger women as sisters. Suitable provision is to be made for those who are really widows. However, a widow's

---

7. Why is Paul encouraging Timothy to stay in Ephesus?
8. What did Paul's being shown mercy emphasize, and what fine warfare does he encourage Timothy to wage?
9. (a) What prayers are to be made, and why? (b) What is said as to women in the congregation?

10. What are the qualifications for overseers and ministerial servants, and why does Paul write these things?
11. (a) What problems will appear later? (b) To what should Timothy give attention, and why?
12. What counsel is given as to dealing with widows and others in the congregation?

family should care for her if possible. To fail in this would be to disown the faith. When at least 60 years of age, a widow may be put on the list if there is "a witness borne to her for fine works." (5:10) On the other hand, younger widows, who let their sexual impulses control them, should be turned down. Rather than gadding about and gossiping, let them marry and bear children, so as to give no inducement to the opposer.

13 The older men who preside in a fine way should be reckoned worthy of double honor, "especially those who work hard in speaking and teaching." (5:17) An accusation is not to be admitted against an older man except on the evidence of two or three witnesses. Persons who practice sin are to be reproved before all onlookers, but there is to be no prejudgment or bias in these things. Slaves should respect their owners, giving good service, especially to brothers, who are "believers and beloved."—6:2.

14 **Counsel on "godly devotion along with self-sufficiency"** (6:3-21). The man that does not assent to healthful words is puffed up with pride and is mentally diseased over questionings, leading to violent disputes over trifles. On the other hand, "godly devotion along with self-sufficiency" is a means of great gain. One should be content with sustenance and covering. The determination to be rich is a snare leading to destruction, and the love of money is "a root of all sorts of injurious things." Paul urges Timothy, as a man of God, to flee from these things, to pursue Christian virtues, to fight the fine fight of the faith, and to "get a firm hold on the everlasting life." (6:6, 10, 12) He must observe the commandment "in a spotless and irreprehensible way" until the manifestation of the Lord Jesus Christ. Those who are rich should "rest their hope, not on uncertain riches, but on God," in order to get a firm hold on the real life. Paul, in closing, encourages Timothy to guard his doctrinal trust and to turn away from defiling speeches and from "the contradictions of the falsely called 'knowledge.'"—6:14, 17, 20.

WHY BENEFICIAL

15 This letter provides a stern warning for those who dabble in vain speculations and philosophical arguments. "Debates about words" are allied to pride and are to be avoided, for Paul tells us that they obstruct Christian growth, furnishing only "questions for research rather than a dispensing of anything by God in connection with faith." (6:3-6; 1:4) Along with the works of the flesh, these disputings are "in opposition to the healthful teaching according to the glorious good news of the happy God."—1:10, 11.

16 The Christians in money-greedy Ephesus apparently needed counsel on fighting materialism and its distractions. Paul gave that counsel. The world has freely quoted him in saying, 'The love of money is the root of all evil,' but how few pay heed to his words! On the contrary, true Christians need to heed this advice all the time. It means life to them. They need to flee from the hurtful snare of materialism, resting their hope, "not on uncertain riches, but on God, who furnishes us all things richly for our enjoyment."—6:6-12, 17-19.

17 Paul's letter shows that Timothy himself was a fine example of what a young Christian should be. Though relatively young in years, he was mature in spiritual growth. He had reached out to qualify as an overseer and was richly blessed in the privileges he enjoyed. But like all zealous young ministers today, he needed to keep pondering over these things and to be absorbed in them so as to make continued advancement. Timely is Paul's advice to all who seek continued joy in making Christian progress: "Pay constant attention to yourself and to your teaching. Stay by these things, for by doing this you will save both yourself and those who listen to you."—4:15, 16.

18 This inspired letter instills appreciation for God's orderly arrangements. It shows how both men and women may do their part in maintaining theocratic harmony in the congregation. (2:8-15) Then it goes on to discuss the qualifications for overseers and ministerial servants. Thus holy spirit indicates the requirements to be met by those who serve in special capacities. The letter also encourages all dedicated ministers to meet these standards, saying: "If any man is reaching out for an office of overseer, he is desirous of a fine work." (3:1-13) The overseer's proper attitude toward the age-groups and sexes in the congregation is appropriately discussed as is the handling of accusations before witnesses. In emphasizing that the older men who work hard in speaking and teaching are worthy of double honor, Paul calls twice on the Hebrew Scriptures as an authority: "For the scripture says: 'You must not muzzle a bull when it

---

13. What consideration should be shown to older men, how are persons who practice sin to be handled, and what responsibility falls upon slaves?
14. What does Paul have to say about pride and the love of money in connection with "godly devotion along with self-sufficiency"?
15. What warning is given against speculations and arguments?

---

16. What counsel did Paul give on materialism?
17. What advice to Timothy is timely for all zealous young ministers today?
18. What orderly arrangements in the congregation are clearly defined, and how does Paul use the Hebrew Scriptures as an authority?

threshes out the grain'; also: 'The workman is worthy of his wages.'"—1 Tim. 5:1-3, 9, 10, 19-21, 17, 18; Deut. 25:4; Lev. 19:13.

[19] After giving all this fine counsel, Paul adds that the commandment should be observed in a spotless and irreprehensible way 'until the manifestation of the Lord Jesus Christ as the King of

those who rule as kings and Lord of those who rule as lords.' On the basis of this Kingdom hope, the letter closes with a powerful exhortation for Christians "to work at good, to be rich in fine works, to be liberal, ready to share, safely treasuring up for themselves a fine foundation for the future, in order that they may get a firm hold on the real life." (1 Tim. 6:14, 15, 18, 19) Beneficial indeed is all the fine instruction of First Timothy!

---

19. How is the Kingdom hope brought to the fore, and what exhortation is given on this basis?

Bible Book Number 55

2 Timothy

Writer: **Paul**

Place Written: **Rome**

Writing Completed: **c. 65 C.E.**

ONCE again Paul was a prisoner in Rome. However, the circumstances of this second imprisonment were much more severe than those of the first. It was approximately 65 C.E. A great fire had swept through Rome in July 64 C.E., causing extensive damage in 10 of the city's 14 regions. According to the Roman historian Tacitus, Emperor Nero was unable to "banish the sinister belief that the conflagration was the result of an order. Consequently, to get rid of the report, Nero fastened the guilt and inflicted the most exquisite tortures on a class hated for their abominations, called Christians by the populace. . . . An immense multitude was convicted, not so much of the crime of firing the city, as of hatred against mankind. Mockery of every sort was added to their deaths. Covered with the skins of beasts, they were torn by dogs and perished, or were nailed to crosses, or were doomed to the flames and burnt, to serve as a nightly illumination, when daylight had expired. Nero offered his gardens for the spectacle . . . There arose a feeling of compassion; for it was not as it seemed, for the public good, but to glut one man's cruelty, that they were being destroyed."*

[2] It was likely about the time of this wave of violent persecution that Paul again found himself a prisoner in Rome. This time he was in chains. He

did not expect to be released but awaited only final judgment and execution. Visitors were few. Indeed, for anyone to identify himself openly as a Christian was to run the risk of arrest and death by torture. Hence Paul could write appreciatively concerning his visitor from Ephesus: "May the Lord grant mercy to the household of Onesiphorus, because he often brought me refreshment, and he did not become ashamed of my chains. On the contrary, when he happened to be in Rome, he diligently looked for me and found me." (2 Tim. 1: 16, 17) Writing under the shadow of death, Paul styles himself "an apostle of Christ Jesus through God's will according to the promise of the life that is in union with Christ Jesus." (1:1) Paul knew that life in union with Christ awaited him. He had preached in many of the chief cities of the known world, from Jerusalem to Rome, and perhaps even as far as Spain. (Rom. 15:24, 28) He had run the course faithfully to the finish.—2 Tim. 4:6-8.

[3] The letter was probably written about 65 C.E., immediately prior to Paul's martyrdom. Timothy was probably still at Ephesus, for Paul had encouraged him to stay there. (1 Tim. 1:3) Now, twice Paul urges Timothy to come to him quickly, and he asks him to bring Mark with him, and also the cloak and scrolls that Paul left at Troas. (2 Tim. 4: 9, 11, 13, 21) Written at so critical a time, this letter contained powerful encouragement for Timothy, and it has continued to provide beneficial encouragement for true Christians in all ages since.

---

* *The Complete Works of Tacitus,* 1942, edited by Moses Hadas, pages 380-1.

---

1. What persecution flared up in Rome about 64 C.E., and for what apparent reason?
2. Under what circumstances did Paul write Second Timothy, and why does he speak appreciatively of Onesiphorus?

---

3. When was Second Timothy written, and how has it benefited Christians through the ages?

⁴ The book of Second Timothy is authentic and canonical for the reasons already discussed under First Timothy. It was recognized and used by early writers and commentators, including Polycarp in the second century C.E.

CONTENTS OF SECOND TIMOTHY

⁵ **"Holding the pattern of healthful words"** (1:1–3:17). Paul tells Timothy that he never forgets him in his prayers and that he is longing to see him. He recollects 'the faith without hypocrisy' that is in Timothy and that dwelt first in his grandmother Lois and his mother Eunice. Timothy should stir up like a fire the gift within him, 'for God gave not a spirit of cowardice, but that of power and of love and of soundness of mind.' Let him therefore be unashamed in witnessing and suffering evil for the good news because God's undeserved kindness has been made clearly evident through the manifestation of the Savior, Christ Jesus. Timothy should "keep holding the pattern of healthful words" that he heard from Paul, guarding it as a fine trust.—1:5, 7, 13.

⁶ Timothy is to commit the things he learned from Paul to "faithful men, who, in turn, will be adequately qualified to teach others." Timothy should prove himself a fine soldier of Christ Jesus. A soldier shuns business entanglements. Moreover, the one crowned at the games contends according to the rules. In order to gain discernment, Timothy should give constant thought to Paul's words. The important things to remember and to remind others of are that "Jesus Christ was raised up from the dead and was of David's seed" and that salvation and everlasting glory in union with Christ, reigning as kings with him, are the rewards for the chosen ones who endure. Timothy is to do his utmost to present himself as an approved workman to God, shunning empty speeches that violate what is holy, which spread like gangrene. Just as in a large house an honorable vessel is kept separate from one lacking honor, so Paul admonishes Timothy to "flee from the desires incidental to youth, but pursue righteousness, faith, love, peace, along with those who call upon the Lord out of a clean heart." The slave of the Lord needs to be gentle toward all, qualified to teach, instructing with mildness.—2:2, 8, 22.

⁷ "In the last days," there will be critical times

hard to deal with and persons who prove false to their show of godly devotion, "always learning and yet never able to come to an accurate knowledge of truth." But Timothy has closely followed Paul's teaching, his course of life, and his persecutions, out of which the Lord delivered him. "In fact," he adds, "all those desiring to live with godly devotion in association with Christ Jesus will also be persecuted." Timothy, however, should continue in the things he learned from infancy, which are able to make him wise for salvation, for *"all Scripture is inspired of God and beneficial."*—3:1, 7, 12, 16.

⁸ **Fully accomplishing the ministry** (4:1-22). Paul charges Timothy to "preach the word" with urgency. (4:2) The time will come when men will not put up with healthful teaching and will turn to false teachers, but let Timothy keep his senses, 'do the work of an evangelizer, fully accomplish his ministry.' Recognizing his death to be imminent, Paul exults that he has fought the fine fight, that he has run the course to the finish and observed the faith. Now he looks confidently forward to the reward, "the crown of righteousness."—4:5, 8.

⁹ Paul urges Timothy to come to him quickly and gives instructions concerning the journey. When Paul made his first defense everyone forsook him, but the Lord infused power into him that the preaching might be fully accomplished among the nations. Yes, he is confident that the Lord will deliver him from every wicked work and save him for His heavenly Kingdom.

WHY BENEFICIAL

¹⁰ "All Scripture is inspired of God and beneficial." Beneficial for what? Paul tells us in his second letter to Timothy: "For teaching, for reproving, for setting things straight, for disciplining in righteousness, that the man of God may be fully competent, completely equipped for every good work." (3:16, 17) Thus the benefit of "teaching" is emphasized in this letter. All lovers of righteousness today will want to heed the letter's wise counsel in striving to become teachers of the Word and in doing their utmost to become God's approved workmen, "handling the word of the truth aright." As in the Ephesus of Timothy's day, so in this modern age, there are those who dabble in "foolish and ignorant questionings," who are "always learning and yet never able to come to an

---

4. What proves that Second Timothy is authentic and canonical?

5. What kind of faith dwells in Timothy, and yet what should he keep doing?

6. What counsel does Paul give on teaching, and how can Timothy be an approved workman and an honorable vessel?

7. Why are the inspired Scriptures to be especially beneficial "in the last days"?

8. What does Paul urge Timothy to do, and in this connection how does Paul exult?

9. What confidence in the Lord's power does Paul express?

10. (a) What particular benefit of "all Scripture" is emphasized in Second Timothy, and what should Christians strive to become? (b) What influence is to be avoided, and how may this be done? (c) For what does there continue to be an urgent need?

accurate knowledge of truth," and who reject "healthful teaching" in favor of teachers who tickle their ears the way they selfishly want it. (2:15, 23; 3:7; 4:3, 4) To avoid this contaminating worldly influence, it is necessary to "keep holding the pattern of healthful words" in faith and love. Moreover, there is the urgent need for more and more persons to become "adequately qualified to teach others" both inside and outside the congregation, like Timothy, "the man of God." Happy are all those who shoulder this responsibility, becoming 'qualified to teach with mildness,' and who preach the word "with all long-suffering and art of teaching"!—1:13; 2:2, 24, 25; 4:2.

[11] As Paul stated, Timothy had known the holy writings "from infancy" because of the loving instruction of Lois and Eunice. "From infancy" also indicates the time to start Bible instruction for children today. But what if, in later years, early fires of zeal start to die out? Paul's advice is to stir up that fire again in the spirit of "power and of love and of soundness of mind," keeping faith without hypocrisy. "In the last days," he said, there will be critical times, with problems of delinquency and false teachings. That is why it is so necessary for

___
11. What advice is given with regard to the young?

young people especially, and all others, to 'keep their senses in all things, and fully accomplish their ministry.'—3:15; 1:5-7; 3:1-5; 4:5.

[12] The prize is worth contending for. (2:3-7) In this connection, Paul calls attention to the Kingdom Seed, saying: "Remember that Jesus Christ was raised up from the dead and was of David's seed, according to the good news." Paul's hope was to remain in union with that Seed. Farther on he speaks of his approaching execution in words of triumph: "From this time on there is reserved for me the crown of righteousness, which the Lord, the righteous judge, will give me as a reward in that day, yet not only to me, but also to all those who have loved his manifestation." (2:8; 4:8) How happy are all those who can look back over many years of faithful service and say the same! However, this requires serving *now* in integrity, with love for the manifestation of Jesus Christ, and demonstrating the same confidence as Paul did when he wrote: "The Lord will deliver me from every wicked work and will save me for his heavenly kingdom. To him be the glory forever and ever. Amen."—4:18.

___
12. (a) How did Paul call attention to the Kingdom Seed, and what hope did he express? (b) How can God's servants today have the same mental attitude as Paul?

Bible Book Number	**56**

Titus

Writer: **Paul**

Place Written: **Macedonia (?)**

Writing Completed:
c. 61–64 C.E.

"PAUL, a slave of God and an apostle of Jesus Christ . . . to Titus, a genuine child according to a faith shared in common." (Titus 1:1, 4) So begins Paul's letter to his coworker and longtime associate Titus, whom he had left on the island of Crete to organize the congregations better. Titus had a big task on his hands. This island, which was said to have been the ancient abode of "the father of gods and men," was the source of the saying, "to Crete a Cretan," meaning "to outwit a knave."* The untruthfulness of its people was proverbial, so that Paul even

___
* McClintock and Strong's *Cyclopedia,* 1981 reprint, Vol. II, page 564; *The New Schaff-Herzog Encyclopedia of Religious Knowledge,* 1958, Vol. III, page 306.

___
1. (a) What task was entrusted to Titus? (b) In what environment had the congregations on Crete sprung up, and what did the Christians in Crete need to do?

quoted their own prophet as saying: "Cretans are always liars, injurious wild beasts, unemployed gluttons." (1:12) The Cretans of Paul's day have also been described as follows: "The character of the people was unsteady, insincere, and quarrelsome; they were given to greediness, licentiousness, falsehood, and drunkenness, in no ordinary degree; and the Jews who had settled among them appear to have gone beyond the natives in immorality."* It was in just such an environment that the congregations of Crete had sprung up; and hence it was especially needful for the believers "to repudiate ungodliness and worldly desires and to live with soundness of mind and righteousness and godly devotion," as Paul exhorted. —2:12.

___
* McClintock and Strong's *Cyclopedia,* 1981 reprint, Vol. X, page 442.

2 The book of Titus itself gives very little information about the association of Paul and Titus. From the references to Titus in Paul's other letters, however, much information can be gleaned. Titus, who was a Greek, often accompanied Paul and on at least one occasion went up to Jerusalem with him. (Gal. 2:1-5) Paul refers to him as "a sharer with me and a fellow worker." It was Titus whom Paul had sent to Corinth after writing his first letter to the Corinthians from Ephesus. While in Corinth, Titus was connected with the collection that was being made for the brothers in Jerusalem, and subsequently he went back at Paul's direction to complete the collection. It was on the return journey to Corinth from his meeting with Paul in Macedonia that Titus was used to carry the second letter from Paul to the Corinthians.—2 Cor. 8: 16-24; 2:13; 7:5-7.

3 After his release from his first imprisonment in Rome, Paul was again associated with Timothy and Titus during the final years of his ministry. This appears to have included service in Crete, Greece, and Macedonia. Finally, Paul is spoken of as going to Nicopolis, in northwest Greece, where he was apparently arrested and taken to Rome for his final imprisonment and execution. It was during the visit to Crete that Paul had left Titus there to "correct the things that were defective and . . . make appointments of older men in city after city," in harmony with the instructions he had given Titus. Paul's letter appears to have been written shortly after he left Titus in Crete, most likely from Macedonia. (Titus 1:5; 3:12; 1 Tim. 1:3; 2 Tim. 4:13, 20) It seems to have served a purpose similar to that of First Timothy, namely, to encourage Paul's colaborer and to give him authoritative backing in his duties.

4 Paul must have written the letter sometime between his first and his second imprisonment at Rome, or about 61 to 64 C.E. The weight of evidence for the authenticity of the letter to Titus is the same as for the contemporary letters to Timothy, the three Bible books often being termed Paul's "pastoral letters." The style of writing is similar. Irenaeus and Origen both quote from Titus, and many other ancient authorities also testify to the book's canonicity. It is found in the Sinaitic and Alexandrine Manuscripts. In the John Rylands Library there is a papyrus fragment, P[32], which is a codex leaf of about the third century C.E. containing Titus 1:11-15 and 2:3-8.* There is no question that the book is an authentic part of the inspired Scriptures.

CONTENTS OF TITUS

5 **Overseers to exhort by healthful teaching** (1: 1-16). After an affectionate greeting, Paul sets out the qualifications for overseers. It is emphasized that an overseer must be "free from accusation," a lover of goodness, righteous, loyal, a man "holding firmly to the faithful word as respects his art of teaching, that he may be able both to exhort by the teaching that is healthful and to reprove those who contradict." This is needful in view of the "deceivers of the mind" who are even subverting entire households for the sake of dishonest gain. So Titus must "keep on reproving them with severity, that they may be healthy in the faith, paying no attention to Jewish fables." Defiled persons may declare publicly that they know God, but they disown him by their works of disobedience.—1:6-10, 13, 14.

6 **Living with soundness of mind, righteousness, and godly devotion** (2:1–3:15). The aged men and aged women should be serious and reverent. The younger women should love their husbands and their children and subject themselves to their husbands "so that the word of God may not be spoken of abusively." The younger men should be an example of fine works and wholesome speech. Slaves in subjection should exhibit "good fidelity to the full." God's undeserved kindness, leading to salvation, has been manifested, encouraging soundness of mind, righteousness, and godly devotion in those whom God has cleansed through Christ Jesus to be "a people peculiarly his own, zealous for fine works."—2:5, 10, 14.

7 Paul stresses the need for subjection and obedience to governments and for "exhibiting all mildness toward all men." Paul and his fellow Christians were once as bad as other men. Not owing to any works of their own, but because of God's kindness, love, and mercy, they have been saved by holy spirit and have become heirs to a hope of everlasting life. So those who believe God should "keep their minds on maintaining fine works." They are to shun foolish questionings and strife over the Law, and as for a man that promotes a sect, they are to reject him after a first and

---

* The Text of the New Testament, by Kurt and Barbara Aland, translated by E. F. Rhodes, 1987, page 98.

5. (a) What qualifications for overseers does Paul emphasize, and why is this needful? (b) Why must Titus reprove with severity, and what is said of defiled persons?
6. What advice is given on Christian conduct?
7. What does Paul stress in connection with subjection, salvation, and fine works?

2, 3. (a) What association did Titus have with Paul? (b) From where did Paul likely write to Titus, and for what purpose?
4. When must the letter to Titus have been written, and what is the evidence for its authenticity?

second admonition. Paul asks Titus to come to him at Nicopolis and, after giving other missionary instructions, stresses again the need for fine works, in order not to be unfruitful.—3:2, 7, 8.

WHY BENEFICIAL

[8] The Cretan Christians lived in an environment of lying, corruption, and greed. Should they just go along with the crowd? Or should they take definite steps to separate themselves completely to serve as a people sanctified to Jehovah God? In making known through Titus that the Cretans should "keep their minds on maintaining fine works," Paul said: "These things are fine and beneficial to men." It is "fine and beneficial" today also, in a world that has sunk into a mire of untruthfulness and dishonest practices, that real Christians "learn to maintain fine works," being fruitful in God's service. (3: 8, 14) All of Paul's condemnation of the immorality and wickedness that threatened the congregations in Crete stands as a warning to us now when 'the undeserved kindness of God instructs us to repudiate ungodliness and worldly desires and to live with soundness of mind and righteousness and godly devotion amid this system of things.' Christians should also be "ready for every good work" in showing obedience to governments, maintaining a good conscience.—2:11, 12; 3:1.

[9] Titus 1:5-9 supplements 1 Timothy 3:2-7 in

---

8. What in Paul's counsel in the letter to Titus is "fine and beneficial" for us today, and why?
9. How is the importance of right teaching underlined, especially as a responsibility of an overseer?

showing what holy spirit requires of overseers. This lays emphasis on the overseer's "holding firmly to the faithful word" and being a teacher in the congregation. How necessary this is in bringing all along to maturity! In fact, this need for right teaching is emphasized several times in the letter to Titus. Paul admonishes Titus to "keep on speaking what things are fitting for healthful teaching." The aged women are to be "teachers of what is good," and slaves are 'to adorn the teaching of their Savior, God, in all things.' (Titus 1:9; 2:1, 3, 10) Stressing the need for Titus as an overseer to be firm and fearless in his teaching, Paul says: "Keep on speaking these things and exhorting and reproving with full authority to command." And in the case of those who disobey, he says: "Keep on reproving them with severity, that they may be healthy in the faith." Thus, Paul's letter to Titus is especially "beneficial for teaching, for reproving, for setting things straight, for disciplining in righteousness."—Titus 2:15; 1:13; 2 Tim. 3:16.

[10] The letter to Titus stimulates our appreciation for the undeserved kindness of God and encourages us to turn from the ungodliness of the world 'while we wait for the happy hope and glorious manifestation of the great God and of our Savior, Christ Jesus.' So doing, those who have been declared righteous through Christ Jesus may become "heirs according to a hope of everlasting life" in the Kingdom of God.—Titus 2:13; 3:7.

---

10. In what does the letter to Titus encourage us, and what happy hope does it stimulate?

Bible Book Number **57**	Writer: **Paul**
Philemon	Place Written: **Rome**
	Writing Completed: **c. 60–61 C.E.**

THIS very tactful and loving letter of Paul is of great interest to Christians today. Not only is it the shortest epistle preserved from the hand of the "apostle to the nations" but in the whole Bible only Second and Third John contain less material. Also, it is the only "private" letter of Paul, in that it was not addressed officially to a congregation or a responsible overseer but was addressed to a private person and dealt solely

with the special problem Paul wanted to discuss with this Christian brother, the apparently well-to-do Philemon, who lived in the Phrygian city of Colossae, in the very heart of Asia Minor.—Rom. 11:13.

[2] The purpose of the letter is clearly revealed: During his first imprisonment in Rome (59-61 C.E.), Paul had great freedom to preach the Kingdom of God. Among those who listened to his

---

1. What are some of the characteristics of the letter to Philemon?

2. Against what background and for what purpose was the letter to Philemon written?

preaching was Onesimus, a runaway slave from the household of Philemon, Paul's friend. As a result, Onesimus became a Christian, and Paul decided, with Onesimus' consent, to send him back to Philemon. It was at this time, also, that Paul wrote letters to the congregations in Ephesus and Colossae. In both of these letters, he gave good counsel to Christian slaves and slave owners on how to conduct themselves properly in this relationship. (Eph. 6:5-9; Col. 3:22–4:1) However, over and above this, Paul composed a letter to Philemon in which he personally pleaded in behalf of Onesimus. It was a letter written with his own hand—an unusual thing for Paul. (Philem. 19) This personal touch added greatly to the weight of his plea.

³ The letter was most likely penned about 60-61 C.E., as Paul had apparently preached in Rome long enough to make converts. Also, because he expresses hope, in verse 22, of being released, we can conclude that the letter was written after some time of his imprisonment had elapsed. It appears that these three letters, one for Philemon and those for the congregations in Ephesus and Colossae, were dispatched with Tychicus and Onesimus.—Eph. 6:21, 22; Col. 4:7-9.

⁴ That Paul was the writer of Philemon is evident from the first verse, where he is mentioned by name. He was acknowledged as such by Origen and Tertullian.* The authenticity of the book is also supported by its being listed, with others of Paul's epistles, in the Muratorian Fragment of the second century C.E.

CONTENTS OF PHILEMON

⁵ **Onesimus sent back to his master "as more than a slave"** (Vss. 1-25). Paul sends warm greetings to Philemon, to Apphia "our sister," to Archippus "our fellow soldier," and to the congregation in Philemon's house. He commends Philemon (whose name means "Loving") for the love and faith he has toward the Lord Jesus and the holy ones. Reports of Philemon's love have brought Paul much joy and comfort. Paul, an aged man and a prisoner, now expresses himself with great freeness of speech concerning his "child" Onesimus, to whom he became "a father" while in prison bonds. Onesimus (whose name means "Profitable") had

formerly been useless to Philemon, but now he is useful to both Philemon and Paul.—Vss. 2, 10.

⁶ The apostle would like to keep Onesimus to minister to him in prison, but he would not do so without Philemon's consent. So he is sending him back, "no longer as a slave but as more than a slave, as a brother beloved." Paul asks that Onesimus be received kindly, the same way Paul himself would be received. If Onesimus has wronged Philemon, let it be charged to Paul's account, for, Paul tells Philemon, "You owe me even yourself." (Vss. 16, 19) Paul hopes he may soon be released and that he may visit Philemon, and he concludes with greetings.

WHY BENEFICIAL

⁷ As is shown by this letter, Paul was not preaching a "social gospel," trying to do away with the existing system of things and its institutions, such as slavery. He did not arbitrarily set even Christian slaves free, but, rather, he sent the runaway slave Onesimus on a journey taking him over 900 miles from Rome to Colossae, right back to his master Philemon. Thus Paul adhered to his high call as an apostle, abiding strictly by his divine commission of "preaching the kingdom of God . . . and teaching the things concerning the Lord Jesus Christ."—Acts 28:31; Philem. 8, 9.

⁸ The letter to Philemon is revealing in that it shows the love and unity that existed among the Christians of the first century. In it we learn that the early Christians called one another "brother" and "sister." (Philem. 2, 20) In addition, it reveals for Christians today the practical application of Christian principles among Christian brothers. On the part of Paul, we find the expression of brotherly love, respect for civil relations and for the property of another, effective tactfulness, and commendable humility. Instead of trying to compel Philemon to forgive Onesimus by the weight of the authority he possessed as a leading overseer in the Christian congregation, Paul humbly appealed to him on the basis of Christian love and his personal friendship. Overseers today can benefit from the tactful manner in which Paul approached Philemon.

⁹ Paul obviously expected Philemon to comply with his request, and Philemon's doing so would be a practical application of what Jesus said at

---

* *The International Standard Bible Encyclopedia,* edited by G. W. Bromiley, Vol. 3, 1986, page 831.

3. When was the letter to Philemon most likely penned, and how was it forwarded?
4. What proves the writership and the authenticity of Philemon?
5. (a) With what greetings and commendation does the letter open? (b) What does Paul tell Philemon of his slave Onesimus?

6. What kind of treatment does Paul recommend for Onesimus, and with what tactful reasoning?
7. As regards Onesimus, how was Paul adhering to his high call as an apostle?
8. What practical application of Christian principles does Philemon illustrate?
9. By complying with Paul's request, what fine precedent that is of interest to Christians today would Philemon set?

Matthew 6:14 and of what Paul said at Ephesians 4:32. Christians today can likewise be expected to be kind and forgiving toward an offending brother. If Philemon could be forgiving toward a slave that he owned and that he was legally free to mistreat as he pleased, Christians today should be able to forgive an offending brother—a far less difficult task.

[10] The operation of Jehovah's spirit is very evi-

dent in this letter to Philemon. It is manifested in the masterful way in which Paul handled a very touchy problem. It is evident in the fellow feeling, the tender affection, and the trust in a fellow Christian that are exhibited by Paul. It is seen in the fact that the letter to Philemon, like the other Scriptures, teaches Christian principles, encourages Christian unity, and magnifies the love and faith that abound among "the holy ones," who hope in God's Kingdom and in whose conduct is reflected the loving-kindness of Jehovah.—Vs. 5.

10. How is the operation of Jehovah's spirit evident in the letter to Philemon?

Bible Book Number 58

Hebrews

Writer: **Paul**

Place Written: **Rome**

Writing Completed: **c. 61 C.E.**

PAUL is best known as the apostle "to the nations." But was his ministry confined to the non-Jews? Not at all! Just before Paul was baptized and commissioned for his work, the Lord Jesus said to Ananias: "This man [Paul] is a chosen vessel to me to bear my name to the nations as well as to kings and *the sons of Israel.*" (Acts 9:15; Gal. 2:8, 9) The writing of the book of Hebrews was truly in line with Paul's commission to bear the name of Jesus to the sons of Israel.

[2] However, some critics doubt Paul's writership of Hebrews. One objection is that Paul's name does not appear in the letter. But this is really no obstacle, as many other canonical books fail to name the writer, who is often identified by internal evidence. Moreover, some feel that Paul may have deliberately omitted his name in writing to the Hebrew Christians in Judea, since his name had been made an object of hatred by the Jews there. (Acts 21:28) Neither is the change of style from his other epistles any real objection to Paul's writership. Whether addressing pagans, Jews, or Christians, Paul always showed his ability to "become all things to people of all sorts." Here his reasoning is presented to Jews as from a Jew, arguments that they could fully understand and appreciate.—1 Cor. 9:22.

[3] The internal evidence of the book is all in support of Paul's writership. The writer was in Italy and was associated with Timothy. These facts fit Paul. (Heb. 13:23, 24) Furthermore, the doctrine is typical of Paul, though the arguments are presented from a Jewish viewpoint, designed to appeal to the strictly Hebrew congregation to which the letter was addressed. On this point Clarke's *Commentary,* Volume 6, page 681, says concerning Hebrews: "That it was written to *Jews,* naturally such, the whole structure of the epistle proves. Had it been written to the *Gentiles,* not one in ten thousand of them could have comprehended the argument, because unacquainted with the Jewish system; the knowledge of which the writer of this epistle everywhere supposes." This helps to account for the difference of style when compared with Paul's other letters.

[4] The discovery in about 1930 of the Chester Beatty Papyrus No. 2 (P[46]) has provided further evidence of Paul's writership. Commenting on this papyrus codex, which was written only about a century and a half after Paul's death, the eminent British textual critic Sir Frederic Kenyon said: "It is noticeable that Hebrews is placed immediately after Romans (an almost unprecedented position),

1. In line with what commission did Paul write the letter to the Hebrews?
2. How may arguments against Paul's writership of Hebrews be refuted?

3. What internal evidence both supports Paul's writership of Hebrews and indicates that he wrote primarily for the Jews?
4. What further evidence is there as to Paul's writership of Hebrews?

which shows that at the early date when this manuscript was written no doubt was felt as to its Pauline authorship."* On this same question, McClintock and Strong's *Cyclopedia* states pointedly: "There is no substantial evidence, external or internal, in favor of any claimant to the authorship of this epistle except Paul."#

⁵ Apart from the book's acceptance by the early Christians, the contents of Hebrews prove that it is "inspired of God." It continually points the reader toward the Hebrew Scripture prophecies, making numerous references to the early writings, and shows how these were all fulfilled in Christ Jesus. In the first chapter alone, no less than seven quotations from the Hebrew Scriptures are used as the point is developed that the Son is now superior to the angels. It constantly magnifies Jehovah's Word and his name, pointing to Jesus as the Chief Agent of life and to God's Kingdom by Christ as mankind's only hope.

⁶ As to the time of writing, it has already been shown that Paul wrote the letter while in Italy. In concluding the letter, he says: "Take note that our brother Timothy has been released, with whom, if he comes quite soon, I shall see you." (13:23) This seems to indicate that Paul was expecting an early release from prison and hoped to accompany Timothy, who had also been imprisoned but who had already been released. Thus, the final year of Paul's first imprisonment in Rome is suggested as the date of writing, namely, 61 C.E.

⁷ During the time of the end of the Jewish system of things, a period of crucial testing came upon the Hebrew Christians in Judea and especially on those in Jerusalem. With the growth and spread of the good news, the Jews were becoming bitter and fanatic in the extreme in their opposition to the Christians. Only a few years earlier, the mere appearance of Paul in Jerusalem had stirred up a riot, with the religious Jews screaming at the top of their voices: "Take such a man away from the earth, for he was not fit to live!" More than 40 Jews had bound themselves with a curse neither to eat nor to drink until they had done away with him, and it required a strong escort of heavily armed troops to bring him down by night to Caesarea. (Acts 22:22; 23:12-15, 23, 24) In this atmosphere of religious fanaticism and hatred of Christians, the congregation had to live, preach, and keep themselves firm in the faith. They had to have sound knowledge and understanding of how

Christ fulfilled the Law that they might keep from falling back to Judaism and its observing of the Mosaic Law with the offering of animal sacrifices, all of it now nothing more than empty ritual.

⁸ No one was better able to understand the pressure and persecution to which the Jewish Christians were exposed than the apostle Paul. No one was better equipped to supply them with powerful arguments and refutations of Jewish tradition than Paul, the former Pharisee. Drawing on his vast knowledge of the Mosaic Law, learned at the feet of Gamaliel, he presented incontestable proof that Christ is the fulfillment of the Law, its ordinances, and its sacrifices. He showed how these had now been replaced by far more glorious realities, bringing inestimably greater benefits under a new and better covenant. His keen mind lined up proof after proof in clear and convincing array. The end of the Law covenant and the coming in of the new covenant, the superiority of Christ's priesthood over the Aaronic priesthood, the real value of Christ's sacrifice compared with the offerings of bulls and goats, the entry of Christ into the very presence of Jehovah in the heavens rather than into a mere earthly tent—all these strikingly new teachings, hateful in the extreme to the unbelieving Jews, were here presented to the Hebrew Christians with such abundant evidence from the Hebrew Scriptures that no reasonable Jew could fail to be convinced.

⁹ Armed with this letter, the Hebrew Christians had a new and powerful weapon to stop the mouths of the persecuting Jews, as well as a persuasive argument with which to convince and convert honest Jews seeking God's truth. The letter shows Paul's deep love for the Hebrew Christians and his burning desire to help them in a practical way in their time of great need.

CONTENTS OF HEBREWS
¹⁰ **The exalted position of Christ** (1:1–3:6). The opening words focus attention on Christ: "God, who long ago spoke on many occasions and in many ways to our forefathers by means of the prophets, has at the end of these days spoken to us by means of a Son." This Son is the appointed Heir of all things and the reflection of his Father's glory. Having made a purification for our sins, he has now "sat down on the right hand of the Majesty in lofty places." (1:1-3) Paul quotes scripture upon scripture to prove Jesus' superiority over the angels.

---

* *The Story of the Bible,* 1964, page 91.
# 1981 reprint, Vol. IV, page 147.

---

5. How do the contents of Hebrews prove it to be inspired?
6. What does the evidence indicate as to place and time of writing of Hebrews?
7. With what kind of opposition were the Jewish Christians in Jerusalem faced, and what did they need?

8. Why was Paul admirably equipped to write this letter to the Hebrews, and what array of arguments did he present?
9. What powerful weapon did the letter of Hebrews become, and how was it a demonstration of Paul's love?
10. What do the opening words of Hebrews state with regard to Christ's position?

[11] Paul writes that "it is necessary for us to pay more than the usual attention." Why so? Because, argues Paul, if there was severe retribution for disobeying "the word spoken through angels, . . . how shall we escape if we have neglected a salvation of such greatness in that it began to be spoken through our Lord?" God made "the son of man" a little lower than angels, but now we behold this Jesus "crowned with glory and honor for having suffered death, that he by God's undeserved kindness might taste death for every man." (2:1-3, 6, 9) In bringing many sons to glory, God first made this Chief Agent of their salvation "perfect through sufferings." He it is who brings the Devil to nothing and emancipates "all those who for fear of death were subject to slavery all through their lives." Jesus thus becomes "a merciful and faithful high priest." And wonderfully, since he himself suffered under test, "he is able to come to the aid of those who are being put to the test." (2:10, 15, 17, 18) Hence, Jesus is counted worthy of more glory than Moses.

[12] **Entering into God's rest by faith and obedience** (3:7–4:13). Christians, of all people, should take warning from the Israelites' example of unfaithfulness, for fear of developing "a wicked heart lacking faith by drawing away from the living God." (Heb. 3:12; Ps. 95:7-11) Because of disobedience and lack of faith, the Israelites who left Egypt failed to enter God's rest, or Sabbath, during which he has desisted from creative works as respects the earth. However, Paul explains: "There remains a sabbath resting for the people of God. For the man that has entered into God's rest has also himself rested from his own works, just as God did from his own." The pattern of disobedience shown by Israel is to be avoided. "For the word of God is alive and exerts power and is sharper than any two-edged sword . . . and is able to discern thoughts and intentions of the heart." —Heb. 4:9, 10, 12.

[13] **Mature view of superiority of Christ's priesthood** (4:14–7:28). Paul urges the Hebrews to hold on to confessing Jesus, the great High Priest who has passed through the heavens, that they may find mercy. The Christ did not glorify himself, but it was the Father who said: "You are a priest forever according to the manner of Melchizedek." (Heb. 5:6; Ps. 110:4) First, Christ was made

perfect for the position of high priest by learning obedience through suffering, in order to become responsible for everlasting salvation to all those obeying him. Paul has "much to say and hard to be explained," but the Hebrews are still babes in need of milk, when, in fact, they ought to be teachers. "Solid food belongs to mature people, to those who through use have their perceptive powers trained to distinguish both right and wrong." The apostle urges them to "press on to maturity." —Heb. 5:11, 14; 6:1.

[14] It is impossible for those who have known the word of God and who have fallen away to be revived again to repentance "because they impale the Son of God afresh for themselves and expose him to public shame." Only through faith and patience can believers inherit the promise made to Abraham—a promise made sure and firm by two unchangeable things: God's word and his oath. Their hope, which is as "an anchor for the soul, both sure and firm," has been established by Jesus' entry "within the curtain" as Forerunner and High Priest according to the manner of Melchizedek.—6:6, 19.

[15] This Melchizedek was both "king of Salem" and "priest of the Most High God." Even the family head Abraham paid tithes to him, and through him Levi, who was still in the loins of Abraham, did so. Melchizedek's blessing of Abraham thus extended to the unborn Levi, and this showed that the Levitical priesthood was inferior to that of Melchizedek. Further, if perfection came through the Levitical priesthood of Aaron, would there be need for another priest "according to the manner of Melchizedek"? Moreover, since there is a change of priesthood, "there comes to be of necessity a change also of the law."—7:1, 11, 12.

[16] The Law, in fact, made nothing perfect but proved to be weak and ineffective. Because they kept dying, its priests were many, but Jesus by "continuing alive forever has his priesthood without any successors. Consequently he is able also to save completely those who are approaching God through him, because he is always alive to plead for them." This High Priest, Jesus, is "loyal, guileless, undefiled, separated from the sinners," whereas the high priests appointed by the Law are weak, having first to offer sacrifices for their own sins before they can intercede for others. So the word of God's sworn oath "appoints a Son, who is perfected forever."—7:24-26, 28.

---

11. (a) Why does Paul counsel paying more than the usual attention to the things heard? (b) Because of his experiences and his exalted position, what things is Jesus able to accomplish?
12. What course must Christians avoid if they are to enter into God's rest?
13. (a) How did Christ become "a priest forever," responsible for everlasting salvation? (b) Why does Paul urge the Hebrews to press on to maturity?

14. How may believers inherit the promise, and how has their hope been established?
15. What shows that Jesus' priesthood, being according to the manner of Melchizedek, would be superior to that of Levi?
16. Why is the priesthood of Jesus superior to the priesthood under the Law?

[17] **The superiority of the new covenant** (8:1–10:31). Jesus is shown to be "the mediator of a correspondingly better covenant, which has been legally established upon better promises." (8:6) Paul quotes in full Jeremiah 31:31-34, showing that those in the new covenant have God's laws written in their minds and hearts, that all will know Jehovah, and that Jehovah will "by no means call their sins to mind anymore." This "new covenant" has made obsolete the former one (the Law covenant), which is "near to vanishing away." —Heb. 8:12, 13.

[18] Paul describes the yearly sacrifices at the tent of the former covenant as "legal requirements . . . imposed until the appointed time to set things straight." However, when Christ came as High Priest, it was with his own precious blood, and not that of goats and of young bulls. Moses' sprinkling of the blood of animals had validated the former covenant and cleansed the typical tent, but better sacrifices were necessary for the heavenly realities in connection with the new covenant. "For Christ entered, not into a holy place made with hands, which is a copy of the reality, but into heaven itself, now to appear before the person of God for us." Christ does not have to make yearly sacrifices, as did Israel's high priest, for "now he has manifested himself once for all time at the conclusion of the systems of things to put sin away through the sacrifice of himself."—9:10, 24, 26.

[19] In summary, Paul says that "since the Law has a shadow of the good things to come," its repetitious sacrifices have not been able to remove the "consciousness of sins." However, Jesus came into the world to do God's will. "By the said 'will,'" says Paul, "we have been sanctified through the offering of the body of Jesus Christ once for all time." Therefore, let the Hebrews hold fast the public declaration of their faith without wavering and "consider one another to incite to love and fine works," not forsaking the gathering of themselves together. If they continue to sin willfully after receiving the accurate knowledge of the truth, "there is no longer any sacrifice for sins left."—10:1, 2, 10, 24, 26.

[20] **Faith explained and illustrated** (10:32–12:3). Paul now tells the Hebrews: "Keep on remembering the former days in which, after you were enlightened, you endured a great contest under sufferings." Let them not throw away their freeness of speech, which has a great reward, but let them endure in order to receive the fulfillment of the promise and "have faith to the preserving alive of the soul." Faith! Yes, that is what is needed. First, Paul defines it: "Faith is the assured expectation of things hoped for, the evident demonstration of realities though not beheld." Then, in one inspiring chapter, he paints in quick succession brief word pictures of men of old who lived, worked, fought, endured, and became heirs of righteousness through faith. "By faith" Abraham, dwelling in tents with Isaac and Jacob, awaited "the city having real foundations," the Builder of which is God. "By faith" Moses continued steadfast, "as seeing the One who is invisible." "What more shall I say?" asks Paul. "For the time will fail me if I go on to relate about Gideon, Barak, Samson, Jephthah, David as well as Samuel and the other prophets, who through faith defeated kingdoms in conflict, effected righteousness, obtained promises." Others too were tried through mockings, scourgings, bonds, and tortures but refused release "in order that they might attain a better resurrection." Truly, "the world was not worthy of them." All of these had witness borne to them through their faith, but they have yet to receive the fulfillment of the promise. "So, then," continues Paul, "because we have so great a cloud of witnesses surrounding us, let us also put off every weight and the sin that easily entangles us, and let us run with endurance the race that is set before us, as we look intently at the Chief Agent and Perfecter of our faith, Jesus."—10:32, 39; 11:1, 8, 10, 27, 32, 33, 35, 38; 12:1, 2.

[21] **Endurance in the contest of faith** (12:4-29). Paul exhorts the Hebrew Christians to endure in the contest of faith, for Jehovah is disciplining them as sons. Now is the time to strengthen enfeebled hands and knees and to keep making straight paths for their feet. They must strictly guard against the entry of any poisonous root or defilement that could cause their rejection, as in the case of Esau, who did not appreciate sacred things. At the literal mountain, Moses said: "I am fearful and trembling" because of the fearsome display of flaming fire, the cloud, and the voice. But they have approached something far more awe-inspiring—Mount Zion and a heavenly Jerusalem, myriads of angels, the congregation of the Firstborn, God the Judge of all, and Jesus the Mediator of a new and better covenant. Now there is all the more reason to listen to divine warning! In Moses' time God's voice shook the earth, but now He has promised to set both heaven and earth in commotion. Paul drives home the point: "Wherefore, see-

---

17. In what is the new covenant superior?
18. What comparison does Paul make on the matter of sacrifice in connection with the two covenants?
19. (a) What has the Law been unable to do, and why? (b) What is God's will in connection with sanctification?
20. (a) What is faith? (b) What glowing word pictures of faith does Paul paint?

---

21. (a) How may Christians endure in the contest of faith? (b) What stronger reason for listening to divine warning does Paul give?

ing that we are to receive a kingdom that cannot be shaken, let us . . . acceptably render God sacred service with godly fear and awe. For our God is also a consuming fire."—12:21, 28, 29.

²² **Various exhortations on matters of worship** (13:1-25). Paul concludes on a note of upbuilding counsel: Let brotherly love continue, do not forget hospitality, let marriage be honorable among all, keep free from the love of money, be obedient to those taking the lead among you, and do not be carried away by strange teachings. Finally, "through him [Jesus] let us always offer to God a sacrifice of praise, that is, the fruit of lips which make public declaration to his name."—13:15.

WHY BENEFICIAL

²³ As a legal argument in support of Christ, the letter to the Hebrews is an unchallengeable masterpiece, perfectly constructed and freely documented with proof from the Hebrew Scriptures. It takes the various features of the Mosaic Law—the covenant, the blood, the mediator, the tent of worship, the priesthood, the offerings—and shows them to have been nothing more than a pattern made by God pointing forward to far greater things to come, all culminating in Christ Jesus and his sacrifice, the fulfillment of the Law. The Law "which is made obsolete and growing old is near to vanishing away," said Paul. But "Jesus Christ is the same yesterday and today, and forever." (8:13; 13:8; 10:1) How joyful those Hebrews must have felt on reading their letter!

²⁴ But of what value is this to us today, in our different circumstances? Since we are not under the Law, can we find anything beneficial in Paul's argument? Most certainly, yes. Here is outlined for us the great new covenant arrangement based on the promise to Abraham that through his Seed all families of the earth would bless themselves. This is our hope for life, our only hope, the fulfillment of Jehovah's ancient promise of blessing through Abraham's Seed, Jesus Christ. Although not under the Law, we are born in sin as Adam's offspring, and we need a merciful high priest, one with a valid sin offering, one who can enter right into Jehovah's presence in heaven and there intercede for us. Here we find him, the High Priest who can lead us to life in Jehovah's new world, who can sympathize with our weaknesses, having "been tested in all respects like ourselves," and who invites us to "approach with freeness of speech to the throne of undeserved kindness, that we may

obtain mercy and find undeserved kindness for help at the right time."—4:15, 16.

²⁵ Furthermore, in Paul's letter to the Hebrews, we find heart-stirring evidence that prophecies recorded long ago in the Hebrew Scriptures were later fulfilled in a marvelous way. All of this is for our instruction and comfort today. For example, in Hebrews, Paul five times applies the words of the Kingdom prophecy at Psalm 110:1 to Jesus Christ as the Kingdom Seed, who "has sat down at the right hand of the throne of God" to wait "until his enemies should be placed as a stool for his feet." (Heb. 12:2; 10:12, 13; 1:3, 13; 8:1) Further, Paul quotes Psalm 110:4 in explaining the important office filled by the Son of God as "a priest forever according to the manner of Melchizedek." Like Melchizedek of old, who in the Bible record is "fatherless, motherless, without genealogy, having neither a beginning of days nor an end of life," Jesus is both King and "a priest perpetually" to administer the everlasting benefits of his ransom sacrifice to all who obediently place themselves under his rule. (Heb. 5:6, 10; 6:20; 7:1-21) It is to this same King-Priest that Paul refers in quoting Psalm 45:6, 7: "God is your throne forever and ever, and the scepter of your kingdom is the scepter of uprightness. You loved righteousness, and you hated lawlessness. That is why God, your God, anointed you with the oil of exultation more than your partners." (Heb. 1:8, 9) As Paul quotes from the Hebrew Scriptures and shows their fulfillment in Christ Jesus, we see the pieces of the divine pattern falling into place for our enlightenment.

²⁶ As the letter to the Hebrews clearly shows, Abraham looked forward to the Kingdom, "the city having real foundations, the builder and maker of which city is God"—the city "belonging to heaven." "By faith" he reached out for the Kingdom, and he made great sacrifices that he might attain its blessings by "a better resurrection." What a striking example we find in Abraham and in all those other men and women of faith—the "so great a cloud of witnesses" that Paul portrays in chapter 11 of Hebrews! As we read this record, our hearts exult and leap for joy, in appreciation of the privilege and hope we have along with such faithful integrity keepers. Thus we are encouraged to "run with endurance the race that is set before us."—11:8, 10, 16, 35; 12:1.

²⁷ Quoting from Haggai's prophecy, Paul calls attention to God's promise: "Yet once more I will

---

22. With what upbuilding counsel does Paul conclude his letter to the Hebrews?
23. What does Paul argue as to the Law, and how does he support his argument?
24. What arrangement is explained in Hebrews that is of immeasurable benefit to us today?

25. What enlightening applications does Paul make of the Hebrew Scriptures?
26. What encouragement does Hebrews give to run the race in faith and with endurance?
27. What glorious Kingdom prospects are highlighted in Hebrews?

set in commotion not only the earth but also the heaven." (Heb. 12:26; Hag. 2:6) However, God's Kingdom by Christ Jesus, the Seed, will remain forever. "Wherefore, seeing that we are to receive a kingdom that cannot be shaken, let us continue to have undeserved kindness, through which we may acceptably render God sacred service with godly fear and awe." This stirring record assures us that Christ appears a second time "apart from sin and to those earnestly looking for him for their salvation." Through him, then, "let us always offer to God a sacrifice of praise, that is, the fruit of lips which make public declaration to his name." May the great name of Jehovah God be forever sanctified through his King-Priest, Jesus Christ!—Heb. 12:28; 9:28; 13:15.

Bible Book Number **59**	Writer: **James**
James	Place Written: **Jerusalem**
	Writing Completed: **Before 62 C.E.**

"HE HAS gone out of his mind." That is what Jesus' relatives thought of him. During the time of his earthly ministry, "his brothers were, in fact, not exercising faith in him," and James, along with Joseph, Simon, and Judas, was not counted as one of Jesus' early disciples. (Mark 3:21; John 7:5; Matt. 13:55) On what grounds can it be said, then, that James the half brother of Jesus wrote the Bible book that bears the name James?

2 The record shows that the resurrected Jesus appeared to James, and this no doubt convinced him beyond question that Jesus was the Messiah. (1 Cor. 15:7) Acts 1:12-14 says that even before Pentecost, Mary and the brothers of Jesus were assembling for prayer with the apostles in an upper chamber in Jerusalem. But did not one of the apostles called James write the letter? No, for at the outset the writer identifies himself, not as an apostle, but as 'a slave of the Lord Jesus Christ.' Moreover, Jude's introductory words, similar to those of James, mention Jude (or Judas) also as "a slave of Jesus Christ, but a brother of James." (Jas. 1:1; Jude 1) From this we can safely conclude that James and Jude, the fleshly half brothers of Jesus, wrote the Bible books that bear their names.

3 James was eminently qualified to write a letter of counsel to the Christian congregation. He was greatly respected as an overseer in the Jerusalem congregation. Paul speaks of "James the brother of the Lord" as one of the "pillars" in the congregation along with Cephas and John. (Gal. 1:19; 2:9) James' prominence is indicated by Peter's sending immediate word to "James and the brothers" after his release from prison. And was it not James who acted as spokesman for "the apostles and the older men" when Paul and Barnabas journeyed to Jerusalem to request a decision regarding circumcision? Incidentally, this decision and the letter of James both start with the identical salutation, "Greetings!"—another indication that they had a common writer.—Acts 12:17; 15:13, 22, 23; Jas. 1:1.

4 The historian Josephus tells us it was High Priest Ananus (Ananias), a Sadducee, who was responsible for the death of James by stoning. This was after the death of the Roman governor Festus, about 62 C.E., and before his successor, Albinus, took office.* But when did James write his letter? James addressed his letter from Jerusalem to "the twelve tribes that are scattered about," literally, "the (ones) in the dispersion." (Jas. 1:1, footnote) It would have required time for Christianity to spread out following the outpouring of holy spirit in 33 C.E., and it would have required time, also, for the alarming conditions mentioned in the letter to develop. Further, the letter indicates that the Christians were no longer small groups but that they were organized into congregations with mature "older men" who could pray for and support the weak. Additionally, sufficient time had elapsed for a measure of complacency and formalism to creep in. (2:1-4; 4:1-3; 5:14; 1:26, 27) It is most probable, therefore, that

---

1. What raises a question as to James' writership of the book that bears the name James?
2. What argues that Jesus' half brother was the writer of James?
3. What were James' qualifications for writing?

---

* *Jewish Antiquities*, XX, 197-200 (ix, 1); *Webster's New Biographical Dictionary*, 1983, page 350.

---

4. What indicates that the letter of James was written shortly before 62 C.E.?

James wrote his letter at a late date, perhaps shortly before 62 C.E., if Josephus' account about the events surrounding the death of Festus and if the sources placing Festus' death in about 62 C.E. are correct.

⁵ As to the authenticity of James, it is contained in the Vatican No. 1209, the Sinaitic, and the Alexandrine manuscripts. It is included in at least ten ancient catalogs prior to the Council of Carthage 397 C.E.* It was widely quoted by early ecclesiastical writers. A deep inner harmony with the rest of the inspired Scriptures is very evident in James' writings.

⁶ Why did James write this letter? A careful consideration of the letter discloses that internal conditions were causing difficulties among the brothers. Christian standards were being lowered, yes, even ignored, so that some had become spiritual adulteresses as regards friendship with the world. Eager to invent supposed contradictions, some have claimed that James' letter encouraging faith by works nullifies Paul's writings regarding salvation by faith and not by works. However, the context reveals that James refers to faith supported by works, not just words, whereas Paul clearly means works of the Law. Actually, James supplements the arguments of Paul, going one step further by defining how faith is made manifest. James' counsel is most practical in its coverage of the day-to-day problems of the Christian.

⁷ Illustrations from everyday life, including animals, boats, farmers, and vegetation, give colorful backing to James' arguments on faith, patience, and endurance. This copying of Jesus' successful teaching methods makes his counsel extremely forceful. This letter impresses one with James' keen discernment of the motives prompting individuals.

CONTENTS OF JAMES

⁸ **Patient endurance as "doers of the word"** (1: 1-27). James opens with words of encouragement: "Consider it all joy, my brothers, when you meet with various trials." Through patient endurance they will be made complete. If a person lacks wisdom, he should keep asking God for it, not in doubt, like a wind-tossed wave of the sea, but in faith. The lowly will be exalted, but the rich will fade away like the flower that perishes. Happy is

---

* See chart, page 303.

---

5. What proves the authenticity of James?
6. (a) What circumstances called for James to write his letter? (b) Rather than contradict, how does James supplement Paul's arguments on faith?
7. How does James copy Jesus' teaching methods, and with what effect?
8. What will result from patient endurance, but what from wrong desire?

the man that endures trial, for "he will receive the crown of life, which Jehovah promised to those who continue loving him." God does not tempt man with evil things to cause his downfall. It is one's own wrong desire that becomes fertile and gives birth to sin, and this, in turn, brings forth death.—1:2, 12, 22.

⁹ From where do all good gifts come? From the never-varying 'Father of celestial lights.' "Because he willed it," says James, "he brought us forth by the word of truth, for us to be a certain firstfruits of his creatures." Christians, then, should be swift about hearing, slow about speaking, slow about wrath, and they should put away all filthiness and moral badness and accept the implanting of the word of salvation. "Become doers of the word, and not hearers only." For he who peers into the mirrorlike law of freedom and persists in it "will be happy in his doing it." The formal worship of the man that does not bridle his tongue is futile, but "the form of worship that is clean and undefiled from the standpoint of our God and Father is this: to look after orphans and widows in their tribulation, and to keep oneself without spot from the world."—1:17, 18, 22, 25, 27.

¹⁰ **Faith perfected by right works** (2:1-26). The brothers are making distinctions, preferring the rich above the poor. But is it not true that "God chose the ones who are poor respecting the world to be rich in faith and heirs of the kingdom"? Are not the rich oppressors? The brothers should practice the kingly law, "You must love your neighbor as yourself," and should shun favoritism. Let them also practice mercy, for as regards the Law, whoever offends in one point offends in all. Faith without works is meaningless, as is telling a needy brother or sister to "keep warm and well fed" without giving practical aid. Can faith be shown apart from works? Was not Abraham's faith perfected by his works in offering Isaac on the altar? Likewise, Rahab the harlot was "declared righteous by works." So faith without works is dead. —2:5, 8, 16, 19, 25.

¹¹ **Controlling the tongue to teach wisdom** (3: 1-18). The brothers should be wary about becoming teachers, lest they receive heavier judgment. Everyone stumbles many times. As a bridle controls a horse's body and a small rudder a large boat, so that little member, the tongue, has great power. It is like a fire that can set a great woodland on fire! Wild animals can be tamed more

---

9. What is involved in being "doers of the word," and what form of worship is approved by God?
10. (a) What distinctions are to be shunned? (b) What is the relationship of works to faith?
11. (a) By use of what illustrations does James warn concerning the tongue? (b) How are wisdom and understanding to be shown?

easily than the tongue. With it men bless Jehovah, yet curse their fellowman. This is not proper. Does a fountain produce both bitter water and sweet? Can a fig tree produce olives? a vine, figs? salt water, sweet water? James asks: "Who is wise and understanding among you?" Let him show his works with meekness and avoid contentiousness, animalistic bragging against the truth. For "the wisdom from above is first of all chaste, then peaceable, reasonable, ready to obey, full of mercy and good fruits, not making partial distinctions, not hypocritical."—3:13, 17.

¹² **Shun sensual pleasure, friendship with the world** (4:1-17). "From what source are there fights among you?" James answers his own question: "Your cravings for sensual pleasure"! The motives of some are wrong. Those who would be friends of the world are "adulteresses," and they become God's enemies. Therefore, he exhorts: "Oppose the Devil, and he will flee from you. Draw close to God, and he will draw close to you." Jehovah will exalt the humble. So the brothers should quit judging one another. And because no one can be sure of his life from one day to the next, they ought to say: "If Jehovah wills, we shall live and also do this or that." Pride is wicked, and it is a sin to know what is right and not do it.—4:1, 4, 7, 8, 15.

¹³ **Happy those who endure in righteousness!** (5:1-20). 'Weep and howl, you rich men!' declares James. 'The rust of your wealth will be witness against you. Jehovah of armies has heard the calls for help from the reapers that you have deprived. You have lived in luxury and sensual pleasure, and you have condemned and murdered the righteous one.' However, in view of the nearness of the Lord's presence, the brothers should exercise patience, like the farmer waiting for his harvest, and consider the pattern of the prophets, "who spoke in the name of Jehovah." Happy are those who have endured! The brothers should recall the endurance of Job and the outcome Jehovah gave, "that Jehovah is very tender in affection and merciful."—5:1-6, 10, 11.

¹⁴ Let them stop swearing oaths. Rather, let their "Yes" mean Yes" and their "No, No." They should openly confess their sins and pray for one another. As is shown by Elijah's prayers, "a righteous man's supplication . . . has much force." If anyone is misled from the truth, the one who

turns him back "will save his soul from death and will cover a multitude of sins."—5:12, 16, 20.

WHY BENEFICIAL

¹⁵ Though James only twice mentions the name Jesus (1:1; 2:1), he makes much practical application of the teachings of the Master, as a careful comparison of James' letter and the Sermon on the Mount reveals. At the same time, Jehovah's name appears 13 times (*New World Translation*), and his promises are emphasized as rewards for faith-keeping Christians. (4:10; 5:11) James draws repeatedly on the Hebrew Scriptures for illustrations and apt quotations in order to develop his practical counsel. He identifies the source by his expressions: "according to the scripture," "the scripture was fulfilled," and "the scripture says"; and he goes on to apply these scriptures to Christian living. (2:8, 23; 4:5) In making plain points of counsel and building faith in God's Word as a harmonious whole, James makes appropriate references to Abraham's works of faith, to Rahab's demonstration of faith by works, to Job's faithful endurance, and to Elijah's reliance on prayer. —Jas. 2:21-25; 5:11, 17, 18; Gen. 22:9-12; Josh. 2:1-21; Job 1:20-22; 42:10; 1 Ki. 17:1; 18:41-45.

¹⁶ Invaluable is James' counsel to be doers of the word and not just hearers, to keep proving faith by works of righteousness, to find joy in enduring various trials, to keep on asking God for wisdom, always to draw close to him in prayer, and to practice the kingly law, "You must love your neighbor as yourself." (Jas. 1:22; 2:24; 1: 2, 5; 4:8; 5:13-18; 2:8) Strong are his warnings against teaching error, injuriously using the tongue, making class distinctions in the congregation, craving sensual pleasure, and trusting in corruptible riches. (3:1, 8; 2:4; 4:3; 5:1, 5) James makes it very plain that friendship with the world amounts to spiritual adultery and enmity with God, and he gives the definition of the practical form of worship that is clean in God's sight: "to look after orphans and widows in their tribulation, and to keep oneself without spot from the world." (4:4; 1:27) All this counsel, so practical and easy to understand, is just what could be expected from this 'pillar' of the early Christian congregation. (Gal. 2:9) Its kindly message continues as a guidepost for Christians in our turbulent times, for it is "wisdom from above," which produces "the fruit of righteousness."—3:17, 18.

¹⁷ James was anxious to help his brothers reach their goal of life in God's Kingdom. So he urges

---

12. (a) What wrong conditions exist in the congregation, and what is their source? (b) What attitude should be avoided and what quality cultivated to gain Jehovah's approval?
13. (a) Why is there woe for the rich? (b) How does James illustrate the need for patience and endurance, and with what results?
14. What closing counsel is given concerning confessing sin and concerning prayer?

---

15. How does James make application of the Hebrew Scriptures? Illustrate.
16. What counsel and warnings does James give, and from what source is such practical wisdom?
17. What strong reason is presented for enduring in faithful works?

them: "You too exercise patience; make your hearts firm, because the presence of the Lord has drawn close." They are happy if they go on enduring trial because God's approval means receiving "the crown of life, which Jehovah promised to those who continue loving him." (5:8; 1:12) Thus God's promise of the crown of life—either immor-

tal life in the heavens or eternal life on earth—is emphasized as strong reason for enduring in faithful works. Surely this wonderful letter will encourage all to reach out for the goal of everlasting life either in heaven or in Jehovah's new world ruled by the Kingdom Seed, our Lord Jesus Christ. —2:5.

Bible Book Number 60

1 Peter

Writer: **Peter**

Place Written: **Babylon**

Writing Completed: **c. 62–64 C.E.**

AS THE early Christians declared abroad the excellencies of God, the Kingdom work prospered and increased throughout the Roman Empire. However, some misunderstandings arose concerning this zealous group. For one thing, their religion had originated from Jerusalem and from among the Jews, and some confused them with the politically minded Jewish zealots who chafed under the Roman yoke and were a constant source of trouble to local governors. Moreover, the Christians were different in that they refused to sacrifice to the emperor or to mix in with the pagan religious ceremonies of the day. They were spoken against and had to undergo many trials on account of the faith. At the right time, and with forethought denoting divine inspiration, Peter wrote his first letter, encouraging the Christians to stand firm and counseling them on how to conduct themselves under Nero, the Caesar of that time. This letter proved to be most timely in view of the storm of persecution that broke out almost immediately thereafter.

² Peter's writership is established by the opening words. Moreover, Irenaeus, Clement of Alexandria, Origen, and Tertullian all quote the letter, naming Peter as writer.* The authenticity of First Peter is as well attested as any of the inspired letters. Eusebius tells us that the elders of the church made free use of the letter; there was no question as to its authenticity in his time

(c. 260-342 C.E.). Ignatius, Hermas, and Barnabas, of the early second century, all make references to it.* First Peter is completely in harmony with the rest of the inspired Scriptures and sets out a powerful message for the Jewish and non-Jewish Christians residing as "temporary residents scattered about in Pontus, Galatia, Cappadocia, Asia, and Bithynia"—regions of Asia Minor.—1 Pet. 1:1.

³ When was the letter written? Its tone indicates that the Christians were experiencing trials, either from the pagans or from unconverted Jews, but that Nero's campaign of persecution, launched in 64 C.E., had not yet begun. It is evident that Peter wrote the letter just prior to this, probably between 62 and 64 C.E. Mark's still being with Peter strengthens this conclusion. During Paul's first imprisonment at Rome (c. 59-61 C.E.), Mark was with Paul but was due to travel to Asia Minor; and at the time of Paul's second imprisonment (c. 65 C.E.), Mark was about to join Paul again in Rome. (1 Pet. 5:13; Col. 4:10; 2 Tim. 4:11) In the interval he would have had the opportunity to be with Peter in Babylon.

⁴ Where was First Peter written? Whereas Bible commentators agree on the authenticity, canonicity, writership, and approximate date of writing, they differ as to the place of writing. According to Peter's own testimony, he wrote his first letter while at Babylon. (1 Pet. 5:13) But some claim that

---

* McClintock and Strong's *Cyclopedia,* 1981 reprint, Vol. VIII, page 15.

* *New Bible Dictionary,* second edition, 1986, edited by J. D. Douglas, page 918.

1. Why did the Christians have to undergo trials, and why was Peter's first letter timely?
2. What proves that Peter was the writer of the letter bearing his name, and to whom was the letter addressed?

3. What evidence is there as to the time of writing of First Peter?
4, 5. (a) What disproves the claim that Peter wrote his first letter from Rome? (b) What indicates that he wrote from the literal Babylon?

he wrote from Rome, saying that "Babylon" was a cryptic name for Rome. The evidence, however, does not support such a view. Nowhere does the Bible indicate that Babylon specifically refers to Rome. Since Peter addressed his letter to those in *literal* Pontus, Galatia, Cappadocia, Asia, and Bithynia, it logically follows that his reference to Babylon was to the literal place of that name. (1:1) There was good reason for Peter to be in Babylon. He was entrusted with 'the good news for those who are circumcised,' and there was a large Jewish population in Babylon. (Gal. 2:7-9) The *Encyclopaedia Judaica,* when discussing the production of the Babylonian Talmud, refers to Judaism's "great academies of Babylon" during the Common Era.*

⁵ The inspired Scriptures, including the two letters written by Peter, make no mention of his going to Rome. Paul speaks of being in Rome but never refers to Peter's being there. Although Paul mentions 35 names in his letter to the Romans and sends greetings by name to 26, why does he fail to mention Peter? Simply because Peter was not there at the time! (Rom. 16:3-15) The "Babylon" from which Peter wrote his first letter was evidently the literal Babylon on the banks of the Euphrates River in Mesopotamia.

CONTENTS OF FIRST PETER
⁶ **The new birth to a living hope through Christ** (1:1-25). At the outset Peter directs his readers' attention to the "new birth to a living hope" and the unfading inheritance reserved for them in the heavens. This is according to God's mercy through the resurrection of Jesus Christ. Therefore "the ones chosen" are greatly rejoicing, though grieved by various trials, so that the tested quality of their faith "may be found a cause for praise and glory and honor at the revelation of Jesus Christ." The prophets of old, and even angels, have inquired concerning this salvation. Hence, the chosen ones should brace up their minds for activity and set their hope on this undeserved kindness, becoming holy in all their conduct. Is this not proper in view of their being delivered, not with corruptible things, but "with precious blood, like that of an unblemished and spotless lamb, even Christ's"? Their "new birth" is through the word of the living and enduring God, Jehovah, which endures forever and which has been declared to them as good news.—1:1, 3, 7, 19, 23.

⁷ **Maintaining fine conduct among the nations** (2:1–3:22). As living stones, Christians are built

up a spiritual house, offering up spiritual sacrifices acceptable to God through Jesus Christ, the foundation cornerstone, who became a stone of stumbling to the disobedient. Those exercising faith have become 'a royal priesthood, a holy nation, to declare abroad the excellencies of the one that called them out of darkness into his wonderful light.' As temporary residents among the nations, let them abstain from fleshly desires and maintain fine conduct. Let them be subject to "every human creation," whether to a king or to his governors. Yes, let them "honor men of all sorts, have love for the whole association of brothers, be in fear of God, have honor for the king." Likewise, let servants be in subjection to their owners, with a good conscience, bearing up under unjust suffering. Even Christ, though sinless, submitted to reviling and suffering, leaving "a model" so that his steps could be followed closely.—2:9, 13, 17, 21.

⁸ Subjection applies also to wives, who through chaste conduct together with deep respect may even win over unbelieving husbands without a word. Their concern should not be external adornment. It should be as it was with the obedient Sarah, "the secret person of the heart in the incorruptible apparel of the quiet and mild spirit, which is of great value in the eyes of God." Husbands should honor wives as 'weaker vessels' and as "heirs with them of the undeserved favor of life." All Christians should show brotherly love. "He that would love life . . . , let him turn away from what is bad and do what is good; let him seek peace and pursue it. For the eyes of Jehovah are upon the righteous ones." Rather than fear men, they should always be ready to make a defense of their hope. It is better to suffer for doing good, if it is God's will, than for doing evil. "Why, even Christ died once for all time concerning sins, a righteous person for unrighteous ones, that he might lead you to God, he being put to death in the flesh, but being made alive in the spirit." Noah's faith, expressed in the constructing of the ark, resulted in preservation for himself and his family. In a corresponding way, those who, on the basis of faith in the resurrected Christ, dedicate themselves to God, get baptized in symbol of that faith, and continue to do God's will are saved and are granted a good conscience by God.—3:4, 7, 10-12, 18.

⁹ **Rejoicing in doing God's will as a Christian, despite suffering** (4:1–5:14). Christians should have the same mental disposition as Christ, living only to do God's will and no longer that of the

---

* Jerusalem, 1971, Vol. 15, col. 755.

6. Of what hope does Peter write, and on what basis is the "new birth" to this hope possible?
7. (a) As what are Christians being built up, and for what purpose? (b) As temporary residents, how should they conduct themselves?

8. (a) What sound admonition is given wives and husbands? (b) What is necessary for one to come into possession of a good conscience before God?
9. What mental disposition should Christians have? Despite what?

nations, even though the nations speak of them abusively for not continuing to run with them "to the same low sink of debauchery." Since the end of all things has drawn close, they should be sound in mind, be prayerful, and have intense love for one another, doing all things that God may be glorified. As trials burn among them, they should not be puzzled, but they should rejoice as sharers in the sufferings of the Christ. However, let no one suffer as an evildoer. Since judgment starts at the house of God, "let those who are suffering in harmony with the will of God keep on commending their souls to a faithful Creator while they are doing good."—4:4, 19.

¹⁰ The older men should shepherd the flock of God willingly, yes, eagerly. Being examples to the flock will assure them of the unfadable crown of glory at the manifestation of the Chief Shepherd. Let younger men be in subjection to the older men, all having lowliness of mind, "because God opposes the haughty ones, but he gives undeserved kindness to the humble ones." Let them be solid in the faith and watchful of that "roaring lion," the Devil. Again, powerful words of assurance ring out as Peter concludes his exhortation: "But, after you have suffered a little while, the God of all undeserved kindness, who called you to his everlasting glory in union with Christ, will himself finish your training, he will make you firm, he will make you strong. To him be the might forever. Amen."—5:5, 8, 10, 11.

WHY BENEFICIAL

¹¹ The first letter of Peter contains sound advice for overseers. Following up on Jesus' own counsel at John 21:15-17 and that of Paul at Acts 20:25-35, Peter again shows the work of the overseer to be a shepherding work, to be done unselfishly, willingly, and eagerly. The overseer is an undershepherd, serving in subjection to "the chief shepherd," Jesus Christ, and is accountable to him for the flock of God, whose interests he must care for as an example and in all humility.—5:2-4.

¹² Many other aspects of Christian subjection are touched on in Peter's letter, and excellent advice is given. At 1 Peter 2:13-17, proper subjection to the rulers, such as a king and governors, is counseled. However, this is to be a relative subjection, being for the Lord's sake and coupled with "fear of God," whose slaves Christians are. House servants are exhorted to be in subjection to their owners and to bear up if they have to suffer "because of conscience toward God." Wives are also given invaluable admonition concerning subjection to husbands, including unbelieving ones, it being shown that their chaste, respectful conduct is "of great value in the eyes of God" and may even win their husbands to the truth. Here Peter uses the illustration of Sarah's faithful submission to Abraham to underscore the point. (1 Pet. 2:17-20; 3:1-6; Gen. 18:12) Husbands, in turn, should exercise their headship with proper consideration for the "weaker vessel." Still on this topic, Peter exhorts: "In like manner, you younger men, be in subjection to the older men." And then he emphasizes the need for lowliness of mind, humility, a Christian quality that is emphasized throughout his letter.—1 Pet. 3:7-9; 5:5-7; 2:21-25.

¹³ At a time when fiery trials and persecutions were beginning to flare up again, Peter provided strengthening encouragement, and his letter is indeed invaluable to all who face such trials today. Notice how he draws on the Hebrew Scriptures in quoting Jehovah's words: "You must be holy, because I am holy." (1 Pet. 1:16; Lev. 11:44) Then, again, in a passage that is rich in its references to other inspired scriptures, he shows how the Christian congregation is built as a spiritual house of living stones on the foundation of Christ. And for what purpose? Peter answers: "You are 'a chosen race, a royal priesthood, a holy nation, a people for special possession, that you should declare abroad the excellencies' of the one that called you out of darkness into his wonderful light." (1 Pet. 2:4-10; Isa. 28:16; Ps. 118:22; Isa. 8:14; Ex. 19:5, 6; Isa. 43:21; Hos. 1:10; 2:23) It is to this "royal priesthood," the general priesthood comprising the entire holy nation of God, that Peter holds forth the Kingdom promise of "an incorruptible and undefiled and unfading inheritance," "the unfadable crown of glory," "everlasting glory in union with Christ." Thus, these are greatly encouraged to go on rejoicing that they may "rejoice and be overjoyed also during the revelation of his glory." —1 Pet. 1:4; 5:4, 10; 4:13.

---

10. What counsel is given to older men and to younger men, and with what powerful assurance does First Peter end?
11. How does Peter follow up Jesus' and Paul's counsel in giving advice to overseers?
12. (a) What relative subjection must be rendered to rulers and to owners? (b) What does Peter admonish regarding wifely submission and the husband's headship? (c) What Christian quality is emphasized throughout the letter?

---

13. (a) How does Peter in his letter make clear the purpose of God's calling out the Christian congregation? (b) To what joyful inheritance does Peter point forward, and who attain to it?

61

2 Peter

Writer: **Peter**

Place Written: **Babylon (?)**

Writing Completed: **c. 64 C.E.**

WHEN Peter composed his second letter, he realized he was to face death soon. He anxiously desired to remind his fellow Christians of the importance of accurate knowledge to help them to maintain steadfastness in their ministry. Would there be any reason to doubt that the apostle Peter was the writer of the second letter bearing his name? The letter itself erases any doubts that may have arisen as to writership. The writer says he is "Simon Peter, a slave and apostle of Jesus Christ." (2 Pet. 1:1) He refers to this as "the second letter I am writing you." (3:1) He speaks of himself as an eyewitness to the transfiguration of Jesus Christ, a privilege that Peter shared with James and John, and he writes of this with all the feeling of an eyewitness. (1:16-21) He mentions that Jesus had foretold his death.—2 Pet. 1:14; John 21:18, 19.

[2] However, some critics have pointed to the difference in style of the two letters as a reason for discounting the second letter as the work of Peter. But this should pose no real problem, for the subject and the purpose in writing were different. In addition, Peter wrote his first letter "through Silvanus, a faithful brother," and if Silvanus were given some latitude in formulating the sentences, this could account for the difference of style in the two letters, since Silvanus apparently did not have a part in writing the second letter. (1 Pet. 5:12) Its canonicity has also been disputed on the grounds that it "is poorly attested in the Fathers." However, as may be observed from the chart "Outstanding Early Catalogs of the Christian Greek Scriptures," Second Peter was regarded as part of the Bible catalog by a number of authorities prior to the Third Council of Carthage.*

[3] When was Peter's second letter written? It is most probable that it was written about 64 C.E. from Babylon or its vicinity, shortly after the first letter, but there is no direct evidence, particularly

---

* See chart on page 303.

1. What facts prove Peter's writership of Second Peter?
2. What argues for the canonicity of Second Peter?
3. When and where was Second Peter apparently written, and to whom was it addressed?

as to the place. At the time of writing, most of Paul's letters were circulating among the congregations and were known to Peter, who regarded them as inspired of God and classed them with "the rest of the Scriptures." Peter's second letter is addressed "to those who have obtained a faith, held in equal privilege with ours," and it includes those to whom the first letter was addressed and others to whom Peter had preached. Just as the first letter had circulated in many areas, so the second letter also took on a general character. —2 Pet. 3:15, 16; 1:1; 3:1; 1 Pet. 1:1.

CONTENTS OF SECOND PETER

[4] **Making sure of the calling to the heavenly Kingdom** (1:1-21). Peter is quick to show loving concern for "those who have obtained a faith." He desires that undeserved kindness and peace be increased to them "by an accurate knowledge of God and of Jesus our Lord." God has freely given them "the precious and very grand promises," through which they may become sharers in divine nature. Therefore, by earnest effort let them supply to their faith virtue, knowledge, self-control, endurance, godly devotion, brotherly affection, and love. If these qualities overflow in them, they will never become inactive or unfruitful with regard to accurate knowledge. The brothers should do their utmost to make sure of their calling and choosing, as well as their entrance into the everlasting Kingdom of their Lord. Knowing that 'the putting off of his tabernacle is soon to be,' Peter is disposed to remind them of these things so that they may make mention of them after his departure. Peter was an eyewitness of Christ's magnificence in the holy mountain when these words "were borne to him by the magnificent glory: 'This is my son, my beloved, whom I myself have approved.'" Thus, the prophetic word is made more sure, and it should be heeded, for it is not by man's will, "but men spoke from God as they were borne along by holy spirit."—1:1, 2, 4, 14, 17, 21.

---

4. (a) How should the brothers strive to become fruitful with regard to accurate knowledge, and what are they promised? (b) How is the prophetic word made more sure, and why should it be heeded?

[5] **Strong warning against false teachers** (2: 1-22). False prophets and teachers will bring in destructive sects, promote loose conduct, and bring reproach upon the truth. But their destruction is not slumbering. God did not hold back from punishing the angels that sinned, from bringing a deluge in Noah's day, or from reducing Sodom and Gomorrah to ashes. But he delivered the preacher Noah and righteous Lot, so "Jehovah knows how to deliver people of godly devotion out of trial, but to reserve unrighteous people for the day of judgment to be cut off." For these are daring, self-willed, like unreasoning animals, ignorant, abusive talkers, delighting in deceptive teachings, adulterous, covetous, and like Balaam in loving the reward of wrongdoing. They promise freedom but are themselves the slaves of corruption. It would have been better for them not to have known the path of righteousness, for the saying has happened to them: "The dog has returned to its own vomit, and the sow that was bathed to rolling in the mire."—2:9, 22.

[6] **Keeping close in mind the day of Jehovah** (3:1-18). Peter is writing to arouse Christians' clear thinking faculties, that they may remember the sayings previously spoken. Ridiculers will come in the last days, saying: "Where is this promised presence" of Christ? It escapes the notice of these men that God destroyed the world of ancient times by water and that "by the same word the heavens and the earth that are now are stored up for fire" and are "reserved to the day of judgment and of destruction of the ungodly men." A thousand years are with Jehovah as one day, so "Jehovah is not slow respecting his promise," but he is patient, not desiring any to be destroyed. Hence, Christians should watch their conduct and should practice deeds of godly devotion as they await and keep close in mind the presence of the day of Jehovah, through which the heavens will be dissolved by fire and the elements will melt with intense heat. But there are to be "new heavens and a new earth" according to God's promise. —3:4, 7, 9, 13.

[7] Hence, they should do their utmost "to be found finally by him spotless and unblemished and in peace." They should consider the patience of their Lord as salvation, just as the beloved Paul wrote them. With this advance knowledge, let them be on guard not to fall from their own

steadfastness. "No," concludes Peter, "but go on growing in the undeserved kindness and knowledge of our Lord and Savior Jesus Christ. To him be the glory both now and to the day of eternity." —3:14, 18.

WHY BENEFICIAL

[8] How essential accurate knowledge is! Peter himself weaves into his arguments accurate knowledge that he has acquired from the Hebrew Scriptures. He testifies that they were inspired by holy spirit: "For prophecy was at no time brought by man's will, but men spoke from God as they were borne along by holy spirit." He points out, also, that Paul's wisdom was "given him." (1:21; 3:15) We benefit greatly by considering all these inspired Scriptures and by holding fast to accurate knowledge. Then we will never become complacent, like those whom Peter describes as saying: "All things are continuing exactly as from creation's beginning." (3:4) Nor will we fall into the traps of the false teachers like those Peter describes in chapter 2 of his letter. Rather, we should constantly consider the reminders provided by Peter and the other Bible writers. These help us to remain "firmly set in the truth" and patiently and steadfastly "go on growing in the undeserved kindness and knowledge of our Lord and Savior Jesus Christ."—1:12; 3:18.

[9] As an aid in increasing in "accurate knowledge of God and of Jesus our Lord," Peter recommends earnest effort to build up those Christian qualities listed in chapter 1, verses 5 to 7. Then, in verse 8, he adds: "For if these things exist in you and overflow, they will prevent you from being either inactive or unfruitful regarding the accurate knowledge of our Lord Jesus Christ." Truly this is splendid encouragement to activity as God's ministers in these critical days!—1:2.

[10] How important it is to exert oneself to the utmost in order to be assured of sharing in "the precious and very grand promises" of Jehovah God! So it is that Peter exhorts the anointed Christians to keep eyes fixed on the Kingdom goal, saying: "Do your utmost to make the calling and choosing of you sure for yourselves; for if you keep on doing these things you will by no means ever fail. In fact, thus there will be richly supplied to you the entrance into the everlasting kingdom of our Lord and Savior Jesus Christ." Then Peter

---

5. What warning does Peter give against false teachers, and what powerful illustrations does he use as to the certainty of God's judgments against such men?
6. (a) Why does Peter write, and what does he say concerning God's promise? (b) In contrast to ridiculers, how must Christians show themselves watchful?
7. Having this advance knowledge, how should Christians exert themselves?

8. (a) How does Peter testify to the inspiration of both the Hebrew and the Greek Scriptures? (b) How will we be benefited by holding fast to accurate knowledge?
9. What earnest effort are we encouraged to make, and why?
10. (a) What promises does Peter emphasize, and what does he exhort in connection with them? (b) What assurance does Peter give concerning the Kingdom prophecies?

calls attention to the magnificence of Jesus' Kingdom glory, of which he had been an eyewitness through the transfiguration vision, and adds: "Consequently we have the prophetic word made more sure." True, every prophecy concerning the magnificent Kingdom of Jehovah will come to certain fulfillment. Thus, it is with confidence that we echo Peter's words quoted from Isaiah's prophecy: "There are new heavens and a new earth that we are awaiting according to his promise, and in these righteousness is to dwell."—2 Pet. 1:4, 10, 11, 19; 3:13; Isa. 65:17, 18.

Bible Book Number 62

1 John

Writer: Apostle John

Place Written: Ephesus, or near

Writing Completed: c. 98 C.E.

JOHN, the beloved apostle of Jesus Christ, had a strong love for righteousness. This helped give him a keen insight into the mind of Jesus. We are therefore not surprised that the theme of love dominates his writings. He was no sentimentalist, however, for Jesus referred to him as one of the "Sons of Thunder [Boanerges]." (Mark 3:17) In fact, it was in defense of truth and righteousness that he wrote his three letters, for the apostasy foretold by the apostle Paul had become evident. John's three letters were indeed timely, for they were an aid in strengthening the early Christians in their fight against the encroachments of "the wicked one."—2 Thess. 2:3, 4; 1 John 2:13, 14; 5:18, 19.

2 Judging from the contents, these letters belong to a period much later than the Gospels of Matthew and Mark—later, also, than the missionary letters of Peter and Paul. Times had changed. There is no reference to Judaism, the big threat to the congregations in the days of their infancy; and there does not appear to be a single direct quotation from the Hebrew Scriptures. On the other hand, John talks about "the last hour" and the appearance of "many antichrists." (1 John 2:18) He refers to his readers by expressions such as "my little children" and to himself as "the older man." (1 John 2:1, 12, 13, 18, 28; 3:7, 18; 4:4; 5:21; 2 John 1; 3 John 1) All of this suggests a late date for his three letters. Also, 1 John 1:3, 4 seems to indicate that John's Gospel was written about the same time. It is generally believed that John's

three letters were completed about 98 C.E., shortly before the apostle's death, and that they were written in the vicinity of Ephesus.

3 That First John was actually written by John the apostle is indicated by its close resemblance to the fourth Gospel, which he unmistakably wrote. For example, he introduces the letter by describing himself as an eyewitness who has seen "the word of life . . . , the everlasting life which was with the Father and was made manifest to us," expressions strikingly similar to those with which John's Gospel opens. Its authenticity is attested by the Muratorian Fragment and by such early writers as Irenaeus, Polycarp, and Papias, all of the second century C.E.* According to Eusebius (c. 260-342 C.E.), the authenticity of First John was never questioned.# However, it is to be noted that some older translations have added to chapter 5 the following words at the end of verse 7 and the beginning of verse 8: "In heaven, the Father, the Word, and the Holy Ghost: and these three are one. And there are three that bear witness in earth." (*King James Version*) But this text is not found in any of the early Greek manuscripts and has obviously been added to bolster the Trinity doctrine. Most modern translations, both Catholic and Protestant, do not include these words in the main body of the text.—1 John 1:1, 2.△

4 John writes to protect his "beloved ones," his

---

* *The International Standard Bible Encyclopedia*, Vol. 2, 1982, edited by G. W. Bromiley, pages 1095-6.
# *The Ecclesiastical History*, III, xxiv, 17.
△ *Insight on the Scriptures*, Vol. 2, page 1019.

---

1. (a) What quality permeates John's writings, yet what shows he was no sentimentalist? (b) Why were his three letters timely?
2. (a) What indicates that John's letters were written much later than Matthew, Mark, and the missionary letters? (b) When and where do the letters appear to have been written?
3. (a) What testifies to the writership and authenticity of First John? (b) What material was added later, but what proves it to be spurious?
4. Against whom is John seeking to protect his fellow Christians, and what false teachings does he refute?

"young children," against the wrong teachings of the "many antichrists" that have gone out from among them and that are trying to seduce them away from the truth. (2:7, 18) These apostate antichrists may have been influenced by Greek philosophy, including early Gnosticism, whose adherents claimed special knowledge of a mystical sort from God.* Taking a firm stand against apostasy, John deals extensively with three themes: sin, love, and the antichrist. His statements on sin, and in support of Jesus' sacrifice for sins, indicate that these antichrists were self-righteously claiming that they were without sin and had no need of Jesus' ransom sacrifice. Their self-centered "knowledge" had made them selfish and loveless, a condition that John exposes as he continually emphasizes true Christian love. Moreover, John is apparently combating their false doctrine as he expounds that Jesus is the Christ, that he had a prehuman existence, and that he came in the flesh as the Son of God to provide salvation for believing men. (1:7-10; 2:1, 2; 4:16-21; 2:22; 1:1, 2; 4:2, 3, 14, 15) John brands these false teachers plainly as "antichrists," and he gives a number of ways in which the children of God and the children of the Devil can be recognized.—2:18, 22; 4:3.

⁵ Since no particular congregation is addressed, the letter was evidently intended for the entire Christian association. The lack of a greeting at the beginning and a salutation at the end would also indicate this. Some have even described this writing as a treatise rather than a letter. The use of the plural "you" throughout (as indicated by capitals in the *New World Translation*) shows that the writer directed his words to a group rather than to an individual.

CONTENTS OF FIRST JOHN

⁶ **Walking in the light, not in the darkness** (1:1–2:29). "We are writing these things," says John, "that our joy may be in full measure." Since "God is light," only those "walking in the light" are having "a sharing with him" and with one another. These are cleansed from sin by "the blood of Jesus his Son." On the other hand, those who "go on walking in the darkness" and who claim, "We have no sin," are misleading themselves, and the truth is not in them. If they confess their sins, God will be faithful and forgive them.—1:4-8.

⁷ Jesus Christ is identified as "a propitiatory

sacrifice" for sins, one who is "a helper with the Father." He that claims to know God but does not observe His commandments is a liar. He that loves his brother remains in the light, but he that hates his brother is walking in the darkness. John strongly counsels not to love the world or the things in the world, for, he says, "If anyone loves the world, the love of the Father is not in him." Many antichrists have come, and "they went out from us," explains John, for "they were not of our sort." The antichrist is the one that denies that Jesus is the Christ. He denies both the Father and the Son. Let the "little children" stay with what they have learned from the beginning so as to "abide in union with the Son and in union with the Father," according to the anointing received from him, which is true.—2:1, 2, 15, 18, 19, 24.

⁸ **Children of God do not practice sin** (3:1-24). Because of the Father's love, they are called "children of God," and at God's manifestation they are to be like him and to "see him just as he is." Sin is lawlessness, and those who are remaining in union with Christ do not practice it. The one who does carry on sin originates with the Devil, whose works the Son of God will break up. The children of God and the children of the Devil are thus evident: Those originating with God have love for one another, but those originating with the wicked one are like Cain, who hated and slew his brother. John tells the "little children" that they have come to know love because "that one surrendered his soul" for them, and he admonishes them not to 'shut the door of tender compassions' on their brothers. Let them "love, neither in word nor with the tongue, but in deed and truth." To determine whether they "originate with the truth," they must check what is in their hearts and see if they "are doing the things that are pleasing in [God's] eyes." They must observe his commandment to "have faith in the name of his Son Jesus Christ and be loving one another." Thus they will know that they are remaining in union with him, and he with them by spirit.—3:1, 2, 16-19, 22, 23.

⁹ **Loving one another in union with God** (4:1–5: 21). The inspired expressions are to be tested. Those expressions that deny that Christ came in the flesh do "not originate with God" but are the antichrist's. They originate with the world and are in union with it, but the inspired expression of truth is from God. John says: "God is love," and

---

* *New Bible Dictionary*, second edition, 1986, edited by J. D. Douglas, pages 426, 604.

5. What indicates that First John was intended for the entire Christian congregation?
6. What contrast does John make between those who walk in the light and those who are in darkness?
7. (a) How does a person show that he knows and loves God? (b) How is the antichrist identified?

8. (a) What distinguishes the children of God from those of the Devil? (b) How have the "little children" come to know love, and what check must they continually make on their hearts?
9. (a) What test is to be made of the inspired expressions? (b) What emphasizes the obligation to love one another?

"the love is in this respect, not that we have loved God, but that he loved us and sent forth his Son as a propitiatory sacrifice for our sins." How great the obligation, then, to love one another! Those who love others have God remain in union with them, and thus love has been made perfect that they "may have freeness of speech," throwing fear outside. "As for us," says John, "we love, because he first loved us." "The one who loves God should be loving his brother also."—4:3, 8, 10, 17, 19, 21.

[10] Showing love as children of God means observing his commandments, and this results in conquering the world, through faith. Concerning those putting faith in the Son of God, God gives witness that He gave them "everlasting life, and this life is in his Son." Thus, they may have confidence that he will hear them in whatever they ask him according to his will. All unrighteousness is sin, yet there is a sin that does not incur death. Everyone born from God does not make a practice of sin. Though "the whole world is lying in the power of the wicked one . . . , the Son of God has come," and he has given his disciples the "intellectual capacity" for gaining knowledge of the true God, with whom they are now in union "by means of his Son Jesus Christ." They must also guard themselves from idols!—5:11, 19, 20.

WHY BENEFICIAL

[11] Just as in the closing years of the first century of the Common Era, so today there are "many antichrists" against whom true Christians must be warned. These true Christians must hold fast to 'the message which they heard from the beginning, have love for one another,' and remain in union with God and the true teaching, practicing righteousness with freeness of speech. (2:18; 3:11; 2:27-29) Most important also is the warning against "the desire of the flesh and the desire of the eyes and the showy display of one's means of life," those materialistic, worldly evils that have engulfed most professing Christians. True Christians will shun the world and its desire, knowing that "he that does the will of God remains forever." In this age of worldly desire, sectarianism, and ha-

tred, how beneficial it is, indeed, to study God's will through the inspired Scriptures and to do that will!—2:15-17.

[12] It is for our benefit that First John makes clear the contrasts between the light that emanates from the Father and the truth-destroying darkness from the evil one, between the life-giving teachings of God and the deceptive lies of the antichrist, between the love that pervades the entire congregation of those in union with the Father along with the Son and the murderous Cainlike hatred that is in those who "went out from us . . . that it might be shown up that not all are of our sort." (2:19; 1:5-7; 2:8-11, 22-25; 3:23, 24, 11, 12) Having this appreciation, it should be our fervent desire to 'conquer the world.' And how may we do this? By having strong faith and by having "the love of God," which means observing his commandments.—5:3, 4.

[13] "The love of God"—how wonderfully is this motivating force highlighted throughout the letter! In chapter 2 we find the sharp contrast made between the love of the world and the love of the Father. Later it is called to our attention that "God is love." (4:8, 16) And what a practical love this is! It found its magnificent expression in the Father's sending forth "his Son as Savior of the world." (4:14) This should stir in our hearts an appreciative, fearless love, in line with the apostle's words: "As for us, we love, because he first loved us." (4:19) Our love should be of the same kind as that of the Father and the Son—a practical, self-sacrificing love. Just as Jesus surrendered his soul for us, so "we are under obligation to surrender our souls for our brothers," yes, to open the door of our tender compassions so as to love our brothers, not in words only, but "in deed and truth." (3:16-18) As John's letter so clearly shows, it is this love, combined with the true knowledge of God, that binds those who go on walking with God in unbreakable union with the Father and the Son. (2: 5, 6) It is to the Kingdom heirs in this blessed bond of love that John says: "And we are in union with the true one, by means of his Son Jesus Christ. This is the true God and life everlasting."—5:20.

10. (a) How may the children of God conquer the world, and what confidence do they have? (b) What attitude must they have toward sin and idolatry?
11. How may Christians today combat antichrists and worldly desires?

12. What contrasts does First John make for our benefit, and how may we conquer the world?
13. (a) How is the love of God highlighted as a practical force? (b) Of what kind should the Christian's love be, resulting in what union?

63
2 John

| Writer: **Apostle John** |
| Place Written: **Ephesus, or near** |
| Writing Completed: **c. 98 C.E.** |

JOHN'S second letter is short—it could have been written on a single sheet of papyrus—but it is full of meaning. It is addressed "to the chosen lady and to her children." Since "Kyria" (Greek for "lady") did exist as a proper name at the time, some Bible scholars feel that an individual by that name was being addressed. On the other hand, it is thought by some that John was writing to a Christian congregation, referring to it as "the chosen lady." This may have been done in order to confuse persecutors. In that case, the greetings of "the children of your sister" mentioned in the last verse would be those of the members of another congregation. So the second letter was not intended to be as general in scope as the first, for it evidently was written either to an individual or to one particular congregation.—Vs. 1.

[2] There is no reason to doubt that John wrote this letter. The writer calls himself "the older man." This certainly fits John not only because of his advanced age but also because, as one of the "pillars" (Gal. 2:9) and the last surviving apostle, he was truly an "older man" in the Christian congregation. He was well-known, and no further identification would be required for his readers. His writership is also indicated by the similarity in style to that of the first letter and John's Gospel. Like the first letter, the second letter appears to have been written in or around Ephesus, about 98 C.E. Concerning Second and Third John, McClintock and Strong's *Cyclopedia* comments: "From their general similarity, we may conjecture that the two epistles were written shortly after the 1st Epistle from Ephesus. They both apply to individual cases of conduct the principles which had been laid down in their fullness in the 1st Epistle."* In support of its authenticity, the letter is quoted by Irenaeus, of the second century, and was

accepted by Clement of Alexandria, of the same period.* Also, John's letters are listed in the Muratorian Fragment.

[3] As was true of First John, the reason for this letter is the onslaught by false teachers against the Christian faith. John wants to warn his readers about such ones so they can recognize them and stay clear of them, while continuing to walk in the truth, in mutual love.

CONTENTS OF SECOND JOHN

[4] **Love one another; reject apostates** (Vss. 1-13). After expressing his love in the truth for 'the chosen lady and her children,' John rejoices that he has found some of them walking in the truth, as commanded by the Father. He requests that they show their love for one another by continuing to walk according to God's commandments. For deceivers and antichrists have gone forth into the world, who do not confess Jesus Christ as coming in the flesh. He that pushes ahead beyond the teaching of Christ does not have God, but he that remains in this teaching "has both the Father and the Son." Anyone that does not bring this teaching is not to be received into their homes, nor is he even to be greeted. John has many things to write them, but instead he hopes to come and speak with them face-to-face, that their joy may be "in full measure."—Vss. 9, 12.

WHY BENEFICIAL

[5] It appears that in John's day, as in modern times, there were some who were not content to stay with the plain, simple teachings of Christ. They wanted something more, something that would tickle their ego, something that would exalt them and put them in a class with worldly

---

* *New Bible Dictionary,* second edition, 1986, edited by J. D. Douglas, page 605.

---

* 1981 reprint, Vol. IV, page 955.

---

1. To whom may Second John have been written?
2. (a) What evidence points to the apostle John as writer of Second John? (b) What suggests that the letter was written in or near Ephesus, about 98 C.E., and what supports its authenticity?

3. Why did John write the letter?
4. Why particularly does John admonish loving one another, and how must those who push ahead beyond the teaching of Christ be treated?
5. (a) What situation arose in John's day that has also arisen in modern times? (b) Like John, how can we today show appreciation for the unity of the congregation?

philosophers, and they were willing to contaminate and divide the Christian congregation in order to gain their selfish ends. John valued the harmony of the congregation that rests in love and in right teaching in union with the Father and the Son. We should place like store on the unity of the congregation today, even refusing fellowship or greetings to those who apostatize to another teaching beyond that received through the inspired Scriptures. By continuing to walk according to God's commandments, and in the full measure of joy to be found in true Christian association, we can be assured that "there will be with us undeserved kindness, mercy and peace from God the Father and from Jesus Christ the Son of the Father, with truth and love." (Vs. 3) Certainly John's second letter underlines the blessedness of such Christian oneness.

Bible Book Number 64

3 John

Writer: Apostle John

Place Written: Ephesus, or near

Writing Completed: c. 98 C.E.

THIS letter is written to Gaius, a faithful Christian whom John truly loved. The name Gaius was a common one in the days of the early congregation. It appears four times in other parts of the Christian Greek Scriptures, referring to at least three and probably four different men. (Acts 19:29; 20:4; Rom. 16:23; 1 Cor. 1:14) There is no information available that would definitely identify the Gaius to whom John wrote with any of these others. All that we know of Gaius is that he was a member of a Christian congregation, that he was a special friend of John's, and that the letter was addressed to him personally, for which reason the word "you" appears always in the singular.

2 Since the style of the opening and closing greetings is the same as that of Second John and the writer again identifies himself as "the older man," there can be no question that the apostle John also wrote this letter. (2 John 1) The similarity of contents and language also suggests that it was written, as in the case of the other two letters, in or near Ephesus, about 98 C.E. Because of its brevity, it was seldom quoted by early writers, but along with Second John, it is to be found in early catalogs of the inspired Scriptures.*

3 In his letter John expresses appreciation for Gaius' hospitality shown toward traveling brothers, and he mentions some trouble with a certain ambitious Diotrephes. The Demetrius mentioned seems to be the one who brought this letter to Gaius, so it is possible he was sent out by John and was in need of Gaius' hospitality on his journey, which the letter should secure. As in the case of Gaius, we know nothing about Diotrephes and Demetrius beyond what we read here. However, the letter gives an interesting glimpse of the close international brotherhood of the early Christians. Among other things, this included the custom of receiving hospitably those traveling 'in behalf of the name,' although these might not be personally known to their hosts.—Vs. 7.

CONTENTS OF THIRD JOHN

4 **The apostle counsels hospitality and good works** (vss. 1-14). John rejoices at hearing that Gaius is still "walking in the truth." He commends him for doing a faithful work, that of showing loving care for visiting brothers. "We . . . are under obligation," says John, "to receive such persons hospitably, that we may become fellow workers in the truth." John wrote previously to the congregation, but the self-exalting Diotrephes receives nothing from John or other responsible ones with

---

* See chart "Outstanding Early Catalogs of the Christian Greek Scriptures," page 303.

1. To whom was Third John addressed, and what is known of him?
2. What identifies the writer, time, and place of the writing of Third John?

3. What does John express through Third John, and what interesting glimpse do we gain of the brotherhood of the early Christians?
4. For what does John commend Gaius, what unruly conduct does he condemn, and what sound advice does he give?

respect. John, if he comes, will call him to account for his 'chattering with wicked words.' The beloved Gaius is advised to "be an imitator, not of what is bad, but of what is good." Demetrius is cited as a praiseworthy example. Rather than write of many things, John expresses the hope of soon seeing Gaius face-to-face.—Vss. 4, 8, 10, 11.

WHY BENEFICIAL

⁵ The apostle John shows himself to be an exemplary overseer in his zeal to safeguard the congregation against contaminating influences. The spirit of love and hospitality that permeated the congregation was commendable, and indeed it was

---

5. (a) How did John show himself to be an exemplary overseer, and what spirit was it important to preserve? (b) Why was John so outspoken against Diotrephes? (c) For what should we be zealous today, in line with what principle stated by John?

their obligation to preserve this happy condition, in order that the local brothers and "strangers" (individuals formerly unknown to their Christian host) who came among them might serve together as "fellow workers in the truth." (Vss. 5, 8) However, Diotrephes had lofty eyes, a thing hateful to Jehovah, and he was disrespectful of theocratic authority, even chattering wickedly about the apostle John. (Prov. 6:16, 17) He was putting a roadblock in the way of the congregation's Christian hospitality. No wonder John was so outspoken against this evil and in favor of genuine Christian love in the congregation. We should be just as zealous today for maintaining humility, walking in the truth, and practicing godly love and generosity, in line with the principle stated by John: "He that does good originates with God. He that does bad has not seen God."—3 John 11.

<table>
<tr><td>Bible
Book
Number</td><td>65

Jude</td><td>Writer: Jude

Place Written: Palestine (?)

Writing Completed: c. 65 C.E.</td></tr>
</table>

THE Christian brothers of Jude were in danger! During the time that had elapsed since the death and resurrection of Christ Jesus, foreign elements had wormed their way into the Christian congregation. The enemy had infiltrated for the purpose of undermining the faith, just as the apostle Paul, about 14 years previously, had warned. (2 Thess. 2:3) How should the brothers be alerted and placed on guard against the danger? The letter of Jude, vigorous and robust in its forthright statement, provided the answer. Jude himself stated his position clearly in verses 3 and 4: 'I found it necessary to write you because certain men have slipped in, ungodly men, turning the undeserved kindness of our God into an excuse for loose conduct.' The very foundations of sound doctrine and morality were being threatened. Jude felt called upon to fight for the interests of his brothers, that they, in turn, might put up a hard fight for the faith.

---

1. Because of what conditions inside the congregation did Jude find it necessary to write his vigorous letter in behalf of his brothers?

² But who was Jude? The opening words tell us that the letter was written by "Jude, a slave of Jesus Christ, but a brother of James, to the called ones." Was Jude, or Judas, an apostle, since 2 of Jesus' original 12 apostles were named Judas? (Luke 6:16) Jude does not speak of himself as an apostle, but instead he speaks of the apostles in the third person as "they," manifestly excluding himself. (Jude 17, 18) Moreover, he calls himself "a brother of James," evidently meaning the writer of the letter of James, who was a half brother of Jesus. (Vs. 1) As one of the "pillars" of the congregation in Jerusalem, this James was well-known, and hence Jude identifies himself with him. This makes Jude also a half brother of Jesus, and he is listed as such. (Gal. 1:19; 2:9; Matt. 13:55; Mark 6:3) However, Jude did not make capital of his fleshly relationship with Jesus, but he humbly placed the emphasis on his spiritual relationship as "a slave of Jesus Christ."—1 Cor. 7:22; 2 Cor. 5:16; Matt. 20:27.

---

2. (a) Who was Jude? (b) What relationship with Jesus did Jude esteem the most?

³ The authenticity of this Bible book is supported by mention of it in the Muratorian Fragment, of the second century C.E. Additionally, Clement of Alexandria (second century C.E.) accepted it as canonical. Origen referred to it as a work of "but a few lines, yet filled with the healthful words of heavenly grace."* Tertullian also considered it to be authentic. There is no doubt that it belongs with the other inspired Scriptures.

⁴ Jude writes "to the called ones," specifying no particular congregation or individual, so his epistle is a general letter to be circulated widely to all Christians. Though it is not stated, the most likely place of writing is Palestine. It is also difficult to fix the date with certainty. However, it must have been well along in the development of the Christian congregation, for Jude calls attention to "the sayings that have been previously spoken by the apostles of our Lord Jesus Christ" and apparently quotes 2 Peter 3:3. (Jude 17, 18) Moreover, there is a strong similarity between Jude and the second chapter of Second Peter. This indicates that he wrote about the same time as Peter, both being deeply concerned over the danger to the congregation at that time. Hence, 65 C.E. is suggested as an approximate date. This date is also supported in that Jude does not mention Cestius Gallus' moving in to put down the Jews' revolt in 66 C.E., nor does he mention the fall of Jerusalem in 70 C.E. Jude in his epistle refers to specific divine judgments executed against sinners, and it is logical that had Jerusalem already fallen, he would have reinforced his argument by mention of this execution of judgment, especially since Jesus foretold the event.—Jude 5-7; Luke 19:41-44.

CONTENTS OF JUDE

⁵ **Warnings against fornication and disregard for lordship** (vss. 1-16). After conveying loving greetings to "the called ones," Jude says he intended to write "about the salvation we hold in common," but he has now found it necessary to write them "to put up a hard fight for the faith." Why so? Because ungodly men have slipped in, turning God's undeserved kindness into an excuse for loose conduct. These men, says Jude, are "proving false to our only Owner and Lord, Jesus Christ." (Vss. 1, 3, 4) He reminds them that though Jehovah saved a people out of Egypt, He afterward "destroyed

those not showing faith." Additionally, Jehovah has reserved "for the judgment of the great day" those angels who forsook their proper dwelling place. Likewise, the everlasting punishment on Sodom and Gomorrah and their neighbor cities is a warning example as to the fate of those who 'commit fornication excessively and go out after flesh for unnatural use.'—Vss. 5-7.

⁶ Now, in like manner, ungodly men "are defiling the flesh and disregarding lordship and speaking abusively of glorious ones." Why, even Michael the archangel did not speak abusively to the Devil when disputing over Moses' body, simply saying: "May Jehovah rebuke you." Yet these men use abusive speech and go on corrupting themselves like unreasoning animals. They have gone in the way of Cain, Balaam, and the rebellious Korah. They are like rocks hidden below water, like waterless clouds, like fruitless trees twice-dead and uprooted, like wild waves that foam up their shame, and like stars with no set course. For these "the blackness of darkness stands reserved forever." (Vss. 8, 9, 13) Enoch prophesied that Jehovah will execute judgment against these ungodly ones. They are murmurers and complainers, and they selfishly admire personalities.

⁷ **Counsel on remaining in God's love** (vss. 17-25). Jude reminds the brothers of how the apostles of the Lord Jesus Christ used to warn that "in the last time there will be ridiculers, proceeding according to their own desires for ungodly things." These troublemakers are "animalistic men, not having spirituality." The "beloved ones," therefore, should build themselves up in the faith and keep themselves in God's love, while they await the mercy of Christ "with everlasting life in view." In turn, let them extend mercy and aid to those who waver. Jude closes by ascribing glory through the Lord Jesus Christ to "God our Savior," the One who can guard them from stumbling.—Vss. 18-21, 25.

WHY BENEFICIAL

⁸ Jude himself found the inspired Scriptures beneficial for warning, exhorting, encouraging, instructing, and admonishing the "beloved ones." In exposing the gross sin of the ungodly intruders, he used expressive illustrations from the Hebrew Scriptures, such as those of the backsliding Israel-

---

* *The Canon of the New Testament,* 1987, by B. M. Metzger, page 138.

---

3. What proves the authenticity of the letter of Jude?
4. What kind of letter is Jude, where was it probably written, and what is suggested as to the time of writing?
5. (a) Why does Jude find it necessary to write the called ones "to put up a hard fight for the faith"? (b) What warning examples does Jude cite?

6. In what are ungodly men indulging, and how does Jude illustrate the wrongness and the outcome of their conduct?
7. (a) How did the apostles warn concerning ridiculers? (b) In view of the hope of everlasting life, what should the "beloved ones" do for themselves and others?
8. What use did Jude make of the inspired Scriptures and of "the book of nature" in admonishing his brothers?

ites, the angels who sinned, and the inhabitants of Sodom and Gomorrah, showing that all who practice like vices will suffer a like punishment. He compared corrupt men to unreasoning animals, and he said that they were going in the path of Cain, rushing into the error of Balaam, and perishing like Korah for their rebellious talk. He also drew vivid pictures from "the book of nature." Jude's forthright letter itself became a part of "all Scripture," to be studied along with the rest of the Scriptures, admonishing right conduct "in the last time."—Jude 17, 18, 5-7, 11-13; Num. 14:35-37; Gen. 6:4; 18:20, 21; 19:4, 5, 24, 25; 4:4, 5, 8; Num. 22:2-7, 21; 31:8; 16:1-7, 31-35.

⁹ Opposition and trials from the outside had failed to check the growth of Christianity, but now the brothers were endangered by corruption from within. Rocks hidden beneath the surface threatened to wreck the entire congregation. Realizing that this danger could be even more devastating, Jude argued strongly in favor of 'putting up a hard fight for the faith.' His letter is as timely today as it was back then. The same warning is still needed. Faith still must be guarded and fought for, immorality uprooted, doubters helped with mercy and

'snatched out of the fire,' if that is possible. In the interest of moral integrity, spiritual effectiveness, and true worship, Christians today must continue to build themselves up in the most holy faith. They must stand by right principles and draw close to God in prayer. They need also to have proper regard for "lordship," respecting God-given authority in the Christian congregation.—Jude 3, 23, 8.

¹⁰ "Animalistic men, not having spirituality," will never enter God's Kingdom and will only endanger others who are on the way to everlasting life. (Jude 19; Gal. 5:19-21) The congregation must be warned against them, and it must get rid of them! Thus, "mercy and peace and love" will be increased toward the beloved ones, and they will keep themselves in God's love, 'while they are waiting for the mercy of their Lord Jesus Christ with everlasting life in view.' God the Savior will set the Kingdom heirs "unblemished in the sight of his glory with great joy." Certainly these join with Jude in ascribing "glory, majesty, might and authority" to Him through Jesus Christ.—Jude 2, 21, 24, 25.

9. Why is Jude's warning still needed at this time, and in what areas must Christians continue to build themselves up?

10. (a) How must the congregation treat animalistic men, and in what will this result? (b) What reward awaits the Kingdom heirs, and in what do these join Jude?

Bible Book Number **66**

Revelation

Writer: **Apostle John**

Place Written: **Patmos**

Writing Completed: **c. 96 C.E.**

ARE the symbolisms of Revelation intended to terrify? Far from it! The fulfillment of the prophecy may bring terror to the wicked, but God's faithful servants will agree with the inspired introduction and the angel's comment at the end: "Happy is he who reads aloud and those who hear the words of this prophecy." "Happy is anyone observing the words of the prophecy of this scroll." (Rev. 1:3; 22:7) Though written before the four other inspired books by John, Revelation is correctly placed last in the collection of 66 inspired books making up our Bible, for it is the

Revelation that takes its readers far into the future, by providing an all-embracing vision of what God purposes for mankind, and that brings the grand theme of the Bible, the sanctification of Jehovah's name and the vindication of his sovereignty by means of the Kingdom under Christ, the Promised Seed, to a glorious climax.

² According to the title verse, this is "a revelation by Jesus Christ, which God gave him . . . And he sent forth his angel and presented it in signs through him to his slave John." So John was merely the writer, not the originator, of the material. Therefore John is not the revelator, nor is the book

1. (a) Regarding the symbolisms of Revelation, with what will God's servants agree? (b) Why is Revelation correctly placed last in the Bible?

2. By what means did the Revelation come to John, and why is the title of the book most appropriate?

a revelation of John. (1:1) This unveiling to God's slave of His wonderful purposes for the future makes its title most appropriate, for the book's Greek name *A·po·ka'ly·psis* (Apocalypse) means "Uncovering" or "Unveiling."

³ Who was this John referred to as the writer of Revelation in its first chapter? We are told that he was a slave of Jesus Christ, as well as a brother and sharer in tribulation, and that he was exiled on the island of Patmos. Obviously he was well-known to his first readers, to whom no further identification was necessary. He must be the apostle John. This conclusion is supported by most ancient historians. Papias, who wrote in the first part of the second century C.E., is said to have held the book to be of apostolic origin. Says Justin Martyr, of the second century, in his "Dialogue With Trypho, a Jew" (LXXXI): "There was a certain man with us, whose name was John, one of the apostles of Christ, who prophesied, by a revelation that was made to him."* Irenaeus speaks explicitly of the apostle John as the writer, as do Clement of Alexandria and Tertullian, of the late second and early third centuries. Origen, noteworthy Biblical scholar of the third century, said: "I speak of him who leaned back on Jesus' breast, John, who has left behind one Gospel, . . . and he wrote also the Apocalypse."#

⁴ The fact that John's other writings put so much emphasis on love does not mean that he could not have written the very forceful and dynamic Revelation. He and his brother James were the ones so filled with indignation against the Samaritans of a certain city that they wanted to call down fire from heaven. That is why they were given the surname "Boanerges," or "Sons of Thunder." (Mark 3:17; Luke 9:54) This divergence in style should cause no difficulty when we remember that in Revelation the subject matter is different. What John saw in these visions was unlike anything he had ever seen before. The outstanding harmony of the book with the rest of the prophetic Scriptures unquestionably proves it to be an authentic part of God's inspired Word.

⁵ According to the earliest testimony, John wrote the Revelation about 96 C.E., approximately 26 years after the destruction of Jerusalem. This would be toward the close of the reign of Emperor

---

* *The Ante-Nicene Fathers,* Vol. I, page 240.
# *The Ecclesiastical History,* Eusebius, VI, xxv, 9, 10.

---

3. Who does Revelation itself indicate the writer named John is, and how do ancient historians support this?
4. (a) What explains the divergence in style in Revelation as compared with John's other writings? (b) What proves Revelation to be an authentic part of the inspired Scriptures?
5. When did John write the Revelation, and under what circumstances?

Domitian. In verification of this, Irenaeus in his "Against Heresies" (V, xxx) says of the Apocalypse: "For that was seen no very long time since, but almost in our day, towards the end of Domitian's reign."* Eusebius and Jerome both agree with this testimony. Domitian was the brother of Titus, who led the Roman armies to destroy Jerusalem. He became emperor at the death of Titus, 15 years before the book of Revelation was written. He demanded that he be worshiped as god and assumed the title *Dominus et Deus noster* (meaning "Our Lord and God").# Emperor worship did not disturb those who worshiped false gods, but it could not be indulged in by the early Christians, who refused to compromise their faith on this point. Thus, toward the close of Domitian's rule (81-96 C.E.), severe persecution came upon the Christians. It is thought that John was exiled to Patmos by Domitian. When Domitian was assassinated in 96 C.E., he was succeeded by the more tolerant emperor Nerva, who evidently released John. It was during this imprisonment on Patmos that John received the visions he wrote down.

⁶ We must appreciate that what John saw and was told to write to the congregations was not just a series of unrelated visions, haphazardly recorded. No, the entire book of Revelation, from beginning to end, gives us a coherent picture of things to come, going from one vision to another until the full disclosure of God's Kingdom purposes is reached at the end of the visions. We should therefore see the book of Revelation as a whole and as made up of related, harmonious parts, transporting us far into the future from John's time. After its introduction (Rev. 1:1-9), the book can be viewed as being divided into 16 visions: (1) 1:10–3:22; (2) 4:1–5:14; (3) 6:1-17; (4) 7:1-17; (5) 8:1–9:21; (6) 10:1–11:19; (7) 12:1-17; (8) 13:1-18; (9) 14:1-20; (10) 15:1–16:21; (11) 17:1-18; (12) 18:1–19:10; (13) 19:11-21; (14) 20:1-10; (15) 20:11–21:8; (16) 21:9–22:5. These visions are followed by a motivating conclusion, in which Jehovah, Jesus, the angel, and John all speak, making their final contribution as the principals in the channel of communication.—22:6-21.

CONTENTS OF REVELATION

⁷ **The introduction** (1:1-9). John explains the divine Source and the angelic part of the channel through which the revelation is given, and he goes

---

* *The Ante-Nicene Fathers,* Vol. I, pages 559-60.
# *The Lives of the Caesars* (Domitian, XIII, 2).

---

6. As what should we see the book of Revelation, and how can it be divided?
7. What does John say about the origin of the Revelation, and what things does he say he shares in common with those in the seven congregations?

on to address those in the seven congregations in the district of Asia. Jesus Christ has made them "to be a kingdom, priests to his God and Father," Jehovah God, the Almighty. John reminds them that he is a sharer with them "in the tribulation and kingdom and endurance in company with Jesus," being in exile on Patmos.—1:6, 9.

8 The messages to the seven congregations (1:10–3:22). As the first vision begins, by inspiration John finds himself in the Lord's day. A strong, trumpetlike voice tells him to write in a scroll what he sees and to send it to the seven congregations, in Ephesus, Smyrna, Pergamum, Thyatira, Sardis, Philadelphia, and Laodicea. Turning toward the voice, John sees "someone like a son of man" in the midst of seven lampstands, having seven stars in his right hand. This One identifies himself as "the First and the Last," the One who became dead but is now living forever and ever and who has the keys of death and of Hades. He is therefore the resurrected Jesus Christ. He explains: "The seven stars mean the angels of the seven congregations, and the seven lampstands mean seven congregations."—1:13, 17, 20.

9 John is told to write to the angel of the congregation of Ephesus, which, despite its labor, endurance, and refusal to put up with bad men, has left its first love and should repent and do the former deeds. The congregation in Smyrna is told that despite tribulation and poverty, it is in fact rich and should not be afraid: "Prove yourself faithful even to death, and I will give you the crown of life." The congregation in Pergamum, dwelling "where the throne of Satan is," keeps holding fast to Christ's name but has apostates in its midst, and these must repent or Christ will war with them with the long sword of his mouth. In Thyatira the congregation has "love and faith and ministry and endurance," yet it tolerates "that woman Jezebel." However, faithful ones who hold fast will receive "authority over the nations."—2:10, 13, 19, 20, 26.

10 The congregation in Sardis has the reputation of being alive, but it is dead because its deeds are not fully performed before God. Those who conquer, however, will not have their names blotted out of the book of life. The congregation in Philadelphia has kept Christ's word, so he promises to keep the congregation "from the hour of test, which is to come upon the whole inhabited earth."

Christ will make the one who conquers to be a pillar in the temple of His God. Christ says: "I will write upon him the name of my God and the name of the city of my God, the new Jerusalem . . . and that new name of mine." Referring to himself as "the beginning of the creation by God," Christ tells the Laodicean congregation that it is neither hot nor cold and will be vomited out of his mouth. Though boasting of riches, those in that congregation are actually poor, blind, and naked. They need white outer garments, and they need eyesalve in order to see. Christ will come in and dine with anyone who opens the door to him. To the one that conquers, Christ will grant to sit down with him on his throne, even as he has sat down with his Father on His throne.—3:10, 12, 14.

11 The vision of Jehovah's holiness and glory (4:1–5:14). The second vision takes us before Jehovah's heavenly throne of splendor. The scene is dazzling in its beauty, like precious gems for brilliance. Around the throne sit 24 elders wearing crowns. Four living creatures ascribe holiness to Jehovah, and he is worshiped as worthy "to receive the glory and the honor and the power" because of being the Creator of all things.—4:11.

12 "The One seated upon the throne" holds a scroll with seven seals. But who is worthy to open the scroll? It is only "the Lion that is of the tribe of Judah, the root of David," that is worthy! This One, who is also "the Lamb that was slaughtered," takes the scroll from Jehovah.—5:1, 5, 12.

13 The Lamb opens six seals of the scroll (6:1–7:17). The third vision now begins. The Lamb proceeds to open the seals. First, a horseman on a white horse goes forth "conquering and to complete his conquest." Then the rider of a fiery-colored horse takes peace away from the earth, and another on a black horse rations out grain. A pale horse is ridden by Death, and Hades follows closely. The fifth seal is opened, and "those slaughtered because of the word of God" are seen calling for the avenging of their blood. (6:2, 9) At the opening of the sixth seal, there is a great earthquake, sun and moon are darkened, and the mighty ones of the earth call upon the mountains to fall over them and hide them from Jehovah and the wrath of the Lamb.

14 After this, the fourth vision begins. Four angels are seen holding back the four winds of the

---

8. (a) What is John instructed to do? (b) Whom does he see in the midst of the lampstands, and what does this One explain?
9. What commendation and counsel are given to the congregations in Ephesus, Smyrna, Pergamum, and Thyatira?
10. What messages are sent to the congregations in Sardis, Philadelphia, and Laodicea?

11. What magnificent vision next comes to John's attention?
12. Who only is worthy to open the scroll with seven seals?
13. What composite vision accompanies the opening of the first six seals?
14. What is seen next with regard to the slaves of God and an innumerable great crowd?

earth until the slaves of God are sealed in their foreheads. Their number is 144,000. Afterward John sees an innumerable great crowd out of all nations, standing before God and the Lamb, to whom they attribute salvation, rendering service day and night in God's temple. The Lamb himself 'will shepherd and guide them to fountains of waters of life.'—7:17.

¹⁵ **The seventh seal is opened** (8:1–12:17). There is silence in heaven. Then seven trumpets are handed to the seven angels. The first six trumpet blasts make up the fifth vision.

¹⁶ As the first three trumpets are successively blown, calamities rain down upon the earth, the sea, and the rivers as well as the fountains of waters. At the fourth trumpet, a third of the sun, moon, and stars is darkened. At the sound of the fifth, a star from heaven releases a plague of locusts that attack those "who do not have the seal of God on their foreheads." This is "one woe," and two more are coming. The sixth trumpet heralds the untying of four angels who come forth to kill. "Two myriads of myriads" of horsemen bring further calamity and slaughter, but still men do not repent of their evil deeds.—9:4, 12, 16.

¹⁷ As the sixth vision begins, another strong angel descends from heaven and declares that "in the days of the sounding of the seventh angel . . . the sacred secret of God according to the good news" is to be brought to a finish. John is given a little scroll to eat. It is "sweet as honey" in his mouth, but it makes his belly bitter. (10:7, 9) Two witnesses prophesy 1,260 days in sackcloth; then they are killed by "the wild beast that ascends out of the abyss," and their corpses are left three and a half days "on the broad way of the great city." Those dwelling on the earth rejoice over them, but this turns to fright when God raises them to life. In that hour, there is a great earthquake. "The second woe is past."—11:7, 8, 14.

¹⁸ Now the seventh angel blows his trumpet. Heavenly voices announce: "The kingdom of the world did become the kingdom of our Lord and of his Christ." The "twenty-four elders" worship God and give thanks, but the nations become wrathful. It is God's appointed time to judge the dead and to reward his holy ones and "to bring to ruin those ruining the earth." His temple sanctuary is opened, and in it is seen the ark of his covenant.—11:15, 16, 18.

¹⁹ Following the announcement of the establishment of the Kingdom, the seventh vision immediately shows "a great sign" in heaven. It is a woman who gives birth to "a son, a male, who is to shepherd all the nations with an iron rod." "A great fiery-colored dragon" stands ready to devour the child, but the child is caught away to God's throne. Michael wars against the dragon, and down to the earth he hurls this "original serpent, the one called Devil and Satan." It is "woe for the earth"! The dragon persecutes the woman and goes off to make war with the remaining ones of her seed.—12:1, 3, 5, 9, 12; 8:13.

²⁰ **The wild beast from the sea** (13:1-18). The eighth vision now shows a wild beast with seven heads and ten horns, ascending out of the sea. It gets its power from the dragon. One of its heads was as though slaughtered to death, but it got healed, and all the earth admired the beast. It utters blasphemies against God and wages war with the holy ones. But, look! John sees another wild beast, this one ascending out of the earth. It has two horns like a lamb, but it begins speaking like a dragon. It misleads earth's inhabitants and tells them to make an image to the first wild beast. All are compelled to worship this image or be killed. Without the mark or number of the wild beast, none can buy or sell. Its number is 666.

²¹ **The "everlasting good news" and related messages** (14:1-20). In happy contrast, in the ninth vision, John sees the Lamb on Mount Zion, and with him are 144,000 who have the names of the Lamb and of the Father on their foreheads. "They are singing as if a new song before the throne," having been "bought from among mankind as firstfruits to God and to the Lamb." Another angel appears in midheaven, bearing "everlasting good news to declare as glad tidings" to every nation and declaring: "Fear God and give him glory." And still another angel announces: "Babylon the Great has fallen!" Another, a third, proclaims that those who worship the wild beast and its image will drink of God's wrath. One "like a son of man" thrusts in his sickle, and another angel too thrusts in his sickle and gathers the vine of the earth, hurling it into "the great winepress of the anger of God." As the winepress is trodden outside the city, blood comes up as high as the bridles of

---

15. What follows the opening of the seventh seal?
16. (a) What attends the successive blowing of the first five trumpets, and what is the first of the three woes? (b) What does the sixth trumpet herald?
17. What events culminate in the announcement that the second woe is past?
18. What important announcement occurs at the sounding of the seventh trumpet, and for what is it now the appointed time?

---

19. What sign and warfare are seen in heaven, and what is the outcome?
20. What two wild beasts next appear in the vision, and how do they influence men on the earth?
21. What does John see on Mount Zion, what do the angels bear and proclaim, and how is the vine of the earth disposed of?

the horses, "for a distance of a thousand six hundred furlongs" (about 184 miles).—14:3, 4, 6-8, 14, 19, 20.

[22] **The angels with the seven last plagues** (15: 1–16:21). The tenth vision begins with another glimpse of the heavenly court. Those who have gained the victory over the wild beast glorify Jehovah, the "King of eternity," for his great and wonderful works. Seven angels come out of the sanctuary in heaven and are given seven golden bowls full of the anger of God. The first six are poured out into the earth, the sea, and the rivers and fountains of waters, as well as upon the sun, the throne of the wild beast, and the river Euphrates, drying up its water to make way for "the kings from the rising of the sun." Demonic expressions gather 'the kings of the entire inhabited earth to the war of the great day of God the Almighty' at Har–Magedon. The seventh bowl is poured out upon the air, and amid terrifying natural phenomena, the great city splits into three parts, the cities of the nations fall, and Babylon receives 'the cup of the wine of the anger of God's wrath.'—15:3; 16: 12, 14, 19.

[23] **God's judgment upon Babylon; the marriage of the Lamb** (17:1–19:10). The 11th vision begins. Look! It is God's judgment upon "Babylon the Great, the mother of the harlots," "with whom the kings of the earth committed fornication." Drunk with the blood of the holy ones, she rides a scarlet-colored wild beast having seven heads and ten horns. This beast "was, but is not, and yet is about to ascend out of the abyss." Its ten horns battle with the Lamb, but because he is "Lord of lords and King of kings," he conquers them. The ten horns turn on and devour the harlot, and with the beginning of the 12th vision, another angel, whose glory lights the earth, declares: "She has fallen! Babylon the Great has fallen!" God's people are commanded to get out of her, lest they share in her plagues. The kings and other mighty ones of the earth weep over her, saying: "Too bad, too bad, you great city, Babylon you strong city, because in one hour your judgment has arrived!" Her great riches have been devastated. As a great millstone is hurled into the sea, so with a swift pitch has Babylon been hurled down, never to be found again. At last the blood of God's holy ones has been avenged! Four times heaven resounds with the call: "Praise Jah, you people!" Praise Jah because

he has executed judgment on the great harlot! Praise Jah because Jehovah has begun to reign as king! Rejoice and be overjoyed because "the marriage of the Lamb has arrived and his wife has prepared herself"!—17:2, 5, 8, 14; 18:2, 10; 19:1, 3, 4, 6, 7.

[24] **The Lamb makes war in righteousness** (19: 11–20:10). In the 13th vision, the "King of kings and Lord of lords" leads heavenly armies in righteous warfare. Kings and strong men become carrion for the birds of heaven, and the wild beast and the false prophet are hurled alive into the fiery lake that burns with sulfur. (19:16) As the 14th vision begins, an angel is seen "coming down out of heaven with the key of the abyss and a great chain in his hand." "The dragon, the original serpent, who is the Devil and Satan," is seized and bound for a thousand years. Those having part in the first resurrection become 'priests of God and of the Christ and rule as kings with him for the thousand years.' Thereafter, Satan will be let loose and will go out to mislead the nations of earth, but he will be hurled, with those who follow him, into the lake of fire.—20:1, 2, 6.

[25] **Judgment Day and the glory of the New Jerusalem** (20:11–22:5). The thrilling 15th vision follows. The dead, great and small, are judged before God's great white throne. Death and Hades are hurled into the lake of fire, which "means the second death," and with them is hurled anyone not found written in the book of life. The New Jerusalem comes down out of heaven, and God tents with mankind, wiping out every tear from their eyes. No more death, mourning, outcry, or pain! Yes, God is "making all things new," and he confirms his promise, saying: "Write, because these words are faithful and true." Those conquering will inherit these things, but the cowards, those lacking faith, and those who are immoral or practice spiritism or idolatry will not.—20:14; 21:1, 5.

[26] John is now shown, in the 16th and final vision, "the Lamb's wife," the New Jerusalem, with its 12 gates and 12 foundation stones bearing the names of the 12 apostles. It is foursquare, and its majestic splendor is represented by the jasper, gold, and pearl in it. Jehovah and the Lamb are the temple of this city, and they are also its light. Only those written in the Lamb's scroll of life may enter into it. (21:9) A pure river of water of life issues

---

22. (a) Who are next seen to glorify Jehovah, and why? (b) Where are the seven bowls of God's anger poured out, and what world-shaking developments follow?
23. (a) How is God's judgment executed on Babylon the Great? (b) What announcements and lament accompany her fall, and what joyful praise resounds throughout heaven?
24. (a) How decisive is the warfare waged by the Lamb? (b) What occurs during the thousand years, and what follows at their end?
25. What thrilling vision follows, and who will inherit the things seen?
26. (a) What description is given of the New Jerusalem? (b) What life-sustaining things are seen in the city, and from where does its light come?

from the throne down the broad way of the city, and on each side are trees of life, which produce new crops of fruit each month and have leaves for healing. The throne of God and of the Lamb will be in the city, and the slaves of God will see His face. "Jehovah God will shed light upon them, and they will rule as kings forever and ever."—22:5.

[27] **The conclusion** (22:6-21). The assurance is given: "These words are faithful and true." Happy, indeed, are all those who observe the words of the prophecy! Having heard and seen these things, John falls down to worship the angel, who reminds him to worship only God. The words of the prophecy are not to be sealed, "for the appointed time is near." Happy are those gaining entrance into the city, for outside are the filthy and "everyone liking and carrying on a lie." Jesus states that he himself sent this witness to the congregations through his angel, and that he is "the root and the offspring of David, and the bright morning star." "And the spirit and the bride keep on saying: 'Come!' And let anyone hearing say: 'Come!' And let anyone thirsting come; let anyone that wishes take life's water free." And let no one add to or take away from the words of this prophecy, lest his portion be taken away "from the trees of life and out of the holy city."—22:6, 10, 15-17, 19.

WHY BENEFICIAL

[28] What a glorious conclusion the book of Revelation does provide for the Bible's inspired collection of 66 books! Nothing has been omitted. There are no loose ends. Now we see clearly the grand finale as well as the beginning. The last part of the Bible closes out the record begun in the first part. As Genesis 1:1 described God's creation of the material heavens and earth, so Revelation 21:1-4 describes a new heaven and a new earth and the untold blessings that will be brought to mankind, as prophesied also at Isaiah 65:17, 18; 66:22; and 2 Peter 3:13. Just as the first man was told he would positively die if disobedient, so God positively guarantees that for the obedient ones, "death will be no more." (Gen. 2:17; Rev. 21:4) When the Serpent first appeared as mankind's deceiver, God foretold the bruising of his head, and the Revelation discloses how the original serpent, who is the Devil and Satan, is finally hurled into destruction. (Gen. 3:1-5, 15; Rev. 20:10) Whereas disobedient man was driven away from the Edenic tree of life, symbolic trees of life appear "for the

curing of the nations" of obedient mankind. (Gen. 3:22-24; Rev. 22:2) Just as a river issued out of Eden to water the garden, so a symbolic river, life-giving and life-sustaining, is pictured as flowing from God's throne. This parallels the earlier vision of Ezekiel, and it also calls to mind Jesus' words about "a fountain of water bubbling up to impart everlasting life." (Gen. 2:10; Rev. 22:1, 2; Ezek. 47:1-12; John 4:13, 14) In contrast to being driven from God's presence, as were the first man and woman, the faithful conquerors will see his face. (Gen. 3:24; Rev. 22:4) It is beneficial indeed to consider these thrilling visions of Revelation!

[29] Note, too, how Revelation ties together the prophecies concerning wicked Babylon. Isaiah had foreseen the fall of the literal Babylon long before it happened, and he had declared: "She has fallen! Babylon has fallen!" (Isa. 21:9) Jeremiah also prophesied against Babylon. (Jer. 51:6-12) But the Revelation speaks in symbol of "Babylon the Great, the mother of the harlots and of the disgusting things of the earth." She too must be overthrown, and John sees it in vision, declaring: "She has fallen! Babylon the Great has fallen!" (Rev. 17:5; 18:2) Do you recall Daniel's vision of a kingdom set up by God that will crush other kingdoms and stand "to times indefinite"? Note how this ties in with the heavenly proclamation in Revelation: "The kingdom of the world did become the kingdom of our Lord and of his Christ, and he will rule as king forever and ever." (Dan. 2:44; Rev. 11:15) And just as Daniel's vision described 'someone like a son of man coming with the clouds of heaven to receive a lasting rulership and dignity and kingdom,' so Revelation identifies Jesus Christ as "The Ruler of the kings of the earth" and as "coming with the clouds," and says that "every eye will see him." (Dan. 7:13, 14; Rev. 1:5, 7) There are certain parallels to be observed, also, between the beasts of Daniel's visions and the beasts of Revelation. (Dan. 7:1-8; Rev. 13:1-3; 17:12) The Revelation provides a vast field, indeed, for faith-strengthening study.

[30] What a wondrous, many-featured vision the Revelation provides concerning God's Kingdom! It brings into brilliant focus what the prophets of old and Jesus and his disciples said concerning the Kingdom. Here we have the completed view of the sanctification of Jehovah's name through the

---

27. (a) What assurance is John given concerning the prophecy? (b) With what pressing invitation and warning does the Revelation conclude?
28. By what examples can we appreciate that Revelation closes out the record begun in the first part of the Bible?

29. (a) How does Revelation tie together the prophecies concerning Babylon? (b) What parallels are to be noted between the visions of the Kingdom, as well as of the beasts, in Daniel and in Revelation?
30. (a) What complete view does Revelation give of the sanctification of Jehovah's name through the Kingdom? (b) What is emphasized with regard to holiness, and whom does this affect?

Kingdom: "Holy, holy, holy is Jehovah God, the Almighty." He is worthy "to receive the glory and the honor and the power." Indeed, he it is that 'takes his great power and begins ruling as king' through Christ. How zealous this regal Son, the "King of kings and Lord of lords," is shown to be as he strikes the nations and treads "the winepress of the anger of the wrath of God the Almighty"! As the grand Bible theme of Jehovah's vindication builds up to its climax, it is emphasized that everyone and everything sharing in his Kingdom purposes must be holy. The Lamb, Jesus Christ, who "has the key of David," is spoken of as holy, and so are the angels of heaven. Those having part in the first resurrection are said to be "happy and holy," and it is stressed that "anything not sacred and anyone that carries on a disgusting thing" will in no way enter "the holy city Jerusalem." Those who have been bought by the blood of the Lamb "to be a kingdom and priests to our God" thus have powerful encouragement to maintain holiness before Jehovah. The "great crowd" too must 'wash their robes and make them white in the blood of the Lamb' that they may render sacred service. —Rev. 4:8, 11; 11:17; 19:15, 16; 3:7; 14:10; 20:6; 21:2, 10, 27; 22:19; 5:9, 10; 7:9, 14, 15.

³¹ The vision of this magnificent and holy Kingdom of God crystallizes in our minds as we note certain features that are called to our attention only in the book of Revelation. Here we have the complete vision of the Kingdom heirs on Mount Zion with the Lamb, singing a new song that only they can master. It is only the Revelation that tells us the number of those bought from the earth to enter the Kingdom—144,000—and that this number is sealed out of the 12 symbolic tribes of spiritual Israel. It is only the Revelation that shows that these 'priests and kings,' who share with Christ in the first resurrection, will also rule with him "for the thousand years." It is only the Revelation that gives us the complete view of "the holy city, New Jerusalem," showing its radiant glory, Jehovah and the Lamb as its temple, its 12 gates and foundation stones, and the kings that reign in it forever by the eternal light that Jehovah sheds upon them.—14:1, 3; 7:4-8; 20:6; 21:2, 10-14, 22; 22:5.

³² It can truly be said that this vision of the "new heaven" and "the holy city, New Jerusalem," sums up all that the Scriptures have foretold from an-

cient times concerning the Kingdom Seed. Abraham looked forward to a seed by which 'all the families of the earth would certainly bless themselves' and to "the city having real foundations, the builder and maker of which city is God." Now, in the Revelation vision, this city of blessing is clearly identified for us as the "new heaven"—a new government, God's Kingdom, made up of the New Jerusalem (the bride of Christ) and her Bridegroom. Together they will administer a righteous government over all the earth. Jehovah promises faithful mankind that they may become "his peoples" in a happy, sinless, deathless condition such as man enjoyed before the rebellion in Eden. And by way of emphasis, the Revelation twice tells us that God will "wipe out every tear from their eyes." —Gen. 12:3; 22:15-18; Heb. 11:10; Rev. 7:17; 21: 1-4.

³³ Yes, what a grand conclusion to the inspired Scriptures! How marvelous are these "things that must shortly take place"! (Rev. 1:1) The name of Jehovah, "the God of the inspired expressions of the prophets," is sanctified. (22:6) The prophetic writings of 16 centuries are shown in fulfillment, and the works of faith of thousands of years are rewarded! "The original serpent" is dead, his hosts are destroyed, and wickedness is no more. (12:9) God's Kingdom rules as "a new heaven" to his praise. The blessings of a restored earth, filled and subdued according to Jehovah's purpose stated in the first chapter of the Bible, stretch for a glorious eternity before mankind. (Gen. 1:28) All Scripture has indeed proved to be "inspired of God and beneficial for teaching, for reproving, for setting things straight, for disciplining in righteousness." Jehovah has used it to lead fully competent, completely equipped men of faith to this marvelous day. Now, therefore, is the time to study these Scriptures to strengthen *your* faith. Obey their commands in order to receive God's blessing. Follow them on the straight path that leads to everlasting life. By doing so, you too can say, in the assured confidence with which the last book of the Bible closes: "Amen! Come, Lord Jesus."—2 Tim. 3:16; Rev. 22:20.

³⁴ What incomparable joy we can now have by hailing "the kingdom of our Lord and of his Christ," the Seed, as this brings eternal sanctification to the matchless name of "Jehovah God, the Almighty"!—Rev. 11:15, 17.

---

31. What features of the Kingdom are called to our attention only in the book of Revelation?
32. (a) How does the vision of the "new heaven" and "the holy city, New Jerusalem," sum up all that had been foretold concerning the Kingdom Seed? (b) What blessings does the Kingdom assure for mankind on earth?

33. (a) What marvelous overall vision does Revelation give of the divine purposes fulfilled? (b) How has "all Scripture" been proved to be "inspired of God and beneficial," and why is it now the time to study and obey God's Word?
34. How can we now have incomparable joy, and why?

Studies on the Inspired Scriptures and Their Background

Study Number 1 — A Visit to the Promised Land

The regions of the land, its physical features, its mountains and valleys, its rivers and lakes, and its climate, soil, and varieties of vegetation.

THE boundaries of the ancient Promised Land were set by Jehovah God. (Ex. 23:31; Num. 34:1-12; Josh. 1:4) For many centuries this area was referred to by some as the land of Palestine, a name derived from the Latin *Palaestina* and the Greek *Pa·lai·sti′ne*. This latter word is drawn from the Hebrew *Pele′sheth.* In the Hebrew Scriptures, *Pele′sheth* is translated "Philistia," and it has reference just to the territory of the Philistines, who were enemies of God's people. (Ex. 15:14) However, since Jehovah promised this land to faithful Abraham and his descendants, the designation "Promised Land," or "Land of Promise," is most appropriate. (Gen. 15:18; Deut. 9: 27, 28; Heb. 11:9) This land is remarkable in the variety of its geography, wrapping up in this small area many of the distinct features and extremes that are to be found throughout the earth. If Jehovah could give as an inheritance to his ancient witnesses such a land of promise with all its beauteous variety, then certainly he can yet give to his dedicated worshipers a glorious new world paradise extending earth wide, with mountains, valleys, rivers, and lakes, to bring them delight. Let us now pay keen attention to the geographic features of the Land of Promise, as we visit on an imaginary tour.*

GENERAL SIZE

[2] According to its God-given boundaries as stated at Numbers 34:1-12, the land promised to Israel was to be a thin strip of territory. It was to be about 300 miles from north to south and about 35 miles wide, on the average. It was not until the reigns of Kings David and Solomon that the entire area promised was occupied militarily, with the placing of many subject peoples under control. However, the portion actually settled by the Jews is generally described as that covering from Dan to Beer-sheba, which was a distance of about 150 miles from north to south. (1 Ki. 4:25) The distance across the country from Mount Carmel to the Sea of Galilee is about 32 miles, and in the south where the Mediterranean shoreline curves gradually to the southwest, it is over 50 miles from Gaza to the Dead Sea. This settled area west of the Jordan River contained only about 6,000 square miles. However, the Israelites additionally settled in lands to the east of the Jordan (lands not included in the original promised boundaries), to make the total of settled territory a little less than 10,000 square miles.

NATURAL REGIONS

[3] Our visit to the Promised Land will take us through the following natural divisions of the country. The outline below provides the key to the accompanying map, which shows the approximate boundaries of the areas discussed.

Geographic Regions
- A. Seacoast of the Great Sea.—Josh. 15:12.
- B. The Plains West of the Jordan
  - 1. Plain of Asher.—Judg. 5:17.

---

* *Insight on the Scriptures,* Vol. 1, pages 332-3.

---

1. (a) Why is the designation "Promised Land" most appropriate? (b) What glorious prospect may we have in mind as we examine the geography of the land?
2. In how much of the Promised Land did the Jews settle, and in what additional territory?

3. Using the map "Natural Regions of the Promised Land" with the paragraph, briefly identify the areas included in the following natural divisions of the land: (a) the plains west of the Jordan, (b) the mountainous regions west of the Jordan, (c) the mountains and tablelands east of the Jordan.

2. The Coastal Strip of Dor.—Josh. 12:23.

3. Pasture Grounds of Sharon.—1 Chron. 5:16.

4. Plain of Philistia.—Gen. 21:32; Ex. 13:17.

5. Central East-West Valley

   a. Plain of Megiddo (Esdraelon).—2 Chron. 35:22.

   b. Low Plain of Jezreel.—Judg. 6:33.

C. The Mountainous Regions West of the Jordan

  1. Hills of Galilee.—Josh. 20:7; Isa. 9:1.

  2. Hills of Carmel.—1 Ki. 18:19, 20, 42.

  3. Hills of Samaria.—Jer. 31:5; Amos 3:9.

  4. Shephelah.—Josh. 11:2; Judg. 1:9.

  5. The Hill Country of Judah.—Josh. 11:21.

  6. Wilderness of Judah (Jeshimon).—Judg. 1:16; 1 Sam. 23:19.

  7. Negeb.—Gen. 12:9; Num. 21:1.

  8. Wilderness of Paran.—Gen. 21:21; Num. 13:1-3.

D. The Great Arabah (the Rift Valley).—2 Sam. 2:29; Jer. 52:7.

  1. Hula Basin

  2. Region Around the Sea of Galilee.—Matt. 14:34; John 6:1.

  3. District of the Jordan Valley (The Ghor).—1 Ki. 7:46; 2 Chron. 4:17; Luke 3:3.

  4. The Salt (Dead) Sea (Sea of the Arabah).—Num. 34:3; Deut. 4:49; Josh. 3:16.

  5. Arabah (southward from the Salt Sea).—Deut. 2:8.

E. Mountains and Tablelands East of the Jordan.—Josh. 13:9, 16, 17, 21; 20:8.

  1. Land of Bashan.—1 Chron. 5:11; Ps. 68:15.

  2. Land of Gilead.—Josh. 22:9.

  3. Land of Ammon and of Moab.—Josh. 13:25; 1 Chron. 19:2; Deut. 1:5.

  4. Mountain Plateau of Edom.—Num. 21:4; Judg. 11:18.

F. Mountains of Lebanon.—Josh. 13:5.

A. SEACOAST OF THE GREAT SEA

⁴ Beginning our visit from the west, we view first the seacoast stretching along the beautiful, blue Mediterranean. Because of large stretches of sand dunes, the only good natural harbor below Mount Carmel is at Joppa; but north of Carmel there are several good natural harbors. The Phoenicians, who lived in the country along this part of the coast, became a famous seafaring people. The average annual temperature along the sunny seacoast is a pleasant 67° F., though the summers are very hot, with an average daytime temperature of about 93° F. in Gaza.

4. What are the characteristics and climate of the seacoast?

B-1 PLAIN OF ASHER

⁵ This coastal plain stretches north from Mount Carmel for about 25 miles. Its greatest width is about eight miles, and it is part of the land that was assigned to the tribe of Asher. (Josh. 19:24-30) It was a fertile strip of plain and produced well, supplying food for Solomon's royal table.—Gen. 49:20; 1 Ki. 4:7, 16.

B-2 THE COASTAL STRIP OF DOR

⁶ This strip of land borders the Carmel Range for about 20 miles. It is only about two and a half miles wide. It actually amounts to a coastal strip of land lying between Carmel and the Mediterranean. In its southern part, there is the harbor city of Dor, and to the south of this, the sand dunes begin. The hills behind Dor produced choice food for Solomon's banquets. One of Solomon's daughters was married to the deputy from this region.—1 Ki. 4:7, 11.

B-3 PASTURE GROUNDS OF SHARON

⁷ In view of the proverbial beauty of its flowers, it is appropriate that Sharon is mentioned in Isaiah's prophetic vision of the restored land of Israel. (Isa. 35:2) This is a fertile, well-watered land. It is a plain that varies from 10 to 12 miles in width, extending for about 40 miles southward from the coastal strip of Dor. In Hebrew times oak forests grew in the northern part of Sharon. Many flocks grazed there after the grain was cut. It is for this reason that it was called the pasture grounds of Sharon. In King David's time, the royal herds were kept in Sharon. (1 Chron. 27:29) Today extensive citrus groves are to be found in this area.

B-4 PLAIN OF PHILISTIA

⁸ This section of land lies south of the pasture grounds of Sharon, extending some 50 miles along the coast and about 15 miles inland. (1 Ki. 4:21) The sand dunes along the shoreline penetrate sometimes as much as three and a half miles. This is a rolling plain, which rises steppelike from 100 feet to as much as 650 feet behind Gaza in the south. The soil is rich; but rain is not very plentiful, and there is always the danger of drought.

B-5 CENTRAL EAST-WEST VALLEY

⁹ The central east-west valley is actually made up of two parts, the Valley Plain of Megiddo, or Esdraelon, to the west, and the Low Plain of Jezreel to the east. (2 Chron. 35:22; Judg. 6:33) This

5, 6. Describe briefly (a) the Plain of Asher, (b) the coastal strip of Dor.

7. (a) How is Sharon referred to in prophecy, and why? (b) In Hebrew times for what was this region used?

8. Where is the Plain of Philistia, and what are its features?

9. (a) What two parts make up the central east-west valley, and of what practical value was it? (b) By using the diagrams of "Typical Cross Sections of the Promised Land," describe the general topography of this area.

KEY TO NUMBERS

A — Seacoast of the Great Sea
B-1 — Plain of Asher
B-2 — The Coastal Strip of Dor
B-3 — Pasture Grounds of Sharon
B-4 — Plain of Philistia
B-5 — Central East-West Valley (Plain of Megiddo, Low Plain of Jezreel)
C-1 — Hills of Galilee
C-2 — Hills of Carmel
C-3 — Hills of Samaria
C-4 — Shephelah
C-5 — The Hill Country of Judah
C-6 — Wilderness of Judah (Jeshimon)
C-7 — Negeb
C-8 — Wilderness of Paran
D-1 — Hula Basin
D-2 — Region Around the Sea of Galilee
D-3 — District of the Jordan Valley (The Ghor)
D-4 — The Salt (Dead) Sea (Sea of the Arabah)
D-5 — Arabah (southward from the Salt Sea)
E-1 — Land of Bashan
E-2 — Land of Gilead
E-3 — Land of Ammon and of Moab
E-4 — Mountain Plateau of Edom
F — Mountains of Lebanon

NATURAL REGIONS of the PROMISED LAND (and adjoining territory)

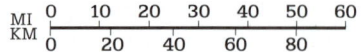

MI 0 10 20 30 40 50 60
KM 0 20 40 60 80

(For cross sections V—V, W—W, X—X, Y—Y, and Z—Z, see opposite page)

Map labels:

MEDITERRANEAN SEA

Sidon
Tyre
Dan
Damascus
Caesarea Philippi
Mt. Hermon
Lebanon Mts.
Chorazin
Capernaum
Bethsaida
Cana
Tiberias
Sea of Galilee
Nazareth
Nain
Edrei
Dor
Beth-shean
Ramoth-gilead
Samaria
Tirzah
Shechem
T. V. of Jabbok
Joppa
Jordan River
Bethel
Jericho
Geba
Rabbah
Ashdod
Ekron
Jerusalem
Heshbon
Gath
Bethlehem
Medeba
Ashkelon
Lachish
Hebron
Gaza
T. V. of Arnon
Salt Sea
Beer-sheba
Kir-hareseth
T. V. of Zered
Kadesh-barnea
Petra
River of Egypt
Ezion-geber
Red Sea

Region labels: A, B-1, B-2, B-3, B-4, C-1, C-2, C-3, C-4, C-5, C-6, C-7, C-8, D-1, D-2, D-3, D-4, D-5, E-1, E-2, E-3, E-4, F

Cross section lines: Y, Z, F, V, W, X

TYPICAL CROSS SECTIONS OF THE PROMISED LAND
(For locations, see map on opposite page)

West-East Section Across Ephraim (V—V)

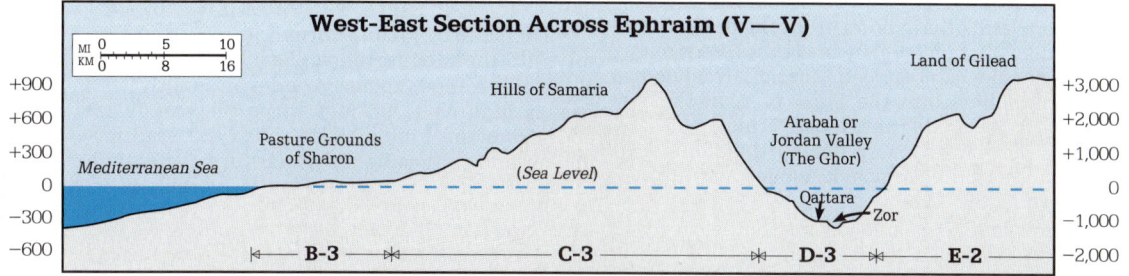

MI 0 — 5 — 10
KM 0 — 8 — 16

Land of Gilead

+900 / +3,000
+600 / +2,000
Hills of Samaria

+300 / +1,000
Pasture Grounds
of Sharon

Arabah or
Jordan Valley
(The Ghor)

Mediterranean Sea

0 / 0
(Sea Level)

Qattara

−300 / −1,000
Zor

−600 / −2,000

|← B-3 →| |← C-3 →| |← D-3 →| |← E-2 →|

West-East Section Across Judah (W—W)

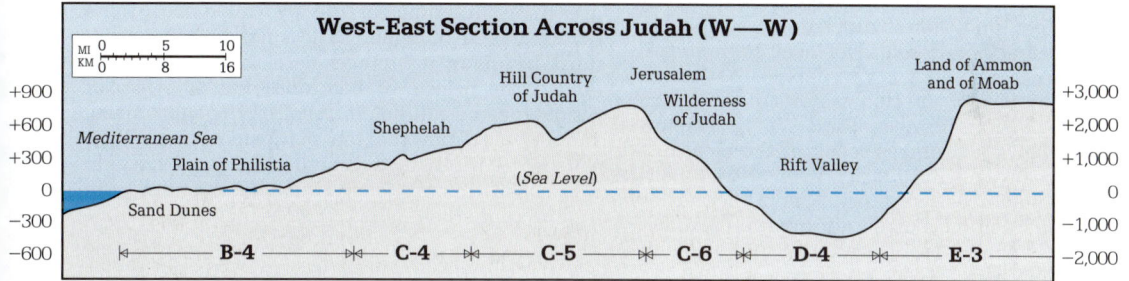

MI 0 — 5 — 10
KM 0 — 8 — 16

Hill Country
of Judah

Jerusalem

Land of Ammon
and of Moab

+900 / +3,000
Wilderness
of Judah

+600 / +2,000
Shephelah

Mediterranean Sea

+300 / +1,000
Plain of Philistia

Rift Valley

0 / 0
(Sea Level)

−300 / −1,000
Sand Dunes

−600 / −2,000

|← B-4 →| |← C-4 →| |← C-5 →| |← C-6 →| |← D-4 →| |← E-3 →|

West-East Section Across Judah (X—X)

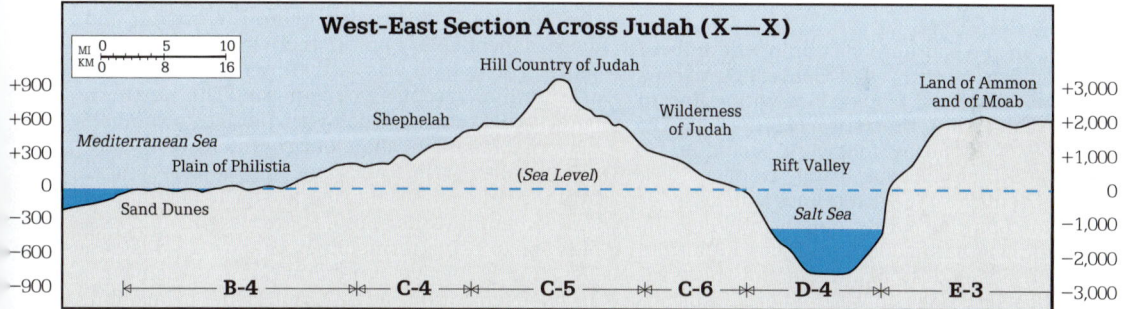

MI 0 — 5 — 10
KM 0 — 8 — 16

Hill Country of Judah

+900 / +3,000
Shephelah

Wilderness
of Judah

Land of Ammon
and of Moab

+600 / +2,000
Mediterranean Sea

Plain of Philistia

+300 / +1,000
Rift Valley

0 / 0
(Sea Level)

−300 / −1,000
Sand Dunes

Salt Sea

−600 / −2,000
−900 / −3,000

|← B-4 →| |← C-4 →| |← C-5 →| |← C-6 →| |← D-4 →| |← E-3 →|

South-North Section Along the Mountains
West of the Jordan (Y—Y)

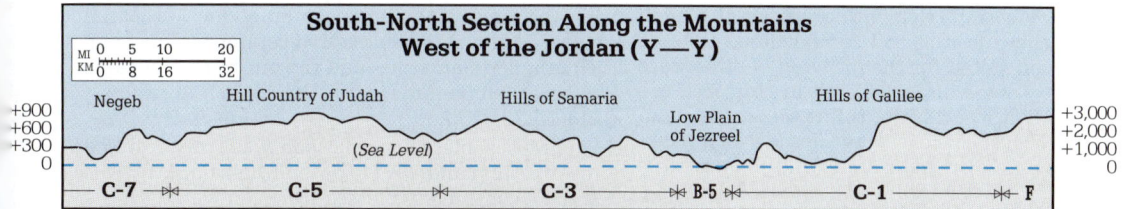

MI 0 — 5 — 10 — 20
KM 0 — 8 — 16 — 32

Negeb   Hill Country of Judah   Hills of Samaria   Hills of Galilee

+900 / +3,000
Low Plain
of Jezreel

+600 / +2,000
+300 / +1,000
0 / 0
(Sea Level)

|← C-7 →| |← C-5 →| |← C-3 →| |← B-5 →| |← C-1 →| |← F →|

South-North Section Along the Arabah
or Rift Valley (Z—Z)

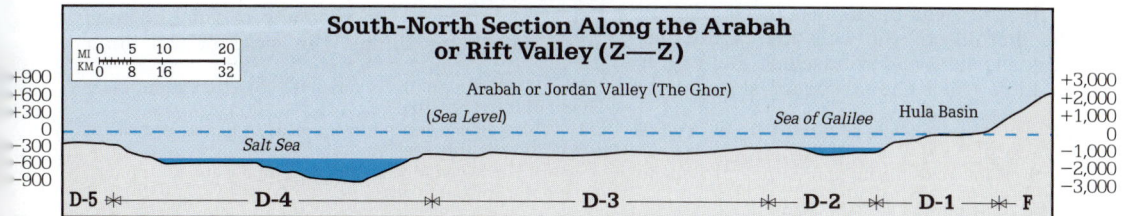

MI 0 — 5 — 10 — 20
KM 0 — 8 — 16 — 32

Arabah or Jordan Valley (The Ghor)

+900 / +3,000
+600 / +2,000
(Sea Level)

+300 / +1,000
Sea of Galilee   Hula Basin

0 / 0
−300 / −1,000
Salt Sea

−600 / −2,000
−900 / −3,000

|← D-5 →| |← D-4 →| |← D-3 →| |← D-2 →| |← D-1 →| |← F →|

Numbers on left are METERS   Elevation is approximately 10 times the linear measurement   Numbers on right are FEET

entire central valley offered easy cross-country travel from the Jordan rift valley to the Mediterranean Coast, and it became an important trade route. The Plain of Megiddo is drained by the torrent valley Kishon, which makes its way out through a narrow gap between Mount Carmel and the hills of Galilee into the Plain of Asher and from there to the Mediterranean. This modest watercourse all but dries up during the summer months, but at other times it wells up into a torrent.—Judg. 5:21.

[10] The Low Plain of Jezreel drains southeasterly toward the Jordan. This valley corridor, the Plain of Jezreel, is about 2 miles wide and covers a distance of nearly 12 miles. The elevation starts at over 300 feet, and then it drops down steadily to about 390 feet below sea level near Beth-shean. The entire central valley is very fertile, the Jezreel section being one of the richest parts of the entire country. Jezreel itself means "God Will Sow Seed." (Hos. 2:22) The Scriptures speak of the pleasantness and beauty of this district. (Gen. 49:15) Both Megiddo and Jezreel were strategic in the battles fought by Israel and surrounding nations, and it was here that Barak, Gideon, King Saul, and Jehu fought.—Judg. 5:19-21; 7:12; 1 Sam. 29:1; 31: 1, 7; 2 Ki. 9:27.

C-1 HILLS OF GALILEE

[11] It was in the southern section of the hills of Galilee (and around the Sea of Galilee) that Jesus did the greater part of his work of witnessing to Jehovah's name and Kingdom. (Matt. 4:15-17; Mark 3:7) Most of Jesus' followers, including all 11 of his faithful apostles, came from Galilee. (Acts 2:7) In this district, sometimes called Lower Galilee, the country is truly delightful, the hills rising no higher than 2,000 feet. From autumn to spring, there is no lack of rain over this pleasant land, and hence it is not a desert region. In springtime every hillside is ablaze with flowers, and every valley basin is rich with grain. On the small plateaus, there is rich soil for farming, and the hills are well suited for the growing of olive trees and vines. Towns of Bible fame in this area are Nazareth, Cana, and Nain. (Matt. 2:22, 23; John 2:1; Luke 7:11) This area gave Jesus a rich background to draw on in framing his illustrations. —Matt. 6:25-32; 9:37, 38.

[12] In the northern section, or Upper Galilee, the hills rise to well over 3,600 feet, becoming, in effect, the foothills of the Lebanon Mountains. Upper Galilee is aloof and windswept, and rain is heavy. In Bible times the westward slopes were thickly forested. This region was assigned to the tribe of Naphtali.—Josh. 20:7.

C-2 HILLS OF CARMEL

[13] The spur of Mount Carmel juts out majestically into the Mediterranean Sea. Carmel is actually a hilly range, about 30 miles in length, that rises as high as 1,790 feet above the sea. It extends from the hills of Samaria to the Mediterranean, and its headland, which forms the main ridge at the northwest end, is unforgettable in its grace and beauty. (Song of Sol. 7:5) The name Carmel means "Orchard," which truly fits this fertile promontory, bedecked with its famous vineyards and fruit and olive trees. Isaiah 35:2 uses it as a symbol of the fruitful glory of the restored land of Israel: 'The splendor of Carmel must be given it.' It was here that Elijah challenged the priests of Baal and that "the fire of Jehovah came falling" in proof of His supremacy, and it was from the top of Carmel that Elijah called attention to the small cloud that became a great downpour, thus miraculously ending the drought on Israel.—1 Ki. 18:17-46.

C-3 HILLS OF SAMARIA

[14] The southern part of this region is the more hilly, rising to above 3,000 feet in the east. (1 Sam. 1:1) In this region, there is a greater and more dependable rainfall than in Judah to the south. This region was settled by the descendants of Ephraim, Joseph's younger son. The northern part of this region, which was allotted to the half tribe of Manasseh, the older son of Joseph, comprises valley basins and small plains surrounded by hills. The hilly land is not so fertile, though there are vineyards and olive groves, made possible by extensive terracing of the lower hillsides. (Jer. 31:5) However, the larger valley basins are excellent for grain growing and general farming. Many cities dotted this region in Bible times. During the time of the northern kingdom, Manasseh supplied the three successive capitals—Shechem, Tirzah, and Samaria—and the entire region came to be called Samaria, after the capital.—1 Ki. 12: 25; 15:33; 16:24.

[15] Moses' blessing on Joseph was truly fulfilled toward this land. "As to Joseph he said: 'May his land be continually blessed from Jehovah with the choice things of heaven, with dew, . . . and with the choice things, the products of the sun, and with the choice things, the yield of the lunar

---

10. (a) Describe the Low Plain of Jezreel. (b) With what Biblical events is this area associated?
11, 12. (a) To what extent did Galilee feature in the ministry of Jesus, and who came from this district? (b) Contrast Lower Galilee with Upper Galilee.

13. (a) What actually is Carmel? (b) What mention is made of it in the Bible?
14. Which tribes settled in the hills of Samaria, and for what crops is this area suitable?
15. (a) How was Moses' blessing on Joseph fulfilled in the region of Samaria? (b) How was this land further blessed during Jesus' time?

months, and with the choicest from the mountains of the east, and with the choice things of the indefinitely lasting hills.'" (Deut. 33:13-15) Yes, this was delightful country. Its mountains were heavily forested, its valleys were productive, and it became filled with prosperous and well-populated cities. (1 Ki. 12:25; 2 Chron. 15:8) In later times Jesus preached in the land of Samaria, as did his disciples, and Christianity found many supporters there.—John 4:4-10; Acts 1:8; 8:1, 14.

C-4 SHEPHELAH

[16] While the name Shephelah means "Lowland," it is actually a hilly area reaching to an altitude of about 1,500 feet in the southern portion and is cut by frequent valleys that run from east to west. (2 Chron. 26:10) It rises due east of the coastal plain of Philistia and is to be considered a lowland only by comparison with the higher hills of Judah farther to the east. (Josh. 12:8) Its hills, which were covered with sycamore trees, now support vineyards and olive groves. (1 Ki. 10:27) It had many cities. In Bible history it served as the buffer zone between Israel and the Philistines or whatever other invading armies tried to enter Judah from the direction of the coastal plain.—2 Ki. 12:17; Obad. 19.

C-5 THE HILL COUNTRY OF JUDAH

[17] This is a high rocky area about 50 miles long and less than 20 miles wide, with elevations varying from 2,000 to over 3,300 feet above sea level. In Bible times the area was covered with timber growth, and especially on the western side, the hills and valleys were rich with grainfields, olive trees, and vineyards. This was a district that produced much good grain, oil, and wine for Israel. Particularly the area around Jerusalem has suffered much deforestation since Bible times and so appears barren in comparison with what it once was. In the winter, snow sometimes falls on the higher elevations in the center, such as at Bethlehem. In ancient times Judah was considered a good place for cities and fortresses, and in troublesome times the people could flee to these mountains for safety.—2 Chron. 27:4.

[18] Outstanding in the history of Judah and of Israel is Jerusalem, also called Zion, after the name of its citadel. (Ps. 48:1, 2) Originally it was the Canaanite city of Jebus, lying on high ground above the junction of the Valley of Hinnom and the Kidron Valley. After David captured it and made it the capital, it was extended to the northwest, and eventually it covered also the Tyropoeon Valley. In time the Valley of Hinnom came to be called Gehenna. Because the Jews made idolatrous sacrifices there, it was declared unclean and was turned into a dump for rubbish and the dead bodies of vile criminals. (2 Ki. 23:10; Jer. 7: 31-33) Thus, its fires became a symbol of total annihilation. (Matt. 10:28; Mark 9:47, 48) Jerusalem drew only a limited water supply from the Pool of Siloam, west of the Kidron Valley, and Hezekiah protected this by building an outer wall to contain it within the city.—Isa. 22:11; 2 Chron. 32:2-5.

C-6 WILDERNESS OF JUDAH (JESHIMON)

[19] Jeshimon is the Bible name for the Wilderness of Judah. It means "Desert." (1 Sam. 23:19, footnote) How descriptive and fitting this name! The wilderness consists of the rugged eastern slopes of barren chalky formations of the Judean hills, which drop in elevation more than 3,000 feet in 15 miles as they approach the Dead Sea, where there is a wall of jagged cliffs. There are no cities and few settlements in Jeshimon. It was to this wilderness of Judah that David fled from King Saul, it was between this wilderness and the Jordan that John the Baptizer preached, and it was to this region that Jesus retired when fasting for 40 days.*—1 Sam. 23:14; Matt. 3:1; Luke 4:1.

C-7 NEGEB

[20] South of the hills of Judah lies the Negeb, where the patriarchs Abraham and Isaac resided for many years. (Gen. 13:1-3; 24:62) The Bible also refers to the southern part of this area as "the wilderness of Zin." (Josh. 15:1) The semiarid Negeb stretches from the district of Beer-sheba in the north to Kadesh-barnea in the south. (Gen. 21:31; Num. 13:1-3, 26; 32:8) The land drops from the hills of Judah by a series of ridges, which run east and west, in such a way as to present a natural barrier against traffic or invasion from the south. The land falls away from the hills in the eastern part of the Negeb to a desert plain in the west, along the seacoast. Summer finds the land as barren as the desert, except near some of the torrent valleys. However, water may be obtained by sinking a well. (Gen. 21:30, 31) The modern State of Israel is irrigating and developing parts of the Negeb. "The river of Egypt" marked the southwestern boundary of the Negeb as well as being part of the southern boundary of the Promised Land.—Gen. 15:18.

---

16. (a) What characterizes the Shephelah? (b) Of what importance was this district in Bible times?

17. (a) How productive was the hill country of Judah in Bible times, and how about today? (b) For what was Judah considered a good place?

18. (a) When did Jerusalem become the capital of Israel and Judah? (b) What are some interesting features of the city?

---

* *Insight on the Scriptures,* Vol. 1, page 335.

---

19. (a) How does Jeshimon fit the meaning of its name? (b) What Bible events took place in this region?

20. Describe the Negeb.

C-8 WILDERNESS OF PARAN

[21] South of the Negeb and merging with the Wilderness of Zin lies the Wilderness of Paran. On leaving Sinai, the Israelites crossed this wilderness on their way to the Promised Land, and it was from Paran that Moses sent out the 12 spies. —Num. 12:16–13:3.

D. THE GREAT ARABAH (THE RIFT VALLEY)

[22] One of the most unusual land formations on this earth is the great Rift Valley. In the Bible, the part that cuts through the Promised Land from north to south is called "the Arabah." (Josh. 18:18) At 2 Samuel 2:29 this split in the earth's crust is described as a gully. To its north is Mount Hermon. (Josh. 12:1) From the foot of Hermon, the Rift Valley drops rapidly southward to about 2,600 feet *below* sea level at the bottom of the Dead Sea. From the southern end of the Dead Sea, the Arabah continues, rising to more than 650 feet above sea level about midway between the Dead Sea and the Gulf of 'Aqaba. Thereafter it descends rapidly into the tepid waters of the eastern prong of the Red Sea. The accompanying section maps show the relation of the Rift Valley to the surrounding country.

D-1 HULA BASIN

[23] Beginning at the foot of Mount Hermon, the Rift Valley quickly falls more than 1,600 feet to the Hula region, which is at about sea level. This district is well watered and remains beautifully green even through the hot summer months. It was in this area that the Danites settled in their city of Dan, which served as an idolatrous center of worship from the time of the judges into the time of the ten-tribe kingdom of Israel. (Judg. 18:29-31; 2 Ki. 10:29) It was at Caesarea Philippi, a town near the location of ancient Dan, that Jesus confirmed to his disciples that he was the Christ, and many believe that it was on nearby Mount Hermon that the transfiguration took place six days later. From Hula, the Rift Valley descends to the Sea of Galilee, which lies about 700 feet below sea level.—Matt. 16:13-20; 17:1-9.

D-2 REGION AROUND THE SEA OF GALILEE

[24] The Sea of Galilee and its surroundings are delightful.* Interest in that region is heightened

---

* *Insight on the Scriptures,* Vol. 1, page 336.

---

21. Where is Paran, and what part did it play in Bible history?
22. By using the map on page 272 and the diagrams on page 273, along with this paragraph, briefly describe the main features of the Arabah (Rift Valley) and their relationship to the surrounding territory.
23. With what was the Hula region associated in Bible times?
24. (a) What other names is the Sea of Galilee called in the Bible? (b) What were its surroundings like in Jesus' day?

because of the many incidents in Jesus' ministry that took place there. (Matt. 4:23) The sea is also called the Lake of Gennesaret, or Chinnereth, and the Sea of Tiberias. (Luke 5:1; Josh. 13:27; John 21:1) It is in reality a heart-shaped lake, almost 13 miles long by about 7 miles wide at its broadest point, and constitutes an important water reservoir for the whole land. It is closely shut in by hills on almost every side. The surface of the lake is about 700 feet below sea level, resulting in pleasant, warm winters and very long, hot summers. In the days of Jesus, it was the center of a highly developed fishing industry, and the thriving cities of Chorazin, Bethsaida, Capernaum, and Tiberias were located on or near the shore of the lake. The peacefulness of the lake can be quickly disturbed by storms. (Luke 8:23) The little plain of Gennesaret, triangular in shape, is located to the northwest of the lake. The soil is rich, producing almost every kind of crop known to the Promised Land. In the spring the gaily colored slopes glow with a brilliance that is nowhere surpassed in the land of Israel.*

D-3 DISTRICT OF THE JORDAN VALLEY (THE GHOR)

[25] This entire gulleylike descending valley is also called "the Arabah." (Deut. 3:17) The Arabs today refer to it as The Ghor, meaning "Depression." The valley starts at the Sea of Galilee and is generally broad—being about 12 miles wide in places. The Jordan River itself lies about 150 feet below the valley plain, turning and twisting in a course of 200 miles to cover the 65 miles to the Dead Sea.# Leaping over and down 27 cascading rapids, it falls about 590 feet by the time it reaches the Dead Sea. The lower Jordan is fringed by a thicket of trees and shrubs, principally tamarisks, oleanders, and willows, among which lions and their cubs lurked in Bible times. This is today known as the *Zor* and is partly flooded in the spring. (Jer. 49:19) Rising above each side of this narrow junglelike strip is the *Qattara,* an inhospitable border of desolate land of little plateaus and dissected slopes leading up to the plains of The Ghor itself. The plains in the northern part of The Ghor, or Arabah, are well cultivated. Even in the southern part, toward the Dead Sea, the plateau of the Arabah, which is today very arid, at one time is said to have produced numerous kinds of dates, as well as many other tropical fruits. Jericho was and still is the most famous city in the Jordan Valley.—Josh. 6:2, 20; Mark 10:46.

---

* *Insight on the Scriptures,* Vol. 2, pages 737-40.
# *Insight on the Scriptures,* Vol. 1, page 334.

---

25. What are the main features of the Jordan Valley?

D-4 THE SALT (DEAD) SEA

[26] This is one of the most remarkable bodies of water on the face of the earth. It is fittingly called dead, for no fish live in the sea and there is little vegetation by its shore. The Bible calls it the Salt Sea, or the Sea of the Arabah, since it is located in the rift valley of the Arabah. (Gen. 14:3; Josh. 12:3) The sea is approximately 47 miles from north to south and 9 miles across. Its surface is about 1,300 feet below that of the Mediterranean Sea, making it the lowest spot on earth. In its northern part, it has a depth of about 1,300 feet. On each side, the sea is shut in by barren hills and steep cliffs. Although the Jordan River brings in fresh water, there is no water outlet except by evaporation, which is as fast as the water intake. The trapped water contains about 25 percent dissolved solid matter, mostly salt, and is poisonous to fish and painful to human eyes. Visitors to most of the area around the Dead Sea are often overwhelmed by a sense of desolation and destruction. It is a place of the dead. Though the entire region was once "a well-watered region . . . like the garden of Jehovah," the area around the Dead Sea is now largely "a desolate waste" and has been such for close to 4,000 years, as striking testimony to the unchangeableness of Jehovah's judgments that were executed there against Sodom and Gomorrah.—Gen. 13:10; 19:27-29; Zeph. 2:9.

D-5 ARABAH (SOUTHWARD FROM THE SALT SEA)

[27] This final section of the Rift Valley runs southward for another 100 miles. This region is virtually all desert. Rain is rare, and the sun beats down without mercy. The Bible also calls this "the Arabah." (Deut. 2:8) About midway, it reaches its highest point at more than 650 feet above sea level and then descends southward again to the Gulf of 'Aqaba, the eastern prong of the Red Sea. It was here, at the port of Ezion-geber, that Solomon built a fleet of ships. (1 Ki. 9:26) For much of the period of the kings of Judah, this part of the Arabah was under the control of the kingdom of Edom.

E. MOUNTAINS AND TABLELANDS EAST OF THE JORDAN

[28] "The side of the Jordan toward the east" rises rapidly from the Rift Valley to form a series of tablelands. (Josh. 18:7; 13:9-12; 20:8) To the north is the land of Bashan (E-1), which, together with half of Gilead, was given to the tribe of Manasseh. (Josh. 13:29-31) This was cattle country, a land for the farmers, a fertile plateau averaging about 2,000 feet above sea level. (Ps. 22:12; Ezek. 39:18; Isa. 2:13; Zech. 11:2) In Jesus' day this area exported much grain, and today it is agriculturally productive. Next, to the south, there lies the land of Gilead (E-2), the lower half of which was assigned to the tribe of Gad. (Josh. 13:24, 25) A mountainous region reaching to 3,300 feet, watered by good rains in the winter and heavy dews in the summer, it was also good livestock country and was specially renowned for its balsam. Today it is noted for its choice grapes. (Num. 32:1; Gen. 37:25; Jer. 46:11) It was to the land of Gilead that David fled from Absalom, and in the western part, Jesus preached in "the regions of Decapolis."—2 Sam. 17:26-29; Mark 7:31.

[29] "The land of the sons of Ammon" (E-3) lies immediately south of Gilead, and half of this was given to the tribe of Gad. (Josh. 13:24, 25; Judg. 11:12-28) It is a rolling tableland, best suited to sheep grazing. (Ezek. 25:5) Still farther to the south is "the land of Moab." (Deut. 1:5) The Moabites themselves were great sheepherders, and to this day sheep raising is the principal occupation of that area. (2 Ki. 3:4) Then, southeast of the Dead Sea, we come to the mountain plateau of Edom (E-4). The ruins of its great trading strongholds, such as Petra, remain to this day.—Gen. 36: 19-21; Obad. 1-4.

[30] To the east of these hills and tablelands lies the extensive rocky wilderness that effectively cut off direct travel between the Promised Land and Mesopotamia, causing the caravan routes to detour many miles northward. To the south this wilderness meets up with the sand dunes of the great Arabian desert.

F. MOUNTAINS OF LEBANON

[31] Dominating the landscape of the Promised Land are the mountains of Lebanon. There are really two ranges of mountains running parallel. The foothills of the Lebanon Range proper continue into Upper Galilee. In many places these hills reach right down to the seacoast. The highest peak in this range is about 10,000 feet above sea level. The highest peak in the adjoining Anti-Lebanon Range is beautiful Mount Hermon, rising 9,232 feet above sea level. Its melting snow provides a major source of water for the Jordan River and a source of dew during the dry period of late spring. (Ps. 133:3) The Lebanon Mountains were specially noted for their gigantic cedars, the wood

---

26. (a) What are some of the remarkable facts about the Dead Sea? (b) What striking testimony does this region give concerning Jehovah's judgments?
27. What kind of territory makes up the southern Arabah, and who controlled this in ancient times?
28. Of what value have the lands of Bashan and Gilead been agriculturally, and how were these regions involved in Bible history?

---

29. East of the Jordan, what lands lay to the south, and for what were they noted?
30. By what are the tablelands bounded on the east?
31. (a) What make up the mountains of Lebanon? (b) What features of Lebanon remain as they were in Bible times?

of which featured in the construction of Solomon's temple. (1 Ki. 5:6-10) While only a few groves of cedars remain today, the lower slopes still support vineyards, olive groves, and fruit orchards, just as they did in Bible times.—Hos. 14:5-7.

³² As we thus conclude our visit to Jehovah's Land of Promise, sandwiched as it is between the forbidding wilderness to the east and the Great Sea, we can form a mental picture of the glory that once clothed it in the days of Israel. Truly, it was "a very, very good land . . . , flowing with milk and honey." (Num. 14:7, 8; 13:23) Moses referred to it in these words: "Jehovah your God is bringing you

into a good land, a land of torrent valleys of water, springs and watery deeps issuing forth in the valley plain and in the mountainous region, a land of wheat and barley and vines and figs and pomegranates, a land of oil olives and honey, a land in which you will not eat bread with scarcity, in which you will lack nothing, a land the stones of which are iron and out of the mountains of which you will mine copper. When you have eaten and satisfied yourself, you must also bless Jehovah your God for the good land that he has given you." (Deut. 8:7-10) May all who love Jehovah now likewise give thanks that he purposes to make the entire earth a glorious paradise, after the pattern of his ancient Land of Promise.—Ps. 104:10-24.

---

32. How did Moses correctly describe the Land of Promise?

Study Number 2

Time and the Holy Scriptures

Describing time divisions used in the Bible, the calendars in common use, pivotal dates for the Bible, and interesting points with regard to "the stream of time."

MAN is deeply conscious of the passing of time. With each tick of the clock, he progresses a step farther down time's corridor. He is wise, indeed, if he makes proper use of his time. As King Solomon wrote: "For everything there is an appointed time, even a time for every affair under the heavens: a time for birth and a time to die; a time to plant and a time to uproot what was planted; a time to kill and a time to heal; a time to break down and a time to build; a time to weep and a time to laugh." (Eccl. 3:1-4) How fleeting is time! The 70 years of the normal life span is far too short a time for a person to take in the abundance of knowledge and to enjoy all the other good things Jehovah has provided for man on this earth. "Everything he has made pretty in its time. Even time indefinite he has put in their heart, that mankind may never find out the work that the true God has made from the start to the finish."—Eccl. 3:11; Ps. 90:10.

² Jehovah himself lives in an eternity of time. As for his creatures, it has pleased him to set them in the stream of time. The angels of heaven, including even the rebellious Satan, are fully aware of the passage of time. (Dan. 10:13; Rev. 12:12) Of mankind it is written, "Time and unforeseen oc-

currence befall them all." (Eccl. 9:11) Happy is the man who at all times includes God in his thoughts and who welcomes God's provision of "food at the proper time"!—Matt. 24:45.

³ **Time Is One-Directional.** Though time is universal, no man living is able to say what it is. It is as unfathomable as space. No one can explain where the stream of time began or where it is flowing. These things belong to the limitless knowledge of Jehovah, who is described as being God "from time indefinite to time indefinite."—Ps. 90:2.

⁴ On the other hand, time has certain characteristics that can be understood. Its apparent rate of flow can be measured. Additionally, it moves in one direction only. Like traffic on a one-way street, time moves relentlessly in that one direction—onward, ever onward. Whatever the speed of its forward movement, time can never be thrown into reverse. We live in a momentary present. However, this present is in motion, flowing continually into the past. There is no stopping it.

⁵ **The Past.** The past is gone, it is history, and it can never be repeated. Any attempt to call back

---

1, 2. What did Solomon write concerning time, and in view of the fleeting nature of time, what should we do with it?

3. What do time and space have in common?
4. What can be said as to the movement of time?
5. Why may it be said that the past has been won or lost?

the past is as impossible as trying to make a waterfall tumble uphill or an arrow fly back to the bow that shot it. Our mistakes have left their mark in the stream of time, a mark that only Jehovah can wipe out. (Isa. 43:25) In like manner, a man's good deeds in the past have made a record that "will come back to him" with blessing from Jehovah. (Prov. 12:14; 13:22) The past has been won or lost. No longer is there any control over it. Of the wicked it is written: "For like grass they will speedily wither, and like green new grass they will fade away."—Ps. 37:2.

⁶ **The Future.** The future is different. It is always flowing toward us. By the help of God's Word, we can identify obstacles that loom ahead of us and prepare to meet them. We can store up for ourselves "treasures in heaven." (Matt. 6:20) These treasures will not be swept away by the stream of time. They will stay with us and will endure into an eternal future of blessing. We are interested in the wise use of time, as it affects that future.—Eph. 5:15, 16.

⁷ **Time Indicators.** Our modern-day watches and clocks are time indicators. They serve as rulers for measuring time. In similar manner Jehovah, the Creator, has set in motion giant time indicators—the earth spinning on its axis, the moon revolving around the earth, and the sun—so that from his standpoint on earth, man may be accurately advised of the time. "And God went on to say: 'Let luminaries come to be in the expanse of the heavens to make a division between the day and the night; and they must serve as signs and for seasons and for days and years.'" (Gen. 1:14) Thus, as a multitude of objects with interlocking purposes, these heavenly bodies move in their perfect cycles, unendingly and unerringly measuring the one-directional movement of time.

⁸ **Day.** The word "day" in the Bible is used with several different meanings, even as it has a variety of applications in modern times. As the earth makes one complete rotation on its axis, it measures out one day of 24 hours. In this sense, a day is made up of daytime and nighttime, a total of 24 hours. (John 20:19) However, the daylight period itself, usually averaging 12 hours, is also called day. "And God began calling the light Day, but the darkness he called Night." (Gen. 1:5) This gives rise to the time term "night," the period usually averaging 12 hours of darkness. (Ex. 10:13) Another sense is where the word "day(s)" refers to a period of time contemporaneous with

some outstanding person. For example, Isaiah saw his vision "in the days of Uzziah, Jotham, Ahaz and Hezekiah" (Isa. 1:1), and the days of Noah and of Lot are mentioned as being prophetic. (Luke 17:26-30) Another example of the flexible or figurative use of the word "day" is Peter's saying that "one day is with Jehovah as a thousand years." (2 Pet. 3:8) In the Genesis account, the creative day is an even longer period of time—millenniums. (Gen. 2:2, 3; Ex. 20:11) The Bible context indicates the sense in which the word "day" applies.

⁹ **Hour.** The division of the day into 24 hours is traced to Egypt. Our modern-day division of the hour into 60 minutes originated from Babylonian mathematics, which was a sexagesimal system (based on the number 60). There is no mention of division into hours in the Hebrew Scriptures.* Instead of dividing the day into specific hours, the Hebrew Scriptures use expressions such as "morning," "noon," "midday," and "evening time" as time indicators. (Gen. 24:11; 43:16; Deut. 28:29; 1 Ki. 18:26) The night was divided into three periods called "the night watches" (Ps. 63:6), two of which are specifically named in the Bible: "the middle night watch" (Judg. 7:19) and "the morning watch."—Ex. 14:24; 1 Sam. 11:11.

¹⁰ There is, however, frequent mention of the "hour" in the Christian Greek Scriptures. (John 12:23; Matt. 20:2-6) Hours were counted from sunrise, or about 6 a.m. The Bible mentions the "third hour," which would be about 9 a.m. The "sixth hour" is mentioned as the time when darkness fell on Jerusalem at Jesus' impalement. This would correspond to our 12 noon. Jesus' expiration in death on the torture stake is stated to have occurred "about the ninth hour," or about 3 p.m.—Mark 15:25; Luke 23:44; Matt. 27:45, 46.#

¹¹ **Week.** It was early in his history that man began to count his days in cycles of seven. In doing this, he followed the example of his Creator, who proceeded to crown his six creative days with a seventh period also called a day. Noah counted

---

* The word "hour" appears in the *King James Version* at Daniel 3:6, 15; 4:19, 33; 5:5, from the Aramaic; however, Strong's *Concordance, Hebrew and Chaldee Dictionary*, gives the meaning of the word as "a look, i.e. a moment." It is translated "moment" in the *New World Translation of the Holy Scriptures.*

See footnotes on these scriptures.

6. How is the future different from the past, and why should we be especially interested in it?
7. What time indicators has Jehovah provided for man?
8. In what different senses is the word "day" used in the Bible?

9. (a) How did the division of the day into 24 hours of 60 minutes each originate? (b) What time indicators are mentioned in the Hebrew Scriptures?
10. How did the Jews count hours in Jesus' time, and how does knowing this help us fix the time of Jesus' death?
11. How old is the use of the "week" as a measurement of time?

days in cycles of seven. In Hebrew, "week" literally refers to a sevenfold unit or period.—Gen. 2: 2, 3; 8:10, 12; 29:27.

¹² **Lunar Months.** The Bible speaks of "lunar months." (Ex. 2:2; Deut. 21:13; 33:14; Ezra 6:15) Our modern months are not lunar months, for they are not determined by the moon. They are merely 12 arbitrary divisions of the solar year. A lunar month is a month that is determined by the new moon. There are four phases of the moon, which make up one lunation averaging 29 days, 12 hours, and 44 minutes. One has only to look at the shape of the moon to tell approximately the day of the lunar month.

¹³ Instead of using strictly lunar months, Noah appears to have recorded events by months of 30 days each. By the log that Noah kept on the ark, we understand that the waters of the Flood kept overwhelming the earth for a period of five months, or "a hundred and fifty days." It was after 12 months and 10 days that the earth had dried off so that the ark's passengers could go out. Thus, those epoch-making events were accurately recorded as to time.—Gen. 7:11, 24; 8:3, 4, 14-19.

¹⁴ **Seasons.** In preparing the earth for habitation, Jehovah made the wise and loving provision of the seasons. (Gen. 1:14) These follow as a consequence of the earth's being tilted, or inclined, at a 23.5° angle to the plane of its travel around the sun. This results in first the Southern Hemisphere's and then, six months later, the Northern Hemisphere's being tilted toward the sun, so that the seasons proceed in order. This change of the seasons provides for variety and contrast and controls the times for planting and harvesting. God's Word assures us that this arrangement for change and contrast of the seasons through the year is to continue forever. "For all the days the earth continues, seed sowing and harvest, and cold and heat, and summer and winter, and day and night, will never cease."—Gen. 8:22.

¹⁵ The year in the Promised Land can generally be divided into the rainy season and the dry season. From about mid-April to mid-October, very little rain falls. The rainy season may be divided into the early, or "autumn," rain (October-November); the heavy winter rains and colder

weather (December-February); and the late, or "spring," rain (March-April). (Deut. 11:14; Joel 2:23) These divisions are approximate, the seasons overlapping because of variations in climate in different parts of the land. The early rain softens up the dry ground, so that October-November is the time for "plowing" and for "the sowing of seed." (Ex. 34:21; Lev. 26:5) During the heavy winter rains from December to February, snowfalls are not uncommon, and in January and February, the temperature may drop below freezing on the higher elevations. The Bible speaks of Benaiah, one of David's mighty men, as killing a lion "on a day of snowfall."—2 Sam. 23:20.

¹⁶ The months of March and April (approximately the Hebrew months of Nisan and Iyyar) are the months of "the spring rain." (Zech. 10:1) This is the late rain, which is needed to make the grain planted in autumn swell, so that a good harvest may result. (Hos. 6:3; Jas. 5:7) This is also the season of the early harvest, and God commanded Israel to offer the firstfruits of the harvest on Nisan 16. (Lev. 23:10; Ruth 1:22) It is a time of beauty and delight. "Blossoms themselves have appeared in the land, the very time of vine trimming has arrived, and the voice of the turtledove itself has been heard in our land. As for the fig tree, it has gained a mature color for its early figs; and the vines are abloom, they have given their fragrance."—Song of Sol. 2:12, 13.

¹⁷ About mid-April the dry season begins, but almost throughout this period, and especially on the coastal plains and the western slopes of the mountains, an abundance of dew sustains the summer crops. (Deut. 33:28) During May, grain is harvested, and it was at the end of this month that the Festival of Weeks (Pentecost) was celebrated. (Lev. 23:15-21) Then, as the weather becomes warmer and the ground drier, the grapes on the vines ripen and are harvested, followed by the other summer fruits, such as olives, dates, and figs. (2 Sam. 16:1) With the ending of the dry season and the beginning of the early rains, all the produce of the land has been harvested, and it was then (about the beginning of October) that the Festival of Booths, or Tabernacles, was held.—Ex. 23:16; Lev. 23:39-43.

¹⁸ **Year.** Our study of time in the Bible now brings us to the expression "year." From the be-

---

12. What is a lunar month, and how does it differ from our modern months?

13. How was the Flood accurately recorded as to time?

14. (a) How did Jehovah make provision for the seasons? (b) How long will the arrangement of seasons continue?

15, 16. (a) How may the rainy season in the Promised Land be subdivided? (b) Describe the seasons of the rains and the relationship of these seasons to agricultural activity.

17. (a) How are the crops sustained during the dry season? (b) Consider the chart "The Year of the Israelites" and divide off the year according to seasons as discussed in paragraphs 15-17. (c) When was the early harvest, the grain harvest, and the time when all the fruits were gathered in, and what festivals coincided with these events?

18. (a) Why is the meaning of the Hebrew word for "year" appropriate? (b) What is the true solar year as regards the earth?

THE YEAR OF THE ISRAELITES

Name of Month	Corresponds to	Sacred Year	Secular Year	Citations	Festivals	
Nisan (Abib)	March - April	1st month	7th month	Ex. 13:4; Neh. 2:1	Nisan 14 Nisan 15-21 Nisan 16	Passover Festival of Unfermented Cakes Offering of firstfruits
Iyyar (Ziv)	April - May	2nd month	8th month	1 Ki. 6:1		
Sivan	May - June	3rd month	9th month	Esther 8:9	Sivan 6	Festival of Weeks (Pentecost)
Tammuz	June - July	4th month	10th month	Jer. 52:6		
Ab	July - August	5th month	11th month	Ezra 7:8		
Elul	August - September	6th month	12th month	Neh. 6:15		
Tishri (Ethanim)	September - October	7th month	1st month	1 Ki. 8:2	Tishri 1 Tishri 10 Tishri 15-21 Tishri 22	Day of the trumpet blast Day of Atonement Festival of Booths Solemn assembly
Heshvan (Bul)	October - November	8th month	2nd month	1 Ki. 6:38		
Chislev	November - December	9th month	3rd month	Neh. 1:1		
Tebeth	December - January	10th month	4th month	Esther 2:16		
Shebat	January - February	11th month	5th month	Zech. 1:7		
Adar	February - March	12th month	6th month	Esther 3:7		
Veadar	(Intercalary month)	13th month				

ginning of man's history, it is mentioned. (Gen. 1:14) The Hebrew word for "year," sha·nah´, comes from a root meaning "repeat; do again" and carries the idea of a cycle of time. This was appropriate, since each year the cycle of seasons was repeated. An earthly year is the time it takes for the earth to make one complete revolution, or trip, around the sun. The actual time that it takes for us here on earth to complete this trip is 365 days 5 hours 48 minutes 46 seconds, or approximately 365 1/4 days. This is called the true solar year.

[19] **Bible Years.** According to the ancient Biblical reckoning, the year ran from autumn to autumn. This was particularly suited to an agricultural life, the year beginning with plowing and sowing, toward the first part of our month of October, and ending with the gathering in of the harvest. Noah counted the year as beginning in the autumn. He recorded the Deluge as beginning "in the second month," which would correspond to the latter half of October and the first half of November. (Gen. 7: 11, footnote) To this day, many peoples of the earth still start their new year in the autumn. At the time of the Exodus from Egypt, in 1513 B.C.E., Jehovah decreed that Abib (Nisan) should become "the start of the months" for the Jews, so that they now had a sacred year, running from spring to spring. (Ex. 12:2) However, Jews in our day observe a secular, or civil, year beginning in the autumn, Tishri being the first month.

[20] **Lunisolar Year.** Until the time of Christ, most nations used lunar years for counting time, em-

ploying various ways of adjusting the year to coincide more or less with the solar year. The common lunar year of 12 lunar months has 354 days, with the months having 29 or 30 days, depending on the appearance of each new moon. The lunar year is therefore about 11 1/4 days short of the true solar year of 365 1/4 days. The Hebrews followed the lunar year. Just how they adjusted this year to coincide with the solar year and the seasons is not explained in the Bible, but they must have added additional, or intercalary, months when needed. The arrangement of intercalary months was later systematized in the fifth century B.C.E. into what is now known as the Metonic cycle. This allowed for the intercalary month to be added seven times every 19 years, and in the Jewish calendar, it was added after the 12th month, Adar, and was called Veadar, or "second Adar." As the lunar calendar is thus adjusted to the sun, the years, which are of 12 or 13 months, are known as lunisolar years.

[21] **Julian and Gregorian Calendars.** A calendar is a system of fixing the beginning, length, and divisions of the year and arranging these divisions in order. The Julian calendar was introduced by Julius Caesar in 46 B.C.E., to give the Roman people a solar-year time arrangement in place of the lunar year. The Julian calendar consists of 365 days in a year, with the exception that on each fourth year (leap year), one day is added, to make it 366 days. However, in the course of time, it was found that the Julian calendar year is actually a little more than 11 minutes longer than the true solar year. By the 16th century C.E., a discrepancy

---

19. (a) How were ancient Bible years reckoned? (b) What "sacred year" did Jehovah later decree?
20. How was the lunar year adjusted to correspond to the solar year, and what are lunisolar years?

21. (a) What is the Julian calendar? (b) Why is the Gregorian calendar more accurate?

of ten full days had accumulated. Thus, in 1582, Pope Gregory XIII introduced a slight revision, instituting what is now known as the Gregorian calendar. By papal bull ten days were omitted from the year 1582, so that the day after October 4 became October 15. The Gregorian calendar provides that centuries not divisible by 400 are not to be considered leap years. For example, unlike the year 2000, the year 1900 was not made a leap year because the number 1,900 is not divisible by 400. The Gregorian calendar is now the one in general use in most parts of the world.

22 **Prophetic "Year."** In Bible prophecy the word "year" is often used in a special sense as the equivalent of 12 months, each month having 30 days, for a total of 360 days. Note what one authority says in commenting on Ezekiel 4:5, 6: "We must suppose that Ezekiel knew a year of 360 days. This is neither a true solar year nor is it a lunar year. It is an 'average' year in which each month has 30 days."*

23 A prophetic year is also called a "time," and a study of Revelation 11:2, 3 and 12:6, 14 reveals how one "time" is reckoned as 360 days. In prophecy a year is occasionally also represented symbolically by a "day."—Ezek. 4:5, 6.

24 **No Zero Year.** Ancient peoples, including the learned Greeks, the Romans, and the Jews, had no concept of zero. To them, everything began counting from one. When you studied Roman numerals in school (I, II, III, IV, V, X, etc.), did you learn a figure for zero? No, because the Romans had none. Since the Romans did not use the number zero, the Common Era began, not with a zero year, but with 1 C.E. This also gave rise to the ordinal arrangement of numbers, such as first (1st), second (2nd), third (3rd), tenth (10th), and hundredth (100th). In modern mathematics, man conceives of everything as starting from nothing, or zero. The zero was probably invented by the Hindus.

25 Thus it is that whenever *ordinal* numbers are used, we must always subtract one to get the full number. For example, when we speak of a date in the 20th century C.E., does it mean that there have been a full 20 centuries? No, it means 19 full centuries plus some years. To express full numbers, the Bible, as well as modern mathematics, employs *cardinal* numbers, such as 1, 2, 3, 10, and 100. These are also called "whole numbers."

26 Now, since the Common Era did not begin with the year zero but began with 1 C.E., and the calendar for the years before the Common Era did not count back from a zero year but began with 1 B.C.E., the figure used for the year in any date is in reality an ordinal number. That is, 1990 C.E. really represents 1989 full years since the beginning of the Common Era, and the date July 1, 1990, represents 1,989 years plus a half year since the beginning of the Common Era. The same principle applies to B.C.E. dates. So to figure how many years elapsed between October 1, 607 B.C.E., and October 1, 1914 C.E., add 606 years (plus the last three months of the previous year) to 1,913 (plus the first nine months of the next year), and the result is 2,519 (plus 12 months), or 2,520 years. Or if you want to figure what date would be 2,520 years after October 1, 607 B.C.E., remember that 607 is an ordinal number—it really represents 606 full years—and since we are counting, not from December 31, 607 B.C.E., but from October 1, 607 B.C.E., we must add to 606 the three months at the end of 607 B.C.E. Now subtract 606 1/4 from 2,520 years. The remainder is 1,913 3/4. That means that 2,520 years from October 1, 607 B.C.E., takes us 1,913 3/4 years into the Common Era—1,913 full years brings us to the beginning of 1914 C.E., and three fourths of a year in addition brings us to October 1, 1914 C.E.*

27 **Pivotal Dates.** Reliable Bible chronology is based on certain pivotal dates. A pivotal date is a calendar date in history that has a sound basis for acceptance and that corresponds to a specific event recorded in the Bible. It can then be used as the starting point from which a series of Bible events can be located on the calendar with certainty. Once this pivotal point is fixed, calculations forward or backward from this date are made from accurate records in the Bible itself, such as the stated life spans of people or the duration of the reigns of kings. Thus, starting from a pegged point, we can use the reliable internal chronology of the Bible itself in dating many Bible events.

28 **Pivotal Date for the Hebrew Scriptures.** A prominent event recorded both in the Bible and in secular history is the overthrow of the city of Babylon by the Medes and Persians under Cyrus. The Bible records this event at Daniel 5:30. Various historical sources (including Diodorus, Afri-

* *Biblical Calendars,* 1961, by J. Van Goudoever, page 75.

22, 23. How long is a prophetic year?
24. How did many ancient peoples start their counting?
25. How do ordinal numbers differ from cardinal numbers?

* *Insight on the Scriptures,* Vol. 1, page 458.

26. How would you figure (a) the years from October 1, 607 B.C.E., to October 1, 1914 C.E.? (b) 2,520 years from October 1, 607 B.C.E.?
27. What are pivotal dates, and why are they of great value?
28. What pivotal date is provided for the Hebrew Scriptures?

canus, Eusebius, Ptolemy, and the Babylonian tablets) support 539 B.C.E. as the year for the overthrow of Babylon by Cyrus. The Nabonidus Chronicle gives the month and day of the city's fall (the year is missing). Secular chronologers have thus set the date for the fall of Babylon as October 11, 539 B.C.E., according to the Julian calendar, or October 5 by the Gregorian calendar.*

²⁹ Following the overthrow of Babylon, and during his first year as ruler of conquered Babylon, Cyrus issued his famous decree permitting the Jews to return to Jerusalem. In view of the Bible record, the decree was likely made late in 538 B.C.E. or toward the spring of 537 B.C.E. This would give ample opportunity for the Jews to resettle in their homeland and to come up to Jerusalem to restore the worship of Jehovah in "the seventh month," Tishri, or about October 1, 537 B.C.E.—Ezra 1:1-4; 3:1-6.#

³⁰ **Pivotal Date for the Christian Greek Scriptures.** A pivotal date for the Christian Greek Scriptures is determined by the date that Tiberius Caesar succeeded Emperor Augustus. Augustus died on August 17, 14 C.E. (Gregorian calendar); Tiberius was named emperor by the Roman Senate on September 15, 14 C.E. It is stated at Luke 3:1, 3 that John the Baptizer began his ministry in the 15th year of Tiberius' reign. If the years were counted from the death of Augustus, the 15th year ran from August of 28 C.E. to August of 29 C.E. If counted from when Tiberius was named emperor by the Senate, the year ran from September of 28 C.E. to September of 29 C.E. Soon after this, Jesus, who was about six months younger than John the Baptizer, came to be baptized, when he was "about thirty years old." (Luke 3:2, 21-23; 1: 34-38) This agrees with the prophecy at Daniel 9:25 that 69 "weeks" (prophetic weeks of 7 years each, thus totaling 483 years) would elapse from "the going forth of the word to restore and to rebuild Jerusalem" and its wall until the appearance of Messiah. (Dan. 9:24, footnote) That "word" was authorized by Artaxerxes (Longimanus) in 455 B.C.E. and was put into effect by Nehemiah in Jerusalem in the latter part of that year. And 483 years later, in the latter part of 29 C.E., when he was baptized by John, Jesus was also anointed by holy spirit from God, thus becoming the Messiah, or Anointed One. That Jesus was baptized and

began his ministry in the latter part of the year also agrees with the prophecy that he was to be cut off "at the half of the week" of years (or after three and a half years). (Dan. 9:27) Since he died in the spring, his ministry of three and a half years must have begun toward the fall of 29 C.E.* Incidentally, these two lines of evidence also prove that Jesus was born in the autumn of 2 B.C.E., since Luke 3:23 shows that Jesus was about 30 years of age when he commenced his work.#

³¹ **How Time Moves Faster.** There is an old saying that "a watched kettle never boils." It is true that when we are watching time, when we are conscious of it, when we are waiting for something to happen, then it seems to pass ever so slowly. However, if we are busy, if we are interested in and preoccupied with what we are doing, then it really appears that "time flies." Moreover, with older people time seems to pass much more quickly than with young children. Why is this? One year added to the life of a one-year-old means a 100-percent increase in life's experiences. One year added to the life of a 50-year-old means just 2 percent more. To the child, a year seems a long, long time. The older person, if busy and in good health, finds that the years seem to fly faster and faster. He comes to a deeper understanding of Solomon's words: "There is nothing new under the sun." On the other hand, young people still have the seemingly slower, formative years with them. Instead of "striving after wind" with a materialistic world, they may use these years profitably in piling up a wealth of godly experience. Timely are Solomon's further words: "Remember, now, your Grand Creator in the days of your young manhood, before the calamitous days proceed to come, or the years have arrived when you will say: 'I have no delight in them.'"—Eccl. 1:9, 14; 12:1.

³² **Time—When People Live Forever.** However, there are joyous days ahead that will be far from calamitous. Lovers of righteousness, whose 'times are in Jehovah's hand,' may look forward to everlasting life in the realm of God's Kingdom. (Ps. 31:14-16; Matt. 25:34, 46) Under the Kingdom, death will be no more. (Rev. 21:4) Idleness, illness, boredom, and vanity will have vanished. There will be work to do, absorbing and intriguing, calling for expression of man's perfect abilities and bringing intense satisfaction in

---

* *Insight on the Scriptures,* Vol. 1, pages 453-4, 458; Vol. 2, page 459.
# *Insight on the Scriptures,* Vol. 1, page 568.

* *Insight on the Scriptures,* Vol. 2, pages 899-902.
# *Insight on the Scriptures,* Vol. 2, pages 56-8.

29. When was Cyrus' decree issued, allowing opportunity for what?
30. How does a pivotal date along with fulfilled prophecy fix the time of Jesus' baptism, and of his birth?

31. (a) Why does the rate of the passage of time appear to vary? (b) What advantage do young people therefore have?
32. How may humans come to appreciate more fully Jehovah's view of time?

accomplishment. The years will seem to flow faster and faster, and appreciative and retentive minds will be continually enriched with memories of happy events. As millenniums pass, humans on this earth will no doubt come to appreciate more fully Jehovah's view of time: 'For a thousand years in Jehovah's eyes are but as yesterday when it is past.'—Ps. 90:4.

[33] Viewing the stream of time from our present human standpoint and taking into account God's promise of a new world of righteousness, how joyous in prospect are the blessings of that day: "For there Jehovah commanded the blessing to be, even life to time indefinite"!—Ps. 133:3.

Study Number *3 Measuring Events in the Stream of Time*

The counting of time in Bible days and a discussion of the chronology of outstanding events of both the Hebrew and Greek Scriptures.

IN GIVING Daniel the vision of "the king of the north" and "the king of the south," Jehovah's angel several times used the expression "the time appointed." (Dan. 11:6, 27, 29, 35) There are many other scriptures too that indicate Jehovah is an accurate timekeeper, who accomplishes his purposes exactly on time. (Luke 21:24; 1 Thess. 5: 1, 2) In his Word, the Bible, he has provided a number of "guideposts" that help us locate important happenings in the stream of time. Much progress has been made in the understanding of Bible chronology. Research by archaeologists and others continues to shed light on various problems, enabling us to determine the timing of key events of the Bible record.—Prov. 4:18.

[2] **Ordinal and Cardinal Numbers.** In the previous study (paragraphs 24 and 25), we learned that there is a difference between cardinal numbers and ordinal numbers. This should be kept in mind when measuring Biblical periods in harmony with modern dating methods. For example, in the reference to "the thirty-seventh year of the exile of Jehoiachin the king of Judah," the term "thirty-seventh" is an ordinal number. It represents 36 full years plus some days, weeks, or months (whatever time had elapsed from the end of the 36th year).—Jer. 52:31.

[3] **Regnal and Accession Years.** The Bible refers to State records of the governments of Judah and Israel, as well as to State matters of Babylon and Persia. In all four of these kingdoms, State chronology was accurately reckoned according to the rulerships of the kings, and the same system of reckoning has been carried over into the Bible. Very often the Bible gives the name of the document quoted, as, for example, "the book of the affairs of Solomon." (1 Ki. 11:41) The reign of a king would cover part of an accession year, to be followed by a complete number of regnal years. Regnal years were the official years in the kingship and were generally counted from Nisan to Nisan, or from spring to spring. When a king succeeded to the throne, the intervening months until the next spring month of Nisan were referred to as his accession year, during which he filled out the regnal term of rulership for his predecessor. However, his own official regnal term was counted as beginning on the next Nisan 1.

[4] As an example, it appears that Solomon began reigning sometime before Nisan of 1037 B.C.E., while David was still living. Shortly afterward, David died. (1 Ki. 1:39, 40; 2:10) However, David's last regnal year continued down to the spring of 1037 B.C.E., still being counted as part of his 40-year administration. The partial year, from the start of Solomon's reign until spring of 1037 B.C.E., is referred to as Solomon's accession year, and it could not be counted as a regnal year for him, as he was still filling out his father's term of administration. Therefore, Solomon's first full regnal year did not begin until Nisan of

---

1. (a) What indicates that Jehovah is an accurate time-keeper? (b) What progress has been made in understanding Bible chronology?
2. Give an example of reckoning with ordinal numbers.
3. (a) What State records assist in determining Bible dates? (b) What was a regnal year, and what was an accession year?

4. Show how Bible chronology may be counted according to regnal years.

1037 B.C.E. (1 Ki. 2:12) Eventually, 40 full regnal years were credited to Solomon's administration as king. (1 Ki. 11:42) By keeping the regnal years apart from accession years in this way, it is possible to calculate Bible chronology accurately.*

COUNTING BACK TO ADAM'S CREATION

⁵ **Starting From the Pivotal Date.** The pivotal date for counting back to Adam's creation is that of Cyrus' overthrow of the Babylonian dynasty, 539 B.C.E.# Cyrus issued his decree of liberation for the Jews during his first year, before the spring of 537 B.C.E. Ezra 3:1 reports that the sons of Israel were back in Jerusalem by the seventh month, Tishri, corresponding to parts of September and October. So the autumn of 537 B.C.E. is reckoned as the date of the restoration of Jehovah's worship in Jerusalem.

⁶ This restoration of Jehovah's worship in the autumn of 537 B.C.E. marked the end of a prophetic period. What period? It was the "seventy years" during which the Promised Land "must become a devastated place" and concerning which Jehovah also said, "In accord with the fulfilling of seventy years at Babylon I shall turn my attention to you people, and I will establish toward you my good word in bringing you back to this place." (Jer. 25:11, 12; 29:10) Daniel, who was well acquainted with this prophecy, acted in harmony with it as the "seventy years" drew to a close. (Dan. 9:1-3) The "seventy years" that ended in the autumn of the year 537 B.C.E. must have begun, then, in the autumn of 607 B.C.E. The facts bear this out. Jeremiah chapter 52 describes the momentous events of the siege of Jerusalem, the Babylonian breakthrough, and the capture of King Zedekiah in 607 B.C.E. Then, as verse 12 states, "in the fifth month, on the tenth day," that is, the tenth day of Ab (corresponding to parts of July and August), the Babylonians burned the temple and the city. However, this was not yet the starting point of the "seventy years." Some vestige of Jewish sovereignty still remained in the person of Gedaliah, whom the king of Babylon had appointed as governor of the remaining Jewish settlements. "In the seventh month," Gedaliah and some others were assassinated, so that the remaining Jews fled in fear to Egypt. Then only, from about October 1, 607 B.C.E., was the land in

the complete sense "lying desolated . . . to fulfill seventy years."—2 Ki. 25:22-26; 2 Chron. 36: 20, 21.

⁷ **From 607 B.C.E. to 997 B.C.E.** The calculation for this period backward from the fall of Jerusalem to the time of the division of the kingdom after Solomon's death presents many difficulties. However, a comparison of the reigns of the kings of Israel and of Judah as recorded in First and Second Kings indicates that this time period covers 390 years. Strong evidence that this is the correct figure is the prophecy of Ezekiel 4:1-13. This prophecy shows that it is pointing to the time when Jerusalem would be besieged and its inhabitants taken captive by the nations, which occurred in 607 B.C.E. So the 40 years spoken of in the case of Judah terminated with Jerusalem's desolation. The 390 years spoken of in the case of Israel did not end when Samaria was destroyed, for that was long past when Ezekiel prophesied, and the prophecy plainly says that it is pointing to the siege and destruction of Jerusalem. Thus, "the error of the house of Israel," too, terminated in 607 B.C.E. Counting back from this date, we see that the period of 390 years began in 997 B.C.E. In that year, Jeroboam, after the death of Solomon, broke with the house of David and "proceeded to part Israel from following Jehovah, and he caused them to sin with a great sin."—2 Ki. 17:21.

⁸ **From 997 B.C.E. to 1513 B.C.E.** Since the last of Solomon's 40 full regnal years ended in the spring of 997 B.C.E., it follows that his first regnal year must have commenced in the spring of 1037 B.C.E. (1 Ki. 11:42) The Bible record, at 1 Kings 6:1, says that Solomon began to build the house of Jehovah in Jerusalem in the second month of the fourth year of his reign. This means three full years and one complete month of his reign had elapsed, bringing us to April-May of 1034 B.C.E. for the start of the temple building. However, the same scripture states that this was also "the four hundred and eightieth year after the sons of Israel came out from the land of Egypt." Again, 480th is an ordinal number, representing 479 complete years. Hence, 479 added to 1034 gives the date 1513 B.C.E. as the year that Israel came out of Egypt. Paragraph 19 of Study 2 explains that from the year 1513 B.C.E., Abib (Nisan) was to be reckoned as "the first of the months of the year" for Israel (Ex. 12:2) and that previously a year beginning in the autumn, with the

---

* In studying this chapter, it may be helpful to refer to *Insight on the Scriptures,* Vol. 1, pages 458-67.
# Study 2, paragraphs 28, 29.

---

5. How is the date for the restoration of Jehovah's worship in Jerusalem determined?
6. (a) What foretold period ended in the autumn of 537 B.C.E.? (b) When must that period have begun, and how do the facts support this?

7. (a) How may the years be calculated back to the division of the kingdom after Solomon's death? (b) What support is supplied by Ezekiel's prophecy?
8. (a) How are the years reckoned back to the Exodus? (b) What change affects Bible chronology about this time?

month Tishri, had been followed. *The New Schaff-Herzog Encyclopedia of Religious Knowledge,* 1957, Vol. 12, page 474, comments: "The reckoning of the regnal years of the kings is based upon the year which began in the spring, and is parallel to the Babylonian method in which this prevailed." Whenever the change of beginning the year in the autumn to beginning the year in the spring began to be applied to periods of time in the Bible, this would involve a loss or gain of six months somewhere in the counting of time.

[9] **From 1513 B.C.E. to 1943 B.C.E.** At Exodus 12:40, 41, Moses records that "the dwelling of the sons of Israel, who had dwelt in Egypt, was four hundred and thirty years." From the above wording, it is apparent that not all this "dwelling" was in Egypt. This time period begins with Abraham's crossing of the Euphrates on his way to Canaan, at which time Jehovah's covenant with Abraham went into effect. The first 215 years of this "dwelling" was in Canaan, and then an equal period was spent in Egypt, until Israel became completely independent of all Egyptian control and dependency, in 1513 B.C.E.* The *New World Translation* footnote on Exodus 12:40 shows that the Greek *Septuagint,* which is based on a Hebrew text older than the Masoretic, adds, after the word "Egypt," the words "and in the land of Canaan." The Samaritan Pentateuch does similarly. Galatians 3:17, which also mentions the 430 years, confirms that this period started with the validating of the Abrahamic covenant, at the time that Abraham crossed the Euphrates on his way to Canaan. This was therefore in 1943 B.C.E., when Abraham was 75 years old.—Gen. 12:4.

[10] Another line of evidence supports the above reckoning: At Acts 7:6 mention is made of the seed of Abraham as being afflicted 400 years. Since Jehovah removed the affliction by Egypt in 1513 B.C.E., the beginning of affliction must have been in 1913 B.C.E. This was five years after the birth of Isaac and corresponds to Ishmael's "poking fun" at Isaac on the occasion of his weaning. —Gen. 15:13; 21:8, 9.

[11] **From 1943 B.C.E. to 2370 B.C.E.** We have

* From Abraham's crossing of the Euphrates to Isaac's birth is 25 years; then to Jacob's birth, 60 years; Jacob was 130 years old when he went down to Egypt.—Gen. 12:4; 21:5; 25:26; 47:9.

9. (a) How is the record dated back to when the Abrahamic covenant went into effect? (b) How are the first 215 years of this period accounted for? (c) How old was Abraham when he crossed the Euphrates on his way to Canaan?
10. What other line of evidence supports the chronology of Abraham's time?
11. How does the Bible timetable carry us back to the date of the Deluge?

seen that Abraham was 75 years old when he entered Canaan in 1943 B.C.E. Now it is possible to date the stream of time farther back, to the days of Noah. This is done by use of the time periods supplied for us in Genesis 11:10 to 12:4. This reckoning, which gives a total of 427 years, is made as follows:

From the beginning of the Deluge to Arpachshad's birth	2	years
Then to the birth of Shelah	35	"
To the birth of Eber	30	"
To the birth of Peleg	34	"
To the birth of Reu	30	"
To the birth of Serug	32	"
To the birth of Nahor	30	"
To the birth of Terah	29	"
To the death of Terah, when Abraham was 75 years old	205	"
Total	427	years

Adding 427 years to 1943 B.C.E. brings us to 2370 B.C.E. Thus the timetable of the Bible shows that the Deluge of Noah's day began in 2370 B.C.E.

[12] **From 2370 B.C.E. to 4026 B.C.E.** Going still farther back in the stream of time, we find that the Bible dates the period from the Deluge all the way to Adam's creation. This is determined by Genesis 5:3-29 and 7:6, 11. The time count is summarized below:

From Adam's creation to the birth of Seth	130	years
Then to the birth of Enosh	105	"
To the birth of Kenan	90	"
To the birth of Mahalalel	70	"
To the birth of Jared	65	"
To the birth of Enoch	162	"
To the birth of Methuselah	65	"
To the birth of Lamech	187	"
To the birth of Noah	182	"
To the Deluge	600	"
Total	1,656	years

Adding 1,656 years to our previous date of 2370 B.C.E., we arrive at 4026 B.C.E. for the creation of Adam, perhaps in the fall, since it is in the fall that the year began on the most ancient calendars.

[13] Of what significance is this today? The first edition of this book, published in 1963, stated: "Does this mean, then, that by 1963 we had progressed 5,988 years into the 'day' on which Jeho-

12. What is the time count back to Adam's creation?
13. (a) How long, then, is the history of mankind on this earth? (b) Why does this not correspond to the length of Jehovah's rest day?

vah 'has been resting from all his work'? (Gen. 2:3) No, for the creation of Adam does not correspond with the beginning of Jehovah's rest day. Following Adam's creation, and still within the sixth creative day, Jehovah appears to have been forming further animal and bird creations. Also, he had Adam name the animals, which would take some time, and he proceeded to create Eve. (Gen. 2:18-22; see also *NW,* 1953 Ed., footnote on vs. 19) Whatever time elapsed between Adam's creation and the end of the 'sixth day' must be subtracted from the 5,988 years in order to give the actual length of time from the beginning of the 'seventh day' until [1963]. It does no good to use Bible chronology for speculating on dates that are still future in the stream of time.—Matt. 24:36."*

¹⁴ How about scientific claims that man has been on this earth for hundreds of thousands or even millions of years? None of them can be substantiated by written records from those early times, as Biblical events are. The fantastic dates given to "prehistoric man" are based on assumptions that cannot be proved. Actually, reliable secular history, together with its chronology, extends back only a few thousand years. The earth has undergone many changes and upheavals, such as the worldwide Deluge of Noah's day, which have

---

* In 1990, this elapsed time must be subtracted from 6,015 years.

14. Why is the Bible account of the origin of mankind to be preferred to the hypotheses and theories of men?

greatly disturbed rock strata and fossil deposits, making any scientific pronouncements on dates prior to the Deluge highly conjectural.* In contrast to all the contradictory hypotheses and theories of men, the Bible appeals to reason through its explicit, harmonious account of the origin of mankind and its carefully documented history of Jehovah's chosen people.

¹⁵ Study of the Bible and contemplation of the works of the Great Timekeeper, Jehovah God, should make us feel very humble. Mortal man is small indeed in comparison with the omnipotent God, whose stupendous act of creation, performed countless millenniums ago, is so simply stated in Scripture: "In the beginning God created the heavens and the earth."—Gen. 1:1.

---

* *Awake!,* September 22, 1986, pages 17-27; April 8, 1972, pages 5-20.

15. How should Bible study affect us?

Questions on chart covering "Main Events of Jesus' Earthly Life": (a) Name some of the outstanding events in Jesus' ministry up to the time of the imprisonment of John the Baptizer. (b) Give the place and year for the following events: ⁽¹⁾ The calling of Simon and Andrew, James and John. ⁽²⁾ The choosing of the 12 apostles. ⁽³⁾ The Sermon on the Mount. ⁽⁴⁾ The transfiguration. ⁽⁵⁾ The raising of Lazarus from the dead. ⁽⁶⁾ Jesus' visit to the home of Zacchaeus. (c) Name some of the outstanding miracles of Jesus; tell when and where they occurred. (d) What are some of the principal events concerning Jesus that occurred from Nisan 8 to Nisan 16, 33 C.E.? (e) What were some of the outstanding illustrations that Jesus gave during his earthly ministry?

MAIN EVENTS OF JESUS' EARTHLY LIFE
The Four Gospels Set in Chronological Order
Symbols: a. for "after"; c. for "circa," or "about."

Time	Place	Event	Matthew	Mark	Luke	John
		Leading Up to Jesus' Ministry				
3 B.C.E.	Jerusalem, temple	Birth of John the Baptizer foretold to Zechariah			1:5-25	
c. 2 B.C.E.	Nazareth; Judea	Birth of Jesus foretold to Mary, who visits Elizabeth			1:26-56	
2 B.C.E.	Judean hill country	Birth of John the Baptizer; later, his desert life			1:57-80	
2 B.C.E., c. Oct. 1	Bethlehem	Birth of Jesus (the Word, through whom all other things had come into existence) as descendant of Abraham and of David	1:1-25		2:1-7	1:1-5, 9-14
	Near Bethlehem	Angel announces good news; shepherds visit babe			2:8-20	
	Bethlehem; Jerusalem	Jesus circumcised (8th day), presented in temple (40th day)			2:21-38	
1 B.C.E. or 1 C.E.	Jerusalem; Bethlehem; Nazareth	Astrologers; flight to Egypt; babes killed; Jesus' return	2:1-23		2:39, 40	
12 C.E.	Jerusalem	Twelve-year-old Jesus at the Passover; goes home			2:41-52	
29, spring	Wilderness, Jordan	Ministry of John the Baptizer	3:1-12	1:1-8	3:1-18	1:6-8, 15-28

Time	Place	Event	Matthew	Mark	Luke	John
		——————— **The Beginning of Jesus' Ministry** ———————				
29, fall	Jordan River	Baptism and anointing of Jesus, born as a human in David's line but declared to be the Son of God	3:13-17	1:9-11	3:21-38	1:32-34
	Judean Wilderness	Fasting and temptation of Jesus	4:1-11	1:12, 13	4:1-13	
	Bethany beyond Jordan	John the Baptizer's testimony concerning Jesus				1:15, 29-34
	Upper Jordan Valley	First disciples of Jesus				1:35-51
	Cana of Galilee; Capernaum	Jesus' first miracle; he visits Capernaum				2:1-12
30, Passover	Jerusalem	Passover celebration; drives traders from temple				2:13-25
	Jerusalem	Jesus' discussion with Nicodemus				3:1-21
	Judea; Aenon	Jesus' disciples baptize; John to decrease				3:22-36
	Tiberias	John imprisoned; Jesus leaves for Galilee	4:12; 14:3-5	1:14; 6:17-20	3:19, 20; 4:14	4:1-3
	Sychar, in Samaria	En route to Galilee, Jesus teaches the Samaritans				4:4-43
		——————— **Jesus' Great Ministry in Galilee** ———————				
	Galilee	First announces, "The kingdom of the heavens has drawn near"	4:17	1:14, 15	4:14, 15	4:44, 45
	Nazareth; Cana; Capernaum	Heals boy; reads commission; rejected; moves to Capernaum	4:13-16		4:16-31	4:46-54
	Sea of Galilee, near Capernaum	Call of Simon and Andrew, James and John	4:18-22	1:16-20	5:1-11	
	Capernaum	Heals demoniac, also Peter's mother-in-law and many others	8:14-17	1:21-34	4:31-41	
	Galilee	First tour of Galilee, with the four now called	4:23-25	1:35-39	4:42, 43	
	Galilee	Leper healed; multitudes flock to Jesus	8:1-4	1:40-45	5:12-16	
	Capernaum	Heals paralytic	9:1-8	2:1-12	5:17-26	
	Capernaum	Call of Matthew; feast with tax collectors	9:9-17	2:13-22	5:27-39	
	Judea	Preaches in Judean synagogues			4:44	
31, Passover	Jerusalem	Attends feast; heals man; rebukes Pharisees				5:1-47
	Returning from Jerusalem (?)	Disciples pluck ears of grain on the Sabbath	12:1-8	2:23-28	6:1-5	
	Galilee; Sea of Galilee	Heals hand on Sabbath; retires to seashore; heals	12:9-21	3:1-12	6:6-11	
	Mountain near Capernaum	The 12 are chosen as apostles		3:13-19	6:12-16	
	Near Capernaum	The Sermon on the Mount	5:1–7:29		6:17-49	
	Capernaum	Heals army officer's servant	8:5-13		7:1-10	
	Nain	Raises widow's son			7:11-17	
	Galilee	John in prison sends disciples to Jesus	11:2-19		7:18-35	
	Galilee	Cities reproached; revelation to babes; yoke kindly	11:20-30			
	Galilee	Feet anointed by sinful woman; illustration of debtors			7:36-50	
	Galilee	Second preaching tour of Galilee, with the 12			8:1-3	
	Galilee	Demoniac healed; league with Beelzebub charged	12:22-37	3:19-30		
	Galilee	Scribes and Pharisees seek a sign	12:38-45			
	Galilee	Christ's disciples his close relatives	12:46-50	3:31-35	8:19-21	
	Sea of Galilee	Illustrations: sower, weeds, others; explanations	13:1-53	4:1-34	8:4-18	
	Sea of Galilee	Windstorm stilled in the crossing of the lake	8:18, 23-27	4:35-41	8:22-25	
	Gadara, SE of Sea of Galilee	Two demoniacs healed; swine possessed by demons	8:28-34	5:1-20	8:26-39	
	Probably Capernaum	Jairus' daughter raised; woman healed	9:18-26	5:21-43	8:40-56	
	Capernaum (?)	Heals two blind men and a mute demoniac	9:27-34			
	Nazareth	Revisits city where reared, and is again rejected	13:54-58	6:1-6		
	Galilee	Third tour of Galilee, expanded as apostles sent	9:35–11:1	6:6-13	9:1-6	
	Tiberias	John the Baptizer beheaded; Herod's guilty fears	14:1-12	6:14-29	9:7-9	

Time	Place	Event	Matthew	Mark	Luke	John
32, near Passover (John 6:4)	Capernaum (?); NE side Sea of Galilee	Apostles return from preaching tour; 5,000 fed	14:13-21	6:30-44	9:10-17	6:1-13
	NE side Sea of Galilee; Gennesaret	Attempt to crown Jesus; he walks on sea; cures	14:22-36	6:45-56		6:14-21
	Capernaum	Identifies "bread of life"; many disciples fall away				6:22-71
32, after Passover	Probably Capernaum	Traditions that make void God's Word	15:1-20	7:1-23		7:1
	Phoenicia; Decapolis	Near Tyre, Sidon; then to Decapolis; 4,000 fed	15:21-38	7:24–8:9		
	Magadan	Sadducees and Pharisees again seek a sign	15:39–16:4	8:10-12		
	NE side Sea of Galilee; Bethsaida	Warns against leaven of Pharisees; heals blind	16:5-12	8:13-26		
	Caesarea Philippi	Jesus the Messiah; foretells death, resurrection	16:13-28	8:27–9:1	9:18-27	
	Probably Mt. Hermon	Transfiguration before Peter, James, and John	17:1-13	9:2-13	9:28-36	
	Caesarea Philippi	Heals demoniac that disciples could not heal	17:14-20	9:14-29	9:37-43	
	Galilee	Again foretells his death and resurrection	17:22, 23	9:30-32	9:43-45	
	Capernaum	Tax money miraculously provided	17:24-27			
	Capernaum	Greatest in Kingdom; settling faults; mercy	18:1-35	9:33-50	9:46-50	
	Galilee; Samaria	Leaves Galilee for Festival of Booths; everything set aside for ministerial service	8:19-22		9:51-62	7:2-10

—————————————— **Jesus' Later Ministry in Judea** ——————————————

Time	Place	Event	Matthew	Mark	Luke	John
32, Festival of Booths	Jerusalem	Jesus' public teaching at Festival of Booths				7:11-52
	Jerusalem	Teaching after Festival; cures blind				8:12–9:41
	Probably Judea	The 70 sent to preach; their return, report			10:1-24	
	Judea; Bethany	Tells of neighborly Samaritan; at home of Martha, Mary			10:25-42	
	Probably Judea	Again teaches model prayer; persistence in asking			11:1-13	
	Probably Judea	Refutes false charge; shows generation condemnable			11:14-36	
	Probably Judea	At Pharisee's table, Jesus denounces hypocrites			11:37-54	
	Probably Judea	Discourse on God's care; faithful steward			12:1-59	
	Probably Judea	Heals crippled woman on Sabbath; three illustrations			13:1-21	
32, Festival of Dedication	Jerusalem	Jesus at Festival of Dedication; Fine Shepherd				10:1-39

—————————————— **Jesus' Later Ministry East of the Jordan** ——————————————

Time	Place	Event	Matthew	Mark	Luke	John
	Beyond Jordan	Many put faith in Jesus				10:40-42
	Perea (beyond Jordan)	Teaches in cities, villages, moving toward Jerusalem			13:22	
	Perea	Kingdom entrance; Herod's threat; house desolate			13:23-35	
	Probably Perea	Humility; illustration of grand evening meal			14:1-24	
	Probably Perea	Counting the cost of discipleship			14:25-35	
	Probably Perea	Illustrations: lost sheep, lost coin, prodigal son			15:1-32	
	Probably Perea	Illustrations: unrighteous steward, rich man and Lazarus			16:1-31	
	Probably Perea	Forgiveness and faith; good-for-nothing slaves			17:1-10	
	Bethany	Lazarus raised from the dead by Jesus				11:1-46
	Jerusalem; Ephraim	Caiaphas' counsel against Jesus; Jesus withdraws				11:47-54
	Samaria; Galilee	Heals and teaches en route through Samaria and Galilee			17:11-37	
	Samaria or Galilee	Illustrations: importunate widow, Pharisee and tax collector			18:1-14	
	Perea	Swings down through Perea; teaches on divorce	19:1-12	10:1-12		
	Perea	Receives and blesses children	19:13-15	10:13-16	18:15-17	

Time	Place	Event	Matthew	Mark	Luke	John
	Perea	Rich young man; illustration of laborers in vineyard	19:16–20:16	10:17-31	18:18-30	
	Probably Perea	Third time Jesus foretells his death, resurrection	20:17-19	10:32-34	18:31-34	
	Probably Perea	Request for James' and John's seating in Kingdom	20:20-28	10:35-45		
	Jericho	Passing through Jericho, he heals two blind men; visits Zacchaeus; illustration of the ten minas	20:29-34	10:46-52	18:35–19:28	

Jesus' Final Ministry at Jerusalem

Time	Place	Event	Matthew	Mark	Luke	John
Nisan 8, 33	Bethany	Arrives at Bethany six days before Passover				11:55–12:1
Nisan 9	Bethany	Feast at Simon the leper's house; Mary anoints Jesus; Jews come to see Jesus and Lazarus	26:6-13	14:3-9		12:2-11
	Bethany-Jerusalem	Christ's triumphal entry into Jerusalem	21:1-11, 14-17	11:1-11	19:29-44	12:12-19
Nisan 10	Bethany-Jerusalem	Barren fig tree cursed; second temple cleansing	21:18, 19, 12, 13	11:12-17	19:45, 46	
	Jerusalem	Chief priests and scribes scheme to destroy Jesus		11:18, 19	19:47, 48	
	Jerusalem	Discussion with Greeks; unbelief of Jews				12:20-50
Nisan 11	Bethany-Jerusalem	Barren fig tree found withered	21:19-22	11:20-25		
	Jerusalem, temple	Christ's authority questioned; illustration of two sons	21:23-32	11:27-33	20:1-8	
	Jerusalem, temple	Illustrations of wicked cultivators, marriage feast	21:33–22:14	12:1-12	20:9-19	
	Jerusalem, temple	Catch questions on tax, resurrection, commandment	22:15-40	12:13-34	20:20-40	
	Jerusalem, temple	Jesus' silencing question on Messiah's descent	22:41-46	12:35-37	20:41-44	
	Jerusalem, temple	Scathing denunciation of scribes and Pharisees	23:1-39	12:38-40	20:45-47	
	Jerusalem, temple	The widow's mite		12:41-44	21:1-4	
	Mount of Olives	Prediction of Jerusalem's fall, Jesus' presence, end of system	24:1-51	13:1-37	21:5-38	
	Mount of Olives	Illustrations: ten virgins, talents, sheep and goats	25:1-46			
Nisan 12	Jerusalem	Religious leaders plot Jesus' death	26:1-5	14:1, 2	22:1, 2	
	Jerusalem	Judas bargains with priests for Jesus' betrayal	26:14-16	14:10, 11	22:3-6	
Nisan 13 (Thursday afternoon)	Near and in Jerusalem	Arrangements for the Passover	26:17-19	14:12-16	22:7-13	
Nisan 14	Jerusalem	Passover feast eaten with the 12	26:20, 21	14:17, 18	22:14-18	
	Jerusalem	Jesus washes the feet of his apostles				13:1-20
	Jerusalem	Judas identified as traitor and is dismissed	26:21-25	14:18-21	22:21-23	13:21-30
	Jerusalem	Memorial supper instituted with the 11	26:26-29	14:22-25	22:19, 20, 24-30	[1 Cor. 11: 23-25]
	Jerusalem	Denial by Peter and dispersion of apostles foretold	26:31-35	14:27-31	22:31-38	13:31-38
	Jerusalem	Helper; mutual love; tribulation; Jesus' prayer				14:1–17:26
	Gethsemane	Agony in the garden; Jesus' betrayal and arrest	26:30, 36-56	14:26, 32-52	22:39-53	18:1-12
	Jerusalem	Questioned by Annas; trial by Caiaphas, Sanhedrin; Peter denies	26:57–27:1	14:53–15:1	22:54-71	18:13-27
	Jerusalem	Judas the betrayer hangs himself	27:3-10		[Acts 1: 18, 19]	
	Jerusalem	Before Pilate, then Herod, and then back to Pilate	27:2, 11-14	15:1-5	23:1-12	18:28-38
	Jerusalem	Delivered to death, after Pilate seeks his release	27:15-30	15:6-19	23:13-25	18:39–19:16
(c. 3:00 p.m., Friday)	Golgotha, Jerusalem	Jesus' death on a torture stake, and accompanying events	27:31-56	15:20-41	23:26-49	19:16-30
	Jerusalem	Jesus' body removed from the torture stake and buried	27:57-61	15:42-47	23:50-56	19:31-42
Nisan 15	Jerusalem	Priests and Pharisees get guard for tomb	27:62-66			
Nisan 16	Jerusalem and vicinity	Jesus' resurrection and events of that day	28:1-15	16:1-8	24:1-49	20:1-25
a. Nisan 16	Jerusalem; Galilee	Subsequent appearances of Jesus Christ	28:16-20	[1 Cor. 15:5-7]	[Acts 1:3-8]	20:26–21:25
Iyyar 25	Mount of Olives, near Bethany	Jesus' ascension, 40th day after his resurrection	[Acts 1:9-12]		24:50-53	

JESUS' EARTHLY RESIDENCE

[16] The four inspired accounts of Jesus' earthly life appear to have been written in this order: Matthew (c. 41 C.E.), Luke (c. 56-58 C.E.), Mark (c. 60-65 C.E.), and John (c. 98 C.E.). As explained in the previous chapter, using the information in Luke 3:1-3 along with the date 14 C.E. for the start of Tiberius Caesar's reign, we arrive at 29 C.E. as the starting point for Jesus' remarkable ministry on this earth. Though the events in Matthew do not always follow in chronological sequence, in most instances the other three books appear to present the actual order of the momentous happenings that occurred. These are epitomized in the accompanying chart. It will be noted that John's account, which was written more than 30 years after the last of the other three, fills in essential gaps in the history that are not covered by the others. Especially noteworthy is John's apparent mention of the four Passovers of Jesus' earthly ministry, which confirms a ministry of three and a half years, ending in 33 C.E.*—John 2:13; 5:1; 6:4; 12:1; and 13:1.

[17] Jesus' death in 33 C.E. is also confirmed by other evidence. According to the Law of Moses, Nisan 15 was always a special Sabbath regardless of the day on which it fell. If it coincided with an ordinary Sabbath, then the day became known as a "great" Sabbath, and John 19:31 shows that such a Sabbath followed the day of Jesus' death, which was therefore a Friday. And not in 31 or 32 but only in 33 C.E. did the 14th of Nisan fall on a Friday. Therefore, it must have been on Nisan 14, 33 C.E., that Jesus died.#

[18] **The 70th "Week," 29-36 C.E.** Time features of Jesus' ministry are also covered by Daniel 9:24-27, which foretells the passage of 69 weeks of years (483 years) "from the going forth of the word to restore and to rebuild Jerusalem until Messiah the Leader." According to Nehemiah 2:1-8, this word went forth "in the twentieth year of Artaxerxes," king of Persia. When did Artaxerxes begin his reign? His father and predecessor, Xerxes, died in the latter part of 475 B.C.E. Artaxerxes' accession year thus began in 475 B.C.E., and this is supported by strong evidence from Greek,

Persian, and Babylonian sources. For example, the Greek historian Thucydides (who has gained fame for his accuracy) writes of the flight of the Greek statesman Themistocles to Persia when Artaxerxes had "lately come to the throne." Another Greek historian of the first century B.C.E., Diodorus Siculus, enables us to establish the date of Themistocles' death as 471/470 B.C.E. After fleeing his country, Themistocles had asked Artaxerxes' permission to study the Persian language for one year before appearing before him, which was carried out. Hence, Themistocles' settlement in Persia must have been not later than 472 B.C.E., and his arrival may reasonably be dated 473 B.C.E. At that time Artaxerxes "had lately come to the throne."*

[19] Thus, "the twentieth year of Artaxerxes" would be 455 B.C.E. Counting 483 years (the 69 "weeks") from this point, and remembering that there was no zero year in crossing into the Common Era, we arrive at 29 C.E. for the appearance of "Messiah the Leader." Jesus became the Messiah when he was baptized and anointed with holy spirit, in the autumn of that year. The prophecy also indicates that "at the half of the [seventieth] week he will cause sacrifice and gift offering to cease." This occurred when the typical Jewish sacrifices lost their validity because of Jesus' sacrifice of himself. "The half" of this "week" of years takes us along three and a half years to the spring of 33 C.E., when Jesus was put to death. However, "he must keep the covenant in force for the many" for the entire 70th week. This shows Jehovah's special favor as continuing with the Jews during the seven years from 29 C.E. to 36 C.E. Then, only, was the way opened for uncircumcised Gentiles to become spiritual Israelites, as is indicated by the conversion of Cornelius in 36 C.E.#—Acts 10:30-33, 44-48; 11:1.

COUNTING THE YEARS IN APOSTOLIC TIMES

[20] **Between 33 C.E. and 49 C.E.** The year 44 C.E. may be accepted as a useful date for this period. According to Josephus (*Jewish Antiquities,* XIX, 351 [viii, 2]), Herod Agrippa I reigned for three years after the accession of Emperor Claudius of Rome (in 41 C.E.). The historical evidence indicates that this Herod died in 44 C.E.△ Looking now

---

* *Insight on the Scriptures,* Vol. 2, pages 57-8.
# *The Watchtower,* 1976, page 247; 1959, pages 489-92.

16. (a) In what order were the four Gospels written? (b) How may we date the start of Jesus' ministry? (c) What sequence do events follow in the different Gospels, and what is to be noted about John's account?
17. What other evidence supports the date of Jesus' death?
18. (a) What did Daniel prophesy in regard to 69 "weeks"? (b) According to Nehemiah, when did this period begin? (c) How do we arrive at the date for the beginning of Artaxerxes' reign?

---

* *Insight on the Scriptures,* Vol. 2, pages 614-16.
# *Insight on the Scriptures,* Vol. 2, pages 899-904.
△ *The New Encyclopædia Britannica,* 1987, Vol. 5, page 880.

19. (a) Counting from "the twentieth year of Artaxerxes," how do we determine the date of Messiah's appearance? (b) How was the prophecy of the 70 "weeks" fulfilled from this date?
20. How does secular history combine with the Bible record in timing Herod's death and preceding events?

at the Bible record, we find it was just prior to Herod's death that Agabus prophesied "through the spirit" concerning a great famine to come, that the apostle James was put to the sword, and that Peter was jailed (at Passover time) and miraculously released. All these events may be dated to 44 C.E.—Acts 11:27, 28; 12:1-11, 20-23.

21 The foretold famine came in about 46 C.E. It must have been about this time, then, that Paul and Barnabas "carried out the relief ministration in Jerusalem." (Acts 12:25) After returning to Syrian Antioch, they were set aside by holy spirit to make the first missionary tour, which covered Cyprus and many cities and districts of Asia Minor.* This probably extended from the spring of 47 C.E. to the autumn of 48 C.E., with one winter spent in Asia Minor. It appears Paul spent the following winter back in Syrian Antioch, and this brings us to the spring of 49 C.E.—Acts 13:1-14:28.

22 The record in Galatians chapters 1 and 2 appears to tie in with this chronology. Here Paul speaks of making two other special visits to Jerusalem after his conversion, the one "three years later" and the other "after fourteen years." (Gal. 1: 17, 18; 2:1) If these two time periods are taken to be ordinals, according to the custom of the day, and if Paul's conversion was early in the apostles' time, as the record seems to indicate, then we may reckon the 3 years and the 14 years consecutively as 34-36 C.E. and 36-49 C.E.

23 Paul's second Jerusalem visit mentioned in Galatians seems to have been concerned with the circumcision issue, as even Titus who accompanied Paul is said not to have been required to be circumcised. If this corresponds to the visit to obtain the ruling on circumcision described in Acts 15:1-35, then 49 C.E. fits nicely as lying between Paul's first and second missionary tours. Moreover, according to Galatians 2:1-10, Paul used this occasion to lay before the "outstanding men" of the Jerusalem congregation the good news that he was preaching, 'for fear he was running in vain.' This he would logically do in reporting to them after his very first missionary tour. Paul made this visit to Jerusalem "as a result of a revelation."

24 **Paul's Second Missionary Journey, c. 49-52 C.E.** After his return from Jerusalem, Paul spent time in Syrian Antioch; hence, it must have been well along in the summer of 49 C.E. that he left there on his second tour. (Acts 15:35, 36) This one was much more extensive than the first and would require him to winter in Asia Minor. It was probably in the spring of 50 C.E. that he answered the Macedonian's call and crossed over into Europe. Then he preached and organized new congregations in Philippi, Thessalonica, Beroea, and Athens. This would bring him to Corinth, in the province of Achaia, in the autumn of 50 C.E., after having made a journey of about 1,300 miles, mostly on foot. (Acts 16:9, 11, 12; 17:1, 2, 10, 11, 15, 16; 18:1) According to Acts 18:11, Paul stayed there 18 months, bringing us to early 52 C.E. With winter ended, Paul could sail for Caesarea, via Ephesus. After going up to greet the congregation, apparently in Jerusalem, he arrived back at his home base of Syrian Antioch, probably in the summer of 52 C.E.*—Acts 18:12-22.

25 An archaeological discovery supports 50-52 C.E. as the dates of Paul's first visit to Corinth. This is a fragment of an inscription, a rescript from Emperor Claudius Caesar to the Delphians of Greece, which contains the words "[Lucius Ju]nius, Gallio, . . . proconsul." Historians are generally agreed that the number 26, which is also found in the text, refers to Claudius' having been acclaimed emperor for the 26th time. Other inscriptions show that Claudius was acclaimed emperor for the 27th time before August 1, 52 C.E. The proconsul's term ran for a year, starting with the beginning of summer. Thus, Gallio's year as proconsul of Achaia appears to have run from the summer of 51 C.E. to the summer of 52 C.E. "Now while Gallio was proconsul of Achaia, the Jews rose up with one accord against Paul and led him to the judgment seat." After Gallio's acquitting Paul, the apostle stayed "quite some days longer," and then he sailed away to Syria. (Acts 18:11, 12, 17, 18) All of this seems to confirm the spring of 52 C.E. as the conclusion of Paul's 18-month stay in Corinth. Another time marker is found in the statement that on arrival in Corinth, Paul "found a certain Jew named Aquila, a native of Pontus who had recently come from Italy, and Priscilla his wife, because of the fact that Claudius had ordered all the Jews to depart from Rome." (Acts 18:2)

---

* Insight on the Scriptures, Vol. 2, page 747.

---

* Insight on the Scriptures, Vol. 2, page 747.

---

21. On what basis can we approximately date Paul's first missionary tour?

22. How may the two visits of Paul to Jerusalem mentioned in Galatians chapters 1 and 2 be dated?

23. What evidence suggests that both Galatians chapter 2 and Acts chapter 15 have reference to Paul's visit to Jerusalem in 49 C.E.?

---

24. During what years did Paul make his second missionary journey, and why, no doubt, did he not reach Corinth till late in 50 C.E.?

25. (a) How does archaeology support 50-52 C.E. for Paul's first visit to Corinth? (b) How does the fact that Aquila and Priscilla "had recently come from Italy" confirm this?

According to the historian Paulus Orosius, of the early fifth century, this expulsion order was given in Claudius' ninth year, that is, in 49 C.E. or early in 50 C.E. Thus, Aquila and Priscilla could have reached Corinth sometime before the autumn of that year, allowing for Paul's stay there from the autumn of 50 C.E. to the spring of 52 C.E.*

²⁶ **Paul's Third Missionary Journey, c. 52-56 C.E.** After the passage of "some time" in Syrian Antioch, Paul was on his way into Asia Minor again, and it is likely that he reached Ephesus by the winter of 52-53 C.E. (Acts 18:23; 19:1) Paul spent "three months" and then "two years" teaching in Ephesus, and after this he left for Macedonia. (Acts 19:8-10) Later, he reminded the overseers from Ephesus that he had served among them "for three years," but this may well be a round figure. (Acts 20:31) It appears that Paul left Ephesus after "the festival of Pentecost" early in 55 C.E., traveling all the way through to Corinth, Greece, in time to spend three winter months there. Then he returned north as far as Philippi by Passover time of 56 C.E. From there he sailed by way of Troas and Miletus to Caesarea and journeyed up to Jerusalem, arriving by Pentecost of 56 C.E.#—1 Cor. 16:5-8; Acts 20:1-3, 6, 15, 16; 21:8, 15-17.

²⁷ **The Closing Years, 56-100 C.E.** It was shortly after his arrival in Jerusalem that Paul was arrested. He was taken to Caesarea and remained in custody there for two years, until Felix was replaced by Festus as governor. (Acts 21:33; 23:23-35; 24:27) The date of Festus' arrival and of Paul's subsequent departure for Rome appears to have been 58 C.E.△ After Paul's shipwreck and wintering in Malta, the journey was completed about 59 C.E., and the record indicates that he remained in captivity in Rome, preaching and teaching, for a period of two years, or until about 61 C.E.—Acts 27:1; 28:1, 11, 16, 30, 31.

²⁸ While the historical record of Acts takes us no farther than this, the indications are that Paul was released and continued his missionary activity, traveling to Crete, Greece, and Macedonia. Whether he reached as far as Spain is not known. Likely Paul suffered martyrdom at the hands of Nero shortly after his final imprisonment at Rome in about 65 C.E. Secular history gives July of 64 C.E. as the date of the great fire in Rome, following which Nero's persecution burst upon the Christians. Paul's imprisonment in "chains" and subsequent execution fit logically into this period. —2 Tim. 1:16; 4:6, 7.

²⁹ The five books by the apostle John were written at the end of a time of persecution brought on by Emperor Domitian. He is said to have acted like a madman during the last three years of his reign, which covered 81-96 C.E. It was while in exile on the island of Patmos that John wrote down the Revelation, about 96 C.E.* His Gospel and three letters followed from Ephesus or its vicinity after his release, and this last of the apostles died about 100 C.E.

³⁰ It is thus seen that by comparing events of secular history with the Bible's internal chronology and prophecy, we are helped to place Bible events more clearly in the stream of time. The harmony of the Bible chronology adds to our confidence in the Holy Scriptures as the Word of God.

* *Notes on the Book of Revelation,* 1852, by Albert Barnes, pages xxix, xxx.

29. When did the apostolic age end, and with the writing of which Bible books?
30. Of what benefit is this study of Bible chronology?

Questions on "Chart of Outstanding Historical Dates" and "Table of the Books of the Bible": (a) By comparing the two charts, name some of the prophets and Bible writers who lived ⁽¹⁾ prior to the setting up of the kingdom of Israel in 1117 B.C.E., ⁽²⁾ during the time of the kingdoms of Israel and Judah, ⁽³⁾ during the time from the beginning of the exile in Babylon until the completion of the Hebrew Scripture canon. (b) Locate the time of the writing of Paul's letters in relation to his missionary tours. (c) What other interesting points do you note as to the time of the writing of other books of the Christian Greek Scriptures? (d) Relate the following persons to some prominent event in Bible history, stating whether they lived before or after the event, or associate them with other persons living at the same time: Shem, Samuel, Methuselah, Lot, King Saul, David, Job, King Hoshea of Israel, Solomon, Aaron, King Zedekiah of Judah. (e) What outstanding events occurred during the lifetime of ⁽¹⁾ Noah, ⁽²⁾ Abraham, ⁽³⁾ Moses? (f) Match the following dates (B.C.E.) with the outstanding events listed below: 4026, 2370, 1943, 1513, 1473, 1117, 997, 740, 607, 539, 537, 455.

Creation of Adam
Law covenant made at Sinai
Jerusalem destroyed
Jews return to Jerusalem after Cyrus' decree
Inspired Bible writing begins
The Flood begins
Babylon falls to Medes and Persians
First king of Israel anointed
Abraham crosses Euphrates; Abrahamic covenant validated
Kingdoms of Israel and Judah split
Northern kingdom subjugated by Assyria
Jerusalem's walls rebuilt by Nehemiah
Israelites delivered from Egypt
Joshua leads Israel into Canaan
Jerusalem's 70-year desolation ends

* *Insight on the Scriptures,* Vol. 1, pages 476, 886.
# *Insight on the Scriptures,* Vol. 2, page 747.
△ Young's *Analytical Concordance to the Bible,* page 342, under "Festus."

26. What dates mark the successive stages of Paul's third missionary journey?
27. What is the timing of events down to the end of Paul's first captivity in Rome?
28. What dates may logically be assigned to the closing events of Paul's life?

CHART OF OUTSTANDING HISTORICAL DATES

Symbols: a. for "after"; b. for "before"; c. for "circa," or "about."

Date	Event	Reference
4026 B.C.E.	Adam's creation	Gen. 2:7
a. 4026 B.C.E.	Edenic covenant made, first prophecy	Gen. 3:15
b. 3896 B.C.E.	Cain slays Abel	Gen. 4:8
3896 B.C.E.	Birth of Seth	Gen. 5:3
3404 B.C.E.	Birth of righteous Enoch	Gen. 5:18
3339 B.C.E.	Birth of Methuselah	Gen. 5:21
3152 B.C.E.	Birth of Lamech	Gen. 5:25
3096 B.C.E.	Death of Adam	Gen. 5:5
3039 B.C.E.	Transference of Enoch; ends his period of prophesying	Gen. 5:23, 24; Jude 14
2970 B.C.E.	Birth of Noah	Gen. 5:28, 29
2490 B.C.E.	God's pronouncement as to mankind	Gen. 6:3
2470 B.C.E.	Birth of Japheth	Gen. 5:32; 9:24; 10:21
2468 B.C.E.	Birth of Shem	Gen. 7:11; 11:10
2370 B.C.E.	Death of Methuselah	Gen. 5:27
	Floodwaters fall (in autumn)	Gen. 7:6, 11
2369 B.C.E.	Making of the covenant after the Flood	Gen. 8:13; 9:16
2368 B.C.E.	Birth of Arpachshad	Gen. 11:10
a. 2269 B.C.E.	Building of the Tower of Babel	Gen. 11:4
2020 B.C.E.	Death of Noah	Gen. 9:28, 29
2018 B.C.E.	Birth of Abraham	Gen. 11:26, 32; 12:4
1943 B.C.E.	Abraham crosses Euphrates on his way to Canaan; Abrahamic covenant validated; beginning of the 430-year period to Law covenant	Gen. 12:4, 7; Ex. 12:40; Gal. 3:17
b. 1933 B.C.E.	Lot rescued; Abraham visits Melchizedek	Gen. 14:16, 18; 16:3
1932 B.C.E.	Ishmael born	Gen. 16:15, 16
1919 B.C.E.	Covenant of circumcision made	Gen. 17:1, 10, 24
	Judgment of Sodom and Gomorrah	Gen. 19:24
1918 B.C.E.	Birth of Isaac, the true heir; beginning of the 'about 450 years'	Gen. 21:2, 5; Acts 13:17-20
1913 B.C.E.	Weaning of Isaac; Ishmael sent away; beginning of the 400-year affliction	Gen. 21:8; 15:13; Acts 7:6
1881 B.C.E.	Death of Sarah	Gen. 17:17; 23:1
1878 B.C.E.	Marriage of Isaac and Rebekah	Gen. 25:20
1868 B.C.E.	Death of Shem	Gen. 11:11
1858 B.C.E.	Birth of Esau and Jacob	Gen. 25:26
1843 B.C.E.	Death of Abraham	Gen. 25:7
1818 B.C.E.	Esau marries first two wives	Gen. 26:34
1795 B.C.E.	Death of Ishmael	Gen. 25:17
1781 B.C.E.	Jacob flees to Haran; his vision at Bethel	Gen. 28:2, 13, 19
1774 B.C.E.	Jacob marries Leah and Rachel	Gen. 29:23-30
1767 B.C.E.	Birth of Joseph	Gen. 30:23, 24
1761 B.C.E.	Jacob returns to Canaan from Haran	Gen. 31:18, 41
c. 1761 B.C.E.	Jacob wrestles angel; is named Israel	Gen. 32:24-28
1750 B.C.E.	Joseph sold as a slave by his brothers	Gen. 37:2, 28
1738 B.C.E.	Death of Isaac	Gen. 35:28, 29
1737 B.C.E.	Joseph made prime minister of Egypt	Gen. 41:40, 46
1728 B.C.E.	Jacob with his whole family enters Egypt	Gen. 45:6; 46:26; 47:9
1711 B.C.E.	Death of Jacob	Gen. 47:28
1657 B.C.E.	Death of Joseph	Gen. 50:26
b. 1613 B.C.E.	Job's trial	Job 1:8; 42:16
a. 1600 B.C.E.	Egypt attains prominence as first world power	Ex. 1:8
1593 B.C.E.	Birth of Moses	Ex. 2:2, 10
1553 B.C.E.	Moses offers himself as a deliverer; flees to Midian	Ex. 2:11, 14, 15; Acts 7:23
c. 1514 B.C.E.	Moses at the burning thornbush	Ex. 3:2

Date	Event	Reference
1513 B.C.E.	Passover; Israelites leave Egypt; Red Sea deliverance; Egypt's power shaken; end of 400-year period of affliction	Ex. 12:12; 14:27, 29, 30; Gen. 15:13, 14
	Law covenant made at Mt. Sinai (Horeb)	Ex. 24:6-8
	End of the 430-year period from validating of Abrahamic covenant	Gal. 3:17; Ex. 12:40
	Moses compiles Genesis in wilderness; Bible writing begins	John 5:46
1512 B.C.E.	Tabernacle construction completed	Ex. 40:17
	Installation of the Aaronic priesthood	Lev. 8:34-36
	Moses completes Exodus and Leviticus	Lev. 27:34; Num. 1:1
c. 1473 B.C.E.	Moses completes the book of Job	Job 42:16, 17
1473 B.C.E.	Moses completes Numbers on Plains of Moab	Num. 35:1; 36:13
	Covenant with Israel at Moab	Deut. 29:1
	Moses writes Deuteronomy	Deut. 1:1, 3
	Moses dies on Mt. Nebo in Moab	Deut. 34:1, 5, 7
	Israel enters Canaan under Joshua	Josh. 4:19
1467 B.C.E.	Major conquest of the land completed; end of the 'about 450 years' of Acts 13:17-20	Josh. 11:23; 14:7, 10-15
c. 1450 B.C.E.	Book of Joshua completed	Josh. 1:1; 24:26
	Death of Joshua	Josh. 24:29
1117 B.C.E.	Samuel anoints Saul as king of Israel	1 Sam. 10:24; Acts 13:21
1107 B.C.E.	Birth of David at Bethlehem	1 Sam. 16:1
c. 1100 B.C.E.	Samuel completes the book of Judges	Judg. 21:25
c. 1090 B.C.E.	Samuel completes the book of Ruth	Ruth 4:18-22
c. 1078 B.C.E.	Book of 1 Samuel completed	1 Sam. 31:6
1077 B.C.E.	David becomes king of Judah at Hebron	2 Sam. 2:4
1070 B.C.E.	David becomes king over all Israel; makes Jerusalem his capital	2 Sam. 5:3-7
a. 1070 B.C.E.	The Ark brought into Jerusalem; covenant for a kingdom made with David	2 Sam. 6:15; 7:12-16
c. 1040 B.C.E.	Gad and Nathan complete 2 Samuel	2 Sam. 24:18
1037 B.C.E.	Solomon succeeds David as king of Israel	1 Ki. 1:39; 2:12
1034 B.C.E.	Construction of temple by Solomon begun	1 Ki. 6:1
1027 B.C.E.	Temple in Jerusalem completed	1 Ki. 6:38
c. 1020 B.C.E.	Solomon completes The Song of Solomon	Song of Sol. 1:1
b. 1000 B.C.E.	Solomon completes the book of Ecclesiastes	Eccl. 1:1
997 B.C.E.	Rehoboam succeeds Solomon; kingdom split; Jeroboam begins reign as king of Israel	1 Ki. 11:43; 12:19, 20
993 B.C.E.	Shishak invades Judah and takes treasures from temple	1 Ki. 14:25, 26
980 B.C.E.	Abijam (Abijah) succeeds Rehoboam as king of Judah	1 Ki. 15:1, 2
977 B.C.E.	Asa succeeds Abijam as king of Judah	1 Ki. 15:9, 10
c. 976 B.C.E.	Nadab succeeds Jeroboam as king of Israel	1 Ki. 14:20
c. 975 B.C.E.	Baasha succeeds Nadab as king of Israel	1 Ki. 15:33
c. 952 B.C.E.	Elah succeeds Baasha as king of Israel	1 Ki. 16:8
c. 951 B.C.E.	Zimri succeeds Elah as king of Israel	1 Ki. 16:15
	Omri and Tibni succeed Zimri as kings of Israel	1 Ki. 16:21
c. 947 B.C.E.	Omri rules as king of Israel alone	1 Ki. 16:22, 23
c. 940 B.C.E.	Ahab succeeds Omri as king of Israel	1 Ki. 16:29
936 B.C.E.	Jehoshaphat succeeds Asa as king of Judah	1 Ki. 22:41, 42
c. 919 B.C.E.	Ahaziah succeeds Ahab as sole king of Israel	1 Ki. 22:51, 52
c. 917 B.C.E.	Jehoram of Israel succeeds Ahaziah as sole king	2 Ki. 3:1
913 B.C.E.	Jehoram of Judah 'becomes king,' with Jehoshaphat	2 Ki. 8:16, 17
c. 906 B.C.E.	Ahaziah succeeds Jehoram as king of Judah	2 Ki. 8:25, 26
c. 905 B.C.E.	Queen Athaliah usurps throne of Judah	2 Ki. 11:1-3
	Jehu succeeds Jehoram as king of Israel	2 Ki. 9:24, 27; 10:36
898 B.C.E.	Jehoash succeeds Ahaziah as king of Judah	2 Ki. 12:1
876 B.C.E.	Jehoahaz succeeds Jehu as king of Israel	2 Ki. 13:1
c. 859 B.C.E.	Jehoash succeeds Jehoahaz as sole king of Israel	2 Ki. 13:10
858 B.C.E.	Amaziah succeeds Jehoash as king of Judah	2 Ki. 14:1, 2
c. 844 B.C.E.	Jeroboam II succeeds Jehoash as king of Israel	2 Ki. 14:23
	Jonah completes the book of Jonah	Jonah 1:1, 2
829 B.C.E.	Uzziah (Azariah) succeeds Amaziah as king of Judah	2 Ki. 15:1, 2

Date	Event	Reference
c. 820 B.C.E.	Book of Joel perhaps written	Joel 1:1
c. 804 B.C.E.	Amos completes the book of Amos	Amos 1:1
c. 792 B.C.E.	Zechariah rules as king of Israel (6 months)	2 Ki. 15:8
c. 791 B.C.E.	Shallum succeeds Zechariah as king of Israel	2 Ki. 15:13, 17
	Menahem succeeds Shallum as king of Israel	
c. 780 B.C.E.	Pekahiah succeeds Menahem as king of Israel	2 Ki. 15:23
c. 778 B.C.E.	Pekah succeeds Pekahiah as king of Israel	2 Ki. 15:27
c. 778 B.C.E.	Isaiah begins to prophesy	Isa. 1:1; 6:1
777 B.C.E.	Jotham succeeds Uzziah (Azariah) as king of Judah	2 Ki. 15:32, 33
c. 761 B.C.E.	Ahaz succeeds Jotham as king of Judah	2 Ki. 16:1, 2
c. 758 B.C.E.	Hoshea 'begins to reign' as king of Israel	2 Ki. 15:30
745 B.C.E.	Hezekiah succeeds Ahaz as king of Judah	2 Ki. 18:1, 2
a. 745 B.C.E.	Hosea completes the book of Hosea	Hos. 1:1
740 B.C.E.	Assyria subjugates Israel, takes Samaria	2 Ki. 17:6, 13, 18
732 B.C.E.	Sennacherib invades Judah	2 Ki. 18:13
a. 732 B.C.E.	Isaiah completes the book of Isaiah	Isa. 1:1
b. 717 B.C.E.	Micah completes the book of Micah	Mic. 1:1
c. 717 B.C.E.	Compiling of Proverbs completed	Prov. 25:1
716 B.C.E.	Manasseh succeeds Hezekiah as king of Judah	2 Ki. 21:1
661 B.C.E.	Amon succeeds Manasseh as king of Judah	2 Ki. 21:19
659 B.C.E.	Josiah succeeds Amon as king of Judah	2 Ki. 22:1
b. 648 B.C.E.	Zephaniah completes the book of Zephaniah	Zeph. 1:1
647 B.C.E.	Jeremiah commissioned as prophet	Jer. 1:1, 2, 9, 10
b. 632 B.C.E.	Nahum completes the book of Nahum	Nah. 1:1
632 B.C.E.	Nineveh falls to Chaldeans and Medes	Nah. 3:7
	Babylon now in line to become third world power	
628 B.C.E.	Jehoahaz, successor of Josiah, rules as king of Judah	2 Ki. 23:31
	Jehoiakim succeeds Jehoahaz as king of Judah	2 Ki. 23:36
c. 628 B.C.E.	Habakkuk completes the book of Habakkuk	Hab. 1:1
625 B.C.E.	Nebuchadnezzar (II) becomes king of Babylon; first regnal year counts from Nisan of 624 B.C.E.	Jer. 25:1
620 B.C.E.	Nebuchadnezzar makes Jehoiakim tributary king	2 Ki. 24:1
618 B.C.E.	Jehoiachin becomes king after Jehoiakim in Judah	2 Ki. 24:6, 8
617 B.C.E.	Nebuchadnezzar takes first Jewish captives to Babylon	Dan. 1:1-4;
	Zedekiah is made king of Judah	2 Ki. 24:12-18
613 B.C.E.	Ezekiel begins prophesying	Ezek. 1:1-3
609 B.C.E.	Nebuchadnezzar comes against Judah a third time; begins siege of Jerusalem	2 Ki. 25:1, 2
607 B.C.E.	Fifth month (Ab), temple razed and Jerusalem destroyed	2 Ki. 25:8-10; Jer. 52:12-14
	Seventh month, Jews abandon Judah; "appointed times of the nations" begin to count	2 Ki. 25:25, 26; Luke 21:24
	Jeremiah writes Lamentations	Lam. introduction, *LXX*
c. 607 B.C.E.	Obadiah writes the book of Obadiah	Obad. 1
c. 591 B.C.E.	Ezekiel completes the book of Ezekiel	Ezek. 40:1; 29:17
580 B.C.E.	Books of 1 and 2 Kings and Jeremiah completed	Jer. 52:31; 2 Ki. 25:27
539 B.C.E.	Babylon falls to the Medes and Persians; Medo-Persia becomes the fourth world power	Dan. 5:30, 31
537 B.C.E.	Decree of Cyrus the Persian permitting Jews to return to Jerusalem takes effect; Jerusalem's 70-year desolation ends	2 Chron. 36:22, 23; Jer. 25:12; 29:10
c. 536 B.C.E.	Daniel completes the book of Daniel	Dan. 10:1
536 B.C.E.	Foundation of temple laid by Zerubbabel	Ezra 3:8-10
522 B.C.E.	Ban put on temple-building work	Ezra 4:23, 24
520 B.C.E.	Haggai completes the book of Haggai	Hag. 1:1
518 B.C.E.	Zechariah completes the book of Zechariah	Zech. 1:1
515 B.C.E.	Zerubbabel completes second temple	Ezra 6:14, 15
c. 475 B.C.E.	Mordecai completes the book of Esther	Esther 3:7; 9:32
468 B.C.E.	Ezra and priests return to Jerusalem	Ezra 7:7

Date	Event	Reference
c. 460 B.C.E.	Ezra completes the books of 1 and 2 Chronicles and Ezra; final compilation of Psalms	Ezra 1:1; 2 Chron. 36:22
455 B.C.E.	Jerusalem's walls rebuilt by Nehemiah; prophecy of 70 weeks begins fulfillment	Neh. 1:1; 2:1, 11; 6:15; Dan. 9:24
a. 443 B.C.E.	Nehemiah completes the book of Nehemiah	Neh. 5:14
	Malachi completes the book of Malachi	Mal. 1:1
406 B.C.E.	Rebuilding of Jerusalem is evidently completed	Dan. 9:25
332 B.C.E.	Greece, fifth world power, rules Judea	Dan. 8:21
c. 280 B.C.E.	The Greek *Septuagint* begun	
165 B.C.E.	Rededication of temple after desecration by Greek idolatry; Festival of Dedication	John 10:22
63 B.C.E.	Rome, sixth world power, rules Jerusalem	John 19:15; Rev. 17:10
c. 37 B.C.E.	Herod (appointed king by Rome) takes Jerusalem by storm	
2 B.C.E.	Birth of John the Baptizer and of Jesus	Luke 1:60; 2:7
29 C.E.	John and Jesus begin their ministries	Luke 3:1, 2, 23
33 C.E.	Nisan 14: Jesus becomes sacrifice providing basis for the new covenant; is impaled	Luke 22:20; 23:33
	Nisan 16: the resurrection of Jesus	Matt. 28:1-10
	Sivan 6, Pentecost: outpouring of spirit; Peter opens the way for Jews to Christian congregation	Acts 2:1-17, 38
36 C.E.	End of the 70 weeks of years; Peter visits Cornelius, the first one of the uncircumcised people of the nations to enter the Christian congregation	Dan. 9:24-27; Acts 10:1, 45
c. 41 C.E.	Matthew writes the Gospel entitled "Matthew"	
c. 47-48 C.E.	Paul begins first missionary tour	Acts 13:1–14:28
c. 49 C.E.	Governing body rules against requiring circumcision for the believers from the nations	Acts 15:28, 29
c. 49-52 C.E.	Paul's second missionary tour	Acts 15:36–18:22
c. 50 C.E.	Paul writes 1 Thessalonians from Corinth	1 Thess. 1:1
c. 51 C.E.	Paul writes 2 Thessalonians from Corinth	2 Thess. 1:1
c. 50-52 C.E.	Paul writes his letter to the Galatians from Corinth or Syrian Antioch	Gal. 1:1
c. 52-56 C.E.	Paul's third missionary tour	Acts 18:23–21:19
c. 55 C.E.	Paul writes 1 Corinthians from Ephesus and 2 Corinthians from Macedonia	1 Cor. 15:32; 2 Cor. 2:12, 13
c. 56 C.E.	Paul writes the letter to the Romans from Corinth	Rom. 16:1
c. 56-58 C.E.	Luke writes the Gospel entitled "Luke"	Luke 1:1, 2
c. 60-61 C.E.	From Rome Paul writes: Ephesians	Eph. 3:1
	Philippians	Phil. 4:22
	Colossians	Col. 4:18
	Philemon	Philem. 1
c. 61 C.E.	Paul writes the letter to the Hebrews from Rome	Heb. 13:24; 10:34
	Luke completes the book of Acts in Rome	
b. 62 C.E.	James, Jesus' brother, writes the letter entitled "James" from Jerusalem	Jas. 1:1
c. 60-65 C.E.	Mark writes the Gospel entitled "Mark"	
c. 61-64 C.E.	Paul writes 1 Timothy from Macedonia	1 Tim. 1:3
	Paul writes Titus from Macedonia (?)	Titus 1:5
c. 62-64 C.E.	Peter writes 1 Peter from Babylon	1 Pet. 1:1; 5:13
c. 64 C.E.	Peter writes 2 Peter from Babylon (?)	2 Pet. 1:1
c. 65 C.E.	Paul writes 2 Timothy from Rome	2 Tim. 4:16-18
	Jude, Jesus' brother, writes "Jude"	Jude 1, 17, 18
70 C.E.	Jerusalem and its temple destroyed by the Romans	Dan. 9:27; Matt. 23:37, 38; Luke 19:42-44
c. 96 C.E.	John, on Patmos, writes Revelation	Rev. 1:9
c. 98 C.E.	John writes the Gospel entitled "John" and his letters 1, 2, and 3 John; Bible writing completed	John 21:22, 23
c. 100 C.E.	John, the last of the apostles, dies	2 Thess. 2:7

NOTE: It should be borne in mind that while many of these dates are firmly established, in the case of some, approximate dates are given, based on the available evidence. The purpose of the chart is not to fix unalterable dates for each event but to help Bible students to locate events in the stream of time and see their relationship to one another.

TABLE OF THE BOOKS OF THE BIBLE

(Some dates [and places written] are uncertain. The symbol a. means "after"; b., "before"; and c., "circa," or "about.")

Books of the Hebrew Scriptures Before the Common Era (B.C.E.)

Name of Book	The Writer	Place Written	Writing Completed	Time Covered
Genesis	Moses	Wilderness	1513	"In the beginning" to 1657
Exodus	Moses	Wilderness	1512	1657-1512
Leviticus	Moses	Wilderness	1512	1 month (1512)
Numbers	Moses	Wilderness/Plains of Moab	1473	1512-1473
Deuteronomy	Moses	Plains of Moab	1473	2 months (1473)
Joshua	Joshua	Canaan	c. 1450	1473-c. 1450
Judges	Samuel	Israel	c. 1100	c. 1450-c. 1120
Ruth	Samuel	Israel	c. 1090	11 years of judges' rule
1 Samuel	Samuel; Gad; Nathan	Israel	c. 1078	c. 1180-1078
2 Samuel	Gad; Nathan	Israel	c. 1040	1077-c. 1040
1 and 2 Kings	Jeremiah	Judah/Egypt	580	c. 1040-580
1 and 2 Chronicles	Ezra	Jerusalem (?)	c. 460	After 1 Chron. 9:44, 1077-537
Ezra	Ezra	Jerusalem	c. 460	537-c. 467
Nehemiah	Nehemiah	Jerusalem	a. 443	456-a. 443
Esther	Mordecai	Shushan, Elam	c. 475	493-c. 475
Job	Moses	Wilderness	c. 1473	Over 140 years between 1657 and 1473
Psalms	David and others		c. 460	
Proverbs	Solomon; Agur; Lemuel	Jerusalem	c. 717	
Ecclesiastes	Solomon	Jerusalem	b. 1000	
Song of Solomon	Solomon	Jerusalem	c. 1020	
Isaiah	Isaiah	Jerusalem	a. 732	c. 778-a. 732
Jeremiah	Jeremiah	Judah/Egypt	580	647-580
Lamentations	Jeremiah	Near Jerusalem	607	
Ezekiel	Ezekiel	Babylon	c. 591	613-c. 591
Daniel	Daniel	Babylon	c. 536	618-c. 536
Hosea	Hosea	Samaria (District)	a. 745	b. 804-a. 745
Joel	Joel	Judah	c. 820 (?)	
Amos	Amos	Judah	c. 804	
Obadiah	Obadiah		c. 607	
Jonah	Jonah		c. 844	
Micah	Micah	Judah	b. 717	c. 777-717
Nahum	Nahum	Judah	b. 632	
Habakkuk	Habakkuk	Judah	c. 628 (?)	
Zephaniah	Zephaniah	Judah	b. 648	
Haggai	Haggai	Jerusalem	520	112 days (520)
Zechariah	Zechariah	Jerusalem	518	520-518
Malachi	Malachi	Jerusalem	a. 443	

Books of the Greek Scriptures Written During the Common Era (C.E.)

Name of Book	The Writer	Place Written	Writing Completed	Time Covered
Matthew	Matthew	Palestine	c. 41	2 B.C.E.-33 C.E.
Mark	Mark	Rome	c. 60-65	29-33 C.E.
Luke	Luke	Caesarea	c. 56-58	3 B.C.E.-33 C.E.
John	Apostle John	Ephesus, or near	c. 98	After prologue, 29-33 C.E.
Acts	Luke	Rome	c. 61	33-c. 61 C.E.
Romans	Paul	Corinth	c. 56	
1 Corinthians	Paul	Ephesus	c. 55	
2 Corinthians	Paul	Macedonia	c. 55	
Galatians	Paul	Corinth or Syrian Antioch	c. 50-52	
Ephesians	Paul	Rome	c. 60-61	
Philippians	Paul	Rome	c. 60-61	
Colossians	Paul	Rome	c. 60-61	
1 Thessalonians	Paul	Corinth	c. 50	
2 Thessalonians	Paul	Corinth	c. 51	
1 Timothy	Paul	Macedonia	c. 61-64	
2 Timothy	Paul	Rome	c. 65	
Titus	Paul	Macedonia (?)	c. 61-64	
Philemon	Paul	Rome	c. 60-61	
Hebrews	Paul	Rome	c. 61	
James	James (Jesus' brother)	Jerusalem	b. 62	
1 Peter	Peter	Babylon	c. 62-64	
2 Peter	Peter	Babylon (?)	c. 64	
1 John	Apostle John	Ephesus, or near	c. 98	
2 John	Apostle John	Ephesus, or near	c. 98	
3 John	Apostle John	Ephesus, or near	c. 98	
Jude	Jude (Jesus' brother)	Palestine (?)	c. 65	
Revelation	Apostle John	Patmos	c. 96	

The Bible and
Its Canon

The origin of the word
"Bible"; determining which
books rightfully belong in
the Divine Library;
rejection of the Apocrypha.

SINCE the inspired Scriptures are commonly referred to as the Bible, it is of interest to inquire into the origin and meaning of the word "Bible." It is derived from the Greek word *bi·bli´a,* which means "little books." This, in turn, is derived from *bi´blos,* a word describing the inner part of the papyrus plant from which, in ancient times, a "paper" for writing was produced. (The Phoenician port of Gebal, through which papyrus was imported from Egypt, came to be called Byblos by the Greeks. See Joshua 13:5, footnote.) Various written communications upon this type of material became known by the word *bi·bli´a.* Thus, *bi·bli´a* came to describe any writings, scrolls, books, documents, or scriptures or even a library collection of little books.

² Surprisingly, the word "Bible" itself generally is not found in the text of English or other-language translations of the Holy Scriptures. However, by the second century B.C.E., the collection of the inspired books of the Hebrew Scriptures was referred to as *ta bi·bli´a* in the Greek language. At Daniel 9:2 the prophet wrote: "I myself, Daniel, discerned by the *books* . . . " Here the *Septuagint* has *bi´blois,* the dative plural form of *bi´blos.* At 2 Timothy 4:13, Paul wrote: "When you come, bring . . . the scrolls [Greek, *bi·bli´a*]." In their several grammatical forms, the Greek words *bi·bli´on* and *bi´blos* occur more than 40 times in the Christian Greek Scriptures and are usually translated "scroll(s)" or "book(s)." *Bi·bli´a* was later used in Latin as a singular word, and from the Latin, the word "Bible" came into the English language.

³ **It Is God's Word.** While various men were used in the inspired writing of it and still others have shared in translating it from the original tongues into the written languages of today, the Bible is, in the fullest sense, *God's* Word, his own inspired revelation to men. The inspired writers themselves viewed it this way, as is evidenced by their use of such phrases as "expression of Jehovah's mouth" (Deut. 8:3), "sayings of Jehovah" (Josh. 24:27), "commandments of Jehovah" (Ezra 7:11), "law of Jehovah" (Ps. 19:7), "word of Jehovah" (Isa. 38:4), 'utterance of Jehovah' (Matt. 4:4), and "Jehovah's word" (1 Thess. 4:15).

THE DIVINE LIBRARY

⁴ What man knows today as the Bible is in fact a collection of ancient divinely inspired documents. These were composed and compiled in written form over a period of 16 centuries. All together this collection of documents forms what Jerome well described in Latin as the *Bibliotheca Divina,* or the Divine Library. This library has a catalog, or official listing of publications, which is limited to those books pertaining to the scope and specialization of that library. All unauthorized books are excluded. Jehovah God is the Great Librarian who sets the standard that determines which writings should be included. So the Bible has a fixed catalog that contains 66 books, all products of God's guiding holy spirit.

⁵ The collection, or list, of books accepted as genuine and inspired Scripture is often referred to as the Bible *canon.* Originally, the reed (Hebrew, *qa·neh´*) served as a measuring rod if a piece of wood was not at hand. The apostle Paul applied the Greek word *ka·non´* to a "rule of conduct" as well as to the "territory" measured out as his assignment. (Gal. 6:16, footnote; 2 Cor. 10:13) So canonical books are those that are true and inspired and worthy to be used as a straightedge in determining the right faith, doctrine, and conduct. If we use books that are not "straight" as a plumb line, our "building" will not be true, and it will fail the test of the Master Surveyor.

⁶ **Determining Canonicity.** What are some of the divine indications that have determined the canonicity of the 66 books of the Bible? First of all,

---

1, 2. (a) What is the general meaning of the Greek word *bi·bli´a?* (b) How are this and associated words used in the Christian Greek Scriptures? (c) How did the word "Bible" come into the English language?
3. How did writers of the Bible testify to its being God's inspired Word?

4. Of what is the Bible composed, and who has determined this?
5. What is the Bible canon, and how did this designation originate?
6. What are some of the factors determining a book's canonicity?

the documents must deal with Jehovah's affairs in the earth, turning men to his worship and stimulating deep respect for his name and for his work and purposes in the earth. They must give evidence of inspiration, that is, that they are products of holy spirit. (2 Pet. 1:21) There must be no appeal to superstition or creature worship but, rather, an appeal to love and service of God. There would have to be nothing in any of the individual writings that would conflict with the internal harmony of the whole, but, rather, each book must, by its unity with the others, support the one authorship, that of Jehovah God. We would also expect the writings to give evidence of accuracy down to the smallest details. In addition to these basic essentials, there are other specific indications of inspiration, and therefore of canonicity, according to the nature of each book's contents, and these have been discussed herein in the introductory material to each of the Bible books. Also, there are special circumstances that apply to the Hebrew Scriptures and others to the Christian Greek Scriptures that help in establishing the Bible canon.

THE HEBREW SCRIPTURES

⁷ It should not be thought that acceptance of what constituted inspired Scripture had to wait till the completion of the Hebrew canon in the fifth century B.C.E. The writings of Moses under the direction of God's spirit were from the very beginning accepted by the Israelites as inspired, of divine authorship. When completed, the Pentateuch constituted the canon up to that time. Further revelations concerning Jehovah's purposes given to men under inspiration would need to follow logically and be in harmony with the fundamental principles concerning true worship that are set forth in the Pentateuch. We have seen this to be true when we considered the different Bible books, especially as these deal directly with that grand theme of the Bible, the sanctification of Jehovah's name and the vindication of his sovereignty by means of the Kingdom under Christ, the Promised Seed.

⁸ The Hebrew Scriptures, especially, abound with prophecy. Jehovah himself, through Moses, provided the basis for establishing the genuineness of prophecy, whether it was really from God or not, and this helped to determine the canonicity of a prophetic book. (Deut. 13:1-3; 18:20-22) An examination of each of the prophetic books of the Hebrew Scriptures along with the Bible as a whole

and secular history establishes beyond doubt that "the word" they spoke was in Jehovah's name, that it did "occur or come true," either completely or in a miniature or partial way when it had to do with things yet future, and that it turned the people toward God. Meeting these requirements established the prophecy as being genuine and inspired.

⁹ Quotations by Jesus and the inspired writers of the Christian Greek Scriptures provide a direct way of establishing the canonicity of many of the books of the Hebrew Scriptures, although this measure is not applicable to all, for example, the books of Esther and Ecclesiastes. In considering the matter of canonicity, then, one other most important factor must be kept in mind, one that applies to the entire Bible canon. Just as Jehovah inspired men to write down his divine communications for their instruction, upbuilding, and encouragement in his worship and service, so it logically follows that Jehovah would direct and guide the collating of the inspired writings and the establishing of the Bible canon. He would do this so that there would be no doubt as to what made up his Word of truth and what would constitute the enduring measuring line of true worship. Indeed, only in this way could creatures on earth continue to be given 'a new birth through the word of God' and be able to testify that "the saying of Jehovah endures forever."—1 Pet. 1:23, 25.

¹⁰ **Establishing the Hebrew Canon.** Jewish tradition credits Ezra with beginning the compiling and cataloging of the canon of the Hebrew Scriptures, and it says that this was completed by Nehemiah. Ezra was certainly well equipped for such a work, being one of the inspired Bible writers himself as well as a priest, scholar, and official copyist of sacred writings. (Ezra 7:1-11) There is no reason to doubt the traditional view that the canon of the Hebrew Scriptures was fixed by the end of the fifth century B.C.E.

¹¹ We today list 39 books of the Hebrew Scriptures; the traditional Jewish canon, while including these same books, counts them as 24. Some authorities, by putting Ruth with Judges and Lamentations with Jeremiah, counted the number of books as 22, though still holding to exactly the same canonical writings.* This made the number of inspired books equal the number of letters in

* *Encyclopaedia Judaica,* 1973, Vol. 4, cols. 826, 827.

---

7. By what progressive steps was the Hebrew canon completed, and with what would any newer portion have to be in harmony?
8. What establishes the canonicity of the prophetic books of the Bible?

9. What important factor must be borne in mind when one considers the question of the Bible canon?
10. By when was the canon of the Hebrew Scriptures fixed?
11. How does the traditional Jewish canon list the Hebrew Scriptures?

the Hebrew alphabet. The following is the list of the 24 books according to the traditional Jewish canon:

The Law (The Pentateuch)	The Writings (Hagiographa)
1. Genesis	14. Psalms
2. Exodus	15. Proverbs
3. Leviticus	16. Job
4. Numbers	17. The Song of Solomon
5. Deuteronomy	18. Ruth
The Prophets	19. Lamentations
6. Joshua	20. Ecclesiastes
7. Judges	21. Esther
8. Samuel (First and Second together as one book)	22. Daniel
	23. Ezra (Nehemiah was included with Ezra)
9. Kings (First and Second together as one book)	24. Chronicles (First and Second together as one book)
10. Isaiah	
11. Jeremiah	
12. Ezekiel	
13. The Twelve Prophets (Hosea, Joel, Amos, Obadiah, Jonah, Micah, Nahum, Habakkuk, Zephaniah, Haggai, Zechariah, and Malachi, as one book)	

¹² This was the catalog, or canon, that was accepted as inspired Scripture by Christ Jesus and the early Christian congregation. It was only from these writings that the inspired writers of the Christian Greek Scriptures quoted, and by introducing such quotations with expressions "as it is written," they confirmed these as being the Word of God. (Rom. 15:9) Jesus, in speaking of the complete inspired Scriptures written up till the time of his ministry, referred to the things recorded in "the law of Moses and in the Prophets and Psalms." (Luke 24:44) Here "Psalms," as the first book of the Hagiographa, is used to refer to this whole section. The last historical book to be included in the Hebrew canon was that of Nehemiah. That this was under the direction of God's spirit is seen in that this book alone provides the starting point for reckoning Daniel's outstanding prophecy that "from the going forth of the word to restore and to rebuild Jerusalem" until the coming of the Messiah there would be a period of 69 prophetic weeks. (Dan. 9:25; Neh. 2:1-8; 6:15) The book of Nehemiah also provides the historical background for the last of the prophetic books, Malachi. That Malachi belongs in the canon of the inspired Scriptures cannot be doubted, since even Jesus, the Son of God, quoted it a number of times. (Matt. 11:10, 14) While similar quotations are made from the majority of the books of the Hebrew canon, all of which were written prior to Nehemiah and Malachi, the writers of the Christian Greek Scriptures make no quotations from any so-called inspired writings written *after* the time of Nehemiah and Malachi down to the time of Christ. This confirms the traditional view of the Jews, and also the belief of the Christian congregation of the first century C.E., that the Hebrew Scripture canon ended with the writings of Nehemiah and Malachi.

APOCRYPHAL BOOKS OF THE HEBREW SCRIPTURES

¹³ What are the Apocryphal books? These are the writings that some have included in certain Bibles but that have been rejected by others because they do not bear evidence of having been inspired by God. The Greek word *a·po′kry·phos* refers to things "carefully concealed." (Mark 4:22; Luke 8:17; Col. 2:3) The term is applied to books of doubtful authorship or authority or those which, while considered to be of some value for personal reading, lacked evidence of divine inspiration. Such books were kept apart and not read publicly, hence the thought of "concealed." At the Council of Carthage, in 397 C.E., it was proposed that seven of the Apocryphal books be added to the Hebrew Scriptures, along with additions to the canonical books of Esther and Daniel. However, it was not until as late as 1546, at the Council of Trent, that the Roman Catholic Church definitely confirmed the acceptance of these additions into its catalog of Bible books. These additions were Tobit, Judith, additions to Esther, Wisdom, Ecclesiasticus, Baruch, three additions to Daniel, First Maccabees, and Second Maccabees.

¹⁴ The book of First Maccabees, while not in any way to be reckoned as an inspired book, contains information that is of historical interest. It gives an account of the struggle of the Jews for independence during the second century B.C.E. under the leadership of the priestly family of the Maccabees. The rest of the Apocryphal books are full of myths and superstitions and abound with errors. They were never referred to or quoted by Jesus or the writers of the Christian Greek Scriptures.

¹⁵ The Jewish historian Flavius Josephus, of the first century C.E., in his work *Against Apion* (I, 38-41 [8]), refers to all the books that were recognized by the Hebrews as sacred. He wrote: "We do not possess myriads of inconsistent books, conflicting with each other. Our books, those which are justly accredited, are but two and twenty [the equivalent of our 39 today, as is shown in paragraph 11], and contain the record of all time. Of these, five are the books of Moses, comprising

---

12. What further confirms the Hebrew canon, and with what writings did it end?

13. (a) What are the Apocryphal books? (b) How did they come to be accepted into the Roman Catholic canon?

14. (a) In what way is First Maccabees of interest? (b) What authorities never referred to the Apocrypha, and why?

15, 16. How did Josephus and Jerome indicate which books are canonical?

the laws and the traditional history from the birth of man down to the death of the lawgiver. . . . From the death of Moses until Artaxerxes, who succeeded Xerxes as king of Persia, the prophets subsequent to Moses wrote the history of the events of their own times in thirteen books. The remaining four books contain hymns to God and precepts for the conduct of human life." Thus Josephus shows that the canon of the Hebrew Scriptures had been fixed long before the first century C.E.

16 Biblical scholar Jerome, who completed the Latin Vulgate translation of the Bible about 405 C.E., was quite definite in his position on the Apocryphal books. After listing the inspired books, using the same counting as Josephus, numbering the 39 inspired books of the Hebrew Scriptures as 22, he writes in his prologue to the books of Samuel and Kings in the *Vulgate:* "Thus there are twenty-two books . . . This prologue of the Scriptures can serve as a fortified approach to all the books which we translate from the Hebrew into Latin; so that we may know that whatever is beyond these must be put in the apocrypha."

THE CHRISTIAN GREEK SCRIPTURES

17 The Roman Catholic Church claims responsibility for the decision as to which books should be included in the Bible canon, and reference is made to the Council of Carthage (397 C.E.), where a catalog of books was formulated. The opposite is true, however, because the canon, including the list of books making up the Christian Greek Scriptures, was already settled by then, that is, not by the decree of any council, but by the direction of God's holy spirit—the same spirit that inspired the writing of those books in the first place. The testimony of later noninspired catalogers is valuable only as an acknowledgment of the Bible canon, which God's spirit had authorized.

18 **The Evidence of Early Catalogs.** A glance at the accompanying chart reveals that a number of fourth-century catalogs of the Christian Scriptures, dated prior to the above-mentioned council, agree exactly with our present canon, and some others omit only Revelation. Before the end of the second century, there is universal acceptance of the four Gospels, Acts, and 12 of the apostle Paul's letters. Only a few of the smaller writings were doubted in certain areas. Likely this was so because such writings were limited in their initial

circulation for one reason or another and thus took longer to become accepted as canonical.

19 One of the most interesting early catalogs is the fragment discovered by L. A. Muratori in the Ambrosian Library, Milan, Italy, and published by him in 1740. Though the beginning is missing, its reference to Luke as the third Gospel indicates that it first mentioned Matthew and Mark. The Muratorian Fragment, which is in Latin, dates to the latter part of the second century C.E. It is a most interesting document, as the following partial translation shows: "The third book of the Gospel is that according to Luke. Luke, the well-known physician, wrote it in his own name . . . The fourth book of the Gospel is that of John, one of the disciples. . . . And so to the faith of believers there is no discord, even although different selections are given from the facts in the individual books of the Gospels, because in all [of them] under the one guiding Spirit all the things relative to his nativity, passion, resurrection, conversation with his disciples, and his twofold advent, the first in the humiliation arising from contempt, which took place, and the second in the glory of kingly power, which is yet to come, have been declared. What marvel is it, then, if John adduces so consistently in his epistles these several things, saying in person: 'what we have seen with our eyes, and heard with our ears, and our hands have handled, those things we have written.' For thus he professes to be not only an eyewitness but also a hearer and narrator of all the wonderful things of the Lord, in their order. Moreover, the acts of all the apostles are written in one book. Luke [so] comprised them for the most excellent Theophilus . . . Now the epistles of Paul, what they are, whence or for what reason they were sent, they themselves make clear to him who will understand. First of all he wrote at length to the Corinthians to prohibit the schism of heresy, then to the Galatians [against] circumcision, and to the Romans on the order of the Scriptures, intimating also that Christ is the chief matter in them—each of which it is necessary for us to discuss, seeing that the blessed Apostle Paul himself, following the example of his predecessor John, writes to no more than seven churches by name in the following order: to the Corinthians (first), to the Ephesians (second), to the Philippians (third), to the Colossians (fourth), to the Galatians (fifth), to the Thessalonians (sixth), to the Romans (seventh). But though he writes twice for the sake of correction to the Corinthians and the Thessalonians, that

---

17. What responsibility does the Roman Catholic Church claim, but who really determined which books make up the Bible canon?
18. What important conclusions can be drawn from the chart showing early catalogs of the Christian Greek Scriptures?

19. (a) What outstanding document has been located in Italy, and what is its date? (b) How does this define the accepted canon of that time?

there is one church diffused throughout the whole earth is shown [?i.e., by this sevenfold writing]; and John also in the Apocalypse, though he writes to seven churches, yet speaks to all. But [he wrote] out of affection and love one to Philemon, and one to Titus, and two to Timothy; [and these] are held sacred in the honorable esteem of the Church. . . . Further, an epistle of Jude and two bearing the name of John are counted . . . We receive the apocalypses of John and Peter only, which [latter] some of us do not wish to be read in church." —*The New Schaff-Herzog Encyclopedia of Religious Knowledge,* 1956, Vol. VIII, page 56.

[20] It is noted that toward the end of the Muratorian Fragment, mention is made of just two

20. (a) How is the omission of one of John's letters and one of Peter's explained? (b) How closely, then, does this catalog correspond to our present-day catalog?

Outstanding Early Catalogs of the Christian Greek Scriptures

Name and Place	Approximate Date C.E.	Matthew	Mark	Luke	John	Acts	Romans	1 Corinthians	2 Corinthians	Galatians	Ephesians	Philippians	Colossians	1 Thessalonians	2 Thessalonians	1 Timothy	2 Timothy	Titus	Philemon	Hebrews	James	1 Peter	2 Peter	1 John	2 John	3 John	Jude	Revelation
Muratorian Fragment, Italy	170	A	A	A	A	A	A	A	A	A	A	A	A	A	A	A	A	A	A			A?	D?	A	A	A?	A	A
Irenaeus, Asia Minor	180	A	A	A	A	A	A	A	A	A	A	A	A	A	A	A	A	A	D	?		A	A	A	A			A
Clement of Alexandria	190	A	A	A	A	A	A	A	A	A	A	A	A	A	A	A	A	A	DA			A		DA	DA		DA	A
Tertullian, N. Africa	207	A	A	A	A	A	A	A	A	A	A	A	A	A	A	A	A	A	A	DA		A		A			A	A
Origen, Alexandria	230	A	A	A	A	A	A	A	A	A	A	A	A	A	A	A	A	A	A	DA	DA	A	DA	A	DA	DA	DA	A
Eusebius, Palestine	320	A	A	A	A	A	A	A	A	A	A	A	A	A	A	A	A	A	A	DA	DA	A	DA	A	DA	DA	DA	DA
Cyril of Jerusalem	348	A	A	A	A	A	A	A	A	A	A	A	A	A	A	A	A	A	A	A	A	A	A	A	A	A	A	
Cheltenham List, N. Africa	365	A	A	A	A	A	A	A	A	A	A	A	A	A	A	A	A	A	A			A	D	A	D	D		A
Athanasius, Alexandria	367	A	A	A	A	A	A	A	A	A	A	A	A	A	A	A	A	A	A	A	A	A	A	A	A	A	A	A
Epiphanius, Palestine	368	A	A	A	A	A	A	A	A	A	A	A	A	A	A	A	A	A	A	A	A	A	A	A	A	A	A	DA
Gregory Nazianzus, Asia Minor	370	A	A	A	A	A	A	A	A	A	A	A	A	A	A	A	A	A	A	A	A	A	A	A	A	A	A	
Amphilocius, Asia Minor	370	A	A	A	A	A	A	A	A	A	A	A	A	A	A	A	A	A	A	DA	A	A	D	A	D	D	D	D
Philaster, Italy	383	A	A	A	A	A	A	A	A	A	A	A	A	A	A	A	A	A	A	DA	A	A	A	A	A	A	A	DA
Jerome, Italy	394	A	A	A	A	A	A	A	A	A	A	A	A	A	A	A	A	A	A	DA	DA	A	DA	A	DA	DA	DA	DA
Augustine, N. Africa	397	A	A	A	A	A	A	A	A	A	A	A	A	A	A	A	A	A	A	A	A	A	A	A	A	A	A	A
Third Council of Carthage, N. Africa	397	A	A	A	A	A	A	A	A	A	A	A	A	A	A	A	A	A	A	A	A	A	A	A	A	A	A	A

A - Accepted without query as Scriptural and canonical
D - Doubted in certain quarters

DA - Doubted in certain quarters, but cataloger accepted it as Scriptural and canonical

? - Scholars uncertain of the reading of the text or how a book mentioned is viewed

□ - A blank space indicates that the book was not used or mentioned by that authority

epistles of John. However, on this point the above-mentioned encyclopedia, page 55, notes that these two epistles of John "can only be the second and third, whose writer calls himself merely 'the elder.' Having already treated the first, though only incidentally, in connection with the Fourth Gospel, and there declared his unquestioning belief in its Johannine origin, the author felt able here to confine himself to the two smaller letters." As to the apparent absence of any mention of Peter's first epistle, this source continues: "The most probable hypothesis is that of the loss of a few words, perhaps a line, in which I Peter and the Apocalypse of John were named as received." Therefore, from the standpoint of the Muratorian Fragment, this encyclopedia, on page 56, concludes: "The New Testament is regarded as definitely made up of the four Gospels, the Acts, thirteen epistles of Paul, the Apocalypse of John, probably three epistles of his, Jude, and probably I Peter, while the opposition to another of Peter's writings was not yet silenced."

21 Origen, about the year 230 C.E., accepted among the inspired Scriptures the books of Hebrews and James, both missing from the Muratorian Fragment. While he indicates that some doubted their canonical quality, this also shows that by this time, the canonicity of most of the Greek Scriptures was accepted, only a few doubting some of the less well-known epistles. Later, Athanasius, Jerome, and Augustine acknowledged the conclusions of earlier lists by defining as the canon the same 27 books that we now have.*

22 The majority of the catalogs in the chart are specific lists showing which books were accepted as canonical. Those of Irenaeus, Clement of Alexandria, Tertullian, and Origen are completed from the quotations they made, which reveal how they regarded the writings referred to. These are further supplemented from the records of the early historian Eusebius. However, the fact that these writers do not mention certain canonical writings does not argue against their canonicity. It is just that they did not happen to refer to them in their writings either by choice or because of the subjects under discussion. But why do we not find exact lists earlier than the Muratorian Fragment?

23 It was not until critics like Marcion came along in the middle of the second century C.E. that an issue arose as to which books Christians should

accept. Marcion constructed his own canon to suit his doctrines, taking only certain of the apostle Paul's letters and an expurgated form of the Gospel of Luke. This, together with the mass of apocryphal literature by then spreading throughout the world, was what led to statements by catalogers as to which books they accepted as canonical.

24 **Apocryphal Writings.** Internal evidence confirms the clear division that was made between the inspired Christian writings and works that were spurious or uninspired. The Apocryphal writings are much inferior and often fanciful and childish. They are frequently inaccurate.* Note the following statements by scholars on these noncanonical books:

"There is no question of any one's having excluded them from the New Testament: they have done that for themselves."—M. R. James, *The Apocryphal New Testament,* pages xi, xii.

"We have only to compare our New Testament books as a whole with other literature of the kind to realize how wide is the gulf which separates them from it. The uncanonical gospels, it is often said, are in reality the best evidence for the canonical."—G. Milligan, *The New Testament Documents,* page 228.

"It cannot be said of a single writing preserved to us from the early period of the Church outside the New Testament that it could properly be added to-day to the Canon." —K. Aland, *The Problem of the New Testament Canon,* page 24.

25 **Inspired Penmen.** This further point is of interest. All the writers of the Christian Greek Scriptures in one way or another were closely associated with the original governing body of the Christian congregation, which included apostles personally selected by Jesus. Matthew, John, and Peter were among the original 12 apostles, and Paul was later selected as an apostle but was not reckoned as one of the 12.# Although Paul was not present at the special outpouring of spirit at Pentecost, Matthew, John, and Peter were there, along with James and Jude and probably Mark. (Acts 1:13, 14) Peter specifically counts the letters of Paul in with "the rest of the Scriptures." (2 Pet. 3:15, 16) Mark and Luke were close associates and traveling companions of Paul and Peter. (Acts 12: 25; 1 Pet. 5:13; Col. 4:14; 2 Tim. 4:11) All these writers were endowed with miraculous abilities

----

* *The Books and the Parchments,* 1963, F. F. Bruce, page 112.

* *Insight on the Scriptures,* Vol. 1, pages 122-5.
# *Insight on the Scriptures,* Vol. 1, pages 129-30.

----

21. (a) Of what interest are Origen's comments on the inspired writings? (b) What did later writers acknowledge?
22, 23. (a) How were the lists of the catalogs in the chart prepared? (b) Why were there apparently no such lists prior to the Muratorian Fragment?

24. (a) What characterizes the Apocryphal "New Testament" writings? (b) What do scholars say of these?
25. What facts about the individual writers of the Christian Greek Scriptures argue for the inspiration of these writings?

by holy spirit, either by special outpouring as occurred at Pentecost and when Paul was converted (Acts 9:17, 18) or, no doubt as in the case of Luke, by the laying on of the apostles' hands. (Acts 8:14-17) All the writing of the Christian Greek Scriptures was completed during the time that the special gifts of the spirit were operative.

26 Faith in the almighty God, who is the Inspirer and Preserver of his Word, makes us confident

that he is the one who has guided the gathering together of its various parts. So we confidently accept the 27 books of the Christian Greek Scriptures along with the 39 of the Hebrew Scriptures as the one Bible, by the one Author, Jehovah God. His Word in its 66 books is our guide, and its entire harmony and balance testify to its completeness. All praise to Jehovah God, the Creator of this incomparable book! It can equip us completely and put our feet on the way to life. Let us use it wisely at every opportunity.

---

26. (a) What do we accept as God's Word, and why? (b) How should we show appreciation for the Bible?

Study Number **5**

The Hebrew Text of the Holy Scriptures

How the Hebrew Scriptures, as part of the inspired Word of God, were copied, preserved as to textual integrity, and transmitted down to this day.

THE 'words of Jehovah' captured in writing may be likened to waters of truth collected in a remarkable reservoir of inspired documents. How grateful we can be that throughout the period of these heavenly communications, Jehovah caused these "waters" to be gathered together in order to become an inexhaustible source of life-giving information! Other treasures of the past, such as regal crowns, heirlooms, and monuments of men, have tarnished, eroded, or collapsed with the passage of time, but the treasurelike sayings of our God will last to time indefinite. (Isa. 40:8) However, questions arise as to whether there has been contamination of these waters of truth after they were taken into the reservoir. Have they remained unadulterated? Have they been transmitted faithfully from the original-language texts, with the result that what is available to peoples of every language on earth today is reliable? We will find it a thrilling study to examine the section of this reservoir known as the Hebrew text, noting the care taken to preserve its accuracy, together with the wonderful provisions made for its transmission and availability to all nations of mankind through versions and new translations.

2 The original documents in the Hebrew and

Aramaic languages were recorded by God's human secretaries, from Moses in 1513 B.C.E. down to shortly after 443 B.C.E. As far as is known today, none of these original writings are now in existence. However, from the beginning, great care was exercised in preserving the inspired writings, including authorized copies of them. About 642 B.C.E., in King Josiah's time, "the very book of the law" of Moses, doubtless the original copy, was found stored away in the house of Jehovah. It had by this time been faithfully preserved for 871 years. Bible writer Jeremiah manifested such great interest in this discovery that he made written record of it at 2 Kings 22:8-10, and about the year 460 B.C.E., Ezra again referred to the same incident. (2 Chron. 34:14-18) He was interested in these things, for "he was a skilled copyist in the law of Moses, which Jehovah the God of Israel had given." (Ezra 7:6) No doubt Ezra had access to other scrolls of the Hebrew Scriptures that had been prepared up to his time, possibly including originals of some of the inspired writings. Indeed, Ezra seems to have been the custodian of the divine writings in his day.—Neh. 8:1, 2.

ERA OF MANUSCRIPT COPYING

3 From Ezra's time forward, there was an increased demand for copies of the Hebrew Scriptures. Not all the Jews returned to Jerusalem and

---

1. (a) How do the 'words of Jehovah' differ from other treasures of the past? (b) What questions arise as to the preservation of God's Word?
2. How were the inspired writings preserved down to Ezra's day?

3. What need arose for additional copies of the Scriptures, and how was this filled?

Palestine in the restoration of 537 B.C.E. and thereafter. Instead, thousands remained in Babylon, while others migrated for business and other reasons, with the result that they were to be found in most of the large commercial centers of the ancient world. Many Jews would make annual pilgrimages back to Jerusalem for the various temple festivals, and there they would share in the worship conducted in Biblical Hebrew. In Ezra's time the Jews in these many faraway lands used local assembly places known as synagogues, where readings and discussions of the Hebrew Scriptures took place.* Because of the many scattered places of worship, copyists had to multiply the supply of handwritten manuscripts.

⁴ These synagogues usually had a storage room known as the genizah. In the course of time, the Jews placed in the genizah discarded manuscripts that had become torn or worn with age, replacing them with new ones for current synagogue use. From time to time, the contents of the genizah would be solemnly buried in the earth, in order that the text—containing the holy name of Jehovah—might not be desecrated. Over the centuries, thousands of old Hebrew Bible manuscripts disappeared from use in this way. However, the well-stocked genizah of the synagogue in Old Cairo was spared this treatment, probably because it was walled up and forgotten until the middle of the 19th century. In 1890, when the synagogue was being repaired, the contents of the genizah were reexamined and its treasures were gradually either sold or donated. From this source, fairly complete manuscripts and thousands of fragments (some said to be of the sixth century C.E.) have found their way to Cambridge University Library and other libraries of Europe and America.

⁵ Today, in various libraries of the world, there have been counted and cataloged perhaps 6,000 manuscripts of all or portions of the Hebrew Scriptures. Until recently there were no such manuscripts (except for a few fragments) older than the tenth century C.E. Then, in 1947, in the area of the Dead Sea, there was discovered a scroll of the book of Isaiah, and in subsequent

years additional priceless scrolls of the Hebrew Scriptures came to light as caves in the Dead Sea area surrendered rich treasures of manuscripts that had been hidden for nearly 1,900 years. Experts have now dated some of these as having been copied in the last few centuries B.C.E. The comparative study of the approximately 6,000 manuscripts of the Hebrew Scriptures gives a sound basis for establishing the Hebrew text and reveals faithfulness in the transmission of the text.

THE HEBREW LANGUAGE

⁶ What men today call the Hebrew language was, in its original form, the language that Adam spoke in the garden of Eden. For this reason it could be referred to as man's language. It was the language spoken in Noah's day, though with a growing vocabulary. In still further expanded form, it was the basic language that survived when Jehovah confused mankind's speech at the Tower of Babel. (Gen. 11:1, 7-9) Hebrew belongs to the Semitic group of languages, of which it is the family head. It appears to be related to the language of Canaan in Abraham's time, and from their Hebraic branch, the Canaanites formed various dialects. At Isaiah 19:18 it is referred to as "the language of Canaan." Moses in his time was a scholar, learned not only in the wisdom of the Egyptians but also in the Hebrew language of his forefathers. For this reason he was in a position to read ancient documents that came into his hands, and these may have provided a basis for some of the information he recorded in what is now known as the Bible book of Genesis.

⁷ Later, in the days of the Jewish kings, Hebrew came to be known as "the Jews' language." (2 Ki. 18:26, 28) In Jesus' time, the Jews spoke a newer or expanded form of Hebrew, and this still later became a rabbinic Hebrew. However, it should be noted that in the Christian Greek Scriptures, the language is still referred to as the "Hebrew" language, not the Aramaic. (John 5:2; 19:13, 17; Acts 22:2; Rev. 9:11) From earliest times, Biblical Hebrew was the binding language of communication, understood by most of Jehovah's pre-Christian witnesses as well as by the Christian witnesses of the first century.

⁸ The Hebrew Scriptures served as a reservoir of crystal-clear waters of truth, communicated and collected under divine inspiration. However,

---

* It is not known when the use of synagogues was instituted. It may have been during the 70-year Babylonian exile when there was no temple in existence, or it may have been shortly following the return from exile, in Ezra's day.

---

4. (a) What was a genizah, and how was it used? (b) What valuable find was made in one of these in the 19th century?
5. (a) What ancient Hebrew manuscripts have now been cataloged, and how old are they? (b) What does a study of them reveal?

6. (a) What was the early history of the Hebrew language? (b) Why was Moses qualified to write Genesis?
7. (a) What later development of Hebrew took place? (b) As what did Biblical Hebrew serve?
8. Having in mind the purpose of the Scriptures, for what can we be truly thankful?

only those able to read Hebrew could avail themselves directly of these divinely provided waters. How could men of the multitongued nations also find a way to imbibe these waters of truth, thus gaining divine guidance and refreshment for their soul? (Rev. 22:17) The only way was by translation from the Hebrew into other languages, thus broadening the flow of the stream of divine truth to all the multitudes of mankind. We can be truly thankful to Jehovah God that from about the fourth or third century B.C.E. down to the present time, portions of the Bible have been translated into more than 1,900 languages. What a boon this has proved to be for all righteously inclined people, who have indeed been enabled to find their "delight" in these precious waters!—Ps. 1:2; 37:3, 4.

⁹ Does the Bible itself give authority or justification for translating its text into other languages? Certainly it does! God's word to Israel, "Be glad, you nations, with his people," and Jesus' prophetic command to Christians, "This good news of the kingdom will be preached in all the inhabited earth for a witness to all the nations," must be fulfilled. For this to take place, translation of the Scriptures is a necessity. Looking back over nearly 24 centuries of Bible translating, it is clear that Jehovah's blessing has accompanied this work. Moreover, ancient translations of the Bible that have survived in manuscript form have also served to confirm the high degree of textual faithfulness of the Hebrew reservoir of truth. —Deut. 32:43; Matt. 24:14.

EARLIEST TRANSLATED VERSIONS

¹⁰ **The Samaritan Pentateuch.** Dating from early times, there is the version known as the Samaritan Pentateuch, which, as the name implies, contains only the first five books of the Hebrew Scriptures. It is really a transliteration of the Hebrew text into Samaritan script, developed from the ancient Hebrew script. It provides a useful pointer to the Hebrew text of the time. This transliteration was made by the Samaritans —descendants of those left in Samaria following the conquest of the ten-tribe kingdom of Israel in 740 B.C.E. and those brought in by the Assyrians at that time. The Samaritans incorporated the worship of Israel with that of their own pagan gods, and they accepted the Pentateuch. It is thought that they made their transcription of it about the fourth century B.C.E., although some

scholars suggest that it may have been as late as the second century B.C.E. As they read its text, they would, in fact, be pronouncing Hebrew. Although the text contains about 6,000 variations from the Hebrew text, many of them are minor details. Few of the existing manuscript copies are older than the 13th century C.E. Some references are made to the Samaritan Pentateuch in footnotes of the *New World Translation.**

¹¹ **The Aramaic Targums.** The Aramaic word for "interpretation" or "paraphrase" is *targum.* From Nehemiah's time forward, Aramaic came to be used as the common language of many of the Jews living in the territory of Persia, and so it was necessary to accompany readings of the Hebrew Scriptures with translations into that language. They likely assumed their present final form no earlier than about the fifth century C.E. Though they are only loose paraphrases of the Hebrew text, and not an accurate translation, they supply a rich background to the text and give aid in determining some difficult passages. Frequent references are made to the Targums in footnotes of the *New World Translation.#*

¹² **The Greek *Septuagint.*** The most important of the early versions of the Hebrew Scriptures, and the first actual written translation from the Hebrew, is the Greek *Septuagint* (meaning, "Seventy"). Its translation began about 280 B.C.E., according to tradition, by 72 Jewish scholars of Alexandria, Egypt. Later, the number 70 somehow came to be used, and thus the version was called the *Septuagint.* Evidently it was completed sometime in the second century B.C.E. It served as Scripture for the Greek-speaking Jews and was used extensively down to the time of Jesus and his apostles. In the Christian Greek Scriptures, most of the 320 direct quotations and the combined total of perhaps 890 quotations and references to the Hebrew Scriptures are based on the *Septuagint.*

¹³ There are still available for study today a considerable number of fragments of the *Septuagint* written on papyrus. They are valuable because they belong to early Christian times, and though often just a few verses or chapters, they help in assessing the text of the *Septuagint.* The

---

* See "Sam" in footnotes, at Genesis 4:8; Exodus 6:2; 7:9; 8:15; and 12:40. This last rendering helps us to understand Galatians 3:17.
# See "T" in footnotes at Numbers 24:17; Deuteronomy 33:13; and Psalm 100:3.

---

9. (a) What authority for translation does the Bible itself give? (b) What further good purpose have ancient Bible translations served?
10. (a) What is the Samaritan Pentateuch, and why is it useful to us today? (b) Give an example of the use of the Samaritan Pentateuch in the *New World Translation.*

11. What are the Targums, and of what benefit are they in connection with the text of the Hebrew Scriptures?
12. What is the *Septuagint,* and why is it so important?
13. What valuable fragments of the *Septuagint* have survived to this day, and of what value are they?

Sources for the Text of the New World Translation
Hebrew Scriptures

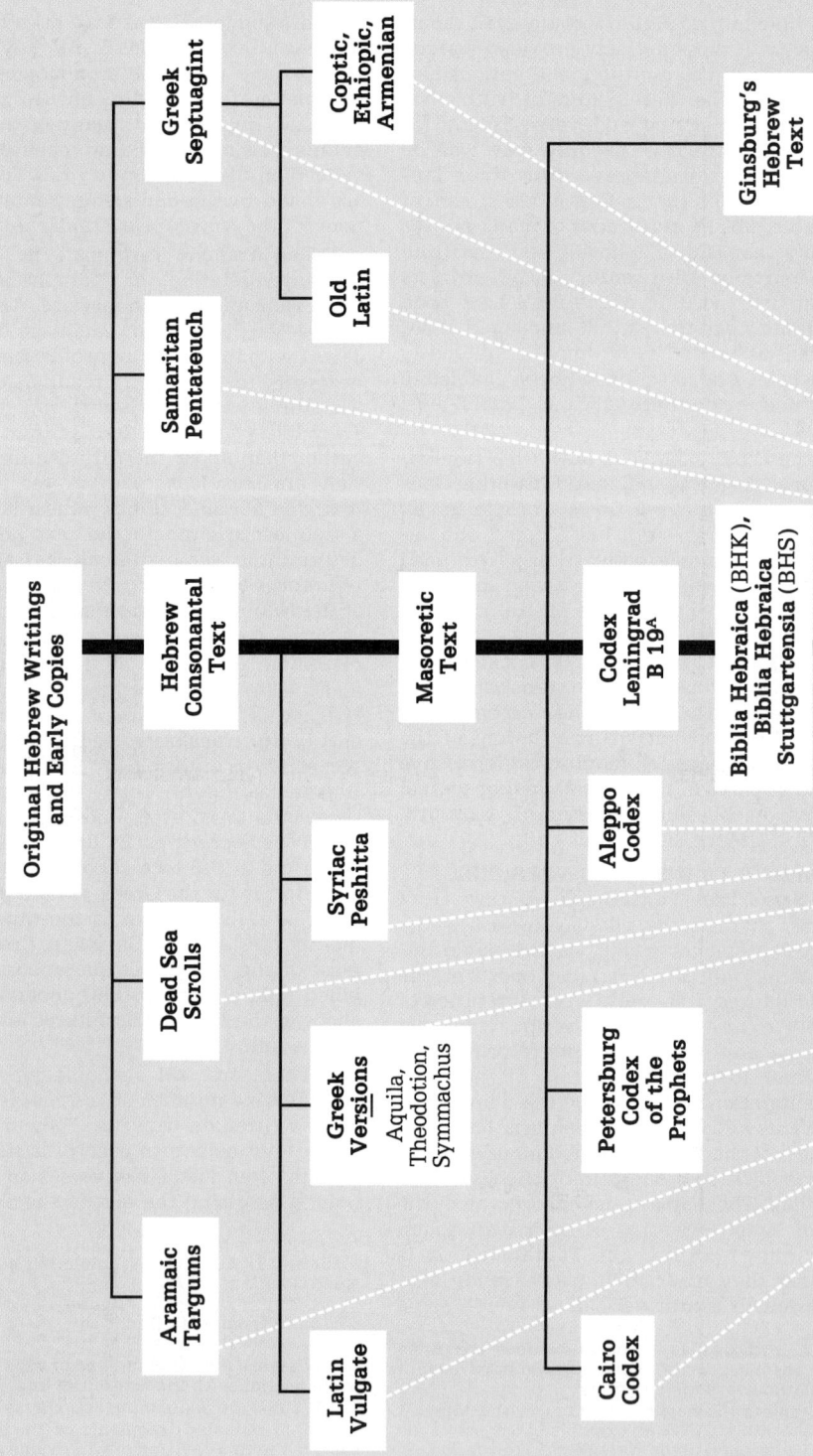

Original Hebrew Writings and Early Copies

- Aramaic Targums
- Dead Sea Scrolls
- Samaritan Pentateuch
- Greek Septuagint
  - Coptic, Ethiopic, Armenian
  - Old Latin
- Hebrew Consonantal Text
- Greek Versions — Aquila, Theodotion, Symmachus
- Latin Vulgate
- Syriac Peshitta

Masoretic Text

- Cairo Codex
- Petersburg Codex of the Prophets
- Aleppo Codex

Codex Leningrad B 19ᴬ

- Ginsburg's Hebrew Text
- Biblia Hebraica (BHK), Biblia Hebraica Stuttgartensia (BHS)

New World Translation

Hebrew Scriptures—English; From English Into Many Other Modern Languages

Sources for the Text of the New World Translation
Christian Greek Scriptures

Original Greek Writings and Early Copies

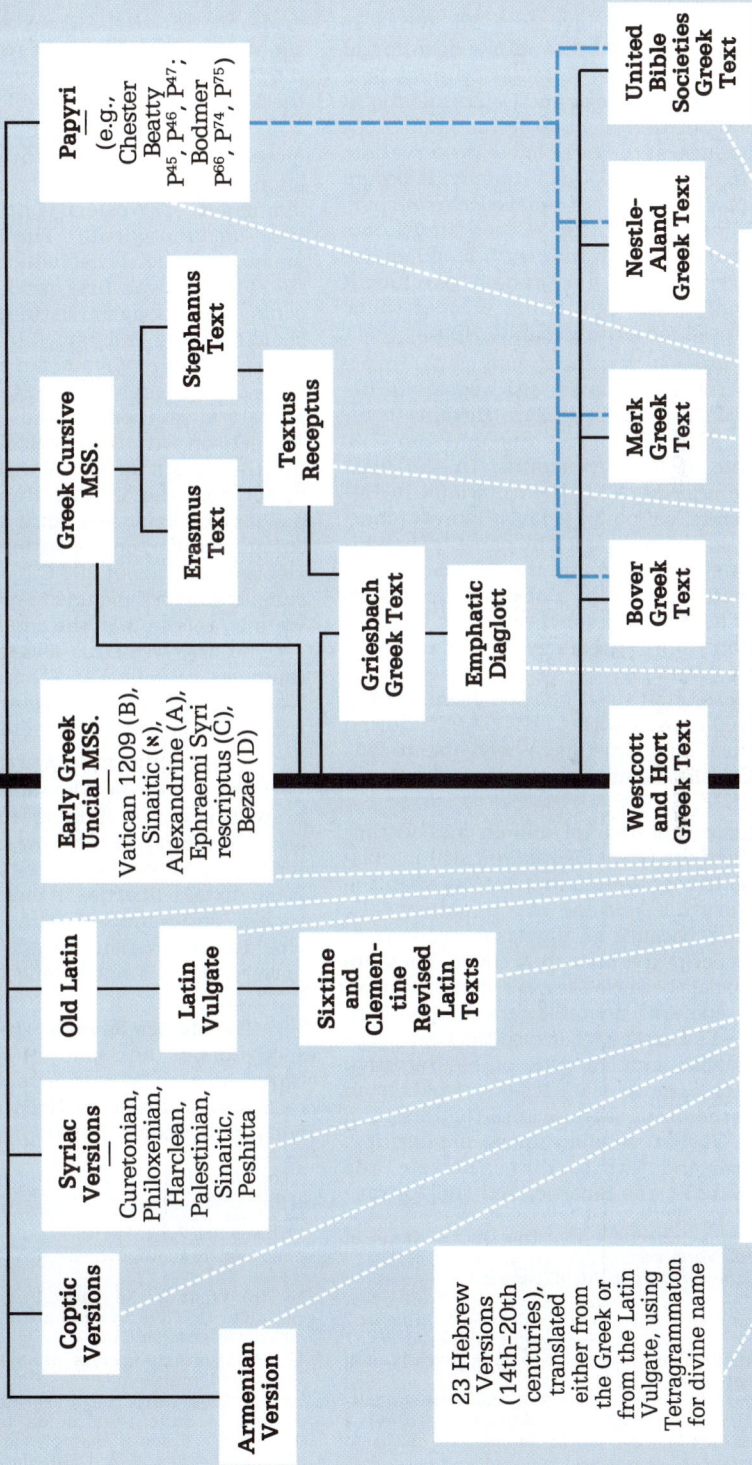

Coptic Versions

Syriac Versions
Curetonian, Philoxenian, Harclean, Palestinian, Sinaitic, Peshitta

Old Latin

Latin Vulgate

Sixtine and Clementine Revised Latin Texts

Armenian Version

23 Hebrew Versions (14th–20th centuries), translated either from the Greek or from the Latin Vulgate, using Tetragrammaton for divine name

Early Greek Uncial MSS.
Vatican 1209 (B), Sinaitic (א), Alexandrine (A), Ephraemi Syri rescriptus (C), Bezae (D)

Papyri (e.g., Chester Beatty P^{45}, P^{46}, P^{47}; Bodmer P^{66}, P^{74}, P^{75})

Greek Cursive MSS.

Stephanus Text

Erasmus Text

Textus Receptus

Griesbach Greek Text

Emphatic Diaglott

Westcott and Hort Greek Text

Bover Greek Text

Merk Greek Text

Nestle-Aland Greek Text

United Bible Societies Greek Text

New World Translation

Christian Greek Scriptures—English; From English Into Many Other Modern Languages

Fouad Papyri collection (Inventory No. 266) was discovered in Egypt in 1939 and has been found to be of the first century B.C.E. It contains portions of the books of Genesis and Deuteronomy. In the fragments of Genesis, the divine name does not occur because of the incomplete preservation. However, in the book of Deuteronomy, it occurs in various places, written in square Hebrew characters within the Greek text.* Other papyri date down to about the fourth century C.E., when the more durable vellum, a fine grade of parchment generally made from calf, lamb, or goat skins, began to be used for writing manuscripts.

[14] It is of interest that the divine name, in the form of the Tetragrammaton, also appears in the *Septuagint* of Origen's six-column *Hexapla,* completed about 245 C.E. Commenting on Psalm 2:2, Origen wrote of the *Septuagint:* "In the most accurate manuscripts THE NAME occurs in Hebrew characters, yet not in today's Hebrew [characters], but in the most ancient ones."[#] The evidence appears conclusive that the *Septuagint* was tampered with at an early date, *Ky′ri·os* (Lord) and *The·os′* (God) being substituted for the Tetragrammaton. Since the early Christians used manuscripts containing the divine name, it cannot be supposed that they followed Jewish tradition in failing to pronounce "THE NAME" during their ministry. They must have been able to witness to Jehovah's name directly from the Greek *Septuagint.*

[15] There are hundreds of vellum and leather manuscripts of the Greek *Septuagint* still in existence. A number of these, produced between the fourth century C.E. and the ninth century C.E., are important because of the large sections of the Hebrew Scriptures that they cover. They are known as uncials because they are written entirely in large, separated capital letters. The remainder are called minuscules because they are written in a smaller, cursive style of handwriting. Minuscule, or cursive, manuscripts remained in vogue from the ninth century until the inception of printing. The outstanding uncial manuscripts of the fourth and fifth centuries, namely, the Vatican No. 1209, the Sinaitic, and the Alexan-

drine, all contain the Greek *Septuagint* with some slight variations. Frequent references are made to the *Septuagint* in the footnotes and comments in the *New World Translation.**

[16] **The Latin *Vulgate.*** This version has been the mother text used by a multitude of Catholic translators in producing other versions in the many languages of Western Christendom. How did the *Vulgate* originate? The Latin word *vulgatus* means "common, that which is popular." When the *Vulgate* was first produced, it was in the common, or popular, Latin of the day so that it could be easily understood by the ordinary people of the Western Roman Empire. The scholar Jerome, who made this translation, had previously made two revisions of the Old Latin Psalms, in comparison with the Greek *Septuagint.* However, his translation of the Vulgate Bible was made direct from the original Hebrew and Greek languages and was thus not a version of a version. Jerome worked on his Latin translation from Hebrew from about 390 C.E. to 405 C.E. While the completed work included Apocryphal books, that were by this time in the copies of the *Septuagint,* Jerome clearly distinguished between the books that were canonical and those that were not. The *New World Translation* refers many times to Jerome's *Vulgate* in its footnotes.[#]

THE HEBREW-LANGUAGE TEXTS

[17] **The Sopherim.** The men who copied the Hebrew Scriptures starting in the days of Ezra and continuing to the time of Jesus were called scribes, or Sopherim. In the course of time, they began to take liberties in making textual changes. In fact, Jesus himself roundly condemned these would-be custodians of the Law for assuming powers that did not belong to them.—Matt. 23: 2, 13.

[18] **The Masora Reveals Alterations.** The scribal successors of the Sopherim in the centuries after Christ came to be known as the Masoretes. These took note of the alterations made by the earlier Sopherim, recording them in the margin or at the

---

* *Reference Bible,* appendix 1c, "The Divine Name in Ancient Greek Versions."
[#] *Insight on the Scriptures,* Vol. 2, page 9.

---

* The *New World Translation* notes these variations by symbol LXX* for Sinaitic, LXX^A for Alexandrine, and LXX^B for Vatican. See footnotes at 1 Kings 14:2 and 1 Chronicles 7:34; 12:19.
[#] See "Vg" in footnote at Exodus 37:6.

---

14. (a) What does Origen testify as to the *Septuagint?* (b) When and how was the *Septuagint* tampered with? (c) What witness must the early Christians have given in using the *Septuagint?*
15. (a) Using the chart on page 314, describe the vellum and leather manuscripts of the *Septuagint.* (b) What references does the *New World Translation* make to these?

16. (a) What is the Latin *Vulgate,* and why is it so valuable? (b) Give an example of the *New World Translation's* reference to it.
17. Who were the scribes, or Sopherim, and for what did Jesus condemn them?
18. (a) Who were the Masoretes, and what valuable comments have they made on the Hebrew text? (b) What are some examples of their corrections, as noted in the *New World Translation?*

end of the Hebrew text. These marginal notes came to be known as the Masora. The Masora listed the 15 extraordinary points of the Sopherim, namely, 15 words or phrases in the Hebrew text that had been marked by dots or strokes. Some of these extraordinary points do not affect the English translation or the interpretation, but others do and are of importance.* The Sopherim allowed their superstitious fear of pronouncing the name Jehovah to ensnare them into altering it to read *'Adho·nai'* (Lord) at 134 places and to read *'Elo·him'* (God) in some instances. The Masora lists these changes.# The Sopherim or early scribes are also charged with making at least 18 emendations (corrections), according to a note in the Masora, though there evidently were even more.△ These emendations were very likely made with good intentions because the original passage appeared to show either irreverence for God or disrespect for his earthly representatives.

19 The Consonantal Text. The Hebrew alphabet is made up of 22 consonants, with no vowels. Originally, the reader had to supply the vowel sounds from his knowledge of the language. Hebrew writing was like an abbreviated script. Even in modern English there are many standard abbreviations that people use in which only consonants appear. For example, there is *ltd.* as an abbreviation for *limited.* Similarly, the Hebrew language comprised a series of words made up only of consonants. Thus, by "consonantal text" is meant the Hebrew text without any vowel markings. The consonantal text of the Hebrew manuscripts became fixed in form between the first and second centuries C.E., although manuscripts with variant texts continued to circulate for some time. Alterations were no longer made, unlike the previous period of the Sopherim.

20 The Masoretic Text. In the second half of the first millennium C.E., the Masoretes (Hebrew, *ba·'aleh' ham·ma·soh·rah',* meaning "the Masters of Tradition") established a system of vowel points and accent marks. These served as a written aid in the reading and pronouncing of vowel sounds, whereas previously the pronunciation had been handed down by oral tradition. The Masoretes made no changes whatsoever in the

texts that they transmitted but recorded marginal notes in the Masora as they saw fit. They exercised great care to take no textual liberties. Additionally, in their Masora, they drew attention to textual peculiarities and gave corrected readings they considered necessary.

21 Three schools of Masoretes were engaged in the development of the vocalizing and accent marking of the consonantal text, namely, the Babylonian, Palestinian, and Tiberian. The Hebrew text now presented in printed editions of the Hebrew Bible is known as the Masoretic text and uses the system devised by the Tiberian school. This system was developed by the Masoretes of Tiberias, a city on the western shore of the Sea of Galilee. Footnotes in the *New World Translation* refer many times to the Masoretic text (under the symbol M) and to its marginal notes, the Masora (under the symbol M^margin).*

22 The Palestinian school placed the vowel signs above the consonants. Only a small number of such manuscripts came down to us, showing that this system of vocalization was imperfect. The Babylonian system of vowel pointing was likewise supralinear. A manuscript exhibiting the Babylonian pointing is the Petersburg Codex of the Prophets, of 916 C.E., preserved in the Leningrad Public Library, U.S.S.R. This codex contains Isaiah, Jeremiah, Ezekiel, and the "minor" prophets, with marginal notes (Masora). Scholars have eagerly examined this manuscript and compared it with the Tiberian text. Although it uses the supralinear system of vocalization, it in fact follows the Tiberian text as regards the consonantal text and its vowels and Masora. The British Museum has a copy of the Babylonian text of the Pentateuch, which has been found to be substantially in agreement with the Tiberian text.

23 Dead Sea Scrolls. In 1947 an exciting new chapter in Hebrew manuscript history began. In a cave at Wadi Qumran (Nahal Qumeran), in the area of the Dead Sea, the first Isaiah scroll, together with other Biblical and non-Biblical scrolls, was discovered. Shortly thereafter, a complete photostatic copy of this well-preserved Isaiah scroll (1QIs^a) was published for scholars to study. It is believed to date toward the end of the second century B.C.E. Here, indeed, was an

---

* *Reference Bible,* appendix 2A, "Extraordinary Points."
# *Reference Bible,* appendix 1B, "Scribal Changes Involving the Divine Name."
△ *Reference Bible,* appendix 2B, "Emendations (Corrections) of the Sopherim."

19. What is the Hebrew consonantal text, and when did it become fixed in form?
20. What did the Masoretes do regarding the Hebrew text?

---

* See footnotes at Psalm 60:5; 71:20; 100:3; and 119:79.

21. What is the Masoretic text?
22. What manuscript of the Babylonian line of texts has become available, and how does it compare with the Tiberian text?
23. What series of Hebrew manuscript finds has been made near the Dead Sea?

incredible find—a Hebrew manuscript about a thousand years older than the oldest existing manuscript of the recognized Masoretic text of Isaiah!* Other caves in Qumran surrendered fragments of over 170 scrolls representing parts of all books of the Hebrew Scriptures except Esther. Studies of such scrolls are still in progress.

[24] One scholar reports that his investigation of the lengthy Psalm 119 in one important Dead Sea Scroll of the Psalms (11QPsᵃ) shows it to be in almost complete verbal agreement with the Masoretic text of Psalm 119. Regarding the Psalms Scroll, Professor J. A. Sanders noted: "Most of [the variants] are orthographic and important only to those scholars who are interested in clues to the pronunciation of Hebrew in antiquity, and such matters."# Other examples of these remarkable ancient manuscripts indicate no great variations in most cases. The Isaiah scroll itself, though it shows some differences in spelling and in grammatical construction, does not vary as to doctrinal points. This published Isaiah scroll was examined as to its variations in the preparation of the *New World Translation,* and references are made to it.△

[25] The major lines of transmission of the Hebrew Scriptures have now been discussed. Principally, these are the Samaritan Pentateuch, the Aramaic Targums, the Greek *Septuagint,* the Tiberian Hebrew text, the Palestinian Hebrew text, the Babylonian Hebrew text, and the Hebrew text of the Dead Sea Scrolls. As a result of study and comparison of these texts, we are assured that the Hebrew Scriptures have come down to us today substantially in the form in which inspired servants of God first recorded them.

THE REFINED HEBREW TEXT

[26] The standard printed edition of the Hebrew Bible right into the 19th century was the Second Rabbinic Bible of Jacob ben Chayyim published in 1524-25. It was not until the 18th century that scholars began to advance the critical study of the Hebrew text. In 1776-80, at Oxford, Benjamin Kennicott published variant readings from over 600 Hebrew manuscripts. Then, in 1784-98, at Parma, the Italian scholar J. B. de Rossi published

variant readings of over 800 more manuscripts. Hebrew scholar S. Baer, of Germany, also produced a master text. In more recent times, C. D. Ginsburg devoted many years to producing a critical master text of the Hebrew Bible. This first appeared in 1894, with a final revision in 1926.* Joseph Rotherham used the 1894 edition of this text in producing his English translation, *The Emphasised Bible,* in 1902, and Professor Max L. Margolis and coworkers used the texts of Ginsburg and of Baer in producing their translation of the Hebrew Scriptures in 1917.

[27] In 1906 Hebrew scholar Rudolf Kittel released in Germany the first edition (and later, a second edition) of his refined Hebrew text entitled *Biblia Hebraica,* or "The Hebrew Bible." In this book Kittel provided a textual apparatus through extended footnotes, which collated or compared the many Hebrew manuscripts of the Masoretic text available at that time. He used the generally accepted text by Jacob ben Chayyim as the basic text. When the far older, superior Ben Asher Masoretic texts, which had been standardized about the 10th century C.E., became available, Kittel set out to produce an entirely different third edition of the *Biblia Hebraica.* This work was completed by his associates after his death.

[28] Kittel's *Biblia Hebraica,* the 7th, 8th, and 9th editions (1951-55), provided the basic text used for the Hebrew section of the *New World Translation* in English. A new edition of the Hebrew text, namely *Biblia Hebraica Stuttgartensia,* dated 1977, was used for updating the information presented in the footnotes of the *New World Translation* published in 1984.

[29] Kittel's presentation of the marginal Masora, which captures many textual alterations of pre-Christian scribes, has contributed to accurate renderings in the *New World Translation,* including restorations of the divine name, Jehovah. The ever-increasing field of Biblical scholarship continues to be made available through the *New World Translation.*

[30] Accompanying this study is a chart that sets

---

* *Insight on the Scriptures,* Vol. 1, page 322.
# *The Dead Sea Psalms Scroll,* 1967, J. A. Sanders, page 15.
△ See "1QIsᵃ" in footnotes at Isaiah 7:1; 14:4.

24. How do these manuscripts compare with the Masoretic text, and what use does the *New World Translation* make of them?
25. What Hebrew texts have now been discussed, and of what does their study assure us?
26. (a) When was a critical study of the Hebrew text advanced, and what are some master texts that have been printed? (b) How has the Ginsburg text been used?

---

* See "Gins." in footnote at Leviticus 11:42.

27, 28. (a) What is the *Biblia Hebraica,* and how has it been developed? (b) How has the *New World Translation* used this text?
29. What feature of the *Biblia Hebraica* was of particular value in restoring the divine name?
30. (a) Using the chart on page 308 showing sources for the Hebrew Scripture portion of the text of the *New World Translation,* trace the history of the Hebrew text through to the *Biblia Hebraica* as the main source of the *New World Translation.* (b) What are some of the other sources to which the New World Bible Translation Committee made reference?

out the sources for the text of the Hebrew Scriptures in the *New World Translation*. This chart briefly shows the development of the Hebrew text leading to Kittel's *Biblia Hebraica,* which was the main source used. The secondary sources that were consulted are shown by the white dotted lines. This is not intended to indicate that in the case of such versions as the Latin *Vulgate* and the Greek *Septuagint,* the original works were consulted. As with the inspired Hebrew writings themselves, the originals of these versions are not now extant. These sources were consulted by means of reliable editions of the texts or from dependable ancient translations and critical commentaries. By consulting these various sources, the New World Bible Translation Committee was able to present an authoritative and reliable translation of the original inspired Hebrew Scriptures. These sources are all indicated in the footnotes of the *New World Translation.*

SOME LEADING PAPYRUS MANUSCRIPTS

Symbol	Name of Manuscript	Date	Language	Located at	Approximate Contents	Examples of Use in *New World Translation* —With References (see footnotes for scriptures cited)
— Of the Hebrew Scriptures —						
	Nash Papyrus	2nd or 1st cent. B.C.E.	Hebrew	Cambridge, England	24 lines of Ten Commandments and some verses of Deuteronomy chaps. 5, 6	
957	Rylands 458	2nd cent. B.C.E.	Greek	Manchester, England	Fragments of Deuteronomy chaps. 23-28	
	Fouad 266	1st cent. B.C.E.	Greek	Cairo, Egypt	Portions of Genesis and Deuteronomy	Deut. 18:5; Acts 3:22; appendix 1C
4Q LXX Lev^b	Dead Sea Leviticus Scroll	1st cent. B.C.E.	Greek	Jerusalem, Israel	Fragments of Leviticus	Lev. 3:12; 4:27
963	Chester Beatty 6	2nd cent. C.E.	Greek	Dublin, Ireland, and Ann Arbor, Mich., U.S.A.	Portions of Numbers and Deuteronomy	
967/ 968	Chester Beatty 9, 10	3rd cent. C.E.	Greek	Dublin, Ireland, and Princeton, N.J., U.S.A.	Portions of Ezekiel, Daniel, and Esther	
— Of the Christian Greek Scriptures —						
P¹	Oxyrhynchus 2	3rd cent. C.E.	Greek	Philadelphia, Pa., U.S.A.	Matt. 1:1-9, 12, 14-20	
P²²	Oxyrhynchus 1228	3rd cent. C.E.	Greek	Glasgow, Scotland	Fragments of John chaps. 15, 16	
P³⁷	Michigan 1570	3rd/4th cent. C.E.	Greek	Ann Arbor, Mich., U.S.A.	Matt. 26:19-52	
P⁴⁵	Chester Beatty 1	3rd cent. C.E.	Greek	Dublin, Ireland; Vienna, Austria	Fragments of Matthew, Mark, Luke, John, and Acts	Luke 10:42; John 10:18
P⁴⁶	Chester Beatty 2	c. 200 C.E.	Greek	Dublin, Ireland; Ann Arbor, Mich., U.S.A.	Nine of Paul's letters	Rom. 8:23, 28; 1 Cor. 2:16
P⁴⁷	Chester Beatty 3	3rd cent. C.E.	Greek	Dublin, Ireland	Rev. 9:10–17:2	Rev. 13:18; 15:3
P⁵²	Rylands 457	c. 125 C.E.	Greek	Manchester, England	John 18:31-33, 37, 38	
P⁶⁶	Bodmer 2	c. 200 C.E.	Greek	Geneva, Switzerland	Most of John	John 1:18; 19:39
P⁷²	Bodmer 7, 8	3rd/4th cent. C.E.	Greek	Geneva, Switzerland, and Vatican Library in Rome, Italy	Jude, 1 Peter, and 2 Peter	
P⁷⁵	Bodmer 14, 15	3rd cent. C.E.	Greek	Geneva, Switzerland	Most of Luke and John	Luke 8:26; John 1:18

31 The Hebrew Scripture portion of the *New World Translation* is thus the product of age-long Biblical scholarship and research. It is founded on a text of great integrity, the richly endowed result of faithful textual transmission. With a flow and

style that are arresting, it offers for serious Bible study a translation that is at once honest and accurate. Thanks be to Jehovah, the communicating God, that his Word is alive and exerts power today! (Heb. 4:12) May honesthearted persons continue to build faith through the study of God's precious Word and be aroused to do Jehovah's will during these momentous days.—2 Pet. 1:12, 13.

---

31. (a) Of what, therefore, is the Hebrew Scripture portion of the *New World Translation* the result? (b) What thanks and hope may we thus express?

SOME LEADING VELLUM AND LEATHER MANUSCRIPTS

Sym-bol	Name of Manuscript	Date	Lan-guage	Located at	Approximate Contents	Examples of Use in *New World Translation* —With References (see footnotes for scriptures cited)
Of the Hebrew Scriptures (in Hebrew)						
Al	Aleppo Codex	930 C.E.	Hebrew	Formerly at Aleppo, Syria. Now in Israel.	Large part of Hebrew Scriptures (Ben Asher text)	Josh. 21:37
	British Museum Codex Or4445	10th cent. C.E.	Hebrew	London, England	Most of Pentateuch	
Ca	Cairo Karaite Codex	895 C.E.	Hebrew	Cairo, Egypt	Earlier and later Prophets	Josh. 21:37; 2 Sam. 8:3
B 19^A	Leningrad Codex	1008 C.E.	Hebrew	Leningrad, U.S.S.R.	Hebrew Scriptures	Josh. 21:37; 2 Sam. 8:3; appendix 1A
B 3	Petersburg Codex of the Prophets	916 C.E.	Hebrew	Leningrad, U.S.S.R.	Later Prophets	appendix 2B
1QIs^a	Dead Sea First Isaiah Scroll	End of 2nd cent. B.C.E.	Hebrew	Jerusalem, Israel	Isaiah	Isa. 11:1; 18:2; 41:29
11QPs^a	Dead Sea Psalms Scroll	1st cent. C.E.	Hebrew	Jerusalem, Israel	Portions of 41 of the last third of the Psalms	
Of the *Septuagint* and Christian Greek Scriptures						
א (01)	Sinaiticus	4th cent. C.E.	Greek	London, England	Part of Hebrew Scriptures and all of Greek Scriptures as well as some Apocryphal writings	1 Chron. 12:19; John 5:2; 2 Cor. 12:4
A (02)	Alexandrinus	5th cent. C.E.	Greek	London, England	All of Hebrew and Greek Scriptures (some small portions lost or damaged) as well as some Apocryphal writings	1 Ki. 14:2; Luke 5:39; Acts 13:20; Heb. 3:6
B (03)	Vatican 1209	4th cent. C.E.	Greek	Vatican Library in Rome, Italy	Originally complete Bible. Now missing: Gen. 1:1–46:28; Ps. 106-137; Hebrews after 9:14; 2 Timothy; Titus; Philemon; Revelation	Mark 6:14; John 1:18; 7:53–8:11
C (04)	Ephraemi Syri rescriptus	5th cent. C.E.	Greek	Paris, France	Parts of Hebrew Scriptures (64 leaves) and of the Greek Scriptures (145 leaves)	Acts 9:12; Rom. 8:23, 28, 34
D^ea (05)	Codex Bezae Cantabrigiensis	5th cent. C.E.	Greek-Latin	Cambridge, England	Most of four Gospels and Acts, a few verses of 3 John	Matt. 24:36; Mark 7:16; Luke 15:21 (reference is shown just to symbol "D")
D^p (06)	Codex Claromontanus	6th cent. C.E.	Greek-Latin	Paris, France	Pauline Epistles (including Hebrews)	Gal. 5:12 (reference is shown just to symbol "D")

The Christian Greek Text of the Holy Scriptures

The copying of the text of the Greek Scriptures; its transmission in Greek and other languages to this day; the reliability of the modern text.

THE early Christians were worldwide educators and publishers of the written 'word of Jehovah.' They took seriously Jesus' words just before his ascension: "You will receive power when the holy spirit arrives upon you, and you will be witnesses of me both in Jerusalem and in all Judea and Samaria and to the most distant part of the earth." (Isa. 40:8; Acts 1:8) As Jesus had foretold, the first 120 disciples received the holy spirit, with its energizing force. That was on the day of Pentecost 33 C.E. The same day, Peter spearheaded the new educational program by giving a thorough witness, with the result that many heartily embraced the message and about 3,000 more were added to the newly founded Christian congregation.—Acts 2:14-42.

² Stirred to action as no other group had been in all history, these disciples of Jesus Christ launched a teaching program that eventually overflowed into every corner of the then known world. (Col. 1:23) Yes, these devoted witnesses of Jehovah were eager to use their feet, walking from house to house, from city to city, and from country to country, declaring "good news of good things." (Rom. 10:15) This good news told about Christ's ransom provision, the resurrection hope, and the promised Kingdom of God. (1 Cor. 15:1-3, 20-22, 50; Jas. 2:5) Never before had such a witness concerning things unseen been presented to mankind. It became an "evident demonstration of realities though not beheld," a display of faith, to the many who now accepted Jehovah as their Sovereign Lord on the basis of Jesus' sacrifice. —Heb. 11:1; Acts 4:24; 1 Tim. 1:14-17.

³ These Christian ministers, men and women, were enlightened ministers of God. They could read and write. They were educated in the Holy Scriptures. They were people informed as to world happenings. They were accustomed to travel. They were locustlike in that they permitted no obstacle to hinder their forward movement in spreading the good news. (Acts 2:7-11, 41; Joel 2: 7-11, 25) In that first century of the Common Era, they worked among people who were in many ways very much like people in modern times.

⁴ As progressive preachers of "the word of life," the early Christians made good use of whatever Bible scrolls they could obtain. (Phil. 2:15, 16; 2 Tim. 4:13) Four of them, namely Matthew, Mark, Luke, and John, were inspired by Jehovah to put "the good news about Jesus Christ" into writing. (Mark 1:1; Matt. 1:1) Some of them, such as Peter, Paul, John, James, and Jude, wrote letters under inspiration. (2 Pet. 3:15, 16) Others became copyists of these inspired communications, which were interchanged with benefit among the multiplying congregations. (Col. 4:16) Further, "the apostles and older men in Jerusalem" made doctrinal decisions under the direction of God's spirit, and these were recorded for later use. This central governing body also sent out letters of instruction to the far-flung congregations. (Acts 5:29-32; 15:2, 6, 22-29; 16:4) And for this, they had to provide their own mail service.

⁵ In order to expedite the distribution of the Scriptures, as well as provide them in a form convenient for reference, the early Christians soon started to use the codex form of manuscript in place of scrolls. The codex is similar in form to the modern book, in which the leaves may readily be turned in looking up a reference, instead of the considerable unrolling that was often required in the case of a scroll. Moreover, the codex form made it possible to bind canonical writings together, whereas those in scroll form were usually kept in separate rolls. The early Christians were pioneers in the use of the codex. They may even have invented it. While the codex was only slowly adopted by non-Christian writers, the great majority of Christian papyri of the second and third centuries are in codex form.*

---

* *Insight on the Scriptures,* Vol. 1, pages 354-5.

---

1. How did the Christian educational program get under way?
2. What good news was now proclaimed, and of what was this work of witnessing a demonstration?
3. What characterized the Christian ministers of the first century C.E.?

4. Under Jehovah's inspiration and leading, what writing was done in the days of the early Christian congregation?
5. (a) What is a codex? (b) To what extent did the early Christians use the codex, and what were its advantages?

[6] **The Medium of Koine (Common Greek).** The so-called classical period of the Greek language extended from the ninth century B.C.E. to the fourth century B.C.E. This was the period of the Attic and Ionic dialects. It was during this time, and especially in the fifth and fourth centuries B.C.E., that many Greek dramatists, poets, orators, historians, philosophers, and scientists flourished, of whom Homer, Herodotus, Socrates, Plato, and others became famous. The period from about the fourth century B.C.E. to about the sixth century C.E. was the age of what is known as Koine, or common Greek. Its development was due largely to the military operations of Alexander the Great, whose army was made up of soldiers from all parts of Greece. They spoke different Greek dialects, and as these mingled together, a common dialect, Koine, developed and came into general use. Alexander's conquest of Egypt, and of Asia as far as India, spread Koine among many peoples, so that it became the international language and remained such for many centuries. The Greek vocabulary of the *Septuagint* was the current Koine of Alexandria, Egypt, during the third and second centuries B.C.E.

[7] In the days of Jesus and his apostles, Koine was the international language of the Roman realm. The Bible itself testifies to this fact. When Jesus was nailed to the stake, it was necessary for the inscription over his head to be posted not only in Hebrew, the language of the Jews, but also in Latin, the official language of the land, and in Greek, which was spoken on the streets of Jerusalem almost as frequently as in Rome, Alexandria, or Athens itself. (John 19:19, 20; Acts 6:1) Acts 9:29 shows that Paul preached the good news in Jerusalem to Jews who spoke the Greek language. Koine was by that time a dynamic, living, well-developed tongue—a language ready at hand and well suited for Jehovah's lofty purpose in further communicating the divine Word.

THE GREEK TEXT AND ITS TRANSMISSION

[8] In the preceding study, we learned that Jehovah preserved his waters of truth in a reservoir of written documents—the inspired Hebrew Scriptures. However, what of the Scriptures written down by the apostles and other disciples of Jesus Christ? Have these been preserved for us with like care? An examination of the vast reservoir of manuscripts preserved in Greek, as well as in other languages, shows that they have. As already explained, this part of the Bible canon comprises 27 books. Consider the lines of textual transmission of these 27 books, which show how the original Greek text has been preserved down to this present day.

[9] **The Fountain of Greek Manuscripts.** The 27 canonical books of the Christian Scriptures were written in the common Greek of the day. However, the book of Matthew was apparently written first in Biblical Hebrew, to serve the Jewish people. The fourth-century Bible translator Jerome states this, saying that it was later translated into Greek.* Matthew himself probably made this translation—having been a Roman civil servant, a tax collector, he without doubt knew Hebrew, Latin, and Greek.—Mark 2:14-17.

[10] The other Christian Bible writers, Mark, Luke, John, Paul, Peter, James, and Jude, all wrote their documents in Koine, the common, living language that was understood by the Christians and most other people of the first century. The last of the original documents was written by John about 98 C.E. As far as is known, none of these 27 original manuscripts in Koine have survived to this day. However, from this original fountainhead, there have flowed to us copies of the originals, copies of copies, and families of copies, to form a vast reservoir of manuscripts of the Christian Greek Scriptures.

[11] **A Reservoir of Over 13,000 Manuscripts.** A tremendous fund of manuscript copies of all 27 canonical books is available today. Some of these cover extensive portions of Scripture; others are mere fragments. According to one calculation, there are over 5,000 manuscripts in the original Greek. In addition, there are over 8,000 manuscripts in various other languages—a total exceeding 13,000 manuscripts all together. Dating from the 2nd century C.E. to the 16th century C.E., they all help in determining the true, original text. The oldest of these many manuscripts is the papyrus fragment of the Gospel of John in the John Rylands Library in Manchester, England, known by the number P[52], which is dated to the first half of the second century, possibly

---

6. (a) When was the period of classical Greek, what did it include, and when did Koine, or common Greek, develop? (b) How and to what extent did Koine come into general use?
7. (a) How does the Bible testify to the use of Koine in the time of Jesus and his apostles? (b) Why was Koine well suited for communicating God's Word?
8. Why do we now examine the reservoir of Greek Scripture manuscripts?

---

* See page 176, paragraph 6.

---

9. (a) In what language were the Christian Scriptures written? (b) What exception is noted with Matthew?
10. How have the Bible writings come down to us?
11. (a) What fund of manuscript copies is available today? (b) How do these contrast with classical works as to quantity and age?

about 125 C.E.* Thus, this copy was written only a quarter of a century or so after the original. When we consider that for ascertaining the text of most classical authors, only a handful of manuscripts are available, and these are seldom within centuries of the original writings, we can appreciate what a wealth of evidence there is to assist in arriving at an authoritative text of the Christian Greek Scriptures.

[12] **Papyrus Manuscripts.** As with early copies of the *Septuagint,* the first manuscripts of the Christian Greek Scriptures were written on papyrus, and this continued to be used for Bible manuscripts until about the fourth century C.E. The Bible writers also apparently used papyrus when they sent letters to the Christian congregations.

[13] Great quantities of papyrus writings have been located in the province of Faiyūm, in Egypt. In the late 19th century, a number of Biblical papyri were brought to light. One of the most important of all modern-day manuscript finds was a discovery made public in 1931. It consisted of parts of 11 codices, containing portions of 8 different books of the inspired Hebrew Scriptures and 15 books of the Christian Greek Scriptures, all in Greek. These papyri range in date of writing from the second century to the fourth century of the Common Era. Much of the Christian Greek Scripture portions of this find are now in the Chester Beatty Collections and are listed as P^{45}, P^{46}, and P^{47}, the symbol "P" standing for "Papyrus."

[14] Papyri of another remarkable collection were published in Geneva, Switzerland, from 1956 to 1961. Known as the Bodmer Papyri, they include early texts of two Gospels (P^{66} and P^{75}) dating from the early third century C.E. The table preceding this study lists some of the outstanding ancient Bible papyri of the Hebrew and Christian Greek Scriptures. In the last column, there are cited passages in the *New World Translation of the Holy Scriptures* where these papyrus manuscripts give support to the renderings made, and this is indicated in the footnotes on those verses.

[15] The discoveries of these papyri supply proof that the Bible canon was completed at a very early date. Among the Chester Beatty Papyri, two codices—one binding together parts of the four Gos-

---

* *Insight on the Scriptures,* Vol. 1, page 323; *New Bible Dictionary,* second edition, 1986, J. D. Douglas, page 1187.

---

12. On what were the first manuscripts written?
13. What important papyrus find was made public in the year 1931?
14, 15. (a) What are some outstanding papyrus manuscripts of the Christian Greek Scriptures listed in the table on page 313? (b) Indicate how the *New World Translation* has made use of these manuscripts. (c) What do the early papyrus codices confirm?

pels and Acts (P^{45}) and another bringing within its covers 9 of the 14 letters of Paul (P^{46})—show that the inspired Christian Greek Scriptures were assembled shortly after the death of the apostles. Since it would have taken time for these codices to circulate widely and find their way down into Egypt, it is apparent that these Scriptures had been collected into their standard form by the second century, at the latest. Thus, by the end of the second century, there was no question but that the canon of the Christian Greek Scriptures was closed, completing the canon of the entire Bible.

[16] **Vellum and Leather Manuscripts.** As we learned in the previous study, the more durable vellum, a fine grade of parchment generally made from calf, lamb, or goat skins, began to be used in place of papyrus in writing manuscripts from about the fourth century C.E. on. Some very important Bible manuscripts in existence today are recorded on vellum. We have already discussed the vellum and leather manuscripts of the Hebrew Scriptures. The table on page 314 lists some of the outstanding vellum and leather manuscripts for both the Christian Greek and the Hebrew Scriptures. Those listed of the Greek Scriptures were written entirely in capital letters and are referred to as uncials. The *New Bible Dictionary* reports 274 uncial manuscripts of the Christian Greek Scriptures, and these date from the fourth century C.E. to the tenth century C.E. Then there are the more than 5,000 cursive, or minuscule, manuscripts, made in a running style of writing.* These, also on vellum, were written during the period from the ninth century C.E. to the inception of printing. Because of their early date and general accuracy, the uncial manuscripts were extensively used by the New World Bible Translation Committee in making careful renderings from the Greek text. This is indicated in the table "Some Leading Vellum and Leather Manuscripts."

ERA OF TEXTUAL CRITICISM AND REFINING

[17] **Erasmus' Text.** Throughout the long centuries of the Dark Ages, when the Latin language dominated and Western Europe was under the iron control of the Roman Catholic Church, scholarship and learning were at a low ebb. However, with the European invention of printing from movable type in the 15th century and the Reformation of the early 16th century, more freedom prevailed, and there was a rebirth of interest in

---

* *New Bible Dictionary,* second edition, page 1187.

---

16. (a) What uncial manuscripts of the Christian Greek Scriptures have survived to this day? (b) To what extent have the uncial manuscripts been used in the *New World Translation,* and why?
17. (a) What two events led to increased study of the Greek text of the Bible? (b) For what work is Erasmus noted? (c) How is a printed master text constructed?

the Greek language. It was during this early revival of learning that the famous Dutch scholar Desiderius Erasmus produced his first edition of a master Greek text of the "New Testament." (Such a printed master text is prepared by carefully comparing a number of manuscripts and using the words most generally agreed upon as original, often including, in an apparatus below, notes about any variant readings in some manuscripts.) This first edition was printed in Basel, Switzerland, in 1516, one year before the Reformation started in Germany. The first edition had many errors, but an improved text was presented in succeeding editions in 1519, 1522, 1527, and 1535. Erasmus had only a few late cursive manuscripts available to him for collating and preparing his master text.

[18] Erasmus' refined Greek text became the basis for better translations into several of the Western European languages. This made possible the production of versions superior to those that had been translated previously from the Latin *Vulgate*. First to use Erasmus' text was Martin Luther of Germany, who completed his translation of the Christian Greek Scriptures into German in 1522. In the face of much persecution, William Tyndale of England followed with his English translation from Erasmus' text, completing this while in exile on the continent of Europe in 1525. Antonio Brucioli of Italy translated Erasmus' text into Italian in 1530. With the advent of Erasmus' Greek text, there was now opening up an era of textual criticism. Textual criticism is the method used for reconstruction and restoration of the original Bible text.

[19] **Division Into Chapters and Verses.** Robert Estienne, or Stephanus, was prominent as a printer and editor in the 16th century in Paris. Being an editor, he saw the practical benefit of using a system of chapters and verses for ready reference, and so he introduced this system in his Greek-Latin New Testament in 1551. Verse divisions were first made for the Hebrew Scriptures by the Masoretes, but it was Stephanus' French Bible of 1553 that first showed the present divisions for the complete Bible. This was followed in subsequent English-language Bibles and made possible the production of Bible concordances such as the one by Alexander Cruden in 1737 and the two exhaustive concordances to the Authorized Version of the English Bible—Robert Young's, first published in Edinburgh in 1873, and James Strong's, published in New York in 1894.

[20] ***Textus Receptus.*** Stephanus also issued several editions of the Greek "New Testament." These were based mainly on Erasmus' text, with corrections according to the Complutensian Polyglott of 1522 and 15 late cursive manuscripts of the previous few centuries. Stephanus' third edition of his Greek text in 1550 became in effect the *Textus Receptus* (Latin for "received text") upon which were based other 16th-century English versions and the *King James Version* of 1611.

[21] **Refined Greek Texts.** Later, Greek scholars produced increasingly refined texts. Outstanding was that produced by J. J. Griesbach, who had access to the hundreds of Greek manuscripts that had become available toward the end of the 18th century. The best edition of Griesbach's entire Greek text was published 1796-1806. His master text was the basis for Sharpe's English translation in 1840 and is the Greek text printed in *The Emphatic Diaglott,* first published complete in 1864. Other excellent texts were produced by Konstantin von Tischendorf (1872) and Hermann von Soden (1910), the latter serving as the basis for Moffatt's English version of 1913.

[22] **Westcott and Hort Text.** A Greek master text that has attained wide acceptance is that produced by the Cambridge University scholars B. F. Westcott and F. J. A. Hort, in 1881. Proofs of Westcott and Hort's Greek text were consulted by the British Revision Committee, of which Westcott and Hort were members, for their revision of the "New Testament" of 1881. This master text is the one that was used principally in translating the Christian Greek Scriptures into English in the *New World Translation.* This text is also the foundation for the following translations into English: *The Emphasised Bible,* the *American Standard Version, An American Translation* (Smith-Goodspeed), and the *Revised Standard Version.** This last translation also used Nestle's text.

[23] Nestle's Greek text (the 18th edition, 1948) was also used by the New World Bible Translation Committee for the purpose of comparison. The committee also referred to those by Catholic Jesuit scholars José M. Bover (1943) and Augustinus Merk (1948). The United Bible Societies text of 1975 and the Nestle-Aland text of 1979 were

---

* See the chart "Some Leading Bible Translations in Seven Principal Languages," on page 322.

---

18. What did Erasmus' text make possible, and who made good use of it?
19. What is the history of the division of the Bible into chapters and verses, and what has this made possible?
20. What was the *Textus Receptus,* and for what did it become the basis?
21. What refined texts have been produced since the 18th century, and how have they been used?
22. (a) What Greek text has attained wide acceptance? (b) As a basis for what English translations has it been used?
23. What other texts were used for the *New World Translation?*

consulted to update the footnotes of the 1984 Reference Edition.*

24 Ancient Versions From the Greek. In addition to the Greek manuscripts, there are also available for study today many manuscripts of translations of the Christian Greek Scriptures into other languages. There are more than 50 manuscripts (or fragments) of Old Latin versions and thousands of manuscripts of Jerome's Latin *Vulgate.* The New World Bible Translation Committee referred to these, as well as to the Coptic, Armenian, and Syriac versions.#

25 From at least the 14th century onward, translations of the Greek Scriptures into the Hebrew language have been produced. These are of interest in that a number of them have made restorations of the divine name into the Christian Scriptures. The *New World Translation* makes many references to these Hebrew versions under the symbol "J" with a superior number. For details, see the foreword of the *New World Translation of the Holy Scriptures—With References,* pages 9-10, and appendix 1D, "The Divine Name in the Christian Greek Scriptures."

TEXTUAL VARIATIONS AND THEIR MEANING

26 Among the more than 13,000 manuscripts of the Christian Greek Scriptures, there are many textual variations. The 5,000 manuscripts in the Greek language alone show many such differences. We can well understand that each copy made from early manuscripts would contain its own distinctive scribal errors. As any one of these early manuscripts was sent to an area for use, these errors would be repeated in the copies in that area and would become characteristic of other manuscripts there. It was in this way that families of similar manuscripts grew up. So are not the thousands of scribal errors to be viewed with alarm? Do they not indicate lack of faithfulness in the transmission of the text? Not at all!

27 F. J. A. Hort, who was coproducer of the Westcott and Hort text, writes: "The great bulk of the words of the New Testament stand out above all discriminative processes of criticism, because they are free from variation, and need only to be

transcribed. . . . If comparative trivialities . . . are set aside, the words in our opinion still subject to doubt can hardly amount to more than a thousandth part of the whole New Testament."*

28 Evaluation of Textual Transmission. What, then, is the net evaluation as to textual integrity and authenticity, after these many centuries of transmission? Not only are there thousands of manuscripts to compare but discoveries of older Bible manuscripts during the past few decades take the Greek text back as far as about the year 125 C.E., just a couple of decades short of the death of the apostle John about 100 C.E. These manuscript evidences provide strong assurance that we now have a dependable Greek text in refined form. Note the evaluation that the former director and librarian of the British Museum, Sir Frederic Kenyon, put on this matter:

29 "The interval then between the dates of original composition and the earliest extant evidence becomes so small as to be in fact negligible, and the last foundation for any doubt that the Scriptures have come down to us substantially as they were written has now been removed. Both the *authenticity* and the *general integrity* of the books of the New Testament may be regarded as finally established. General integrity, however, is one thing, and certainty as to details is another."#

30 As to the last observation on "certainty as to details," the quotation in paragraph 27 by Dr. Hort covers this. It is the work of the textual refiners to rectify details, and this they have done to a large degree. For this reason, the Westcott and Hort refined Greek text is generally accepted as one of high excellence. The Christian Greek Scripture portion of the *New World Translation,* being based on this excellent Greek text, is thus able to give its readers the faithful "saying of Jehovah," as this has been so wonderfully preserved for us in the Greek reservoir of manuscripts.—1 Pet. 1:24, 25.

31 Of further interest are the comments of Sir Frederic Kenyon in his book *Our Bible and the Ancient Manuscripts,* 1962, on page 249: "We must be content to know that the general

---

* *The Kingdom Interlinear Translation of the Greek Scriptures,* 1985, pages 8-9.
# See footnotes at Luke 24:40; John 5:4; Acts 19:23; 27:37; and Revelation 3:16.

---

24. To what ancient versions has the *New World Translation* also referred? What are some examples?
25. Of what special interest are the Hebrew-language versions that are referred to in the *New World Translation?*
26. How did textual variations and manuscript families arise?
27. What assurance do we have as to the integrity of the Greek text?

---

* *The New Testament in the Original Greek,* 1974, Vol. I, page 561.
# *The Bible and Archaeology,* 1940, pages 288-9.

28, 29. (a) What must be our net evaluation of the refined Greek text? (b) What authoritative statement do we have on this?
30. Why can we be confident that the *New World Translation* is providing for its readers the faithful "saying of Jehovah"?
31. (a) What have modern discoveries shown as to the text of the Greek Scriptures? (b) How does the chart on page 309 indicate the principal source for the Christian Greek Scripture portion of the *New World Translation,* and what are some of the secondary sources that were used?

authenticity of the New Testament text has been remarkably supported by the modern discoveries which have so greatly reduced the interval between the original autographs and our earliest extant manuscripts, and that the differences of reading, interesting as they are, do not affect the fundamental doctrines of the Christian faith." As shown on page 309 in the chart, "Sources for the Text of the New World Translation—Christian Greek Scriptures," all related documents have been drawn on to provide an accurately translated English text. Valuable footnotes back up all these faithful renderings. The New World Bible Translation Committee used the best results of Bible scholarship developed through the centuries in producing its fine translation. What confidence we may have today that the Christian Greek Scriptures, as they are now available to us, do indeed contain "the pattern of healthful words" as written down by the inspired disciples of Jesus Christ. May we keep holding to these precious words in faith and in love!—2 Tim. 1:13.

32 Both this and the preceding study have been devoted to a discussion of the manuscripts and text of the Holy Scriptures. Why has this been given such exhaustive treatment? The purpose has been to show conclusively that the texts of both the Hebrew and the Greek Scriptures are essentially the same as the authentic, original text that Jehovah inspired faithful men of old to record. Those original writings were inspired. The copyists, though skilled, were not inspired. (Ps. 45:1; 2 Pet. 1:20, 21; 3:16) Hence, it has been necessary to sift through the vast reservoir of manuscript copies in order to identify clearly and unmistakably the pure waters of truth as they originally poured forth from the Great Fountainhead, Jehovah. All thanks go to Jehovah for the marvelous gift of his Word, the inspired Bible, and the refreshing Kingdom message that flows forth from its pages!

32. Why has considerable space been devoted here to a discussion of the manuscripts and text of the Holy Scriptures, and with what satisfying result?

Study Number 7

The Bible in Modern Times

The history of Bible societies; the Watch Tower Society's work in printing and publishing Bibles; the production of the *New World Translation*.

THE Holy Scriptures, the 66 inspired books that we know today as the Bible, contain "the word of Jehovah" put down in writing. (Isa. 66:5) Through many centuries this "word" flowed freely from Jehovah to his prophets and servants on earth. These divine communications accomplished their immediate purpose and also gave powerful foregleams of events certain to take place in the then distant future. It was not always required of God's prophets that they put down in writing "the word of Jehovah" that was relayed to them. For example, some of the utterances of Elijah and Elisha that were made for the generation of their time have not been preserved in written form. On the other hand, the prophets Moses, Isaiah, Jeremiah, Habakkuk, and others received specific orders to "write down" or to 'write in a book or scroll' "the word of Jehovah"

that was revealed to them. (Ex. 17:14; Isa. 30:8; Jer. 30:2; Hab. 2:2; Rev. 1:11) "The sayings previously spoken by the holy prophets" were thus preserved, along with other holy writings, to arouse the clear thinking faculties of Jehovah's servants and especially to provide guidance concerning "the last days."—2 Pet. 3:1-3.

2 Much copying of the inspired Hebrew Scriptures was done from Ezra's time forward. Beginning in the first century of the Common Era, the Bible was copied and recopied by the early Christians and was used in witnessing concerning Jehovah's purposes with regard to His Christ throughout the length and breadth of the then known world. When printing from movable type became common (from the 15th century onward), further impetus was given to multiplying and distributing copies of the Bible. Much translation as well as printing was undertaken by private groups in the

1. (a) For what purposes were divine communications given, and why were some therefore not recorded? (b) What specific orders did Jehovah give to many of the prophets, and with what benefit for us in "the last days"?

2. What periods in history have been noted for increased activity in Bible copying and translation?

16th and 17th centuries. As early as 1800, the Bible had appeared in whole or in part in 71 languages.

BIBLE SOCIETIES

³ Greater momentum was given this work in the 19th and 20th centuries, when newly formed Bible societies began to take a hand in the gigantic task of distributing the Bible. One of the earliest of these Bible societies was the British and Foreign Bible Society, which was organized in London in 1804. The organizing of this Bible society triggered the establishment of many more such societies.*

⁴ With so many Bible societies operating, the work of spreading the Bible flourished. By the year 1900, the Bible had appeared in whole or in part in 567 languages, and by 1928, in 856 languages. By 1938 the thousand mark was passed, and now the Bible is available in more than 1,900 languages. Jehovah's refreshing word of life has overspread the earth! Thus, it has become possible for men of all nations to answer the call: "Praise Jehovah, all you nations, and let all the peoples praise him." (Rom. 15:11) The chart on page 322, "Some Leading Bible Translations in Seven Principal Languages," gives further information on modern-day Bible distribution.

⁵ Though making the Bible available to the multitudes of the earth is a commendable work, the putting of these Bibles to use in giving the people Bible understanding is an even more important task. It was the conveying of "the sense" of the word that was important in Jewish and early Christian times, when few Bibles were available, and this is still the most important thing. (Matt. 13:23; Neh. 8:8) However, this work of teaching God's Word to the peoples of all the earth has been speeded up by the wide distribution of the Bible. As Jehovah's Witnesses today press forward with their globe-encircling work of Bible education,

they are grateful that millions of Bibles are now available in many lands and languages.

JEHOVAH'S WITNESSES AS BIBLE PUBLISHERS

⁶ Witnesses of Jehovah are Bible-publishing people. This was so in the days of Ezra. It was so in the days of the early disciples of Jesus Christ, who saturated the ancient world with their handwritten copies of the Bible to such an extent that the rich legacy we have received of their manuscript writings surpasses that of any other ancient literature. Now, in these modern times, the same kind of energetic Bible-publishing activity characterizes Jehovah's Witnesses.

⁷ In 1884 Jehovah's Witnesses formed a corporation for carrying on their Bible-publishing work, the corporation being now known as the Watch Tower Bible and Tract Society of Pennsylvania. At first Bibles were purchased from other Bible societies for redistribution by these Witnesses, who were even then developing their characteristic house-to-house ministry. The *King James Version* of 1611 in English was used as their basic version for Bible study.

⁸ True to its name, the Watch Tower Bible and Tract Society has engaged in distributing Bibles, as well as publishing books, tracts, and other Christian literature. This has been for the purpose of instruction in the correct teachings of God's Word. Its Bible education has helped lovers of righteousness to break away from false religious tradition and worldly philosophy and to return to the freedom of Bible truth as revealed through Jesus and other devoted spokesmen for Jehovah. (John 8:31, 32) From the time that the magazine *The Watchtower* began to be published in 1879, the publications of the Watch Tower Society have quoted, cited, and referred to scores of different Bible translations. Thus, the Society has recognized the value of all of them and has made use of the good in all of them as being of value in clearing away religious confusion and setting forth the message of God.

⁹ **Rotherham and Holman Bibles.** In 1896 Jehovah's Witnesses, by means of the Watch Tower Society, entered directly into the field as publishers and distributors of the Bible. In that year

---

* Among the many Bible societies formed since 1804 are the American Bible Society (1816), formed out of already existing local societies, as well as the Edinburgh Bible Society (1809) and the Glasgow Bible Society (1812), both later incorporated (1861) into the National Bible Society of Scotland. By 1820 Bible societies had also been formed in Switzerland, Ireland, France, Finland, Sweden, Denmark, Norway, the Netherlands, Iceland, Russia, and Germany.

---

3. What factor has greatly contributed to the increase in Bible distribution since the beginning of the 19th century?
4. (a) What statistics prove that the word of life has indeed overspread the earth? (b) What helpful information is supplied on the chart on page 322 about the different Bible versions listed? Illustrate this by reference to some specific Bible version.
5. What is even more important than Bible distribution, yet for what are Jehovah's Witnesses thankful?

6. Witnesses of Jehovah have been characterized by what activity today as well as in ancient times?
7. What corporation did Jehovah's Witnesses form? when? and how did they start to develop their ministry at that time?
8. (a) How has the Watch Tower Bible and Tract Society been true to its name? (b) How has the Society made use of many Bible translations, and to what end?
9. How did the Society enter the field of Bible publishing?

SOME LEADING BIBLE TRANSLATIONS IN SEVEN PRINCIPAL LANGUAGES

Name of Version	Originally Published	Basic Text for Hebrew Scriptures	Divine Name Rendered	Basic Text for Greek Scriptures
ENGLISH				
Rheims-Douay*	1582-1610	Vulgate	Lord (ADONAI, twice)	Vulgate
King James Version*	1611	M	LORD (Jehovah, few)	Received Text
Young	1862-98	M	Jehovah	Received Text
English Revised*	1881-95	M	LORD (Jehovah, few)	Westcott and Hort
Emphasised Bible	1878-1902	M (Ginsburg)	Yahweh	Westcott and Hort, Tregelles
American Standard	1901	M	Jehovah	Westcott and Hort
An American Translation (Smith-Goodspeed)*	1923-39	M	LORD (Yahweh, few)	Westcott and Hort
Revised Standard*	1946-52	M	LORD	Westcott and Hort, Nestle
New English Bible*	1961-70	M (BHK)	LORD (Jehovah, few)	New eclectic text
Today's English Version	1966-76	M (BHK)	LORD	UBS
New King James Bible/ Revised Authorised Version	1979-82	M (BHS)	LORD (YAH, few)	Majority Text
New Jerusalem Bible*	1985	M	Yahweh	Greek
SPANISH				
Valera	1602	M	Jehová	Received Text
Moderna	1893	M	Jehová	Scrivener
Nácar-Colunga*	1944	M	Yavé	Greek
Evaristo Martín Nieto*	1964	M	Yavé	Greek
Serafín de Ausejo*	1965	M (BHK)	Yahvéh, Señor	Nestle-Aland
Biblia de Jerusalén*	1967	M	Yahveh	Greek
Cantera-Iglesias*	1975	M (BHK)	Yahveh	Greek
Nueva Biblia Española*	1975	M	Señor	Greek
PORTUGUESE				
Almeida	1681, 1750	M	Jehovah	Received Text
Figueiredo*	1778-90	Vulgate	Senhor	Vulgate
Matos Soares*	1927-30	Vulgate	Senhor	Vulgate
Pontifício Instituto Bíblico*	1967	M	Javé	Merk
Jerusalém*	1976, 1981	M	Iahweh	Greek
GERMAN				
Luther*	1522, 1534	M	HErr	Erasmus
Zürcher	1531	M	Herr, Jahwe	Greek
Elberfelder	1855, 1871	M	Jehova	Received Text
Menge	1926	M	HErr	Greek
Luther (revised)*	1964, 1984	M	HERR	Greek
Bibel in heutigem Deutsch (Gute Nachricht)*	1967	M (BHS)	Herr	Nestle-Aland, UBS
Einheitsübersetzung*	1972, 1974	M	Herr, Jahwe	Greek
Revidierte Elberfelder	1975, 1985	M	HERR, Jahwe	Greek
FRENCH				
Darby	1859, 1885	M	Eternel	Greek
Crampon*	1894-1904	M	Jéhovah	Merk
Jérusalem*	1948-54	Vulgate, Hebrew	Yahvé	Vulgate, Greek
TOB Ecumenical Bible*	1971-75	M (BHS)	Seigneur	Nestle, UBS
Osty*	1973	M	Yahvé	Greek
Segond Revised	1978	M (BHS)	Eternel	Nestle-Aland, Black, Metzger, Wikgren
Français courant	1982	M (BHS)	Seigneur	Nestle, UBS
DUTCH (NETHERLANDS)				
Statenvertaling	1637	M	HEERE	Received Text
Leidse Vertaling	1899-1912	M	Jahwe	Nestle
Petrus-Canisiusvertaling*	1929-39	M	Jahweh	Nestle
NBG-vertaling	1939-51	M	HERE	Nestle
Willibrordvertaling*	1961-75	M	Jahwe	Nestle
Groot Nieuws Bijbel*	1972-83	M	Heer	Nestle
ITALIAN				
Diodati	1607, 1641	M	Signore	Greek
Riveduta (Luzzi)	1921-30	M	Eterno	Greek
Nardoni*	1960	M	Signore, Jahweh	Greek
Pontificio Istituto Biblico*	1923-58	M	Signore, Jahve	Merk
Garofalo*	1960	M	Jahve, Signore	Greek
Concordata*	1968	M (BHK)	Signore, Iavè	Nestle, Merk
CEI*	1971	M	Signore	Greek
Parola del Signore*	1976-85	M (BHS)	Signore	UBS

* An asterisk denotes that the Apocrypha was included but may not appear in all editions.
"M" refers to the Masoretic text. When it stands alone, no special edition of the Masoretic text is specified.
"BHK" refers to Kittel's *Biblia Hebraica*.
"UBS" refers to *The Greek New Testament*, by United Bible Societies.
"BHS" refers to *Biblia Hebraica Stuttgartensia*.
"Greek" indicates translation made from the Greek, but no special text indicated.

printing rights were obtained from the British Bible translator Joseph B. Rotherham to publish in the United States the revised twelfth edition of his *New Testament.* On the title page of these printed copies, there appeared the name of the Watch Tower Bible and Tract Society, Allegheny, Pennsylvania, the Society's headquarters being located there at the time. In 1901 arrangements were made for a special printing of the *Holman Linear Bible,* containing marginal explanatory notes from the Society's publications of 1895 to 1901. The Bible text itself presented the *King James Version* and the *Revised Version* of the Hebrew and Greek Scriptures. The entire edition of 5,000 copies had been distributed by the year 1903.

¹⁰ **The Emphatic Diaglott.** In 1902 the Watch Tower Society came to be the copyright owners, sole publishers, and distributors of *The Emphatic Diaglott.* This version of the Christian Greek Scriptures was prepared by the English-born Bible translator Benjamin Wilson, of Geneva, Illinois. It was completed in 1864. It used the Greek text of J. J. Griesbach, with a literal interlinear English translation and Wilson's own version to the right using his special signs of emphasis.

¹¹ **A Bible Students Edition.** In 1907 the Watch Tower Society published a "Bible Students Edition" of the Bible. This volume contained a clear printing of the King James Version of the Bible and included excellent marginal notes, together with a valuable appendix designed by Jehovah's Witnesses. The appendix, which was later enlarged to over 550 pages, was called the "Berean Bible Teachers Manual" and was also published in separate book form. It contained brief comments on many of the verses of the Bible, with references to *The Watchtower* and to the Society's textbooks, and an epitome of doctrinal topics with key scriptures to facilitate their presentation to others. This was similar in form to the Society's later publication *"Make Sure of All Things."* Also included were a topical index, explanations of difficult texts, a list of spurious passages, a Scripture index, a comparative chronology, and 12 maps. This excellent Bible served Jehovah's Witnesses for decades in their public preaching work.

A BIBLE PRINTING SOCIETY

¹² For 30 years the Watch Tower Society engaged outside firms to do the actual printing of its Bibles. However, in December 1926, *The Emphat-*

ic Diaglott became the first Bible version to be printed on the Society's own presses at Brooklyn, New York. The printing of this edition of the Christian Greek Scriptures stimulated the hope that a complete Bible would someday be printed on the Society's presses.

¹³ **The King James Version.** World War II underlined the need for independent publication of the Bible itself. While the global conflict was at its height, the Society succeeded in purchasing plates of the complete King James Version of the Bible. It was on September 18, 1942, at the New World Theocratic Assembly of Jehovah's Witnesses, with key assembly point at Cleveland, Ohio, that the Society's president spoke on the subject "Presenting 'the Sword of the Spirit.'" As the climax to this address, he released this first complete Bible printed in the Watch Tower Society's Brooklyn factory. In its appendix it provided a list of proper names with their meanings, a specially prepared "Concordance of Bible Words and Expressions," and other helps. An appropriate running head was provided at the top of each page. For example, "Jephthah's earnest vow" replaced the traditional "Jephthah's rash vow" at Judges 11, and "Prehuman existence and human birth of God's Word" appeared at John chapter 1.

¹⁴ **The American Standard Version.** Another important Bible translation is the *American Standard Version* of 1901. It has the most commendable feature of rendering God's name as "Jehovah" nearly 7,000 times in the Hebrew Scriptures. After long negotiations, the Watch Tower Society was able to purchase, in 1944, the *use* of the plates of the complete American Standard Version of the Bible for printing on its own presses. On August 10, 1944, at Buffalo, New York, the key city of 17 simultaneous assemblies of Jehovah's Witnesses linked together by private telephone lines, the Society's president delighted his large audience by releasing the Watch Tower edition of the *American Standard Version.* The appendix includes a most helpful expanded "Concordance of Bible Words, Names, and Expressions." A pocket edition of the same Bible was published in 1958.

¹⁵ **The Bible in Living English.** In 1972 the Watch Tower Society produced *The Bible in Living English,* by the late Steven T. Byington. It consistently renders the divine name as "Jehovah."

---

10. What version of the Greek Scriptures did the Society become publishers of in 1902?
11. When did the Society publish the "Bible Students Edition," and what did this contain?
12. When did the Society enter the field of Bible printing?

---

13. (a) What was the first complete Bible printed by the Society, and when was it released? (b) What helps did it contain?
14. What improved translation of the Bible was printed by the Society in 1944, and what features does this Bible have?
15. What translation was produced by the Society in 1972?

[16] Thus, not only are Jehovah's Witnesses preaching the good news of God's established Kingdom in more than 200 countries and islands throughout the earth but they have also become printers and publishers, on a large scale, of the priceless Book that contains that Kingdom message, the Holy Scriptures inspired by Jehovah God.

NEW WORLD TRANSLATION OF THE HOLY SCRIPTURES

[17] Jehovah's Witnesses acknowledge their indebtedness to all the many Bible versions that they have used in studying the truth of the Word of God. However, all these translations, even down to the very latest, have their defects. There are inconsistencies or unsatisfactory renderings, which are infected with sectarian traditions or worldly philosophies and hence are not in full harmony with the sacred truths that Jehovah has recorded in his Word. Particularly since 1946, the president of the Watch Tower Bible and Tract Society had been in quest of a faithful translation of the Scriptures from the original languages —a translation just as understandable to modern readers as the original writings were understandable to intelligent, ordinary people of the Bible-writing era itself.

[18] On September 3, 1949, at the Brooklyn headquarters of the Society, the president announced to the Board of Directors the existence of the New World Bible Translation Committee and that it had completed a modern translation of the Christian Greek Scriptures. The committee's document was read, by which the committee assigned the possession, control, and publication of the translation manuscript to the Society, in recognition of the Society's unsectarian work of promoting Bible education throughout the earth. Portions of the manuscript were also read, as examples of the nature and quality of the translation. The directors were unanimous in accepting the gift of the translation, and arrangements were made for its immediate printing. Typesetting began on September 29, 1949, and by early summer of 1950, tens of thousands of copies were completed in bound form.

[19] **Releasing the New World Translation in Its Parts.** It was on Wednesday, August 2, 1950, on the fourth day of their international assembly at Yankee Stadium, New York, that a totally surprised audience of 82,075 of Jehovah's Witnesses heartily accepted the release of the New World Translation of the Christian Greek Scriptures. Encouraged by the initial enthusiastic reception, as well as by later expressions of appreciation for the translation's merits, the Committee next undertook the extensive work of translating the Hebrew Scriptures. This appeared in five additional volumes, released successively from 1953 to 1960. The set of six volumes formed a library of the entire Bible in modern English. Each volume also contained valuable aids to Bible study. A vast storehouse of Scriptural information was thus made available to the modern-day student of the Bible. Diligent effort had been made to draw on every reliable source of textual information so that the New World Translation would express clearly and accurately the powerful message of the original inspired Scriptures.

[20] Among the Bible study aids in the six-part first edition of the New World Translation was the invaluable collection of textual footnotes, giving background to the renderings. In these notes powerful arguments in defense of the Scriptures were made available. A valuable chain-reference system was also included. These chains of important doctrinal words were designed to direct the student to a series of key texts on these subjects. There were numerous cross-references in the margins of the pages. These directed the reader to (a) parallel words, (b) parallel thoughts, ideas, and events, (c) biographic information, (d) geographic information, (e) fulfillments of prophecies, and (f) direct quotations in or from other parts of the Bible. In the volumes were also important forewords, illustrations of some ancient manuscripts, helpful appendixes and indexes, and maps of Bible lands and locations. This first edition of the New World Translation provided a gold mine for personal Bible study and for beneficial teaching of honesthearted persons by Jehovah's Witnesses. A special student's edition, published in one volume in a printing of 150,000 copies, was later released on June 30, 1963, at the opening of the "Everlasting Good News" Assembly of Jehovah's Witnesses at Milwaukee, Wisconsin, U.S.A.

[21] **One-Volume Revised Edition.** In the summer of 1961, at a series of assemblies of Jehovah's Witnesses held in the United States and Europe, a revised edition of the complete New World Trans-

---

16. In what twofold work are Jehovah's Witnesses thus engaged?
17. (a) How have the many Bible versions been useful, and yet what defects do they contain? (b) Since 1946, what had the president of the Watch Tower Society been seeking?
18. How did the Society come to be publishers and printers of the New World Translation?
19. (a) How did the New World Translation appear in its parts? (b) What effort had been made in preparing these volumes?

---

20. What valuable aids did the first edition of the New World Translation contain in its (a) footnotes, (b) marginal references, and (c) forewords and appendixes?
21. (a) What were the circumstances of the release of the revised New World Translation? (b) What were some of its features?

lation of the Holy Scriptures in one handy volume was released for distribution. It was accepted with joy by the hundreds of thousands who attended these assemblies. Bound in green cloth, it contained 1,472 pages and had an excellent concordance, an appendix on Bible topics, and maps.

22 **Further Editions.** In 1969 *The Kingdom Interlinear Translation of the Greek Scriptures* was released, with a second edition issued in 1985. This volume provides a literal English translation of the Greek text edited by Westcott and Hort as well as the modern-English rendering of the 1984 edition of the *New World Translation*. It thus opens up to the serious Bible student what the original Greek basically or literally says.

23 A second revision of the *New World Translation* was released in 1970, and a third revision with footnotes followed in 1971. At the "Kingdom Increase" District Conventions of Jehovah's Witnesses, held in 1984, a revised reference edition was issued in English. It includes a complete updating and revision of the marginal (cross) references that were initially presented in English from 1950 to 1960. Designed for the serious Bible student, it contains over 125,000 marginal references, more than 11,000 footnotes, an extensive concordance, maps, and 43 appendix articles. Also in 1984, a regular-size edition of the 1984 revision, with marginal references but without footnotes, was made available.

24 **Some Advantages.** In order to aid the reader in quickly locating any desired material, both the regular and reference editions contain a carefully designed running head at the top of each page. These running heads describe the material below, and they are especially planned to aid the Kingdom publisher in quickly locating texts in answer to questions that may be put to him. For example, he may be trying to locate counsel on the training of children. Coming to page 860 (regular edition) in the Proverbs, he sees the last key phrase, "A good name." Since this is the last phrase of the heading, it indicates that the subject will appear late on that page, and that is where he finds it, at Proverbs 22:1. The scripture identified by the first part of the running head on page 861, "Train up a boy," he finds early on the page, at verse 6. The next element of the heading reads, "Not spare the rod." This material is located near the bottom of the first column, in verse 15. These running heads at the tops of the pages can be a great aid to the Kingdom publisher who knows the general loca-

tion of texts for which he is searching. They can open up the Bible for quick action.

25 At the back of both the regular and reference editions of this Bible, there is a feature called "Bible Words Indexed." Here are to be found thousands of important Bible words together with lines of context. A concordance service is thus made available, including the wide range of new, descriptive words used in the text. For those accustomed to the *King James Version* renderings, help is given in making scores of transitions from older English Bible words to the more modern Bible terms. Take, for example, the word "grace" in the *King James Version.* This is listed in the index, referring the student to "undeserved kindness," the up-to-date expression used in the new translation. The word index makes it possible to locate Scripture texts on key doctrinal subjects, such as "soul" or "ransom," supporting detailed study directly from the Bible texts. A Kingdom publisher who is called upon to preach on any of these outstanding subjects could immediately use the brief portions of context supplied in this concordance. Additionally, principal citations are listed for outstanding proper names, including geographic places as well as prominent Bible characters. Invaluable aid is thus rendered to all Bible students using this translation.

26 A scholarly appendix offers further accurate information beneficial for teaching. The appendix articles are arranged in such a way that they can be used as an aid in explaining basic Bible doctrines and related matters. For example, in dealing with the subject "soul," the appendix, under eight different headings, lists Scripture texts that show the various ways in which the word "soul" (Hebrew, *ne'phesh*) is used. Diagrams and maps are also provided in the appendix articles. The *Reference Bible* contains a more extensive appendix as well as helpful footnotes that supply important textual information in a simple way. Thus, the *New World Translation* is outstanding for the range of services that it provides for placing accurate knowledge quickly at the disposal of its readers.

27 **Aid in Pronouncing Bible Names.** In the English text itself, all editions of the *New World Translation* render aid in the pronunciation of proper names. The system is the same as that designed by an expert for the *Revised Standard*

22, 23. What further editions have been released, and what are some of their features?
24. (a) What are some of the advantages of both the regular and reference editions? (b) Illustrate the use of the running heads.

25. What concordance service is provided, and to what practical uses may this be put?
26. Illustrate one of the ways in which the appendix to the *New World Translation* is of help.
27, 28. Explain and illustrate how the *New World Translation* indicates the pronunciation of proper names.

Version of 1952. The proper name is broken down into syllables that are kept apart by a dot or by the accent mark ('). The accent mark follows the syllable on which major emphasis should be put in pronouncing the word. If the accented syllable ends in a vowel, then the vowel is long in its pronunciation. If a syllable ends in a consonant, then the vowel in that syllable is short in its pronunciation.

[28] As an example, note Job 4:1. Here it speaks of "El'i·phaz the Te'man·ite." While the accent in both cases falls on the first syllable, the letter "e" is to be pronounced differently in these two cases. In "El'i·phaz" the accent mark falling after the consonant "l" makes the vowel "e" short, as in "end." Whereas, in "Te'man·ite" the accent falling directly after the vowel "e" makes it long, as the first "e" in "Eden." When the two vowels "a" and "i" are combined, as in "Mor'de·cai" at Esther 2:5 and "Si'nai" at Exodus 19:1, the "ai" is pronounced simply as a long "i."

[29] **A Fresh Translation.** The *New World Translation* is a fresh translation from the original Bible languages of Hebrew, Aramaic, and Greek. By no means is it a revision of any other English translation, nor does it copy any other version as to style, vocabulary, or rhythm. For the Hebrew-Aramaic section, the well-refined and universally accepted text of Rudolf Kittel's *Biblia Hebraica,* the 7th, 8th, and 9th editions (1951-55), was used. A new edition of the Hebrew text known as *Biblia Hebraica Stuttgartensia,* dated 1977, was used for updating the information presented in the footnotes of the *New World Translation—With References.* The Greek section was translated principally from the Greek master text prepared by Westcott and Hort, published in 1881. However, the New World Bible Translation Committee also consulted other Greek texts, including Nestle's Greek text (1948). Descriptions of these excellent master texts are presented in Studies 5 and 6 of this volume. The translation committee has made a vigorous and accurate translation of the Bible, and this has resulted in a clear and living text, opening up the way to a deeper, more satisfying understanding of the Word of God.

[30] Note one critic's evaluation of this translation: "Original renderings of the Hebrew Scriptures into the English language are extremely few. It therefore gives us much pleasure to welcome the publication of the first part of the New World Translation [of the Hebrew Scriptures], Genesis to Ruth. . . . This version has evidently made a special effort to be thoroughly readable.

No one could say it is deficient in freshness and originality. Its terminology is by no means based upon that of previous versions."[*]

[31] The Hebrew scholar Professor Dr. Benjamin Kedar of Israel, in an interview with a representative of the Watch Tower Society, evaluated the *New World Translation* as follows: "In my linguistic research in connection with the Hebrew Bible and translations, I often refer to the English edition of what is known as the *New World Translation.* In so doing, I find my feeling repeatedly confirmed that this work reflects an honest endeavor to achieve an understanding of the text that is as accurate as possible. Giving evidence of a broad command of the original language, it renders the original words into a second language understandably without deviating unnecessarily from the specific structure of the Hebrew. . . . Every statement of language allows for a certain latitude in interpreting or translating. So the linguistic solution in any given case may be open to debate. But I have never discovered in the *New World Translation* any biased intent to read something into the text that it does not contain."[#]

[32] **A Literal Translation.** Faithfulness as to translation is also demonstrated in its being literal. This requires an almost word-for-word correspondency between the rendering in English and the Hebrew and Greek texts. In the presentation of the text in the language into which it is translated, the degree of literalness should be as high as the original-language idiom permits. Furthermore, literalness requires that the word order of most of the renderings be the same as in the Hebrew or Greek, thus preserving the emphasis of the original writings. Through literal translation, the flavor, color, and rhythm of the original writings may be accurately communicated.

[33] There have been occasional departures from the literal text, for the purpose of conveying in understandable terms the difficult Hebrew or Greek idioms. However, in the reference edition of the *New World Translation,* these have been called to the reader's attention by means of footnotes that give the literal rendering.

[34] Many Bible translators have abandoned liter-

---

[*] Alexander Thomson, *The Differentiator,* June 1954, page 131.
[#] June 12, 1989, translated from the German.

---

29. Is the *New World Translation* simply a revision of earlier translations, and what features support your answer?
30. What is one critic's evaluation of this translation?
31. How did one Hebrew scholar evaluate the *New World Translation?*
32. To what extent is the *New World Translation* literal, and with what benefit?
33. How have occasional departures from the literal text been noted?
34. (a) What results from abandoning literal translation? (b) Illustrate.

alness for what they consider to be elegance of language and form. They argue that literal renderings are wooden, stiff, and confining. However, their abandonment of literal translation has brought about, by the introduction of paraphrase and interpretation, many departures from the accurate original statements of truth. They have, in effect, watered down the very thoughts of God. For example, the dean emeritus of a large American university once charged Jehovah's Witnesses with destroying the beauty and elegance of the Bible. By the Bible he meant the *King James Version,* which had long been venerated as a standard of beautiful English. He said: 'Look what you have done to Psalm 23. You have destroyed its swing and beauty by your "Je/ho/vah is/ my/ shep/herd." Seven syllables instead of six. It is shocking. It is off balance. There is no rhythm. The King James has it right with its six balanced syllables—"The/ Lord/ is/ my/ shep/herd."' It was protested to the professor that it was more important to put it the way that David, the Bible writer, put it. Did David use the general term "Lord," or did he use the divine name? The professor admitted that David used the divine name, but he still argued that for the sake of beauty and elegance, the word "Lord" would be warranted. What a lame excuse for removing Jehovah's illustrious name from this psalm to his praise!

35 Thousands of renderings have been sacrificed in this way on the altar of man's concept of language beauty, resulting in inaccuracies in the many Bible versions. Thanks be to God that he has provided the *New World Translation,* with its clear and accurate Bible text! May his great name, Jehovah, be sanctified in the hearts of all who read it!

---

35. For what may we thank God, and what is our hope and prayer?

Advantages of the "New World Translation"

A discussion of its modern language, its uniformity, its careful verb renderings, and its dynamic expression of the inspired Word of God.

IN RECENT years a number of modern Bible translations have been published that have done much to help lovers of God's Word to get to the sense of the original writings quickly. However, many translations have eliminated the use of the divine name from the sacred record. On the other hand, the *New World Translation* dignifies and honors the worthy name of the Most High God by restoring it to its rightful place in the text. The name now appears in 6,973 places in the Hebrew Scripture section, as well as in 237 places in the Greek Scripture section, a total of 7,210 places all together. The form *Yahweh* is generally preferred by Hebrew scholars, but certainty of pronunciation is not now attainable. Therefore, the Latinized form *Jehovah* continues to be used because it has been in use for centuries and is the most commonly accepted English rendering of the Tetragrammaton, or four-letter Hebrew name יהוה. Hebrew scholar R. H. Pfeiffer observed: "What-ever may be said of its dubious pedigree, 'Jehovah' is and should remain the proper English rendering of *Yahweh.*"*

2 The *New World Translation* is not the first version to restore the divine name in the Christian Greek Scriptures. From at least the 14th century onward, many translators have felt forced to restore God's name to the text, particularly in places where the Christian Greek Scripture writers quote from Hebrew Scripture texts that contain the divine name. Many modern-language missionary versions, including African, Asian, American, and Pacific-island versions of the Greek Scriptures, use the name Jehovah liberally, as do some European-language versions. Wherever the divine name is rendered, there is no longer any doubt as to which "lord" is indicated. It is the Lord of heaven and earth, Jehovah, whose name is sanctified by being

---

* *Introduction to the Old Testament,* Robert H. Pfeiffer, 1952, page 94.

---

1. (a) What trend does the *New World Translation* correct, and how? (b) In English, why is *Jehovah* used rather than *Yahweh* or some other form of the name?

2. (a) Are there precedents for restoring the divine name in the Christian Greek Scriptures? (b) What doubt is thus removed?

kept unique and distinct in the *New World Translation of the Holy Scriptures.**

[3] The *New World Translation* adds further to the sanctification of Jehovah's name by presenting his inspired Scriptures in clear, understandable language that brings the intended meaning plainly to the reader's mind. It uses simple, modern language, is as uniform as possible in its renderings, conveys accurately the action or state expressed in the Hebrew and Greek verbs, and distinguishes between the plural and singular in its use of the pronoun "you" and when using the imperative form of the verb where the context does not make it apparent. In these and other ways, the *New World Translation* brings to light in modern speech, as much as possible, the force, beauty, and sense of the original writings.

RENDERED IN MODERN LANGUAGE

[4] The older Bible translations contain many obsolete words that belong to the 16th and 17th centuries. Though not understood now, they were readily understood then. For example, one man who had much to do with putting them in the English Bible was William Tyndale, who is reported as saying to one of his religious opponents: 'If God spare my life, ere many years I will cause a boy who drives the plow to know more of the Scriptures than you do.' Tyndale's translation of the Greek Scriptures was easy enough for a plowboy to understand in his time. However, many of the words he used have now become archaic, so that 'a boy who drives the plow' can no longer clearly grasp the meaning of many words in the King James and other older versions of the Bible. Thus, it has become necessary to remove the shrouds of archaic language and to restore the Bible to the ordinary language of the common man.

[5] It was the language of the common man that was used in writing the inspired Scriptures. The apostles and other early Christians did not use the classical Greek of philosophers such as Plato. They used everyday Greek, that is, Koine, or common Greek. Hence, the Greek Scriptures, like the Hebrew Scriptures before them, were written in the language of the people. It is highly important, then, that translations of the original Scriptures should also be in the language of the people, in order to be readily understood. It is for this reason

---

* *Kingdom Interlinear Translation,* 1985 Edition, pages 1133-8.

---

3. By what means does the *New World Translation* help to convey the force, beauty, and sense of the original writings?
4. (a) What noble purpose did one early Bible translator express? (b) What has become necessary with the passage of time?
5. In what language should the Bible appear, and why?

that the *New World Translation* uses, not the archaic language of three or four centuries ago, but clear, expressive modern speech so that readers will really get to know what the Bible is saying.

[6] To give some idea of the extent of change in the English language from the 17th century to the 20th century, note the following comparisons from the *King James Version* and the *New World Translation.* "Suffered" in the *King James Version* becomes "allowed" in the *New World Translation* (Gen. 31:7), "was bolled" becomes "had flower buds" (Ex. 9:31), "spoilers" becomes "pillagers" (Judg. 2:14), "ear his ground" becomes "do his plowing" (1 Sam. 8:12), "when thou prayest" becomes "when you pray" (Matt. 6:6), "sick of the palsy" becomes "paralytic" (Mark 2:3), "quickeneth" becomes "makes . . . alive" (Rom. 4:17), "shambles" becomes "meat market" (1 Cor. 10:25), "letteth" becomes "acting as a restraint" (2 Thess. 2:7), and so on. From this the value of the *New World Translation* in using current words in place of obsolete words can well be appreciated.

UNIFORMITY OF RENDERINGS

[7] The *New World Translation* makes every effort to be consistent in its renderings. For a given Hebrew or Greek word, there has been assigned one English word, and this has been used as uniformly as the idiom or context permits in giving the full English understanding. For example, the Hebrew word *ne'phesh* is consistently translated "soul." The corresponding Greek word, *psy·khe',* is translated "soul" in every occurrence.

[8] At some places a problem has arisen over the translation of homographs. These are words in the original language that are spelled the same but that have different basic meanings. Hence, the challenge is to supply the word with the correct meaning when translating. In English there are homographs such as "Polish" and "polish" and "lead" (the sheep) and "lead" (pipe), which are spelled identically but are distinctly different words. One Bible example is the Hebrew *rav,* which represents distinctly different root words, and these are therefore rendered differently in the *New World Translation. Rav* most commonly has the meaning "many," as at Exodus 5:5. However, the word *rav* that is used in titles, as in "Rabshakeh" (Heb., *Rav-sha·qeh'*) at 2 Kings 18:17, means "chief," as when rendered "his *chief* court official" at Daniel 1:3. (See also Jeremiah 39:3, footnote.) The word *rav,* identical in form, means "archer,"

---

6. Illustrate the benefit of using current expressions in place of obsolete words.
7. How is the *New World Translation* consistent in its renderings?
8. (a) Give examples of homographs. (b) How have these been handled in the translation?

which accounts for the rendering at Jeremiah 50:29. Word experts, such as L. Koehler and W. Baumgartner, have been accepted as authorities by the translators in separating these identically spelled words.

⁹ As to this feature of uniformity, note what Hebrew and Greek commentator Alexander Thomson had to say in his review on the *New World Translation of the Christian Greek Scriptures:* "The translation is evidently the work of skilled and clever scholars, who have sought to bring out as much of the true sense of the Greek text as the English language is capable of expressing. The version aims to keep to one English meaning for each major Greek word, and to be as literal as possible. . . . The word usually rendered 'justify' is generally translated very correctly as 'declare righteous.' . . . The word for the Cross is rendered 'torture stake' which is another improvement. . . . Luke 23:43 is well rendered, 'Truly I tell you today, You will be with me in Paradise.' This is a big improvement upon the reading of most versions." On the translation of the Hebrew Scriptures, the same reviewer made this comment: "The New World Version is well worth acquiring. It is lively and lifelike, and makes the reader think and study. It is not the work of Higher Critics, but of scholars who honour God and His Word." —*The Differentiator,* April 1952, pages 52-7, and June 1954, page 136.

¹⁰ The consistency of the *New World Translation* has won many a technical Bible discussion in the field. For example, some years ago, a society of freethinkers in New York asked the Watch Tower Society to send two speakers to address their group on Biblical matters, which request was granted. These learned men held to a Latin maxim, *falsum in uno falsum in toto,* meaning that an argument proved false in one point is totally false. During the discussion, one man challenged Jehovah's Witnesses on the reliability of the Bible. He asked that Genesis 1:3 be read to the audience, and this was done, from the *New World Translation:* "And God proceeded to say: 'Let light come to be.' Then there came to be light." Confidently, he next called for Genesis 1:14, and this also was read from the *New World Translation:* "And God went on to say: 'Let luminaries come to be in the expanse of the heavens.'" "Stop," he said, "what are you reading? My Bible says God made light on the first day, and again on the fourth day, and that is inconsistent." Though he claimed to know Hebrew, it had to be pointed out to him that the Hebrew word translated "light" in verse 3 was

'ohr, whereas the word in verse 14 was different, being ma·'ohr', which refers to a luminary, or source of light. The learned man sat down defeated.* The faithful consistency of the *New World Translation* had won the point, upholding the Bible as reliable and beneficial.

CAREFUL VERB RENDERINGS

¹¹ The *New World Translation* gives special attention to conveying the sense of the action of the Greek and Hebrew verbs. In doing so, the *New World Translation* endeavors to preserve the special charm, simplicity, forcefulness, and manner of expression of the original-language writings. It has thus been necessary to use auxiliary verbs in English to convey carefully the actual states of the actions. Because of the power of their verbs, the original Scriptures are so dynamic and so expressive of action.

¹² The Hebrew verb does not have "tenses" in the way the term "tense" is applied to most languages of the West. In English, verbs are viewed particularly from the standpoint of tense, or time: past, present, and future. The Hebrew verb, on the other hand, basically expresses the condition of the action, that is, the action is viewed as either complete (the perfect state) or incomplete (the imperfect state). These states of the Hebrew verb may be used to indicate actions in the past or in the future, the context determining the time. For example, the perfect, or completed, state of the verb naturally represents actions in the past, but it is also used to speak of a future happening as if it had already occurred and were past, showing its future certainty or the obligation of it to occur.

¹³ Accurately conveying the state of the Hebrew verb into English is most important; otherwise, the meaning may be distorted and a completely different thought expressed. For an example of this, consider the verbal expressions in Genesis 2:2, 3. In many translations, speaking of God's resting on the seventh day, expressions such as "he rested," "he desisted," "he had desisted," "he then rested," "God rested," and "he had rested" are used. From these readings one would conclude that God's resting on the seventh day was completed in the past. But note how the *New World Translation* brings out the sense of the verbs used in the passage at Genesis 2:2, 3: "And by the seventh day God came to the completion of his

---

* *Insight on the Scriptures,* Vol. 1, page 528.

11. What dynamic feature of the original Scriptures is preserved in the *New World Translation?* How?
12. (a) What is one way in which Hebrew differs from Western languages? (b) Explain the two states of the Hebrew verb.
13. Why is proper regard for the state of the Hebrew verb important in reaching a correct understanding of Genesis 2:2, 3?

---

9. How did one Hebrew and Greek commentator appraise the *New World Translation?*
10. Illustrate how the consistency of the *New World Translation* upholds Bible truth.

work that he had made, and *he proceeded to rest* on the seventh day from all his work that he had made. And God proceeded to bless the seventh day and make it sacred, because on it *he has been resting* from all his work that God has created for the purpose of making." The expression in verse 2 "he proceeded to rest" is a verb in the imperfect state in Hebrew and so expresses the idea of an incomplete or continuing action. The rendering "he proceeded to rest" is in harmony with what is said at Hebrews 4:4-7. On the other hand, the verb in Genesis 2:3 is in the perfect state, but in order to harmonize with verse 2 and Hebrews 4:4-7, it is translated "he has been resting."

[14] One of the reasons for inaccuracies in translating the Hebrew verbal forms is the grammatical theory today called *waw* consecutive. *Waw* (ו) is the Hebrew conjunction that basically means "and." It never stands alone but is always joined with some other word, frequently with the Hebrew verb, in order to form one word with it. It has been, and still is, claimed by some that this relationship has the power to convert the verb from one state to another, that is, from the imperfect to the perfect (as has been done in many translations, including modern ones, at Genesis 2:2, 3) or from the perfect to the imperfect. This effect has been described also by the term *"waw* conversive." This incorrect application of the verbal form has led to much confusion and to mistranslation of the Hebrew text. The *New World Translation* does not recognize that the letter *waw* has any power to change the state of the verb. Rather, the attempt is made to bring out the proper and distinctive force of the Hebrew verb, thus preserving the meaning of the original accurately.*

[15] Similar care has been exercised in the translating of the Greek verbs. In Greek the verb tenses express not only the *time* of an action or state but also the *kind* of action, whether momentary, starting out, continuing, repetitious, or completed. Attention to such senses in the Greek verb forms leads to a precise translation with the full force of the action described. For example, giving the sense of the continuative idea where this occurs in the Greek verb not only brings out the true color of a situation but also makes admonition and counsel more forceful. For instance, the *continuing* disbelief of the Pharisees and Sadducees is

brought home by Jesus' words: "A wicked and adulterous generation *keeps on seeking* for a sign." And the need for continuing action in right things is well expressed by the words of Jesus: *"Continue to love* your enemies." *"Keep on,* then, *seeking* first the kingdom." *"Keep on asking,* and it will be given you; *keep on seeking,* and you will find; *keep on knocking,* and it will be opened to you."—Matt. 16:4; 5:44; 6:33; 7:7.

[16] The Greek has an unusual tense called the aorist, which refers to action that is punctiliar, or momentary. Verbs in the aorist may be rendered in a variety of ways, according to their context. One way in which it is used is to denote *one act* of a certain kind, though not related to any particular time. Such an example is found at 1 John 2:1, where many versions render the verb for "sin" so as to allow for a continuing course of sin, whereas the *New World Translation* reads, "commit a sin," that is, a single act of sin. This conveys the correct meaning that if a Christian should commit an act of sin, he has Jesus Christ, who acts as an advocate, or helper, with the heavenly Father. Thus, 1 John 2:1 in no way contradicts but only contrasts with the condemnation of the 'practice of sin' found at 1 John 3:6-8 and 5:18.*

[17] The imperfect tense in Greek may express not only an action that continues but also an action attempted but not accomplished. Note how Hebrews 11:17 in the *King James Version* reads: "By faith Abraham, when he was tried, *offered up* Isaac: and he that had received the promises *offered up* his only begotten son." The verb "offered up" differs in form in these two occurrences in the Greek. The first occurrence is in the perfect (completed) tense, whereas the second is in the imperfect (past continuous) form. The *New World Translation,* taking into account the different tenses, translates the verse: "Abraham, when he was tested, *as good as offered up* Isaac, and the man . . . *attempted to offer up* his only-begotten son." The completed sense of the first verb is thus retained, while the imperfect tense of the second verb indicates that the action was intended or attempted but not carried out to completion. —Gen. 22:9-14.

[18] Careful attention to the function of other parts of speech, such as to the cases of nouns, has led to the clearing up of apparent contradictions.

---

* *Reference Bible,* appendix 3C, "Hebrew Verbs Indicating Continuous or Progressive Action."

---

14. Avoiding the mistaken view of the *waw* consecutive, what does the *New World Translation* endeavor to do as to the Hebrew verbs?
15. (a) With what care have the Greek verbs been translated? (b) Illustrate the benefit of presenting the continuative idea correctly.

---

* *Insight on the Scriptures,* Vol. 1, page 1008.

---

16. By taking into account the Greek aorist tense, how is John's comment on "sin" at 1 John 2:1 correctly expressed?
17. Besides showing continuing action, what else may the Greek imperfect tense express? Illustrate.
18. What has resulted from careful attention to the function of other parts of speech? Give an example.

For example, at Acts 9:7, in recounting the remarkable experience of Saul on the road to Damascus, a number of translations say that his traveling companions 'heard the voice' but did not see anyone. Then, at Acts 22:9, where Paul is relating this incident, the same translations read that although they saw the light, 'they did not hear the voice.' However, in the first reference, the Greek word for "voice" is in the genitive case, but in the second instance, it is in the accusative case, as it is at Acts 9:4. Why the difference? None is conveyed in the above translations into English, yet the Greek, by the change of case, indicates something different. The men heard literally "of the voice" but did not hear it the way Paul did, that is, hear the words and understand them. Thus, the *New World Translation,* noting the use of the genitive at Acts 9:7, reads that the men who were with him were "hearing, indeed, the *sound* of a voice, but not beholding any man."

PLURAL "YOU" INDICATED

¹⁹ The older English forms of the second person singular, "thee," "thou," and "thy," have been retained in some modern translations in cases where God is being addressed. However, in the languages in which the Bible was written, there was no special form of the personal pronoun for use in address to God, but the same form was used as when addressing one's fellowman. So the *New World Translation* has dropped these now sanctimonious usages and employs the normal conversational "you" in all cases. In order to distinguish the second person plural "you" and verbs whose plural number is not readily apparent in English, the words are printed entirely in small capital letters. Often it is helpful to the reader to know whether a given Scripture text refers to "you" as an individual, or to "YOU" as a group of persons, a congregation.

²⁰ For example, at Romans 11:13 Paul is speaking to the many: "Now I speak to YOU who are people of the nations." But at verse 17 the Greek changes to the singular "you," and the application is brought down pointedly to the individual: "However, if some of the branches were broken off but you . . . were grafted in . . . "

NEW WORLD TRANSLATION IN OTHER LANGUAGES

²¹ In 1961 it was announced that the Watch Tower Society was proceeding to render the *New World Translation* into six more widely used languages, namely, Dutch, French, German, Italian, Portuguese, and Spanish. This translation work was entrusted to skilled and dedicated translators, all working together at the Watch Tower Society's headquarters in Brooklyn, New York. They served as a large international committee working under competent direction. It was in July 1963, at the "Everlasting Good News" Assembly of Jehovah's Witnesses at Milwaukee, Wisconsin, U.S.A., that the firstfruits of this translation work became available when the *New World Translation of the Christian Greek Scriptures* was released simultaneously in the above six languages. Now inhabitants of the earth who speak languages other than English could begin to enjoy the advantages of this modern translation. Since then, translation work has continued, so that by 1989 the *New World Translation of the Holy Scriptures* had appeared in 11 languages, with more than 56,000,000 copies having been printed.*

GRATITUDE FOR POWERFUL INSTRUMENT

²² The *New World Translation* is indeed a powerful instrument for demonstrating that "all Scripture is inspired of God and beneficial." From the points discussed in this study, we can appreciate that it is accurate and reliable and that it can provide genuine enjoyment to those who desire to hear God speak to man stirringly in modern, living language. The language of the *New World Translation* is spiritually arousing, and it quickly puts the reader in tune with the dynamic expression of the original inspired Scriptures. We no longer need to read and reread verses in order to understand obscure phrases. It speaks out with power and clarity from the very first reading.

²³ The *New World Translation of the Holy Scriptures* is a faithful translation of God's Word, "the sword of the spirit." As such, it is indeed an effective weapon in the spiritual warfare of the Christian, an aid in 'overturning strongly entrenched false teachings and reasonings raised up against the knowledge of God.' How well it enables us to declare with better understanding the things beneficial and upbuilding, the glorious things related to God's Kingdom of righteousness —yes, "the magnificent things of God"!—Eph. 6:17; 2 Cor. 10:4, 5; Acts 2:11.

19, 20. (a) What has the *New World Translation* done as to sanctimonious forms of address, and why? (b) Illustrate how the singular "you" may be distinguished from the plural.

21. (a) How has it become possible for more and more of earth's population to enjoy the benefits of the *New World Translation?* (b) What is the total number of copies of the *New World Translation* printed by the Watch Tower Society by 1989?

---

* Complete editions published in Danish, Dutch, English, French, German, Italian, Japanese, Portuguese, and Spanish (also in part in Finnish and Swedish).

22, 23. In what outstanding ways does this translation of the inspired Scriptures benefit the Christian?

Archaeology
and the Inspired Record

A study of archaeological discoveries and of ancient records of secular history that corroborate the Bible record.

BIBLE archaeology is the study of the peoples and events of Bible times through writings, implements, buildings, and other remains that are found in the earth. The search for ancient remains, or artifacts, at ancient Bible locations has involved much exploration and the moving of millions of tons of dirt. An artifact is any object that shows human workmanship and that gives evidence of man's activity and life. Artifacts may include such items as pottery, ruins of buildings, clay tablets, written inscriptions, documents, monuments, and chronicles recorded on stone.

² By the early 20th century, archaeology had been developed into a careful field of study, with expeditions to Bible lands being sponsored by major universities and museums in Europe and America. As a result, archaeologists have uncovered a wealth of information that sheds light on the way things were in Bible times. Sometimes archaeological finds have demonstrated the Bible's authenticity, showing its accuracy right down to the tiniest detail.

ARCHAEOLOGY AND
THE HEBREW SCRIPTURES

³ **The Tower of Babel.** According to the Bible, the Tower of Babel was a mighty construction work. (Gen. 11:1-9) Interestingly, archaeologists have uncovered in and around the ruins of ancient Babylon the sites of several ziggurats, or pyramid-like, staged temple-towers, including the ruined temple of Etemenanki, which was within Babylon's walls. Ancient records concerning such temples often contain the words, "Its top shall reach the heavens." King Nebuchadnezzar is reported to have said, "I raised the summit of the Tower of stages at Etemenanki so that its top rivalled the heavens." One fragment relates the fall of such a ziggurat in these words: "The building of this temple offended the gods. In a night they threw down what had been built. They scattered them abroad, and made strange their speech. The progress they impeded."*

---

* *Bible and Spade,* 1938, S. L. Caiger, page 29.

⁴ **The Water Tunnels at the Spring of Gihon.** In 1867 in the Jerusalem area, Charles Warren discovered a water channel running from the Spring of Gihon back into the hill, with a shaft leading upward toward the City of David. Here, apparently, was the way in which David's men first penetrated the city. (2 Sam. 5:6-10) It was in 1909-11 that the entire system of tunnels leading from the Gihon spring was cleared. One massive tunnel, averaging 6 feet in height, was chiseled for 1,749 feet through solid rock. It led from Gihon to the Pool of Siloam in the Tyropoeon Valley (within the city) and is apparently the one that Hezekiah built. An inscription in early Hebrew script was found on the wall of the narrow tunnel. It reads, in part: "And this was the way in which it was cut through:—While [. . .] (were) still [. . .] axe(s), each man toward his fellow, and while there were still three cubits to be cut through, [there was heard] the voice of a man calling to his fellow, for there was *an overlap* in the rock on the right [and on the left]. And when the tunnel was driven through, the quarrymen hewed (the rock), each man toward his fellow, axe against axe; and the water flowed from the spring toward the reservoir for 1,200 cubits, and the height of the rock above the head(s) of the quarrymen was 100 cubits." What a remarkable feat of engineering for those times!*—2 Ki. 20:20; 2 Chron. 32:30.

⁵ **Shishak's Victory Relief.** Shishak, king of Egypt, is mentioned seven times in the Bible. Because King Rehoboam left the law of Jehovah, Jehovah permitted Shishak to invade Judah, in 993 B.C.E., but not to bring it to complete ruin. (1 Ki. 14:25-28; 2 Chron. 12:1-12) Until recent years, there appeared to be only the Bible record of this invasion. Then there came to light a large document of the Pharaoh whom the Bible calls

---

* *Ancient Near Eastern Texts,* 1974, J. B. Pritchard, page 321; *Insight on the Scriptures,* Vol. 1, pages 941-2, 1104.

1. What is meant by (a) Bible archaeology? (b) artifacts?
2. Of what value is Bible archaeology?
3. What ancient ruins and records confirm the existence of ziggurats in ancient Babylon?

4. What archaeological discoveries were made at Gihon, and what connection may these have with the Bible record?
5. What archaeological evidence found at Karnak is there of Shishak's invasion and Bible place-names?

Shishak (Sheshonk I). This was in the form of an imposing relief in hieroglyphics and pictures on the south wall of a vast Egyptian temple at Karnak (ancient Thebes). On this gigantic relief, there is depicted the Egyptian god Amon, who is holding in his right hand a sickle-shaped sword. He is bringing to Pharaoh Shishak 156 manacled Palestinian prisoners, who are attached by cords to his left hand. Each prisoner represents a city or village, the name of which is shown in hieroglyphics. Among those that can still be read and identified are Rabbith (Josh. 19:20); Taanach, Beth-shean, and Megiddo (Josh. 17:11); Shunem (Josh. 19:18); Rehob (Josh. 19:28); Hapharaim (Josh. 19:19); Gibeon (Josh. 18:25); Beth-horon (Josh. 21:22); Aijalon (Josh. 21:24); Socoh (Josh. 15:35); and Arad (Josh. 12:14). The document also makes reference to the "Field of Abram," this being the earliest mention of Abraham in Egyptian records.*

⁶ **The Moabite Stone.** In 1868 the German missionary F. A. Klein made a remarkable discovery of an ancient inscription at Dhiban (Dibon). This has become known as the Moabite Stone. A cast was made of its writing, but the stone itself was broken up by the Bedouin before it could be moved. However, most of the pieces were recovered, and the

---

* *Light From the Ancient Past,* 1959, J. Finegan, pages 91, 126.

6, 7. What is the history of the Moabite Stone, and what information does it give concerning the warfare between Israel and Moab?

stone is now preserved in the Louvre, Paris, with a copy in the British Museum, London. It was originally erected at Dibon, in Moab, and gives King Mesha's version of his revolt against Israel. (2 Ki. 1:1; 3:4, 5) It reads, in part: "I (am) Mesha, son of Chemosh-[. . .], king of Moab, the Dibonite . . . As for Omri, king of Israel, he humbled Moab many years (lit., days), for Chemosh [the god of Moab] was angry at his land. And his son followed him and he also said, 'I will humble Moab.' In my time he spoke (thus), but I have triumphed over him and over his house, while Israel hath perished for ever! . . . And Chemosh said to me, 'Go, take Nebo from Israel!' So I went by night and fought against it from the break of dawn until noon, taking it and slaying all . . . And I took from there the [vessels] of Yahweh, dragging them before Chemosh."* Note the mention of the divine name in the last sentence. This can be seen in the accompanying picture of the Moabite Stone. It is in the form of the Tetragrammaton, to the right of the document, in line 18.

⁷ The Moabite Stone also mentions the following Bible places: Ataroth and Nebo (Num. 32: 34, 38); the Arnon, Aroer, Medeba, and Dibon (Josh. 13:9); Bamoth-baal, Beth-baal-meon, Jahaz, and Kiriathaim (Josh. 13:17-19); Bezer (Josh. 20:8), Horonaim (Isa. 15:5); and Beth-diblathaim and Kerioth (Jer. 48:22, 24). It thus supports the historicity of these places.

---

* *Ancient Near Eastern Texts,* page 320.

The Moabite Stone

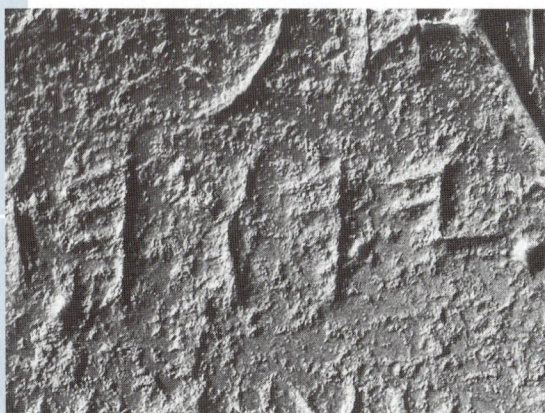

An enlargement of the Tetragrammaton, which appears in an ancient lettering, in the 18th line, to the right

King
Sennacherib's
Prism

horses, mules, donkeys, camels, big and small cattle beyond counting, and considered (them) booty. Himself [Hezekiah] I made a prisoner in Jerusalem, his royal residence, like a bird in a cage. . . . His towns which I had plundered, I took away from his country and gave them (over) to Mitinti, king of Ashdod, Padi, king of Ekron, and Sillibel, king of Gaza. . . . Hezekiah himself . . . did send me, later, to Nineveh, my lordly city, together with 30 talents of gold, 800 talents of silver, precious stones, antimony, large cuts of red stone, couches (inlaid) with ivory, *nimedu* -chairs (inlaid) with ivory, elephant-hides, ebony-wood, boxwood (and) all kinds of valuable treasures, his (own) daughters, concubines, male and female musicians. In order to deliver the tribute and to do obeisance as a slave he sent his (personal) messenger."* As for this tribute imposed by Sennacherib upon Hezekiah, the Bible confirms the 30 talents of gold but mentions only 300 talents of silver. Moreover, it shows that this was *before* Sennacherib threatened Jerusalem with siege. In Sennacherib's slanted report for Assyrian history, he purposely omits mention of his crushing defeat in Judah, when in one night Jehovah's angel destroyed 185,-000 of his soldiers, thus forcing him to flee back to Nineveh like a whipped dog. Nevertheless, this boastful written record on Sennacherib's Prism indicates an immense invasion of Judah before Jehovah turned the Assyrians back after they threatened Jerusalem.—2 Ki. 18:14; 19:35, 36.

⁸ **King Sennacherib's Prism.** The Bible records in considerable detail the invasion by the Assyrians under King Sennacherib in the year 732 B.C.E. (2 Ki. 18:13–19:37; 2 Chron. 32:1-22; Isa. 36:1–37:38) It was during 1847-51 that the English archaeologist A. H. Layard excavated the ruins of Sennacherib's great palace at Nineveh in the territory of ancient Assyria. The palace was found to have about 70 rooms, with nearly 10,000 feet of walls lined with sculptured slabs. The yearly reports of events, or annals, of Sennacherib were recorded on clay cylinders, or prisms. The final edition of these annals, apparently made shortly before his death, appears on what is known as the Taylor Prism, preserved in the British Museum, but the Oriental Institute of the University of Chicago has an even finer copy on a prism that was discovered near the site of ancient Nineveh, the capital of the Assyrian Empire.

⁹ In these last annals, Sennacherib gives his own boastful version of his invasion of Judah: "As to Hezekiah, the Jew, he did not submit to my yoke, I laid siege to 46 of his strong cities, walled forts and to the countless small villages in their vicinity, and conquered (them) by means of well-stamped (earth-)ramps, and battering-rams brought (thus) near (to the walls) (combined with) the attack by foot soldiers, (using) mines, breeches as well as sapper work. I drove out (of them) 200,150 people, young and old, male and female,

¹⁰ **The Lachish Letters.** The famous fortress city of Lachish is mentioned more than 20 times in the Bible. It was located 27 miles west-southwest of Jerusalem. The ruins have been extensively excavated. In 1935, in a guardroom of the double gatehouse, there were found 18 ostraca, or pieces of pottery inscribed with writing (3 more were found in 1938). These turned out to be a number of letters written in ancient Hebrew characters. This collection of 21 is now known as the Lachish Letters. Lachish was one of the last strongholds of Judah to hold out against Nebuchadnezzar, being reduced to a pile of charred ruins during the period of 609-607 B.C.E. The letters reflect the urgency of the times. They appear to be letters written from remaining outposts of Judean troops to Yaosh, a military commander at Lachish. One of these (number IV) reads in part: "May YHWH [Tetragrammaton, "Jehovah"] let my lord hear even now tidings of good. . . . we are watching for the fire signals of Lachish, according to all the signs which

---

8. What does the Bible record concerning Sennacherib, and what have excavations of his palace revealed?
9. What does Sennacherib record, in harmony with the Bible account, but what does he fail to mention, and why?

---

* *Ancient Near Eastern Texts,* page 288.

10, 11. (a) What are the Lachish Letters, and what do they reflect? (b) How do they support Jeremiah's writings?

my lord gives, because we do not see Azekah." This is a striking confirmation of Jeremiah 34:7, which mentions Lachish and Azekah as the last two fortified cities left remaining. This letter apparently indicates that Azekah had now fallen. The divine name, in the form of the Tetragrammaton, appears frequently in the letters, showing that the name Jehovah enjoyed everyday usage among the Jews at that time.

[11] Another letter (number III) commences as follows: "May YHWH [that is, Jehovah] cause my lord to hear tidings of peace! . . . And it has been reported to your servant saying, 'The commander of the army, Coniah son of Elnathan, has come down in order to go into Egypt and to Hodaviah son of Ahijah and his men he has sent to obtain [supplies] from him.'" This letter appears to confirm that Judah went down to Egypt for assistance, in violation of Jehovah's command and to her own destruction. (Isa. 31:1; Jer. 46:25, 26) The names Elnathan and Hoshaiah, appearing in the complete text of this letter, are also found at Jeremiah 36:12 and Jeremiah 42:1. Three other names mentioned in the letters are also found in the Bible book of Jeremiah. They are Gemariah, Neriah, and Jaazaniah.—Jer. 32:12; 35:3; 36:10.*

[12] **The Nabonidus Chronicle.** In the latter half of the 19th century, excavations near Baghdad produced many finds of clay tablets and cylinders that threw much light on the history of ancient Babylon. One of these was the very valuable document known as the Nabonidus Chronicle, which is now in the British Museum. King Nabonidus of Babylon was the father of his coregent, Belshazzar. He outlived his son, who was killed on the night that troops of Cyrus the Persian took Babylon, October 5, 539 B.C.E. (Dan. 5:30, 31) The Nabonidus Chronicle, a remarkably well-dated record of the fall of Babylon, helps to establish on what day this event occurred. Following is a translation of a small part of the Nabonidus Chronicle: "In the month of Tashritu [Tishri (September-October)], when Cyrus attacked the army of Akkad in Opis on the Tigris . . . the 14th day, Sippar was seized without battle. Nabonidus fled. The 16th day [October 11, 539 B.C.E., Julian, or October 5, Gregorian] Gobryas (*Ugbaru*), the governor of Gutium and the army of Cyrus entered Babylon without battle. Afterwards Nabonidus was arrested in Babylon when he returned (there). . . . In the month of Arahshamnu [Marchesvan (October-November)], the 3rd day [October 28, Julian], Cyrus entered Babylon, green twigs were spread in front of

---

* *Insight on the Scriptures,* Vol. 1, pages 151-2; *Light From the Ancient Past,* pages 192-5.

12, 13. What does the Nabonidus Chronicle describe, and why is it of special value?

him—the state of 'Peace' (*sulmu*) was imposed upon the city. Cyrus sent greetings to all Babylon. Gobryas, his governor, installed (sub-)governors in Babylon."*

[13] It may be noted that Darius the Mede is not mentioned in this chronicle, and thus far, no mention has been found of this Darius in any non-Biblical inscription, nor is he mentioned in any secular historical document prior to the time of Josephus (Jewish historian of the first century C.E.). Some have therefore suggested that he might be the Gobryas mentioned in the above account. While the information available concerning Gobryas seems to parallel that regarding Darius, such identification cannot be considered conclusive.# In any event, secular history definitely establishes that Cyrus was a key figure in the conquest of Babylon and that he thereafter ruled there as king.

[14] **The Cyrus Cylinder.** Some time after he began ruling as king of the Persian World Power, Cyrus' capture of Babylon in 539 B.C.E. was recorded on a clay cylinder. This outstanding document is also preserved in the British Museum. A part of the translated text follows: "I am Cyrus, king of the world, great king, legitimate king, king of Babylon, king of Sumer and Akkad, king of the four rims (of the earth), . . . I returned to [certain previously named] sacred cities on the other side of the Tigris, the sanctuaries of which have been ruins for a long time, the images which (used) to live therein and established for them permanent

---

* *Ancient Near Eastern Texts,* page 306.
# *Insight on the Scriptures,* Vol. 1, pages 581-3.

---

14. What is recorded on the Cyrus Cylinder?

The Nabonidus Chronicle

sanctuaries. I (also) gathered all their (former) inhabitants and returned (to them) their habitations."*

[15] The Cyrus Cylinder thus makes known the king's policy of restoring captive peoples to their former places. In harmony with this, Cyrus issued his decree for the Jews to return to Jerusalem and rebuild the house of Jehovah there. Interestingly, 200 years previously, Jehovah had prophetically named Cyrus as the one who would take Babylon and bring about the restoration of Jehovah's people.—Isa. 44:28; 45:1; 2 Chron. 36:23.

ARCHAEOLOGY AND THE CHRISTIAN GREEK SCRIPTURES

[16] As it did with the Hebrew Scriptures, archaeology has brought to light many interesting artifacts in support of the inspired record contained in the Christian Greek Scriptures.

[17] **Denarius Coin With Tiberius' Inscription.** The Bible shows clearly that Jesus' ministry took place during the rule of Tiberius Caesar. Some of Jesus' opposers tried to trap him by asking about the matter of paying head tax to Caesar. The record reads: "Detecting their hypocrisy, he said to them: 'Why do you put me to the test? Bring me a denarius to look at.' They brought one. And he said to them: 'Whose image and inscription is this?' They said to him: 'Caesar's.' Jesus then said: 'Pay back Caesar's things to Caesar, but God's things to God.' And they began to marvel at him." (Mark 12: 15-17) Archaeologists have found a silver denarius coin bearing the head of Tiberius Caesar! It was put in circulation about 15 C.E. This is consistent with Tiberius' period of rule as emperor, which began in 14 C.E., and it brings added support to the record stating that John the Baptizer's ministry commenced in the 15th year of Tiberius, or the spring of 29 C.E.—Luke 3:1, 2.

[18] **Pontius Pilate Inscription.** It was in 1961 that the first archaeological find was made with reference to Pontius Pilate. This was a stone slab located at Caesarea, which bore in Latin the name of Pontius Pilate.

[19] **The Areopagus.** Paul delivered one of his most famous recorded speeches in Athens, Greece,

Denarius coin with Tiberius' inscription

in 50 C.E. (Acts 17:16-34) This was when certain Athenians laid hold of Paul and led him to the Areopagus. The Areopagus, or Hill of Ares (Mars' Hill), is the name of a bare, rocky hill, about 370 feet high, immediately northwest of the Acropolis of Athens. Steps cut in the rock lead to the top, where rough, rock-hewn benches, forming three sides of a square, can still be seen. The Areopagus still remains, confirming the Bible's recorded setting for Paul's historic speech.

[20] **The Arch of Titus.** Jerusalem and its temple were destroyed by the Romans under Titus, in 70 C.E. The next year, in Rome, Titus celebrated his triumph, together with his father, Emperor Vespasian. Seven hundred selected Jewish prisoners were marched in the triumphal procession. Loads of the spoils of war were also paraded, including temple treasures. Titus himself became emperor, serving as such from 79 to 81 C.E., and after his death a large monument, the Arch of Titus, was completed and dedicated *divo Tito* (to the deified Titus). His triumphant procession is represented in bas-relief, carved on each side of the passage through the arch. On the one side, there are depicted the Roman soldiers, holding headless spears and crowned with laurels, carrying the sacred furniture from Jerusalem's temple. This includes the seven-branched lampstand and the table of showbread, upon which the sacred trumpets are seen resting. The relief on the other side of the passage shows the victorious Titus standing in a chariot drawn by four horses and conducted by a woman representing the city of Rome.* Each year thousands of sightseers view this triumphal Arch of Titus, which still stands in Rome as silent testimony to the fulfillment of Jesus' prophecy and the terrible execution of Jehovah's judgment upon rebellious Jerusalem.—Matt. 23:37–24:2; Luke 19:43, 44; 21:20-24.

[21] In the same way that the discovery of ancient

---

* *Ancient Near Eastern Texts,* page 316.

---

15. What does the Cyrus Cylinder reveal about Cyrus, and how does this harmonize with the Bible?
16. What has archaeology brought to light in connection with the Greek Scriptures?
17. How does archaeology support Jesus' discussion of the tax question?
18. What find has been made with reference to Pontius Pilate?
19. What still remains in Athens, confirming the setting of Acts 17:16-34?

---

* *Light From the Ancient Past,* page 329.

---

20. To what does the Arch of Titus continue to testify, and how?
21. (a) In what way has archaeology worked hand in hand with the discovery of manuscripts? (b) What is the proper attitude to have concerning archaeology?

The Arch of Titus

manuscripts has helped to restore the pure, original text of the Bible, so the discovery of the multitude of artifacts has often demonstrated that the things stated in the Bible text are historically, chronologically, and geographically reliable, right down to the minutest details. However, it would be a mistake to conclude that archaeology agrees with the Bible in every case. It must be remembered that archaeology is not an infallible field of study. Archaeological findings are subject to human interpretations, and some of these interpretations have changed from time to time. Archaeology has at times provided unrequired support for the truthfulness of God's Word. Further, as stated by the late Sir Frederic Kenyon, director and principal librarian of the British Museum for many years, archaeology has rendered the Bible "more intelligible through a fuller knowledge of its background and setting."* But faith must rest on the Bible, not on archaeology.—Rom. 10:9; Heb. 11:6.

²² The Bible contains within itself incontrovertible evidence that it is indeed the authentic "word of the living and enduring God," as we will see in the next study.—1 Pet. 1:23.

———
* *The Bible and Archaeology*, 1940, page 279.

22. What evidence will be considered in the next study?

Study Number **10**

The Bible —Authentic and True

The Bible's coverage of history, geography, and human origins; its accuracy as to science, culture, and customs; the candor, harmony, and integrity of its writers; and its prophecy.

THE Bible is generally accepted as a great literary masterpiece of transcendent poetic beauty and a remarkable accomplishment for the men who were its writers. But it is much more than that. The writers themselves testified that what they wrote originated with Jehovah, the almighty God himself. This is the underlying reason for the Bible's beauty of expression and, more important, its surpassing value as the book of life-giving knowledge and wisdom. Jesus, the Son of God, testified that the words he spoke "are spirit and are life," and he quoted copiously from the ancient Hebrew Scriptures. "All Scripture is inspired of God," said the apostle Paul, who spoke of the Hebrew Scriptures as "the sacred pronouncements of God."—John 6:63; 2 Tim. 3:16; Rom. 3: 1, 2.

² The apostle Peter testified that the prophets of God were moved by holy spirit. King David wrote: "The spirit of Jehovah it was that spoke by me, and

1. (a) As what is the Bible generally accepted? (b) What is the underlying reason for the Bible's preeminence?

2, 3. How did the Bible's writers testify to its inspiration?

his word was upon my tongue." (2 Sam. 23:2) The prophets credited their utterances to Jehovah. Moses warned against making any addition to or taking away from the sacred words given him by Jehovah. Peter counted Paul's writings as inspired, and Jude seemingly quoted Peter's statement as inspired authority. Finally, John, the writer of Revelation, wrote as he was directed by the spirit of God and warned that anyone adding to or taking away from this prophetic revelation would be accountable, not to man, but directly to God.—1 Pet. 1:10-12; 2 Pet. 1:19-21; Deut. 4:2; 2 Pet. 3:15, 16; Jude 17, 18; Rev. 1:1, 10; 21:5; 22:18, 19.

[3] These devoted slaves of God all testified that the Bible is inspired and true. There are many other proofs of the authenticity of the Holy Scriptures, some of which we will discuss under the 12 headings that follow.

[4] **(1) Historical Accuracy.** From the earliest times, the canonical books of the Hebrew Scriptures have been received by the Jews as inspired and as wholly trustworthy documents. Thus, in David's time, the events recorded from Genesis to First Samuel were fully accepted as the true history of the nation and God's dealings with them, and this is illustrated by the 78th Psalm, which refers to more than 35 of these details.

[5] Opponents of the Bible have strongly attacked the Pentateuch, especially as to authenticity and authorship. However, to the Jews' acceptance of Moses as writer of the Pentateuch may be added the testimony of ancient writers, some of whom were enemies of the Jews. Hecataeus of Abdera, the Egyptian historian Manetho, Lysimachus of Alexandria, Eupolemus, Tacitus, and Juvenal all ascribe to Moses the institution of the code of laws distinguishing the Jews from other nations, and the majority distinctly note that he committed his laws to writing. Numenius, the Pythagorean philosopher, even mentions Jannes and Jambres as the Egyptian priests who withstood Moses. (2 Tim. 3:8) These authors cover a period extending from the time of Alexander (fourth century B.C.E.), when the Greeks first became curious about Jewish history, to that of Emperor Aurelian (third century C.E.). Many other ancient writers mention Moses as a leader, ruler, or lawgiver.* As we have seen from the previous study, archaeological discoveries often support the historical accuracy of events recorded in the Bible where God's people became involved with the surrounding nations.

___

* *The Historical Evidences of the Truth of the Scripture Records,* 1862, George Rawlinson, pages 54, 254-8.

4. How were the books of the Hebrew Scriptures always viewed by the Jews?
5. What have ancient writers testified concerning Moses and the Law code of the Jews?

[6] But what of the Christian Greek Scriptures? Not only do they verify the Hebrew Scripture account but they themselves are proved to be historically accurate as well as authentic and of equal inspiration with the Hebrew Scriptures. The writers declare to us what they heard and saw, for they were eyewitnesses of and often participants in the very events that they recorded. They were believed by thousands of their contemporaries. Their testimony finds abundant confirmation in references by ancient writers, among whom are Juvenal, Tacitus, Seneca, Suetonius, Pliny the Younger, Lucian, Celsus, and the Jewish historian Josephus.

[7] Writing in *The Union Bible Companion,* S. Austin Allibone says: "Sir Isaac Newton . . . was also eminent as a critic of ancient writings, and examined with great care the Holy Scriptures. What is his verdict on this point? 'I find,' says he, 'more sure marks of authenticity in the New Testament than in any profane [secular] history whatever.' Dr. Johnson says that we have more evidence that Jesus Christ died on Calvary, as stated in the Gospels, than we have that Julius Caesar died in the Capitol. We have, indeed, far more. Ask anyone who professes to doubt the truth of the Gospel history what reason he has for believing that Caesar died in the Capitol, or that the Emperor Charlemagne was crowned Emperor of the West by Pope Leo III. in 800 . . . How do you know that such a man as Charles I. ever lived, and was beheaded, and that Oliver Cromwell became ruler in his stead? . . . Sir Isaac Newton is credited with the discovery of the law of gravitation . . . We believe all the assertions just made respecting these men; and that because we have historical evidence of their truth. . . . If, on the production of such proof as this, any still refuse to believe, we abandon them as stupidly perverse or hopelessly ignorant. What shall we say, then, of those who, notwithstanding the abundant evidence now produced of the authenticity of the Holy Scriptures, profess themselves unconvinced? . . . Surely we have reason to conclude that it is the heart rather than the head which is at fault;—that they do not wish to believe that which humbles their pride, and will force them to lead different lives.'"*

[8] The superiority of Christianity as a religion whose followers worship with truth is highlighted

___

* 1871, pages 29-31.

6. What testimony supports the historical accuracy of the Greek Scriptures?
7. (a) What argument does S. A. Allibone present as to the Bible's superior claims to authenticity? (b) What does he say is at fault with those who refuse the evidence?
8. In what way is the Christianity of the Bible shown to be distinguished from all other religions?

by George Rawlinson, who wrote: "Christianity —including therein the dispensation of the Old Testament, which was its first stage—is in nothing more distinguished from the other religions of the world than in its objective or historical character. The religions of Greece and Rome, of Egypt, India, Persia, and the East generally, were speculative systems, which did not even seriously postulate an historical basis. . . . But it is otherwise with the religion of the Bible. There, whether we look to the Old or the New Testament, to the Jewish dispensation or to the Christian, we find a scheme of doctrine which is bound up with facts; which depends absolutely upon them; which is null and void without them; and which may be regarded as for all practical purposes established if they are shown to deserve acceptance."*

⁹ **(2) Geographic and Geologic Accuracy.** Many writers have commented on the remarkable accuracy of the Bible description of the Promised Land and neighboring territories. As an example, an Oriental traveler, Dr. A. P. Stanley, said concerning the Israelites' wilderness trek: "Even if their precise route were unknown, yet the peculiar features of the country have so much in common that the history would still receive many remarkable illustrations. . . . The occasional springs, and wells, and brooks, are in accordance with the notices of the 'waters' of Marah; the 'springs' of . . . Elim; the 'brook' of Horeb; the 'well' of Jethro's daughters, with its 'trough' or tanks, in Midian. The vegetation is still that which we should infer from the Mosaic history."# In the account of Egypt, the accuracy is seen not only in the general description of the territory—its rich grain lands, its Nile River edged with reeds (Gen. 41:47-49; Ex. 2:3), its waters derived from 'rivers, canals, reedy pools, and impounded waters' (Ex. 7:19), its 'flax, barley, wheat, and spelt' (Ex. 9:31, 32)—but also in the names and sites of towns.

¹⁰ Such is the reliance placed on the geologic and geographic record in the Bible by some modern-day scientists that they have followed it as a guide and have been well rewarded. Some years ago, a noted geologist, Dr. Ben Tor, followed through on the scripture: "For Jehovah your God is bringing you into a good land, . . . a land the stones of which are iron." (Deut. 8:7, 9) A few miles from Beersheba, he found immense cliffs saturated with red-black ore. Here was an estimated 15 million

tons of low-grade iron ore. Later, engineers discovered a mile-long outcrop of excellent ore, 60 to 65 percent pure iron. Dr. Joseph Weitz, Israel's noted authority on reforestation, said: "The first tree Abraham put in the soil of Beersheba was a tamarisk." "Following his lead, four years ago we put out two million in the same area. Abraham was right. The tamarisk is one of the few trees we have found that thrives in the south where yearly rainfall is less than six inches."* The book *Tree and Shrub in Our Biblical Heritage,* by Nogah Hareuveni, adds: "It appears that the Patriarch Abraham did not simply plant any tree upon arriving in Beersheva. . . . He chose the tree whose shade is cooler than that of other trees. Moreover, the [tamarisk] can withstand heat and long dry spells by sending its roots deep down to find underground water. Not surprisingly, the [tamarisk] remains to this day in the vicinity of Beersheva."# —Gen. 21:33.

¹¹ As to details such as chronological and geographic statements in the Bible, Professor R. D. Wilson writes in *A Scientific Investigation of the Old Testament,* pages 213-14: "The chronological and geographical statements are more accurate and reliable than those afforded by any other ancient documents; and the biographical and other historical narratives harmonize marvelously with the evidence afforded by extra-biblical documents."

¹² **(3) Races and Languages of Mankind.** In the book *After Its Kind,* Byron C. Nelson says: "It was *man* that was made, not the Negro, the Chinese, the European. Two human beings whom the Bible knows as Adam and Eve were created, out of whom by natural descent and variation have come all the varieties of men that are on the face of the earth. All races of men, regardless of color or size, are one natural species. They all think alike, feel alike, are alike in physical structure, readily intermarry, and are capable of reproducing others of the same character. All races are descended from two common ancestors who came full-formed from the hand of the Creator."△ This is the testimony of Genesis 1:27, 28; 2:7, 20-23; 3:20; Acts 17:26; and Romans 5:12.

¹³ As to the Bible's account of the focal point

---

* *The Historical Evidences of the Truth of the Scripture Records,* pages 25-6.
# *Sinai and Palestine,* 1885, pages 82-3.

---

9. Illustrate the accuracy of the Bible's geographic references.
10. How have modern scientists been rewarded in following the Bible record?

---

* *Reader's Digest,* March 1954, pages 27, 30.
# 1984, page 24.
△ 1968, pages 4-5.

---

11. How does Professor Wilson testify concerning Bible accuracy?
12. How do the facts fit the Bible record of the origin of mankind?
13. What did one archaeologist say about the focal point from which ancient languages spread?

from which the spreading of ancient languages began, the archaeologist Sir Henry Rawlinson said that "if we were to be thus guided by the mere intersection of linguistic paths, and independently of all reference to the scriptural record, we should still be led to fix on the plains of Shinar, as the focus from which the various lines had radiated."* —Gen. 11:1-9.

[14] **(4) Practicality.** If there were no other proofs of authenticity available, the Bible's righteous principles and moral standards would set it apart as a product of the divine mind. Additionally, its practicality extends to every phase of daily living. No other book gives us a rational view of the origin of all things, including mankind, and of the Creator's purpose toward the earth and man. (Gen., chap. 1; Isa. 45:18) The Bible tells us why man dies and why wickedness exists. (Gen., chap. 3; Rom. 5:12; Job, chaps. 1, 2; Ex. 9:16) It sets out the highest standard of justice. (Ex. 23:1, 2, 6, 7; Deut. 19:15-21) It gives right counsel on business dealings (Lev. 19:35, 36; Prov. 20:10; 22:22, 23; Matt. 7:12); clean moral conduct (Lev. 20:10-16; Gal. 5: 19-23; Heb. 13:4); relationships with others (Lev. 19:18; Prov. 12:15; 15:1; 27:1, 2, 5, 6; 29:11; Matt. 7:12; 1 Tim. 5:1, 2); marriage (Gen. 2: 22-24; Matt. 19:4, 5, 9; 1 Cor. 7:2, 9, 10, 39); family relationships and duties of husband, wife, and children (Deut. 6:4-9; Prov. 13:24; Eph. 5: 21-33; 6:1-4; Col. 3:18-21; 1 Pet. 3:1-6); proper attitude toward rulers (Rom. 13:1-10; Titus 3:1; 1 Tim. 2:1, 2; 1 Pet. 2:13, 14); honest work as well as master-slave and employer-employee relationships (Eph. 4:28; Col. 3:22-24; 4:1; 1 Pet. 2: 18-21); proper associations (Prov. 1:10-16; 5: 3-11; 1 Cor. 15:33; 2 Tim. 2:22; Heb. 10:24, 25); settling disputes (Matt. 18:15-17; Eph. 4:26); and many other things that vitally affect our everyday lives.

[15] The Bible also provides valuable pointers regarding physical and mental health. (Prov. 15:17; 17:22) In recent years, medical research has demonstrated that a person's physical health is indeed affected by his mental attitude. For example, studies have shown that persons who are prone to express anger often have the highest levels of blood pressure. Some reported that anger produced cardiac sensations, headaches, nosebleeds, dizziness, or inability to vocalize. However, the

Bible long ago explained: "A calm heart is the life of the fleshly organism."—Prov. 14:30; compare Matthew 5:9.

[16] **(5) Scientific Accuracy.** Though the Bible is not a treatise on science, where it touches on scientific matters, it is found to be accurate and in harmony with true scientific discovery and knowledge. Its record of the order of creation, including animal life (Gen., chap. 1); the earth's being round, or spherical (Isa. 40:22); and the earth's hanging in space on "nothing" antedate scientific discoveries of these truths. (Job 26:7) Modern physiology has demonstrated the truth of the Scriptural statement that "not all flesh is the same flesh," the cellular structure of the flesh of one kind being different from that of another, man having his own unique "flesh." (1 Cor. 15:39)* In the field of zoology, Leviticus 11:6 classes the hare with the cud-chewing animals. This was once scoffed at, but science now finds that the rabbit reingests its food.#

[17] The statement that the 'life of the flesh is in the blood' has in modern times come to be recognized as a basic truth of medical science. (Lev. 17: 11-14) The Mosaic Law indicated which animals, birds, and fish were "clean" for human consumption, and it excluded risky foods. (Lev., chap. 11) The Law required that at a military encampment, human excrement be covered over, thus providing considerable protection from fly-borne infectious diseases, such as dysentery and typhoid fever. (Deut. 23:9-14) Even today, in some lands severe health problems exist because of improper disposal of human wastes. People in such lands would be much healthier if they followed the Bible's counsel on hygiene.

[18] The Bible recommends a little wine for "the sake of your stomach" and for "sickness." (1 Tim. 5:23) Dr. Salvatore P. Lucia, professor of medicine at the University of California School of Medicine, writes: "Wine is the most ancient dietary beverage and the most important medicinal agent in continuous use throughout the history of mankind."△

[19] **(6) Culture and Customs.** A. Rendle Short writes in *Modern Discovery and the Bible,* about

---

* *The Journal of the Royal Asiatic Society of Great Britain and Ireland,* London, 1855, Vol. 15, page 232.

---

14. (a) What alone would set the Bible apart as inspired of God? (b) What rational view is presented only in the Bible, and how does its practicality extend to every phase of daily living?
15. What Bible counsel on mental and physical health has been shown to be practical?

---

* *Insight on the Scriptures,* Vol. 2, page 246.
# *Insight on the Scriptures,* Vol. 1, pages 555-6, 1035.
△ *Wine as Food and Medicine,* 1954, page 5.

---

16. What are some of the Bible statements of truth that far predate their discovery by science?
17. How has the Bible been shown to be medically sound?
18. What other illustration of the Bible's scientific accuracy is given?
19. How may the accuracy of Luke's writings be illustrated?

the book of Acts: "It was the Roman custom to govern the provinces of their far-flung empire by continuing as far as they safely could the local system of administration, and consequently the authorities in different districts went by many different names. No one, unless he were either an observant traveller or a painstaking student of records, could possibly give all these gentry their correct denomination. It is one of the most searching tests of Luke's historical sense that he always manages to achieve perfect accuracy. In several cases it is only the evidence of a coin, or an inscription, that has given us the necessary information to check him; the recognized Roman historians do not adventure themselves on such a difficult terrain. Thus Luke calls Herod and Lysanias tetrarchs; so does Josephus. Herod Agrippa, who slew James with the sword and cast Peter into prison, is called a king; Josephus tells us how he became friendly at Rome with Gaius Cæsar (Caligula) and was rewarded with a royal title when Caligula came to be emperor. The governor of Cyprus, Sergius Paulus, is called proconsul. . . . Not long before, Cyprus had been an imperial province, and governed by a proprætor or legatus, but in Paul's time, as is shown by Cyprian coins, both in Greek and Latin, the correct title was proconsul. A Greek inscription found at Soloi on the north coast of Cyprus is dated 'in the proconsulship of Paulus' . . . At Thessalonica the city magnates took the quite unusual title of politarchs [city rulers, Acts 17:6, footnote], a name unknown to classical literature. It would be quite unfamiliar to us, except from Luke's use of it, if it were not for the fact that it appears in inscriptions. . . . Achaia under Augustus was a senatorial province, under Tiberius it was directly under the emperor, but under Claudius, as Tacitus tells us, it reverted to the senate, and therefore Gallio's correct title [Acts 18:12] was proconsul. . . . Luke is equally happy, equally accurate, in his geography and his travel experiences."*

20 Paul's letters accurately reflect the background of his time and indicate that he was an eyewitness of the things written. For example, Philippi was a military colony whose citizens were especially proud of their Roman citizenship. Paul admonished the Christians there that their citizenship was in the heavens. (Acts 16:12, 21, 37; Phil. 3:20) Ephesus was a city noted for magical arts and spiritistic practices. Paul instructed Christians there as to how to arm themselves against becoming prey to the demons, and at the same time, he gave an accurate description of the armor of a Roman soldier. (Acts 19:19; Eph. 6:13-17) The custom of Roman victors of leading a triumphant march with a procession of captives, some naked, is used in illustration. (2 Cor. 2:14; Col. 2:15) At 1 Corinthians 1:22, the differing outlooks of Jews and Greeks are pointed out. In such matters the Christian writers reflect the accuracy of Moses, the writer of the Pentateuch, of which George Rawlinson says: "The *ethological* accuracy of the Pentateuch as respects Oriental manners and customs generally, has never been questioned."*

21 **(7) Candor of Bible Writers.** Throughout the Bible, the unhesitating candor of its writers is strong proof of its reliability. Moses, for example, straightforwardly tells of his own sin and God's judgment that he and his brother, Aaron, should not enter the Promised Land. (Num. 20:7-13; Deut. 3:23-27) The sins of David on two occasions as well as the apostasy of his son Solomon are openly exposed. (2 Sam., chaps. 11, 12, 24; 1 Ki. 11:1-13) Jonah writes about his own disobedience and its result. The entire nation of Israel was condemned by nearly all the writers of the Hebrew Scriptures, all of whom were Jews, for its disobedience to God, in the very record the Jews cherished and accepted as the pronouncements of God and the true history of their nation. The Christian writers were no less candid. All four of the Gospel writers revealed Peter's denial of Christ. And Paul called attention to Peter's serious error on a matter of faith in making a separation between Jews and Gentiles in the Christian congregation at Antioch. It builds confidence in the Bible as truth when we realize that its writers spared no one, not even themselves, in the interests of making a faithful record.—Matt. 26:69-75; Mark 14:66-72; Luke 22:54-62; John 18:15-27; Gal. 2:11-14; John 17:17.

22 **(8) Harmony of Writers.** The Bible was written over a period of more than 1,600 years by about 40 writers, with no disharmony. It has been widely distributed in tremendous numbers despite the fiercest opposition and the most energetic efforts to destroy it. These facts help to prove that it is what it claims to be, the Word of the almighty God, and that it is indeed "beneficial for teaching, for reproving, for setting things straight, for disciplining in righteousness."—2 Tim. 3:16.#

---

* *The Historical Evidences of the Truth of the Scripture Records,* page 290.
# *The Bible—God's Word or Man's?,* pages 12-36.

---

* 1955, pages 211-13.

---

20. How do Paul's writings accurately reflect the times in which he lived and wrote?

21. (a) Give examples of the candor of the Bible writers. (b) How does this build confidence in the Bible as truth?
22. What else proves that the Bible is indeed God's Word, and for what purpose was it written?

23 Its inspiration is shown by the thorough consistency with which it emphasizes the theme of sanctification of Jehovah's name by his Kingdom under Christ. A few of the outstanding instances are:

Gen. 3:15	Promise of the Seed that will destroy the Serpent
Gen. 22:15-18	All nations will bless themselves by means of Abraham's seed
Ex. 3:15; 6:3	God emphasizes his memorial name, Jehovah
Ex. 9:16; Rom. 9:17	God states purpose to have his name declared
Ex. 18:11; Isa. 36:18-20; 37:20, 36-38; Jer. 10:10, 11	Jehovah greater than all other gods
Ex. 20:3-7	God respects name, demands exclusive devotion
Job, chaps. 1, 2	Jehovah's rightful sovereignty and man's attitude and integrity toward it
Job 32:2; 35:2; 36:24; 40:8	God's vindication brought to the fore
Isa. 9:7	God zealously supports everlasting Kingdom of his Son
Dan. 2:44; 4: 17, 34; 7:13, 14	The importance of God's Kingdom by the "son of man"
Ezek. 6:10; 38:23	People "will have to know that I am Jehovah." This statement appears more than 60 times in the prophecy of Ezekiel
Mal. 1:11	God's name to be great among the nations
Matt. 6:9, 10, 33	Sanctification of God's name by his Kingdom is of primary importance
John 17:6, 26	Jesus declared God's name
Acts 2:21; Rom. 10:13	Jehovah's name to be called on for salvation
Rom. 3:4	God to be proved true, though every man a liar
1 Cor. 15:24-28	Kingdom to be handed back to God; God to be all things to everyone
Heb. 13:15	Christians must make public declaration to Jehovah's name
Rev. 15:4	Jehovah's name to be glorified by all nations
Rev. 19:6	Jehovah's name praised after devastation of Babylon the Great

24 **(9) Integrity of Witnesses.** Of the weight that may be accorded the testimony of early Christians —the writers of the Christian Scriptures as well as others—George Rawlinson says: "The early converts knew that they might at any time be called upon to undergo death for their religion. . . . Every early writer advocating Christianity, by the fact of his advocacy, braved the civil power, and rendered himself liable to a similar fate. When faith is a matter of life and death, men do not lightly take up with the first creed which happens to hit their fancy; nor do they place themselves openly in the ranks of a persecuted sect, unless they have well weighed the claims of the religion which it professes, and convinced themselves of its being the truth. It is clear that the early converts had means of ascertaining the historic accuracy of the Christian narrative very much beyond ourselves; they could examine and cross-question the witnesses —compare their several accounts—inquire how their statements were met by their adversaries —consult Heathen documents of the time—thoroughly and completely sift the evidence. . . . All this together—and it must be remembered that the evidence is *cumulative*—constitutes a body of proof such as is seldom producible with respect to any events belonging to remote times; and establishes beyond all reasonable doubt the truth of the Christian Story. In no single respect . . . has that story a mythic character. It is a single story, told without variation, whereas myths are fluctuating and multiform; it is blended inextricably with the civil history of the times, which it every where represents with extraordinary accuracy, whereas myths distort or supersede civil history; it is full of prosaic detail, which myths studiously eschew; it abounds with practical instruction of the plainest and simplest kind, whereas myths teach by allegory. . . . Simple earnestness, fidelity, painstaking accuracy, pure love of truth, are the most patent characteristics of the New Testament writers, who evidently deal with facts, not with fancies . . . They write 'that we may know the certainty of those things' which were 'most surely believed' in their day."*—Compare Luke 1:1, 4.

25 An enthralling field covered by the Bible is that of divine prophecy. The authenticity of the Bible has been in no way as strikingly demonstrated as in the fulfillment of numerous prophecies, all showing the remarkable forevision of Jehovah in foretelling the future. This prophetic Word is indeed "a lamp shining in a dark place," and paying attention to it will strengthen the faith of those who desire to survive until all Kingdom prophecy

---

23. What consistent theme also proves the Bible's inspiration? Illustrate.
24. (a) How does the integrity of the early Christians establish the truthfulness of "the Christian Story"? (b) What other proof is there that the Bible writers recorded facts, not myths?

---

* *The Historical Evidences of the Truth of the Scripture Records,* pages 225, 227-8.

---

25. What outstandingly demonstrates the authenticity of the Bible?

is fulfilled in God's everlasting new world of righteousness. The three tables that follow add further proof of the Bible's authenticity in showing many of these prophetic fulfillments, as well as the harmony of the entire Hebrew and Greek Scriptures.

———

Questions on chart "Outstanding Prophecies Concerning Jesus and Their Fulfillment": (a) What prophecies concerning his birth put Jesus in line for Messiahship? (b) What prophecies were fulfilled at the beginning of Jesus' ministry? (c) How did Jesus fulfill prophecy by the way he carried on his ministry? (d) What prophecies were fulfilled during the last few days before Jesus' trial? (e) How was prophecy fulfilled at the time of his trial? (f) What prophecies marked his actual impalement, his death, and his resurrection?

Questions on chart "Examples of Other Bible Prophecies Fulfilled": (a) What foretold events occurred after the nation of Israel came into the land of Canaan? (b) What prophecies of judgment against Israel and Judah came to pass, and when? (c) What was foretold of a restoration? Was this fulfilled? (d) Which nations are listed against whom specific messages of judgment came, and how were these prophetic judgments fulfilled? (e) What are some of the outstanding events of history foretold by Daniel? by Jesus?

With the passage of time, the Bible shines forth more and more brilliantly as being truly "inspired of God and beneficial."—2 Pet. 1:19; 2 Tim. 3:16.

———

Questions on chart "Some Quotations and Applications of the Hebrew Scriptures by Writers of the Greek Scriptures": (a) How do references to Genesis in the Greek Scriptures support its account of creation? (b) What applications are made of references in Genesis to Abraham and to Abraham's seed? (c) What quotations are made from the book of Exodus as to the Ten Commandments and other aspects of the Law? (d) Where do we find the original declarations of the two great commandments, to love Jehovah with one's whole heart and soul and to love one's neighbor as oneself? (e) Name some of the basic principles stated in the Pentateuch that are quoted in the Greek Scriptures. How are they applied? (f) What passages in the Psalms, quoted in the Greek Scriptures, magnify Jehovah [1] as Creator and Owner of the earth? [2] as the One who shows interest in the righteous and cares for them? (g) How do the Christian Greek Scriptures apply passages from Isaiah and the other prophets to [1] the preaching of the good news? [2] the rejection of the good news by some? [3] people of the nations, in addition to a remnant of Israel, becoming believers? [4] the benefits of exercising faith in the good news?

(10) OUTSTANDING PROPHECIES CONCERNING JESUS AND THEIR FULFILLMENT

Prophecy	Event	Fulfillment
Gen. 49:10	Born of the tribe of Judah	Matt. 1:2-16; Luke 3:23-33; Heb. 7:14
Ps. 132:11; Isa. 9:7; 11:1, 10	From the family of David the son of Jesse	Matt. 1:1, 6-16; 9:27; 15:22; 20:30, 31; 21:9, 15; 22:42; Mark 10:47, 48; Luke 1:32; 2:4; 3:23-32; 18:38, 39; Acts 2:29-31; 13:22, 23; Rom. 1:3; 15:8, 12
Mic. 5:2	Born in Bethlehem	Luke 2:4-11; John 7:42
Isa. 7:14	Born of a virgin	Matt. 1:18-23; Luke 1:30-35
Jer. 31:15	Babes killed after his birth	Matt. 2:16-18
Hos. 11:1	Called out of Egypt	Matt. 2:15
Mal. 3:1; 4:5; Isa. 40:3	Way prepared before	Matt. 3:1-3; 11:10-14; 17:10-13; Mark 1:2-4; Luke 1:17, 76; 3:3-6; 7:27; John 1:20-23; 3:25-28; Acts 13:24; 19:4
Dan. 9:25	Appeared as Messiah at end of 69 "weeks"	Presented himself for baptism and was anointed on schedule in 29 C.E. (Luke 3:1, 21, 22)
Isa. 61:1, 2	Commissioned	Luke 4:18-21
Isa. 9:1, 2	Ministry caused people in Naphtali and Zebulun to see great light	Matt. 4:13-16
Ps. 78:2	Spoke with illustrations	Matt. 13:11-13, 31-35
Isa. 53:4	Carried our sicknesses	Matt. 8:16, 17
Ps. 69:9	Zealous for Jehovah's house	Matt. 21:12, 13; Mark 11:15-18; Luke 19:45, 46; John 2:13-17
Isa. 42:1-4	As Jehovah's servant, would not wrangle in streets	Matt. 12:14-21
Isa. 53:1	Not believed in	John 12:37, 38; Rom. 10:11, 16
Zech. 9:9; Ps. 118:26	Entry into Jerusalem on colt of an ass; hailed as king and the one coming in Jehovah's name	Matt. 21:1-9; Mark 11:7-11; Luke 19:28-38; John 12:12-15

Prophecy	Event	Fulfillment
Isa. 28:16; 53:3; Ps. 69:8; 118:22, 23	Rejected, but becomes chief cornerstone	Matt. 21:42, 45, 46; Acts 3:14; 4:11; 1 Pet. 2:7
Isa. 8:14, 15	Becomes stone of stumbling	Luke 20:17, 18; Rom. 9:31-33; 1 Pet. 2:8
Ps. 41:9; 109:8	One apostle unfaithful; betrays Jesus	Matt. 26:47-50; John 13:18, 26-30; 17:12; 18:2-5; Acts 1:16-20
Zech. 11:12	Betrayed for 30 pieces of silver	Matt. 26:15; 27:3-10; Mark 14:10, 11
Zech. 13:7	Disciples scatter	Matt. 26:31, 56; John 16:32
Ps. 2:1, 2	Roman powers and leaders of Israel act together against anointed of Jehovah	Matt. 27:1, 2; Mark 15:1, 15; Luke 23:10-12; Acts 4:25-28
Isa. 53:8	Tried and condemned	Matt. 26:57-68; 27:1, 2, 11-26; John 18:12-14, 19-24, 28-40; 19:1-16
Ps. 27:12	Use of false witnesses	Matt. 26:59-61; Mark 14:56-59
Isa. 53:7	Silent before accusers	Matt. 27:12-14; Mark 14:61; 15:4, 5; Luke 23:9; John 19:9
Ps. 69:4	Hated without cause	Luke 23:13-25; John 15:24, 25; 1 Pet. 2:22
Isa. 50:6; Mic. 5:1	Struck, spit on	Matt. 26:67; 27:26, 30; John 18:22; 19:3
Ps. 22:16, ftn.	Impaled	Matt. 27:35; Mark 15:24, 25; Luke 23:33; John 19:18, 23; 20:25, 27
Ps. 22:18	Lots cast for garments	Matt. 27:35; John 19:23, 24
Isa. 53:12	Numbered with sinners	Matt. 26:55, 56; 27:38; Luke 22:37
Ps. 22:7, 8	Reviled while on stake	Matt. 27:39-43; Mark 15:29-32
Ps. 69:21	Given vinegar and gall	Matt. 27:34, 48; Mark 15:23, 36
Ps. 22:1	Forsaken by God to enemies	Matt. 27:46; Mark 15:34
Ps. 34:20; Ex. 12:46	No bones broken	John 19:33, 36
Isa. 53:5; Zech. 12:10	Pierced	Matt. 27:49; John 19:34, 37; Rev. 1:7
Isa. 53:5, 8, 11, 12	Dies sacrificial death to carry away sins and open way to righteous standing with God	Matt. 20:28; John 1:29; Rom. 3:24; 4:25; 1 Cor. 15:3; Heb. 9:12-15; 1 Pet. 2:24; 1 John 2:2
Isa. 53:9	Buried with the rich	Matt. 27:57-60; John 19:38-42
Jonah 1:17; 2:10	In grave for parts of three days, then resurrected	Matt. 12:39, 40; 16:21; 17:23; 20:19; 27:64; 28:1-7; Acts 10:40; 1 Cor. 15:3-8
Ps. 16:8-11, ftn.	Raised before corruption	Acts 2:25-31; 13:34-37
Ps. 2:7	Jehovah declares him His Son by spirit begettal and by resurrection	Matt. 3:16, 17; Mark 1:9-11; Luke 3:21, 22; Acts 13:33; Rom. 1:4; Heb. 1:5; 5:5

(11) EXAMPLES OF OTHER BIBLE PROPHECIES FULFILLED

Prophecy	Event	Fulfillment
Gen. 9:25	Canaanites to become servants to Israel	Josh. 9:23, 27; Judg. 1:28; 1 Ki. 9:20, 21
Gen. 15:13, 14; Ex. 3:21, 22	Israel to come out of Egypt with much property when God judges enslaving nation	Ex. 12:35, 36; Ps. 105:37
Gen. 17:20; 21:13, 18	Ishmael to produce 12 chieftains and become a great nation	Gen. 25:13-16; 1 Chron. 1:29-31
Gen. 25:23; 27:39, 40	Edomites to dwell away from fertile soils, to serve Israelites, and at times to revolt	Gen. 36:8; Deut. 2:4, 5; 2 Sam. 8:14; 2 Ki. 8:20; 1 Chron. 18:13; 2 Chron. 21:8-10
Gen. 48:19, 22	Ephraim to become greater than Manasseh, and each tribe to have an inheritance	Num. 1:33-35; Deut. 33:17; Josh. 16:4-9; 17:1-4

Prophecy	Event	Fulfillment
Gen. 49:7	Simeon and Levi to become scattered in Israel	Josh. 19:1-9; 21:41, 42
Gen. 49:10	Kingly leadership to come from Judah	2 Sam. 2:4; 1 Chron. 5:2; Matt. 1:1-16; Luke 3:23-33; Heb. 7:14
Deut. 17:14	Israel to request a monarchy	1 Sam. 8:4, 5, 19, 20
Deut. 28:52, 53, 64-66, 68	Israel to be punished for unfaithfulness; cities besieged, sent into slavery	Fulfilled on Samaria in 740 B.C.E. (2 Ki. 17:5-23), on Jerusalem in 607 B.C.E. (Jer. 52:1-27), and on Jerusalem again in 70 C.E.
Josh. 6:26	Penalty for rebuilding Jericho	1 Ki. 16:34
1 Sam. 2:31, 34; 3:12-14	Eli's line cursed	1 Sam. 4:11, 17, 18; 1 Ki. 2:26, 27, 35
1 Ki. 9:7, 8; 2 Chron. 7:20, 21	Temple to be destroyed if Israel turned apostate	2 Ki. 25:9; 2 Chron. 36:19; Jer. 52:13; Lam. 2:6, 7
1 Ki. 13:1-3	Jeroboam's altar to be polluted	2 Ki. 23:16-18
1 Ki. 14:15	Overthrow of ten-tribe kingdom of Israel	2 Ki. 17:6-23; 18:11, 12
Isa. 13:17-22; 45:1, 2; Jer. 50:35-46; 51:37-43	Destruction of Babylon; gates of Babylon to be left open; Medes and Persians to conquer under Cyrus	Dan. 5:22-31; secular history corroborates. Cyrus took Babylon when gates left open*
Isa. 23:1, 8, 13, 14; Ezek. 26:4, 7-12	City of Tyre to be destroyed by Chaldeans under Nebuchadnezzar	Secular history records mainland part of city destroyed and island part submitted to Nebuchadnezzar after 13-year siege#
Isa. 44:26-28	Rebuilding of Jerusalem and temple by the returning Jewish exiles; Cyrus' part in it	2 Chron. 36:22, 23; Ezra 1:1-4
Jer. 25:11; 29:10	Restoration of a remnant would be after 70 years' desolation	Dan. 9:1, 2; Zech. 7:5; 2 Chron. 36:21-23
Jer. 48:15-24; Ezek. 25:8-11; Zeph. 2:8, 9	Moab to be laid waste	Moab now an extinct nation△
Jer. 49:2; Ezek. 25:1-7; Zeph. 2:8, 9	Ammonite cities to become desolate heaps	Ammon now an extinct nation⊠
Jer. 49:17, 18; Ezek. 25:12-14; 35:7, 15; Obad. 16, 18	Edom to be cut off as though it had never been	Edom became extinct as a nation after destruction of Jerusalem in 70 C.E.▢
Dan. 2:31-40; 7:2-7	Four kingdoms depicted: Babylon, Persia, Greece, and Rome. Many prophetic details foretold	Secular history confirms fulfillments in rise and fall of these powers+
Dan. 8:1-8, 20-22; 11:1-19	After kingdom of Persia, a mighty one, Greece, would rule. That kingdom to be divided into four, out of which would come two powers, the king of the north and the king of the south	Alexander the Great conquered Persian Empire. After his death four generals took over. Eventually Seleucid and Ptolemaic powers developed and were continually at war with each other◇
Dan. 11:20-24	Ruler to decree registration. In days of his successor, "the Leader of the covenant" would be broken	Registration decree in Palestine during reign of Caesar Augustus; Jesus killed during reign of his successor, Tiberius Caesar☉
Zeph. 2:13-15; Nah. 3:1-7	Nineveh to become a desolation	Became a mound of rubbish⊿
Zech. 9:3, 4	Island city of Tyre to be destroyed	Accomplished by Alexander in 332 B.C.E.☉

* *Herodotus* I, 191, 192; *Insight on the Scriptures*, Vol. 1, page 567.
# McClintock and Strong's *Cyclopedia*, 1981 reprint, Vol. X, page 617; *Insight on the Scriptures*, Vol. 2, pages 531, 1136.
△ *Insight on the Scriptures*, Vol. 2, pages 421-2.
⊠ *Insight on the Scriptures*, Vol. 1, page 95.
▢ *Insight on the Scriptures*, Vol. 1, pages 681-2.
+ *"Your Will Be Done on Earth,"* pages 104-25, 166-77, 188-95, 220-9.
◇ *"Your Will Be Done on Earth,"* pages 121-2, 172-4, 194-5, 220-63; *Insight on the Scriptures*, Vol. 1, pages 70-1.
☉ *"Your Will Be Done on Earth,"* pages 248-53; *Insight on the Scriptures*, Vol. 1, page 220.
⊿ See page 159, paragraphs 5, 6.
☉ McClintock and Strong's *Cyclopedia*, 1981 reprint, Vol. X, pages 618-19.

Prophecy	Event	Fulfillment
Matt. 24:2, 16-18; Luke 19:41-44	Jerusalem to be surrounded by staked fortifications and destroyed	Fulfilled by Romans in 70 C.E.*
Matt. 24:7-14; Mark 13:8; Luke 21:10, 11, 25-28; 2 Tim. 3:1-5	Great time of trouble foretold before complete end of this system of things; to include wars, food shortages, earthquakes, pestilence, lawlessness, preaching of Kingdom good news to all the nations	Unprecedented time of trouble on earth since first world war in 1914. Kingdom preaching now being done in over 200 lands

* See page 188, paragraph 9.

(12) SOME QUOTATIONS AND APPLICATIONS OF THE HEBREW SCRIPTURES BY WRITERS OF THE GREEK SCRIPTURES

(NOTE: This list does not include references that are listed in the "Outstanding Prophecies Concerning Jesus," on the preceding pages.)

Quotation	Statement	Application
Gen. 1:3	God commands light to shine	2 Cor. 4:6
Gen. 1:26, 27	Man made in God's likeness, male and female	Jas. 3:9; Mark 10:6
Gen. 2:2	God rests from earthly creative work	Heb. 4:4
Gen. 2:7	Adam made a living soul	1 Cor. 15:45
Gen. 2:24	Man to leave his parents and stick to his wife; the two become one flesh	Matt. 19:5; Mark 10:7, 8; 1 Cor. 6:16; Eph. 5:31
Gen. 12:3; 18:18	All nations to be blessed by means of Abraham	Gal. 3:8
Gen. 15:5	Abraham's seed to be many	Rom. 4:18
Gen. 15:6	Faith counted to Abraham as righteousness	Rom. 4:3; Gal. 3:6; Jas. 2:23
Gen. 17:5	Abraham father of those with faith out of "many nations"	Rom. 4:16, 17
Gen. 18:10, 14	A son promised to Sarah	Rom. 9:9
Gen. 18:12	Sarah calls Abraham "lord"	1 Pet. 3:6
Gen. 21:10	Symbolic drama involving Sarah, Hagar, Isaac, and Ishmael	Gal. 4:30
Gen. 21:12	Seed of Abraham to be through Isaac	Rom. 9:7; Heb. 11:18
Gen. 22:16, 17	God swears by himself to bless Abraham	Heb. 6:13, 14
Gen. 25:23	God's favor to Jacob over Esau foretold	Rom. 9:12
Ex. 3:6	God is the God, not of the dead, but of the living	Matt. 22:32; Mark 12:26; Luke 20:37
Ex. 9:16	God's reason for allowing Pharaoh to remain	Rom. 9:17
Ex. 13:2, 12	Firstborn dedicated to Jehovah	Luke 2:23
Ex. 16:18	God equalizes matters in the gathering of manna	2 Cor. 8:15
Ex. 19:5, 6	Israel in line to be kingdom of priests	1 Pet. 2:9
Ex. 19:12, 13	The awesomeness of Jehovah at Mount Sinai	Heb. 12:18-20
Ex. 20:12-17	Fifth, sixth, seventh, eighth, ninth, and tenth commandments	Matt. 5:21, 27; 15:4; 19:18, 19; Mark 10:19; Luke 18:20; Rom. 13:9; Eph. 6:2, 3; Jas. 2:11
Ex. 21:17	Penalty for breaking fifth commandment	Matt. 15:4; Mark 7:10
Ex. 21:24	Eye for eye and tooth for tooth	Matt. 5:38
Ex. 22:28	"You must not speak injuriously of a ruler of your people"	Acts 23:5
Ex. 24:8	The making of the Law covenant—"the blood of the covenant"	Heb. 9:20; Matt. 26:28; Mark 14:24
Ex. 25:40	Moses instructed in the pattern of the tabernacle and its furnishings	Heb. 8:5
Ex. 32:6	Israelites rise up to revel and have a good time	1 Cor. 10:7

Quotation	Statement	Application
Ex. 33:19	God has mercy upon whomever he pleases	Rom. 9:15
Lev. 11:44	"You must be holy, because I am holy"	1 Pet. 1:16
Lev. 12:8	Offering by a poor person after birth of a son	Luke 2:24
Lev. 18:5	He that keeps the Law will live by it	Gal. 3:12
Lev. 19:18	Love your neighbor as yourself	Matt. 19:19; 22:39; Mark 12:31; Rom. 13:9; Gal. 5:14; Jas. 2:8
Lev. 26:12	Jehovah was God of Israel	2 Cor. 6:16
Num. 16:5	Jehovah knows those who belong to him	2 Tim. 2:19
Deut. 6:4, 5	Love Jehovah with whole heart and soul	Matt. 22:37; Mark 12: 29, 30; Luke 10:27
Deut. 6:13	"It is Jehovah your God you must worship"	Matt. 4:10; Luke 4:8
Deut. 6:16	"You must not put Jehovah your God to the test"	Matt. 4:7; Luke 4:12
Deut. 8:3	Man must not live by bread alone	Matt. 4:4; Luke 4:4
Deut. 18:15-19	God to raise up a prophet like Moses	Acts 3:22, 23
Deut. 19:15	Every matter must be established by two or three witnesses	John 8:17; 2 Cor. 13:1
Deut. 23:21	"You must pay your vows to Jehovah"	Matt. 5:33
Deut. 24:1	Mosaic Law provision for divorce	Matt. 5:31
Deut. 25:4	"You must not muzzle a bull when it is threshing"	1 Cor. 9:9; 1 Tim. 5:18
Deut. 27:26	Israelites who did not abide by Law were cursed	Gal. 3:10
Deut. 29:4	Not many Jews listened to the good news	Rom. 11:8
Deut. 30:11-14	The need to have "the 'word' of faith" in one's heart and preach it	Rom. 10:6-8
Deut. 31:6, 8	God will by no means forsake his people	Heb. 13:5
Deut. 32:17, 21	God incited jealousy of Jews by inviting Gentiles. Israelites incited Jehovah to jealousy through idolatry	Rom. 10:19; 1 Cor. 10: 20-22
Deut. 32:35, 36	Vengeance is Jehovah's	Heb. 10:30
Deut. 32:43	"Be glad, you nations, with his people"	Rom. 15:10
1 Sam. 13:14; 16:1	David, a man agreeable to God's own heart	Acts 13:22
1 Sam. 21:6	David and his men eat loaves of presentation	Matt. 12:3, 4; Mark 2:25, 26; Luke 6:3, 4
1 Ki. 19:14, 18	Only a remnant of Jews remained faithful to God	Rom. 11:3, 4
2 Chron. 20:7	Abraham called God's "friend" ("lover")	Jas. 2:23
Job 41:11	"Who has first given to [God]?"	Rom. 11:35
Ps. 5:9	"Their throat is an opened grave"	Rom. 3:13
Ps. 8:2	God furnishes praise "out of the mouth of babes"	Matt. 21:16
Ps. 8:4-6	"What is man that you keep him in mind?" God subjected all things under Christ's feet	Heb. 2:6, 7; 1 Cor. 15:27
Ps. 10:7	"Their mouth is full of cursing"	Rom. 3:14
Ps. 14:1-3	"There is not a righteous man"	Rom. 3:10-12
Ps. 18:49	People of the nations to glorify God	Rom. 15:9
Ps. 19:4, ftn.	No lack of opportunity to hear the truth of God's existence as testified to by all creation	Rom. 10:18
Ps. 22:22	"I will declare your name to my brothers"	Heb. 2:12
Ps. 24:1	The earth belongs to Jehovah	1 Cor. 10:26
Ps. 32:1, 2	"Happy is the man whose sin Jehovah will by no means take into account"	Rom. 4:7, 8
Ps. 34:12-16	"The eyes of Jehovah are upon the righteous"	1 Pet. 3:10-12
Ps. 36:1	"There is no fear of God before their eyes"	Rom. 3:18
Ps. 40:6-8	God no longer approved of sacrifices under the Law; one offering of body of Jesus, according to God's will, brings sanctification	Heb. 10:6-10
Ps. 44:22	"We have been accounted as sheep for slaughtering"	Rom. 8:36
Ps. 45:6, 7	"God is [Christ's] throne forever"	Heb. 1:8, 9

Quotation	Statement	Application
Ps. 51:4	God vindicated in his words and judgments	Rom. 3:4
Ps. 68:18	When Christ ascended on high, he gave gifts in men	Eph. 4:8
Ps. 69:22, 23	Peace table of Israelites becomes a trap	Rom. 11:9, 10
Ps. 78:24	The bread from heaven	John 6:31-33
Ps. 82:6	"You are gods"	John 10:34
Ps. 94:11	"Jehovah knows that the reasonings of the wise men are futile"	1 Cor. 3:20
Ps. 95:7-11	Disobedient Israelites did not enter into God's rest	Heb. 3:7-11; 4:3, 5, 7
Ps. 102:25-27	"You . . . , O Lord, laid the foundations of the earth"	Heb. 1:10-12
Ps. 104:4	"He makes his angels spirits"	Heb. 1:7
Ps. 110:1	The Lord to sit at Jehovah's right hand	Matt. 22:43-45; Mark 12:36, 37; Luke 20: 42-44; Heb. 1:13
Ps. 110:4	Christ a priest forever according to the manner of Melchizedek	Heb. 7:17
Ps. 112:9	"He has distributed widely . . . His righteousness continues forever"	2 Cor. 9:9
Ps. 116:10	"I exercised faith, therefore I spoke"	2 Cor. 4:13
Ps. 117:1	"Praise Jehovah, all you nations"	Rom. 15:11
Ps. 118:6	"Jehovah is my helper; I will not be afraid"	Heb. 13:6
Ps. 140:3	"Poison of asps is behind their lips"	Rom. 3:13
Prov. 26:11	"The dog has returned to its own vomit"	2 Pet. 2:22
Isa. 1:9	Except for a remnant, Israel would have been like Sodom	Rom. 9:29
Isa. 6:9, 10	Israelites did not pay attention to the good news	Matt. 13:13-15; Mark 4:12; Luke 8:10; Acts 28:25-27
Isa. 8:17, 18	"Look! I and the young children, whom Jehovah gave me"	Heb. 2:13
Isa. 10:22, 23	Only a remnant of Israel to be saved	Rom. 9:27, 28
Isa. 22:13	"Let us eat and drink, for tomorrow we are to die"	1 Cor. 15:32
Isa. 25:8	"Death is swallowed up forever"	1 Cor. 15:54
Isa. 28:11, 12	People did not believe even though spoken to "with the tongues of foreigners"	1 Cor. 14:21
Isa. 28:16	No disappointment for those who rest their faith on Christ, the foundation in Zion	1 Pet. 2:6; Rom. 10:11
Isa. 29:13	Hypocrisy of scribes and Pharisees described	Matt. 15:7-9; Mark 7:6-8
Isa. 29:14	God makes the wisdom of wise men perish	1 Cor. 1:19
Isa. 40:6-8	The word spoken by Jehovah endures forever	1 Pet. 1:24, 25
Isa. 40:13	'Who has become Jehovah's counselor?'	Rom. 11:34
Isa. 42:6; 49:6	"I have appointed you as a light of nations"	Acts 13:47
Isa. 45:23	Every knee shall bend to Jehovah	Rom. 14:11
Isa. 49:8	The acceptable time to be heard, in "the day of salvation"	2 Cor. 6:2
Isa. 52:7	Feet of carriers of good news beautiful	Rom. 10:15
Isa. 52:11	"Get out from among them, and separate yourselves"	2 Cor. 6:17
Isa. 52:15	Good news announced to the Gentiles	Rom. 15:21
Isa. 54:1	"Be glad, you barren woman who does not give birth"	Gal. 4:27
Isa. 54:13	"And they will all be taught by Jehovah"	John 6:45
Isa. 56:7	Jehovah's house to be a house of prayer for all nations	Matt. 21:13; Mark 11: 17; Luke 19:46
Isa. 59:7, 8	Wickedness of men described	Rom. 3:15-17
Isa. 65:1, 2	Jehovah became manifest to Gentile nations	Rom. 10:20, 21
Isa. 66:1, 2	"The heaven is my throne, and the earth is my footstool"	Acts 7:49, 50

Quotation	Statement	Application
Jer. 5:21	Having eyes, but not seeing	Mark 8:18
Jer. 9:24	"He that boasts, let him boast in Jehovah"	1 Cor. 1:31; 2 Cor. 10:17
Jer. 31:31-34	God to make a new covenant	Heb. 8:8-12; 10:16, 17
Dan. 9:27; 11:31	"The disgusting thing that causes desolation"	Matt. 24:15
Hos. 1:10; 2:23	Gentiles also to become God's people	Rom. 9:24-26
Hos. 6:6	"I want mercy, and not sacrifice"	Matt. 9:13; 12:7
Hos. 13:14	"Death, where is your sting?"	1 Cor. 15:54, 55
Joel 2:28-32	"Everyone who calls on the name of Jehovah will be saved"	Acts 2:17-21; Rom. 10:13
Amos 9:11, 12	God to rebuild the booth of David	Acts 15:16-18
Hab. 1:5	"Behold it, you scorners, and wonder at it"	Acts 13:40, 41
Hab. 2:4	"My righteous one will live by reason of faith"	Heb. 10:38; Rom. 1:17
Hag. 2:6	Heavens and earth to be shaken	Heb. 12:26, 27
Mal. 1:2, 3	Jacob loved, Esau hated	Rom. 9:13

The Inspired Scriptures Bring Eternal Benefits

OUR review of "all Scripture . . . inspired of God" has opened before our eyes a glorious vision of Jehovah's sovereignty and his Kingdom purpose. We have noted that the Bible is one Book, with one powerful theme—the vindication of Jehovah's sovereignty and the ultimate fulfillment of his purpose for the earth by means of his Kingdom under Christ, the Promised Seed. From the Bible's opening pages, this one theme is developed and explained through the writings that follow, until, in its closing chapters, the glorious reality of God's grand purpose by means of his Kingdom is made clear. What a remarkable book the Bible is! Starting from the awe-inspiring creation of the material heavens and of the earth with its creature life, the Bible gives us the one inspired and authentic account of God's dealings with humankind until our time and carries us through to the complete realization of Jehovah's glorious creation of "a new heaven and a new earth." (Rev. 21:1) With his grand purpose fully accomplished by means of the Kingdom of the Seed, Jehovah God is seen in the relationship of a kind Father to a happy united human family, which joins in with all the heavenly hosts in praising him and sanctifying his holy name.

[2] How wonderfully this theme involving the Seed is developed throughout the Scriptures! Expressing the first inspired prophecy, God gives the promise that 'the seed of the woman' will bruise the serpent in the head. (Gen. 3:15) More than 2,000 years pass, and God tells faithful Abraham: "By means of your seed all nations of the earth will certainly bless themselves." Over 800 years later, Jehovah gives a like promise to one of Abraham's descendants, loyal King David, showing that the Seed will be a kingly one. As time passes, Jehovah's prophets thrillingly join in to foretell the glories of Kingdom rule. (Gen. 22:18; 2 Sam. 7: 12, 16; Isa. 9:6, 7; Dan. 2:44; 7:13, 14) Then the Seed himself appears, more than 4,000 years after the first promise in Eden. This One, who is also 'the seed of Abraham,' is Jesus Christ, "Son of the Most High," and to him Jehovah gives "the throne of David his father."—Gal. 3:16; Luke 1:31-33.

[3] Though this Seed, God's anointed King, is bruised in death by the Serpent's earthly seed, God raises him from the dead and exalts him to His own right hand, where he awaits God's due time to 'crush Satan's head.' (Gen. 3:15; Heb. 10:13; Rom. 16:20) Then the Revelation brings the entire vision to its glorious climax. Christ enters into

1. What glorious vision has our review of "all Scripture" opened before our eyes?

2, 3. How is the theme involving the Seed developed throughout the Scriptures?

Kingdom power and hurls "the original serpent, the one called Devil and Satan," from heaven down to earth. For a short time, the Devil brings woe to the earth and wages war with 'the remaining ones of the seed of God's woman.' But Christ, as "King of kings," smites the nations. The original Serpent, Satan, is abyssed and then is to be finally destroyed forever. Meanwhile, by means of New Jerusalem, the Lamb's bride, the benefits of Christ's sacrifice are applied to mankind for the blessing of all the families of the earth. Thus, the magnificent theme of the inspired Scriptures unfolds before us in all its thrilling grandeur!—Rev. 11:15; 12:1-12, 17; 19:11-16; 20:1-3, 7-10; 21: 1-5, 9; 22:3-5.

BENEFITING
FROM THIS INSPIRED RECORD

⁴ How can we gain the greatest benefit from the Holy Scriptures? We can benefit by letting the Bible go to work in our lives. By daily study and application of the inspired Scriptures, we can get guidance from God. "The word of God is alive and exerts power," and it can be a marvelous power for righteousness in our lives. (Heb. 4:12) If we continually study and follow the leadings of God's Word, we will come to "put on the new personality which was created according to God's will in true righteousness and loyalty." We will be made new in the force actuating our minds, and we will be transformed by making our minds over, so as to prove to ourselves "the good and acceptable and perfect will of God."—Eph. 4:23, 24; Rom. 12:2.

⁵ We can learn much by observing how other faithful servants of God have benefited from studying God's Word and meditating upon it. For example, there was Moses, 'the meekest of all men,' who was always teachable and willing to learn. (Num. 12:3) We should always have the same prayerful appreciation of Jehovah's sovereignty as he had. It was Moses who said: "O Jehovah, you yourself have proved to be a real dwelling for us during generation after generation. Before the mountains themselves were born, or you proceeded to bring forth as with labor pains the earth and the productive land, even from time indefinite to time indefinite you are God." Moses was thoroughly acquainted with God's wisdom, for he was used by Jehovah in writing the opening books of the Bible. Hence, he understood the importance of daily seeking wisdom from Jehovah. Thus, he prayed to God: "Show us just how to count our days in such a way that we may bring a heart of wisdom in." Since "the days of our years" may be few, just

70 years, or 80 in the case of "special mightiness," we are wise if we feast daily upon his Word, for then "the pleasantness of Jehovah our God" will "prove to be upon us," as it was upon his faithful servant Moses.—Ps. 90:1, 2, 10, 12, 17.

⁶ How necessary it is to meditate daily on God's Word! Jehovah made this plain to Moses' successor, Joshua, telling him: "Only be courageous and very strong to take care to do according to all the law that Moses my servant commanded you. Do not turn aside from it to the right or to the left, in order that you may act wisely everywhere you go. This book of the law should not depart from your mouth, and you must in an undertone read in it day and night, in order that you may take care to do according to all that is written in it; for then you will make your way successful and then you will act wisely." Did Joshua's continual reading of Jehovah's Law 'make his way successful'? Jehovah's blessing on his courageous campaign in Canaan supplies the answer.—Josh. 1:7, 8; 12:7-24.

⁷ Consider, too, the beloved David, another who deeply treasured wisdom from Jehovah. What heartfelt appreciation he showed for Jehovah's "law," "reminder," "orders," "commandment," and "judicial decisions"! As David expressed it: "They are more to be desired than gold, yes, than much refined gold; and sweeter than honey and the flowing honey of the combs." (Ps. 19:7-10) This exulting theme is expanded and repeated by another psalmist with soul-stirring beauty throughout the 119th Psalm. As we daily study God's Word and abide by its wise counsel, may we ever be able to say to Jehovah: "Your word is a lamp to my foot, and a light to my roadway. Your reminders are wonderful. That is why my soul has observed them."—Ps. 119:105, 129.

⁸ In the days of his faithfulness, David's son Solomon also lived by God's Word, and in his sayings too, we can find moving expressions of appreciation that we do well to make our very own. Through daily reading and application of the Bible, we will come to understand fully the inner depth of meaning of Solomon's words: "Happy is the man that has found wisdom, and the man that gets discernment. Length of days is in its right hand; in its left hand there are riches and glory. Its ways are ways of pleasantness, and all its roadways are peace. It is a tree of life to those taking hold of it, and those keeping fast hold of it are to be called happy." (Prov. 3:13, 16-18) Daily study and obedience to God's Word lead to the greatest hap-

---

6. How may we, like Joshua, make our way successful?
7. How did David express his appreciation for the wisdom from God, and how is the same appreciation expressed in Psalm 119?
8. What sayings of Solomon should we make our very own?

---

4. How can we gain the greatest benefit from the Holy Scriptures, and why?
5. What can we learn from the attitude and example of Moses?

piness now, together with the assurance of "length of days"—eternal life in Jehovah's new world.

⁹ Not to be overlooked among those who have cherished and obeyed the inspired Scriptures are God's faithful prophets. Jeremiah, for example, had a very difficult assignment. (Jer. 6:28) As he said: "The word of Jehovah became for me a cause for reproach and for jeering all day long." But he had been well fortified by his studies of God's Word, and in fact, he himself was used to write four books of the inspired Scriptures—First and Second Kings, Jeremiah, and Lamentations. So, what happened when discouragement seemed to envelop Jeremiah and he thought he would desist from preaching "the word of Jehovah"? Let Jeremiah himself answer: "In my heart it proved to be like a burning fire shut up in my bones; and I got tired of holding in, and I was unable to endure it." He was compelled to speak out Jehovah's words, and in doing so, he found that Jehovah was with him "like a terrible mighty one." If we study and keep studying God's Word, so that it becomes just as much a part of us as it was of Jeremiah, then Jehovah's invincible power will likewise be with us, and we will be able to triumph over every obstacle in continuing to speak of His glorious Kingdom purpose.—Jer. 20:8, 9, 11.

¹⁰ Now, what of our greatest example, "the Chief Agent and Perfecter of our faith, Jesus"? Was he familiar with the inspired Scriptures after the manner of all the prophets and other faithful men before him? Certainly he was, as his many quotations and his course of life in harmony with the Scriptures clearly show. It was with God's Word in mind that he presented himself to do his Father's will here on this earth: "Here I have come, in the roll of the book it being written about me. To do your will, O my God, I have delighted, and your law is within my inward parts." (Heb. 12:2; Ps. 40: 7, 8; Heb. 10:5-7) Thus, God's Word played a key role in Jehovah's sanctifying of Jesus, or setting him apart for his service. Jesus prayed that his followers might likewise be sanctified: "Sanctify them by means of the truth; your word is truth. Just as you sent me forth into the world, I also sent them forth into the world. And I am sanctifying myself in their behalf, that they also may be sanctified by means of truth."—John 17:17-19.

¹¹ Being sanctified "by means of the truth," the spirit-begotten and anointed footstep followers of Jesus must 'remain in his word' in order to be really his disciples. (John 8:31) Thus, Peter, in writing to "those who have obtained a faith," stressed the need for continued study and attention to God's Word: "For this reason I shall be disposed always to remind you of these things, although you know them and are firmly set in the truth that is present in you." (2 Pet. 1:1, 12) Continual reminders, such as are found in the daily reading and study of God's Word, are important also to all who hope to be of the "great crowd" whom John saw in vision after describing the 144,000 sealed ones of the tribes of spiritual Israel. For unless they keep on taking in life's water of truth, how can this great crowd intelligently "keep on crying with a loud voice, saying: 'Salvation we owe to our God, who is seated on the throne, and to the Lamb'"?—Rev. 7:9, 10; 22:17.

¹² We cannot escape it! The way to gain the greatest benefit from the inspired Scriptures, the way to find salvation to everlasting life, is to study those Scriptures and live by them every day of our lives. We must constantly meditate on God's Word, with the same prayerful attitude of appreciation as expressed by the psalmist: "I shall remember the practices of Jah; for I will remember your marvelous doing of long ago. And I shall certainly meditate on all your activity." (Ps. 77:11, 12) Meditating on Jehovah's 'marvelous doing and activity' will stir us also to be active in fine works, with everlasting life in view. The purpose of this book, *"All Scripture Is Inspired of God and Beneficial,"* is to encourage everyone who loves righteousness to share in the eternal and satisfying benefits that accrue from continued study and application of the Word of God.

IN "CRITICAL TIMES"

¹³ This modern age is the most critical time in human history. It is explosive with awesome possibilities. Indeed, it can truly be said that the very survival of the human race is in peril. Most appropriate, then, are the words of the apostle Paul: "But know this, that in the last days critical times hard to deal with will be here. For men will be lovers of themselves, lovers of money, self-assuming, haughty, blasphemers, disobedient to parents, unthankful, disloyal, having no natural affection, not open to any agreement, slanderers, without self-control, fierce, without love of goodness, betrayers, headstrong, puffed up with pride, lovers of pleasures rather than lovers of God, having a form of godly devotion but proving false to its power; and from these turn away."—2 Tim. 3:1-5.

¹⁴ Why turn away from such ones? Because their godless way is soon to end in destruction!

---

9. What encouragement may we draw from the example of Jeremiah?
10. What role did the Scriptures play in Jesus' life, and what did he pray in behalf of his disciples?
11. (a) What did Peter stress to anointed Christians regarding God's Word? (b) Why is study of the Bible also important to the great crowd?

12. Why must we constantly meditate on God's Word?
13. In what "critical times" are we living?
14. In view of the times, what advice of Paul should we heed?

Rather, let us, along with all honesthearted ones, turn to the healthful teaching of the inspired Scriptures, making these Scriptures the very foundation of our daily living. Let us heed the words of Paul to young Timothy: "You, however, continue in the things that you learned and were persuaded to believe." (2 Tim. 3:14) Yes, "continue" in them, says Paul. Doing so, we must humbly let the Scriptures teach us, reprove us, set things straight for us, and discipline us in righteousness. Jehovah knows what we need, for his thoughts are so much higher than our thoughts. By his inspired Scriptures, he tells us what is beneficial for us so that we may be fully equipped and competent for the good work of witnessing to his name and Kingdom. Paul gives this outstanding advice in the context of describing the "critical times" that come "in the last days": "All Scripture is inspired of God and beneficial for teaching, for reproving, for setting things straight, for disciplining in righteousness, that the man of God may be fully competent, completely equipped for every good work." May all of us survive these critical times by giving heed to this inspired advice!—2 Tim. 3:16, 17; Isa. 55: 8-11.

¹⁵ Obedience to the inspired Scriptures should be our goal. It was through disobedience to the word and command of Jehovah that the first man fell into sin and death, "and thus death spread to all men." So man lost the opportunity that might

---

15. (a) What has resulted from disobedience? (b) What glorious opportunity has been opened up by the obedience of Christ?

have been his in the Edenic Paradise to "actually take fruit also from the tree of life and eat and live to time indefinite." (Rom. 5:12; Gen. 2:17; 3:6, 22-24) But it is through the obedience of Christ and on the basis of the sacrifice of this "Lamb of God" that Jehovah will cause "a river of water of life, clear as crystal," to flow forth for the benefit of all those of mankind who dedicate themselves to Him in obedience. As the apostle John saw it in vision: "On this side of the river and on that side there were trees of life producing twelve crops of fruit, yielding their fruits each month. And the leaves of the trees were for the curing of the nations."—John 1:29; Rev. 22:1, 2; Rom. 5:18, 19.

¹⁶ Once again the way to everlasting life lies open to mankind. Happy, then, are those who heed the inspired scripture: "You must choose life in order that you may keep alive, you and your offspring, by loving Jehovah your God, by listening to his voice and by sticking to him; for he is your life and the length of your days." (Deut. 30:19, 20) Blessed is Jehovah, the God and Father of our Lord Jesus Christ, who makes this grand provision for life through the sacrifice of his Son and by means of his everlasting Kingdom. How great is our joy and gratitude that we can read and reread, study and restudy, and meditate on these precious truths, for truly "all Scripture is inspired of God and beneficial," leading on to eternal life either in heaven or on a paradise earth. (John 17:3; Eph 1: 9-11) Then everything will be 'holiness to Jehovah.'—Zech. 14:20; Rev. 4:8.

---

16. Of what eternal benefit are the inspired Scriptures?

PALESTINE
in the Time of Christ

MEDITERRANEAN SEA
(GREAT SEA)

ABILENE

Damascus

ITURAEA

DECAP

Dion

Mt. Hermon

Caesarea Philippi

Gadara

Sidon

Chorazin

Bethsaida

SEA OF GALILEE

GALILEE

Capernaum

Magadan

Tiberias

PHOENICIA

Tyre

Cana

Nain

Nazareth

Dor

Caesarea